AFGHANISTAN

AFGHANISTAN
The Great Game Revisited

Edited by
Rosanne Klass

FREEDOM HOUSE

First published in 1987.

Library of Congress Cataloging-in-Publication Data

Afghanistan, the great game revisited.

Bibliography: p.
Includes index.
1. Afghanistan—Foreign relations—Soviet Union.
2. Soviet Union—Foreign relations—Afghanistan.
3. Afghanistan—Strategic aspects. 4. Afghanistan—History—Soviet occupation, 1979-   I. Klass, Rosanne.
DS357.6.S65A35 1987 958'.1044 87-25140
ISBN 0-932088-16-3 (alk. paper)
ISBN 0-932088-15-5 (pbk. : alk. paper)

Distributed by arrangement with

UPA, Inc.
4720 Boston Way
Lanham, MD 20706

3 Henrietta Street
London WC2E 8LU England

Contents

FREEDOM HOUSE

Freedom House is an independent organization that places human freedom in the broad context of individual rights and global politics. Freedom House believes that civil rights at home and advocacy of human rights abroad depend upon American power, its prestige, and its human values.

In international affairs, these values concentrate our attention on violations of human rights by tyrants on the right as well as the left of the political spectrum. At home, our values stress the need to provide all citizens equality of opportunity, not only in law but in daily civic and private performance.

Freedom House has a very active program that includes bimonthly and annual publications, public advocacy, press conferences, lecture series, and research of political rights and civil liberties in every country.

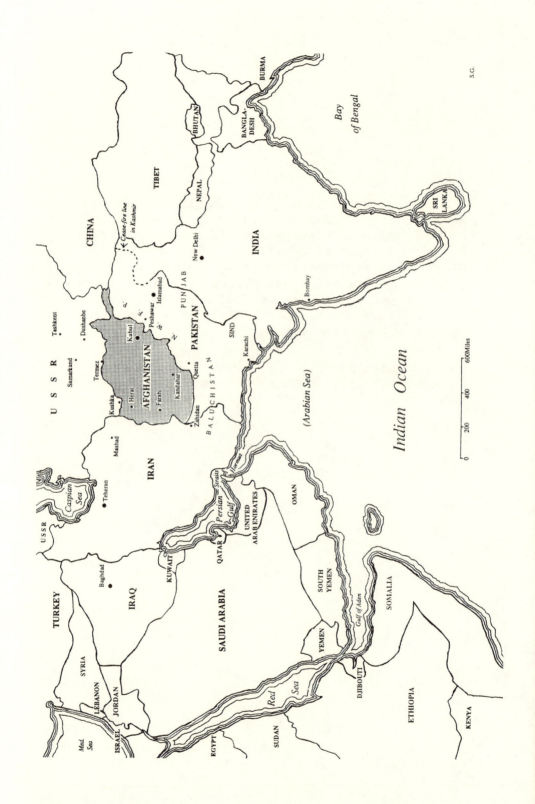

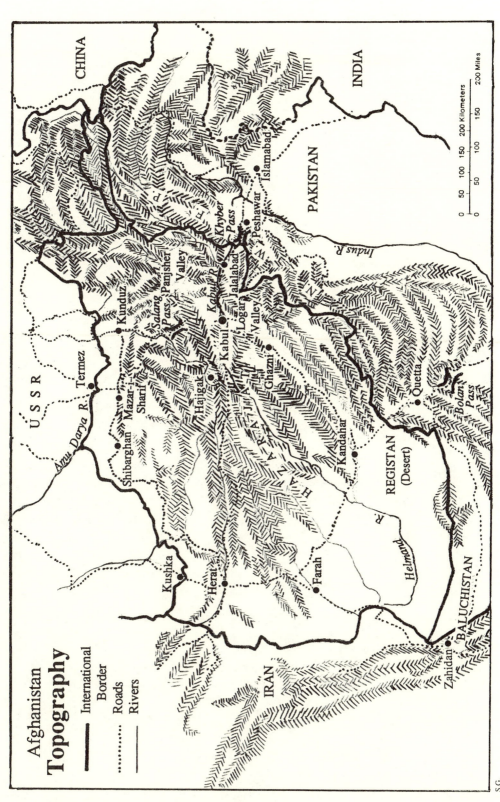

Afghanistan
Topography

— International
    Border
········· Roads
——— Rivers

CHINA

USSR

Amu Darya R.

Termez

Kushka

Kunduz

Shibarghan

Mazar-i-Sharif

Herat

Salang Pass

Panjsher Valley

Kabul

Haugak

HAZARAJAT

Logar Valley

Ghazni

Kandahar

Farah

Helmand R.

REGISTAN
(Desert)

Khyber Pass

Jalalabad

Peshawar

Islamabad

Indus R.

PAKISTAN

INDIA

Quetta

Bolan Pass

BALUCHISTAN

Zahidan

IRAN

0   50 100   200 Kilometers
0   50   100 150 200 Miles

S.G.

*"Turkistan, Afghanistan, Transcaspia, Persia...are the
pieces on a chessboard upon which is being played
out a game for the dominance of the world."*
    ---Lord Curzon (Viceroy of India, 1899-1905)

The Great Game Revisited

Rosanne Klass

"THE FRIENDSHIP of Afghanistan is of no service to Russia whatsoever,
beyond allowing her to pass through the country to India, which means
placing Afghanistan under the foot of Russia."

So wrote Abdur Rahman, Amir of Afghanistan, nearly a century ago, in
an autobiography which was published in London in 1900.[1] He knew
whereof he spoke: he had spent years of exile in Russia as the honored
guest of the Tsar. During those years he had been the interested recipient of
numerous confidences from high officials who hoped to enlist his aid in
bringing Afghanistan into the Russian orbit. Kipling called it "The Great
Game"---Russia's pursuit of access to the Indian Ocean and control of the
Indian subcontinent, which began at least as early as 1791, when invasion
plans were drawn up under Catherine the Great, and British efforts to foil it.

"Throughout my twelve years in Russia," the Amir wrote, "I discovered
that there is not the slightest doubt that Russia is always plotting toward
India...determined to attack India sooner or later, when she can find a
favorable opportunity...hence she does require to pass through my
country...but also to take Afghanistan if she can."

Abdur Rahman, the "iron amir" who ruled Afghanistan from 1880 till
his death in 1901 and laid the groundwork for its entry into the modern
world, was a remarkably astute and prescient figure. Dying in the same year
as Queen Victoria, he already perceived the shape of many of the social and
economic, as well as political and technological, changes that were to

emerge after World War I. He had come to the throne in the wake of the Second Anglo-Afghan War, with British troops occupying Kabul for the second time in forty years. By then he had spent much of his life in Russia and its Asian territories, journeying as far as the Chinese border. The British allowed him to take power in Afghanistan simply because no one else could do it. Concerned for their Indian empire, they feared that he was pro-Russian; the Russians, expanding steadily across Central Asia, confidently expected him to be so.

But like most Afghans, then and since, Abdur Rahman was single-mindedly concerned with the interests of his own country, which he defined as independence plus economic and social development---and those interests, he saw, lay with the West. "Personally," he wrote, "I am under great obligations to [the Russians], and shall never forget their kindness, because ingratitude is the very worst of sins. But...I am not entitled to sell my country and my people to the Russians in compensation for my personal gratitude toward them."

Referring to his many confidential discussions with Russian officials during the years of his exile, he wryly noted the freedom with which they had confided to him their intentions, hopeful of winning his assistance. "How very little Russia expected at that time that I should be king of Afghanistan and the strongest opponent of that policy at some future date!"

His autobiography, begun in the 1880s, was intended to spell out publicly his policy recommendations "to my sons and successors." He also used it as a forum through which he could urge Britain, then the world's leading power, to provide a counterweight to Russian pressures: for without such a counterweight from the West---steady, steadfast, quiet but firm---he was sure that his nation would be swallowed up, not by the British who had twice invaded it but had twice withdrawn, but by the colossus to the north, whose more permanent intentions he knew all too well.

> The Russian policy in Asia [he wrote] is that in any way, rightly or wrongly, friendly or unfriendly, with peace or war, the Islamic kingdoms should be washed away...They would be glad if Turkey [then the Ottoman Empire, encompassing modern Turkey, Iraq, Syria, Jordan, Lebanon, Israel, and all of Arabia], Persia and Afghanistan ceased to exist as kingdoms but were maintained merely to be used as tools in the service of Russia herself, in which case it would be a matter of indifference whether they existed or not, and their duration would simply depend on the length of time that Russia required them to serve her purpose.
>
> I think it is necessary to mention here that the Russian policy of aggression is slow and steady, but firm and unchangeable. If once

they make up their minds to do a thing, there is no stopping them, and no changing their policy. It is not the case with them, as with some other countries, that every party that comes into power can undo the work that has been done by the party before itself. Their habit of forward movement resembles the habit of the elephant, who examines a spot thoroughly before he places his foot upon it, and when once he puts his weight there is no going back, and no taking another step in a hurry until he has put his full weight on the first foot, and has smashed everything that lies under it. Russia has moved and marched toward India during the last sixty years [i.e., since the 1820s] very slowly but firmly. She has not occupied a place without first being certain of success. And after taking a place she makes announcements and a great noise about keeping the peace; and signs new treaties and agreements, swearing all vows and oaths that she will never proceed any further. These vows last until, but no longer than, the time when the newly annexed place is strongly fortified for reinforcements and the Russian influence has spread all over it. After this, Russia takes another place...lying near to the first, without either going very far or retreating again. When this place is properly absorbed, she moves on...

Faced with the necessity for friendly relations with his powerful northern neighbor (Afghanistan has a thousand-mile border with Russia), Abdur Rahman urged an Afghan policy of formal neutrality, nonalignment, and friendship with all, buttressed by expanding ties to the West---not only England but the United States and Japan, whose importance he foresaw---while keeping the Russians at polite arm's-length. And for the next fifty years, as Russia, Tsarist and Soviet, moved ever closer, even snipping off a bit of Afghan territory north of the Oxus River, Afghan rulers attempted to sustain this policy, despite a brief third war with British India.

With equal passion, Abdur Rahman exhorted England to provide the steadfast counterweight which he considered necessary to frustrate Russian designs. The West, he insisted, must make clear its interest in Afghanistan's continuing independence and must help Afghans to strengthen their own country's stability. The British pursued such a policy---unevenly, but adequately---as long as they held their Indian Empire and were willing to defend it, and (notwithstanding recent statements to the contrary) Afghanistan did not slip within the Russian sphere of influence until the 1950s or even later; the Afghans made strenuous efforts to stay outside that sphere despite persistent Soviet manipulation and enticements.

But after World War II, Britain no longer had either the strength or the will to hold on to its Indian Empire. In 1947, the British withdrew forever from an India newly divided into the successor states of India and Pakistan, which were preoccupied by fratricidal antagonisms. The United States, now the paramount Western power, was left to take over the protective role. It chose not to do so. Washington viewed Afghanistan as strategically negligible, a relic of out-dated imperialist strategies, and the Afghans as annoyingly intractable, their independent stance verging on the uppity. The conventional wisdom of post-war American policy assumed that the mountain ranges and the passes that had guarded the Indian subcontinent for three thousand years had been rendered obsolete by the air age.

In 1953, then-Prime Minister (and Prince) Mohammed Daoud asked for American aid to update an army which consisted of a few World War I biplanes and horse-drawn artillery. The Eisenhower Administration, annoyed by Afghanistan's insistence on its historic nonalignment, its refusal to sign a formal treaty like the Baghdad Pact, and its dispute with Pakistan over the Pushtun border areas, not only turned him down but, in Daoud's eyes, slapped him down. Furious, rejecting the policy of a century, Daoud turned to Moscow for arms, and the patient Russian pachyderm, after more than 150 years of trying, at last began to edge its way into Kabul. Daoud thought he could ride it---and so did Washington.

For the next two decades, the United States watched with remarkable equanimity as the Soviets gradually increased their inroads: equipping the Afghan armed forces---creating them, almost---and penetrating the officer corps, getting a foothold in the educational system, building a strategic highway system, gaining control of resource development and ultimately achieving an economic hammerlock on the country. The United States, with its modest aid programs and Peace Corps volunteers, complacently pronounced increasing Soviet involvement in Afghanistan to be the very model of a new spirit of Soviet-American cooperation in the underdeveloped nations of the Third World, a showcase of détente. The first result was not merely the enlargement but the legitimization of Soviet penetration. If the Americans were not disturbed, the Afghans finally were---enough to force Daoud to step down in 1963. But later, when a constitutional experiment began to show hope of some modest success, "the Red Prince" seized power again in 1973 via a Soviet-backed coup carried out by Afghans who had been subverted, enabling the Soviets to establish, behind his nationalist facade, a Communist-manipulated, pro-Soviet regime---though one not yet fully secured for Moscow.

During these years, Washington not merely ignored but rejected the warnings of anti-Communist Afghans. The ten-year effort (1963-1973) to replace Daoud's earlier dictatorship with a modest step toward constitutional democratic government received nothing more than cosmetic support from the United States.   When Daoud overthrew the king and the liberal constitution, Washington turned a blind eye to his Soviet backing, while presumed experts declared his dictatorship eminently suited to Afghan psychological needs and identified his Communist associates as merely over-eager young reformers.

But by 1976 even Daoud was alarmed at the growth of Soviet influence. And so, at last, were the unwatchful Americans---and the very watchful Shah of Iran.   With American encouragement (some of it probably transmitted by the Shah), Daoud abruptly tried to reverse course, ousting the Communists in his regime.   The result was the Communist coup of April 1978---"the Great Saur Revolution."   Now at last, almost a century after Abdur Rahman's warnings, the persistent colossus to the north had finally achieved its Afghan base, installing a catspaw in Kabul through which to subvert and eventually control Pakistan and Iran by manipulating old regional and ethnic disputes, another step on the path to its long-sought goal: the Persian Gulf and the Indian Ocean.   Still Washington and the rest of the world paid little or no attention, even though thousands of Soviet troops were quietly moved into Afghanistan (15,000 to 20,000 of them *before* the invasion, according to a French Communist source later confirmed by Babrak Karmal[2]) and an American ambassador was kidnapped and killed in Kabul.

Only twenty months later---when the open use of the Soviet Army was deemed necessary to consolidate Communist control over a people who risen against the puppet regime, its foreign controllers, its reign of terror and its frontal attack on their religion and their society---did the world finally take notice; and even then, only because the Soviet Army was used.   Why Afghanistan was the target of this move was a question neither the press nor policy makers seemed able to explain.

For with neglect had come ignorance, and ignorance increased the lack of interest, reinforcing neglect.   If the major Western governments had no interest in contemporary Afghanistan, then neither did the press, policy analysts, or scholars.   For nearly a century Afghanistan had been dismissed as a remote non-place of only minor exotic interest; indeed, for the press the term "an Afghanistan story" was journalistic slang for a news item from any far-off place devoid of interest, routinely destined for the wastebasket. Only a few months before the invasion, an important editor could flatly state, "The Soviets aren't going to invade Afghanistan.   Afghanistan is of absolutely no importance to anyone. The Soviets don't want it---and if they do want it, they can have it. Nobody cares."[3]

Scholars too ignored Afghanistan, aside from a tiny handful pursuing recondite research in esoteric fields. A crossroads, Afghanistan fell outside of designated areas of study: the Middle East, the Indian subcontinent, Central Asia, Iranian and Soviet studies. Specialists in each of these fields left it to the others; as a result it slipped unnoticed between the cracks, examined by none. In short, Afghanistan was regarded as a historic appendage that had outlived any significance, much as doctors regard the appendix---until it erupts with a poisonous infection. Yet even a casual look at a topographical map should have reminded everyone that, so long as geography plays a role in history, Afghanistan will remain what it has been since prehistoric times---the defense perimeter of the Indian subcontinent, crucial to access between the Eurasian land mass to the Indic plains, the Persian Gulf, and the Indian Ocean. For 4,000 years, no power that has controlled the mountains and passes of Afghanistan and wanted to move on southward has been prevented.

However, when the Soviet invasion came and government officials, foreign policy specialists, scholars, journalists, commentators and the concerned public scrambled for information that could provide perspective on a world crisis, there was almost nothing available---and certainly no sources that were comprehensive, reliable and in-depth. For lack of better alternatives, the press turned to prestigious all-purpose foreign policy pundits, who, whatever their qualifications in other fields, were grossly uninformed about Afghanistan and could only grope and guess in their efforts to explain events. Because Brezhnev was then in poor health and seldom in view, some leaped to the conclusion that unidentified underlings had blundered into a hasty and ill-considered decision to invade. This is still widely believed, despite subsequent reports that, at least from October 1979 on, decisions on Afghanistan were controlled by a special task force made up of Defense Minister Dmitri Ustinov, then-KGB chief Yuri Andropov and Boris Ponamarev, secretary of the Central Committee's International Department.[4]

A number of "experts" suggested that the invasion was a defensive Soviet move undertaken to protect the southern borders of the USSR from a tidal wave of fanatic Islamic revivalism. Such speculation was possible only for those completely ignorant of the history of Afghan-Soviet relations as well as the nature of Islam in Afghanistan (which, as detailed elsewhere in this volume, posed no threat whatsoever to Soviet Central Asia until well after the invasion). Other experts---and many editors---announced with relief, less than a month after the invasion, that since Soviet forces had not immediately pressed on into Pakistan, the USSR obviously had no further regional ambitions.

These are only a few examples of the torrent of uninformed---and misinformed---speculation that was rushed into print[5] (to be seized on, cited and supported by Soviet apologists, particularly in the British and American press). Once set in print, these uninformed speculations became set in concrete, widely quoted, repeated, and accepted as fact and wisdom---and in the absence of more accurate correctives, their errors continue to be widely reported as fact to this day. The problem of ignorance has thus been made worse by the addition of a great deal of "information" that is in reality a jumble of errors, half-truths and distortions.

Interestingly enough, in 1980 (and since), almost none of these experts considered the possibility that the Afghan people themselves might play a part in deciding their own fate. Aside from a handful of those who knew the Afghans well, it occurred to no one that they had already influenced events or might do so in future, least of all that they might choose to fight against the overwhelming power of the Soviet Union. As a result, once the international shock of the invasion had been absorbed and world attention returned to other matters, Afghanistan was once again ignored. Nearly two years later, the press and policy makers alike were surprised to realize that there was still a war going on between the Afghan nation and its would-be conquerors. Only then did they begin to pay it some modest attention, but they still found few sources of accurate information or backgrounding.

In fact, in the nearly seven years since the Soviet invasion forced the Afghanistan crisis upon world attention, this lack of the essential basic information which is needed to understand events and their implications has hardly improved---at least, not outside the growing but still small international circle of specialists whose work is often unpublished or appears only in obscure or specialized publications. The result has been a longstanding, continuing international crisis of major importance, the significance of which remains a puzzle even to many of those who must deal with it, let alone those who want to study it. Everyone agrees that Afghanistan is indeed a crisis of major international significance---but very few can explain precisely why.

This book was conceived and designed to help remedy that problem by providing in succinct form the data necessary for a basic understanding of the Afghanistan issue, including the historical and geopolitical contexts in which it can be better understood.

The leading experts on each aspect of the issue were asked to write the chapters on their respective areas of expertise, and in each case to distill and encapsulate the essential information needed to provide a basis for public understanding not only of what has already occurred but of future developments. They were asked to avoid speculation and theorizing, and to focus instead on providing confirmed data and clearcut analysis. Since this book is not designed primarily for specialists and academic scholars, they were also asked to keep the scholarly apparatus to the minimum necessary for documentation and as guidelines for those who wish to pursue various aspects of the issue further.

Each of the contributors brings to his subject not only extended research but active involvement, hands-on experience and firsthand observation. Moreover, with few exceptions, the contributors are not professionally associated or in contact and in several cases are not even familiar with one another's work, which is in diverse specialized fields: they meet for the first time in these pages. In other words, this book is not the result of a consensus. Each author reached his conclusions independently on the basis of data in his own area of specialization. The extent to which they agree is therefore indicative of the compelling nature of the data. To whatever degree they may differ in detail or conclusions, taken together they provide a coherent picture of the issue. Much of this material has never before appeared in print; much has been available until now only in bits and pieces scattered in specialized publications in several countries and several languages, and is here brought together for the first time. Many of the subjects discussed have received little public attention until now.

This volume can be read as a unified work which lays the foundation for a broad understanding of the Afghanistan issue in a regional and world context. At the same time, it has been organized to aid research on specific topics, and the appendices should help readers find their way through unfamiliar territory. Many subjects are discussed from a different angles in several chapters, and researchers are advised to make thorough use of the index.

A number of frequently asked questions are answered here. As one example, many journalists puzzle over the lack of organizational unity in the Afghan Resistance, attributing it simplistically (on the basis of fragmentary personal observations further limited by their inability to speak the local languages) to "tribal differences." The sections on the Resistance, the culture, sovietization, Soviet operations and several "Who's Who" entries, in combination, reveal a far more complex situation in which cultural, political, technical and topographical factors, outside interference and Soviet manipulations all play a part.

Equally important, a number of widespread fictions and misconceptions are demolished. The portrait of the Afghan people that emerges here differs significantly from that in the popular press, which too often portrays them as ignorant primitives, religious fanatics eager to immolate themselves as martyrs in an effort to impose medieval restrictions on their own society. Western observers with little understanding of Islam or the peoples involved have seized upon a facile but highly inaccurate parallel with Iran's revolutionaries (of whom they also may have only superficial knowledge). For that matter, the very use of the words "tribe" and "tribal" in connection with the Afghans evokes in many minds an image of semi-savage primitives, whereas the equally appropriate term "clan" would evoke an analogy (and a more accurate one) with the tough gallantry of Scottish Highlanders---whom in fact the Afghans in many ways resemble. Far from being uncivilized and primitive, the Afghans are heirs to a high culture of historic importance, particularly rich in literature, philosophy and art. They fell behind when historical forces cut them off from the scientific and technological revolution that began in the sixteenth century--- comparatively recently, as history goes.* Nor are they particularly xenophobic or fanatical---labels put on them by foreigners who attempted to take over their country and were met by entrenched defiance.† Indeed, the general absence of religious fanaticism in Afghan society throws an interesting light on Soviet efforts to manipulate and even promote the most extreme elements in the Resistance (which have little ideological support among the Afghan people),†† and raises questions about the reported favor of these elements with outside supporters. It is true that illiteracy is widespread in Afghanistan, but this does not mean that

---

* See Appendix II.

† Visitors to Afghanistan uniformly testify to Afghan hospitality. The British regularly described the warmth with which they were welcomed as guests when their armies were no longer on Afghan soil. Jewish refugees from Nazi Germany were given haven in Kabul during World War II.

†† Since 1978 the Communist regimes in Kabul have consistently identified Gulbuddin Hekhmatyar, the most radical figure, as the primary or even the sole leader of the entire Resistance; discussions elsewhere in this book and in references cited raise interesting questions about possible motivations for this special attention. In the event that the Communist regimes in Kabul were ever to be replaced or joined by the most radical elements in the Resistance and these elements attempted to implement their extremist programs, it appears certain that they would meet with massive public opposition, setting off disorders which would provide the Soviets with an opportunity to return in the guise of providing stability. In such a case, an international community convinced that the Afghans are "incapable" of self-government would hardly protest.

Afghans did not want education. They hungered for it, as I can personally attest.*

Lack of education was the result of national poverty and, as the chapters on Soviet economic manipulation and resource control reveal, that poverty was in significant part the result of outside pressures that prevented the Afghans from developing their resources for their own benefit. It is quite clear that Afghanistan has the resources to prosper; it is also quite clear that since at least the 1920s, Soviet policies played a role in keeping it poor.

Perhaps the single most widespread and persistent myth about Afghanistan is that it is "the Soviet Vietnam," a facile analogy based on a number of unexamined assumptions which, in the light of the facts, prove to be supported misconceptions. The analogy originated in the fact that the Soviets expected a short campaign in Afghanistan but have found themselves engaged in a long one; it is sustained by wishful thinking. The resulting assumptions require careful examination and rethinking. A number of them spring from the analogy itself, first and foremost the assumption (nurtured by Moscow) that the Soviet Union blundered into Afghanistan unintentionally and by mistake; that the USSR has no permanent ambitions in Afghanistan and no further ambitions in the region; that the campaign in Afghanistan is costing the USSR heavily in lives and treasure, a drain it can ill afford; that the war is a stalemate Moscow cannot win; and that the Soviet Union is eager to withdraw but needs international help to find a face-saving means of doing so (another assumption carefully nurtured by Soviet officials). Each of these assumptions should be re-examined in the light of the facts in the following chapters and additional sources to which they point.

While it is clear that Moscow preferred, and at first attempted, to achieve its goals in Afghanistan without using Soviet military forces overtly, the history of Soviet (and earlier Tsarist) political, economic and military efforts to gain control of Afghanistan, as detailed from a variety of perspectives in the following chapters, refutes the suggestion that Soviet moves were accidental, unwilling or inadvertent---or that they are regretted. On the contrary, the data indicates that Moscow was prepared to use whatever measures were required to achieve its goals over a period of many years---and still is.

As detailed in chapter ten, Soviet deployment, strategy and tactics have

---

* Illiteracy is often confused with ignorance or even lack of intelligence. Nobody who has experience of a nonliterate society will make that mistake. In the specific case of Afghanistan, its people, educated or not, are notably intelligent, dynamic and worldly.

been misunderstood and misreported; their losses have been minimal, while the military benefits, both strategic and operational, have been enormous. Since Soviet military planning is based not on cost-effectiveness but on goal-achievement, their assessment of the war is likely to differ greatly from those of Western observers.

The economic cost, widely estimated at about $2 billion per year (a fraction of U.S. expenditures in Vietnam) is only a very small percent of the total Soviet military budget and would not present a significant problem in terms of the total Soviet economy, even if the USSR were bearing the total cost. But, as detailed elsewhere in this book, the Soviet Union is *not* bearing the total cost: at least one-quarter and possibly much more of the cost of the Soviet occupation of Afghanistan has been transferred to the Afghan economy and is being paid for by Afghan natural gas and other resources. Given the resources already developed and those marked for future exploitation, Moscow can view the costs of its campaign as a longterm investment in gas, iron, copper, chrome, uranium, possibly oil, and other resources which will in time more than repay that initial investment---if indeed it is not doing so already.*

In short, the USSR is following the classic pattern of colonial exploitation, and is doing so with a crudeness seldom seen among other imperialist powers after the nineteenth century; one must look back to the Belgian Congo under Leopold II to find its like. (In a 1985 speech to Party members, Babrak Karmal described Afghan workers in the gas fields as living in caves, without shoes, adequate clothing, or sufficient food;[7] corvée labor, disguised as voluntary service, is common in areas under DRA control.)

Moreover, estimates of the economic drain on the Soviet Union make no allowance for that part of the cost which is being borne by East bloc and satellite states at Soviet demand. The amounts are unknown, but in 1986 East German officials complained bitterly to a Western visitor about the size of the contribution they were required to make to the occupation of

---

*In an interview in New Delhi in November 1986, Yuri Gankovsky, head of the Near and Middle East Department of the Institute of Oriental Studies in the Soviet Academy of Sciences and a member of the official delegation accompanying Mikhail Gorbachev on his visit to India, declared that the war in Afghanistan is not costing Moscow "one cent." "We are paid for everything we are sending to Afghanistan," he said. "All our expenses---I state 'all' twice---are paid by Afghanistan...There is a giant gas field in the northern part of Afghanistan, and by supplying the gas, Afghanistan is paying us for everything...Afghanistan is supplying us not only with gas... but also with fruit, with skins and agriculture, cotton."[6]

Afghanistan,[8] where East Germany is involved in police training and operations and other projects. Given the heavy involvement of East Germany, Bulgaria, Czechoslovakia, Hungary, Romania, Cuba, Yugoslavia, and, since about 1985, Poland, in various aspects of the Afghan regime and its economy, their contributions may significantly reduce Soviet costs. India has been providing economic aid to the DRA for years and announced in the spring of 1987 that its aid and trade with Kabul would be increased. The USSR is therefore bearing much less of the total cost of the invasion, war and occupation than is commonly believed.

After visiting Moscow in April 1987, Senator Gordon J. Humphrey, chairman of the joint Congressional Task Force on Afghanistan, reported that Soviet foreign ministry officials with whom he spoke seemed "confident and cocky" about Afghanistan. He added: "The Soviets were quite pleased with the way things are going in Afghanistan....They feel that they have time on their side and they will succeed...The cost to the Soviets is just not high enough yet...They expressed no real discomfort about losses in men or material."[9]

The supposition that the Soviet Union has no permanent ambitions in Afghanistan is belied, directly or by implication, by data in almost every chapter of this book. This illusion is related to one of the most widespread assumptions---the conclusion that, because Soviet forces did not immediately press on into Iran or Pakistan when they invaded Afghanistan, the Soviet Union has no further ambitions in the region. Such assumptions can be explained only by ignorance of history in general and the history of Russian/Soviet imperialism and strategies in Central Asia in particular.

Obviously those commentators who in 1980 heaved such audible sighs of relief at the lack of any further Soviet ambitions were unfamiliar with the history which lay behind Abdur Rahman's simile of the elephant. The implications of an entrenched Soviet presence in Afghanistan for the future of Iran, Pakistan, and the region are specifically discussed below in several chapters and can be broadly inferred from others and from additional sources listed in the bibliography. Suffice it here to point out the immediacy of Pakistan as a target. Without sanctuary and logistical support via Pakistan, the Afghan Resistance could be swiftly crushed, as were the Central Asian insurgents sixty years ago once they had been isolated. Pakistan's harbors would offer Moscow the long-sought warm-water ports and facilities for the growing Soviet fleet (which already has access to facilities in Vietnam, South Yemen and Africa) giving it effective control of the Indian Ocean. Pakistan's transport and communication systems need only short links to those in Afghanistan to provide the USSR with a direct line from Termez to those ports. And Pakistan is the only remaining U.S. ally in South Asia between Turkey and Thailand.

In addition to the subversive activities directed against Pakistan detailed elsewhere in this book, the science and engineering divisions of Kabul University, now integrated with the Soviet-run Polytechnic Institute, are reliably reported to have been transformed into a terrorist training center similar to Lumumba University in Moscow (whose alumni include "Carlos the Jackal") and it is reportedly expanding. The "student body" is believed to be almost entirely Baluchis from Pakistan, Iranians of various parties, and Palestinians, with a sprinkling of Syrians, Libyans and Yemenis. The PLO established ties with the DRA early on, and maintains an office in Kabul; in 1981 the PFLP, a PLO component specializing in terrorism, published a photo of its representative pinning a medal on Babrak Karmal and a statement proclaiming the identity of DRA and PFLP goals.

Pushtun tribesmen from Pakistan are trained and supplied with weapons at a center in Jalalabad initially run by the al-Zulfikar terrorist organization set up by the sons of the late Pakistani President Zulfikar Ali Bhutto;* al-Zulfikar is sworn to destroy Pakistani President Zia ul-Haq, who ousted Bhutto from power, put him on trial, and refused to commute his death sentence. Al-Zulfikar originally had its headquarters in Kabul; they were later moved to New Delhi and then, reportedly, to Libya, but it reportedly still maintains offices and training camps in Afghanistan as well as in Libya and South Yemen. Selected students from these several programs and others mentioned below are sent on to the Soviet Union itself for advanced training.

Pakistan has always been internally vulnerable. Since its creation in 1947, it has been spasmodically beset by provincial separatist movements in the Northwest Frontier Province, Baluchistan, East Pakistan, and Sind. With Indian assistance, East Pakistan broke away in 1971 to form the new country of Bangladesh; the Pushtun and Baluchi movements are discussed elsewhere below in considerable detail. Suffice it to say here that since 1978, the DRA has consistently proclaimed its support for Pushtun and Baluchi independence as well as for the domestic political parties opposing the Zia government (the MRD and the PPP), which have indicated willingness to recognize the DRA and cut off support for the Afghan

---

* Shahnawaz Bhutto died in Cannes in 1985 under mysterious circumstances; after investigation the French police took his Afghan widow into custody for several days. His brother, Murtaza, remains head of al-Zulfikar, shuttling between Paris and his primary base in London, where he works through the offices of his father's party, the PPP, now headed by his sister, Benazir.

Resistance. The London-based Baluchi leader, Ataullah Mangal, who in 1983 declared that Pakistan must cease to exist "in its present form," is a frequent visitor to Kabul, as are the Pushtun separatist leaders Khan Abdul Ghaffar Khan, now 97 years old but still active, and his son Khan Abdul Wali Khan. In 1983 an official of Indira Gandhi's Congress-I Party told a "World Sind" meeting in New Delhi that the time had come for India to annex Sind.[10]

These movements have for years repeatedly risen and subsided on waves of outside support and stimulus from Kabul, Moscow and New Delhi. DRA embassies in London, Washington, Paris, New York and elsewhere now serve as liaison and facilitators for these and other activities.* As noted above and detailed below, preparations are in readiness to set operations in motion to destroy Pakistan if and when the decision is taken. In The Northwest Frontier Province alone, it is said that there is not a Pushtun tribe that has not had some of its members trained, armed and bribed by the DRA and its associates. The first hints are also visible of a press campaign to undermine international support for the Zia government, similar to the campaign that destroyed support for the Shah of Iran in 1979.

The references to India---here and elsewhere---may come as a surprise to many, but extended and growing Indian military and economic ties to the Soviet Union, especially since 1971, can be readily documented. U.S. military aid to Pakistan since the invasion of Afghanistan has been made the occasion for further beefing up India's military forces with the most advanced Soviet weaponry, although by 1984 they were already the world's fourth largest. India is the paramount regional power and, should a crisis occur in Pakistan, it would be unreasonable to expect New Delhi to remain aloof and uninvolved. Its refusal to condemn the Soviet invasion of Afghanistan, and its active and increasing support of the DRA, must therefore be taken into consideration.

As for Moscow's purported regrets and declared eagerness to withdraw its forces from Afghanistan, it should be kept in mind---but is all too often forgotten---that Soviet spokesmen at the highest levels began disseminating these reports as early as February 1980, when Armand Hammer reported that his friend Leonid Brezhnev had confided to him that the USSR was anxious

---

* DRA agents, including KhAD agents, who in at least some cases are known to maintain contact with these embassies, also attempt to pressure and manipulate Afghan refugee communities in Europe, the United States and elsewhere, with some success. In the guise of refugees and Resistance supporters, some of them also attempt to influence international opinion.

to withdraw its forces but would need international assistance to do so. Since then, under all of Brezhnev's successors, hardly a distinguished visitor has returned from Moscow without a similar message, usually received as a private confidence from an unnamed high Soviet official.[11]   In 1986 Mikhail Gorbachev, in conformity with his more public style, gave it dramatic form in his Vladivostok speech when he called Afghanistan "a bleeding wound."

Despite their frequency and their similarity, each of these messages is hailed as a new development and a potential breakthrough. In 1987 the acknowledgement by a Soviet consular official in New York that the invasion of Afghanistan was a "mistake" (a comment which he subsequently hedged as "his personal opinion") was greeted as the first such admission by any Soviet official.[12] One can only wonder at the shortness of human and institutional memories.

More important, however, is the fact that the implications of these "confidences" and "revelations" go unexamined: they invariably suggest that in order for the USSR to withdraw from Afghanistan, the world community must stop all aid to the Resistance, minimize attention and make concessions, i.e., enable the Soviet Union to achieve its goals without need for its military forces. Nor is attention paid to the disparity between what the Soviet leadership says and what it is actually doing in Afghanistan. Actions do speak louder than words, and Soviet statements should be measured against ongoing Soviet policies and actions.

And finally, in assessing the Vietnam analogy one cannot ignore the fact that the United States was forced to withdraw from Vietnam in large part as a result of enormous political costs, not only at home but throughout the world. One cannot expect massive domestic protests in the Soviet Union. Discontent at casualties in Afghanistan does surface here and there from time to time, visible through samizdat and other subterranean channels, but as yet there is no indication that it presents a significant problem except, potentially, in Soviet Central Asia. The Soviet media seem to be conditioning the public to think of involvement in Afghanistan as a parallel to the defense of "our great Socialist motherland" in World War II, and perhaps even to think of Afghanistan as part of that motherland. In late 1985, one newspaper quoted the bereaved mother of a soldier killed in action as saying, "My son's blood was shed on Afghan soil, *which I can no longer consider to be foreign.* [emphasis added]"[13] In late 1986, Pravda quoted Mikhail Gorbachev as saying, "Our international solidarity with the Afghan people is as exclusively and equally important as the security of the Soviet Union."[14]

And what political price is the Soviet Union in fact paying in the world?

Where are the massive international demonstrations, the thousands marching in the streets of New York, Berkeley, Paris, Stockholm, Amsterdam, Sydney, and Bonn? Not even in the Muslim world are there mass protests. Where are the thundering editorials? Where is the drumbeat of daily reproach on radio and television? Where are the dozens of documentaries?* In October 1984, when the Soviet ambassador to Pakistan threatened that journalists trying to cover the war would be killed[15], there was no cry of outrage in the world press. In fact, the Western media, ordinarily sensitive to any restrictions and attacks on the press, have barely reported the death of three journalists in Afghanistan: a Norwegian, an Australian, and in 1985 an American.

What international negotiations are suspended? What sanctions imposed? At the time of the invasion, many governments and much of the public indicated reluctance even to boycott the Moscow Olympics. Today, after seven years of destruction, oppression and genocide, the few modest measures taken by the U.S. and others in response to the invasion have been universally lifted, and the mention of Afghanistan in the course of international negotiations with the Soviet Union in no way prevents those negotiations from proceeding unhindered.

In 1985, the U.S. State Department agreed in writing that the United States would serve as co-guarantor (with the Soviet Union) of any settlement reached in the U.N.-sponsored proximity talks between Pakistan and the DRA---that is, committed the United States in advance to support sight unseen a result the nature and terms of which could not yet be known. In response to criticism, the State Department said that its letter represented no change in U.S. policy, but high-level U.S. officials privately characterized it as a radical change.

If the political price was initially somewhat higher than the near-zero Moscow expected, it has nevertheless not been high.

All this is not to say that Afghanistan *could not* be transformed into something approaching an international political disaster for the Soviet Union if the will to do so existed. The international political price could unquestionably be very significantly upped, particularly in the so-called Third World---Asia, Latin America, Africa, and especially the Muslim world--- where the Soviet Union seeks expanded political and economic connections and where the history and nature of its relations with Afghanistan are of specific relevance, as well as in the United States and Europe. This could

---

* Film exists, often obtained at significant risk. Most of it sits unused in cans on the shelf.

most assuredly be done, and might well begin with the widespread dissemination of both accurate information about Soviet actions in Afghanistan and the history of Soviet-Afghan relations.

For twenty-five years, the Soviet Union proclaimed Afghanistan to be the model of its relationships with developing countries in what is now called the Third World, and it has never repudiated that claim. It could therefore be useful to take the Soviets at their word and examine Soviet economic, military, trade, aid, and cultural programs in other countries of Asia, Africa, Latin America, and the Pacific in the light of the Afghan model, as outlined below in the chapters discussing Soviet military and economic agreements, resource development and aid programs. Both governments and the public in developing countries might benefit from knowledge of the true nature of those model relations.

The world also could and should be told loudly and clearly about the genocide being conducted by Soviet and DRA forces in Afghanistan. Thus far the international silence regarding that genocide is deafening. No preachers thunder about Afghanistan from their pulpits, few editors in their columns and those only rarely. Only handfuls, not thousands, demonstrate in the streets of a few of the world's cities. International spokesmen of human rights who speak out eloquently on other atrocities are silent on this one. Entertainers not only fail to use their talents to raise aid funds and public consciousness on behalf of the Afghans but refuse to do so.[16] As late as 1982, an influential editor could dismiss atrocities in Afghanistan with the comment, "Torture is not news."[17]

Even today, when the facts have been documented and spread before the world by half-a-dozen sources, including the U.N., and it is no longer possible to claim ignorance, the voices of conscience remain silent. Pope John Paul II has met with Resistance figures and has issued a few statements, but aside from a handful, other religious leaders have said nothing. In the United States, it was not until 1985 that two major denominations finally condemned the Soviet invasion. The rest, including the National Council of Churches, have not only remained silent but in several cases have actually *refused* to issue a condemnation,[18] as has the World Council of Churches, in which the Soviet-appointed representatives of the Russian Orthodox Church exert significant influence. Even those church organizations that provide assistance to Afghan refugees maintain a carefully "nonpolitical," noncondemnatory stance, in vivid contrast to their active, outspoken positions concerning Cambodia, South Africa, Central America, and elsewhere. The media have not rushed to the refugee camps to locate and interview survivors or glutted the screen with testimonies of Afghan suffering.

If silence in the face of known genocide is complicity, then today the world and its self-proclaimed moral leadership are accomplice to the destruction of the Afghan people. The facts are available; it cannot be said that events are unknown and unknowable. The four reports of the United Nations Special Rapporteur on Afghanistan are relatively brief and are couched in the most cautious and bloodless diplomatic language, yet they are utterly damning. It is clear that Soviet and DRA action in Afghanistan resemble, equal, and in many cases may outstrip those of the Nazis against the general civilian population* of Europe and the USSR itself in World War II.

The Soviet and DRA response to these and other revelations of genocidal atrocities and even the limited attention given them indicates that international obloquy is a price they are not eager to pay. Not only are these revelations denounced by their diplomats and in their press, but strenuous efforts are made to twist and escape them, even to the point of accusing Afghans in the Resistance of killing their own children for propaganda purposes.[19]   Soviet/DRA sensitivity to this embarrassment to the "national reconciliation" campaign was indicated in early 1987 when the DRA, in an effort to defuse the issue, agreed to permit the International Committee for the Red Cross, forbidden to work in Afghanistan since 1981, to open a small clinic in Kabul. When the U.N. Special Rapporteur was appointed in 1984, the DRA announced that they would not accept his reports, refused to respond to his requests to visit Afghanistan, and subsequently attempted to smear his personal reputation. In 1987, as part of their "national reconciliation" campaign for international acceptance, they suddenly announced that he could visit Kabul. In March 1987 the DRA released the only political prisoner to have gained international attention, Prof. Hasan Kakar.

Clearly, the political results of international awareness of atrocities are potentially damaging. These and other political costs can be significantly raised, if there is a will to do so; and if the international political costs begin to rise and become high enough, then---but only then---a more serious Soviet interest in withdrawal might possibly emerge. But this has not yet happened.

If the Soviet Union is paying a minimal economic and political price, the same is true of its puppet regimes in Kabul. The DRA has not been treated as a pariah state: it boasts of its diplomatic relations with more

---

* Excepting the special cases of Gypsies, the Jewish "final solution" and the death camps.

than eighty countries. Aside from the Islamic conference, where Afghanistan's seat has remained empty since 1980, the DRA has not been ousted from any international organization. Each year the U.N. General Assembly votes to condemn the presence of (unnamed) foreign forces in Afghanistan but representatives of the DRA continue to hold Afghanistan's seat not only in the General Assembly but in all other organs of the United Nations, while representatives of the Resistance have not been permitted to set foot on the grounds of the United Nations.* U.N. Agencies provide assistance and support as usual to the DRA, and in 1986 UNICEF awarded a medal and diploma to the DRA in recognition of its work "in combating illiteracy."[21]

No major nation has embargoed trade with the DRA. Afghan goods---particularly carpets, karakul and dried fruits, but possibly also urea and other products---are sold in Western Europe by the Soviet Union as well as the DRA. Saudi Arabia permits the DRA to display its piety by sending large numbers of Afghans to Mecca for the annual religious pilgrimage although it is known that a high proportion of them are KhAD agents and all are selected and vetted by KhAD.[22] Swiss experts are currently installing a new power-generating system in Kabul that will help relieve DRA dependency on power lines repeatedly destroyed by the Resistance. India, leader of the nonaligned movement and to many a voice of conscience in the world, has consistently refused to condemn the Soviet invasion and has long combined economic aid to the DRA with increasing trade, economic, scientific and technical cooperation, cultural, and other exchanges, now to be expanded.

In 1986 there was an international outcry for sanctions against South Africa, where hundreds, perhaps several thousand, were killed by an oppressive government. There has been no such outcry for sanctions against the DRA, where the number of dead is approaching one million. In fact, when in 1985 the U.S. Congress moved to withdraw "most favored nation" trading status from the DRA, the U.S. State Department objected.

Kabul banks and the Kabul money market are reportedly doing a brisk trade, and turning a brisk profit in hard currency, by handling currency exchanges for citizens of a number of countries. One recent report suggested a turnover of $2 million a day.[23] Much of this comes from handling the

---

* In November 1986, when a leadership group arrived at the U.N. press room for a press conference arranged by the Saudi Arabian delegation---literally the first time Resistance representatives were permitted to step inside the iron fence surrounding U.N. headquarters in New York---they were physically attacked by members of the DRA delegation armed with knives and guns, who subsequently received not even a reprimand from the Secretary General.[20]

transmission and currency exchange transactions for millions of dollars sent home to India by Indian nationals and emigrants living in the United States and Europe.[24] The Kabul bazaars remain awash with Japanese and Western goods, commonplace in most of the world but rare luxuries in the USSR, access to which is one of the inducements for the thousands of Soviet and East European personnel running the puppet regime in Kabul. These goods, and liquor and drugs, are also smuggled into Pakistan and sold there.[25]

The question of Soviet and DRA involvement in the international traffic in Afghan-produced opium, heroin and hashish has been almost entirely ignored, at least publicly. When the question of the drug trade has surfaced at all in the world press, it has almost invariably been couched in terms of possible Resistance involvement.*   No journalists have investigated possible Soviet/DRA involvement, in part perhaps because open sources of information are hard to come by and others are risky to pursue. It is, however, known and confirmed that Soviet/DRA aircraft systematically destroy Afghan grain crops. Obviously, then, they could similarly destroy the highly visible fields of scarlet poppies. The continuing traffic in narcotics of Afghan origin indicates that they do not do so. At least one Western journalist has privately reported seeing Soviet tanks guarding poppy fields.[26] Yet there has been no public comment on the implications of these facts, nor have the media paid attention to available information. A French medical volunteer based in northern Afghanistan between April 1983 and August 1985 reported that the Soviets controlled the opium trade, fixing prices and buying the entire crop, first offering prices which encouraged the local farmers to substitute opium poppies for other crops, then cutting prices by half, thereby leaving the peasants with neither food crops nor the money to buy food.[27]

In June 1986 Dutch police discovered a cache of 220 kilos of heroin with a street value of $13-$20 million secreted in a shipment of Afghan raisins loaded in Riga that arrived in Rotterdam on board a Soviet freighter, the *Kapitan Tonson*.[28]   The incident initially made headlines in northern

---

* While individual Afghans may be involved in drug smuggling, there has been no indication of the involvement of any responsible Resistance leaders or organizations; indeed they have strongly denounced the drug trade. In this connection as in others the penetration and manipulation of the Resistance by Communist agents disguised as mujahideen has gone unexamined (see relevant discussions elsewhere below). Knowledgeable sources indicate that the bulk of the drug trade moves through PLO and related Soviet-connected channels across Baluchistan to the Eastern Mediterranean and thence to Europe.

Europe but suddenly vanished from the news; in the United States it received only a brief mention a year later. (In an apparent move to deflect any potential scandal, the DRA, though making no reference to the Rotterdam incident, announced that a few corrupt individuals in the customs service had been weeded out; but since the incident quickly dropped from public attention, this cover story was never exploited.)

The movement of Afghan heroin and hashish into Pakistan (which has in the last few years experienced a sudden upsurge in addiction despite extensive efforts to eradicate domestic production) has also gone unexamined, but the few reports available suggest that narcotics, along with smuggled liquor, are among the weapons used by the DRA in its campaign to undermine and pressure Pakistan.[29] In the absence of detailed public information, it is impossible to factor into any estimate of Soviet costs in Afghanistan the potentially massive profits that may be coming from the international drug trade, but obviously, given the profit margin, Afghan-produced narcotics could defray a significant percentage of these costs.

Nor have the world media given significant attention to the looting and destruction of art in Afghanistan. Most journalists are unaware of its existence and importance. Yet the objects involved are of the highest merit and international importance, long since identified as major treasures of the world's artistic heritage---for example, the Bagram ivories; the great architectual monuments at Herat (declared a world art city by UNESCO), Ghazni, Ghor, Mazar-i-Sharif and elsewhere; the Alexandrian city excavated by French archeologists near the Oxus River; and numerous Buddhist relics, among many others. Hundreds of unexcavated sites give promise of more treasures to be found in this palimpsest of history.

The Kabul Museum was suddenly dismantled in 1979.[30] Following a brief flurry of international attention, the post-invasion regime announced its restoration with all the collections not only intact but improved but there has been no reliable independent verification of this claim by unconstrained, disinterested sources familiar with the prewar collections.* Informed sources, including Western scholars and observers present in Kabul at the time, suspect that many of the most important objects and rare manuscripts have been secretly transported to the Soviet Union then and since. Certainly there are indications that the spectacular 1978 finds of Bactrian gold and

_____

* All UNESCO experts sent to Afghanistan since 1980 have been Soviet or East bloc nationals.

other objects unearthed by Soviet archeologists working in areas under Soviet/DRA control have been sent to the USSR (aside from the negligible number of minor objects displayed by the DRA as the collection of the Kabul Museum). Recent reports in the French press reinforce these suspicions.

Many of the architectural monuments are believed or known to have been severely damaged.* French and Swedish journalists have brought out photographs and eyewitness reports of damage and destruction of many of the greatest monuments of Herat (located in the outskirts, which are off-limits to journalists officially admitted by the DRA) and it may be that enough evidence will soon exist to make a reliable estimate of these cultural losses.[31] Periodic DRA accusations that art objects have been and are being stolen and smuggled out for sale by the staff of the Kabul Museum and Resistance members and supporters, and that monuments have been attacked by Resistance fire, suggest an attempt to prepare a preemptive ex-planation for major losses. No curators, art historians or scholars have spoken out on this question. In fact, there are indications that some European scholars are actively cooperating with the Soviet officials involved. (See bibliography).

In sum, it can hardly be said that the DRA, let alone the Soviet Union, has paid a significant political price---yet.

Political and economic efforts are of course discussed as additions to, not substitutes for, ongoing military and humanitarian assistance to the Resistance and the Afghan people. Whatever the flaws of the Resistance, only its courageous struggle has prevented the consolidation of Soviet control in Afghanistan and slowed down further Soviet ambitions in the region. The discussion of the military aspects of the issue in later chapters indicates the complexity and sensitivity of the problems involved in providing military aid, and the summary surveys of Soviet/DRA intelligence and penetration efforts suffice to indicate the complicated nature of these problems.

This volume does not include an extended discussion of the indirect negotiations for a "political solution" to the Afghanistan issue---the so-

---

* One site, the Buddhist monuments at Hadda, was apparently destroyed as heathen idols by a Radical Resistance group, the Hezb-i-Islami/Hekhmatyar, and others may have been damaged in the general warfare; but there are reliable reports of major damage by Soviet/DRA longrange artillery and aircraft, and of deliberate Soviet/DRA use of monumental buildings for military purposes.

called proximity talks conducted in Geneva since 1982 under the auspices of the United Nations.* There are several reasons for this omission:

These talks---like many other such efforts, both governmental and private, since 1980---are conducted in secrecy; the details of their content are not available except in unconfirmed rumors. In the absence of specific and accurate information, any detailed discussion would be purely speculation, which this volume tries to avoid. As developments occur, readers can assess them independently on the basis of the data provided in this book and other sources indicated. However, certain aspects of the negotiations which are rarely mentioned in reports and commentary should be called to specific attention:

In Geneva---as in the international responses to the Soviet invasion---the Afghan people are not consulted: officially only the government of Pakistan and the puppet DRA regime are involved in the proximity talks. The representatives of the Afghan people---i.e., the Resistance---are not only excluded from the decision-making process, they are not even officially kept informed of its progress. The United States and the Soviet Union are not formally participants (although Soviet "advisers" are always present in Geneva and, since they are the actual decision-makers, are constantly consulted by their DRA proxies), but they are systematically and officially informed and are frequently consulted by the U.N. negotiatior, Diego Cordovez. So is the government of Iran, which was invited to participate in the talks but has refused to do so until the Resistance is represented. But the Afghan people whose fate is being negotiated are not represented. Nor is this simply due to the lack of agreed representation or Resistance disunity: the inclusion of representatives of the Afghan people---whether the Resistance or the millions of refugees---has never been seriously considered or even acknowledged as a possibility.

In short, the Geneva negotiations on Afghanistan present one of the few precise parallels in recent history to the Munich conference of 1938 in

---

* More specifically, they are conducted by the UN Department of Security Council and Political Affairs, which is headed by Undersecretary-General Vasily S. Safronchuk, a Soviet career diplomat who spent the years 1978-1980 in Kabul as chief Soviet adviser to the new DRA. Safronchuk arrived in Afghanistan shortly after the April 1978 Communist coup to direct the PDPA in the successful installation of a Communist system. While in Kabul he was in effective control of the Afghan foreign ministry. He remained there through the Taraki and Amin regimes and until well after the Soviet invasion and the installation of Babrak Karmal, and he presumably played a part in the preparations for both.[32]

which the representatives of several major powers determined the fate of a small nation without consulting the representatives of that nation.

This is particularly interesting in view of the propaganda value of the Geneva proximity talks to both the Soviet Union and the DRA. Firstly, they are used to legitimize the DRA regime in Kabul. Pakistan specifically refuses to negotiate directly with the DRA because direct talks would imply recognition, thereby necessitating the format of proximity talks facilitated by a U.N. go-between, but neither the Soviets nor the DRA refer to this fact. Instead they imply that the talks are direct and even state that the Geneva talks demonstrate Pakistani recognition of the DRA.

Secondly, and more subtly, neither Soviet nor DRA sources acknowledge that the negotiations have anything to do with any issues *in Afghanistan itself;* in fact, they specifically deny it. Without exception, all Soviet and DRA comments on these and other international efforts specify that they deal with the problems *"surrounding"* Afghanistan,[33] identified as issues whose locus is in Pakistan and Iran, instigated by more distant "imperialist" and "hegemonist" powers (i.e., the United States, China and sometimes also Britain, West Germany, Egypt, and "Zionists").[34] DRA and Soviet sources without exception define the presence of Soviet forces in Afghanistan as an "internal" question to be determined only by the DRA and the Soviet Union bilaterally. The nature of any future government is similarly delimited. Until recently DRA and Soviet statements constantly reiterated "the irreversible nature of the revolution," a phrase softened to "the revolutionary process" when the "national reconciliation" campaign was launched in 1986 (and thereafter soft-pedaled).[35] While Moscow may be prepared to sacrifice Dr. Najibullah (as they did Taraki, Amin and Babrak Karmal), it is quite clear that the PDPA, under Soviet tutelage, is to retain control of any "government of reconciliation" that might be put in place;[36] any non-Communists included would be window-dressing. In this connection it should be noted that the four issues mandated for negotiation by the United Nations General Assembly have now been reduced to only three: a cutoff of all international support for the Resistance, the return of the Afghan refugees, and the withdrawal of Soviet forces. The fourth mandated issue---self-determination for Afghanistan---has been unobtrusively dropped from the agenda.

In assessing the proximity talks, it is also necessary to keep in mind the many issues *not* under discussion in Geneva, including, among others: the dismantling of permanent Soviet military installations in Afghanistan and the return of the annexed Wakhan salient; the permanent withdrawal of the estimated 9,000 Soviet "advisers" who actually direct the ministries, educational institutions and all other agencies of the DRA government, along with their East European and Cuban counterparts; the dismantling of terrorist training centers; the return of thousands of Afghan children transported to the Soviet Union for indoctrination; the ending of extensive Sovietization efforts in all aspects of Afghan society; and the abrogation of hundreds of unequal treaties and agreements between the DRA and the Soviet Union and its satellites (and recently between individual Afghan provinces and individual Soviet republics) which give the Soviet Union, directly and through its satellites, effective control over Afghan police and military, press, broadcasting, education, films and cultural institutions, economic development, natural resource exploitation, trade, and, in sum, the whole of Afghan society and its future development. Also omitted from discussion is the Soviet-Afghan Friendship Treaty of 1978, one clause of which would enable a legitimized DRA (as a recognized sovereign state) to invite the return of Soviet forces and agree to Soviet bases in Afghanistan, this time in tidy conformity with diplomatic niceties, thereby forestalling any international response.

In short, the negotiations, as presently structured, could be reasonably interpreted as a discussion of arrangements for the Soviet control of Afghanistan without the active use of Soviet military forces and in a manner satisfactory to international public opinion. While other interpretations can and surely will be argued, they will have to take into account and explain Soviet and DRA actions and not only rhetoric, gestures and declarations of intent if they are to be argued seriously. Such official Soviet pronouncements as Mr. Gorbachev's recent statement[37] that the Soviet Union would not insist on continued political influence over the Afghan government, that the PDPA "national reconciliation program" and "government of reconciliation" could be neutral, and that "the Soviet Union does not and will not interfere" should be evaluated in the light of the verifiable data in the chapters that follow, not least that on Sovietization.

Those who would put their faith in a future coalition "government of reconciliation" should be prepared to specify means by which a repetition of the experience of Czechoslovakia can be prevented, particularly in view of Dr. Najib's statement to the PDPA Central Committee on 30 December 1986, in which he said, "...the aims of reconciliation...are, most importantly, peace and security, the future development of the gains of the revolution, the complete implementation of the PDPA Action Program...and the consolidation of a regime friendly with the Soviet Union,"[38] and Prime Minister Keshtmand's statement in Moscow in February 1987 that any coalition government would have policies similar to the present regime and that "Life itself bears out the irreversible character of the revolutionary process in Afghanistan."[39]

Having taken advantage of the editor's prerogative to editorialize---a privilege denied to other contributors to this volume---it is necessary to recognize that other analysts may disagree significantly with these conclusions---and others which are inferred from the data that follows and additional sources. They are invited to do so---but, that said, it should be added that in order to be persuasive they will have to come up with a coherent body of facts pointing systematically in directions significantly different from those indicated by the mass of reliable information which is now available and which is summarized in the following chapters.

Notes

1. Abdur Rahman Khan, *The Life of Abdur Rahman, Amir of Afghanistan,* 2 Vols. Ed. by Sultan Mohammed Khan, (London: John Murray, 1900)

2. "Geneve accueille çe week-end un colloque sur le sort des refugies afghans," *Tribune de Geneve* (Geneva, Switzerland, 3 November 1983); also Babrak Karmal interview, *Al-Ahali* (Cairo, 15 January [FBIS *South Asia* 23 January] 1986).

3. Conversation with the author.

4. Anthony Arnold, *Afghanistan's Two-Party Communism* (Stanford: Hoover Institution Press, 1983): 99.

5. See, for example: George F. Kennan, "Is mature statemanship shown in Afghan crisis?" *Sentinal Star* (Orlando, Florida, 17 February 1980); Selig Harrison, "Did Moscow fear another Tito?" *New York Times* (13 January 1980); Harrison, "The Shah, not the Kremlin, touched off Afghan coup," *Washington Post* (13 May 1979); Ralph S. Clem, "Moscow's stake in Afghanistan," *New York Times* [letter] (29 August 1979); Abel Baker (pseud.), "A needed White Paper," *New York Times* (22 June 1980); John Sommerville, "The truth about the Afghanistan crisis," *New York Times Week in Review* [advertisement] (10 August 1980); Fred Halliday, *Soviet Policy in the Arc of Crisis,* (Washington, D.C.: Institute for Policy Studies); Halliday, "Wrong moves on Afghanistan," *The Nation* (26 January 1980); I. F. Stone, "Reaping invasion's rewards," *New York Times* (24 February 1980); Leslie H. Gelb, "An Afghan-Polish scenario," *The News* (New York, 13 September 1980); *The Defense Monitor* (Washington, D.C.: Center for Defense Information, January 1980); and additional editorials, analyses and commentary by these and others.

6. Washington Times News Service, 5 December 1986. Gankovsky later denied making these statements but according to the news service, the interview was taped and is verifiable. Also: Richard Ehrlich, *Pakistan Times* (11 December 1986), in FBIS *South Asia* (19 December 1986): F1.

7. Speech at the 15th PDPA Plenum, 19 March 1985 (FBIS *South Asia* 3 April 1985: C3). Reproaching his audience for lack of sufficient political zeal and devotion, Babrak said, "Unfortunately we see in practice serious and crude deviations from the high principle of our party and revolutionary sovereignty... I would like to cite a specific case in this regard. The majority of workers engaged in the work of extraction and tunneling for gas in Jowzjan Province live underground; they have no suitable clothes or shoes for work, and no beds to sleep on; their food is inadequate and they lack health care...Unfortunately such examples exist in other ministries too."

8. Personal communication to the author.

9. Richard M. Weintraub, "Sen. Humphrey visits Moscow, Kabul," *Washington Post* (15 April 1987). Sen. Humphrey stated that he "saw no indication that the Kremlin is worried about its position in Afghanistan."

10. FBIS *South Asia Report* (8 November 1983): F2.

11. See, inter alia: "Dobrynin said to assure pullout," *New York Times* (31 January 1980); "Soviets hint at readiness to leave Afghanistan," *Washington Post* (28 February 1980); "Armand Hammer sees Brezhnev, affirms Afghan Bid," *New York Times* (28 February 1980); Andrew Young, "Afghanistan: Do the Soviets want out?" *Washington Post* (6 July 1980).

12. James S. Newton, "Russian faults Afghan invasion," *New York Times* (3 March 1987).

13. *Krasnaya Zveada* (5 September 1985); quoted in Radio Liberty Research RL 306/85 (11 September 1985): 2.

14. *Pravda* (10 October 1986), cited in *Soviet Muslims Brief*, vol. 2, no. 4 (November-December 1986).

15. Jeri Laber and Barnett R. Rubin, *Tears, Blood and Cries* (New York: Helsinki Watch, 1984): 186.

16. Personal observations of the author, as well as communications from individuals who have tried to set up fundraising events in Europe and the U.S.

17. Conversation with the author.

18. Personal communications to the author by observers present for the debates and votes.

19. FBIS *Soviet Union* (6 January 1987): "Washington Post resorts to forgery," *Izvestia* (Moscow, 30 December 1986): 4.

20. The incident was widely reported. The presence of weapons was confirmed to the author by an employee of a U.N. delegation who was present, glimpsed the weapons and helped disarm the attackers.

21. Kabul Radio Domestic Service (7 October 1986) [FBIS South Asia (10 October 1986): C3.]

22. Personal communication from Col. Mohammed Ayub Asil of NIFA, a former police official working under cover for the Resistance who was assigned by the DRA in 1982 to escort several hundred pilgrims to Mecca. Also: Col. Asil's public testimony at the Oslo Hearings on Afghanistan, March 1983, and interviews and public statements in Europe and the United States in April 1983.

23. Steven R. Weisman, "Afghans mix 'Sovietization' and free market," *New York Times* (15 May 1987).

24. Personal communication from former Afghan businessman with banking connections.

25. Faiz M. Khairzada, "Western goods a Soviet weapon in Southwest Asia," *Wall Street Journal* (19 January 1984).

26. Personal communication to the author.

27. Ann-Marie Le Magorou, "Deux ans dans les vallées du Badakhchan," *Les Nouvelles d'Afghanistan* (No. 29/30, October 1986): 22. Mlle. Le Magorou was in Badakhshan for Médecins Sans Frontières.

28. Colin Smith, "Heroin: The Red Route," *The Observer* (London, 24 August 1986); "World News" column *Financial Times* (18 August 1986); "Sowjets an Heroin-Schumuggel beteiligt," *Die Welt* (19 August 1986).

29. Khairzada, op. cit.

30. Rosanne Klass, "Missing in action: treasures of Afghanistan," *Asia* (March-April, 1981): 27 ff.

31. "La destruction des monuments d'Hérat" and "L'UNESCO détournée," Les Nouvelles d'Afghanistan (No. 31, Paris, December 1986): 11-15. Maps, photographs of destruction, and a detailed report with bibliography.

32. See: Henry S. Bradsher, *Afghanistan and the Soviet Union* (Durham: Duke University Press, 2d ed., 1985); also Arnold, op. cit.

33. See numerous DRA publications; also DRA and Soviet statements, numerous FBIS reports, South Asia and Soviet Union editions, 1980 to date.

34. Ibid.

35. Ibid.

36. Ibid.

37. Interview with *L'Unita*, Rome, quoted in the *New York Times* (21 May 1987).

38. FBIS *South Asia* (2 January 1987): C1.

39. United Press International (19 February 1987), quoting Tass. Also, FBIS Soviet Union (20 February 1987): D6-7. For an attempt to rationalize such a position, see: Selig Harrison, "A route out of Afghanistan," *New York Times* (20 May 1987). Under the Law on Political Parties promulgated in July 1987, no political party other than the PDPA can be established without the advance approval of the Presidium of the Revolutionary Council. In order to apply for such permission, the would-be party must submit the names of its members and its sources of financing. See Press Release No. 09/87, *Law on Political Parties in the DRA*, Permanent Mission of the Democratic Republic of Afghanistan to the United Nations.

A Soviet Ambassador in Kabul Writes Us a Letter--- Sixty Years Ago?...Or Today?*

MEMBERS OF the Afghan Resistance with access to Afghan Government archives have been distributing around Kabul a most interesting Soviet document, and have just [1981] sent us a copy. This is an official letter sent almost sixty years ago by [Soviet] Ambassador Roskolnikov to the Afghan Ministry of Foreign Affairs, on February 20th, 1922 (Official Soviet Document no. 165). The Ambassador had sent this letter in reply to the Afghan Government's protest over the entry of Soviet troops into the two small independent Muslim states of Khiva and Bukhara, in Central Asia.

Raskolnikov's letter sounds almost word for word like some of Mr. Brezhnev's latest declarations concerning the presence of Soviet troops in Afghanistan.† After nearly sixty years, we should note, Soviet troops still occupy Khiva and Bukhara, which were dissolved as national entities and officially annexed to the USSR in 1924. (Their territories were partitioned between the present Soviet Socialist "Republics" of Uzbekistan, Turkmenistan and Tajikistan.) The Russian Ambassador wrote:

> Concerning the question of the independent status of Khiva and Bukhara, this has been provided for in the treaty agreed to and signed by the two Governments of Russia and Afghanistan. The Government which I represent has always recognized and respected

---

* From *Afghan Realities*, No. 3 (Paris, August-September 1981).
† This applies equally to subsequent statements by Messrs. Andropov, Chernenko, and Gorbachev, including the latter's remarks at Vladivostok in 1986, as well as to almost every statement made by any DRA official since 1980. Even a cursory review of press reports of their ongoing statements regarding Afghanistan reveals their consistency. -ed.

the independence of the two Governments of Khiva and Bukhara. The presence of a limited contingent of troops belonging to my Government is due to temporary requirements expressed and made known to us by the Bukharan Government. This arrangement has been agreed to with the provision that whenever the Bukharan Government so requests, not a single Russian soldier will remain on Bukharan soil. The extension of our friendly assistance in no way constitutes an interference against the independence of the sovereign State of Bukhara. If the Government of Bukhara should cease to formulate its request and should prove dissatisfied with the continuation of such brotherly assistance, then the Government I represent shall most immediately withdraw its troops.[1]

A few historical notes may clarify the matter for the reader:

When Tsarist Russia in 1868 conquered the ancient civilized Muslim lands of Central Asia, it directly annexed large portions of territory, but allowed two Emirates to survive as protectorates: these were the kingdoms of Khiva and Bukhara, famous for centuries as hearths of Islamic culture. In the years 1868-1917, a powerful nationalist and reform-minded movement gripped Central Asian Muslim intellectuals, both in the annexed territories and in the "protected" Emirates: these intellectuals, who called themselves *Jadid* or "Renewed," agitated against Russian rule but also criticized the Emirs for their perceived subservience to Russian interests. Because of common hatred for the Tsar, Muslim *Jadids* came to forge ties with numerous Russian revolutionaries.

The Bolshevik Revolution of 1917 aroused great hopes among the Muslim population of Russian or "protected" Central Asia. Colonized Muslims were convinced that the new regime would grant them full independence. Lenin multiplied assurances to this effect; thus, on 24 November 1917, the Soviet government issued the following proclamation to the Empire's Muslims: "Your beliefs and customs, your national and cultural institutions are henceforth free and not to be violated. You may freely and without hindrance organize your national life."

At the same time, the USSR supported the Afghan struggle for independence against Great Britain: In a letter to King Amanullah of Afghanistan dated 27 November 1919, Lenin discussed the possibility of joint Russian and Afghan action against the British in India: "Your country is the only independent Muslim state in the world, and fate sends the Afghan people the great historic task of uniting about itself all enslaved Muslim people and leading them on the road to freedom and independence." Afghanistan had established diplomatic relations with the USSR on 7 April

1919, and signed treaties of friendship in September 1920 and August 1921. The text of the treaties, however, stipulated that the Soviet Union pledged itself to recognize the independence of Khiva and Bukhara.

The development of events in Russian Central Asia was indeed beginning to worry the Afghans, who share close religious, cultural and often linguistic ties with the Muslims on the other side of the Amu Darya [Oxus River]. Indeed many Central Asian intellectuals of the *Jadid* movement had been directly influenced before the 1917 Revolution by ideas found in Afghan newspapers such as Mahmud Tarzi's *Seraj-ol-Akhbar*. It is not entirely surprising if, in the very beginning, Afghan officials entertained the same illusions about the new Soviet regime's ultimate intentions as did many of the Central Asia *Jadid* intellectuals themselves. But Soviet determination to maintain Muslim Central Asians under Russian domination came quickly and brutally to light.

In November 1917, in the portion of Central Asia which had been directly annexed to Russia under the Tsar, a Muslim People's Council convened in the city of Kokand and proclaimed the autonomy of the region. In January 1918, having qualified this demand as "bourgeois" and "anti-proletarian," the Soviets occupied Kokand and massacred its people. (Statistical evidence indicates that roughly half of the city's population was killed.) The repression provoked a guerrilla uprising against the new regime on the part of numerous Muslim peasants (derisively referred to in Russian historiography as *basmachi*---"bandits").

Nevertheless, many intellectuals of the *Jadid* movement remained convinced of the necessity of temporary cooperation with the Bolsheviks; in exchange for their mass adherence to the Soviet Communist Party, notably at the Baku Congress of September 1920, the *Jadids* demanded national independence and the retention of Islam for its moral and cultural values; one of the movement's main theoreticians, the Tatar Sultan Galiev (Sultan Ali), argued that the Muslim peoples as a whole constituted an exploited class.

Thanks to the involuntary assistance of these *Jadids,* now more or less provisionally turned Communists, the Soviets were able to liquidate Central Asian national resistance. In 1917, the former protectorates of Khiva and Bukhara had claimed full independence and even repulsed a Soviet offensive launched from Tashkent in March 1918. The Russians then decided to support local factions of the *Jadid* movement, the "Young Khivans" and "Young Bukharans," who were in political opposition to the Emirs. On 1 February 1919, Soviet troops invaded Khiva and installed the "Young Khivans" in power; Lenin solemnly proclaimed Khiva to be an independent State, but did not withdraw the Red Army.

In Bukhara, the "Young Bukharans" indicated their opposition to the idea of a Soviet invasion of the Emirate. But when Soviet troops invaded Bukhara in the Autumn of 1920 and put the Emir to flight, the "Young Bukharans" made the fateful decision of agreeing to form a new government, in the hope of preserving a measure of political autonomy. As in the case of Khiva, the Soviet Union formally recognized the full sovereignty of the Bukharan State---without, however, withdrawing its troops.

As indicated above, the USSR pledged to respect the independence of Khiva and Bukhara in treaties signed with Afghanistan in September 1920 and August 1921, while the Russian Ambassador's letter dated 20 November 1922, promised the withdrawal of Soviet troops. But in 1924, the USSR annexed Khiva and Bukhara; their languages---Turkish and Persian---were abolished, and were replaced by pseudo-languages fabricated by Soviet linguists: i.e., "Uzbek" and "Tadzhik," which were merely local dialects of Turkish and Persian transcribed into Latin and later Cyrillic script. Mosques were closed or changed into museums, and Koranic education was abolished. (As of 1981, only two *madrasas* or Koranic seminaries were allowed to function to serve the needs of more than 40 million Soviet Muslims.) Soviet insistence on cotton production at the expense of food crops in Central Asia caused malnutrition in the region in the 1930s, but Uzbek and Tajik peasants who protested that they couldn't eat cotton were shot.

And finally, between 1918 and 1939, virtually all surviving members of the *Jadid*, young Khivan, and Young Bukharan movements, having served their purpose, were executed---on charges of "bourgeois nationalist deviationism"---and were replaced by young bureaucrats trained in new Soviet schools.

Notes

1. Cf., "In the circumstances, we were compelled to render military aid requested by a friendly country...As for the limited Soviet military contingent, we will be prepared to withdraw it with the agreement of the Afghan Government." (Report of the Central Committee, 26th Congress of the Communist Party of the Soviet Union, 1981.) The terms "limited military contingent" and "brotherly assistance" ("of the great Soviet Union") are repeated endlessly in almost every speech by officials of the Kabul regime, and in most statements by Soviet officials referring to Afghanistan.

2. From 1879 until the brief third Anglo-Afghan war of May 1919, Afghanistan's foreign relations were conducted through the Viceroy of India, although in other respects the country was independent. See Poullada.

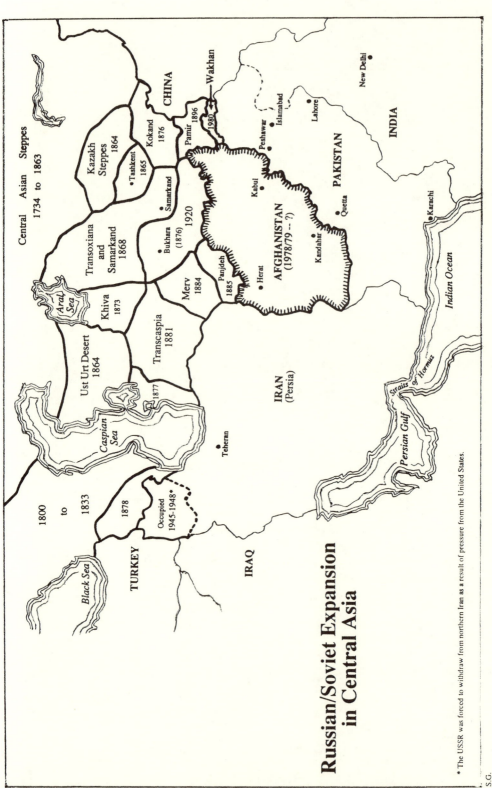

Russian/Soviet Expansion in Central Asia

Central Asian Steppes 1734 to 1863

CHINA

Kazakh Steppes 1864

Kokand 1876

Tashkent 1865

Pamir 1896

1980 → Wakhan

New Delhi

Islamabad

Lahore

Peshawar

INDIA

PAKISTAN

Transoxiana and Samarkand 1868

Samarkand 1920

Bukhara (1876)

Kabul

Quetta

Aral Sea

Khiva 1873

Merv 1884

Panjdeh 1885

Herat

AFGHANISTAN (1978/79 -- ?)

Kandahar

Ust Urt Desert 1864

Transcaspia 1881

1877

Karachi

Caspian Sea

IRAN (Persia)

Teheran

Straits of Hormuz

Persian Gulf

Indian Ocean

1800 to 1833

1878

Occupied 1945-1948*

Black Sea

TURKEY

IRAQ

* The USSR was forced to withdraw from northern Iran as a result of pressure from the United States.

S.G.

When you get home tell them in Washington, they're always too late."
---Afghan official in conversation with the editor, Kabul, 1966

The Road to Crisis 1919-1980---American Failures, Afghan Errors and Soviet Successes

Leon B. Poullada

The Russian policy of aggression is slow and steady but firm and unchangeable...Their habit of forward movement resembles the habit of the elephant, who examines a spot thoroughly before he places his foot upon it and when he once puts his weight there is no going back and no taking another step in a hurry until he has put his full weight on the first foot and smashed everything that lies under it.[1]

--Abdur Rahman, Amir of Afghanistan, 1880-1901

THE SEIZURE of Afghanistan represents, in one audacious but carefully planned act of rapine, the long-sought Russian breakthrough of the great Hindu Kush mountain barrier to South Asia and the advance of the Soviet Union's strategic power to within 500 miles of the Persian Gulf and the Straits of Hormuz. If the Soviets succeed in consolidating Afghanistan as a forward base, they can intimidate the entire region and blackmail Japan and the Western alliance, which cannot long survive the pressure from a superpower with geopolitical ambitions that controls its essential oil supplies.

In short, the Soviet presence in Afghanistan has completely altered the geostrategic balance of power in an area which has been, for many centuries, the gateway to the Indian subcontinent and the Middle East.

Some analysts try to explain the Soviet action without looking beyond the 1970s, even dismissing earlier history as irrelevant. Some suggest that it was merely a fulfillment of the Brezhnev Doctrine, a move to protect a crumbling Communist regime. Others, confusing Afghanistan with Iran,

try to explain it as a defensive move against a putative Islamic fundamentalist penetration of Moscow's own Muslim republics. Those who most
insistently ignore history suggest that the invasion was an unplanned
reaction to circumstances, an aberration of Soviet policy. Since it is
impossible to examine the inside of the little black box of Soviet
intentions, these speculations are futile. The fact is that the Soviets are
now in Afghanistan and that their presence there puts them in a position to
exploit a wide range of alternative options from political subversion to
military occupation of countries beyond Afghanistan.

In order to understand Soviet maneuvers and successes in Afghanistan,
we must consider simultaneously the failures of American diplomacy there
because the two are inversely related: the successes of one were the failures
of the other. This essay is a comparative case study of Soviet and American
diplomacy in Afghanistan, starting with the first official American contacts
in the 1920s.

Historical background

Russia has had designs on Afghanistan for many years; the invasion was
a logical extension of Russia's ancient claims to a "manifest destiny" which
have for centuries impelled it toward the Indian Ocean and more recently
toward the oil resources of the Persian Gulf.

During the nineteenth century Tsarist armies spread south from their
major military bases in Orenburg in the Urals, cut through the Kazakh
steppes, and swallowed, one after the other, the independent Muslim
kingdoms of Central Asia. By the 1870s they were probing the then-ill-
defined borders of Afghanistan but were halted temporarily by countervailing
British power. In 1879 Britain, after two unsuccessful invasions of
Afghanistan, made the country a *de facto* protectorate as a buffer for the
defense of India.

In the 1880s the Russians continued their expansion, moving into Merv
and seizing the Afghan territory of Panjdeh; but the Afghan Amir Abdur
Rahman, with British support, managed to delimit the borders of
Afghanistan (including the troublesome Durand Line separating Afghanistan
from British India) and thus checked further Russian nibbling at Afghan
territory for the remainder of the century.

The Russians waited, consolidating their conquests as a base for the next
step in confirmation of Abdur Rahman's pachydermal analogy. Their next
opportunity came in 1919, when a change of government in Afghanistan
brought to power the reformer King Amanullah. Amanullah had strong anti-
British sentiments and a frantic desire to modernize his country. The
Soviets, picking up where the Tsars had left off, lured him with offers of

economic and military aid as well as political support in his quarrels with Britain,[2] thereby gaining a substantial, if temporary, foothold. In Afghanistan in collusion with Amanullah they organized Indian revolutionaries, operating from Kabul, to stir up trouble in British India, and infiltrated agents into the tribal areas to foster revolts along the Indian border (now Pakistan's Northwest Frontier Province and Baluchistan).[3] Their activities were checked by the strong British presence and by the tribal revolt that overthrew Amanullah in 1929 and drove him into exile in Italy.

But, demonstrably, the Russian/Soviet drive to the south was only dormant. It was revived in 1953 when the rise to power in Afghanistan of Mohammed Daoud presented new opportunities. A careful study of history from that period to the present reveals that the 1979 Soviet invasion, far from being a casual, random or defensive move, was the culmination of a calculated process which has, thus far at least, involved five stages:

Stage 1: (1953*---1963) The establishment of a subversive infrastructure inside Afghanistan, especially during Daoud's first period of power.

Stage 2: (1963---1973) The formation of a secret communist party and the subversion and destruction of nascent Afghan democratic institutions.

Stage 3: (1973---1978) The return of Daoud to power with Communist support in order to destroy the Afghan monarchy and as a figurehead for behind-the-scenes Soviet control via his Afghan Communist supporters.

(The activation of the next well-planned stages was probably optional, as needed).

Stage 4: (1978---1979) The overthrow of Daoud when he was no longer useful and the installation of an openly Communist government completely subservient to Moscow.

Stage 5: (1979 to the present)---When Stage Four proved inadequate, the physical invasion, installation of totally controlled puppets and absorption of Afghanistan into the Soviet bloc.

At each of these stages American diplomacy had opportunities to foil the Soviet plan but did not use them effectively.

Early American mistakes

During Amanullah's reign the United States had its first official contacts with Afghanistan. From the beginning, American diplomacy was shortsighted. In 1919, after initiating a short war with British India, Amanullah recaptured the right to conduct his own foreign relations, a British prerogative since 1879. (Afghans consider the day of the signing of the 1919 treaty their Day of Independence.) Amanullah sent an official

---

* Or even much earlier; see: Bodansky, also Noorzoy.

mission to secure recognition of his newly-won independence from a number of countries. The mission was given a warm welcome by the new Bolshevik regime, and the USSR, by its prompt action, became the first nation to recognize Afghan independence. This made a strong favorable impression on Amanullah and laid the groundwork for the close Soviet-Afghan collaboration during his ten-year reign.

In contrast, the United States snubbed the mission: President Harding, at first reluctant even to receive it, did so only after consulting the British; he conveyed a deliberately deceptive and ambiguous reply to the request for recognition, deeply offending the Afghans.[4]

In 1922, Cornelius Van H. Engert, an American diplomat stationed in Persia, made an unofficial visit to Amanullah's court and was accorded a friendly welcome as the first American official to visit Afghanistan. He wrote a detailed report to the State Department, strongly recommending recognition of Afghanistan. It was filed away and ignored.[5]

After Amanullah's overthrow in 1929, Soviet moves were held in abeyance by his pro-British successor, Nadir Shah, and, after Nadir's assassination in 1933, by his brothers who, as prime ministers, effectively ruled during the first twenty years of the reign of his youthful son, Zahir Shah. From 1933 to 1953 the Afghan government was consistently conservative and pro-West.

Nevertheless, the United States withheld recognition until 1934, a dozen years after Engert's recommendation; even then, State Department officials in charge of Afghan affairs, whose ignorance about Afghanistan was abysmal, persisted in dealing with Afghanistan as an extension of British India. Wallace Murray, the leading "expert" during much of this period, assured an American Congressman that the United States could not extend recognition to Afghanistan because "Afghanistan is doubtless the most fanatic hostile country in the world today."[6] This attitude prevented the U.S. government from opening a diplomatic mission in Kabul until 1942; even then, it was done only as a wartime measure to prepare the way for possible transit of Lend-Lease supplies to the Soviet Union.[7]

Nevertheless, Afghan relations with the United States became very cordial during the war when Engert, who had returned to Kabul as the first American resident representative, mounted a rescue operation to prevent the collapse of the Afghan economy. Landlocked, neutral Afghanistan had been unable to export its commodities or import essential goods such as medicines, spare parts, tires and petroleum products because the Allies would not allocate priorities or shipping space. Minister Engert and his British colleague together battled the wartime Allied bureaucracy and eventually succeeded in alleviating the distress of the Afghan people.[8] As a result of the goodwill generated during this period, the immediate postwar years presented a great opportunity for the United States to cement close relations with Afghanistan---an opportunity that was wasted through ignorance, apathy, and bumbling diplomacy.

During this period top Afghan officials time and again offered full Afghan cooperation and friendship. They wanted to modernize their country in a gradual, conservative way---principally through foreign investment and domestic private enterprise---and to strengthen their foreign defense and internal security. Their top choice to provide the counsel and aid they needed was the United States. Consequently they invited American companies to do business in Afghanistan, offering oil exploration concessions, aviation development rights, and other investment opportunities. To prove their sincerity they used their own meagre resources to employ American teachers for the best Kabul schools and contracted with the Morrison-Knudsen Construction Company of Boise, Idaho, to develop a large multi-purpose irrigation project in the Helmand Valley.

American officialdom was indifferent to these friendly Afghan overtures. In 1949, Afghan Minister of National Economy Abdul Majid Zabuli was sent to Washington to obtain a loan for a modest, well-conceived, integrated economic development plan. He was shunted by the State Department to the Export-Import Bank. National economic planning had not yet become popular: the Ex-Im Bank completely failed to understand the sophistication of the Majid plan and offered instead to finance new contracts for Morrison-Knudsen (which had domestic American political clout). Majid protested that so much investment in longterm irrigation projects would result in un-balanced development and would cause serious problems. Indeed, he wanted to refuse the loan; but his superiors overruled him because they wanted to establish close economic relations with the United States for political reasons. During a conversation with President Truman, Afghan Prime Minister Shah Mahmud noted: "The Afghan government tends to think of the loan as of political as well as of economic importance, possibly increasingly so in the light of Soviet interest and offers of assistance to Afghanistan."[9]

Majid ultimately resigned. His predictions proved true: The Helmand was for many years a white elephant and a constant source of friction in Afghan-American relations. By rejecting the broad economic role in the future of Afghanistan which the Afghans had offered, American diplomacy frittered away an important political asset and opened the way for the Soviet economic offensive of the 1950s.

Even more disappointing to Afghan leaders was the American rejection of requests for military aid. Shortly after World War II, internal security in Afghanistan became more fragile, in part because of the fractious tribes.

The military weakness of the central government hampered orderly political and economic development. It also invited Soviet pressure.

The condition of the Afghan armed forces at this time was pitiful: they consisted mostly of tribal levies owing primary allegiance to their kinsmen rather than to the government. Clad in ragged, ill-fitting uniforms and armed with a motley variety of antiquated weapons, they were a ridiculous caricature of a defense force.[10] Afghan leaders wanted to create a loyal, well-trained and equipped gendarmerie. They offered to *buy* surplus American military equipment in India. American officials demurred and delayed, finding many bureaucratic reasons why such sales could not be approved: Afghanistan had not been an ally during the war; legislation did not authorize such sales; the U.S. was opposed in principle to the sale of arms; and so forth. In the end the Afghans gave up and bought Czech arms. Once again American short-sighted obstructionism wasted an opportunity to gain Afghan friendship.

Still, the Afghans did not give up. All during the 1940s and early 1950s Afghan officials repeatedly approached Americans at all levels---from the military attaché in Kabul to the president in Washington---and persisted in requests for a military relationship with the United States. They did not ask for handouts. They were willing to use their meager foreign exchange to pay for arms and training. In December 1948 Abdul Majid Zabuli told American officials in Washington that his government feared a Soviet attack now that the British were withdrawing from India, and repeated that his country needed weapons to defend its territory and maintain internal security against tribal insurrections.[11]

These urgent Afghan requests were parried with more American bureaucratic evasiveness, and the Afghans lacked sophistication about ways to steer through the labyrinthine channels of the American decision-making process. By the mid-1950s a more powerful obstacle had emerged: the strong objections of Pakistan, our new ally, to military aid for Afghanistan, with whom strained relations had developed over the issue of "Pushtunistan."

This vexing problem involving the status of the Pushtuns,* a large, tribal ethnic group that straddles the Pakistan-Afghanistan border, is extremely complex, with ramifications rooted in history and in the dynamics of internal Afghan politics. Long dormant, it reemerged when Britain's withdrawal from the sub-continent created the states of India and Pakistan.[12]

To Pakistani and American officials the issue was deceptively simple: a matter of Afghan irredentism and territorial ambitions. American diplomats found the constant harping of Afghan officials obscure and annoying. To

---

* Also known as Pukhtuns or Pathans. See Barth and Glossary.

them the problem was a bore and it did not seem worth the effort to study and understand its complexities. The Pakistani position was easy to understand and support. Moreover, the United States, entering the era of Dulles' "pactomania," was courting Pakistan to join military alliances such as CENTO and SEATO, the so-called Northern Tier of defense against the USSR.

In October 1954, the new Afghan prime minister, Prince Mohammed Daoud, sent his brother, Foreign Minister Mohammed Naim, to Secretary of State Dulles to make a final appeal for military aid. In December, Dulles replied: "After careful consideration, extending military aid to Afghanistan would create problems not offset by the strength it would generate. Instead of asking for arms, Afghanistan should settle the Pushtunistan dispute with Pakistan."[13]   To underline what "problems" Dulles had in mind, he sent a copy of his reply to the Pakistan government.

The Afghans were outraged by this flagrant breach of confidence and diplomatic practice. *Just one month later,* in January 1955, Daoud accepted the long-standing Soviet offer of military aid, which Afghanistan had previously rejected.   That same year, 1955, the Pushtunistan dispute brought Pakistan and Afghanistan to the edge of war and Afghanistan's highest political authority, the *Loya Jirga* (Great Tribal Council), approved Daoud's acceptance of Soviet military aid; and in December, Bulganin and Khrushchev visited Afghanistan, offering to support Pushtunistan and to re-equip the Afghan army and air force.

American failure between 1946 and 1954 to respond to the genuine economic and security needs of a friendly and pro-Western Afghanistan and to understand the internal Afghan political imperatives of the Pushtunistan problem, had set the stage for the successful Soviet penetration of Afghanistan.

The first Daoud period

Meanwhile, in 1953, seven factors coalesced to precipitate a Soviet diplomatic offensive in Afghanistan of unprecedented scope and intensity:[14]

1. The King's cousin, General Mohammed Daud---an imperious, ego-centric, autocratic, relatively young (44) Pushtun nationalist prince---came to power as prime minister through a palace coup, replacing the conservative, pro-Western and sagacious rule of the King's uncles. Daud wanted to modernize rapidly, and to win the Pushtunistan dispute with Pakistan.

2. The death of Stalin brought to power in the USSR the new Khrushchev regime, which was prepared, as Stalin had not been, to use economic and military aid to penetrate Third World countries.

3. Inside Afghanistan, the number of foreign-trained, dissatisfied

intellectuals eager to support radical changes to achieve development reached a critical mass.

4. Because of Pushtunistan, Afghanistan had voted against Pakistan's admission to the United Nations in 1947. Pakistan retaliated by a series of blockades and slow-downs of goods in transit to landlocked Afghanistan. Daoud, an army general and former defense minister, bitterly resented the cut-off of petroleum products which immobilized the Afghan army.

5. In the United States, Eisenhower became president, and Truman's Point Four Doctrine of combatting communism through economic assistance to poor countries was transformed into the Kennan/Dulles doctrine of containment and cold war.

6. The American embassy in Kabul could not cope with the new challenges presented by the Daoud regime. There were personal animosities between Ambassador Angus Ward and Prime Minister Daoud. The U.S. Foreign Service had been emasculated by congressional economies and Senator Joseph McCarthy's attacks on its loyalty; in any case it was essentially Europe-oriented and ill-equipped to deal with new problems of remote Third World countries. In the Kabul embassy there was not a single officer who had an adequate background on Afghan affairs and only one who could do more than mumble a few words of bazaar Farsi.[15]

7. Washington's assessment of the strategic importance of Afghanistan was totally inadequate.

The coincidence and interplay of these seven factors made the Daoud régime ripe for Soviet exploitation. They gave Soviet diplomacy the opportunity to apply its technique of using regional disputes to its advantage. The Soviets made brilliant use of the Pakistani-Afghan dispute to drive a wedge between Pakistan, Afghanistan and the United States.[16] By supporting the Afghan case on Pushtunistan and catering to Daud's obsessive drive for hasty economic development and increased military power, the USSR insinuated itself into a preponderant position in Afghanistan.

The Soviet program

The Soviet aid program in Afghanistan was the first such Soviet program in the Third World. It has been described in detail in other places.[17] What should be noted here is that Soviet diplomacy was designed so that each aid project achieved some specific political and/or strategic objective.* For example:

1. To gain maximum psychological advantage, certain project offers

---

* See: Noorzoy.

were timed to coincide with moments of maximum pressure and distress felt by Afghans in their quarrel with Pakistan:
• Coinciding with Pakistani blockades, Moscow
---offered free transit through the USSR
---airlifted perishable exports
---constructed gasoline and grain storage facilities for the blockaded Afghans.
• Coinciding with the 1955 "flag incident," which almost led to war between Pakistan and Afghanistan , Moscow
---offered political support for Pushtunistan
---offered extensively military aid.

2. Soviet programs (usually undertaken in Kabul, where they achieved maximum visibility) were devised to win the gratitude of the Afghan public and impress them with Soviet benevolence, so as to lull them into a false sense of security and overcome deep-rooted Afghan suspicion of the Russians:
• The Soviets provided the machinery and materials for paving the streets of Kabul.
• They gave attention to people-oriented projects like grain silos, a bakery, and housing projects.
• They donated a 100-bed hospital.
• Soviet propaganda, representing the USSR as the champion of anticolonialism and the friend of developing nations, used Afghanistan as a prime example of disinterested benevolence.
• The Soviets flattered the Afghan leaders and the public, making them feel important, through state visits of top Russian leaders such as Bulganin and Khrushchev, who stayed several days. Afghan leaders were given special treatment in Moscow and busy Soviet officials found time to discuss Afghan problems in detail. In contrast, Eisenhower managed to spare only a few hours for Kabul on his way to somewhere else.
• Afghan leaders visiting Moscow always came back with gifts. In August 1957, for example, King Zahir was given an interest-free $15 million loan.

3. Aid offers were aimed at increasing Soviet potential for political leverage:
• Army and air force officers were trained in the USSR.
• Extensive scholarships and technical training programs were set up for civilians in the USSR.
• Campaigns of cultural and propaganda events were lavishly financed.

4. Economic aid was designed to increase Afghan dependence on the USSR:

• Transit agreements disrupted traditional trade patterns and redirected them through the USSR.

• Barter agreements absorbed major Afghan commodities.

• A gas pipeline was built to the USSR.

• A $100 million line of credit---which in one stroke absorbed the total debt-service capacity of Afghanistan---made the country a poor credit risk for non-Soviet bloc loans.

• Offers were made to finance successive Five Year Plans.

5. The Soviet program was designed to improve the long-term strategic value of Afghanistan if and when a Soviet occupation should take place:

• A chain of logistical supply depots---grain, petroleum, machine shops, etc.---was established between the Soviet border and Kabul.

• Improved military communications were set up with the construction of roads, bridges, and the Salang Pass tunnel through the Hindu Kush mountain massif, the historical barrier between the northern plains (and Soviet Central Asia) and the capital.

• Major military airfields were constructed at Bagram and Shindand; the runways at Kabul airport were improved and extended.

A careful analysis of the extensive Soviet economic, military, and cultural programs set in motion during the first Daoud regime, 1953-1963, reveals a coherent, integrated and premeditated plan, disguised as something the Afghans themselves wanted and needed but in fact serving first and foremost Soviet political, economic and strategic interests. The size and scope of the Soviet effort was overwhelming in a small (in population) and poor country like Afghanistan.

By 1978 the Soviets had completed seventy-one separate projects, of which fifty-two were still being operated by Soviet technicians. Sixty more projects had been agreed upon and the Soviet Union had invested more than 3 billion dollars in Afghanistan. By 1978 they had also trained 5,000 students in Soviet academic institutions and 1,600 in technical schools, plus 3,725 Afghan military personnel, of whom some had been coopted by the KGB.[18] Long before they ever sent a single soldier over the border, the Soviet presence in Afghanistan was already overpowering. Stage One, begun in the 1950s---the creation of a subversive infrastructure within Afghanistan---was long since in place.

The Daoud regimes made all this possible, and the inadequate American diplomatic reponse failed to prevent it. Daoud paid with his life for his megalomania and his over-confidence that he could manipulate Soviet and American competition to his own ends. He must carry the burden of historical responsibility for leading his country into the Russian snare.* Unfortunately all Afghans are paying the price for the mistakes of their leaders. The price to be paid by the United States for its diplomatic failure remains to be seen.

The American response

American policy-makers were slow to realize the potential of the Soviet diplomatic offensive. This was partly due to the inadequate operations of the American embassy in Kabul in the 1950s under the direction of Ambassador Angus Ward.[19] When Daoud began to succumb to Soviet seduction, the embassy did little to alert Washington.

Ward, who was personally an admirable and upright man of impeccable integrity, had been a hostage of the Chinese Communists when he was Consul General in Mukden. He hated Communism passionately, and was convinced that Daoud had sold out to the Soviets. But, blinded by his personal animus toward Daoud, Ward failed to correctly assess or report the extent of the Soviet danger. He was greatly influenced by the King's uncles, whom Daoud had ousted from power, and by a free-wheeling, pistol-packing CIA station chief who, under diplomatic cover, constantly plotted with the Pakistanis to "destabilize" the Daoud regime. Through his intelligence service, Daoud was aware of the embassy's hostile activities (though Washington was not) and naturally believed that they represented official policy. This, combined with the personal animosity between Daoud and Ward, produced a period of strong anti-American feeling in Kabul. The embassy was cut off from effective government contacts and for nearly two critical years American diplomacy operated blindly. The resulting paralysis and loss of American influence gave the Soviets a clear start with no American competition.

Inadequate embassy operations and reporting contributed to top-level Washington attitudes, which were primarily based on erroneous

---

*But Daoud could not have done it without the support of large segments of the intellectual elite, who, basking in Soviet blandishments and heedless of American warnings, chuckled at their own cleverness in extracting dollars and rubles from the rival superpowers. Today, in exile, many of those who survive bitterly condemn the Soviet invasion and complain that the United States is not doing enough to extricate Afghanistan from the Russian grip. But they themselves contributed largely to the extinction of their freedom.

assessments. In 1953, a secret study by the Joint Chiefs of Staff had concluded that:

Afghanistan is of little or no strategic importance to the United States. Its geographic location, coupled with the realization by Afghan leaders of Soviet capabilities, presages Soviet control of the country whenever the situation so dictates. It would be desirable for Afghanistan to remain neutral because otherwise it might be overrun as an avenue to the Indian subcontinent. *Such neutrality will remain a stronger possibility if there is no Western-sponsored opposition to communism* in Afghanistan, which opposition in itself might precipitate Soviet moves to take control of the country.[20] (Emphasis added).

The National Security Council took a similar position:

The Kremlin apparently does not consider Afghanistan's relatively meager assets to be worthy of serious attention and probably believes that it can take Afghanistan easily whenever its broader objectives would be served. There is little doubt that Afghanistan could be conquered regardless of its will to resist. In the event of an invasion, it is possible that certain elements, particularly the Afghan tribesmen, would continue to resist.[21]

Top officials of the American government were thus being advised that Afghanistan could be written off without a struggle because it had no value to American security interests. The Soviet thrust, according to these assessments, presented no real danger to the United States, and in any case, there was little that the United States could do to counter it. Moreover, it was argued, the United States should do nothing to offend the Russians or cause them to escalate their campaign of penetration. In addition to ignorance and apathy, then, appeasement became a dominant theme of American diplomacy in Afghanistan.[22] This counsel of appeasement demonstrated a profound ignorance not only about Afghanistan but about Russia. As Henry Kissinger once warned, the Russians have historically expanded into "any vacuums created by irresolution or weakness . . . since communist ideology has no rationale for *not* exploiting a favorable power balance."[23]

The appeasement counseled by the Joint Chiefs and the NSC in the early 1950s was not subjected to the corrective scrutiny of area specialists in Washington: for the most part they were not interested in Afghanistan. Soviet specialists considered Afghanistan to lie on a remote fringe of the Soviet empire. South Asia specialists were obsessed with India and, marginally, Pakistan; to them, Afghanistan with its boring Pushtunistan propaganda was merely a nuisance. Middle East specialists were preoccupied with Arab-Israeli problems: the thought that Afghanistan might one day present a Soviet threat to the Strait of Hormuz and to the supply of oil for Japan and the West did not even cross their minds. The academic community was equally uninformed and uninterested: the first book on Afghanistan by an American scholar did not appear until 1965, and few others followed.[24]

Finally, in mid-1955, when Angus Ward was replaced by Sheldon T. Mills, supported by a new strong deputy chief of mission, Armin Meyer, the embassy began to communicate with the Afghan government and to formulate a plan to counter Soviet penetration. The plan called for an integrated program of aid to education and civil aviation, road links to Pakistan, and a rescue operation of the Helmand project.[25] The most difficult part was to sell it to Washington.

The plan was well-conceived but poorly executed. It took months to modify Washington's mistaken view that Afghanistan was not important to American security and to convince top American leaders that such an aid program should be initiated. Many more months elapsed before cumbersome aid machinery could be put in place. American aid technicians and administrators sent to Afghanistan were, with rare exceptions, unfamiliar with the country, its languages and customs; in too many cases they had never served abroad before. Bureaucratic snarls and red tape were endemic. In contrast to the Soviet projects, which were completed speedily and placed only a modest burden on the Afghan economy,* the American projects dragged on interminably and were more costly, with a high proportion of expenditures going for American salaries and expensive housing---which aid administrators insisted (probably correctly) were necessary to lure American technicians to far-off Afghanistan.

The inefficiency of the American aid program in those crucial early years was compounded by Pakistan's refusal to even talk with the Afghans about what the Pakistanis called "the Pushtunistan stunt." On several occasions this hard line resulted in economic blockades that affected supplies for American projects, increasing the already intolerable costs and delays.

On top of all this, the Afghans themselves were not very helpful. They are a notoriously proud people. The residue of the Ward era, and the memories of the humiliating years when they pleaded vainly for American aid, caused many influential Afghans to look on the sudden American interest with suspicion. They felt that belated American action was intended, not to help Afghanistan, but only to bring the Cold War into their country. Their wounded pride often caused them to be secretive and

---

* For a differing view, see: Noorzoy, also Shroder and Assifi.

uncooperative.   Most Americans working in Afghanistan, including officials, knew nothing about the history of thwarted Afghan efforts to obtain American assistance and were frustrated by what they perceived as Afghan ingratitude and hostility. Years of clumsy American diplomacy now reaped a harvest of misunderstanding that gave the Soviet program a psychological advantage.

By 1957, after the Soviets had had nearly three years' head start on American competition, the National Security Council at last began to assess the situation more realistically:

> Afghanistan has incurred so huge a burden of debt to the Communist bloc as to threaten its future independence. The Afghans hope to have the best of both worlds in aid but the capability of the United States to shape events in South Asia is severely limited. The United States should try to resolve the Afghan dispute with Pakistan and encourage Afghanistan to minimize its reliance upon the Communist bloc for military training and equipment and *to look to the United States* and other free world sources for military training and assistance.[26] (Emphasis added).

Apparently the NSC found no inconsistency between this startling recommendation and the long history of rebuffed Afghan pleas for help in solving the Pushtunistan dispute and for American military aid. But this new assessment was helpful to the few American officials who were trying to blunt the Soviet offensive in Afghanistan. The American aid program nonetheless limped along in a losing competition with the strong, steady Soviet effort.

At that point Washington made a serious effort to reverse the trend, sending Henry Byroade, an energetic troubleshooter and crackerjack operator, as ambassador to Kabul with a mandate to stop the Soviets and get the American program going. He did manage to breathe some new life into the aid program, but he had to battle both the recalcitrant Afghans and the Washington AID bureaucracy---his most formidable adversary. At one point Byroade became so frustrated with the incompetence and delays of the aid administration that he imported the Army Corps of Engineers to finish a lagging road program. Moreover, the American ambassador in Pakistan, William Rountree, fought a masterful rearguard battle to prevent any American pressure on Pakistan to take a more reasonable attitude toward Afghanistan. In spite of Byroade's herculean efforts, the rescue operation was too little and too late.

In 1963, after a decade of misrule and deepening hostilities with Pakistan, Daoud was forced to resign by a royal family conclave; but by then the USSR had established a firm base of operations in Afghanistan and the belated, incompetent American aid effort had failed to counteract Soviet influence or preserve a true independence for the country.

The American failure to stop Soviet penetration of Afghanistan produced a series of rationalizations that conditioned American diplomacy until the Soviet invasion---and which, to a considerable extent, still prevail. It was said that the preponderant Soviet influence in Afghanistan was the natural corollary of its geographic position; that the Soviet presence was beneficial because it was developing the country at no cost to the American taxpayer; that Afghan support of Soviet positions in international forums was the logical position for a weak Third World nonaligned country to take; that the USSR would not attack Afghanistan because it already controlled the Afghan economy and was using Afghanistan as a showcase for "peaceful coexistence." It was further said that by maintaining a low profile the United States was diminishing the risk of a Soviet invasion because the USSR did not feel threatened; that an invasion would damage Soviet relations with Third World (especially Islamic) countries; that superpower aid competition had evolved into a cooperative relationship in which Soviet and American aid programs complemented each other. (Examples given for this were the Soviet construction of runways and buildings at the Kabul airport for which the United States had supplied all the communications equipment. One could also point to the Russian silos filled with American wheat.)

The Soviets encouraged these views with amiable talk of detente, the end of the cold war, and similar tranquilizing propaganda. But they were busy working underground, subverting Afghan military officers during their training tours in the USSR and plotting to install a communist government in Afghanistan.

The democratic experiment

The last chance for American diplomacy in Afghanistan occurred during the democratic experiment which followed the deposition of Daoud in 1963. Afghanistan got a new liberal constitution transforming the political system from an oligarchy into a constitutional monarchy. The new constitution, drafted by an elite committee of intellectuals chaired by Mohammed Moussa Shafiq, a lawyer trained in Egypt and the United States and later prime minister, provided for a popularly elected parliament. It barred all members of the immediate royal family from public office (a measure aimed principally at Daoud but also designed to broaden the base of political participation). National elections were carried out by universal secret ballot. Broad human rights including those of women were prescribed. The constitution also mandated the parliament to pass a law authorizing the formation of political parties.[27]

Afghanistan was thus thrust full tilt into an experiment in parliamentary democracy. It failed for three basic reasons:

First, the "separation of powers" doctrine was carried to an absurd extreme: the executive, headed by a prime minister appointed by the king, could be immobilized by the parliament.

Second, the new and inexperienced parliament was transformed by the few Communist deputies (including Babrak Karmal) and their leftist dupes secretly directed by the USSR, into a forum for irresponsible criticism of the government and the royal family. Students, secretly instigated by the Communists,* agitated in the streets against the government, and at least one riot resulted in a number of deaths. The student riots so frightened the timid king---who had to approve all laws---that he would not sign the law creating legal political parties, believing it would result in political chaos. In fact, legal political parties might have saved the situation by introducing party discipline and a loyal opposition, creating groupings around which moderates could rally.

Third, failure to create legal parties did not hamper the tiny Communist party [the PDPA], which worked underground and was secretly advised and subsidized by the Soviets.† The Russians instructed the Afghan Communists to sabotage the democratic experiment because they rightly feared that the success of democracy in Afghanistan would spell the end of their hard-bought influence. They also actively worked to reconcile the two warring factions of the Communist Peoples' Democratic Party of Afghanistan (PDPA): Khalq (Masses) headed by Nur Mohammed Taraki and Parcham (Flag) led by Babrak Karmal.[28]

There has been considerable debate among scholars and American officials as to whether the Afghan Communists were indeed from the start under the control of Moscow. A former Afghan Minister of the Interior has stated categorically that he examined the extensive dossiers resulting from close surveillance by the Afghan intelligence service and that these documents proved beyond a doubt that Afghan Communist leaders were controlled, paid, and ordered directly by KGB officers in the Soviet embassy in Kabul. They were trained in detail in how to eventually seize the government by force.[29]

These important subversive developments escaped the notice of American policymakers because information about them would have required a considerable covert intelligence-gathering capability. The CIA, however,

---

* A key student agent was Najibullah, then a protegé of Karmal, whom he replaced as head of the puppet regime in May 1986.

† See: Arnold.

both in Afghanistan and Washington, had for years concentrated all its effort and interest on Soviet bloc activities *and deliberately ignored internal Afghan matters.* During the critical period after Daoud's departure, a time of intense underground political activity, American diplomacy was in effect flying blind. It was in America's security interest to know what the Afghan Communists were up to, and to support and encourage the democratic political development of Afghanistan---but again American diplomacy failed to rise to the occasion. A measure of this failure is the fact that *in every year of the democratic experiment, American economic aid declined.* No special effort was made to give strong visible support to the several prime ministers between 1963 and 1973, after which date Daoud recaptured power.[30]

During the decade of the constitutional period, only one prime minister was ever invited to visit the United States, and that was because he had been ambassador in Washington. Needless to say all were repeatedly invited to make official visits to the Soviet Union.

During a major portion of the constitutional period a political appointee served as American ambassador in Kabul. He had excellent academic qualifications and managed to establish close personal relations with the King, but tended to concentrate on the top man to the neglect of the new and struggling political leaders. His messages to Washington indicated that he accepted the "low American profile" theory with respect to Soviet-American competition in Afghanistan. He was also apparently unable to persuade the King to legalize political parties---the key to the success of the parliamentary experiment---or to persuade Washington to increase its political and economic support for the fledgling democracy. Thus, through Communist machinations and American neglect, the infant liberal Afghan constitution was strangled in its cradle. Stage Two of the Soviet plan was now complete.

The destruction of the monarchy

The failure of the democratic experiment also spelled the end of the Afghan monarchy. The deadlock in parliament and the absence of parties and party discipline caused the government to grind slowly to a halt. In the early 1970s, severe droughts and famine struck part of the country and the government's slow and incompetent response aroused popular indignation and disappointment with democracy. American food aid belatedly came to the rescue, but it was clear that the days of democratic government were numbered.

This was what the Communists had been working and waiting for. In 1973 they went to Daoud, who, like Achilles, was sulking in his tent, fuming against the constitutional prohibition which prevented his return to political activities.   The Communists, under Soviet tutelage, played on his ego, urging him to seize power with their support, depose his cousin the King, and proclaim a republic. They wanted to destroy the monarchy, the one institution of national unity in a multilingual, multi-ethnic country. Daoud's hubris and vaulting ambition led him for the second time into the Communist trap: he thought he could seize power with Communist help and, after entrenching himself, discard his leftist supporters. In July 1973, while the King was abroad, a handful of military officers, among whom were some trained in the Soviet Union, instigated by local Afghan Communists, executed an almost bloodless coup and installed Daoud as president of the new Afghan Republic.

American diplomacy now gave to the autocrat, Daoud, stronger support than Washington had given to the struggling prime ministers of the democratic period. Whereas support for the democratic governments had been indifferent and laggard, the United States lost no time in recognizing and offering increased economic aid to Daoud. It thus placed its seal of approval on the overthrow of the monarchy and the demise of democracy. The United States emphasized this move by replacing Ambassador Robert G. Neumann, the confidante of the King, with Theodore L. Eliot, who as Executive Secretary of the State Department was considered to be close to the Secretary of State.[31]

Daoud, still remembering the Ward period, was at first suspicious and cool to friendly overtures, but the State Department went to great lengths to soothe his feelings. Eliot requested a full historical review of the documents of the Ward period and used it to convince Daoud that the U.S. government had never officially approved the local activities of the embassy or the CIA. He told Daoud that the U.S. looked forward to close collaboration with him. To prove the point, American aid programs were substantially increased, particularly in the troubled Helmand Valley project, and political support was offered to improve Afghan-Pakistani relations. All this may not have been intended as signs of approval for Daoud's autocratic regime but it certainly looked that way to most Afghans. To them, the message from America was clear: forget your king and your democracy and be happy under your dictator.

With the end of the monarchy, which had always been a symbol of unity to the diverse Afghan tribes and nationalists, Stage Three of the Russian plan was accomplished.

The Communist coup

The Soviets apparently expected that the aging, ailing Daoud would be a willing instrument, permitting the Communists, who had participated in his coup and joined his government, to become the effective power behind his throne (obviating the need for stages 4 and 5), but Moscow had misjudged the strong-willed, bull-headed Daoud: he refused to play by their rules. During the five years that he was to remain in power, Daoud obtained *Loya Jirga* approval for a new constitution that made him head of a single-party state for life. By 1976 he had discarded most of his leftist supporters, and had embarked on the delicate task of trying to loosen the smothering Soviet embrace. He tried to diversify his sources of aid by turning to the wealthy Islamic oil states. His preferred instrument for regaining Afghan independence was the Shah of Iran, who responded with generous offers of economic aid and political support and tried, with some success, to improve relations between Pakistan and Afghanistan.

If Daoud would not play their game, the Russians were ready to discard him and move to the fourth stage: the installation of an openly Communist government in Afghanistan. They reacted to Daoud's efforts to disengage from them by secretly strengthening the Afghan Communists. In 1976 they achieved the long-sought reconciliation between the bitterly opposed Parcham and Khalq factions of the PDPA. Under Soviet direction the now-unified PDPA established close liaison with the secret Soviet-trained subversive cells in the Afghan armed forces and developed plans for the overthrow of Daoud.

Of these important developments American officials were blissfully ignorant. Their surprise knew no bounds when in April 1978 the Khalq leadership, using as a pretext the mysterious assassination of a popular leftist labor leader and PDPA ideologue, staged a huge illegal demonstration in Kabul. Daoud responded by arresting the Khalq leaders, who immediately activated the subverted military units in accordance with the prearranged plan. Daoud, members of his family, and his cabinet were murdered and the Khalq faction headed by Nur Mohammed Taraki and Hafizullah Amin, in a brief collaboration with Karmal and the Parcham faction, seized power. Judging from what is known about the links between the PDPA and the Soviet KGB, there can be little doubt that the operation was meticulously planned by Soviet experts.[32]

With Khalq heading the new government, a secondary position was given to the Parcham leader, Babrak Karmal. The temporary unity of these two factions quickly fell apart. The Khalqis purged the Parchamis and took over. Babrak, Najibullah and others were sent off as ambassadors. They were later recalled to Kabul but refused to return, remaining under Soviet protection in Moscow and Eastern Europe until the Russians produced Babrak as their puppet during the Soviet invasion the following year.

The Taraki/Amin government immediately launched a program of ruthless repression, jailing and killing thousands. Its so-called "reform" measures in land ownership, education, and the change of the Afghan flag to communist red deeply offended the anti-communist Afghan people, who rose in revolt. Further repressive measures only fueled popular resistance and soon the entire country was up in arms. The army deserted in droves, and the Taraki government was in danger of falling. In September 1979, Hafizullah Amin, Taraki's deputy, had Taraki killed, seized power, and resorted to even more repressive measures.

The American diplomatic response to the Communist coup of 1978 had been mushy as usual. No attempt was made to break relations with the Communist usurpers, nor to express revulsion for the bloodbath which ended the Daoud regime and the gross violations of human rights which ensued. There was no official American disapproval of the shift in political power in a strategic country. On the contrary, the United States applied the doctrine of "automatic recognition"[33] and sent a new ambassador, Adolph "Spike" Dubs, a top expert on Soviet affairs, to deal with the new Communist regime on the basis of "business as usual." American aid programs were continued without a hitch. In contrast, although fierce resistance by the people of Afghanistan began soon after the Communists seized power in April 1978, the United States gave them no help at this stage.

In February 1979 Dubs was kidnapped by "dissidents," and under the pretext of a rescue by an Afghan military unit with Soviet advisers, was in effect murdered. (The report on the official investigation into Dubs' death has never been made public.) At last the United States issued a vigorous protest and began to wind down its aid program. But in effect the United States had quietly acquiesced in the establishment of an avowedly Communist government in Afghanistan---Stage Four of the Russian plan.

The Soviet invasion

American official softness toward the Communist coup and the regime of terror that followed sent the wrong signals to Moscow. At the time of the 1978 coup, Secretary of State Cyrus Vance was in Moscow working on an arms limitation treaty, and the Soviets, to cover up their activities in Afghanistan, put on their usual peace offensive. Vance declared himself "pleasantly surprised" at how forthcoming they were on the arms question and praised their cooperation. His naïveté was only one of the signs of American weakness which misled the Kremlin into assuming American acquiescence in the outright seizure of Afghanistan. American complacence over the years in the face of progressive Communist penetration and influence convinced the Politburo that Washington considered Afghanistan of little value to American security and considered it to be within the Soviet sphere of domination.

In addition, American reaction to earlier events in other Third World areas such as Angola, Ethiopia, South Yemen and Cambodia, where Communist governments had seized power with direct or indirect Soviet military intervention, convinced the Kremlin planners that the Vietnam syndrome had paralyzed American capacity to oppose such moves. These factors---including American preoccupation with the Iranian hostage crisis---must have entered into Politburo calculations as it pondered the "correlation of forces" at the time of the decision to invade Afghanistan.

According to the Soviet doctrine of "correlation of forces," global historical events produce situations in which the capitalist world is overwhelmed and weakened, providing opportunities for the expansion of Communist power. By mid-1979 the Soviets were already deeply involved in Afghanistan with thousands of troops and advisers on the ground,* and the correlation of forces favored a forward Russian move. The United States seemed to have abandoned the field and, in Soviet perception, the occupation of Afghanistan was the logical response to American appeasement.

So in December 1979, noting the precarious position of the Communist regime in Kabul, the USSR, in accord with the Brezhnev Doctrine and claiming falsely that they had been invited in by the Afghan government, invaded Afghanistan, killed Amin and installed Babrak Karmal in his place. This, then, was the ultimate "fulfillment" of the promise made by Bulganin in 1955 and sanctified in several solemn treaties: "In relations with Afghanistan, the Soviet Union has invariably been guided---and will continue to be guided in the future---by the principles of respect for territorial integrity and sovereignty, non-aggression, non-interference in internal affairs, equality and mutual benefit, peaceful co-existence and economic cooperation."[34]

The invasion set in motion Stage Five of the Soviet program---the conquest and absorption of Afghanistan into the Soviet bloc. But here the Soviets grossly underestimated the Afghans. The mighty Red Army failed to impress them: what should have been a quick, surgical pacification operation soon turned into a military quagmire for the Soviets and a war of national liberation as well as a *jihad* for the Afghans. After almost eight years of bloody fighting, Stage Five is still very much incomplete and the final outcome remains in doubt.

---

* See: Bodansky, also Klass.

American diplomacy since the invasion

The Soviets had expected to pay a moderate political price for their direct intervention in Afghanistan, a Third World nonaligned country. They must have known that most Islamic nations would protest vigorously and that there would be the usual United Nations resolutions. The Kremlin had been through all that when Soviet troops quelled national movements in Hungary and Czechoslovakia. Moscow was not prepared, however, for the violent American reaction. The Politburo naturally assumed that the American President and his advisers could read a map and that they must have already considered the strategic position of Afghanistan and deliberately discounted it. In fact, however, such had not been the case.

American officials, from the President on down, expressed shock, surprise, horror and outrage over the invasion. The fact that it had been in the making for several decades, and that a glance at a map of the region would have revealed at once the dangers of a Soviet thrust into a country that lies like a wedge between the strategic Persian Gulf and South Asia, had escaped the attention of the top American political leaders. Those few Afghans and American diplomats who had been aware of the danger for years, and had blunted their lances trying to penetrate the consciousness of high American officials, were not surprised---either at the Soviet invasion or at the astonishment of the president and his advisers.[35] Nevertheless, official American reaction to the invasion seemed to border on hysteria and the new round of diplomacy it set off was just as ineffective as the previous one had been tragic.[36]

The United States government had little reason to be caught off guard. Not only had diplomatic reporting raised many danger flags but, in the months preceding the invasion, American intelligence had accurately warned about the warlike preparations going on in the USSR. First alarms were sounded in April 1979---fully eight months before the invasion---when the Soviets sent General Shepilev, who had masterminded the invasion of Czechoslovakia in 1969, as head of a large military mission to Kabul. Shepilev lingered on in Kabul for a very long time. Soon, suspicious troop movements began inside the USSR. Members of the Soviet Army reserve in Central Asia were called to active duty. Two divisions near the Afghan border were reinforced and issued new weapons. A battalion of the elite 105th Guards Airborne division stationed at Ferghana in Soviet Uzbekistan was flown secretly into Bagram airbase north of Kabul. A reinforced armored unit soon joined them and was deployed to guard the strategic Salang Pass. A satellite communications ground station appeared in Termez just north of the Afghan border. Other motorized divisions were placed on an alert status.[37]

These intelligence warnings were passed up the line in Washington but were not taken seriously at cabinet or presidential level. Some mild warnings against interfering in the internal affairs of Afghanistan, indistinguishable from the many routine protests filed for the bureaucratic record, were issued to the Soviets. *But no warnings or alerts were sent to the American embassy in Kabul nor to the Afghan government.* The embassy was therefore taken completely by surprise when the invasion came, and Soviet military advisers were able to nullify any resistance by Afghan forces by disarming them in advance on the pretext that the equipment had to be "winterized."[38]

Despite this casual attitude in Washington beforehand, the actual invasion was greeted with howls of protest and near-hysteria by American officials. President Carter immediately issued a statement calling it "a grave threat to peace," and a few days later, "the greatest threat to peace since the Second World War."[39] On December 28, 1979, he wrote an angry letter to Brezhnev demanding troop withdrawal and warning that the invasion could have "serious consequences for U.S.-Soviet relations." Carter characterized Brezhnev's reply as completely inaccurate and misleading (a diplomatic term for a lie), adding, "This action of the Soviets has made a more dramatic change in my own opinion of what the Soviets' ultimate goals are than anything they've done in the previous time I've been in office."[40]

Moreover, no one in the American government had prepared in advance a considered position as to what the U.S. would do if and when Moscow actually moved. So when the invasion occurred---in the middle of the Christmas holidays, when most top officials were out of Washington---the U.S. was caught completely unprepared. Responses were thrown together hastily and without carefully consulting staff experts. According to one top official, even the formulation of the so-called Carter Doctrine, announced a month later in the President's State of the Union message, "grew out of last-minute pressures for a presidential speech. As far as is known...the Carter administration...(never) conducted a detailed study of the implications of the policy or its alternatives."[41] As formulated, the Carter Doctrine stated: "An attempt by any outside force to gain control of the Persian Gulf regions will be regarded as an assault on the vital interests of the United States and such assault will be repelled by any means necessary, including military force." In a sense, this somewhat hazy formulation invited the USSR to remain in Afghanistan so long as it did not reach out for the Persian Gulf.[42]

The confused and explosive American reaction to the invasion was in fact the result of a long ongoing struggle inside the Carter administration between "hardliners" led by presidential National Security Adviser Zbigniew Brzezinski, and "softliners" led by Secretary of State Vance, prompted by his

Soviet affairs adviser, Marshall Shulman.[43]   The invasion unleashed the hardliners who were told to come up with an effective riposte. Diplomatic niceties were cast to the winds and Carter was urged to leap on his white steed and ride in all directions at once.

The response recommended by the hardliners was couched primarily as a military short-term reaction to what was perceived as an immediate Soviet threat to American national security (rather than than a concern for Afghanistan and its people.)   Carter summed it up well: "The Soviet invasion is a direct threat to U.S. national security.   It places the Soviets within aircraft striking range of the vital oil resources of the Persian Gulf; it threatens a strategically located country, Pakistan; and it poses the prospect of increased Soviet pressure on Iran and other nations of the Middle East."[44]

Carter struck out in all directions wherever he thought the USSR could be hurt. In quick succession, and with little consideration of the political realities or economic consequences, he announced the formation of a Rapid Deployment Force to defend the Persian Gulf, withdrew the SALT II treaty from Senate consideration, cancelled a new American consulate in Kiev and a Soviet consulate in New York, rescinded existing cultural exchanges, and imposed trade restrictions on the USSR, especially in high technology and oil drilling equipment. He also curtailed Soviet fishing rights in American waters, cancelled an agreement to sell Moscow 17 million tons of livestock feed grain and embargoed future shipments. In addition he blocked Occidental Petroleum's $20 billion barter deal to exchange liquid phosphate concentrate for Soviet anhydrous ammonia, potash and urea and finally, he announced a boycott of the 1980 Olympics in Moscow by the U.S. and as many of its allies as could be persuaded.[45]

These sanctions were, on the whole, hastily conceived and not very effective. Some were actually counterproductive. Most eventually had to be rescinded, even though the Soviet army remained in Afghanistan. Carter did, however, take certain actions which had far greater long-term significance. He initiated a massive rearmament program, which was continued and expanded by the Reagan administration. He initiated a program of covert military aid to the Afghan Resistance. He rearmed Pakistan as a frontline state. Although Pakistan refused the initial Carter offer as "peanuts," the military aid program was subsequently developed under the Reagan administration.[46]

Carter also took one other diplomatic initiative which, though not much noticed at the time, may have been the most effective of all: he sent Secretary of Defense Harold Brown to China to discuss joint action. While the Brown conversations remain secret, there is no doubt that the mere fact that they occurred severely shook Kremlin planners, for whom China is the *bête noir*. Subsequently, China has strongly backed Pakistan in resisting Soviet pressures and has supplied arms to the Afghan Resistance. More importantly, it has firmly maintained that Sino-Soviet relations cannot be normalized until the Soviet army withdraws from Afghanistan. This represents powerful leverage on the Soviet Union.

The other programs which Carter initiated and which have been continued by the Reagan administration have created a variety of problems. American rearmament has strengthened U.S. diplomacy but, domestically, it is politically controversial. Military aid to Pakistan aroused opposition from India (and its Congressional supporters) and, in Pakistan, increased internal political opposition to President Zia-ul-Haq's government.[47] Aid to the *mujahideen*, which was supposed to be covert in order to protect Pakistan, was promptly leaked to the press and debated publicly, embarrassing Pakistan and subjecting that country to Soviet pressures and threats.

The Reagan administration has, on the whole, been supportive of the Afghan Resistance. The "Reagan Doctrine" was formulated to extend American aid to "freedom fighters" who resist Communist governments in their own countries. Unfortunately the doctrine covers such diverse groups as the contras in Nicaragua and insurgents in Cambodia, Ethiopia and Angola, along with the Afghan mujahideen, but in the United States the people and Congress do not support all these groups with equal enthusiasm. There is a danger that the Afghans will get lumped in with the other, less popular insurgents. So far aid to the Afghans was (and is) strongly supported by the American people and by Congress with bipartisan approval. Indeed, since 1984, the Congress and particularly the joint task force headed by Senator Gordon J. Humphrey and Representative Robert J. Lagormarsino, have urged even stronger efforts.

Within the U.S. government, however, there were---and still are---skeptics who oppose Afghan aid. Immediately following the invasion, most American military and intelligence "experts" believed that the Afghan Resistance had no chance against the mighty Soviet army and would be overrun in a matter of weeks. Only the few who really knew Afghanistan and were familiar with its stout people and intimidating terrain predicted a long and bitter war.[48] Eight years later the Afghans are still fighting and the skeptics are more cautious in voicing their views. Nevertheless many of them continue to argue that collapse of the Resistance is imminent and consequently that military aid is wasted and will only prolong the agony and increase the slaughter. Another type of critic argues that the United States does not really want the Afghans to win but only to make the Soviets bleed. They point to the inadequacy of the weapons supplied to the Resistance, especially the failure---at least until recently---to give them adequate air defense. In their view it is better to stop this policy of "fighting to the last Afghan" by cutting off military aid.

In spite of these contrary views there is little evidence that the Reagan administration doubts the capacity of the Afghans to resist or is helping them only in order to bleed the Russians. In fact the Deputy Director of the CIA, John McMahon, was reportedly forced to resign in 1986 because he opposed the Reagan policy of helping the freedom fighters. Nevertheless, the long period of uncertainty and continuing debate have affected the effectiveness of the aid program.

Thus far the Afghan Resistance has received substantial military and economic aid from the Reagan administration. Much of the economic aid is channeled to the Afghan refugees in Pakistan through international and private agencies. The military aid passes through Pakistan into the hands of the Afghan political parties in Peshawar and is distributed by them to their field commanders. This arrangement had not been altogether satisfactory and most experts agree that there is substantial leakage in the pipeline: there are credible charges of weapons diversion and corruption. The Reagan administration is constrained in remedying this situation by the need to use Pakistan as a conduit. Pakistan in turn prefers certain Afghan groups to others because of domestic political considerations and is wary of provoking the Soviets beyond a certain point.

At times Reagan's rhetoric has exceeded his actions. He has given general political and diplomatic support to the Afghan Resistance. He has continued to give and even increase military aid to the mujahideen. He has personally received Resistance leaders, celebrated Afghanistan Day each year at a White House ceremony, and told Gorbachev at a summit meeting in November 1985 that Soviet-American relations could not be normalized so long as Soviet troops remained in Afghanistan. On the other hand one of his first acts in office was to cancel the grain embargo and recently he has even approved subsidized grain sales to the Soviet Union. The administration has also declined thus far to extend diplomatic recognition to the Resistance Alliance or withdraw recognition from the Kabul regime.

The United States has strongly supported the negotiations between Pakistan and the Kabul regime conducted in Geneva through the United Nations since 1982. This effort grew out of annual General Assembly resolutions calling for the withdrawal of unnamed "foreign troops," for the restoration of Afghan non-aligned independence, for the right of Afghans to choose their own government, and for the return of the refugees with peace and honor.[49]

The General Assembly instructed the U.N. Secretary General to arrange peace negotiations. The proximity talks supervised by Diego Cordovez, a Deputy Secretary General of the UN, have made slow progress on lesser points but have encountered a principal stumbling block in Soviet refusal to specify an acceptable withdrawal schedule. According to some observers, the Soviets have been using the Geneva talks to gain time, to obtain legitimacy for the Kabul regime and to weaken support for the mujahideen by pressuring Pakistan.

Following his first summit meeting with Reagan, Gorbachev stated that the Soviet Union wanted to reach a political settlement in Afghanistan.[50]

Shortly thereafter the U.S., which had previously declined to provide an advance written guarantee of a U.N.-negotiated agreement, sent a letter stating that it was indeed prepared to guarantee such an agreement provided it complied with the conditions laid down in U.N.` General Assembly resolutions. Issuance of the letter was justified as being a goodwill gesture intended to encourage Gorbachev's stated desire to find a political solution. Soon after, however, the talks in Geneva reached a dead end when it turned out the Soviets, through their Afghan surrogates, were offering to withdraw only four years *after all aid to the resistance was cut off*.

Once again, the Soviets had achieved a significant change in U.S. policy with nothing but words. (Although Washington claimed that the letter did not constitute a change of policy, knowledgeable former American officials said it was indeed a major shift.) Even assuming that the Soviets are sincere in wanting a political settlement, an American guarantee of a Geneva agreement is dangerous because the principal parties to the conflict---the USSR and the Afghan people---are not directly involved in Geneva. Iran refused to participate and Afghan Resistance leaders have unanimously and vigorously stated that they refuse to be bound by any agreement made over their heads.

Moreover, the Geneva negotiations seem to have dropped the General Assembly resolution requirement for self-determination. If a Geneva agreement permitted Soviet troops to remain in Afghanistan even for a transitional period, or permitted Communists to remain in power, the Afghan people would surely reject it. Any attempt by Pakistan or the United States to enforce the guarantee of such an agreement would lead to open conflict with the Afghan Resistance. The United States would find itself trapped in an imbroglio worse than Lebanon, while Pakistan might be similarly destroyed.

Conclusion

By 1978 the United States had invested a total of 523.9 million dollars in economic aid to Afghanistan but these vast sums were largely wasted by incompetent American diplomacy. During the same period the USSR invested $1.265 billion in economic aid and $1.250 billion in military aid in Afghanistan. Moscow's investment remains intact under Soviet control; the American investment is lost.[51]

The Soviet Union is now in a commanding geostrategic position, threatening South Asia, the Middle East with its vital oil, and the Indian Ocean.

In gauging the Soviet threat presented by the invasion of Afghanistan, American leaders have once again made a fundamental error. The Carter Doctrine assumed that a Soviet attack on the Persian Gulf was imminent. The Soviet threat to the Gulf, however is neither immediate nor solely military. It may take two years, or ten, or twenty years for the Russians to consolidate their position in Afghanistan. In the meantime they will make all sorts of peaceful noises, sign disarmament agreements, and offer fragrant promises, in the hope that their position in Afghanistan will come to be accepted by a forgetful world as it has been in the Baltic states and Eastern Europe. Then slowly they will prepare the way by peaceful economic penetration and political subversion, until in the ripeness of time they will be "invited" into Tehran or Kuwait, Karachi or Oman, and they will then bring down the other foot as the elephant did in Abdur Rahman's analogy. This is the long-range nature of the Soviet threat and it is the principal lesson of Afghanistan, where it took fifty years to prepare the ground.

The gains made by Soviet diplomacy in Afghanistan were not so much a tribute to its quality, nor to its advantages of geography and contiguity, as to its steadfastness, consistency, cunning, perseverance, opportunism, long-range planning and astute exploitation of a regional quarrel.

Conversely, they are an indictment of the ignorance, vacillation, pusillanimity, incoherence, inconstancy, and appeasement of American diplomacy. This does not derogate from the efforts of many fine diplomats and AID employees who, over the years, wrestled with the Afghan problem. Even the incompetent were well-intentioned and respected the courage and dignity of the Afghans. There were some outstanding officials who fought courageously for recognition of the strategic importance of Afghanistan and for the need to help the Afghan people. A debt of admiration and gratitude is owed to such men as Engert, Mills, Meyer, Byroade and others, who went beyond the call of duty to try to avoid the present tragedy.

But ever since the erroneous security assessments of the 1950s, ignorance, apathy and appeasement have been the dominant themes of American diplomacy in Afghanistan.

Fear of offending the Russians and hope that American restraint would evoke a similar response from the Soviets in fact only drew them deeper into Afghanistan. It led them to believe that they could trample with impunity on the freedom of their neighbors. Even today---after the naked aggression against Afghanistan, the bestial rape of the Afghan people, and many years of unremitting Afghan resistance---the United States still hesitates to provide the Afghan freedom fighters with adequate and sufficient arms for fear that it will provoke the Soviets into escalating the conflict. The only thing that prevents the total conquest of Afghanistan is the epic courage and resourcefulness of its national liberation resistance.

The noble Afghan people have taken everything the Soviets, with their superior weapons, have thrown at them. They have stood up against the special SPETSNAZ troops which are considered by military experts to be the most highly trained elite units in the world. The Afghans have pinned down Soviet power, humiliating it before the entire world, restraining its spread in Poland and buying precious time for the free world to organize the defenses of the Persian Gulf. One would think that American diplomacy would recognize instantly the need to strengthen the Afghan Resistance in every possible way---but once again American support for the Afghans is timorous, rhetorical and vacillating.

The moment of truth for American diplomacy in Afghanistan has come. It must work actively for a realistic peace that will restore freedom to the Afghan nation. But to do this it must first shake off its paralysis of appeasement and forsake the naive belief that if the United States does nothing to provoke the Soviets they will see the error of their ways and quietly fade away from their commanding position in the Middle East and South Asia, abandoning any further geopolitical expansion and leaving the region peaceful, secure and free. The possibility of such an outcome is denied by history. The hope for it is the grand illusion of our time.

Notes

1. Abdur Rahman Khan, *The Life of Abdur Rahman, Amir of Afghanistan*, 2 vols., ed. by Sultan Mohammed Khan, (London: John Murray, 1900).

2. Leon B. Poullada, *Reform and Rebellion in Afghanistan, 1919-1929: King Amanullah's Failure to Modernize a Tribal Society* (Ithaca: Cornell University Press, 1973).

3. Milan Hauner, "The Soviet Threat to Afghanistan and India," *Modern Asian Studies* (London, 15; 1981): 287-309. (A recent manifestation of Afghan trouble-making in the sub-continent is the al-Zulfikar terrorist movement, based in Kabul, South Yemen, Tripoli and New Delhi; headed by the son of the late Pakistani prime minister, Zulfikar

Ali Bhutto, it is dedicated to the overthrow of the Zia government in Pakistan and reportedly linked to Bhutto's PPP in Pakistan.)

4. Letter from President Harding to King Amanullah, *United States National Archives*, 890H.001 (29 July 1921).

5. Cornelius Van H. Engert, "A Report on Afghanistan," U.S. Department of State, Division of Publications, Series C., No. 53, Afghanistan No. 1, 1924.

6. *U.S. National Archives*, NEA Memorandum of conversation, file 890H.00/122, 1930.

7. Interview with Cornelius Van H. Engert, 3 October 1975.

8. Ibid.

9. *Foreign Relations of the United States*, Vols. 5 and 6, 1948, 1949.

10. Personal observations by the author and conversations with American military attaches in Kabul, 1953-1956.

11. *Foreign Relations of the United States*, Vol. 5, Part 1, 1948. Majid felt that, if attacked, Afghanistan would be overrun but that the Russians would be unable to pacify the country and that with arms, the Afghans could conduct guerilla tactics for an indefinite period. As in the Helmand case, Majid was prescient of the situation in Afghanistan today.

12. For a full exposition of the Pushtunistan problem see: Louis Dupree, "Pushtunistan," *American Universities Field Staff Reports*, 5 no. 2 (November 1961); D. Franck, "Pushtunistan," *Middle East Journal*, 6, no. 1 (1952); Leon B. Poullada, "Pushtunistan," *Pakistan's Western Borderlands*, Ainsley T. Embree, ed. (Durham, N.C.: Carolina Academic Press, 1977).

13. Interview on 12 December 1976 with Prince Mohammed Naim, Daoud's brother and foreign minister, who showed the author a copy of the note sent by Dulles.

14. The events which occurred during Daoud's first regime (1953-1956), the Soviet economic offensive, and the American response are recounted from the author's personal experience as Economic Counselor of the American embassy in Kabul during this period, and the author's contemporary journals.

15. The lack of competent language officers forced the embassy to rely entirely on native translators. One of these, employed by the USIS but frequently used by the embassy in the early 1950s, was the secret Communist leader Nur Mohammed Taraki. He was in a position to feed the USIS and the embassy slanted reports and distorted translations regarding public opinion and events. He could also influence the hiring of other Communists as translators. In short, the embassy was to some extent relying on Soviet agents for its information.

16. The development of this Soviet diplomatic gambit has now been observed in the

exploitation of other regional quarrels: for example, Pakistan/India, Ethiopia/Somalia, North/South Yemen, Angola/South Africa, Israel/Arab states, Iran/Iraq, etc. By espousing the cause of one of the hard-pressed parties to the dispute, the USSR ingratiates itself and acquires enormous leverage on its protégé.

17. Soviet aid programs and projects in Afghanistan have been described and analyzed in: Nake Kamrany, *Peaceful Competition in Afghanistan* (Washington, D.C.: Communication Service Corp., 1969). Also in Peter G. Franck, *Afghanistan Between East and West* (Washington, D.C.: National Planning Association, 1960). Also see Louis Dupree, *Afghanistan* (Princeton: Princeton University Press, 1973); 490-558; Noorzoy, also Shroder and Assifi, this volume; and listings in bibliography.

18. Central Intelligence Agency, "Communist Aid Activities in Non-Communist Less-Developed Countries, 1954-1979" (Washington D.C., 1980).

19. Leon B. Poullada, "Afghanistan and the United States: The Crucial Years," *Middle East Journal*, Vol. 35, No.2 (Spring 1981).

20. *Index of Declassified Documents*, No. 33A (Arlington, Virginia, 1979).

21. Ibid., No. 377A (1978) Regarding Soviet assessment of "meager assets," see Shroder and Assifi, this volume.

22. These early documents prepared by the highest security agencies of the American government contain the seeds of all the ineffective American diplomacy that followed and that continues even now.

23. Henry Kissinger interview in *Newsweek* (29 November 1982): 31.

24. Arnold Fletcher, *Afghanistan: Highway of Conquest* (Ithaca: Cornell University Press, 1965).

25. See Leon B. Poullada, *Middle East Journal* op. cit. The entire embassy and USIS staff was expanded and fortified at this time. Four out of six officers on this staff, including the author, later achieved ambassadorial rank.

26. *Declassified Documents Quarterly Catalog*, 5, No. 1 (1979) No. 448.

27. Richard S. Newell, *The Politics of Afghanistan*, (Ithaca: Cornell University Press, 1972): 162-180. Shafiq was later murdered in jail by the Communist regime immediately following the 1978 coup.

28. Anthony Arnold, *Afghanistan's Two-Party Communism: Parcham and Khalq*, (Palo Alto: Hoover Institution Press, 1983.) See also Arnold, this volume.

29. Interview with a former Afghan Minister of the Interior who requested anonymity, on 21 June 1978.

30. In separate interviews in 1967, 1976 and 1977, with three of these prime ministers---

Maiwandwal, Shafiq, and Etemadi---all complained bitterly to the author that they had not been able to elicit encouragement or support from American officials during the period of democratic reform.

31. Interview with Theodore L. Eliot, United States ambassador to Afghanistan, 8 March 1976.

32. Interview with former Afghan Minister of the Interior, 23 June 1978. Partial confirmation has come from Vladimir Kuzichkin, a defecting KGB major, who revealed that Babrak Karmal has been a KGB agent for many years. [*Time* (22 November 1982): 33)] These revelations increase the credibility of reports, current at the time of the coup, that some of the rebel air force planes, on which success of the coup finally hinged, were flown by Russian pilots.

33. In the past the granting or withholding of diplomatic recognition by the U.S. implied approval or disapproval of a new government and of its legitimacy. With so many coups and sudden changes of government around the world, the United States now simply continues to do business with the new leaders without a formal act of recognition. I have termed this the doctrine of *automatic recognition*. A curious crepuscular situation has arisen regarding the American embassy in Kabul since the Soviet invasion. The U.S. withdrew its ambassador and the mission is headed by a chargé d'affaires. The U.S. does not officially recognize the Kabul regime, yet the embassy remains in operation and does business at an administrative level with the Afghan foreign ministry. This constitutes not a pragmatic solution but a puzzle for international lawyers.

34. Speech by Premier Bulganin reported in the *Times of India* (19 December 1955).

35. As early as 1955 the author predicted just such an outcome. See his declassified despatch from Kabul to the State Department, Number 93, 17 October 1955, available on request from the Department of State and the National Archives.

36. For excellent summaries of the American reaction see: Thomas T. Hammond, *Red Flag Over Afghanistan*, (Boulder, Colorado: Westview Press, 1984); Henry S. Bradsher, *Afghanistan and the Soviet Union*, (Durham, N.C.: Duke University Press, 1983).

37. U.S. State Department, "Chronology of Recent Events Related to Afghanistan," 1980.

38. U.S. State Department *Press Briefing Record* (23 March 1979) and "Chronology of Recent Developments Related to Afghanistan," 1980.

39. *Presidential Documents*, No. 15 (31 December 1979): 2287 and No. 16 (14 January 1980): 25.

40. *New York Times* (1 January 1980).

41. David D. Newsom, "America Engulfed," *Foreign Policy*, 43 (Summer 1981): 17-32.

42. State of the Union Address, 23 January 1980.

43. *New York Times* (1 January 1980). See also Hammond, op. cit.: 107.

44. *Presidential Documents*, No. 16 (28 January 1980): 41.

45. Bradsher fully discusses the Carter sanctions in op. cit: 189-199.

46. *Presidential Documents*, 16 (14 January 1981): 27.

47. G.S. Bhargava, *South Asian Security After Afghanistan* (Toronto: Heath and Co., 1983): 91-106.

48. Rosanne Klass, "Afghans Battle On," *New York Times* (30 July 1981).

49. *New York Times* (14 December 1985).

50. *Washington Post* (28 November 1985): A47.

51. Central Intelligence Agency, "Communist Aid to Non-Communist Less Developed Countries, 1954-1979," (Washington, D.C., 1980).

"Unlike the leading capitalist power, the USSR gives extensive aid to other countries without imposing terms incompatible with their national interests and dignity. There are no military and political strings attached."

    ---V. Rymalov, Soviet economist

Soviet Economic Interests and Policies in Afghanistan

M. Siddieq Noorzoy

SOVIET ECONOMIC interests and policies in Afghanistan, evident for a period of more than sixty years, should be viewed in the context of overall Soviet policies and interests in similar small developing countries. To attempt to view Afghanistan in isolation is to don blinders that block out a fuller understanding of long-term Soviet policies in the Third World. It also reduces any understanding of the Soviet threat to Afghanistan itself, contributing to the naïve analyses of Soviet motives as merely defensive responses to an unexpected threat to its southern borders. Soviet behavior toward Less Developed Countries (LDCs) in general, and toward Afghanistan in particular, has demonstrably been based on economic as well as political and military elements, projected for long-term achievement.

Afghanistan can therefore be usefully viewed as a paradigm of Soviet economic policies in underdeveloped countries, policies that fit into long range Soviet geopolitical plans. In any case, an analysis of Soviet policies regarding Afghanistan refutes any theories that the Soviet takeover and invasion were historical accidents, unintended misadventures or hasty defensive responses to unexpected circumstances.

A distinct set of consistent Soviet economic policies in Afghanistan, leading to penetration, manipulation, control and eventually exploitation, can be traced back to the very beginning of Afghan-Soviet relations in the 1920s. After a setback in the 1930s and 1940s, these policies were revived and took on more complexity from the 1950s on through the 1970s, with the clear objective of penetrating the Afghan economy at different levels for multiple purposes.

Finally, the post-invasion economic policies must be distinguished from these pre-invasion "softer" approaches. Since 1979, Soviet activities have focussed on the exploitation of important Afghan natural resources (almost unknown to the rest of the world, but well-known for many years to Moscow) and the integration of Afghanistan into the Soviet economy for the benefit of the latter. Even the limited data available undermine the almost universal assumption that the war in Afghanistan is financially expensive to the Soviet Union and demonstrate that, on the contrary, the Soviets are shifting the costs of the war to the Afghan people and eventually expect to make economic gains.

To understand events in Afghanistan, it is useful first to review briefly overall Soviet international economic policies, some of which are not widely known or understood; then to assess the Soviet economic strategy in Afghanistan; and then to look at some of their specific plans for exploiting Afghan resources.

The nature of Soviet economic policies

Since World War II, Soviet foreign economic policies have been projected on a global basis with complexities and workings that, because of the nature of the Soviet bureaucratic system, are still in large part uncomprehended.[1]   It is known, however, that Soviet foreign economic policies and their implementations are rarely ad hoc decisions. Since the 1920s, Moscow's basic economic decisions have been based on intermediate (five-year) and long-term (25-year) plans.

It is well known, of course, that the USSR is a monolithic state. It is less widely recognized that, as a monolithic state, the USSR (or its agencies in international trade) forms not only one of the world's largest *monopoly* (single seller) suppliers of commodities but also one of the world's largest *monopsony* (single buyer) purchasers of imports from certain individual countries and even world markets. In these situations, comparable offsetting market forces are not necessarily present.

This singular *combination* of long-term planning, monolithism, and combined monopoly/monopsony market powers provides the Soviet Union with a unique set of tools for foreign economic policy-making and implementation. These achieve high degrees of effectiveness which have not been commonly recognized.

Such effectiveness becomes even more pronounced when trading is done on a bilateral basis---which is the basic Soviet method for trade with small, underdeveloped countries. Moreover, a significant portion of this trade is carried out on a barter basis for which only implicit, unannounced prices may exist. Such Soviet-Afghan bilateral barter agreements have existed for agricultural products since the 1950s. In addition, even when nominal price agreements for traded goods do exist, the Soviet government is often able to isolate its price agreements from world market prices (as in the case of Afghan natural gas).

Finally, it should be pointed out that the Soviets reject the theory of comparative (cost) advantage in international trade, i.e., the idea that comparative production costs in two countries (or multilaterally in world markets) determine the pattern of trade. Since international trade also serves Soviet political objectives, they can dismiss the role of even those criteria they do use, depending on circumstances and political priorities.

In the global context, Soviet foreign economic policies aim at the following objectives:

• To expand economic relations through international trade, preferably bilateral;

• To expand Soviet economic and political influence by creating economic dependency;

• To create economic complementarity with the Soviet economy, i.e., exporting domestic surplus goods and importing scarce commodities.

When it comes to trade in mineral resources, the Soviet Union also pursues specific political as well as economic goals:[2]

• To obtain imports of high technology from industrial countries in exchange for exports of Soviet raw materials;

• To enhance its desired world monopoly in various mineral resource categories by obtaining exclusive access to the mineral resources of underdeveloped countries;

• To use such access in an overall zero-sum game in order to deny access to those resources to the United States and other free world economies.

Soviet policies are designed to make underdeveloped countries dependent on the Soviet economy not only through bilateral trade agreements but also by extending long-term credit, usually at nominally low interest rates and low-bid contract offers which non-communist lenders cannot or will not match.

Finally, Soviet foreign economic policies include the dumping of goods on LDC markets at prices below *local domestic* production costs, thereby increasing dependency and reinforcing other means of pursuing policy objectives. All of these objectives and methods can be seen in the history of Soviet-Afghan economic relations.

The spectrum of policy tools that a large country can apply to influence economic decision-making in a small country includes aspects of trade, loans, and technical assistance programs. In the bilateral economic relations between Afghanistan and the Soviet Union all of these tools were used over a period of several decades to achieve the set of interrelated economic objectives discussed above, viz., making the Afghan economy dependent on the USSR and thereby subjecting Afghanistan to Soviet influence. In essence this dependency became a de facto part of bilateral Soviet/Afghan relations as a result of the magnitudes of Soviet trade, capital loans and technical assistance programs, and the integration of the Afghan economy with the Soviet economy.

The goal of Soviet economic integration was achieved by carefully offering loans and assistance programs (which had to be repaid) almost entirely for the development of those sectors of the Afghan economy and products which would meet Soviet production needs (e.g., minerals) and consumption demands (e.g., agricultural products), or those projects which fitted Soviet political and military interests. Thus, the structure of production in the Afghan economy became---as intended---complementary with that of the Soviet economy.

To accomplish the objectives of dependency and economic integration (as well as repayment of Soviet debt) an overall mechanism was needed between the two countries. This mechanism was the volume of bilateral trade.

In general, the larger the volume of trade between a large economy and a small economy *as a proportion of the total trade of the small economy,* the greater the degrees of dependency and integration of the small economy with the large one. From the mid-1950s historical trends in this direction are observable in bilateral Afghan and Soviet trade.

Afghanistan before 1978

Soviet economic efforts in Afghanistan before 1978 can be roughly divided into two periods:

Between 1921 and 1955, the Soviet Union tried, but on the whole failed, to obtain trade concessions from the Afghans and to penetrate the Afghan economy for political as well as economic gains.

From 1955 to 1978, the Soviets finally gained a foothold in Afghanistan and utilized complex and multifaceted techniques to achieve the following goals:

1. To penetrate the Afghan economy in various sectors and at multiple levels by diverting Afghan trade from free world markets; by granting large-scale credits at unrealistically low, nominal interest rates of 2 percent or

less[3]; and by insinuating direct Soviet participation into Afghan economic planning and policy formulation for sectoral allotments of government investments.

2. To increase Afghan dependency on the Soviet economy through a rising volume of bilateral trade; through increased transit trade via the USSR to other markets[4] (skillfully taking advantage of Afghan-Pakistani friction to encourage the Afghans to rely on Soviet transit alternatives); through growing Afghan debt obligations; and through complex monetary and barter arrangements (whose term structures are still unknown).

1919 to 1955

Inheriting the empire of tsarist Russia and its expansionist ambitions, the new Soviet government was determined not merely to regain and hold the old imperial territories but to extend them. Despite rhetoric denouncing colonialism and exploitation, the Communist regime ruthlessly crushed independence movements in Central Asia.

Soviet relations with Afghanistan and Muslim Central Asia during the reign of King Amanullah---which roughly coincided with the first decade of Soviet government, and was a period of extraordinary good will toward that still-unknown new regime because of Bolshevik liberal rhetoric---are highly revelatory of long-term Soviet intentions regarding their neighbors, Afghanistan in particular, and are a more accurate reflection of Soviet policy than Lenin's effusions of friendship.

Direct evidence that the new Soviet regime shared old tsarist ambitions in Afghanistan soon became available in connection with Panjdeh, an Afghan territory north of Mazar-i-Sharif and Herat which had been invaded and annexed by tsarist Russia in 1885 in violation of treaty commitments [See map, p. 36].

In February 1921, the Soviets signed a treaty with Amanullah providing for the lawful return of this Afghan territory.[5] But Panjdeh was never returned; it was instead incorporated into the Turkmen SSR.

That same 1921 treaty acknowledged the independence of the Muslim states of Bukhara and Khiva, in accordance with Lenin's assurances of good intentions toward the Muslim kingdoms and his encouragement of Amanullah's pan-Islamic leadership ambitions. Yet even as the treaty was being signed, the Muslims in Bukhara, Khiva, and other independent states in Turkestan were under attack by Communist forces.

For some years Afghanistan supported those Muslims, accepting more than 200,000 refugees and providing assistance to the fighting men, the so-called "Basmachi."[6]   Eventually the Soviets, by a combination of inducements and threats, were able to persuade Afghanistan to cut off its support. Thus isolated, the Muslim states were eventually subdued by a ruthless war of attrition. Subsequently the Soviets settled more Slavs in these regions,[7] where economic dependency was increased by encouraging the population to concentrate on the production of raw agricultural commodities such as cotton to be exported to the European part of the USSR in exchange for manufactured goods. Essentially, with some exceptions this economic pattern still continues.[8]

Meanwhile, the Soviets were already attempting to penetrate Afghanistan economically. Moscow proposed that the 1921 treaty, which provided for an exchange of consulates, should permit Soviet trade with private merchants as well as with the Afghan government.[9] Had this proposal been accepted, the Soviets would have had wide access to Afghan citizens through consulates in the key cities of Herat, Kandahar, Mazar-i-Sharif, Maimana and Ghazni, as well as through their embassy in Kabul. Soviet officials could have used their overwhelming state-based monopoly/monopsony power in direct trade with individuals and private firms, and trade access would, of course, have facilitated political access.

Although this project was rejected, the treaty did allow Afghan goods to enter the USSR duty-free, while Afghan duty on Soviet goods was cut to 5 percent. The result was a substantial increase in bilateral trade: Afghan exports to the USSR rose from 1.3 million rubles in 1923/24 to 11.7 million rubles in 1928/29, while imports from the USSR in the same period jumped from a mere 69,000 rubles to 7 million rubles.[10] After Amanullah's abdication in 1929, the few Soviet consulates that had been opened during his reign were closed and trade stagnated, but the Soviets did not give up. When a new commercial treaty was under negotiation in 1936, they again proposed to open consulates with trading privileges in all major Afghan cities. Again they were turned down.

1955 to 1978

In late 1954 the United States refused to provide military assistance to Afghanistan, and Daoud turned to the Soviets. In addition to opening a major avenue of penetration and dependency via the military, this also opened an equally important avenue of penetration through bilateral economic relations. In December 1955, Nikita Khrushchev and Nikolai Bulganin visited Kabul and offered the Afghans a $100 million loan at a nominal interest of 2 percent. This time Afghanistan, under Daoud, accepted.

By 1967, Soviet credits to Afghanistan totalled $570 million. By 1978, the total committed and uncommitted Soviet credit to Afghanistan had climbed to $1.265 *billion.* A comparison with U.S. credit and grants, which started before 1955 but totaled only $470 million by 1977, makes it clear that the Soviet strategy was to outperform U.S. financial aid in the development process, thereby gaining wider political as well as economic influence.

From the Afghan perspective, both the absolute magnitude of Soviet credit and its sectoral size distribution were important. As foreign debt grew, so did Afghanistan's repayment burden, as indicated by the need to reschedule debt repayments. Moreover, the greater the concentration of Soviet loans in any given sector of the Afghan economy, the greater the dependency of Afghan policymaking in that particular sector on Soviet decisions and influence.

Soviet influence was exerted through the loan term structure, the repayment schedules, and the introduction of barter payment in commodities, the price structure of which depended perforce on negotiated arrangements rather than world markets. (This seems to have been applied especially to the development, pricing, and export of natural gas to the Soviet Union: the price and value of the exports were determined by the schedule of debt repayments to Moscow.*) Increasingly the Afghan government found it difficult to argue for better terms of trade such as an increase in the price of gas exports.

It would be a mistake to isolate Soviet economic moves from Soviet political interests in Afghanistan, for how else can Soviet emphasis on loans to Afghanistan be explained? For two decades, from 1955 to 1975, Afghanistan was the third largest LDC recipient of Soviet largesse, outstripped only by Egypt and India.[11] And this, despite the weak Afghan economy and its repayment difficulties.

Those repayment difficulties could be, and were, converted into tools of Soviet policy, enabling the Soviets to increase pressure on the Afghan government. Foreign economic influence on national decision-making and national priorities can be cumulative: the larger the amount of foreign debt and the larger the foreign involvement in technical and policy areas *deriving from one single source,* the greater the total weight of influence that single source can exert. Between 1955 and 1978, the Soviet economic presence and influence on the formulation of Afghan planning and policy became pervasive. By 1978, Afghanistan had more than 2,000 Soviet technical and economic advisers in its midst.

This widespread Soviet involvement in the Afghan economy, structured and applied to complement the simultaneous growth of Afghan military

---

* See: Shroder and Assifi.

dependency,[12] was used to promote political influence both externally (Afghanistan's foreign policy) and internally (penetration of Afghan political and military organizations for long-range Soviet objectives). The pervasive Soviet influence provided an opportunity for large numbers of Soviet personnel to work freely inside Afghanistan as never before to achieve a multiplicity of goals.

Arguably, the short-run goal of many of the Soviet economic programs--- mainly consumer-oriented---was to disarm traditional Afghan suspicion of Russian intentions and to generate acceptance of a Soviet presence.[13] Long-term objectives were more complex, consisting of policies that were deliberately concealed. Two significant aspects of Soviet economic policies in Afghanistan from 1955 to 1978 indicate their long-term nature and the subtlety of their application:

During the formalized planning period that began with the First Five-year Plan (initiated under Daoud in 1956/57*), the USSR gradually became Afghanistan's largest supplier of capital and technical advice. Not surprisingly, Soviet aid did not aim at promoting private investment and private participation in the Afghan economy: it was in Moscow's interest to promote the government's share in the economy and increase its participation. And, indeed, quantitative evidence for the years 1956-1972 indicates that private investment (and therefore private capital formation) was in fact minimized.[14] To some extent this can be blamed on the constraints operating in the economy in general, but in large part, reduced levels of investment in the private sector by both private investors and the government were caused by the deliberate under-utilization of private sector resources and the misallocation of aggregate public investment in disregard of national priorities---that is, the transformation of what had hitherto been a largely private-sector economy into a state-controlled one.

This was nowhere more obvious than in agriculture, which was almost entirely privately owned and operated, primarily by small farmers. Although agriculture was the most important single economic sector, it received a disproportionately small share of public investment.[15] As a result, nearly 50 percent of the arable land, most of which is dependent on irrigation, received little water and/or no cultivation during the three five-year plans (1956-1972), despite a two-year drought-induced famine in some areas. It is typical, hence perhaps noteworthy, that the sole Soviet aid involvement in the agricultural sector before 1978 was the establishment of

---

* The Afghan fiscal year begins 21 March and overlaps the international calendar year.

a model state-owned farm in Nangrahar province, the crops of which were entirely exported to the USSR.

Since the invasion, agriculture has been singled out by Soviet forces for a war of attrition and destruction. Long-term trends indicate two distinct Soviet policies: the forced depopulation of rural areas and the gradual extension of government control to private farmland. These policies and their consequences are discussed below. The point to note here is this: if, before the invasion and even before the Communist takeover, Soviet policy anticipated eventual de-privatization and collectivization of Afghan farming, it would be plausible for them to have influenced planning policy against allocating a greater share of total investment to privately owned agriculture during the planning years. Actual planning investment patterns support this argument.

Second, in the manufacturing sector and, in particular, in the sector that offered the greatest potential for a rapidly growing Afghan economy, the development of mining and mineral exploitation, Soviet economic aid was almost entirely limited to projects that were linked, directly or indirectly, with the Soviet economy. This policy prevented the development of an Afghan industrial base that would not only have raised national income but would also have led to the training and development of skilled labor and would have utilized the often-wasted capacities of Afghanistan's new educated class. The Soviets formally agreed to help finance and develop basic industries---but reneged when it came to implementing the agreements.

These dependency policies parallel those applied directly in Soviet Central Asia, which has been kept in a colonial dependency relationship to Russia and the Slavic SSRs, i.e., providing raw materials and minerals in exchange for manufactured goods.[16] It seems clear that the Soviets were extending this policy to the Afghan economy long before the Communist coup or the invasion.

As noted above, the mechanism used by the Soviet Union in creating Afghan economic dependency was bilateral trade. The growing Afghan debt to Moscow had to be repaid; and long before the Afghan Communists seized power in 1978, the Afghan economy was increasingly tied into that of the Soviet Union.[17]

Since the Communist takeover and Soviet invasion

It has been widely assumed that the invasion of Afghanistan has burdened the Soviet Union with an ongoing economic drain; indeed, this is part of the rationale for the frequent description of Afghanistan as "Moscow's Vietnam." An examination of the economic data suggests

Table 1

Selected Soviet Exports to Afghanistan Since the Communist Takeover
(in U.S. dollars)

Year*	Machinery, equipment, vehicles (code 10-19)	Geological equipment: drilling and extraction (code 12860)	Aircraft (code 193)	Trucks (code 1910-19110)	Petroleum, petroleum products (code 21.22)
1979	$128,113,680	$31,367,400	$1,052,940	$17,825,460	$54,429,960
1980	156,425,840	36,790,800	963,240	28,426,620	102,884,000
1981	223,298,400	50,407,040	78,616,100	30,799,920	97,578,640
1982	299,219,040	27,563,120	125,110,480	46,087,680	98,396,000
1983	246,158,640	23,372,960	57,685,760	42,943,360	157,862,000
1984	455,744,160	22,679,360	222,470,160	66,450,960	162,684,560
Totals	$1,307,991,200	$192,180,680	$485,898,740	$232,534,000	$673,835,160

Source: Foreign Trade of the USSR in 1980, 1982, 1983 and 1984, Statistical Compendiums. Ministry of Foreign Trade, Moscow 1981, 1983 and 1985.

Domestic dollar/ruble rates are different from foreign trade rates. Conversion rates applied here are $1.38 per ruble for 1979/80 and $1.36 thereafter.

* The figures in this table are for the international calendar year, not the Afghan fiscal year.

however that, far from facing an economic drain in Afghanistan, the Soviet Union is forcing the Afghan economy to bear much of the military cost--- and that in any case, the Soviets expect to make economic gains in the long run.

Information on the Afghan economy and trade since the invasion---and for that matter since the Communist takeover in 1978---is perforce based in part on data provided by Moscow, Comecon countries and the puppet regime in Kabul---data that are limited and in the case of Kabul, unreliable---plus extrapolations from announcements of trade agreements, new loans, etc., as well as data provided by international organizations. But even these limited data indicate that what pass for "economic development" and "trade relations" are far from the international norm. They indicate that under the rubric of international trade, the Afghans are being forced to pay for the invasion and occupation of their country. They also indicate that the Soviets are giving priority to the implementation of what can only be a long-planned exploitation of Afghanistan's major mineral resources in ways that will benefit only the Soviet economy. They further indicate that the Afghans are also being forced to pay for the despoliation of their natural resources.

An indicated in Table 1, between 1979 and 1984 alone, the Soviets "sold" to Afghanistan more than 2 billion dollars worth of heavy equipment, much of it military, including more than $718 million in aircraft and trucks. These include of course the aircraft which bomb and strafe Afghan villages and spray incendiaries over the crops, and the trucks on which the Soviet and Afghan armies and their supplies move.* (By way of comparison, in the two years preceding the Communist takeover, Afghanistan imported a total of $4.2 million worth of trucks, most of them for ordinary commercial use; and international trade figures for the years 1974-1979 show no aircraft purchases at all.)

Equally important is the nature of what are seemingly non-military items, and their intended use. "Machinery, equipment and transportation vehicles" totaled $456 million for 1984 alone, and $1.3 billion for 1979-84. The exact nature of these items is not specified, and is not readily ascertainable; but almost certainly a significant part of them---"equipment and transportation vehicles"---is military in nature, for there is no sector of the Afghan economy that could absorb such large imports on a continuing basis. Moreover, this is not even the complete story, for Soviet exports

---

* The figures on aircraft, trucks and petroleum also serve to indicate the intensification of the war, e.g., the four-fold increase in aircraft between 1983 and 1984.

of machinery and equipment to the main sectors of the Afghan economy are listed separately---agricultural equipment, manufacturing machinery for textile, chemical, and other industries, road construction equipment, the geological equipment included in Table 1, and several other categories of vehicles, such as passenger cars and tractors.

Some of these items may be equipment for the building and enlargement of the massive Soviet air bases at Shindand, Bagram, Kabul, and elsewhere, and for the underground installations reportedly being built in several areas. Some may be for the construction of housing for Soviet personnel (which goes on apace), for the repair of major highways damaged by the ongoing war, or for the missile emplacements which have reportedly been constructed. It is likely that some of it may be intended for use in constructing railroads: the Soviets have announced their intention to run rail lines from their border to key supply depots. Only the mujahideen have thus far prevented the construction of these lines.

Soviet sales of petroleum and petroleum products reveal again the exploitative, colonialist Soviet approach to developmental aid. Under the rubric of Afghanistan's Seven Year Plan (initiated in 1976), the Soviets agreed to build a petroleum refinery in Afghanistan[18]---but never began it. Although the fact is not shown in Soviet trade statistics, as late as 1982 Afghanistan exported $44.66 million of crude oil to the USSR while purchasing $98.4 million in refined petroleum and petroleum products. Since prices were not made public for either transaction, there is at least room for a presumption of exploitation: low prices for Afghan crude (as is the case with Afghan natural gas), high prices for Soviet refined products.

In fact, neither Soviet trade data nor international trade statistics show *any* exports of mineral resources other than natural gas from Afghanistan to the Soviet Union, *although these are known to occur.* In addition to the crude oil mentioned above, there are widespread reports of Soviet mining of uranium and the seizure of government stores of lapis lazuli and emerald. Efforts to begin mining copper at Ainak have begun, though fighting has hampered them.

Meanwhile, of the petroleum products being "sold" to Afghanistan, a high proportion must be flowing through the Soviet-made pipeline to Soviet military installations for use by the invading forces, since civilian usage is much diminished by the war conditions and population flight and it is known that kerosene and bottled gas, used for cooking and heating in the major cities, is often in short supply.

As for the geological equipment for drilling and extraction, that is a clear-cut indication of Soviet intentions to exploit Afghanistan's known major mineral resources and its potentially significant hydrocarbon resources, as discussed in more detail below. Suffice it here to say that Afghan natural gas, at prices well below world market rates, is being exported steadily into the Soviet Union to pay for these new "purchases"---in other words, to pay the cost of the Soviet invasion, occupation and exploitation of the country (reportedly, the gas fields in the north, in the Shibarghan area, are among the most heavily guarded Soviet installations); and that it is obvious that similar exploitation of other resources can be expected. In short, the cost of the war is being shifted to the Afghan economy, and those sectors of the economy which are not significantly useful to Soviet policy are being treated as expendable.

Agriculture

Agriculture is the most severely affected sector of the economy, rapidly approaching large-scale economic disaster. Before the war, Afghanistan was essentially self-sustaining in food production except for sporadic problems resulting from regional droughts. Indeed, it was a food-exporting country, selling fresh and dried fruits and nuts throughout the region.

Before 1978, more than 87 percent of the Afghan population lived in some 22,750 rural villages. The basic values of Afghan society are found in their purest form in these communities: a strong faith in Islam and a firm belief in freedom, private property rights and private enterprise, along with a largely self-sufficient structure of production which also produced surplus for the cities and exports. Most of the rural population were small independent farmers. Large land holdings were rare, especially for irrigated land where an average holding did not exceed five or six hectares (twelve to fifteen acres); for dry farming, land holdings might be large *by Afghan standards,* i.e., as much as 200 acres or more.

The first large-scale dislocations in the agricultural sector occurred after the Communist takeover in 1978, the result of forced land redistribution (labeled "reforms") carried out in accordance with a doctrinaire Marxist approach by the Taraki and Amin regimes. Indeed, this is what led to the initial rural resistance. Since the Soviet invasion and the installation of the Parcham faction in Kabul, Communist policies on land redistribution have remained unclear; but several other major developments of a dramatic and cataclysmic nature have severely damaged agriculture and the rural communities.[19]

It is clear that from the beginning of their open involvement in December 1979, the Soviets have carried out a policy of depopulating much of rural Afghanistan through a campaign of massive bombardments, crop destruction, the destruction of the intricate underground irrigation systems *(karez)* on which production depends, the slaughter of livestock, the destruction of orchards and vineyards, and above all through a terror campaign of massacres and atrocities committed in many areas. This policy was pointed out as early as December 1980.[20] The result has been the large-scale abandonment of farming and farmland, much of which will revert to desert without continuous care and maintenance.

The losses are revealed by figures published by the Kabul regime itself; though not reliable, they are indicative. In 1975/76, three years before the Communist takeover, 3.882 million hectares (9.59 million acres) were under cultivation. In 1984, the Kabul regime reported that 2.9 million hectares (7.16 million acres) were under cultivation.[21] Assuming that this figure is correct, then by their own account *more than one-quarter of existing arable land had already been abandoned by 1984*. Since the attacks on villages have intensified since then and the number of refugees continues to increase, one can assume that by now well over 50 percent of the arable land has been abandoned, as commonly reported.

Recent studies show some of the concentrated effects on agriculture:[22] an estimated five million animals were destroyed by the Soviet/DRA troops between 1980-84; percentage reductions estimated in outputs are: for wheat 80; for corn 77; for barley and rice, 74 each; for cotton, 88. The farm labor supply is estimated to have fallen by 52 percent between 1978 and 1987. The policy of rural depopulation is further evidenced by the composition of the refugee population, the overwhelming majority of whom were farmers and rural villagers before the invasion. The deliberate attacks on the agricultural structure, coupled with drought conditions in some provinces in 1983/84 and again in 1984/85, have led to what have been described as pre-famine conditions in some areas.[23]

There are two basic reasons for the Soviet policies of depopulating rural Afghanistan and destroying rural life: since 1978, the rural communities have been the strongholds of opposition to communism and have provided the support base for the mujahideen. Moreover, agricultural land is largely privately owned and farmed, and the farmers who resisted land redistribution[24] will also resist collectivization.

The motivation for policies of massive depopulation and the destruction of the rural infrastructure is therefore obvious. The Soviets and the regime are unconcerned about the possibility of famine in these areas; indeed famine serves their purposes. As for Kabul and the few other major towns or selected districts either under regime control or wooed by them, any food shortages are met through imports of wheat from the Soviet Union. By destroying food supplies in the rural areas---as well as purchasing any available local surpluses at inflated prices---the Soviets also exert economic pressure on the mujahideen and the resisting population as a whole.

Surviving Afghan fruit crops are used to help pay the bill for Soviet "aid": dried fruits and nuts are shipped to the USSR and Eastern Europe, and sometimes resold to Western Europe.

Manufacturing

Before 1978, manufacturing was only a small sector of the Afghan economy. Cement, urea, and a few other products produced on a modest scale had been added to earlier Afghan textile manufacturing, largely for domestic consumption. Despite rather grandiose pronouncements in the Five Year Plan announced by the Afghan Communists since they seized power in 1978, and more recent (1985) extensive projections of proposed developments in manufacturing and other sectors, by April 1986 only a disjointed list of unrelated projects had been announced as major manufacturing development projects.[25]

Soviet policies toward manufacturing in Afghanistan appear to have two objectives:

1. To discourage the development of heavy and light industries that (a) require large capital investment and/or (b) would result in substitution for Soviet-produced goods;

2. To promote the development of certain consumer goods, such as prefabricated housing and bakeries; and also to develop certain other industries, such as cement, that involve high transport costs for Soviet products. Even in this case, some Afghan cement has been exported in exchange for Soviet cement; the higher quality of Afghan cement presumably subsumes the transport costs.

The general picture in manufacturing indicates that this sector is suffering from labor shortages, shortages of raw materials, outages of power, and idle capacity even in the small manufacturing base that existed before 1978. Consumer needs such as textiles and sugar, previously largely met by domestic production, are now met by imports from the USSR. By 1986, in some provinces (Balkh), up to 50 percent of the manufacturing industries were inactive. Some industries such as textiles were severely affected even earlier: between 1978-1982, output of textiles fell by 70 percent, from Afs. 5,463 billion to Afs. 1,651 billion. By 1984, one third of the population had either been killed or had left the country, so consumer demand had fallen by one third; nevertheless, in 1982-1984, imports of textiles from the Soviet Union rose by 180 percent from 3.3 to 9.26 million meters. What proportion of this is due to trade diversion from the free markets is not known.

In general this kind of trend is repeated in other manufacturing industries with different degrees of severity. The overall trend is clear; only the actual magnitudes are unknown.

The expected pay-offs

As noted, by 1978 the Soviet Union had advanced to Afghanistan a total of $1.265 billion in credits. In April 1985, the Kabul regime announced that since 1978 Moscow had provided an additional $946.64 million, for a total of more than $2.2 billion. According to Kabul, $448.47 million of this was a generous "grant"; but even if this is true, it would still leave Afghanistan in debt to Moscow to the tune of $1.763 billion dollars as of 1985, with more "aid" to be paid for every day as the war continues.

On the basis of published Soviet trade statistics, it appears that in the years 1979-1984, Afghanistan's cumulative balance-of-trade deficit with the USSR (value of imports from the Soviet Union minus the value of exports to the Soviet Union) amounted to an additional $849.19 million, which confirms 90 percent of the above credit extension. This deficit grew by another $372 million in 1985-1986, thus adding an equivalent amount to the debt structure, bringing the total debt to $2.135 billion by the end of 1986.

How is such a debt to be paid off, ever, by a country that was poor to begin with and is now ruined, depopulated, and destitute? There are clear indications that the Soviet Union has been thinking of that for many years and knows exactly what payment it wants.

In any ranking of Soviet economic interests in Afghanistan, direct and unlimited access to Afghan mineral and energy resources must head the list. For decades, the Soviets worked to gather information about those resources and, in the process, they have made sure that neither Afghanistan nor any international investors developed them. It is quite clear that they planned to control their exploitation for the benefit of the Soviet economy and Soviet policies.

Northern Afghanistan is geologically related to areas of Turkestan in which are found some of the Soviet Union's richest and most accessible mineral and hydrocarbon resources. The Soviets therefore had good reason to expect that a survey of Afghan resources would yield significant discoveries, and for decades they pressured the Afghan government to make sure that, especially north of the Hindu Kush, nobody but themselves would be allowed to explore or develop them.* Eventually the Soviets were instrumental in conducting the most comprehensive survey of mineral resources ever made in Afghanistan. The survey report completed in 1977 indicates that Afghanistan is rich in mineral resources. The survey showed the presence of 1,432 minerals of significance, including many of

---

* Indeed, for decades foreigners were forbidden even to visit certain areas of the north as tourists without special permission from the Afghan Ministry of Interior.---ed.

international economic or strategic importance, pinpointing the locations and categorizing them as deposits, occurrences, and showings, with detailed maps.[26]

The results of this survey, and the details of Soviet dealings with Afghanistan in this connection as well as Soviet moves to exploit the massive resources discovered, are significant in assessing the economic aspects of Soviet policy toward Afghanistan.

From the Soviet perspective, the exploitation of these and any other subsequent discoveries can meet policy needs in several possible ways:

• Some resources would be useful to the Soviet economy if their production and transportation costs would be comparable to or lower than other existing sources, including Soviet domestic sources. Afghanistan's copper ores and possibly its massive deposits of high-grade iron ores, among others, fall into this category.

• For strategic minerals such as uranium and rare earths, costs are not a primary consideration. High content deposits of rare earths, uranium and strontium, among others, were discovered in Helmand province; since 1980 there have been persistent reports of secret Soviet mining of uranium there and near Kabul.[27]

• The Soviet Union may not itself need some of Afghanistan's rich mineral resources. But it may want control of specific resources to be used in the overall framework of a zero-sum game that the USSR plays with the free enterprise economies, particularly with the United States. Moreover, the Soviet Union may want the control and development of essential resources in negotiating for economic-cum-political gains with developing economies that require such resources for their own industrial growth. How any of the large number of minerals found in Afghanistan might fit into such a schema is uncertain.

Whatever the particular purposes of specific programs, however, it is clear that Soviet economic policies toward Afghanistan, both before and since the invasion, include the application of cost-benefit analysis. While economic interests may be only one element of overall Soviet strategic policies toward Afghanistan, economic gains are neverthless maximized whenever possible.

At the least, the Soviets shift the cost of their involvement in Afghanistan to the Afghan economy whenever possible. This is apparent from the list of Soviet exports to Afghanistan in Table 1 (page 80), in which shipments of military equipment *that is used against the Afghan people* are charged to the Afghan economy: even if some parts of the listed expenditures are allocated as so-called "grants" to the DRA, it is clear that the balance is charged to the economy.

As noted, the small and declining manufacturing sector of the Afghan economy and the agricultural sector, which has undergone substantial destruction and neglect since 1979 and is in addition subject to drought, cannot generate enough output to meet Afghanistan's debt payments to the USSR. Even though reported exports of Afghan textiles, cement, chemical fertilizer (urea), raisins and fruits are mentioned from time to time in the press or even in Soviet trade data, these are relatively modest quantities and their exports cannot be applied to reduce the growing trade deficit, let alone pay off the large debt to the USSR. In fact, except for natural gas, the value of total Afghan exports to the Soviet Union steadily declined from 1981 to 1985 (the last period for which consistent data are available). This is hardly surprising: it reflects the decline in agricultural production since the invasion.

While it is of course possible that much unrecorded bilateral trade occurs, it is clear from the flows of recorded commodity trade, and from the damage known to have been done to agriculture and other sectors of the Afghan economy by the war, that Afghanistan can hope to pay off its growing deficit with the Soviet Union only from that sector of the economy which offers the greatest potential for increased output, namely the mining sector.

Except for natural gas, Soviet trade statistics show no other minerals as being imported from Afghanistan. Occasional press reports of exports of crude oil, uranium, coal, gems and precious stones mentioned above are sporadic and unconfirmable. That does not mean that unrecorded exports of these and other minerals to the USSR are not taking place---only that there is no clear evidence yet. In any case, however, the question remains: to what area of the mining sector will the substantial imports of geological equipment contained in Table 1 be applied? Between 1979 and 1984, these imports of mineral exploration, extraction and drilling equipment amounted to more than $192 million. If there are no payoffs from these investments, why are they occurring?

Clearly, payoffs for the Soviets either exist or are expected. But another question arises: if these exports of geological equipment are part of the trade balance that Afghanistan is paying for, why are the outputs of the mineral sector not recorded in domestic production in Afghanistan? And if they are exported to the Soviet Union, why are such exports not recorded?

A look at the exploitation of Afghan natural gas---the first major resource development undertaken in Afghanistan---offers some answers to these questions, and indicates the economic benefits the Soviet Union expects to reap.

The example of natural gas

The Soviet development of natural gas in northern Afghanistan exclusively for export to the Soviet Union is of exemplary interest in this connection. These gas supplies, exported into Soviet Central Asia at very low prices, release Soviet supplies for transmission to European Russia, Eastern and Western Europe. Afghanistan's exports of natural gas, initially intended to pay off import requirements for developments, now are being used not only to pay the cost of the Soviet occupation but may indirectly be generating hard currency for the USSR. The integration of Afghan gas reserves into the Soviet supply network seems to be part of long-run Soviet energy strategy.[28]

The exports and pricing of natural gas to the Soviet Union are important not only because gas has become the largest item among Afghan exports but also because at least some statistics on gas are available, including Soviet trade statistics. These confirm the longstanding Afghan complaint that the Soviets have been exploiting this important Afghan resource without appropriate compensation.

There is significant reason to believe that reported figures do not tell the full story of Afghan losses on natural gas, since various factors---including the location of the gas meters in the Soviet Union, and the barring of Afghan access to them---make it likely that for years the USSR has been taking more and paying less than acknowledged figures indicate. Nevertheless, even on the basis of published figures, it is possible to estimate some part of the loss of revenue to Afghanistan:

According to the Soviet data, during the period 1979-1981 the Soviets imported 5.2 billion cubic meters (cm) of Afghan gas for which they paid about $48 per 1000 cm. This compared to the international price of $114.78 per 1000 cm at that time. On this basis, the loss of revenue to Afghanistan for those two years alone was approximately $335.8 million. In fact, in 1979 the USSR agreed to pay Afghanistan $83.37 per 1000 cm (25 percent below world prices); if the loss is calculated merely on the difference between the agreed below-market price and the actual Soviet payment, it still amounts to a sum of $172.5 million.[29]

This does not of course take into account other costs, including the cost to Afghanistan, both directly and in terms of economic growth, because it does not have access to its own gas for internal use and development. If complete figures were available, therefore, the Afghan loss would have to be significantly larger---and this covers a period of only two years out of almost twenty years in which Afghan gas has flowed northward.

It is therefore clear that, whatever prices are applied to measure losses, Afghanistan has been experiencing substantial losses in revenue from the exports of Afghan gas to the Soviet Union over a period of two decades; and these losses are cumulative. The Afghan economic losses are, of course,

Soviet economic gains. Given what has taken place in the development and export of Afghan natural gas, it is not unreasonable to assume that the Soviet Union will apply a similar approach to the development of other major Afghan natural resources.

Conclusions

For nearly seventy years, economic policies have been one of the main Soviet vehicles for developing economic and political influence in Afghanistan. These policies are intended to develop Afghan economic dependency on the USSR and to integrate the small Afghan economy with the overwhelming Soviet economy.

Some of these are not recent policies; they extend back beyond the 1950s. In fact, they go back to the very establishment of the Soviet Union and the first contacts of the Bolshevik government with Afghanistan, and to the 1920s, when the core of Soviet policies toward Afghanistan was formulated. These policies met with a degree of success under King Amanullah, were then rebuffed and set back by his successors in the 1930s and 1940s, and finally found opportunity with the ascension of Prime Minister Daoud in 1953.

Beginning in 1955, the Soviet Union undertook a multi-faceted economic offensive, utilizing a "soft" approach that involved increasing complexities in bilateral economic transactions. The magnitude of those transactions became pervasive: between 1955 and 1975, Afghanistan was the third largest recipient of Soviet loans to developing countries, and for the Afghans, the Soviet Union became the largest source of economic aid. The Soviets used these loans to influence political as well as economic decisions of the Afghan government; to create economic dependency through transactions (loans and the scheduling of debt repayment); to divert Afghan commodity trade from the free world markets to the Soviet economy, thereby bringing about greater integration of the small Afghan economy with that of the USSR; and to ensure that Afghan resources were not developed independently for the benefit of the Afghan nation itself but were either exploited for the economic benefit of the USSR or left undeveloped to await the opportunity for such exploitation in future.

Economic integration was designed along lines complementary to Soviet production and consumption structures. Using the sectoral distribution of the large loans to Afghanistan, the increasing volume of trade, and Soviet participation in planning formulations (as well as actually reneging on several agreements), Soviet strategy was designed to produce an Afghan production structure geared to the production of primary goods, including mineral and agricultural products, for the Soviet market. (None of the major industrial projects that the Soviets agreed to finance and develop under the 1976 Seven Year Plan has materialized.)

In the manufacturing sector, Soviet economic policies toward Afghanistan since the invasion remain unchanged. Those focussed on Afghan agriculture---i.e., the rural communities that provide the basis of resistance to Soviet aggression---have been actively destructive: the depopulation of entire districts through massive bombardments; massacres of the civilian population, including women and children; destruction of crops, orchards, animal stock, and the essential irrigation systems. The result has been the world's largest social dislocation and refugee population, more than five million refugees (approximately 34 percent of the prewar population) now in Pakistan and Iran* and another estimated two million living as displaced persons inside Afghanistan---largely in Kabul, which has grown from about 900,000 to approximately 1.3 million† since 1979, but many also in the mountains and valleys that are relatively secure under Resistance control. Coupled with the estimated loss of one million lives, this means that more than 52 percent of the pre-invasion population have disappeared from their homes, villages and towns throughout Afghanistan. The full implications of these primary areas of concern on other areas in the economy are not known.

But, given the effects of these massive population dislocations and losses and the effects of the rising casualties and continued outflows of refugees, the Afghan economy is clearly pressured toward eventual collapse. The Soviets are destroying the economic infrastructure that supports the mujahideen, and the balance of the economy still under production cannot meet the requirements of the remaining civilian population. Coupled with the effects of the recent drought, pre-famine conditions are occurring in many parts of the country.

In view of the fact that the manufacturing sector in Afghanistan is small and dwindling, and that the agricultural sector has lost both labor and land (an estimated one million hectares, about 26 percent of the prewar cultivable land, had been ruined by 1984), it is obvious that any large economic gains to the Soviets can come only from the mining and hydrocarbon sector.

The Soviets, involved in mining exploration and development as well as

---

* According to UNHCR, Iran reported between 2-2.5 million Afghan refugees as of late 1986, and UNHCR data indicate approximately 3.2 million registered in Pakistan by the end of that year. Approximately 50,000 others are scattered elsewhere, mostly in Europe, the U.S. and India.

† According to official DRA figures.

natural gas before the invasion, have substantially increased their activities in these fields since 1980. As noted, the prices paid to Afghanistan for natural gas have been substantially below world prices, about 60 percent below prices paid to Iran, and much below Soviet internal prices. The loss in revenue to Afghanistan was $336 million in just two years. These losses for natural gas create a strong presumption of similar losses in other areas of mineral production and exports, now and in future---losses to Afghanistan, but clearly benefits to the Soviet economy.

These facts do not support the facile and all-too-common assumption that the Soviets are paying all the economic costs of their aggression in Afghanistan themselves, and that it must necessarily be a drain they can ill-afford. In economic terms, Afghanistan is certainly not "Moscow's Vietnam," as it is commonly referred to. Any analysis of Soviet actions, intentions, strategy or tactics regarding Afghanistan that fails to take into consideration these economic realities cannot be taken seriously.

Notes

1. Cf., for example, P. Gruzinov, *The USSR's Management of Foreign Trade* (New York: M.E. Sharpe, Inc., 1979).

2. John R. Thomas has recently argued that natural resources, both within the Soviet Union and in the LDCs, play an important and special role in Soviet foreign policy. In the case of Siberian resources, the Soviets are trying to entice and intimidate Japan into trading technology for resources; in the case of LDCs, Soviet policy is twofold: obtaining access to LDC resources and denying such access to the United States and its allies. See Thomas, *Natural Resources in Soviet Foreign Policy* (New York: National Strategy Information Center, Agenda Paper No. 15, 1985).

3. This interest rate was applied to the first major Soviet loan to Afghanistan---$100 million in 1955. The USSR easily converted such a low nominal rate of interest to a much higher real rate of cost of borrowing by raising export prices of the goods that such a capital loan was to be spent on, by lowering the monetary or barter prices of Afghan exports to the Soviet Union and by raising the costs of the services that accompany the transfer of capital loans, e.g., the salary, benefits, etc. for Soviet technical workers. See also: Shroder and Assifi, this volume.

4. Observable transit trade through the Soviet Union to markets in Europe has substantially increased since the invasion, though the actual volume cannot be determined from available trade data. Earlier diversions in transit trade to the Soviet Union were due to political disputes between landlocked Afghanistan and Pakistan, on which the Soviets capitalized.

5. For the provisions of this treaty, see: Ludwig W. Adamec, *Afghanistan 1900-1923: A Diplomatic History* (Los Angeles: University of California, Near Eastern Center, 1967): 188-191. Item no. IX states that "...Russia agrees to hand over to Afghanistan the frontier districts which belonged to the latter in the last century..."

6. See: Michael Rywkin, *Moscow's Muslim Challenge* (New York: M.E. Sharpe, Inc.): 40-43.

7. Ibid., 59-64.

8. For a discussion of Russian economic policies in these Muslim republics see: Francis Newton, "Soviet Central Asia: Economic Progress and Problems," *The Middle East Economy* (Elie Kedouri, ed. London: Frank Cass, 1976): 87-107.

9. See: Ludwig W. Adamec, *Afghanistan's Foreign Affairs to the Mid-Twentieth Century* (Tucson: University of Arizona Press, 1974): 56.

10. No appropriate afghani/ruble exchange rate is available for the period under discussion.   Even the trade data are available only for some years.   See: Vartan Gregorian, *The Emergence of Modern Afghanistan: 1880-1946* (Palo Alto: Stanford University Press, 1969): 146, 196 and 254.

11. Orah Cooper and Carol Fogarty, "Soviet Economic and Military Aid to the Less Developed Countries 1954-78," Fourth Economic Committee of the U.S. Congress (10 October 1979): 648-662.

12. See: M.S. Noorzoy, "Long Term Economic Relations between Afghanistan and the Soviet Union: An Interpretive Study," *International Journal of Middle East Studies,* vol. 17, no. 2 (1985): 151-173 and sources cited therein.   In the post-invasion period the patterns of building more airports and enlarging existing ones, road construction and the construction of a railroad through Hairatan (1983) all complement military usage even though these are ostensibly constructed for economic reasons.

13. Ibid.: 160-161.

14. See: M.S. Noorzoy, "Planning and Growth in Afghanistan," *World Development,* vol. 4, no. 9 (1976): 761-773.

15. See: M.S. Noorzoy, "Alternative Economic Systems for Afghanistan" *International Journal of Middle East Studies,* vol. 15, no. 1 (1983): 25-45.

16. Cf. Francis Newton, op. cit.

17. Trade figures give the trends which correlate closely with political developments:

Percent of total Afghan imports from the Soviet Union		Percent of total Afghan exports to the Soviet Union	
1957/58 (1st Daoud period)	29%	42%1958/59 (1st Daoud period)	42%
1977/78 (2nd Daoud period)	37%	1962/63 " " "	58%
1978/79 (1st year under Communist regime)	64%	1972/73 (last year of constitutional period)	8.5%
1981-1986 (post-invasion)	68%	1977/78 (last year of 2nd Daoud period)	34%
		1979/80 (Communist regime)	87%

94

Direct imports from the Soviet Union, as a proportion of total imports, have declined from the high of 1979/80. Taken together, in 1985/86 the USSR/East Bloc received 76 percent of Afghanistan's total exports and provided 67 percent of its total imports.

For trade data up to 1981/82 see: Noorzoy, "Long Term Economic Relations between Afghanistan and the Soviet Union," op. cit: Table 2, 164 and 163-166. More recent data are reported on an ongoing basis in FBIS Daily Reports, *South Asia* edition.

18. See: *First Seven Year Plan* [March 1976-March 1983], vol. II (Kabul: Ministry of Planning, 1976): 71.

19. For details see: Noorzoy, "Alternative Economic Systems for Afghanistan," op. cit., 34-38, 43-44 and "Long Term Economic Relations..." op. cit.: 166-169. See also widespread general press reports, and reports of the UN Special Rapporteur, Dr. Claude Malhuret, and others listed in the bibliography of this volume.

20. This was pointed out by the author in the paper "Alternative Economic Sytems for Afghanistan," presented to the annual meeting of the American Anthropological Association in Washington, D.C., in December 1980. Published op. cit. See: pp. 38 and 42.

21. See: FBIS (28 July 1982).

22. See: M. Qasim Yusufi, "Effects of the War on the Agricultural Situation in Afghanistan," in *The Sovietization of Afghanistan*, S.B. Majrooh and S.M.Y. Elmi (Eds.), Peshawar Afghan Jehad Works Translation Centre, (1986): pp. 157-78. See also Azam Gul and Grant Farr, "Decline in Afghan Agricultural Production 1978 to 1982," mimeographed (1983).

23. See: Michael Barry, Johan Lagerfelt and Marie-Odile Terrenoire, *Mission to Afghanistan and Pakistan* (Oxford: Central Asian Survey Incidental Papers No. 4, 1986). "Field Mission Inside Afghanistan." Also see: Frances D'Souza, *The Threat of Famine in Afghanistan* (London: Afghan Aid Committee, 1984), see also: *Monthly Bulletin* (Peshawar: Afghan Information Centre, various issues.)

24. Many small farmers and landless refused to accept redistributed lands.

25. See: FBIS (1 April 1985).

26. Abdullah Shareq, et al. *Mineral Resources of Afghanistan: Afghanistan Geological and Mines Survey* (Kabul: Ministry of Mines, 1977): 419. 2d ed. Translated from Russian by G.M. Bezulov. 12 maps.

27. See: *New York City Tribune* (12 January 1984) and *The Economist* (2 February 1984).

28. Cf. J.B. Hannigan and C.H. McMillan, *The Soviet Energy Stake in Afghanistan and Iran* (Ottawa, Canada: Institute of Soviet and East European Studies, Carlton University, August 1981).

29. Noorzoy, "Long Term Relations..." op. cit., 161-162.

Mineral Resources in Afghanistan
As Compiled by Afghan and Soviet Geologists
As of 1977 (Deposits, Occurrences and Showings)

58 solid combustible materials: 45 coal, 3 lignite, 9 peat, 1 shale.

898 metallic minerals:
  85 ferrous metals, 69 iron, 2 manganese, 14 chromium, 241 copper, 92 lead and zinc, 7 aluminum, 4 molybdenum, 136 tungsten, 174 tin, 12 bismuth, 141 mercury, 1 cadmium, 27 beryllium, 44 lithium, 11 cesium and ribidium, 32 tantalum and niobium.

4 radioactive elements: uranium, thorium and rare earths.

105 precious metals: 95 lode gold, 5 placer gold, 5 silver.

Total of 118 non-metallic minerals, including 36 chemical raw materials:
  8 sulphur, 7 fluorite, 17 barite, 2 celestite, 2 borosilicate.

2 mineral fertilizers.

80 other non-metallic minerals:
  22 muscovite, 26 asbestos, 7 talc, 2 magnesite, 6 graphite, 17 gypsum.

14 salts.

20 precious and semi-precious stones:
  1 ruby, 7 emerald, 2 kunzite, 1 garnet, 1 lazarite,
  4 serpentine, 5 tourmaline.

23 electronic and optical minerals:
  18 quartz, 5 calcite.

69 industrial materials:
  5 limestone, dolomite and marble quarries;
  20 facing and ornamental quarries;
  15 sand and gravel quarries;
  29 cement raw materials:
    8 limestone and marl quarries; 4 limestone and dolomite fluxes;
    3 refractory clays; 7 clays for brick, roofing tile, etc.;
    4 porcelain and pottery clays; 3 glass raw material and siliceous sandstone.

Prepared by M.S. Noorzoy.
Source: Abdullah Shareq et al., eds. *Mineral Resources of Afghanistan*
(Kabul: Ministry of Mines, 1977): 73-79.2d. ed. Translated from Russian by G.M. Bezulov.

"The policy and mentality of colonialism are alien to us. We do not covet the lands or wealth of others. It is the colonialists who are attracted by the smell of oil."
   ---Leonid Brezhnev, 1980

Afghan Resources and Soviet Exploitation

John F. Shroder, Jr. and Abdul Tawab Assifi

AFGHANISTAN IS a land whose spectacular scenery contains a stark and dynamic geology. The frequent earthquakes and floods, dust storms and avalanches, are merely surface indicators of long eons of intense mineral-resource generation below the surface. To see this land as a geologist is to know that beleaguered, backward Afghanistan does not have to remain war-torn and economically devastated for long; instead, the rich resource-base there could contribute to rapid development and economic growth.

Some recognition of Soviet military and geopolitical motives in Afghanistan has begun to appear, but thus far almost no attention has been paid to their economic motives. Yet, just as Moscow spent decades preparing the way for a political takeover and military control, so they also spent decades preparing to exploit Afghanistan's many resources---especially its highly valuable minerals---for the Soviet Union's economic benefit. That preparation---and that exploitation---were and still are couched in terminology the Soviets filched from the Marshall Plan and its successors: "developmental aid," "technical assistance," "economic assistance," and similar terms well-suited to the sensibilities of Third World countries. In reality, it has taken the form of the crudest and crassest colonial exploitation--- of a kind abandoned by the other colonial powers long before they gave up their empires. The Soviets repeatedly declared Afghanistan to be the model of their friendly or "fraternal" economic aid programs. Ironically, it is also a fine model of their exploitative practices, and a paradigm of their use of economic and resource techniques.

Their economic policy vis á vis Afghanistan should be viewed in its overall policy context: in all aspects of their foreign policy, the Soviets use a comprehensive approach, coordinating all of their foreign activities and relying on a combination of patient long-term planning and opportunism to attain their goals. Diplomacy, trade, economic and technical assistance, cultural programs and exchanges, military aid, training and educational programs, and ideological penetration are all subservient to the long-range achievement of their strategic geopolitical objectives.

The style of their operation changes, of course, depending on the situation and the phase of their dealings in a given country. Initially, all is amiable: agreements and contracts are wrapped in the language of friendship, noninterference, and sympathetic Soviet protection of the client country against the ambition of others. All is done behind a facade of legality, validity, and correctness. Behind the benevolent terminology, however, the contracts and agreements signed with the Russians have another face which emerges as they are actually implemented. In practice, they are ruthlessly and methodically manipulated for Soviet purposes. As time goes on and the Soviet economic grip on its beneficiary grows tighter, its dealings are handled in an increasingly domineering fashion. The Soviets' intrusive power grows until Moscow attains a position in which it can invalidate past contracts or demand new ones.

Afghanistan is not only a model of what happens when a country becomes entangled in Soviet economic aid programs; it is also, tragically, an example of what actions the Soviets take when such a nation attempts to extricate itself, even slightly, from that heavy-handed grip. Such an effort on the part of the Afghans helped precipitate the Communist coup of 1978, the subsequent failure of which led to the invasion.

It is impossible, in brief compass, to detail all aspects of the Soviet economic program through which Moscow gradually gained control of the Afghan economy, but representative examples will demonstrate Soviet methods of economic penetration, subversion, and exploitation used in Afghanistan (as elsewhere) and the anticipated economic benefits that the Soviet Union expects to reap.

World resource confrontation

Recently the concepts of resource war as applied to the USSR and its foreign policy have been hotly debated among scholars. Some reject the possibility of the Soviets waging a resource war[1] while others are convinced that they not only can, but do.[2]   As long as the USSR had plentiful resources and largely remained out of world markets, the Soviets appeared to be nonthreatening, at least economically speaking.   But a number of changes have led some observers to reverse this assessment:

(a) Increased Soviet import shopping for some materials of which they seemed to have a surplus, e.g., natural gas, lead, copper, zinc, aluminum, molybdenum, cobalt and chromium;

(b) Exports of some of these and other natural resources, e.g., chromium, manganese, lead, titanium, iron, vanadium, nickle, diamonds and precious metals;

(c) Increased fears of the massive export of some materials and cut-off of others as a *threat potential* of the Soviets;

(d) Diplomatic and military maneuvers to disrupt---or to control---other resource-rich areas, particularly Afghanistan, Angola, South Africa, and the Persian Gulf, potentially enabling the USSR to at least deny those resources to the West.

There is indeed little evidence that the USSR would as yet actually be capable of controlling world prices to its advantage by market manipulation. However, Moscow is currently seeking to enter OPEC (Organization of Petroleum Exporting Countries), GATT (General Agreement on Trades and Tariffs), the World Bank and the IMF (International Monetary Fund); these would certainly increase their ability to influence world commerce in materials.[3] Moreover, to discount the desire and ability of the Soviets to pursue some resource acquisition/denial strategies seems rather foolish, given both the reality of their continuing imperial expansion throughout an era when all other empires have been dissolving and the statements of their leadership since 1917. Furthermore the Soviets are unlikely to be blind to the fact that resource insecurity was a significant factor in German and Japanese initiation of both World Wars, and that explosive modern population growth is producing extreme demands upon the world's resources.

Thus, while it would be excessive to suggest that the control of valuable resources is Moscow's primary goal in Afghanistan and elsewhere, it would be most unwise to dismiss their economic aims as insignificant.[4]   A foremost specialist on Soviet resources points especially to two crescent-shaped areas in the Eastern Hemisphere. One, running from North Africa through the Middle East into the Central USSR, contains 74 percent of the world's proven oil and gas reserves; the second, including central and southern Africa, Afghanistan, and the USSR's Kazakhstan and Yakutia mineral belts, contains 61 percent of the world's other proved minerals (excepting coal).[5] In recent years, Soviet activities and those of its Cuban proxy have been heavily concentrated in these two crescents.

In any case, whether Soviet moves are structurally planned, defensive, or opportunistic, they are obviously dependent upon the resources available to further their influence and power. The element of economic opportunism--- i.e., the acquisition of resources for use or even merely for their own sake--- is supported by a defector from Moscow's Institute of United States Studies: "The Soviet government behaves like an ordinary Soviet consumer. He grabs anything which happens to be on the counter, even if he doesn't need it, knowing that tomorrow it may no longer be available."[6] The ever-present *defitsitnye materialy* (commodities shortages) in the USSR,[7] is likely to lead the Soviets to see the world differently than do Americans or Europeans. Thus an essential dimension of conflict with the USSR includes access to the resources of the world as one of the chief prizes.

The hydrocarbons of the Middle East and the minerals of South Africa are only the most obvious resources in Soviet maneuvers toward acquisition and control. Afghanistan is pivotal to the Soviets for both internal and external access to resources:

• *internally*, because Afghanistan can provide additional resources for the development of Central Asia;

• *externally*, because Afghanistan could provide one of the best routes through which to move toward the Indian Ocean and the Straits of Hormuz to fulfill their presumed strategic interests. This, of course, is a continuation of the classic Russian expansion "from heartland to rimland,"[8] which formed the theoretical basis for British efforts to block Russian movements into the area in the nineteenth century.

The significant elements in Soviet mineral resources policy are:

• awareness that between them, the Soviet Union and South Africa conduct much of the world trade in chrome ore, manganese ore, platinum group metals, asbestos and gold;

• limited regard for environmental concerns;

• a centrally planned economy in which consumption is tightly limited by controlled production;

• self-sufficiency as a primary objective with economic cost as only a secondary factor; and

• little encouragement for minerals trade with developing nations.[9]

These factors can be usefully applied as background to the development of the economic relationship between Afghanistan and the Soviet Union.

Afghanistan, Central Asia and the "Soviet Midlands"

Excellent new detail is now available on the regional position and economic integration of Central Asia, Kazakhstan and the Western Siberian economic region in the overall Soviet economic picture, indicating that the geographic mean center of population of the USSR is moving southeastward from the Slavic heartland into Central Asia, near Afghanistan, as a result of high population growth and high soil fertility in the latter areas and their relative accessibility to the country's economic core.[10] There has been intensive economic integration of Western Siberia and northern Kazakhstan into the national mainstream; their resources have been transported mostly westward across the Urals to the Slavic heartland. These areas, in short, constitute the primary Russian energy colony in which a "robber economy" (*Raubwirtschaft*) has been practiced: much is taken, little is returned. Elsewhere in the same areas a plantation economy has been instituted, turning this area into a significant producer of agricultural and mineral raw materials that are consumed and used in the Slavic heartland. In addition, in Central Asia, the ratio of Slavic colonists (who have settled there since the Russian conquest) to the indigenous population has dropped as the Muslim birthrate has skyrocketed, and the limited contacts between the two groups have apparently not changed significantly. Robber and plantation economies are clearly indicated for Afghanistan's future if Soviet control there is consolidated.

The development program for the area seems to be a significant addition to all previously planned projects of water diversion, which include the so-called "Green Bridge" program to ship agricultural products from this area to other parts of the Soviet empire, centrally planned cooperation between districts in some industries, and integration into the national fuel-energy systems. The recent shelving of plans to divert massive amounts of Arctic waters south into Central Asia may have already shifted attention south to the water of the Oxus River and other rivers rising in Afghanistan's Hindu Kush. The lack of iron ore and coking coal in Soviet Central Asia makes that region dependent on outside sources. This potentially further shifts emphasis south towards Afghanistan's rich Hajigak iron deposits, and the plentiful natural gas (on both sides of the border) that can be used for coking.

Furthermore, the position of what has been called "the Soviet Midlands" between European Russia, Siberia and the Far East makes this area a bridge between these widely separated parts of the Soviet empire. All transport links pass through this region: Afghanistan, at the southern edge, can therefore be neatly fitted into future development schemes, as well as opening the way southward.

Afghanistan also offers a potential outlet for the large labor surplus indicated by Soviet Central Asian population growth. Afghanistan's population was low even before the war---only 15 million in a country larger than France. Since 1980 it has been subject to catastrophic larger than France. Since 1980 it has been subject to catastrophic depopulation. A post-war resettlement of Afghanistan by surplus Uzbeks, Tajiks, Turks and others from Soviet Central Asia may be among Soviet plans. (Around 1982 there were rumors that the Soviets were already sending settlers into certain areas in northeastern Afghanistan.) Finally, population pressure within southern Central Asia, and ethnic assertiveness there, have thus far been successfully checked by income maintenance, a vigorous if often corrupt private economy, and a less-than optimal use of labor.[11] The delicate balance could be upset by a number of factors; resettlement in Afghanistan could serve as a safety valve.

Soviet interest in Afghan resources: before 1978

As early as 1927, Moscow indicated its interest in Afghanistan's mineral resources,[12] but it was not until after World War II that the Soviets began to pressure the Government of Afghanistan to let them search for and develop its resources. By then, the Afghans had had some unfortunate diplomatic and resource exploration experiences with the United States,[13] but were reluctant to admit the Soviets. The Afghans instead chose in 1949 to ask the United Nations for assistance in oil exploration; but nothing came of this. In 1950 the USSR offered to undertake the exploration, but Afghanistan rejected the offer, instead asking the French to explore for oil in the north. Meanwhile, the Afghans continued to seek U.S. development aid but, aside from the Helmand Valley irrigation and hydroelectric project, nearly all projects proposed to Washington by the Afghans at that time were rejected. Moscow stepped in with offers to undertake them. In 1953 the Afghan government changed: Daoud came to power and Afghanistan became the first non-Communist country to accept Soviet economic aid.* In 1955 Moscow offered a loan of $100 million at 2 percent interest, part of it earmarked for hydrocarbon exploration, and moved into the leading role in Afghan development.

The Soviet aid was supposedly to be used for projects jointly determined by Afghan-Soviet survey teams. Moreover, the terms of the loan ostensibly left Afghanistan free to spend the money anywhere in the world market, although in practice all contracts went to the Soviets. Ostensibly this was because they were cheaper; in fact, under credit and loan contract pricing methods, they actually cost more and couldn't compete in open international bidding. Nevertheless, Soviet pressures won them the contracts---but that was just the beginning of the hidden costs.

---

* See Poullada; also Noorzoy.

exploitation, for example---did not have the efficiency and productivity of their Western counterparts. The overall development package was enormous, and cannot be fully discussed here, but a few examples will demonstrate: a Soviet drill bit used for hydrocarbon exploration could produce only one-fifth or even one-tenth as much as an American, French, or other bit under the same conditions. Further, the Soviet-made drilling rigs sold to Afghanistan under the economic assistance agreements were clumsy and very much outmoded. When drilling operations had to be moved to an adjacent area---an operation that would take American rigs less than a week---the Russian rigs took a month.

Thus, even leaving aside the subsequent gross exploitation outlined below, ostensibly low-cost Soviet aid actually cost Afghanistan more in return for relatively smaller amounts of services and production; it took longer to achieve results; and the ratio of credit to the value of Afghan natural gas to the USSR was much higher.[14]

Throughout the late 1950s the USSR also made several offers to take over the entire Helmand Valley project from the Americans. These offers were refused, but in 1960 the Soviet pressure enabled Moscow to take over construction of a power plant on the Kabul River begun by West Germany.

Soviet objections to French oil exploration (France then being in NATO) forced the Afghans to cancel the French contract. In 1954, despite continued Soviet requests to take over the exploration, the Afghans replaced the French with a (neutral, non-NATO) Swedish group which began drilling in 1956, but Moscow continued to exert pressure against Afghan use of aid from any other source for oil exploration, even the U.N. or a neutral country. In 1957 Afghanistan was finally pressured into accepting a Soviet loan of $15 million for petroleum exploration to be carried out by Czechoslovakia. Shortly thereafter, the Afghans arranged for the U.S. Geological Survey to provide two geologists to write a new Petroleum Law that was meant to provide background for legislation to help private business.[15] (How this was arranged despite Soviet pressure has not been publicly explained, but the new law was apparently ignored.)

The Czechs took over drilling from the Swedes and very soon (in 1958) they reported oil strikes. In short order, they were replaced by personnel from Soviet Techno-Export, an engineering/development organization with KGB involvement and intelligence capability. By 1960, the Soviets were reporting rich oil finds around Shibarghan in the north of Afghanistan. In 1961 Moscow provided $200 million in additional credit for further gas and oil exploration and development, and in April 1963, the Soviets got a final agreement for the surveying and exploration of other mineral resources.

Thus by 1963, the Soviets had forced out all others and had almost completely taken over the means of resource acquisition and exploration in Afghanistan---not only from other outside competitors but from the Afghans themselves.

At about the same time, the increasing recognition of Afghanistan's resource potential created a need for high quality, large-scale topographical maps to improve geological surveys and mapping for development. For this the Afghans turned to the United States. In 1958/59 American topographers began to fly the entire country for stereographic aerial photography. The Soviets objected and took over the mapping of the northern third of the country in order to keep Western observers away from their borders. Although ground survey and altitude controls were used carefully, overlap between the two sets of maps was incompatible.[16] Nevertheless, a complete topographical map series at various detailed scales was produced in the early 1960s, with only a narrow gap between incompatible maps of some areas. These maps were generally available for about a decade thereafter---until Soviet advisors to the Afghanistan Cartographic Institute gradually transformed the maps into low-level state secrets.

Increasing fears of the Soviet presence in Afghanistan led to Prime Minister Daoud's ouster in March 1963 and his replacement by Dr. Mohammed Yussof, the German-educated former Minister of Mines and Industries. Dr. Yussof inaugurated a decade-long attempt to institute a freer, more democratic system, and to reduce the degree of Afghan dependency on economic aid from the USSR. Throughout this period, and the subsequent second Daoud regime (1973-78), the United States tried in a limited fashion to keep track of the resource question in Afghanistan. In 1963 an internal State Department document suggested that Afghanistan probably had few resources of interest to the U.S. but that further detailed investigations should be made.[17] The U.S. Embassy in Kabul sought to provide some of this information,[18] but by the late 1960s Soviet control over the Ministry of Mines and Industries was sufficient to block full disclosure and stymie progress in resource assessment.

In 1973 the Daoud coup tilted Afghanistan further to the left. Many Western advisors were forced out of the ministeries---in particular the Ministry of Mines and Industries and the Afghanistan Cartographic Institute. A booklet on the Soviet work on Afghan resources was published in English in Kabul,[19] but it was so small and superficial, and the translation so poor and laden with mistakes, that the idea of a scanty resource base was perpetuated. In 1974-1976, however, the United Nations sponsored a resource assessment project and two Canadian geologists were brought in to oversee exploration progress. They reported favorably about potential resources, but were highly critical about concealed documents and attempts to impede their research. Their report was ultimately rejected by the Afghan government and was subsequently suppressed; we may presume that this was done with the encouragement of the many Soviet advisors to the government.

In 1977 a 419-page resource survey was finally published under United Nations authorization. It was identified as the work of Soviet and Afghan geologists, condensed and translated into English by a Russian and edited by one of the Canadians, but even this was held as highly confidential (see below).

Furthermore, we now know from several Afghan defectors that throughout this period Soviet advisors were systematically deluding *the Afghan government itself* about its own resource base. In many cases the results of Russian geological investigations were not communicated to the Afghan government at all---not even to Mr. H. Afzali, the Director of the Afghanistan Geological Survey.[20] In other cases, two sets of reports seem to have been filed: a pessimistic one for Afghan consumption and another, more accurate one for use only in the USSR. By 1976 important maps on geology, mineral resources, tectonics, metallogenesis, hydrogeology and magmatics had been compiled by the Soviets but had not been released.

In fact, as retrospective assessment now reveals, the field data that had been accumulating documented a certain richness in a wide variety of resources for so small a country, and several world-class deposits as well---in iron, copper, emeralds, lapis lazuli, and perhaps rare earth elements.

Apparently, as the geological exploration proceeded, progressive Soviet control of Afghan resources was achieved by political maneuver. The case of the rich Ainak copper deposit is only one example of Soviet manipulation of the Afghan government to gain control of Afghan resources. Exact details are uncertain, but the Deputy Foreign Minister in the Daoud government indicated in 1976 that Soviet threats concerning Afghan debts for economic and military assistance forced Daoud to assign the deposit to the USSR over other higher bids.[21] Similar cases are cited below.

Since the 1978 takeover

Following the Marxist coup in 1978, Soviet involvement in Afghanistan, charged to the Afghans as aid, further increased. In 1978-79, Soviet military technicians (not troops) increased to 4,000, the highest anywhere in the world. More than 4,500 Afghan students were sent to Soviet and East

European institutions (many of them against their will), pushing Communist training programs to record heights. At this time---before the invasion---Afghanistan became fifth among underdeveloped countries in the number of Soviet economic technicians present. In twenty-three years---between 1954 and the 1978 coup---Soviet aid totalled about $1.3 billion. In April 1985, the Kabul regime reported (with effusive expressions of gratitude) that in the seven years since the coup the Soviets had provided $946.64 million more. Although these figures cannot be considered trustworthy (they were not explained, and even if accurate may include military costs), they are at least indicative: in the first seven years of Communist rule, Moscow poured in 73 percent again as much as it had provided in the previous quarter-century.[22]

It was not until after the 1978 coup that a copy of the detailed and optimistic 1977 resource inventory, never publicly released, became available in the West.[23] A World Bank report[24] on the favorable economics of future Afghan resource development, ready to be released in 1978, was held back after the coup. Taken together, the resource inventory and the economic report presented a tremendously positive assessment of potential future development in Afghanistan: unfortunately, the political realities changed abruptly.

The 1978 coup and the Soviet invasion set off a new spate of resource-development rhetoric in Afghanistan. The Taraki-Amin regime immediately indicated its desire to exploit Afghan natural resources, designating the northern petroliferous area near Shibarghan as the principle base for industrial expansion. [25] In addition, they planned to implement a number of resource-exploitation contracts negotiated with the Soviet Union by the previous Daoud regime. These included:

• $30 million of petroleum equipment

• Studies and designs for the $600 million Ainak copper smelter and a second large natural-gas fertilizer plant near Mazar-i-Sharif (the first having been built by the Soviets and opened in 1971)

• $22 million for detailed mapping of northern Afghanistan

• $50 million for the first rail-and-vehicle bridge over the Amu Darya, to be built from Termez in Soviet Uzbekistan to Hairatan

• $5 million for renovation of the nearby Sher Khan river port. New oil discoveries in the north also led to planning for the construction of a new oil refinery.[26]

All of these were designed to meet Soviet, not Afghan, priorities.

In sum, Taraki and Amin had taken over a country with a newly recognized resource potential, but with an economy totally penetrated and controlled by the USSR and a bureaucracy stymied by a combination of its own inadequacy and deliberate manipulation. Since the 1979 invasion, the Soviet-installed regime---headed first by Babrak Karmal and then by Dr. Najib but controlled by Soviet advisors---has continued to emphasize the importance of mineral resources and has changed the government structure so as to gain greater control of them.[27] Meanwhile, Western powers have responded cautiously, uncertain in the face of political instability in Kabul and fearful of Soviet ambitions toward the Persian Gulf. On the whole, they largely ignored the significance of the Afghan resource base until the securing of a copy of the 1977 mineral-resource inventory provided final confirmation of what had long been suspected in some circles.[28]

Afghanistan's rich resource base

The 419-page, 1977 mineral-resource inventory of Afghanistan begins with a forty-eight-page discussion of the main geologic features, including stratigraphy, tectonics, and igneous rocks, followed by twenty-two pages on the metallogenetic features.

Part II summarizes 1,432 specific mineral resources which are precisely located, described and classified in three categories: (1) *deposits*, (2) *occurrences*, and (3) *showings*. In addition, 306 broadly defined areas are identified in which *mechanical mineralogical haloes* occur, suggesting potential occurrences of specific minerals. This exhaustive catalog of mineral locations occupies 70 percent of the report.

Part III defines the different ground-water aquifers in the country stratigraphically and describes 198 specific water localities, including 112 mineralized waters and 86 fresh-water wells and springs in desert regions. Eleven excellent maps are included:

1. Geologic map (1:2,500,000)
2. Tectonic map (1:2,500,000)
3. Magmatic complexes (1:2,000,000)
4. Metallogenetic zones (1:5,000,000)
5. Mineral deposits, occurrences and showings (1:2,000,000)
6. Maps showing: a. Fuel minerals and ferrous metals
                    b. Nonferrous metals
                    c. Tungsten and tin
                    d. Rare and precious metals
                    e. Nonmetallic minerals
                    f. Hydrogeologic map
                    g. Fresh and mineral waters.

These maps, prepared according to international standards, contain a wealth of information in visual form. In aggregate, the five mineral-deposit

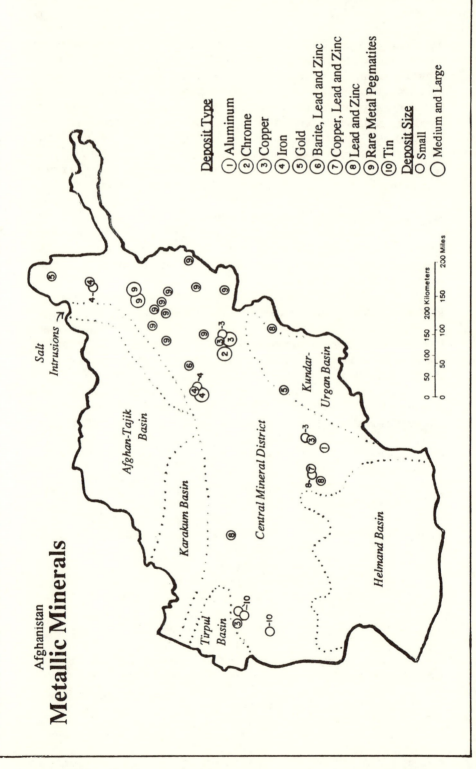

Afghanistan
Metallic Minerals

Deposit Type

① Aluminum
② Chrome
③ Copper
④ Iron
⑤ Gold
⑥ Barite, Lead and Zinc
⑦ Copper, Lead and Zinc
⑧ Lead and Zinc
⑨ Rare Metal Pegmatites
⑩ Tin

Deposit Size

○ Small
◯ Medium and Large

Salt
Intrusions

Afghan-Tajik
Basin

Karakum Basin

Central Mineral District

Tirpul
Basin

Helmand Basin

Kundar-
Urgan Basin

0	50	100	150	200 Kilometers
0	50	100	150	200 Miles

S.G.- adapted from Marvin Barton

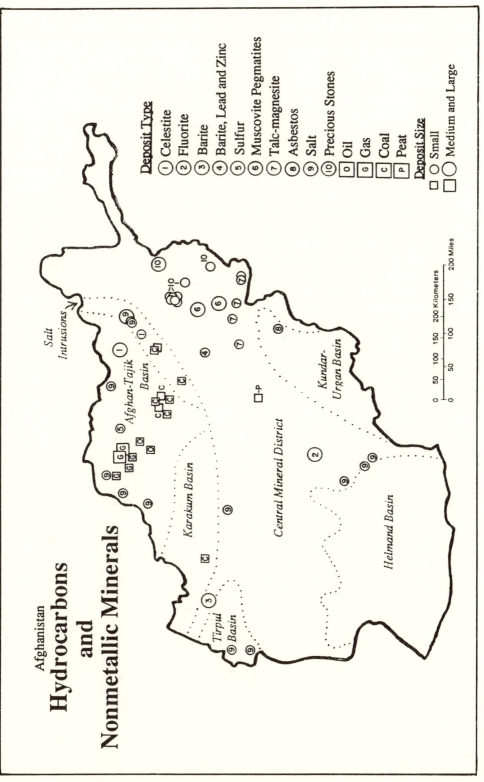

Afghanistan

Hydrocarbons
and
Nonmetallic Minerals

Deposit Type
① Celestite
② Fluorite
③ Barite
④ Barite, Lead and Zinc
⑤ Sulfur
⑥ Muscovite Pegmatites
⑦ Talc-magnesite
⑧ Asbestos
⑨ Salt
⑩ Precious Stones
⊙ Oil
Ⓖ Gas
Ⓒ Coal
Ⓟ Peat

Deposit Size
□ ○ Small
□ ○ Medium and Large

Salt Intrusions

Afghan-Tajik Basin

Karakum Basin

Tirpul Basin

Central Mineral District

Kundar-Urgan Basin

Helmand Basin

0 50 100 150 200 Kilometers
0   50   100   150   200 Miles

S.G.: adapted from Marvin Barton

and mineral-occurrence maps show the following: 58 solid combustible materials, 898 metallic minerals, 114 rare metals, 4 radioactive elements and rare earths, 105 precious metals, 118 nonmetallic minerals, 14 salts, 21 precious and semiprecious stones, 23 electronic and optical minerals, and 69 industrial materials, with 67 of the latter already quarries at the time of the report. The total number of recognized industrial mineral *deposits* was 78, which is therefore about the number judged to be of commercial significance. Some of these are much better than others, however, and in 1974-76 a few had been judged by the Canadian consulting team to be world-class deposits, i.e., deposits that would be immediately commercial if brought on stream, and which could affect the world price of the resource. (See maps, pp. 108-109, and Tables of Mineral Resources, p.95)

The precise characteristics of the major resources are still poorly known: either not enough close-spaced sampling has been done or else the detailed reports are held as state secrets by the Soviets---and the Afghans, if they have access to them. Nevertheless, some definition of the best deposits is now possible, especially through analysis of the historical details of the exploration.

Natural gas

Russian hydrocarbon exploration at first focused primarily on natural gas. In 1963, gas was discovered at Khwaja Gugirak, near Shibarghan---an area that has subsequently revealed several large natural gas fields with reserves estimated (as of 1977) in excess of 500 trillion cubic feet. The Soviets promptly set about directing these finds to their own use, and denying them to the Afghans.

A sixty-mile-long pipeline carrying large volumes of Afghan natural gas into Soviet Central Asia was completed in 1967 and opened in 1968. Afghanistan's use of its first developed resource was limited to what could be obtained from a subsidiary pipeline feeding gas to a 36,000 kw thermal power plant in Mazar-i-Sharif and a 100,000-ton-per-year fertilizer plant (also built with Soviet credit, and using only about 250 million cubic meters per year). Aside from these two small plants, and the use of gas for cooking and heating in the camps of Soviet technicians in the Shibarghan area, Soviet planners did not allow for *any* use of Afghan natural gas *inside Afghanistan itself.*[29]

In February 1978, shortly before the Communist coup, Kennedy Nahas, a development expert for the United Nations, drafted a letter for Engineer Salah, the Afghan Deputy Minister of Mines and Industries, detailing proposals for the construction of a new gas pipeline running south from the gasfields to Kabul, further thermal generation of electricity using gas, and its transmission by power lines to all sections of the country needing power. A Soviet engineer at the Ministry of Planning immediately called Mr. Nahas in and called him on the carpet, demanding to know why his proposal had been prepared and issued. Three months later, just one week after the April coup, the Soviet embassy in Kabul executed a host of agreements with the new Communist regime on minerals, gas and oil. The integrated energy project for Afghanistan was dead.

In May 1979, a new group of 200 Soviet geologists arrived in northern Afghanistan to look for gas. A short time later they announced the discovery of another gas-bearing zone capable of producing one quarter million cubic meters per day. In early 1980, more Russian experts appeared in Afghanistan to increase gas production by 65 percent.[30] Afghan/Soviet agreements called for the average annual export of 2.5 billion cubic meters of gas to the USSR up to the year 1985, with any reduction of deliveries from Khwaja Gugirak to be made up by adding in desulfurized gas from Jarquduq. The revenues from the sale of gas were not, however, to be returned to the Afghan government: they were to be applied as repayment for Soviet loans and the interest on those loans, including those funds spent by the Soviets for Soviet-assisted projects. The repayment of loans was detailed in Article 5 of the 6 February 1968 Agreement for Economic and Technical Assistance in the years 1967-1972: [31]

> The repayment of the loans and the payment of interest on loans... by the Royal Afghan Government with the export of natural gas and delivery of other Afghan goods from Afghanistan to the Soviet Union in accordance with the accredited Afghan-Soviet Trade Agreement, shall be made as follows:
>
> The quantity of natural gas and the kinds of other Afghan goods and their prices, quantities, and time of delivery for each calendar year, will be determined by the two sides three months before the beginning of the year of the repayment of the loan and the payment of interest on the loan.
>
> In the event the value of the natural gas delivered and other Afghans goods does not suffice for the repayment of the loans and interests coming to maturity during the calendar year, the remainder shall be paid in internationally exchangeable currencies of [sic] the currencies of each side at the exchange rates that will be established by the two sides in accordance with Article 13, Afghan-Soviet Trade and Payments Agreement dated July 17, 1950. The exchange of rubles to other currencies shall be done on the basis of the worth of that currency in gold, on the day of payment.
>
> The expenses of Soviet institutions related to the technical

assistance of the construction of the projects...shall be paid by the export of natural gas and other Afghan goods...under the conditions of the accredited Afghan-Soviet Trade Agreement.

Although the 1968 Agreement spoke of prices "determined by the two sides," in practice the Soviet Union determined the price it would pay and controlled all information regarding the amount of gas imported, the payment due Afghanistan, and other such details. Despite Afghan protests, the gas has always been metered for accounting and crediting purposes on the Soviet side of the border and by Soviet personnel. Afghan officials were and are forced to accept Moscow's word as to the amount being transported into the USSR and the amount of credit due Afghanistan, as well as accepting a price schedule unilaterally determined by the Soviets. This raises a question about all figures involved in Soviet importation of Afghan natural gas; the amounts imported could differ significantly from those published.

In fact, *even on the basis of their own figures, the Soviet Union never paid Afghanistan more than a fraction of the going world market price for natural gas.* The original price from the 1960s to 1974 was 17 cents per thousand cubic feet (tcf), (which was finally doubled to 34 cents per tcf) in spite of the supposed annual fixing of the price specified in the agreement quoted above. By 1976, the scheduled revision and redetermination of the price schedule for Afghan natural gas was already two years overdue, and the Russians showed no inclination to work on it. Even assuming that they were providing an accurate report of the amount of gas they were receiving, the price they were then paying (i.e., crediting against Afghanistan's debt) was only about 46 cents per tcf. At the same time, Moscow was paying *three times as much* for Iranian natural gas. (The Iranians were instructed to keep secret the price they were getting from the USSR for their gas, but Iranian officials privately informed the Afghan government.) Pressed on this price differential, the Russians answered that Iranian gas has a higher caloric content, which is true; but the difference is about 15-20 percent, not 200 percent!

Afghanistan's repeated attempts to reschedule and increase gas prices met with a steady Soviet *nyet* for two more years. Moscow finally agreed to raise the price from 46 cents to about 59 cents per tcf, or about 30 percent. Then, just a few days before the Communist coup of 28 April 1978 (of which they probably had foreknowledge), they raised it to $1.05 per tcf, making that price retroactive for three years. Thus in 1977-78, before the coup, the Afghans received credits of $54 million; which jumped to $97 million for 1978-79, by which time a Communist regime had been installed in Kabul. Nevertheless, even with a Communist regime, the Afghans still received *only about one-fifth of the comparable international price.* As of 1982, after the Soviet army had installed a totally subservient puppet whose rule they were trying to consolidate, Moscow was reportedly pricing Afghan gas at $2.35 per tcf---which was still well below world market prices: a year earlier, in 1981, Moscow was *selling Soviet gas* to Europe at about $5.10 per tcf.

By way of comparison, in 1980 bargaining, Moscow offered Iran $3.11-$3.97 per tcf; the Iranians refused, holding out for $4.81-$4.53 (lowest)---roughly the same price which the United States pays to Mexico and Canada---and when the Russians declined to meet their price, Iran cut off gas shipments to the USSR. In short, at that time the Soviet gas bill was reduced by $100 to $600 million per year because of their low payments to Afghanistan.[32] As noted above, they are now saving even more by not applying any amounts to Afghan debt service and using Afghan gas to pay a significant share of military costs. (They may eventually also be able to sell it to Western Europe or at least use it domestically in order to release other supplies for profitable sale.) In response to Afghan requests for better prices, Soviet negotiators persistently argued that Moscow was entitled to lower prices because the exploration and extraction of Afghan natural gas had been done with the help of favorable Soviet credit terms. They argued further that, since Afghan gas was tied to a specific Soviet region, it did not have comparable international value. Over Afghan protests, the Russians had constructed a monopoly situation for themselves. They were in fact charging many times the nominal 2 percent interest rates on their loans, using the crushing burden of Afghanistan's indebtedness to them to force extortionate terms upon the Afghans. Their dealings amounted to rapacious colonial exploitation, comparable to the worst abuses of the sharecropper arrangement in the American South three generations ago. Yet, as always, those dealings were conducted behind an amiable facade of friendly development assistance.

In 1980, the Soviets took the uniquely obscene step of crediting its imports of Afghan natural gas against the cost of maintaining the "friendly, fraternal assistance" of its "limited military contingent" in Afghanistan. In other words, since 1980 the Afghans have been forced to pay with their natural resources for the brutal invasion and occupation of their own country and the destruction of their own people, characterized by the UN Special Rapporteur as genocide.

Reports since 1979 indicate that from 70 billion cubic feet to as much as 105 billion cubic feet have been going to the USSR annually to pay for the military occupation, and a subsequent 65 percent additional increase was planned. The International Petroleum Encyclopedia even reported 158 billion cubic feet produced in 1982, although, because the pipelines were repeatedly blown up by the Resistance from 1980 to 1985, this high figure is suspect: other reports indicated that attacks and sabotage had decreased production to only 41 billion cubic feet per year. In 1985, however, the Resistance reported that the pipeline was buried 15-20 feet deep and "hardened" against attack; since then, some have even estimated that production is now five times what it was in the late 1970s.[33]

Importation of natural gas into the Soviet Union may seem something of a contradiction in terms for a country that possesses the largest gas reserves in the world, approximately 40 percent of the total world supply. These imports, however, are important to the gas-supply logistics of the USSR: they enter the southern part of the Central Asian region, the most difficult area for the Soviets to supply from their own trunkline systems. For this reason, exports from Afghanistan might even increase somewhat in the next ten years and will remain logistically important in the southern USSR.[34] The large number of anticlines and other possible sedimentologic traps at the southern edge of the great Kopet Dagh trough in Afghanistan indicate further potential there. This trough is known to be rich in hydrocarbons in its northern sector, which is in the USSR; and in fact, at its north end, near the Caspian Sea, it is the site of the world-famous Baku fields where major Russian oil and gas production first started.

Oil

Afghanistan continues to be totally dependent on foreign supplies of oil---mostly gasoline, diesel, and kerosene--coming from Iran and the Soviet Union. This dependence on foreign supplies has always cost the country much of its actual and potential foreign currency resources. Once again, Soviet manipulation contributed to this problem.

Afghanistan initiated oil exploration as early as 1925, and in 1937 granted an American consortium (Texaco and Seabord) an exclusive 25-year concession, but this was abruptly terminated at the onset of World War II. After the War, the Swedes found oil in the Angot hills of Saripul; but then, as indicated above, the Soviets stepped in with their massive credits, took over hydrocarbon exploration and diverted attention from oil to natural gas. They managed to persuade the responsible government officials that gas exports were the most profitable and they argued that in any case Afghanistan was not endowed with major oil reserves. They repeatedly emphasized that the exploitable reserves at Angot (2 million tons) did not justify the construction of a refinery, and they did not look elsewhere at that time.

When Daoud came to power for the second time in 1973, he renewed efforts to find oil. Since the Russians showed little interest, Afghan engineers, geologists, and technical personnel undertook the assignment. Their exploration soon met with one success after another. In 1975, twenty-five years after the Swedes had been forced out, reserves equal to those of Angot were discovered at Aq-Darya. A year later, better quality oil was found in three layers at Qashqari, with reserves estimated at 12 million tons. Soon additional strikes were made at Bazar Kami and Biland Ghor; like the others, these were all in the Saripul-Shibarghan area.[35] While drilling for natural gas, a larger oil strike was made at Ali Gul, approximately 200 kilometers west of Saripul, opening the possibility of other and possible larger strikes that might be made in the intervening territory.

The geological history of the region leaves open the possibility of major reserves in Afghanistan. We now know, for example, that five major sedimentary basins with hydrocarbon-exploration interest occur in Afghanistan at the southeast end of the main Kopet Dagh basin. The Karakum Basin in the northwest contains present production, but the Afghan-Tajik basin to the northeast is also petroliferous and has several undrilled salt domes in likely areas. Both basins have over 30 large anticlines and other geological structures of considerable interest.[36]

Meanwhile, oil exploration was going on in other parts of the country in the 1970s and there, at last, non-Soviet companies were doing the work. The Kundar-Urgun basin in the Katawaz area in the southeast was judged by German geologists[37] to be a likely hydrocarbon zone, and around 1974-75 the French company Total contracted to do hydrocarbon explorations there. Total did not complete its contract obligations, forfeiting its contract rights prematurely and giving as its reasons geological formations that presumably made a significant strike unlikely. Afghan specialists found these explanations unconvincing, and two separate reports from high-level Afghan administrators indicated that a combination of Soviet machinations and bureaucratic corruption was responsible.

In any case, Afghanistan was interested not only in major strikes for export purposes but in developing supplies to meet domestic needs, a purpose that could be served by smaller strikes. The Afghans themselves continued the work in Katawaz. The Helmand Basin in the southwest is virtually unexplored because of the thick cover of non-petroliferous young sediments, but in 1976 British Tri-Central contracted for exploration in the adjoining western province of Farah. Next, the American Cities Service showed interest in explorations in the Dasht-i-Margo and Registan areas of the southwest; negotiations had reached the contract stage when the 1978 coup occurred, putting an end to these efforts. Since 1978, additional oil has been found in the Tirpul basin to the west of Herat, although the basin is small.

Oil production of a few thousand tons per year in the north, in the existing fields alone, rose slowly but steadily by about 20 percent a year throughout the 1970s. In 1977 proven oil reserves were reported to be only about 10-15 million tons---an insignificant 5 percent of, say, those of Brunei or Dubai, and a mere thousandth of Kuwait's, but at least enough for domestic needs. While Daoud's Seven-Year Plan for 1976-1983 was being prepared, the Russians were repeatedly asked to provide credits for the construction of a refinery. They stalled, claiming that the Angot reserves could not justify it. That argument was undercut when the new reserves were discovered; it was hoped that Afghanistan might be helped to develop its oil resources for internal use, even if they ultimately proved too small for significant export. A search for oil in 1978 was reported to be unfruitful. Nevertheless, some of the 200 geologists who arrived from the USSR in 1979 were supposed to initiate construction of three oil fields and a 500,000-ton refinery shortly thereafter, although the aid was never forthcoming, the war intervened and Afghanistan's oil is still in the ground. Since 1980, the Soviets have built two pipelines from the USSR to supply the petroleum needs of their military operations in Afghanistan.

Coal

Coal deposits in Afghanistan are vast[38] and have barely begun to be exploited. There are about 100 million tons in high-grade proven reserves, with another 400 million tons in the "probable" category. Coal occurs across northern Afghanistan from Herat to Badakshan in nine major deposits plus 36 coal occurrences.[39] Except for the millenia of extensive wood-cutting (which deforested the country), coal mining is the oldest established modern fuel industry in Afghanistan, begun some sixty years ago. In 1954, about 17,000 tons of coal were produced; in 1965, about 80,000 tons. From 1965 to the present, production has fluctuated erratically because of management problems, a desperate manpower situation caused by abysmally low pay scales for arduous and unpleasant work and, since 1979, war. The coal is used in cement plants, textile mills, a cotton mill, a sugar refinery, the government bakery in Kabul, and in briquettes of compressed fragments for domestic use. In the late 1970s, six complete briquette-manufacturing units were planned; one was under construction by the Bulgarians in 1980. Extensive development of the coal deposits has been planned by the regime in Kabul. The Czechs first laid out the mines in 1954, and a new Czech group that arrived in 1978 succeeded in tripling production in two years. In 1979, annual production was up to 190,000 tons.[40]

Coal production is significant to Afghanistan and its Communist bosses because it represents a "proletarian" labor-intensive industry which provides essential fuel for other industry and for domestic consumption in a country without any other available energy resources---and with all Afghan natural gas flowing into the Soviet Union, Afghanistan is indeed effectively without other *available* energy resources. Coal production also helps decrease domestic demand for access to gas production which can then be kept flowing to the USSR.

Copper

There is evidence that the copper deposits at Ainak in eastern Logar province, south of Kabul, were mined as long as 4,000 years ago. The use of copper in Afghanistan goes back to the Bronze age, and indeed some scholars have speculated that bronze may have been invented there. Copper was used for coins, spears, cooking utensils, and other objects, and Ainak's copper is mentioned in a Chinese manuscript of the third or fourth century A.D.

In the 1970s, as plans developed for an industrial infrastructure in Afghanistan, planning also began for the exploitation of Ainak copper. Once again, the Soviets willingly provided financing for geological surveys to determine the extent of the reserves. The original estimates indicated that the Ainak reserves total more than 6 million tons of copper metal in comparatively high-grade 0.7 percent to 1.2 percent grade ore.[41] Afghan planning proceeded for the development of the mines and the creation of a smelting and refinery complex to produce copper for export as well as domestic use, using power generated by the American-built Kajakai hydroelectric project in the Helmand Valley, the thermal power plant at Mazar-i-Sharif, and other generating stations around Kabul.

But as negotiations for funding and contracts for this development program neared their conclusion, it became obvious that, although Soviet planners had participated in the formulation of the Afghans' original Ainak Development Plan, they had very different ideas about its actual implementation. Indeed, Soviet proposals for Ainak copper were remarkably similar to those for Hajigak iron ore discussed below: only the mining of the ore and its concentration were to be done in Afghanistan. The concentrate would then be shipped into the Soviet Union, where it would be smelted and refined.[42]

In an interesting recent development, Soviet documents captured by the Afghan Resistance show the importance attached to these deposits. One such document (translated from the Russian) reads as follows: [43]

> To Comrade Mirsahib Karval from 19.07.81 in charge of the Central Zone of the City of Kabul and Kabul Province, Copy to Major-General Comrade Boyarov IM.
>
> Workers, State employees and techno-engineering workers of the Ainak Group, comprising about 400 persons in all, inspired by the decision of the PDPA [People's Democratic Republic of Afghanistan], have, during the course of the years following the April Revolution, in spite of the complicated situation in the Province, been prospecting for copper ore in the Ainak deposits. Thanks to the selfless work carried out by the collective, as directed by the Group, deposits of some 11.5 million tons of copper metal have been discovered as part of the mineral wealth of Ainak. *In size, richness and copper content the deposits appear to be the largest in the world.* [Emphasis added]   Prospecting for the deposit continues.   At present work around the clock with boring installations has permitted bore holes up to 1,000 meters to be drilled.   With the aim of keeping the drilling installations working non-stop, it is essential twice a month to introduce hot lubrication materials (ICM) into the drilling pipes, provide spare parts and provisions, and at the same time send drilling brigades away for a rest and at the appropriate time arrange for their relief.   The Department of Geological Prospecting at the Ministry of Mines and Industry is preparing to deliver to Ainak essential materials and move drilling brigades there.   A column of eight motor vehicles will be ready to leave Kabul for Ainak on Monday, 20 July, at 9:00 am. The Ministry requests you to provide the necessary protection for the column en route to Ainak and facilitate the unloading of the materials brought there and transfer of the ICM to the containers which the Group possesses.   It is necessary to allow some two to two-and-a-half hours to perform this operation and escort the column returning to Kabul with the relieved drilling brigade.
>
> With respect, Ministry of Mines and Industry, 18 July, 1981.
>
> M.E. Danesh.
No. 2155 27.04.13607

Thus Mr. Danesh, then the Minister of Mines and Industry, inadvertently let us know that the Ainak deposit appears twice as large as originally described: Ainak appears capable of producing 11.5 million tons of copper. This should be compared with the world's largest open pit mine, the Bingham Canyon Pit in Utah, which produced about 9 million tons during its entire life. The Dzhezkazgan copper deposits in Kazakhstan, one of the two largest in the USSR, are only one-quarter to one-third as large as Ainak. The Ainak deposit is quite large enough to warrant great interest by the Soviets: even though copper is not strictly a strategic material (at least not from the point of view of the United States) because it is widely available in the U.S. and elsewhere, it is of greater significance to Moscow. The Soviets have expended considerable effort to bring the mine on stream: as recently as July 1986 they proposed to bring power transmission lines from the Soviet border "to benefit Ainak."

The Afghan freedom fighters are well aware of the significance of Ainak, however, and have brought considerable force against it. (In May 1986, for example, they brought down a helicopter gunship protecting a convoy there, killed five Soviet engineers and captured one.) At present, therefore, Ainak is only an isolated military outpost with little development activity,[44] but big plans for it are mentioned constantly in the Afghan press.

Iron

Geologic reports show 5 deposits, 52 occurrences, and 12 showings of iron in Afghanistan. By far the most prominent is the Hajigak iron ore reserve in the central massif. (This rich deposit was first discovered more than 150 years ago but its inaccessible location high in the eastern end of the Koh-i-Baba range discouraged interest until its rediscovery in the early 1960s.) Preliminary surveys---carried out by the Soviets, as usual---quickly determined the size and purity of the deposits: the ore is largely high-grade, directly shippable pyrite-magnetite with an unusually high grade of 67 percent iron. Measured reserves are about 111 million tons and speculative reserves (based on reasonable geologic inference) are more than two billion tons. As a comparison, the total production of ore from Minnesota's Mesabi Range---the foundation of the American steel industry---during the seventy-three years from its development till the mid-1960s amounted to 2.4 billion tons.[45] Thus, in reserves, Hajigak may represent the third-largest known iron ore deposit in the world; meanwhile, both U.S. and European sources are in decline. Dolomitic limestone, required in the preparation for industrial iron, is available nearby, and both coking coal and natural gas for coking are potentially available.

Until the Communist takeover, international markets showed considerable interest in the development of Hajigak, particularly if better roads, a railway, or a slurry pipeline could be constructed to solve the problem of access. With a steel mill under construction in Karachi, its regional economic significance was further increased. A Franco-German company prepared development and exploitation studies for Hajigak, recommending that after a concentration process, the ore should be transported to Doab, less than 31 miles (50 km.) to the north, where the blast furnace complex would be located; the necessary coking coal would come from Shah Bashek and Dara-i-Suf, northwest of Doab.[46]

The development of Hajigak became a major component of Daoud's Seven-Year Plan. An infrastructure of roads, railroads, and other transport facilities for mining, processing, and marketing would have to be created, along with the manufacturing plants, housing and storage. To be economically feasible, the blast furnace would have to have a capacity of one million tons per year. Electric power and energy sources such as coke, coal and gas would have to be developed as well. Financing would be necessary to make it all possible.

By 1975-76, Daoud and others in the Afghan government had at last decided to reduce, not increase, Afghan economic dependency on the Soviet Union. They therefore looked elsewhere for help with Hajigak. Iran agreed to provide credit for railroad construction, a project that would cost nearly a billion dollars. The French company SOFRERAIL did the surveys and designs for an integrated rail network that was to extend eventually from Herat to Kandahar and Kabul (near the routes of the present roads), with a spur to Hajigak and connecting links to the Iranian, Soviet and Pakistani borders. In 1976-77, Afghan departments began work on roads. It was hoped that eventually the remaining funding would come through a consortium of French, German, American, and Japanese companies, and that iron billets would be exported to Iran, Pakistan (where the Soviets were building the Karachi steel mill, since completed), the USSR, and other possible world markets.

It was an enormous project, initially putting a heavy burden on national resources but with great potential benefits. The project was therefore planned to develop along with the development of the infrastructure and energy resources, gradually increasing production capacity according to the availability of export markets. Newer and more advanced reaction techniques were to be used for the production of sponge iron, utilizing Afghan natural gas instead of coke in order to make initial smaller-scale sponge iron production---as little as 200,000 tons per year or less---economically feasible.

Needless to say, Russian advisors had participated in the early planning; they had even earmarked loan funds for it. As the Seven-Year Plan progressed, however, their economic aid failed to materialize. Negotiations pursuing this question revealed that the Russians had different plans for Hajigak: as they saw it, at Hajigak as at Ainak, only the mining of the ore should be done in Afghanistan. The ore would then be transported into the

Soviet Union, to the area of its coke and electric power sources, and the production of iron and steel would be done entirely in the Soviet Union. In short, the Russians wanted a total monopoly of Hajigak's iron ore, like their monopoly of Afghan natural gas. Indeed, if colonialism is defined as the exploitation of raw materials and the sale of finished goods, one could hardly find a more classic example.

Reasons for the Soviet plan are not hard to find: conditions for iron-ore development, and the quantity and ore grade of available resources in the USSR, have deteriorated in recent years.[47] High-grade direct-shipping ores have been gradually depleted, necessitating costly development and the enrichment of lower grade ores, often located far from industrial core areas. Not surprisingly, soon after their invasion of Afghanistan the Soviets announced their intention to exploit and develop the iron deposits at Hajigak and to build a railroad from the north into the area in order to do so.

Cement

Afghanistan has huge supplies of limestone and coal with which to produce plentiful cement. The demands of modern development led to the first Afghan cement production in 1958. By 1966, production had risen to 158,000 tons per year, though production was erratic and frequent scarcities resulted in a flourishing black market. By 1977, eight quarries and two plants were in operation, at Pul-i-Khumri and near Kandahar, and the Pul-i-Khumri plant was being enlarged by a Czech group. Two other major plants were planned to come on stream in the 1980s: one in Herat with a 210,000-ton capacity and a second Kandahar plant of 840,000 tons. These plants were expected to provide a sizeable export surplus after domestic demands were met.[48]

In 1981, a most peculiar trade protocol for cement was signed between Afghanistan and the Soviet Union: an agreement to exchange each other's cement production ton for ton. This odd arrangement can be understood when it is realized that Soviet cement is of inferior quality and cannot be sold on world markets, whereas Afghan cement is manufactured according to international standards and can be sold on world markets to the hard currency benefits of the Soviets.[49]

Chromium

The Logar deposit near Kabul is not large, only about 180,000 tons of 42 percent ore (although unpublished work by German geologists indicated tonnages two and one-half times greater than this), but its presence has been of interest to many for some time,[50] primarily because it is a strategic mineral, essential to high-grade steel manufacture including all military steel. The United States and the West are without significant supplies of chromium and are dependent on those of southern Africa, which is an unstable region; indeed, the U.S. has on occasion been forced to buy its chrome from the USSR, the other significant source.

In the 1970s, Soviet production was second only to South Africa (which had an annual output of about three million metric tons), but by the 1980s, the USSR's deteriorating chromite position had led to widespread Soviet prospecting and exploration.[51] Thus, despite its limited size, the Logar chrome deposit may be important to the Soviets---both as a resource for themselves and for potential denial to a dependent West.

Precious stones

Gem-quality emerald, ruby, lapis lazuli, kunzite, tourmaline, aquamarine, serpentine, and garnet are known, and some deposits are of considerable significance.[52] Large numbers of these stones, which had been put on display in Kabul by the Taraki regime and had an estimated value of $60 million, were seized by the Soviets shortly after their invasion. At present, as a result of the war, most of the precious stone deposits are under Resistance control and off-limits to the DRA regime in Kabul. The extreme portability and salability of the gems is helping the war effort of the Afghan freedom fighters. But in the event of a Soviet victory, the high quality and rarity of many of the stones (especially lapis lazuli and emerald) represent a future hard-currency revenue source for Moscow if mined carefully and marketed properly. They similarly represent a potentially significant economic resource for a free Afghanistan.

Other strategic minerals

Numerous other important mineral deposits occur in Afghanistan, some of which are strategic, others merely useful for Afghan development or for balance of payments. The deposits of lead, zinc, molybdenum, tin, beryllium, cesium, rubidium, lithium, tantalum, barite, celestite, asbestos, magnesite, muscovite, and gold all look potentially attractive. Both gold and silver were mined in ancient times.

Among the most strategic resources, and therefore among those most difficult to assess from afar, are the reported uranium deposits. The Khanneshin volcanic complex on the lower Helmand has been reported to be rich in uranium and other rare earths, but quantities are unknown and, until recently, reports and maps of the deposits were unavailable.[53] Other uranium-rich deposits have reportedly been looted by the Soviets from time to time since the invasion, but little in the way of unclassified data is available.

Water and hydroelectric power

In assessing motivations for the Soviet takeover of Afghanistan, the role of vital water supplies in arid and energy deficient south-central Asia has largely been overlooked.

Three main drainage basins originate in Afghanistan:

• the Turkestan drainages of the Amu Darya (Oxus River) and other small peripheral drainages, all of which flow northward toward or into the USSR;

• south and eastward-flowing Indus River drainages of the Kabul, Kurram and Gumal Rivers;

• the westward Afghan-Iranian Plateau drainages of the Helmand and other small systems that flow into the Seistan depression.

It is significant that of these three, all significant to Afghanistan and its neighbors, only the Turkestan basin of the Oxus seems to be receiving much development attention at present from the Soviets in Afghanistan; projects there will affect both northern Afghanistan and Soviet Turkestan.*

The nineteenth century choice of a major river, the Amu Darya, as the boundary between the Russian empire and Afghanistan caused many development problems later for both countries; at one time the border had to be renegotiated because of river channel changes. The Afghans were never allowed to use much of the river water: both Tsarist and Soviet regimes wanted as much of it as possible downstream and had problems because they did not control the headwaters, which are in Afghanistan.

Along its course, the Amu Darya is fed by a variety of rivers from both the USSR and Afghanistan. Approximately 25-30 percent of the total runoff is contributed by the Afghan part of the basin. The mean water flow of the river where it turns north into the Soviet Union is about 1,740-2,000 cubic meters per second, similar to that of the Nile.[54] Attempts to gain control of this considerable resource have been a major element in postwar Soviet domestic policy: since 1950, they have proposed at least three major dam and irrigation canals. The great Kara-Kum Canal, 1,500 km (932 miles) long, is the longest and largest canal in the world and carries water for irrigation from a point just downstream from Afghanistan across the Kara-Kum desert in the USSR toward the Caspian Sea. Completion of the vast $1.5-2 billion scheme is obviously important to Moscow, and their desire to control the entire Amu Darya watershed can therefore be assumed.[55]

In addition to using the Amu Darya water for irrigation in the USSR,

* See Krakowski.

the Soviets have many other hydroelectric and irrigation schemes also either under construction or planned for that part of the Turkestan basin inside northern Afghanistan. The Kalagay dam on the Kunduz River, an Afghan tributary of the Amu Darya, will produce 60 megawatts and irrigate more than 90,000 hectares of Afghan land. In May 1980---a mere five months after the invasion---Mohammed Asimoy, President of the Tajikistan SSR Academy of Sciences, announced that the USSR planned to construct a cascade of hydroelectric stations on the Kunduz River in Afghanistan and that Soviet engineers *had already determined* the sites of the future dams. A 40-megawatt dam then in construction on the Hari Rud River above Herat would, he said, irrigate another 73,000 hectares. Meanwhile, the Yugoslavs are also planning dams on the Murghab, the Kaisar, and the Sar-i-Pul rivers that will permit irrigation of an additional 250,000 hectares.[56] The absence of any large new projects south of the Hindu Kush watershed (aside from plans to bring Soviet power lines to the copper mines at Ainak and insignificant work in Kabul and Jalalabad) is noteworthy.

Afghanistan's estimated total hydroelectric potential is 2,500 Mw, not including the massive canyons of Badakshan through which the Amu Darya flows and which greatly increase the hydroelectric potential of the region. As of 1975, only about 9 percent of that potential---240 Mw---had been developed. Ten hydroelectric plants had been built, more than half of them on the Kabul River system (which contains 30 percent of the total potential excluding the Amu). Two more were on the Helmand (28 percent of the potential) and two in the north (38 percent of the potential). The problem, as always, was financing.

General resource development and Afghanistan's future

By 1977, Soviet geologists were able to divide Afghanistan into twenty-one metallogenetic zones, defined on the basis of tectonic division and representing convenient areal divisions with similar geology and mineral-emplacement mechanisms.[57] These represent a strategy of subdivision for further mineral exploration and development convenient to the Soviet group responsible for the design.

It is clear that the Soviets have great economic interest in maintaining their access to the resources in Afghanistan even if they should, in future, agree to troop withdrawals. One possible scenario would involve partition of Afghanistan. A repeatedly rumored renegotiation of the border between Afghanistan and the Soviet Union, combined with the secret annexation in 1980 of the Wakhan Corridor where the Oxus originates, could serve Moscow's interests very well, economically as well as strategically. From an historical and even a technical perspective, the current boundary along the

Amu Darya River and the Kara-Kum desert, negotiated between 1885 and 1895 by the British and Russian governments, has been and remains problematical because even at the outset it was viewed as a purely artificial and temporary frontier possessing no elements of stability of duration. During the delimitation process Russia claimed sections of territory belonging to Afghanistan on the grounds that they were occupied by Turkomans, the majority of whom resided in Russian-controlled territory. On many occasions military representatives from Russia (as well as Britain) suggested a boundary running much further south through the mountains of the Hindu Kush. The Amir of Afghanistan, Abdur Rahman, demurred, not wishing to lose any more territory.

In 1885, however, shortly after the lengthy Anglo-Russian negotiations began, Russian forces simply attacked Panjdeh, a section of Afghan territory north of the Oxus, and seized it, in order to gain ground while the border negotiations were in progress. The British protested, but accepted the *fait accompli* on the Russian promise to go no further. (Internal Russian documents of the time expressed great glee not only on the acquisition of territory but, even more emphatically, on the humiliation of Great Britain.) The British ultimately achieved a boundary formed by the Amu Darya River plus a line extended westward from the Amu across the Kara-Kum desert. The border, which was neither militarily defensible nor ethnically propitious, remained until 1980. As far as the Russians (Tsarist and Soviet), are concerned, excellent economic, political and cultural reasons have always existed for the weakening of that border. In fact, one of the Tsarist generals participating in the original border delimitation discussions is reported to have said to his British counterparts: The Oxus is a river, and rivers are bad boundaries; therefore, we want the Hindu Kush as a real wall to divide our possessions from yours in Central Asia.[58] This idea was certainly repeated more than once during the negotiations, and events since 1980 suggest that a century later it may remain current in Soviet thinking.

In order to counter the Afghan Resistance, the Soviets have apparently been building both a physical infrastructure geared toward rapid transportation and resource extraction and political mechanisms viewed as essential for either long-term control or a negotiated settlement on satisfactory terms. The Soviet-DRA regime in Kabul, for example, has attempted to give the appearance of even-handed and beneficial treatment of all the diverse population groups in the country, while simultaneously ensuring that it own best interests are maintained by means of a traditional imperialist-style divide-and-rule strategy. Various development projects have been created---or at least announced---to achieve these nominally beneficial goals. However, all of them are concentrated in the north and, propaganda to the contrary notwithstanding, seem geared to benefit the Soviet economy first.

The Amu Darya is navigable for much of its length once it reaches the northern plains: hovercraft have been installed and new ports are being built to further utilize the river.[59] In 1982, a combined road and rail bridge across the Amu carrying fuel pipelines south was completed and Afghanistan's first railroad is being constructed from the Soviet border south to the coal mines in the northern foothills of the Hindu Kush. A new town and extensive warehousing are also planned for this northern area. Another railroad extension has now crossed the border at Kushka, north of Herat. In addition, other bridges have been built or are planned across the upper Amu in Badakshan---one between Shigan in Afghanistan and Khorog in the Tajik SSR and another, possibly at Qadzi Deh or Khandud, which will connect with the improved Soviet road network across the border.[60] A new strategic highway has been built from Murghab in Soviet Tajikistan to the extreme northeast of the Wakhan corridor which, since its secret annexation by Moscow, gives the USSR a direct border with Pakistan. A new tunnel on this highway runs beneath the Andemin Pass,* allowing the Soviets much greater ease of access to Pakistan and menacing the highly strategic Karakorum Highway from Pakistan to China.

A new barter market at Khwahan in Badakshan, just across the Amu border from Soviet Tajikistan, has been set up to provide consumer items such as household appliances, not available in northern Afghanistan, in exchange for local Afghan agricultural products. Afghan Tajiks can travel to the USSR for medical treatment without visas, while Soviet Tajik doctors travel through Badakhshan.[61] (Soviet citizens no longer need visas to enter Afghanistan; travel to Afghanistan is treated like travel within the Soviet Union.)

The rich loessic soils of northern Afghanistan, similar to those of the Ukraine and the American Middle West, and the fact that the highest *insolation* (i.e., maximum amount of sunlight) in the entire Soviet Union is received throughout this border region, mean that with proper irrigation the agricultural potential here is large and of significant value in Soviet planning.

The strong physical infrastructure now being built or in planning for the north also may be a precondition for an eventual partition of the country along a renegotiated boundary, as implied above. A new border drawn along

---

* The altitude of the pass is 15,130; the altitude of the tunnel is unknown at this writing.

the axis of the Hindu Kush would provide the Soviets with complete control of the rich energy resources of the north as well as the vital northern watershed, and would split the country along ethnic lines. Northern Afghanistan abuts directly on Soviet Turkestan, Uzbekistan, and Tajikistan, and the contiguous populations are ethnically similar on both sides of the border. Such a boundary change would cut off the Pushtuns in the south, paving the way for Pushtun elements to exert pressure on Pakistan for Pushtun unity---the old "Pashtunistan" demand--- as well as limiting the flow of aid to the Afghan resistance in the north. A north-south partition would provide also a northern haven for the much-despised Communist accomplices of the present Soviet-DRA regime in Kabul in the event of a Soviet withdrawal from Kabul and southern Afghanistan (which would presumably be promoted as a "compromise"). The high mountain border of the Hindu Kush would be much more easily defended than the border now in existence. The similarity of such shifting borders to those forced on Poland and others by the Soviets at the end of World War II is obvious.

Partition of Afghanistan obviously was not the Soviet intention when they invaded. Yet more than seven years of reasonably successful resistance by the Afghan freedom fighters, with no end in sight, plus continued international pressure on the Soviets to withdraw their armed forces, have undoubtedly led Moscow to consider alternatives. The partition of Afghanistan into a potentially rich Soviet-controlled (or even annexed) north and a ruined, impoverished---and dependent---south, useful as a threat to Pakistan, might be forced upon the Afghans as part of the price for a partial Russian exit and as a solution for the Afghan issue in international relations.

In sum, although it cannot be said that economic benefits were the sole or even the primary goal of the Soviet takeover and subsequent invasion of Afghanistan, which primarily sought to replace a fatally incompetent Marxist regime and improve the strategic position on their southern flank, it is clear that economic benefits were among the significant side results that the Soviet Union expected to achieve.

It is very clear that the Soviets were well aware of significant resources available in Afghanistan, and that over a period of many decades and especially from the 1950s on they actively sought to gain control of those resources, both known and potential, and to exploit them for the benefit of the USSR at the expense of Afghanistan---or, if they could not do that, to at least make sure that the Afghans themselves did not develop their own resources for their own benefit but instead let them lie untouched until

Soviet exploitation could be imposed in one way or another. In short, if Afghanistan remained a poor and underdeveloped country, dependent on outside aid, it was in no small part due to deliberate Soviet manipulation of Afghan economic potential, particularly since the 1960s when Soviet resource specialists began to assume control in the Ministry of Mines and Industry.

It is also clear that since 1978, despite a war situation, the Soviets have moved rapidly to develop those resources for their own benefit, doing so with a speed and organization that could only be possible on the basis of previous planning, and that they intend to continue to do in the future.

In December 1986, a senior Soviet official, visiting New Delhi as a member of the official delegation accompanying Chairman Mikhail Gorbachev, told an interviewer that the war in Afghanistan is not costing Moscow "one cent" because of the natural gas and other products the Soviet Union is getting from Afghanistan. While this may be an exaggeration, it is nevertheless clear that the Soviet exploitation of Afghan resources is paying a significant part of the cost of the seizure of Afghanistan and the resulting war, and that if the Soviets are not already doing so now, they eventually expect to make a long-range and ongoing profit from their rape of that nation.

Finally it should be noted that landlocked Afghanistan's search for a route to the sea in the twentieth century led to a number of publications in Kabul from the 1950s-1970s that spoke of "natural rights" of access to the Indian Ocean. This issue is likely to reemerge in any future pacified, Sovietized Afghanistan, and to be directed more skillfully than before at Pakistan, possibly through exploitation of the Baluchistan issue.[62]

Afghan and Pakistani resource exploitation and joint development, combined with Soviet funding and aid projects, could purchase an overland rail transit through Baluchistan and construction of a new harbor on Pakistan's Makran coast that would provide a direct corrider from the USSR to port facilities on the Arabian Sea. Integration of resource extraction and refinement might work well in this context: e.g., Soviet-mined iron from Hajigak might go to the Soviet-built steel mill in Karachi, and copper from the Chagai lode in Pakistani Baluchistan might be combined with that of the Ainak deposit and smelter in Afghanistan.

Plentiful evidence exists to indicate that the Soviets intend to assimilate, if not to ultimately annex, northern Afghanistan into Soviet Central Asia while continuing to foment alternately or simultaneously unrest in Pakistan and put pressure on that country. Soviet economic aid offers to Pakistan today resemble those made decades ago to Afghanistan and in many cases dovetail with Soviet plans for Afghanistan, as noted above. Unless the international community takes further steps and exerts greater pressures than they have to date, it is ever more likely that the USSR will consolidate its takeover and further direct the rich resources of Afghanistan to its own benefit. If that should occur, the effect on the entire region---and far beyond--- will be incalculable.

Notes

Note: Rare items marked "UNO Library" are in the Afghanistan Collection of the Library of the University of Nebraska at Omaha.

1.   M. Shafer, "Mineral Myths," *Foreign Policy* (Summer 1982): 154-171.
 R.G. Jensen, T. Shabad, and A.W. Wright, eds., *Soviet Natural Resources in the World Economy* (University of Chicago Press, 1983).

2. A.E. Eckes Jr., *The United States and the Global Struggle for Minerals* (University of Texas Press, 1979).
 ----"The global struggle for minerals: a historian's perspective," *International Minerals: A National Perspective* (A.F. Agnew, ed., Boulder, Colorado: Westview Press, 1983): 155-164.
 J.A. Miller, D.I. Fine and R.D. McMichael, "The Resource War in 3-D--- Dependency, Diplomacy, Defense," (World Affairs Council of Pittsburgh, 1980).
 Anonymous, "'Resource war' against U.S. is charged," *Geotimes* (December 1980): 22.

3. J. Yemma, "Soviets rethink economic ties," *The Christian Science Monitor* (28 August 1986): 21.

4. M.I. Goldman, "The changing role of raw-material exports and Soviet foreign trade," *Soviet Natural Resources in the World Economy* (R.G. Jensen, T. Shabad and A.W. Wright, eds., 1983): 623-638.
 L.H. Bullis, "A Congressional Handbook on U.S. Materials Import Dependency/Vulnerability: Report to House Banking, Finance, and Urban Affairs Subcommittee on Economic Stabilization," U.S. 97th Congress First Session Committee Print 97-6 (September 1981).

5. A.A. Meyerhoff, "Soviet petroleum: history, technology, geology, reserves, potential and policy," *Soviet Natural Resources in the World Economy* (R.G. Jensen, T. Shabad and A.W. Wright, eds. University of Chicago Press, 1983).

6. G. Orinova, "Commentary," *Forum for a Healthier Society*, vol. 3, no. 1 (Philadelphia: Smithkline Co., 1981): 4

130

7. S. Bailer, *The Soviet Paradox: External Expansion, Internal Decline* (New York: Alfred Knopf, 1986).

8. This formulation, the so-called "Mackinder model," can be found in most basic geography textbooks.

9. S.D. Strauss, "Mineral self-sufficiency---the contrast between the Soviet Union and the United States," *Mining Congress Journal* (November 1979): 49-54 and 59.
    A.F. Agnew, "International minerals: problems and opportunities," *International Minerals: A National Perspective* (A.F. Agnew, ed. AAAS Selected Symposium 90. Boulder, Colorado: Westview Press, 1983): 115-153.

10. Leslie Dienes, "Central Asia and the Soviet Midland: Regional Position and Economic Integration," (Presentation at Foreign Policy Research Institute conference on "Implications of Soviet Presence in Afghanistan," Arlington, Va. 25 September 1986); proceedings to be published in a forthcoming book edited by M. Hauner and R. Canfield.

11. Ibid.

12. J.F. Shroder Jr., "Physical resources and the development of Afghanistan," *Studies in Comparative International Development* vol. XVI (1981): 3-4, 36-63.
    --- "The USSR and Afghanistan mineral resources," *International Minerals; A National Perspective* (A.F. Agnew, ed. AAAS Selected Symposium 90. Boulder, Colorado: Westview Press, 1983): 115-153.

13. L. Poullada, "Afghanistan and the United States: the crucial years," *The Middle East Journal,* vol. 35, no.2 (1981): 178-190. See also Poullada, this volume.

14. A.T. Assifi, "The Russian Rope: Soviet economic motives and the subversion of Afghanistan," *World Affairs,* vol. 145 (winter 1982): 253-266.

15. D. Cerkel and R.L. Miller, Petroleum law for Afghanistan. Prepared under the auspices of the Ministry of Mines and Industries of Afghanistan and the International Cooperation Administration of the U.S.A. (U.S. Geological Survey, Kabul, Afghanistan, 27 May 1958): 49 [Available UNO Library].

16. M. Glicken,"Making a map of Afghanistan," *Photogrammetric Engineering*, vol. 26 (1960): 743-745.

17. A.A. Michel, "The Natural Resources of Afghanistan," Internal position paper of U.S. Department of State, 1963. [Available UNO Library].

18. C.W. Sweetwood, *Afghanistan: important mineral occurrences.* Office of Mineral and Petroleum Attaché (American Embassy, Kabul, 1968) Map. [Available UNO Library].

19. *Geology and Mineral Resources of Afghanistan.* Department of Geological Survey, Ministry of Mines and Industries of the Republic of Afghanistan (Kabul, 1973): 103. [Available UNO Library].

20. H. Afzali, "Les ressources d'hydrocarbures, de metaux et de substances utiles de l'Afghanistan: aperçu général," *Chronique de la recherche miniere Paris* no. 460 (1984): 29-51.

21. Shroder, op. cit.

22. *Communist aid activities in non-Communist less developed countries; Afghanistan.* United States Central Intelligence Agency, National Foreign Assessment Center (September 1979) ER 79-1004126: 36-38.

23. Abdulllah Shareq, V.M. Chmyriov, K.F. Stazhilo-Alekseev, V.I. Dronov, P.J. Gannon, B.K. Lubemov, A. Kh. Kafarskiy, E.P. Malyarov, and L.N. Rossovskiy (Translated from Russian by G.H. Bezulov) *Mineral Resources of Afghanistan.* 2d ed. (Kabul: Ministry of Mines). United Nations Development Program Project AFG/74/012 (1977): 419. [Available UNO Library].

24. B.G. Kavalsky, J. Borthwick, W. Haddad, H. Imam, A. Kundu, J. Meerman, C. Remy, S. Taylor, *Afghanistan: The Journey to Economic Development* (1978) World Bank Document report no. 1777a-AF; vol. 1, The main report: 358; vol. 11, Source material and statistics on the economy of Afghanistan: 255. [Available UNO Library].

25. "Afghanistan steps up drive for oil production," *The Oil and Gas Journal,* vol. 77, no. 14 (2 April 1979): 64.

26. U.S. CIA report cited above (Note 22).

27. "Soviets turning Afghanistan into permanent client state," *Omaha World-Herald* editorial. (Saturday, 6 June 1981).

28. Shroder, op. cit.

29. Assifi, op. cit.

30. "Afghanistan gas production capacity rises 65%," *The Oil and Gas Journal,* vol. 78, no. 7 (18 February 1980): 66.

31. Assifi, op. cit.

32. Assifi, op. cit.

33. "Afghan rebels blow pipeline," (Reuters News Agency) *Omaha World-Herald* (9

132

October 1980); Edward Girardet, "Afghan rebels strong despite losses," *The Christian Science Monitor* (16 March 1982); "Rebels disrupt Soviet plans in Afghanistan," *The Oil and Gas Journal*, vol. 80, no. 37 (1982): 34; *International Petroleum Encyclopedia.* (Tulsa, Oklahoma: Pennwell Publishing Co., 1983); *World Gas Report* vol. 3, no. 17 (London, 13 September 1983): 11; vol. 5, no. 4 (20 February 1984): 5; vol. 5, no. 5 (5 March 1984): 4; vol. 5, no. 8 (16 April 1984): 4; vol. 5, no. 18 (3 September 1984): 3; vol. 6, no. 7 (1 April 1985): 4-5.

34. J.P. Stern, "Soviet natural gas in the world economy," *Soviet Natural Resources in the World Economy* (R.G. Jensen, T. Shabad and A.W. Wright, eds., 1983): 363-384.

35. "Afghanistan steps up drive for oil production," *The Oil and Gas Journal,* vol. 77, no. 14 (2 April 1979): 64.

36. "Survey finds gas propects good in northern Afghanistan," *The Oil and Gas Journal,* vol. 75, no. 15 (11 April 1977): 40; "Good potential seen for more Afghanistan gas finds," *The Oil and Gas Journal* , vol. 76, no. 29 (17 July 1978): 100.

37. A. Schreiber, D. Weippert, H.P. Wittenkindt, and R. Wolfart, "Geology and petroleum potentials of central and southern Afghanistan," *American Association of Petroleum Geologists Bulletin* vol. 56, 1972: 1494-1519.

38. Kavalsky, et al., op. cit.

39. Shroder, op. cit.

40. Shroder, op. cit.

41. Shroder, op. cit.

42. Assifi, op. cit.

43. "Rich spoils of Russia's war," *The Sunday Telegraph* Sunday Magazine (London, 9 June 1985).

44. J. Rupert, "The Soviet's underground war," *Washington Post* (20 October 1986).

45. R.W. Marsden, J.W. Emanuelson, J.S. Owens, N.E. Walker and R.F. Werner, "The Mesabi iron range, Minnesota," *Ore Deposits of the United States, 1933-1967* (J.W. Ridge, ed. American Institute of Mining, Metallurgical and Petroleum Engineers, Inc. 1976): 521.

46. Assifi, op. cit.

133

47. T. Shabad, "The Soviet potential in natural resources: an overview," (Jensen, Shabad and Wright, op. cit.): 263.

48. Kavalsky, et al., op.cit.

49. *Wall Street Journal* (16 September 1981) op. cit.

50. M.E. Volin, "Chromite deposits in Logar Valley, Kabul Province, Afghanistan," Unpublished report, U.S. Department of Interior, Bureau of Mines (Washington, D.C., 1950). (United Nations Library, Kabul, and UNO Library.)
    M. Vejlupek, "Geologie a Nerostne Suroviny Afghanistanu" [Geology and unexploited resources of Afghanistan], *Geologicky Pruzkum* vol. 22 (Prague, 1980): 16-18.
    P. Gentelle, "Du non-développement et sous-développement. Afghanistan," *Les Temps Modernes* no. 408-409 (Paris, July-August, 1980): 281-307.

51. W.A.D. Jackson, "Soviet chromite ores: Output and export," Jensen, Shabad and Wright, op. cit.

52. Shareq, op. cit.

53. Ibid.

54. N.C. Field, "The Amu Darya: a study in resource geography," *Geographical Review* vol. 44, no. 4 (October 1954): 528-542.

55. D.K. Willis, "World's largest canal inches across Russia," *The Christian Science Monitor* (Thursday, 8 November 1979): 3.

56. Shroder, op. cit.

57. Shroder, op. cit.

58. George N. Curzon, "The fluctuating frontier of Russia in Asia," *The Nineteenth Century* vol. 25 (February 1889): 144 and 267-283.

59. N. Temko, "Soviets' second front in Afghanistan," *The Christian Science Monitor* (Friday, 4 December 1982): 1 and 22.

60. Azmat Hayat Khan, "Sovietization of Afghanistan," *Defence Journal* (Pakistan), vol. X, no. 1-2 (1984): 15-22; "The Role of Turkestan in the Sovietization of Afghanistan," *Defence Journal* (Pakistan), vol. XII, no. 12: 39-43.

61. Azmat, op. cit.

62. See: A.H. Tabibi, *The Right of Transit of Land-locked Countries* (Kabul: Afghan Book Publishing House, 1970): 140. [Available, UNO Library].

134

M. I. Glassner, *Access to the Sea for Developing Land-locked States* (The Hague, Netherlands: Martinus Nijhoff Publishers, 1970): 39-83.

"...There are---and can be---no antagonisms among different Communist parties...Any differences can be resolved in the course of discussion."
USSR, Questions and Answers, Moscow, 1965

Afghanistan's Communist Party: The Fragmented PDPA

Anthony Arnold and Rosanne Klass

POLITICS IN Afghanistan cannot be understood if they are viewed in the context of a modern party system. Except for the embryonic constitutional monarchy that existed from 1964 to 1973, no such system has ever existed in Afghanistan.

With illiteracy widespread, and with a topography that rules out easy communications, the overwhelming majority of Afghans were, until recent years, unconcerned with events further away than the next village or valley---and even then, for the most part, only as their own community was affected. The village has always been the basic Afghan social, political and economic unit, and local leaders have traditionally operated independently of provincial or national control. Outside of Kabul, modern roads and communications only began to impinge upon these traditional attitudes in the late 1950s. Even today, life goes on according to age-old customs and traditions that are extremely resistant to change.

For Afghans, the significant politics are those of the village, tribal or communal level, in which an ancient tradition of rough-hewn, town-meeting-type democracy prevails. All males in the community participate in formal decision-making through a form of open meeting known as a *jirga*. Although only men actually participate and vote in a jirga, they do so only after consultations within their families, where women exercise an influence that is powerful even though it may not be publicly visible. (These family discussions can be so lively that husbands and wives are forbidden to argue an issue with each other, although they can do so indirectly through all the other relatives.)

Essentially, the traditional Afghan system of self-government aims at local autonomy, with as little interference from the national government and its provincial representatives as possible. When it becomes necessary from time to time to decide on matters of overriding national importance---e.g., the adoption of a constitution---a *Loya Jirga* (Great Council) of representatives from every part of the country is convened. No new directions in Afghan national policy can be considered legitimate until they have been approved and confirmed by this supreme referendum.

In such a system, political issues are immediate and concrete, and loyalties are highly personal. An Afghan may be loyal or even obedient to a family member, a friend, a village elder or even on occasion a tribal leader, but this is a personal commitment of one individual to another, not a pledge to an abstract cause or ideology. Such support will not be extended to strangers, no matter what their office or rank. In any case, even personal loyalties are transcended by the immutable codes of religion and culture, which every Afghan is expected to absorb in infancy and abide by for life.

Historically, the Afghans have coalesced politically only when an alien power invades their own territory or otherwise intrudes upon their concerns. It has been accepted practice among the Pushtuns, whose tribal connections straddle the Afghan/Pakistani border, to interrupt their intra-tribal feuds and forge temporary alliances against efforts by either Kabul or Islamabad (or its predecessor, British India) to exert authority over the tribes on either side of the border. Invariably these alliances soon break down; in any case, once the external threat passes, normal internal rivalries always reemerge. It is worth noting, however, that when outside forces---the British in bygone times or the Russians today---connive to exploit this pattern for their own purposes, they get little benefit from it. A client tribe will accept money and arms and use them, as intended, to defeat a troublesome rival---but they will then turn against their alien patrons. In short, whatever the temporary alliances, the ultimate pattern constantly reemerges: it is the basic social unit against all outsiders, whether domestic or foreign.*

In sum, the Afghans incline to a high degree of individualism, community independence and self-sufficiency, family loyalty, resistance to change and, among the Pushtuns, strong traditions of feuding.† They are

---

* See: Barth.

† In this they resemble many other mountain peoples, e.g., the Highland Scots, the Montenegrans, the Basques, etc.

Democratic Party of Afghanistan (PDPA---Moscow's surrogate rulers in Kabul). These realities have shaped many of the developments in that party.

egalitarian, and do not subordinate themselves easily to collective endeavors---especially if the leader of such an endeavor has not earned their personal respect and does not exhibit the traits they prize. In many ways their values resemble those of the pioneering American rugged individualist; "Don't tread on me" could easily serve as their motto.

Traditionally, Afghans have not banded together in organizations that extended beyond local, tribal or ethnic boundaries. Issues that transcend local concerns have been for the most part of interest only to a tiny---if vociferous---educated minority, most of them in Kabul and many of them connected in one way or another with the government.

Within this context, modern political parties, ideologies, political philosophies and party loyalties are still largely alien concepts. They are a comparatively shallow overlay, a veneer, even among those who have nominally adopted them, including most members of the People's Democratic Party of Afghanistan (PDPA---Moscow's surrogate rulers in Kabul). These realities have shaped many of the developments in that party.

The beginnings of modern Afghan politics

Modern Afghan politics had their origins in the decade-long reign of King Amanullah.* When he came to the throne in 1919, the Ottoman empire had just collapsed in the wake of World War I. New Muslim states had been created, and in Turkey, Kemal Ataturk was wrenching a traditional Muslim society into the modern world. To the north, the new Soviet government was proclaiming lofty ideals, denouncing colonialism, and promising restored independence to the Tsar's subject peoples in Central Asia. To the south, Gandhi was challenging the permanence of Britain's Indian empire.

The heady winds of change began to reach Kabul. Amanullah, inspired to emulate Ataturk, sent numbers of students to Turkey and Europe where they picked up new ideas. Meanwhile, he was impetuously trying to transform Afghanistan overnight. After his downfall in 1929, followed by turmoil and civil war, his successor, Nadir Shah, put on the brakes; but the seeds of new political ideas---some of them only half-digested---had been sown.

During Amanullah's reign, a political organization called *Jawanan Afghan* [Afghan Youth] emerged, initially promoting the idea of a constitutional monarchy. (In fact, both Amanullah and Nadir Shah promulgated constitutions in 1923 and 1931, respectively.) By the early

---

* See: Poullada.

1930s, however, the organization had become so radicalized that it was urging the subversion of the royal government and even of the Islamic code. This brought on resolute government action that dispersed Jawanan Afghan as an organization. Some of its former members then carried out a rash of political assassinations, culminating in the murder of Nadir Shah himself in November 1933.

His 19-year-old son took the throne as Zahir Shah, but by Afghan tradition he was too young to rule; for the next twenty years, actual power was wielded by his three paternal uncles. In 1947, the most liberal of these, Shah Mahmud, as prime minister oversaw the formation of the seventh National Assembly, a 120-member nominal parliament which had never wielded significant political power. Shah Mahmoud tried to strengthen the Assembly by appointing more than forty new members who were committed to political reform and cautious democratization.

The new members tried zealously to root out what they and many foreign observers perceived as corruption, but which was to its practioners merely the traditional system of gifts, patronage and nepotism by which Afghanistan, like the rest of the Near East, had operated since time immemorial. The result was several years of considerable political ferment. In early 1951, when a liberalized press law permitted the publication of independent newspapers, five new journals sprang up, each representing a political trend and several of them radical.

One was the organ of *Wikh-e-Zalmayan* [Awakened Youth], a Pushtun nationalist party that succeeded *Jawanan Afghan* but did not resort to violence in advocating a multi-party constitutional monarchy. Although the party was not Marxist-Leninist, it numbered among its members some who toyed with Marxist ideas and at least one---Nur Mohammad Taraki--- who had already worked with the Communist party in India and would eventually found the PDPA. Among its other members and associates were the king's cousin and brother-in-law, Prince Daoud, an army general and minister of defense; the astute former minister of national economy, international businessman and founder of the Afghan National Bank, Abdul Majid Zabuli; and the young Babrak Karmal.

Another journal was *Watan* [Homeland], published by an organization with the same name headed by Mir Mohammed Ghobar, a historian and a former member of Jawanan Afghan. Ghobar had been jailed by Nadir Shah and later wrote a history of Afghanistan from a socialist perspective. His associate, Mir Mohammed Siddiq Farhang, later became a member of the elected parliament in the 1960s and subsequently collaborated with the government of Babrak Karmal for some months following the Soviet invasion.

Nidya-i-Khalq [Voice of the Masses], edited by Dr. Abdur Rahman Mahmudi, was the organ of *Khalq* [Masses], an organization more overtly radical and antimonarchical than the others, which should not however be confused with the Khalq Communist faction that emerged many years later.

Another important organization, *Cloob-i-Melli* [National Club], issued no publication, nor did it agitate for sweeping internal reforms. It was headed by Prince Mohammed Daoud; the name of its youth wing, *Ittehadya Pakhtunistan*, [Pushtunistan Alliance] indicated its primary interest: the demand for autonomy for the Pushtuns of Pakistan (and their eventual union with Afghanistan, though this was not emphasized publicly). Domestically, Daoud's organization seemed most interested in keeping a finger on the pulse of what all other organizations were doing. One of its more active members was Babrak Karmal.

There were extensive connections and relationships among these various groups and their members, but they were not formalized or overt and their exact nature remains unclear.

In the eyes of Kabul's conservative ruling circles, these groups and their publications eventually went too far. Even though political ferment was largely confined to a narrow group of students and intellectuals in the capital, the potential for serious unrest provoked a sudden strong government response: shortly before the 1952 parliamentary elections, Shah Mahmoud's government---probably acting at the insistence of other royal family members---closed down the opposition papers and jailed their editors and some of their associates.

A year later, however, Prince Daoud replaced Shah Mahmud as prime minister. His ascension to power was a mixed blessing for the activists: some, like Taraki, escaped imprisonment altogether and found immediate jobs with the government;* others, including Babrak, were eventually released from jail, and some of these also received official posts; still others, including Ghobar and Mahmudi, remained behind bars. Unlike his predecessor, Daoud had no intention of democratizing or liberalizing Afghanistan; but neither did he want to see the royal family---of which he was a prominent member---overthrown. After a decade of his rule that saw Afghanistan establish closer relations with the USSR and estrange itself from Pakistan, the king secured his resignation and appointed a new prime minister.

---

* Taraki was sent as press attaché to Washington, where he promptly resigned and denounced the Afghan government.

The decade of democratization and the founding of the Communist party

The mild-mannered king's dismissal of his intimidating cousin and his choice of a new prime minister from outside the royal family surprised many observers (including Daoud). So did his immediate business-like approach to drawing up a modern constitution that would bring about a democratic constitutional monarchy. Moreover, when the draft constitution was debated by a Loya Jirga in 1964, the king insisted on a provision that would deny important government posts to members of the immediate royal family, including Daoud.

The new constitution also envisaged the formation of political parties, but the hesitant king never got around to signing the law legalizing them. Nevertheless, with national parliamentary elections by universal suffrage and secret ballot scheduled for September 1965, a number of unofficial political organizations sprang up (or emerged from underground), mostly visible through their numerous publications---seven of them in the first year, two dozen in the next few years (although not all of them survived). If not quite parties, these groups were organized in some degree and covered the spectrum from the Maoist *Shola-i-Jawid* and the Marxist-Leninist PDPA on the left to the virulently chauvinistic *Afghan Mellat* on the right.

Most of these movements tended to be radical but except for the PDPA, all were more or less content to bide their time, awaiting the legalization of parties that never came. They were never able to take their case to the people, and, except for the conservative Islamic groups, none of these new movements carried much political weight save in the rarefied intellectual circles of Kabul's bureaucracy and academe; the rest of the country was almost entirely unaware of them.

Remnants of most of them still exist, although they are now mostly outside of Afghanistan. [See Appendix V for the most important groups and personalities aside from the PDPA.] Some have taken a major role in the Afghan resistance; others are collaborating with today's Communist regime in some degree. And of course one of them, the PDPA itself, seized power in 1978.

The People's Democratic Party of Afghanistan

The founding party congress of the PDPA---and so far the only one---took place secretly at the home of Nur Mohammad Taraki on 1 January 1965. According to official Party sources and Dr. Anahita Ratebzad, there were twenty-seven founding fathers and one founding mother (Anahita, discreetly concealed behind a curtain). As has been standard practice in

Communist parties since Lenin's day, the Party did not enlist in its ranks any of the workers or peasants in whose name it was preparing to seize power. All of the founders were members of the educated élite---writers, civil servants, teachers, bureaucrats, doctors---many of them ambitious and frustrated.

Whether or not the Soviet embassy was involved in the founding of the PDPA is unknown, but there are indications that it may have been, at least indirectly. If KGB defector Vladimir Kuzichkin is correct, Babrak Karmal may already have been a KGB agent at that time.[1]

From the outset, the PDPA tried to conceal its total ideological subservience to Moscow. The overt Party platform, released in 1965, was a relatively bland document that called only for a "national democratic" form of government, a line previously developed in Moscow for the use of other pro-Soviet parties in Islamic countries. Simultaneously, however, the Party had also drafted a secret constitution which spelled out its unswerving loyalty and dedication to Marxism-Leninism.

The PDPA founding congress saw a carefully balanced union between two equally pro-Soviet but mutually antagonistic factions that probably existed before the Party's official founding. These two groups eventually became known by the names of their official publications:

---*Parcham* ["Banner" or "Flag"] whose members for the most part came from successful, educated, urban (primarily Kabul) families, was led by Babrak Karmal, the son of an army general. Although many Parchami were of Pushtun origin, the urban, Kabul-oriented makeup of the group included a number of non-Pushtuns.

---*Khalq* ["Masses" or "People"] was made up almost entirely of Pushtun intellectuals who, like their leader, Nur Mohammad Taraki, came from village backgrounds. They tended to be significantly less well-off economically than the Parchami.

The doctrinal differences between the two factions were only tactical: Parcham was ready to pursue a "common front" approach, i.e., outward and temporary collaboration with non-Marxists, pending seizure of power. Khalq on the other hand rejected such collaboration and demanded loyalty to "pure," uncompromising revolutionary socialism. But the origins of the bitter conflict between them actually lay less in doctrine than in traditional cultural sources: ethnic differences, social differences, the enduring mutual contempt between Kabuli and provincials, personal loyalties to individual leaders, and the competition for power among those leaders.

Of the twenty-eight founders, twenty-one have been identified: ten were Parchamis and eleven were Khalqis* [See Appendix IV].

The founding of the Party may well have been designed to exploit the opportunity offered by the forthcoming 1965 parliamentary elections in which the PDPA fielded eight candidates, all of them in Kabul and, of course, none of them bearing a Party identification. Four Parchamis (but no Khalqis) won: Babrak, his reputed mistress Anahita Ratebzad, Nur Ahmad Nur, and a shadowy figure, Fezan alHaq, who soon vanished from the political scene. As soon as the new parliament convened, PDPA agents instigated mass student riots which Karmal and other Parchamis in the parliament successfully manipulated, forcing the government to resign and setting a pattern of destabilizing the new constitutional process that continued for the next ten years.

It is important to realize that at this time---even before its factions split--- the PDPA was still very small. Among Afghans inclined to the left, the Maoist Shola-i-Jawid attracted more members.[†] As late as 1973, after both Parcham and Khalq had spent eight years actively recruiting, one estimate put membership at only a few hundred in each group.

Within eighteen months, the uneasy Parcham-Khalq union began to crack. In mid-1966, Babrak criticized the Khalqis for being too openly and outspokenly socialist. The Khalqis in turn accused him of betraying sacred socialist goals, and a year later were able to expel Babrak and his followers, who made up half of the Central Committee, from the Party. The Parchamis proceeded to organize their own party, with the identical name (People's Democratic Party of Afghanistan), rules, and classic organization.

Now completely separate and competing, each of the two parties--- Parcham and Khalq---began a frantic recruitment campaign, focusing especially on teachers and students. The first target was teachers, particularly those specializing in teacher training: the long-range goal was to establish an infrastructure in the schools that would first influence and then recruit the youth who would form the power élite in the next generation. And students of course were the most vulnerable segment of the population.

The focus of each party reflected the background of its own members. In

---

* Hafizullah Amin, later the key figure in the 1978 coup, was not among them. He was then studying for an advanced degree in education in the United States. He returned in time to run for parliament a few months later, but lost--- as did the other Khalqi candidates, Taraki and Jauzjani.

† It developed a sizable following among students as well as in a small but influential group of doctors, lawyers and other professionals.

Khalq, Hafizullah Amin and many others came from the provinces, and they targeted students of the same background. This was a rich lode because, after primary school, the best students from each village were sent to boarding schools in Kabul (as Amin and his associates had been twenty years earlier). Homesick, cut off from their families and structured communal environments, dazzled by a relatively modern big city, these students were comparatively easy prey for Khalqi recruiters who concentrated primarily on developing personal relationships to establish allegiances. Conveniently, some of the largest of these boarding schools were teacher-training institutions where Amin had extensive contacts, influence and even power, having himself been first a student, then a teacher, and finally principal of one of the largest schools.

The Parchamis were equally active among students, but they targeted a different group---again, those like themselves: students at the Kabul lycees which catered to city youth, in large part the offspring of prosperous middle class families headed by professionals and bureaucrats, and also students at Kabul University, where Najibullah was a key Parcham agent. Although Parcham's target groups were less isolated and therefore less emotionally susceptible, they came from urban families that tended to be more cosmopolitan, ambitious, deracinated, and less rooted in traditional Afghan and Muslim values.*

In any case, for most of the student targets the ideological appeal of Parcham or Khalq (or any other alien ideology, for that matter) was of minor importance. The two organizations were more like trendy fraternities and the loyalties they inspired were equally non-intellectual. The nonparticipating followings they attracted have been compared to the fans of professional sports teams; according to some sources, many novitiate Khalqis, at least, did not know the politics of the organization until after they had joined.

Other PDPA targets consisted of journalists and media personalities, bureaucrats and military officers, particularly those trained in the Soviet Union, some of whom had probably already been singled out and co-opted by the KGB or GRU. Both Parcham and Khalq, however, carefully avoided recruiting openly among state employees in sensitive positions (though both developed cadres of secret adherents) in order not to alarm the authorities.

The 1973 coup: the end of the monarchy and democratization

The ten-year Afghan experiment in constitutional monarchy faced a great many problems, many of which defied easy or speedy solution, and several

---

* See: Barth on urban vs. rural values in Afghanistan.

elements were antagonized by the failure to resolve their often-conflicting interests.

On the one hand, King Zahir's effort to divorce the royal family from politics and governance annoyed family members with political ambitions (not least among them Daoud). At the same time, the growing urban educated class chafed at the royal family's continued behind-the-scenes influence, and at the limits on upward mobility imposed by the steady shrinkage of foreign aid from the two superpowers who had once seemed ready to finance Afghanistan's leap into progress and prosperity.*

The ordinary Afghan villager, of course, paid little heed to such problems; but in 1971-72, a combination of drought and mismanagement brought on a serious famine in the central mountains. Then the villagers too turned on the government for its failure to take action swiftly enough.

In the second national elections, held in 1969, the two PDPA organizations saw their support slip, lessening their hopes of gaining power through the ballot box: among the Parchamis, only Karmal was reelected, though Amin of Khalq also won a seat this time.

Meanwhile, Daoud, though publicly appearing to acquiesce in his permanent loss of power, had clandestinely begun working with Parcham and its members in the military.

At the end of 1972 an energetic new prime minister began to attack many long-standing problems, offering a possibility that the constitutional system might succeed, and the third round of national parliamentary elections was scheduled for late 1973.

On 17 July 1973, however, Gen. Mohammed Daoud, with the aid of key Parchamis, deposed his cousin the king in a virtually bloodless coup, abolished the monarchy, and proclaimed a republic with himself as president.

The Parchami---and presumably the Soviet---intention had been for Daoud to front for them while they edged Afghanistan into Moscow's camp: the population knew him as a national leader, and to most Afghans his coup seemed merely a fight within the royal family, hence acceptable. Daoud, however, did not intend to become anyone's figurehead. In a series of remarkably deft maneuvers he transferred his erstwhile Parchami allies into positions of political impotence. By 1976, he had purged virtually all Parchamis---at least those he knew of---from his inner councils.

For the Parchamis, Daoud's bureaucratic musical chairs were particularly galling because, as the price for staying in his good graces, their party had

---

* See: Noorzoy on political effects of Soviet aid sectoral distribution.

been forced to cease recruiting. No such inhibitions hampered their rivals, the Khalqis, whose insistence on doctrinaire purity kept them outside the government. As a result of their aggressive recruitment efforts they now outnumbered the Parchamis by about three to one (although, as noted above, both parties were still very small). Even more significant than their numerical superiority was the concentration of military officers they brought into Khalq from 1973 on.

But Daoud had offended not only the Parchamis: Moscow was not amused when he began distancing himself from the USSR and cultivating new foreign aid donors such as Egypt, India, Saudi Arabia and Iran. In 1975 Daoud mended his political fences with Pakistan and shelved the Pushtunistan issue, a perennial source of friction in Afghan-Pakistani relations that had benefited Soviet interests. Perhaps worst of all, Daoud declared his intention of making the Non-Aligned Nations Movement (which was scheduled to hold a meeting in Kabul 6-9 May 1978) truly nonaligned.

The 1978 coup: The PDPA takes over

In 1976 and 1977, the Communist Party of the Soviet Union (CPSU), working via the Communist Party of India (CPI) and the Awami National Party of Pakistan, began efforts to heal the breach between Parcham and Khalq as a necessary first step toward a coup d'etat to unseat Daoud. A first reunification pact broke down but on 3 July 1977, the two sides reached an agreement on cooperation and began laying plans to seize power. Over the next several months, preparations for the coup proceeded apace, including (according to subsequent official accounts) ten rehearsals involving key military officers. Few knew the purpose of these exercises: even the participants believed in the carefully crafted cover story, i.e., that they were designed as defensive moves to protect the republic from any coup attempts by royalists or rightists.

These rehearsals belie assertions by some analysts that the coup on 27 April 1978 was "accidental." The same analysts assert that the USSR had nothing to do with it, but there is abundant documentary evidence of Moscow's involvement in at least the first step (healing the Parcham-Khalq split), and circumstantial evidence of complicity in the planning and possibly the execution of the coup itself. There is also Babrak's own blunt acknowledgment to an Indian journalist friend of long standing that "Russia wanted that there should be revolution here."[2]

This is not to say that the April 1978 coup ("The Great Saur

Revolution") necessarily occurred exactly as and when the Soviets---or the Parchamis, for that matter---had planned. On the contrary, Khalqis and Parchamis alike concur that it had been planned for the Afghan month of Assad (August), but the timetable was accelerated when Daoud arrested Communist leaders in the wake of demonstrations protesting the murder of a senior Parchami ideologue, possibly by Khalqis. Daoud's net missed the one key figure: Hafizullah Amin, the Khalqi coordinator for coup planning. Probably thanks to the connivance of Lt. Col. Pacha Sarbaz, a high-ranking member of Daoud's military counterintelligence and, unknown to Daoud, a secret Khalqi, Amin was not jailed until eleven hours after he was alerted, during which time he activated his secret military contacts.

The coup rehearsals paid off. After forty-eight hours of bitter and very bloody fighting, Daoud and his family lay dead and the country's rule ostensibly passed into the hands of a "Military Revolutionary Council" under Air Force Colonel (later General) Abdul Qader. Only a day or two later, after it was certain that organized opposition had ceased, did Qader turn over the reins of power to Nur Mohammed Taraki and take up a lesser position as minister of defense. Taraki proclaimed the founding of the Democratic Republic of Afghanistan (DRA), dedicated, he declared, to nonalignment and "positive" neutrality. He vigorously denied any connections with communism or Communist thinking. Oddly enough, despite the PDPA's well-known political positions---and the fact that, in its first month of existence, the DRA signed more than twenty new agreements with Moscow while Soviet advisers began pouring into Afghanistan---he seems to have been believed by a good many people who should have known better.

Parcham and Khalq split again

In the new DRA cabinet, as in the PDPA founding congress, the careful balance between Parcham and Khalq was preserved. If anything, Parcham appeared to have the edge because both the minister of interior (police) and the minister of defense were Parchami; between them, they controlled most of the government's guns, and thus enjoyed a weighty political advantage. But Khalq's Hafizullah Amin had the real power in the army through the numerous Khalqi officers, and the ineffectual Abdul Qader soon found himself outmaneuvered.

Less than two months after the coup, Babrak, five other ranking Parchami leaders, and several lesser followers were packed off into diplomatic exile as ambassadors,* while those left at home were eliminated

---

* The traditional Afghan way of getting rid of political opponents.

from the party and state bureaucracies. Only weeks later, the exiles were accused of attempting an anti-Khalq coup from abroad; they abandoned their posts and allegedly took refuge in Czechoslovakia with at least one of them, Najibullah, absconding with the embassy funds. In fact, the dismissed ambassadors are believed to have gone straight to Moscow.

The purge of Parchamis remaining in Afghanistan intensified: many were jailed and tortured, and some were executed. Subsequently, circumstantial evidence and broad Khalqi hints indicated that the USSR had been involved in assisting the plotters---a circumstance unlikely to improve Khalq's relations with Moscow.

Afghanistan under Khalq

Meanwhile, immediately after the April coup, a reign of terror had begun in Kabul and other cities as the new regime moved to eliminate any potential non-Communist opposition by arresting, jailing, and in many cases killing all who might offer leadership. First went the experienced political figures, religious leaders, and important civil servants, judges, army officers. Eventually the net spread to include lesser figures---teachers, writers, artists, students, bureaucrats, lawyers, merchants. Anyone in the educated classes who did not demonstrate support for the new regime was in danger of the midnight knock on the door. It was also a convenient way to pay off personal grudges: the property of those imprisoned was seized and often handed out to Party members.

The still incomplete Pul-i-Charki prison, designed to hold five thousand common criminals, was put to immediate use, crammed with three or four times that number of political prisoners of all ages and both sexes. A secret police was set up (known first by the Farsi acronym AGSA, later as KAM, after the Soviet invasion reorganized as KhAD under Najibullah and in 1986 raised to a ministry, WAD). Torture was introduced under the tutelage of East German and Soviet KGB officers, who also reportedly provided modern electrical torture devices. Mass secret executions without trial began. Thousands disappeared. (In September 1979, Amin published an avowedly partial list of those executed; it contained twelve thousand names. Estimates of those executed in the first eighteen months alone run as high as fifty thousand or even more.)*

After the initial period in which they furiously denied their Communist sympathies, the Khalqis undertook to recast Afghanistan in the Soviet mold, bringing home to the majority of the population---the villagers throughout

---

* See: Rubin. Also see: Rubin; Laber and Rubin; Roy; and Barry, in bibliography.

148

the provinces---the reality of the new regime. Though labeled "reforms," the new programs---land redistribution, Marxist indoctrination in the guise of literacy classes, the denunciation of religion, the replacement of the tricolor flag with an all-red one almost identical with the Soviet flag, and other steps--- brought an immediate reaction. Spontaneous resistance to the regime spread rapidly, becoming all but universal.

By mid-1979 Amin had taken over effective power from Taraki, who was increasingly a figurehead. Rejecting Soviet advice to slow down and move less openly until control was consolidated, Amin and his doctrinaire purist associates continued to antagonize the Afghan people.

In December 1978, Moscow got Taraki's signature on a Treaty of Friendship and Cooperation, one of whose clauses was later cited by Moscow as justification for the invasion. In mid-1979, the USSR stopped referring to Afghanistan as "socialist."† In September 1979, they attempted to get rid of Amin, inducing Taraki to invite him to an ambush. Amin got wind of the plot and arrived surrounded by bodyguards; when the shooting died down, it was Taraki who was gone, leaving Amin in full control but caught in a hopeless dilemma. On the one hand he neither could nor would abandon his total ideological commitment to Moscow; on the other hand he had to deal with Moscow's obvious intent to abandon him. His solution was to become ideologically "more holy than the Pope" in order to get back into the Kremlin's good graces, but that tactic only hastened his own downfall.

The Afghan people, slowly awakening to the reality of an ever more openly atheist Communist regime, were resisting it more and more forcefully. By the autumn of 1979, the DRA controlled only perhaps a third of the provinces, power was obviously slipping from its hands, and Soviet preparations for the invasion were already well under way.

The Soviet invasion, the downfall of the Khalqis, and since

In December 1979, faced with the prospect of losing decades of economic, political and ideological investment in the country, Moscow invaded in massive force and replaced Amin with the more obedient Babrak and his Parchami associates. In addition to Amin (who was killed by a special Soviet commando unit), seven other ranking Khalqis were executed

---

† The Soviets resumed the use of the term in justifying the invasion and installation of the Babrak Karmal regime, which accused Amin of betraying the revolution.

either during the invasion or within a few months; many others simply vanished, including four founding members of the PDPA. Some of these are rumored to survive in prison; if so, it is not impossible that the Soviets may one day try to resurrect some of them in yet another new Afghan government. Several were released in 1987. [See Appendix IV].

Political tactics and strategies

In the immediate wake of the invasion, Soviet political tactics involved trying to undo some of the political damage that the openly Marxist Khalqis had visited on the PDPA. Afghan media stopped calling the DRA a socialist country, or even holding out socialism as an eventual goal. Under its new leadership, the DRA proclaimed itself ready to respect, observe and preserve Islam as a "sacred religion." The national flag, dyed blood red under the Khalqis, reverted to a less provocative traditional red, green and black tricolor. Land redistribution was downplayed and even reversed. An appeal was made to persons who only a short time before had been labeled class enemies, including independent entrepreneurs, landowners, religious figures and traders. A number of political prisoners---most though not all of them Parchamis---were ostentatiously released in the presence of the international press, though secret arrests of potential opponents continued unabated.

Within the PDPA---almost certainly at Soviet insistence---some Khalqis were preserved at the top level in order to promote the image of party unity. These were for the most part opportunists who had abstained from Khalq-Parcham feuding, plus several others who are believed to owe primary allegiance directly to the USSR, possibly as KGB agents, rather than to Khalq. The most important ones were First Deputy Prime Minister Assadullah Sarwari and Minister of Interior Sayed Mohammed Gulabzoy. (Sarwari, in particular, was anathema to the Parchamis for his previous personal participation, as chief of Taraki's security service, in torturing such Parchamis as Second Deputy Prime Minister [later, Prime Minister] Sultan Ali Keshtmand.)

"Broadening the base"

Great publicity was given to the non-Party status of certain figures who were being brought into the government in important positions, e.g., Minister of Commerce Mohammed Khan Jalalar, who had served in pre-Communist cabinets; Minister of Agriculture and Land Reform Fazel Rahim Momand; and Minister of Public Health Mohammed Ibrahim Azim. All had been known as leftist in the past (Jalalar is widely assumed to have been a Soviet agent since long before the 1978 coup) but none had any known formal PDPA ties.

At the same time, eight other Afghans who had served in past non-Communist governments were given positions as advisers in various ministries: Mir Mohammed Siddiq Farhang, Ghulam Jailani Bakhtari, Abdur Rauf Benawa, Abdul Ghafoor Rawan Farhadi, Abdulhai Habibi, Abdul Hakim, Abdul Walid Hoquqi and Abdul Wahid Sorabi. The objectivity of some of these individuals might be questioned (Bakhtari is both a brother-in-law and cousin of Babrak, for example, and Habibi was a delegate to the Soviet-controlled World Peace Council), but an effort was being made to dilute at least the appearance of a total PDPA monoply of power.

This policy was called "broadening the base" of government. Unfortunately for its architects, a handful of Afghans without Communist credentials scarcely balanced the presence of 85,000 Soviet occupation troops. As 1980 wore on and popular outrage against the invasion gained strength, the occupation forces swelled, while talk of non-Communist participation in government became muted. Approaches to prominent exiles were widely rumored, but all such efforts fizzled out.

By the end of 1981, the various non-Communist ministers and advisers had almost all vanished from the scene. Jalalar remained as minister of commerce and Sorabi was still an adviser, but if there were other ostensible non-Communists involved in running the DRA's domestic affairs, the media were not boasting about it. "Base broadening" in its first phase had clearly proven to be a failure.*

In place of direct non-Party involvement in the regime, a "National Fatherland Front" (NFF) was set up in June 1981.† The NFF was intended to attract non-Party individuals who would carry out tasks on behalf of the DRA, and it was also to serve as an umbrella group for various subfronts like the Democratic Youth Organization of Afghanistan (DYOA), Democratic Women's Organization of Afghanistan (DWOA) and others. Although claiming a huge membership, the NFF has come under periodic criticism for not having fulfilled its tasks.

Parcham/Khalq hostilities and concentrations of strength

The Parchamis had a knottier problem in dealing with the presence of the Khalqis, in part because the latter had killed and tortured so many Parchamis during their eighteen months of ascendancy. It is understandably

---

* New efforts of a similar sort, begun in 1985 and intensified from 1986 on, were embodied in a wider "national reconciliation" campaign that was supposed to coopt even those opposed to the PDPA.

† Its name was changed to simply "National Front" at the beginning of 1987.

difficult for a man who has been tortured to work amicably with the man who tortured him. At the same time, there was a need, underlined by Soviet pressure, to present a united front both to internal enemies---the Resistance and the populace---and to the outside world. Accordingly, Party unity was listed as the main task at consecutive Party plenums in the first several post-invasion years. After a hiatus during which "conquering the counter-revolution" took top honors, unity again became the main goal in 1986, indicating that the problem persisted.

The most egregious Khalqi offender, Sarwari, was shipped off to Moscow in June 1980 "for medical treatment," and thence to Mongolia as ambassador; officially, he lost his various Party and state titles only in 1986, but after 1980 his name was never mentioned in the official press, even during DRA state visits to Mongolia.

However, Gulabzoy, Amin's minister of communications, remains in the cabinet (as of this writing) and was elevated to the more important post of minister of interior, probably at Soviet insistence. The *sarandoy* (police) come under Gulabzoy's command, and recruitment into that service still virtually requires allegiance to Khalq, as it did in Taraki's and Amin's day. As one of the three main security services, the others being the army and the secret intelligence agency (now WAD), the police carry considerable political weight.

The main armed group under Parcham control is WAD, formerly KhAD,* presided over from its establishment immediately after the invasion until November 1985 by Dr. Najibullah, who was reportedly trained by the KGB.[3] KhAD replaced Amin's secret police (KAM), whose persecution of Parchamis probably led to wholesale retribution when Parcham regained power. Over the post-invasion years, KhAD has gained power in step with the KGB's own increased influence in the USSR itself under Andropov and his successors, and now represents a dominant force within the DRA (see below).

The third force, the army (including the air force), still has the Khalqi heritage of the Amin era, but there too the Parchamis have made inroads in the years since the invasion. Overall, however, the army probably still has more Khalqi than Parchami sympathizers among the officer corps; among enlisted men, most of whom are unwilling conscripts, probably neither faction has much influence.

Factional rivalry is not confined to intellectual discussion. Babrak's exhortation to a sarandoy audience in 1984 not to use the weapons they had

---

* Still almost universally called KhAD. The two acronyms are therefore used interchangeably in this volume for the post-1986 period.

been issued in intra-Party disputes reflects the depth of hostility that continues to exist. Armed clashes between Parchamis and Khalqis even at high levels continue to be reported by nonofficial sources. Since the replacement of Babrak Karmal by Najibullah in mid-1986, there have been reports of additional splits and conflict within Parcham itself. Babrak supporters have demonstrated openly in the streets. According to some sources, there may be other factions as well.[4]

PDPA membership

Since the invasion, it is estimated that the Parchamis have increased their relative strength from about 25 percent of the PDPA to about 40 percent, but reliable statistics on absolute numbers of party members are not available. Non-Communist sources estimate a membership of perhaps 5,000 at the time of the 1978 coup, with a subsequent see-saw growth to perhaps 11,000 by 1982. In January 1979, the Taraki government claimed 50,000 Party members; but various figures given by Karmal after the invasion suggest that in April 1982 the Party still had, at most, fewer than 20,000 members. Nevertheless, when the Babrak regime began giving figures, they claimed a steady rise from 63,000 members and candidate-members in 1982 to 170,000 in early 1987.[5]

These figures are unquestionably exaggerated, but there probably has been a significant increase in Party membership since 1980. In the first place, there has been an intensive, ongoing recruitment drive to sign up new Party members, by coercion if necessary. Second, there are many who have collaborated with the regime and hope to gain a measure of protection by signing up; it is significant that, according to the DRA's own figures, 60 to 65 percent of Party membership is in various security forces (militias, sarandoy, WAD and the military) and, in turn, 60 to 65 percent of those forces are Party members. Many of those who have borne arms against the Resistance doubtless feel that there is now no turning back. Third, DRA figures in 1986 stated that 60 percent of the Party is under thirty years old, indicating that much pressure for joining is being applied to the young, whose education and careers hang on their response to the call.[6]

In any case, it is clear that, on the basis of their own, probably exaggerated figures, the PDPA at the time of the 1978 coup could claim to represent a mere one-quarter of one percent of the pre-war population, and that even today it claims to represent barely one percent.

Insofar as the recruiting has been successful, moreover, it seems to have been confined to the cities, particularly Kabul, and to concentrations of security forces. As the Resistance has stepped up its activities in the outlying towns and countryside where more than 90 percent of Afghanistan's people live, PDPA members' existence there has become ever more precarious. It is significant that between 1983 and 1984 the number of Party committees for the DRA's 89 cities, towns, and large administrative districts actually fell from 70 to 61, indicating that 35 percent of these major units no longer had even nominal Party representation. Figures for later years have not been published, but Babrak Karmal's plea in December 1985 for the establishment of DRA power in "most of the villages and all of the districts" reflects the Party's continued weakness.[7]

The PDPA/DRA impotence in rural Afghanistan, already apparent before the invasion, became more marked immediately afterwards. Therefore, in about 1982, without making any formal announcement, the Kabul authorities divided the country into nine zones---one for each major compass direction (north, northwest, west, etc.), and one for the center---through which tighter control could be developed. The precise subordination and administrative responsibilities of these zones have never been clarified, but they may be Ministry of Defense regions similar to the USSR's own "Theater of Military Activities" (*teatr voyennikh deystviy*---TVD) military districts. The precise borders of the zones are also unknown, but they probably coincide to some degree with preexisting provincial borders. With nine zones for twenty-nine provinces, however, the zones are clearly larger units, and the zonal chiefs appear to outrank provincial governors, formerly the highest-ranking officials outside Kabul itself.

Zonal chiefs are usually appointed without fanfare; their designation becomes publicly known only incidentally, in connection with publicity about some aspect of their activities. Some zonal chiefs are known to hold military rank (usually major general or brigadier general), but others have no known connection with the military. They are, however, important persons, invariably being at least candidate if not full members of the PDPA's Central Committee.

Reflection of Soviet politics in Afghanistan

Former KGB chief Andropov's inheritance of Brezhnev's mantle of leadership in late 1982 had eventual repercussions in Afghanistan. Andropov died little more than a year after assuming power, but after an interregnum under the ineffectual Konstantin Chernenko, Andropov's chosen heir, Mikhail Gorbachev, took the reins in early 1985. In November 1985, Dr. Najibullah,* who had been in charge of KhAD since the Soviet occupation began, quit his job as security chief to take up fulltime Party work. Retaining his seat

---

* Who has shortened his name to Najib.

on the Politburo, he also became a Party secretary. In early May, 1986, he replaced Babrak as PDPA chief.[8] In abandoning, retaining, and assuming these various responsiblities in just under six months, Najib in Afghanistan followed precisely the same path Andropov had earlier followed to the top of the Kremlin hierarchy between June and November 1982.

From late 1985 through 1986 and up to the date of this writing, DRA leaders' open admission of selected shortcomings paralleled Gorbachev's campaign of "glasnost" [openness] in the USSR. Babrak and Najib had plenty to be open about, from the security forces' incompetence in dealing with the Resistance to Party factionalism to corruption in high places, and, selectively, they let it all hang out. One of the favorite charges was against resorting to words not deeds, an accusation repeated so often and at such length by both leaders as to prove its own point. Clearly, bombast as a substitute for efficiency was rife throughout the system, starting at the top.[9]

"Broadening the base" returns

Before Najib had taken the first steps along the path to ultimate power, there was an apparent shift in the DRA's course. In late 1985, for the first time since 1981, a policy of "broadening the base" by admitting non-Party figures to the ruling circles was back in vogue, now labelled "a government of national reconciliation." From December 1985 through February 1986, 70 non-Party individuals were named in Afghan media as having received top level appointments, including 9 out of 13 civil service supergrade appointments, 56 of 79 new Revolutionary Council (RC) members, 6 of 18 RC presidium members, 15 of 21 newly appointed ministers and deputy ministers, 10 of the 37 members of the Election Commission, and 27 of 74 members of a Constitutional Drafting Commission.[10]

The admission of so many non-Party faces to high level posts was unprecedented in the short history of the DRA, but its significance should not be overrated. Many of the appointees wear more than one government hat (hence the total of more than 70 in the above statistics), which probably indicates a dearth of willing volunteers. Also, many are widely known to have already compromised themselves by previous collaboration, including Nehmatullah Pazhwak, a longtime associate of Karmal; and the same is doubtless true of many others who have merely taken this opportunity to go public. Finally, there is considerable doubt about how much authority the new officeholders really enjoy. For example, there are a number of non-Party ministers without portfolio with ostensible responsibility for such matters as tribal affairs, yet the PDPA ministers for each of these fields continues to hold his title and exert whatever authority remains after the

Soviet advisors have had their say. As far as the PDPA is concerned, its "leading role" remains sacrosanct for the indefinite future, and this view is unquestionably endorsed by Moscow.[11]

Nevertheless, the government claims that non-Party representation within their ranks is growing. During 1986, the DRA undertook provincial elections and claimed to have completed the process by autumn. The first results, from areas where Soviet/PDPA control is perhaps firmer than elsewhere, indicated that 4,120 representatives had been chosen for 381 councils, and of those elected, only 40.8 percent were PDPA members.[12] Like other DRA statistics, these are open to considerable skepticism, but they are intriguing, especially because the "elections" were so obviously sham. The announcement that elections would be held in a given district, for example, would appear only a day before the results were published. One victor at the polls claimed ignorance of his own nomination until after the results were announced.[13] Still, at year's end the acting president of the Council of Ministers---succeeding Babrak Karmal---was Haji Mohammed Chamkani, who had been a member of parliament and senator under the king and was not formally a PDPA member.

Intra-Party changes

Before the DRA had completed these changes, Najib had already replaced Babrak, and the Party was undertaking its own broadening program. In mid-1986, the Central Committee (CC) was expanded from 50 to 96, with 31 of the newcomers bypassing the candidate member stage. Only five of the old candidates failed to be promoted to full membership, and there were 38 new candidates as well. By the end of the year, 13 new candidates and 11 new full members had been added.[14] The expansion may well have served Parcham's interests in its ongoing conflict with Khalq, although hard evidence to that effect is still missing.

PDPA propaganda during 1986 made much of plans to merge the Party with five unnamed groups that previously had been independent. In July, it was revealed that one of these was Ofuq's "Revolutionary Society of Afghan Toilers."* This was followed by an utterly confusing array of nearly identical names: Vanguard Organization of the Working People of Afghanistan, Vanguard Workers' Organization of Afghanistan, Revolutionary Organization of the Working People of Afghanistan, Vanguard Organization

---

* Mohammed Zaher Ofuq is the son of the founder of "Awakened Youth." He became an alternate CC member in 1966 and sided with Khalq over the Babrak split in 1967. Thereafter he went into eclipse for nearly two decades, surfacing for the first time as head of this otherwise unknown group.

of Young Afghan Workers, and Revolutionary Association of the Working People of Afghanistan.[15] How many---if any---of these supposed organizations existed in more than name remains in considerable doubt.

"Everybody says I'm such a disagreeable man, and I can't think why"

The transition from Babrak to Najib did not proceed without ripples. Soviet security forces disarmed their Afghan colleagues in Kabul and shut down the media for a day as a precautionary measure during the transition. Pro-Babrak demonstrations were reported in various Kabul and Jalalabad schools and later confirmed by Najib in bitter comments about undisciplined female students. Whether they were really pro-Babrak or merely anti-Najib is an open question: given the record of KhAD abuses against those unfortunate enough to fall into its hands, the popularity of its former chief was predictably low.[16]

For the first few months after Najib's takeover, Babrak continued as president of the Council of Ministers and a ranking Politburo member. In November 1986, however, he was stripped of all remaining Party and state positions. The political fate of those close to Babrak, such as Baryalai and Anahita, is still in question at this writing.

Changes in December 1986

At the end of 1986, Najib flew to Moscow at the head of a large delegation of PDPA functionaries. He was received by an equally impressive array of Soviet Party notables, headed by Mikhail Gorbachev himself. This was the most prestigious Soviet recognition of any DRA delegation since Taraki flew in to sign the friendship treaty in 1978. For better or worse, Gorbachev, for the first time since coming to power in early 1985, had come down unequivocally in support of the PDPA/DRA.[17]

On the other hand, when Najib returned to Kabul it was with the concept of a "government of national reconciliation," designed to include even some of those who had been active Resistance fighters. Najib claimed to be holding talks with 417 groups encompassing some 37,000 members, for the purpose of setting up a coalition government. At the same time, he announced a unilateral DRA ceasefire, to last from 15 January to 15 July 1987.[18]

After only a short pause for consultation, the Resistance unanimously rejected Najib's proffered initiatives, which they roundly denounced as a fraud designed to perpetuate PDPA rule.[19] This is undoubtedly what the maneuvers were expected to secure if the Resistance had been naïve enough to accept them, but it is still unclear whether that unlikely outcome had really been anticipated. Whatever the possible hidden motives, the short-term effect was increased unity and confidence among the various Resistance groups, which saw in Najib's offers only another indication of Soviet deception and DRA weakness.

A glance to the future

In the short space of a year, there has been a notable shift in the Soviet/DRA negotiating position. Like the second-hand car dealer who quickly offers a compromise instead of insisting on his original price, the Communists have seemingly undercut themselves. Through 1985, the Soviets said they were in favor of a negotiated political settlement but that no timetable for withdrawal was possible until all outside aid to the mujahideen had ceased. Then came ever stronger hints about an existing timetable, again pegged to a political settlement. Finally, the head of a prestigious Soviet think tank, Yury Primakov, told Western correspondents that the USSR was bent on getting out of Afghanistan whether or not a political settlement was negotiated.[20]

When first talking about broadening the base of government, DRA officials said that "bandits" would be excluded. That position has steadily eroded, until in early 1987 persons who had been in armed opposition to the DRA were invited as a class to join the government, if they accept "the irreversability of the revolutionary process."[21]

These and other examples of Communist backpedaling, regardless of whatever ulterior motives they may conceal, are psychologically cheering to the Resistance, which has not budged from its original positions, including insistence on an unconditional, rapid and total Soviet withdrawal. Nevertheless, there is a serious question about Soviet intentions in all this maneuvering. The red carpet treatment given Najib by Gorbachev in December 1986 reinforces the view that Moscow remains committed to preserving the PDPA in power in Kabul come what may.

There is some doubt about the degree to which today's Soviet "reasonableness" might be part of a massive deception program. Their publicly-stated positions must always be viewed in the context of their actions---military, economic, social and political. Certainly the emergence of a dominant secret police role in both the USSR and Afghanistan has already had a profound effect on both countries' internal and external policies. Internally, the proclaimed "glasnost" campaign is an effort to reestablish the state's credibility by a new approach to information management. No longer able to control the spread of negative information, both the Soviet and Afghan states now resort to admitting certain faults that everyone   knows exist, hoping to limit the damage and preserve the last bastion, the legitimacy of Communist rule: in the DRA as in the USSR, individuals may be criticized, shortcomings may be aired, but state policies and the official ideology remain unassailable.   These ground rules will probably remain in effect.

Externally, it can be anticipated that the KGB/WAD penchant for information manipulation will be manifested in renewed efforts to split the Resistance internally and to alienate it from its international supporters.*   Already, the reconciliation program is being interpreted in some quarters as such a ploy. Forgeries and orchestrated disinformation programs, not all of which may be immediately detectable, will probably play an ever-greater role.

Efforts to assassinate Resistance leaders and to place secret collaborators in high positions in Resistance and refugee circles will probably increase. Career enhancement maneuvers, including the sacrifice of lower level agents in order to ensure promotions of agents within the security apparatus of the Resistance, can be anticipated.

In the arcane world of intra-PDPA politics, it may be that those Afghans with long careers of KGB collaboration are now in an even more favorable position than before. Appendix IV identifies some individuals who, based on open information, appear to have the closest probable KGB connections, and who thus might play a leading role in the future if the Soviets consider Najib inadequate to the job.

---

* See: Bodansky.

Notes

The information in the first part of this chapter, dealing with the period before 1965, derives from general readings, personal observations, and conversations with Afghans over many years.

The material regarding the PDPA and the period since 1965 is largely a distillation of *Afghanistan's Two-Party Communism* (see bibliography), which is fully documented; Notes 1 and 2 below are included here only to support assertions that have been the subject of controversy.

Additional citations (Notes 3-21) are given for statements regarding the period since that book was published.

1. *Time Magazine* (22 November 1982): 33.

2. *New Delhi* 3 no. 24 (27 April-10 May 1981): 10.

3. *New York Times* (16 January 1987): 6. Also: interview with confidential source.

4. Anthony Arnold, "The Situation in Afghanistan: How Much of a Threat to the Soviet State?," *The World and I* (January 1986): 355-356; *Afghan Realities* (16 July 1986): 4-5.

5. *Pravda* (5 January 1987).

6. According to U.S. State Department estimates, at the end of 1986 there were about 80,000 Afghans under arms in various DRA security services---the army, WAD (KhAD), the sarandoy, and the various militias and border guards. If the percentages of Party membership released by the DRA are at all accurate, this would imply that the maximum number of full and candidate PDPA members is about that same number. Judging on the basis of earlier official PDPA statistics, 50 percent or more of these are probably candidates rather than full members. Moreover, it must be emphasized that those serving in any of the security services have little option but to sign up if their superiors exert sufficient pressure on them; complaints in the Party press that Party recruitment in the army is not meeting planned   goals therefore indicate the degree of resistance that exists even under these circumstances. Finally, the reliability of those signed up under pressure is at best question- able, and it seems likely that any man forced into this situation might well seek reinsurance by secretly signing up as a mujahideen informant. [See: U.S. Department of State, "Afghanistan: Seven Years of Occupation," Special Report 155 (December 1986): 9.] For pressures to join, see Amin, this volume.

7. Arnold, "The Situation in Afghanistan," op. cit., 356.

8. Radio Kabul, 5 May [FBIS 6 May] 1986.

9. Ibid., 30 March [FBIS 3 April] 1986 and 11 July [FBIS, 14 July] 1986.

10.   Ibid., 26 December [FBIS 27 December] 1985; 17 January [FBIS 21 and 22 January] 1986; *Kabul New Times* (29 December 1985, 23 January 1986, 11 and 22 February 1986).

11. Radio Kabul, 22 November [FBIS 25 November] 1986.

12. *Kabul New Times* (5 October 1986).

13. U.S. Department of State, *Afghanistan: Seven Years of Soviet Occupation* Special Report No. 155 (December 1986): 14.

14.   *Kabul New Times* (12 July 1986); Radio Kabul 20 November [FBIS 21 November] 1986; and Bakhtar News Agency 31 December [FBIS 31 December] 1986.

15. Bakhtar News Agency, 17 September [FBIS 17 September] 1986; *Kabul New Times* (23 November 1986). Even the DRA English-language versions of these names were inconsistent.

16. *BBC World Service* (6 May [FBIS 7 May] 1986); Radio Kabul 10 July [FBIS 15 July] 1986.

17. *Pravda* (14 December [FBIS 15 December] 1986).

18. Radio Kabul, 3 January [FBIS 5 January] 1987.

19. *Daily Telegraph* (London: 3 January [FBIS 5 January] 1987).

20. *San Francisco Chronicle* (27 December 1986): 6.

21. *Pravda* (5 January [FBIS 5 January] 1987).

"Of all the elements that make up history, geography is the one that never changes."
   ---Bismarck

Afghanistan: The Geopolitical Implications of Soviet Control

Elie Krakowski

IT IS GENERALLY acknowledged that the Soviet invasion of Afghanistan in December 1979 changed the geostrategic significance of the region. Confusion remains, however, about Soviet objectives and intentions. Is Moscow solely interested in consolidating its control of Afghanistan? Was the invasion an isolated act, designed to crush a Muslim rebellion that threatened an established Communist regime? Or was it part of a larger Soviet plan for control of the region? In other words, what is the relative importance of Afghanistan in the context of Soviet global interests?

In order to set these questions in their appropriate larger context, it is helpful to look at the determining factors of Soviet foreign policy: Soviet foreign policy can be described as a composite of three key factors: ideology, strategic interests, and opportunity. Communist ideology, in South Asia as elsewhere, provides the overall sense of direction and sets the long-term Soviet goals---which are themselves superimposed on traditional Russian aspirations. Strategic interests and conditions at any particular time give to this general sense of direction a more concrete set of objectives.

These first two factors---ideology and strategic interests---have been determined long since by Soviet policy-makers. But it is Moscow's perception of the third factor---opportunity---which at any point actually sets policy in motion and endows Soviet foreign policy with this or that

---

* The views expressed here do not necessarily reflect those of the U.S. government.

immediate direction. Thus the end result, whether success or failure, is the byproduct of the encounter between Soviet moves and those of other actors and forces on the international stage.

How does this interaction of ideology, geostrategic considerations, constraints and opportunities manifest itself in the case of Afghanistan? A useful way to tackle these questions is to approach the problem from several different but complementary angles. The analysis that follows starts from the relatively narrow focus of Soviet-Afghan relationships before the invasion, moves on to the question of how those relationships and later ones fitted into overall Soviet foreign policy, and then takes up the larger context of Soviet global geostrategic relationships, interests, and objectives. Finally, Soviet behavior since the invasion---both in Afghanistan itself and towards Pakistan---will be examined within this overall context.

This approach throws into relief a number of activities and trends that otherwise appear to be disjointed both before but especially since the invasion, and which in many cases have gone unnoticed. In other words, this step-by-step approach makes it possible to assess more clearly the trends in Soviet policy in Afghanistan and South Asia, throws light on the strategic importance of events in Afghanistan itself, and makes it possible to answer the questions of Soviet intentions with which we began.

Soviet-Afghan relations

The invasion has often been viewed primarily in terms of the events immediately preceding it. The Soviet Union, it is said, reacted defensively to protect its interests. According to this analysis, Moscow was faced with a growing Muslim rebellion against recently imposed Afghan Communist rule, and decided that it had to invade in order to avoid a complete collapse of the Afghan Communist regime, the loss of Soviet control, and the establishment of a hostile government as its neighbor.

Seen in the larger, longer-term context, however, the invasion appears as the logical culmination of decades of Soviet policies aimed at achieving ever-greater control of Afghanistan. In particular, the sequence and direction of events reflect the Soviet predilection for ideological subservience over simple control---i.e., Moscow's belief that its only reliable allies are "socialist" subject states.

Soviet influence in Afghanistan goes back to the period following the Bolshevik revolution. The first Soviet-Afghan friendship treaty was signed in 1921. But it was not until Moscow began paying increasing attention to Third World countries in the 1950s that a more active and permanent Soviet role became manifest. In 1955, in part as a result of American neglect, Kabul turned for assistance to the Soviet Union and accepted Moscow's longstanding offer of aid. It was at the initiative of then-Prime Minister Daoud Khan that Soviet military assistance, including the training of Afghan officers in the USSR, was started.

Thereafter, throughout the 1950s and 1960s, Moscow's influence in Kabul developed into a position of pre-eminence that was never threatened--- or even challenged---by any outside powers. The United States never, seriously attempted to develop significant influence there. Yet, for Moscow, that deepening relationship apparently was not sufficient. The Soviet objective---to bring about an ever-more-subservient Afghanistan--- required more than that; and the groundwork was being laid through the penetration of the Afghan infrastructure made possible by Soviet military, economic and other assistance.*

Moscow encouraged the development and growth of a local Communist movement and worked to insure its pre-eminence. In 1965 the Afghan Communist party---the PDPA---was created, no doubt to take advantage of opportunities under the new constitution. When former Prime Minister Daoud seized power through a military coup in 1973 and proclaimed himself head of a new republic, he relied for support on pro-Moscow army and air force officers and the Parcham ("Banner") faction of the Afghan Communist party. With his long pro-Soviet credentials, Daoud appeared to be well-suited to carry out Soviet wishes. Outwardly, his takeover presented a not-too-abrupt change, well in keeping with modern, "progressive" trends: it appeared to be a transition from an increasingly anachronistic form of government, monarchy, to the more popular republican form of rule, under a familiar nationalist leader. Moreover, since Daoud was both a cousin and a brother-in-law of the deposed king, Zahir Shah, the change was acceptable to the Afghan people, to whom it looked simply like a power struggle within the royal family. It all appeared made to order: Soviet control would be increased but the façade of independence remained intact.

Daoud, like the King before him, was keenly aware of the need for good relations with the Soviet Union. But, also like the King, he was first and foremost an Afghan. Both men thought that they could develop and maintain good relations with the USSR, as well as control their own local Communists, while at the same time avoiding total dependence on, or control by, Moscow. In short, both no doubt thought they could use Moscow without being used themselves. Moscow was rapidly to become

---

* For detailed descriptions of American and Soviet policies toward Afghanistan, esp. between 1955 and 1978, see: Poullada; Noorzoy; and Shroder and Assifi.

disappointed with Daoud. Internally, he gradually proceeded to eliminate his Communist supporters from positions of influence. In foreign affairs, he began to improve relations with neighboring states as well as with other deeply religious Muslim countries. He began to send Afghan military officers to Egypt and India for training and, shortly before his overthrow, to Pakistan as well.

There is a striking parallel between the overthrow of the King in 1973 and the assassination of Daoud in 1978, aside from the involvement of the same pro-Soviet officers in both. In both cases, an Afghan leader's serious attempt to improve relations with neighboring states---in particular, with Pakistan---was soon followed by his removal from power.

Having been disappointed twice with non-Communists, the Soviets next relied on the Khalq ("Masses") wing of the Afghan Communist party which took power in the April 1978 coup. The Khalqis soon established their party dominance and quickly proceeded to implement their Marxist program, down to the replacement of the traditional national flag with the Communist red banner. As long as traditional societal patterns had been left untouched, the Afghan people had remained by and large indifferent to the exact form of the central government. It was the attempt by a minority regime to drastically alter the existing Afghan value system and social structure, and the brutality associated with this attempt, that finally provoked large-scale resistance.

When faced with such a clear-cut response to the attempt to impose Marxism in Afghanistan, Moscow had another option besides invasion: it could have backtracked and installed a more pliable non-Communist frontman as leader while adopting at the very least a more gradual approach to the implementation of the Marxist-Leninist agenda. Through such a step Moscow could have conveyed the idea that Islam and its associated traditions would no longer be targets---at least, not openly. But this would have gone against the oft-proclaimed Soviet principle of the "irreversability" of the revolutionary process: it would have been an admission of failure. Instead, Moscow chose to send in large numbers of Soviet troops in December 1979, and to install another, even more subservient leader, Babrak Karmal. (When Babrak proved inadequate he was replaced in 1986 by the KGB's man, Dr. Najibullah.) In other words, given a choice between control with communism or control without it, Moscow chose the former.

The strategy and tactics adopted by the Soviet Union in Afghanistan throw additional light on the importance of the stakes. Moscow no doubt expected that a massive show of force---70,000 to 80,000 in the initial invasion---would quickly destroy any opposition and induce submission. When this did not materialize, Moscow dug in for the long haul, adopting a long-term strategy of outlasting the resistance---through a terror campaign designed to co-opt, drive out, or kill the population---while minimizing international interest and attention. All of this was also formulated in such a way as to keep the Soviet military commitment relatively limited in cost, in numbers of men, and in casualties.

Global trends and Soviet policy

While an examination of Soviet behavior in Afghanistan from the perspective of bilateral Soviet-Afghan relations is important, it represents only a part of the total picture. Another element in that picture emerges when the unfolding of Soviet-Afghan relations is seen in the larger context of Soviet foreign policy. This overview throws into relief the degree to which the Soviet decision to invade in 1979, as well as subsequent Soviet actions in Afghanistan and in the region, are in fact a part of that larger policy and strategy and not simply an isolated case in relations with one particular neighboring country.

The Soviet invasion can be seen simultaneously as a culmination point, a watershed, and the beginning of a new phase in Soviet foreign policy. The invasion was Moscow's first *direct* use of force in support of its objectives outside the Soviet bloc since World War II. For the first time since that war, Soviet forces were invading an independent, non-aligned, Third World state. The applicability of the so-called "Brezhnev Doctrine," by which Moscow had arrogated unto itself the right to intervene militarily in a "socialist" state, was apparently being extended beyond the Soviet bloc.

In the 1950s, when Moscow began its active participation in the Third World, the Soviet Union was militarily inferior to the West both in the significant area of nuclear weapons and in the ability to project power far from its own borders. A massive Soviet military buildup over the next two decades substantially altered that equation.

In the political arena, the proclamation of the Brezhnev Doctrine in 1968 indicated the change that was already occurring by then in Soviet self-perception. Since then---and up to the present---Soviet statements about the "correlation of forces" have reflected increasing confidence about that self-perception as well as increasing arrogance toward the non-Soviet world. The typical Soviet statement on this subject declares that, since World War II, "a radical change in the balance of world forces" has occurred "in favor of socialism," and that this change has "created new conditions for solving the problem of war and peace." The West, according to Moscow, "has lost the historical initiative. It can no longer reverse the course of world development." Or, as stated somewhat more bluntly by Yuri Andropov in September 1983, "No one will ever be able to reverse the course of history"---

the "course of history" being the well-known Marxist euphemism for ultimate complete Communist world domination.

This change in the "correlation of forces" in favor of "the camp of socialism" has been ascribed by Soviet analysts to what they describe as "their [the West's] defeats in social battles, to the loss of their colonial possessions, to the abandonment of the capitalist system by more and more countries, to the achievements of world socialism and the mounting influence of Communist parties in the bourgeois countries."[1] Those who recognize the might of the Soviet Union, who are willing to appease it and who, in general, accede to its demands and its view of the world, are labelled "realists," while those who insist on resisting those same demands are described as "increasing the danger of war" and attempting to go "against the tide of history." The arrogance and the threatening tone of many recent Soviet pronouncements are not only revelatory of their increasing self-confidence, but also parallel more and more closely their actual behavior.

When Moscow became an active participant in Third World affairs in the mid-1950s, the process of decolonization was getting seriously under way. By 1960, many if not most of the former colonies were becoming independent, and the Soviet Union proceeded to take advantage of strong anti-Western sentiments in many of these newly independent states. But Moscow by and large advanced with caution for some years. The Cuban crisis of 1962 had revealed most embarrassingly the gap between Soviet bluff and Soviet capabilities. Moscow's need to concentrate on correcting that "imbalance"---the reality of American power, and the will to use that power, evident in Vietnam and, in 1965, in the Dominican Republic---militated against any approach drastically different from one guided by caution. The following years---the early and middle 1970s---were the height of "detente." In this period Moscow's agenda included developing a set of agreements and understandings with the United States meant to seriously restrict future American freedom of movement in various areas, and Soviet leaders were reluctant to jeopardize such gains.

Moscow's more aggressive involvement in the Third World coincided with the United States' withdrawal from Vietnam and that country's fall to the North Vietnamese Communists in April 1975. America's disillusionment with the trappings of global interests and responsibilities occurred as rapidly as had its rise to active interventionism. Long before the fall of Saigon, American unwillingness to undertake new international commitments that entailed any degree of risk was made manifest in many ways by the U.S. Congress. In late 1975, the passage of the Clark Amendment, forbidding any U.S. assistance to the democratic resistance in Angola, ratified that emotional reaction.

The Soviet Union was not slow in taking notice of this new reality. Moscow had provided assistance to the small Angolan Marxist-Leninist party before Angola became independent, but not on the scale that followed the Clark Amendment. Now, at the moment of independence, Moscow poured massive aid into Angola in the form of material, weapons, and men (Cuban troops), thereby assuring the success of the Communists. In those years, active Soviet intervention, often utilizing willing proxies, also occurred in a number of other countries--- North Yemen, South Yemen, Somalia, Ethiopia, and Mozambique in Africa and the Mideast, and, in South Asia, Cambodia and Laos, where the Soviets supported Vietnamese attempts to colonize all of IndoChina. While in the 1960s only three regimes outside the Soviet bloc---Cuba, North Korea, and North Vietnam---openly identified themselves as Marxist-Leninist, by 1980 six others had been added to the list: Angola, Mozambique, Ethiopia, the People's Republic of Yemen, Nicaragua, and Afghanistan.

Soviet brazenness in the Third World did not go entirely unmatched by its moves in Europe. There, the campaign to dictate Soviet terms to West Europeans on their own defense---i.e., basically, to pressure them into advocating unilateral disarmament by the West---included fairly open interference in the domestic politics of several countries (most blatantly in West Germany), replete with threats of dire consequences should the Europeans dare to oppose Moscow. And it should be remembered that European discussions about modernizing Europe's nuclear deterrent, which led to this Soviet campaign, were themselves the result of Soviet attempts at nuclear blackmail and intimidation by means of the deployment of the new SS-20 missiles targeted at Western Europe.

When it comes to Moscow's overall Soviet policy and attitudes, the Soviet approach to members of NATO is one thing, but the approach to European neutrals is even more illuminating. In 1981, incursions by Soviet submarines in the territorial waters of Sweden, a neutral state, became public knowledge when one such submarine was grounded near a sensitive Swedish naval base. Far from apologizing and promising to discontinue these flagrant violations, (which, it turns out, had been going on for years), Moscow adopted a threatening tone toward Sweden and actually *increased* the number of such penetrations. There are other instances: for example, the shooting down of the Korean commercial airliner by Soviet fighter planes in 1983, or the cold-blooded murder of the American official observer Maj. Arthur Nicholson in Germany in 1985. Far from apologizing for these events, Moscow accused the victims of being responsible for them. These events underscore the use of intimidation as one of the major components of Soviet policy. They demonstrate how the Soviets now see themselves, how they see the outside world, and what they believe they can do to it.

In summary, the invasion of Afghanistan---however significant it may have been in itself---occurred in a context of increasingly assertive and aggressive Soviet international behavior.

The geostrategic environment and Soviet policy

Soviet intervention in Afghanistan is, then, both a product of long-term Soviet bilateral policies and a reflection of broader trends in the conduct of Soviet foreign policy, combined with perceived opportunities. But what is the relative significance of Afghanistan, and of South Asia, within that larger context of Soviet foreign policy? And how important is Afghanistan itself within that larger context? What priorities, if any, have been established in Moscow's activities and designs throughout the region and the world?

It is generally recognized that the United States remains the primary target of Soviet policy, and that dividing Western Europe from the United States is a key Soviet objective. As seen by Moscow, the Soviet Union has two major strategic fronts---Western Europe on the one hand, the Far East and the Pacific on the other. On both the Western and Eastern fronts, however, things have remained frozen for some time now and seem unlikely to change in the near future; the ratio of opportunity to risk has been too insignificant to allow meaningful Soviet advances, or even attempts to alter the status quo more than peripherally. Opportunity must therefore be sought elsewhere.

A quick comparison of threat-perception maps of both the U.S. and the Soviet Union reveals something about the where---and the why---of Soviet pressure points.[2] Wherever the West has developed a strong military presence and has indicated a will to prevent further Soviet encroachments, the freezing of such encroachments has occurred. While this is most visibly true in the West, it is also true in the East where, in Moscow's calculations, the presence of the Chinese giant must be coupled with the U.S. presence and commitments.

Soviet attempts at expansion have therefore focused on strategic chokepoints, and on perceived soft spots in Western or Third World positions. Soviet activities in a number of areas illustrate this approach. For example, in the Horn of Africa (which controls the strategic approaches to the Red Sea and Suez Canal, and much of the Indian Ocean), they have worked to establish new Soviet outposts or to outflank existing Western positions. In southern Africa (which commands major sea lanes) they have been active in a variety of ways, overt and covert---in Angola, Mozambique, South Africa and Southwest Africa/Namibia, among others. They have been similarly active in Southeast Asia, through the Vietnamese. In Central America, they have been exploiting local conditions and an apparent lack of firm will in Washington regarding an appropriate American response,* to distract the United States and undermine its ability to cope with crisis situations elsewhere. In this context, the perceptiveness of the Chinese interpretation of the strategic map can be appreciated.

Beijing's analysts start from the premise that Moscow has a well-integrated geostrategic design whose ultimate objective is the total triumph of Soviet communism over the rest of the world. Like the assessment generally shared by Western analysts, the Chinese view begins with the premise that Moscow realizes that it cannot, for the foreseeable future, afford a direct confrontation with Washington, and that its approach must therefore be an indirect one that seeks to progressively isolate the United States from the rest of the world. As the Chinese have put it, "Soviet hegemonism needs at first to edge out the United States from the old Euro-Asian-African continent."

As the Chinese see it, the very existence of nuclear deterrence makes conventional forces "the only applicable military power against nuclear-armed enemies." (Although Moscow has been improving its naval forces significantly, the Chinese believe that these will continue to remain secondary to Soviet land power.) Moscow's superiority in conventional land forces is well known; but the effectiveness of conventional forces, unlike the effectiveness of nuclear weapons, diminishes with distance. Given the above factors, as well as the conditions prevailing both in the West and on the Soviet-Chinese border which limit Soviet opportunity, "a least expensive way for the Soviets to achieve their strategic objectives with low risk and high certainty of success is 'pushing forward the strategy of a southward thrust' while maintaining 'a stalemate on both the Eastern and Western fronts.'"[3]

This "southward thrust strategy" entails a multifaceted approach in which various regional substrategies are related to each other in order to converge toward the ultimate objective of "final domination over the world." The "strategic deployment," required for this ultimate result---and based initially on the southward thrust---is usually described as being composed of three basic objectives:

---

* As evidenced in the close Congressional votes on aid to the democratic Nicaraguan resistance.

(a) control of the oil resources in the Middle East, North Africa, and the Persian Gulf region;

(b) control of southeast Asia and the Strait of Malacca, through which shipping to Japan and the Far East must pass;

(c) Moscow's ability to have its own way in southern Africa, the key to major sea lanes, and on the African east coast along the Indian Ocean.

Were the Soviet Union to achieve these objectives, Moscow would control the economic lifelines of both Europe and Japan, with predictable consequences for their international relationships.*

The Vietnamese invasion of Cambodia, which occurred the year before the invasion of Afghanistan, is seen in the context of Vietnamese colonization of the whole of Indochina and as being intimately connected to this overall Soviet design. So is the series of "friendship" treaties signed between Moscow and India, Vietnam, and Mongolia--- all of which border on China. Moscow is seen as moving from north to south while its Vietnamese proxy moves from east to west across Southeast Asia, together carrying out this southward strategy. Control of Afghanistan and Indochina are only the first two steps in that strategy.

And, just as the steps outlined above are military and political moves on the strategic chessboard, so "detente" represents, on the diplomatic side, the attempt to lull and divide the target nations, serving as a smokescreen to mask the real intentions of the "new Tsars."[4]

The flanking-movement character of overall Soviet strategy is not, in essence, the result of theoretical prescription for an ideal strategy; rather, it is Moscow's response to a world situation that limits its options elsewhere. But the southward thrust *per se*, though it may have been activated in order to circumvent these same obstacles, is also the result of other, more positive, considerations.†

Soviet movement in the region to the south of Soviet Central Asia can occur in an area where the U.S. "does not have pre-stationed forward bases and thus will have to count on lines of communication prolonged and susceptible to interruption."[5] Conversely, this is a region in which Moscow can make use of its superior conventional capabilities. Another significant factor that makes the region to the south of its Central Asian

---

* This does not exclude other benefits such as resource control.

† Beijing sees the strategic importance to Moscow of the Northern Pacific and Central Pacific regions as essentially derivative, i.e., as potential bases for intercepting and blocking American Rapid Deployment Forces. Moscow would have to break out of the northern Pacific before it could intercept American forces in transit through the Central Pacific region.

territories attractive for Soviet exploitation is that this area is, in the Chinese description, "economically backward, sociopolitically unstable, and not steadfastly leaning to the West." Moscow can therefore engage here in "fishing in troubled waters."[6]

Pakistani analysis of the situation---at least insofar as it has been put forward by President Zia ul-Haq---seems to coincide squarely with the above-described Chinese world view. In an interview published in the *Washington Post*, President Zia defined the nature of the Soviet threat in the South Asia region:

> If they (the Soviets) move here (Pakistan) over the bodies of Pakistanis, they are at the mouth of the Gulf, and whoever controls the Straits of Hormuz controls the Gulf. In one move they have threatened to secure the Straits of Hormuz, encircle Iran and tell the Chinese, "We are on your flank."[7]

Zia's statement was part of his explanation of the strategic context of the Soviet invasion of Afghanistan. The Soviets clearly intend, he said, to follow the consolidation of their control in Afghanistan with the absorption of Pakistan into the Soviet empire in one way or another. While taking some pains to indicate that he would not allow a Soviet invasion of his country---it would occur only "over the bodies of Pakistanis"---Zia pointed clearly to the main axis of the Soviet thrust. For the West, the implications of further Soviet progress in the region are obvious. The threat to the security of the sea lanes, both in the Persian Gulf area and around South Africa, and to Western access to Middle Eastern oil would be significantly increased.

Of yet greater importance would be the opportunities for effective Soviet blackmail and intimidation. The political mileage Moscow might derive from a successful use of force in Afghanistan could diminish the need for its actual denial of the sea lanes or for actual direct Soviet control in the region. Were regional states to be so intimidated, Western European access to the region might suddenly become limited by Soviet *diktat*. Moscow's objective of dividing Western Europe from the U.S. would then be significantly advanced.

Existing Soviet pressures on Iran, the result in part of the flanking movement achieved by the Soviet presence in Afghanistan, would be immeasurably increased if Moscow gained control of Pakistan as well, whether directly or indirectly. Close Soviet ties with India already exist. The Moscow-Kabul-Islamabad-New Delhi axis would also send a clear message to the Chinese.

It might be argued that Moscow would not pursue such a course because of the potential negative impact it would have on its Indian friends. According to this argument, eliminating Pakistan as an independent entity would deprive Moscow of a useful tool in developing ever-stronger ties with India; Moscow would no longer be able to exacerbate tensions between India and Pakistan in order then to either support India or play the peacemaker. Moreover, such a development---the argument goes---would alienate a now-friendly India, which would not particularly appreciate becoming a neighbor of the Soviet Union.

This argument, however, misses the essence of the Soviet approach. Soviet moves do not appear to be dictated by a desire to please India or even by a wish to avoid antagonizing New Delhi. Rather, they seem to be the result of opportunities that arise for fulfilling broad Soviet objectives. Control of Pakistan would clearly further those goals. Furthermore, it is entirely possible that in Moscow's calculus---as well as in the reality, if one is to judge by current Indian behavior---Soviet control of Pakistan would produce a more, not less, compliant India. (One could, of course, postulate all sorts of hypothetical moves to escape such consequences: New Delhi might try to achieve closer relations with both Washington and Beijing. But in realistic terms, that is highly unlikely. Such a major gain would advance the Soviet strategy of encircling China. If such a gain occurred, and if Washington had allowed such a situation to develop, the strength of the Soviet position would make any such Indian efforts fruitless. In that case, neither Washington nor Beijing would look like a credible counterbalance.)

The recent establishment of diplomatic relations with Moscow by both Oman and the United Arab Emirates may be a good indicator of ways in which those in the region actually perceive current trends and respond to them. No doubt there were several reasons for these diplomatic moves, but fear of things to come if their governments do not develop "good relations" with the Soviets---i.e., appease them---must have been a dominant factor. Comments reportedly made by an Omani official about the new relationship with Moscow support this assumption: "The foreign policy of the Soviet Union has changed a lot for the better since Gorbachev came," he said---a somewhat surprising statement coming from a Muslim, particularly in the light of the increasingly brutal Soviet policy in Islamic Afghanistan since Gorbachev's ascent to power. Revealing that his government was "helping" in talks between Moscow and Saudi Arabia, he added that the Soviets had "become more flexible. They have promised us that they wouldn't help our enemies (particularly South Yemen) against us."[8]   Again,   a somewhat disingenuous statement in view of the clear

Soviet record and of Moscow's manipulation of both sides in the nearby Iran-Iraq conflict.

The Soviet push toward the Persian Gulf

Within this context, it now remains to look at what Soviet policy in Afghanistan and the region has actually been since the invasion. To what degree is it an attempt merely to consolidate Afghanistan? To what degree does it represent preparation to go beyond Afghanistan toward the possible dismemberment of Pakistan, and toward the next phase in the geostrategic objectives described above?

In the seven years since the invasion, Soviet policy in Afghanistan---and in Pakistan---has undergone some modifications and adjustment, but it has remain unchanged in its essence. Except for the initial period immediately following the invasion, when Moscow thought it would be able to crush the Resistance swiftly, the basis of Soviet strategy has been a long-term, relatively limited commitment designed to minimize costs and casualties. The Soviet approach has had two basic components:

1) to outlast the Resistance; and at the same time

2) to keep international interest and attention to a minimum.

The wearing down of the Resistance has been pursued via a strategy of terror which includes indiscriminate killing, driving the population out of the country or at least into the cities where they can be better controlled, and co-opting the people.

While co-optation has not, on the whole, been very successful, the other methods have been more effective: Afghanistan's pre-war population has been reduced by fully one third. There are some 4.5 to 5 million refugees in Pakistan and Iran (3.5 to 4 million of them in Pakistan alone, the world's largest refugee population). There are an additional 2 million internal refugees, most of whom have fled to Kabul and several other cities. And, although figures on Afghanistan have never been precise, it is possible that as much as 9 percent of the total pre-invasion population has been killed.

The other component in Moscow's strategy---minimizing international interest in, and attention to, Afghanistan---has been no less crucial to the successful pursuit of Soviet objectives, although it has perhaps been underestimated in the West. Outside attention to the war translates into active material and moral support for the Resistance; and while the importance of material support is obvious, the value of other kinds of support should not be underestimated. Because the guerrilla character of the war, almost by definition, diminishes the importance of the purely military aspect, the psychological component and the political, propaganda, and diplomatic aspects play a role that is perhaps equally significant in achieving ultimate victory---or in ultimate defeat.

Moscow has understood from the beginning that the final elimination of the Resistance depends on those two tracks proceeding together. They have pursued this second aspect of their strategy---minimizing world attention---in a number of ways. They have attempted outright intimidation of independent journalists. This has included the threat, made publicly by the Soviet ambassador to Pakistan in 1984, to kill those journalists who might dare to venture into Afghanistan.[9] It has also included chasing and kidnapping reporters (although the latter seems to have produced results more negative than positive) and killing them, as threatened. It has also involved bombing clinics and hospitals---even when clearly marked with a red cross---and attempting to capture medical personnel in order to dissuade French and other voluntary medical and humanitarian organizations from operating inside Afghanistan, reporting their observations, and thus generating interest in the war among their compatriots and the world at large.

Moscow has also used negotiations to the same end. The so-called "proximity talks" between Pakistan and the Soviet puppet regime in Kabul held under United Nations auspices in Geneva since 1983 have been encouraged by the Soviet Union as a means of deceiving the West into thinking that a solution is attainable through negotiations alone. The objective is to make the outside world believe that some "minor" concessions on its part would resolve the problem, and that the West can therefore forget Afghanistan and return to business as usual. Underlying such an approach is a keen Soviet understanding that once democracies lose interest in an issue, "recommitting" themselves to it again becomes a difficult, it not an impossible, proposition.

Of the several paths followed by the Soviets in pursuit of their goals, the military dimension has received the most attention in the Western media. The military effort has not been designed to seize and hold ground but, as pointed out above, to terrorize the people, to kill them, to drive them out of the country or co-opt them. Militarily, the Soviets have concentrated on periodic sweeps essentially intended to keep the Resistance off balance and to wear it out. This has entailed keeping Soviet forces in the major cities and a number of garrisons. The military effort has concentrated on protecting these Soviet/puppet bases and the single major road network in the country, as well as on the progressive elimination of the Resistance.

To use Mao's comparison of guerrillas supported by the population to fish swimming in water, the basic Soviet approach in Afghanistan has been to progressively empty the water out of the bowl, thereby ultimately killing the fish. Whereas, at the beginning of the war, the Resistance could rely on the local population to provide it with food, the situation has now been reversed in a number of areas where the population---if indeed it still remains---expects the Resistance to provide it with the means of sustenance.*

The other side of the coin, however, is that the Resistance, far from becoming demoralized, has become increasingly effective despite the continuing pressure brought to bear on it. It has been able to inflict increasingly heavy losses on the Soviets in both materiel and men. The Afghan puppet army on which the Soviets initially attempted to rely has, despite some improvements, remained largely incompetent and unreliable. The apparent decision to rely on Soviet special forces (including *SPETSNAZ*) as the key to Soviet counter-insurgency strategy, reflected in the large increase of such forces in Afghanistan since 1985, is no doubt in part related to the growing Resistance capabilities.

The more purely military dimension---especially as it concerns various tactical adjustments, gains, reverses, and losses---could be viewed as the more short-term component of the Soviet approach. Moscow has at the same time been paying careful attention to the underlying bases of long-term control. Some of the measures and policies adopted appear to apply equally to all of Afghanistan. Others, however, reveal another more differentiated approach to the absorption of Afghanistan within the Soviet system.

Early in the war, Soviet authorities in Afghanistan began to reshape the Afghan educational system along Soviet lines.[†] The Afghan curriculum now strongly resembles that of the USSR. In order to increase divisions among Afghans along ethnic lines, thus facilitating control, the Soviets have introduced the use of local languages in the schools, replacing the Farsi *lingua franca*. Russian has replaced all other foreign languages in the curriculum and has become the requisite for any advancement in Afghan society, as it is for non-Russian nationalities in the USSR.

---

* Here, as elsewhere in this chapter, when Soviet intentions, objectives, and tactics are discussed, it is important to distinguish between these and the ultimate reality. Thus, depopulation, while in some respects a clearly negative development, also makes it possible for the Resistance to worry less about Soviet retaliation against the civilian population. With appropriate logistical improvements, the Resistance would now be able to operate in areas heretofore avoided.

[†] See: Amin

In part because of the Afghan public's resistance to these educational changes, Soviet authorities have undertaken what can only be described as extensive kidnappings of large numbers of young children, forcibly sending them to the Soviet Union for "education" for periods of "at least ten years." According to the Resistance and other sources, between 1980 and 1985 more than 50,000 Afghans were sent to the Soviet Union for training. Of these, almost 24,000 were young people, and the majority of those---20,000---were children between the ages of four and eight.[10] In addition to worrying about the Marxist indoctrination of the Afghans, Moscow has been building up and strengthening WAD (formerly KhAD), the Afghan equivalent of the KGB, the Soviet secret police. These measures reflect single-minded Soviet concentration on the building of cadres which will ultimately---or so the Soviets hope---take over on behalf of their masters.

Dividing the country

There is growing evidence that, in planning for the long term, Moscow early on adopted a gradual approach to the absorption of Afghanistan, and one differentiating between different parts of the country. Although clearly seeking the pacification and control of Afghanistan in its entirety, Moscow has applied a differentiated, regional approach to the incorporation of various sections of Afghanistan within the Soviet empire. For the purposes of this strategy, which is based on both the military dimension and the longterm measures being applied to the whole country, the north is viewed as distinct from the south and southwest, and different policies are applied to the two parts of the country.*

Such a distinction had already been established in Tsarist times---by the Russians if not by others---when the Hindu Kush was being described by Tsarist officials as the "natural" boundary between the Russian and British empires. This view, then mere wishful thinking, now constitutes an integral part of Soviet encroachment efforts. Topography, ethnicity, and natural resources all favor such a distinction. Northern Afghanistan is contiguous to Soviet territory and readily accessible; it is also flatter than the terrain further south and therefore easier to pacify. A large portion of the people in the north are of the same ethnic stock as the people in contiguous areas of Soviet Central Asia---Tajiks, Turkomans, and Uzbeks. This is not the case south of Hindu Kush, where the majority are overwhelmingly

---

* The north is here understood to include the following provinces: Badakhshan, Takhar, Kunduz, Baghlan, Samangan, Balkh (sometimes called Mazar), Jowzjan, Fariyab, and possibly Badghis---but not Herat.

ethnically linked to the Pushtuns of Pakistan.* Moreover, most of Afghanistan's natural resources are also to be found in the northern part of the country. [See maps, pp. 108-109.]

A strategy designed solely to restore Soviet control at the pre-invasion level, or even one intended to consolidate a more direct kind of Soviet power over the entire country, would aim at developing resources south of the Hindu Kush as well as north of it. Such a strategy would also seek to apply a more or less even-handed approach to the various key cities of the country in terms of establishing Soviet control over urban populations. But instead, Moscow has sought both to exploit and to build up the northern region while at the same time wreaking havoc, destruction and desolation on the rest of the country.

Soviet policies in the north have taken many forms, reaching into virtually every aspect of life. Economic development and exploitation have been almost exclusively concentrated in the north. Moscow has promoted the development of the Amu Darya (Oxus River) separating the Soviet Union from Afghanistan. Gas and electricity projects have been undertaken. Two dams have been built for irrigation purposes in the Kunduz and Herat areas, and several others are planned. The economic effort has also included the exploitation of natural resources and the construction of factories.

These economic policies have been integrated into a multidimensional approach to control in the north, going hand in hand with actions aimed at the retention of the population and the establishment of total control. Whereas in the rest of the country the Soviet occupiers have actively sought to depopulate the land, in the north they have actively and systematically sought to retain and co-opt the population.

That this has been a matter of policy is evident from a number of indicators: Moscow has sought to "buy" the ethnic groups of the north by playing up to their strong sense of ethnic pride and identification and encouraging the use of their mother tongues, heretofore given less prominence. Moscow constantly emphasizes the common traditions, culture and languages shared by the northern ethnic groups and their "brethren" in Soviet Central Asia. There have been a significant number of exchanges of delegations---especially cultural---with Soviet Central Asia, particularly in the last two or three years. Soviet media in both Russian and Central Asian languages have frequently emphasized the high degree of "well-being" and "achievement" attained by the same ethnic groups "under Soviet sovereignty."

Soviet military operations in the north have for the most part been

---

* See: Barth.

small-scale (in contrast to the sweeps in other areas) and have relied more heavily on KhAD and the regime's militias rather than on Soviet troops. In contrast to other areas, where villages are attacked seemingly almost at random in terror operations, in the north the Soviets appear to attack only mujahideen positions and those villages and cities which actively support the Resistance.

The ratio of police/militia to regular Afghan forces in the northern zone appears to differ markedly from that in the rest of the country. In the north, there are only two Afghan army divisions, each with a limited strength of 3,000; the police forces, on the other hand, number about 30,000, and the *Mohafiz* (the locally-raised militia---literally, "Protection"), number 12,000 to 13,000, organized into eleven guards brigades. Whereas the army represents the Kabul regime, the guards brigades are equated with local control---and it appears that they are meant to provide the northern zone with a separate force.

Sayyed Nassim Shah (Maihanparast), the Afghan who headed the northern zone from 1983 through 1985, reportedly spent sixteen years in Tashkent and Moscow for training before he was brought back to Afghanistan in 1982 and made a member of the Central Committee of the PDPA. As far as is known, no other provincial Afghan official in any other part of the country has been given this kind of prominence. His unique position is further highlighted by the fact that at the November 1985 Afghan Communist party plenum, he was the only official singled out by name and praised by Babrak Karmal for his "effective leadership" in the pacification of the north.

Yet a further barometer of Soviet intentions is represented by the changing fortunes of the Setem-i-Milli, an organization which has long sought the separation of northern Afghanistan from the rest of the country. Under the King and later under Daoud, the Setem-i-Milli was demanding only regional autonomy within the Afghan state; now it is calling for complete separation from "Pushtun domination." Apparently a number of members of Setem-i-Milli are in the upper echelons of the northern zone Communist administrative structure.

Soviet policy in the northern zone takes on even greater significance when it is compared with policies in the rest of the country and with actions directed across the border at Pakistan itself since 1985. In the north, as mentioned above, the Soviets and their puppets have avoided destruction of cities, villages, and the countryside except when confronted by active resistance. In the rest of the country, however, Moscow has actively sought to destroy not only opposition to its rule but the very existence of the population and it means of support and subsistence. Thus, such major cities as Herat in the West and Kandahar in the south have been subjected to attacks and heavy bombardment that have reduced significant portions of these cities to rubble.* Similarly, outside of the northern zone, irrigation networks, crops and villages have been destroyed, and the land depopulated and turned to desert, making it difficult for the population to return.[11] In sum, these patterns suggest that in the north, Moscow is creating a gradual accretion to its Central Asian empire, while through the systematic devastation of the other major areas it is insuring that a weak vacuum will exist in the rest of the country.

Meanwhile, starting in 1985, the gradual escalation in the intensity and sophistication of the war, as well as in the diplomatic aspects involving other states, have taken what appears to be a new twist. Militarily, the Soviets began to increase the level and intensity of their operations more significantly than they had done previously.† The continuation of military operations during the winter months, which had already begun the year before, became more pronounced in 1985. Efforts to interdict Resistance supply routes became less haphazard, much more frequent, and more intense in both ferocity and firepower.

Military operations began to involve the frequent use of special forces (SPETSNAZ and others). Indeed, 1985 saw a significant increase in the numbers of Soviet special-purpose forces in Afghanistan. Emphasis on small-scale operations and night ambushes, often involving thirty to fifty men, increased significantly. In general it would appear that Moscow decided in 1985 that these special forces would henceforth constitute the key to their counterinsurgency military strategy.

Accompanying these shifts has been a greater emphasis on placing a bigger share of the fighting on the Afghan Communists. Moscow has increased its attention to the training and use of Afghan Communist commando forces; these, supported by heavy Soviet air support and firepower, have been used with increasing frequency

Pressure on Pakistan

To the steady integration of northern Afghanistan into the Soviet system and to the destruction of the rest of the country through intensified military activity and other techniques, the expanded focus on Pakistan must be added as another essential element in the equation.

---

* In 1985, a Swedish observer who visited Herat described it as looking like Hiroshima. In early 1986, a Resistance commander in Kandahar told a German doctor there that the prewar population of 250,000 had been reduced to about 35,000.---ed.

† See: Bodansky.

In mid-September 1985, the Kabul regime held a jirga, or assembly, of the Pushtun border tribes---*from both sides of the border.* That assembly, in addition to reflecting regime efforts to gain legitimacy, marked the revival of the Pushtunistan/Baluchistan issue. The Durand line---the border between Afghanistan and what is now Pakistan---was drawn artificially through the territory of the Pushtun tribes (and, to a lesser degree, the Baluch) in1893, splitting them up. It has constituted a source of periodic friction between Afghan and Pakistani governments since 1947.* Babrak Karmal, in a major address to the 1985 jirga, openly called for the reunification of the separated ethnic group---*under Afghan sovereignty.*

His speech, directed at tribes stretching across both sides of the existing border, represented an open call for the subversion of Pakistan. The Pushtun and Baluch territories not now within Afghanistan---i.e., the provinces of Baluchistan and the Northwest Frontier, more than half the territory of Pakistan---he referred to as "a part of sacred land...left in the hands of the British colonialists and their inheritors" (read 'Pakistan').

Arguing for "reunification"---i.e., Afghan annexation---he stated that "it was the policy of divide and rule which subjected the Pushtuns and Baluchis to the domination of imperialism and reaction, and which disturbed their unity and freedom and brought them under suppression." Calling for "reunification," Babrak asked the tribes in the meantime to help defeat the Afghan resistance to Communist rule, to help cut the Resistance supply routes: "Pushtun and Baluchi brothers, unite," he exhorted them. "Wherever you live, defend the honor and dignity of the borders of your sacred land---the free, independent, and new revolutionary Afghanistan." His appeal was neither gratuitous nor poetic license. Afghan subversion of Pakistan has begun to manifest itself in an increasing number of ways. To the training and arming of Baluch and Pushtuns in Afghanistan for armed actions in Pakistan---which began several years earlier---are now added large-scale payments to tribal leaders in the border areas of Pakistan as well as in Afghanistan, to buy their cooperation in interdicting Afghan Resistance supply routes and to pay for various terrorist acts in cities and towns in the border regions of Pakistan.

It is of no small relevance to note that the Afghan Communist implementer of these subversion programs was none other than Dr. Najib/Najibullah, then the head of KhAD, the Afghan KGB, and since May 1986 the new Soviet-picked puppet "ruler" of Afghanistan. These acts of subversion, using Pushtuns, Baluchis, and other tribes, have in turn been accompanied by steadily increasing military violations of Pakistani territory---

---

* See: Poullada; Barth; Bodansky.

hundreds of aerial incursions and bombing runs on Pakistani border towns as well as cross-border artillery shelling. In 1986 alone, by late November, air violations numbered more than 700 (compared to more than 200 for the entire year of 1985) and artillery shellings more than 150 (compared to a total of 25 in 1985). As 1987 began, air shellings in January alone were several times higher than in January 1986. While such activities can be linked to the clear Soviet attempt to intimidate Pakistan into agreeing to a virtual surrender on the Afghanistan question, their objective is also part of their wider strategic plan.

There is little doubt that in 1979 Moscow expected a somewhat different development in the war than the one that did occur. And, although they were no doubt surprised by the initially strong international reaction to the invasion, Soviet authorities nevertheless probably assumed that international interest and attention would die down and that the Resistance would be gradually worn out, its morale destroyed. Instead, the opposite has happened. Interest, attention, and support from the outside world have steadily increased, particularly since about 1982---and the Resistance, while hit hard and persistently, has increased its effectiveness and its ability to inflict damage on the Soviets and their Afghan puppets.

Hence Soviet attempts since 1983 to deceive the West into believing that a diplomatic solution may be at hand. Hence the heightened level of military activity and pressure on Pakistan. So far, responding to the challenge in characteristically Soviet terms, Moscow has chosen to go further on the offense rather than limit itself to consolidating existing gains.

Conclusions---and, what next?

Soviet strategy in the region has moved from being essentially concerned with the consolidation of Soviet power in Afghanistan itself (as was the case at the time of the invasion) to the insuring of favorable conditions for the further expansion of Moscow's influence in South Asia as a whole.

Soviet strategy can be seen as consisting of two distinct but related steps:

• The eventual absorption of the northern half of Afghanistan, whether through formal annexation or through less formal means.

• The creation of small, dependent buffer states between India and the Soviet empire.

Under such a scheme, Afghanistan as such would disappear---or, to use the Soviet lexicon, it would finally "reflect the national aspirations of the peoples" of the area. The Uzbeks, Tajiks, and others in the north would be "reunited" with their "brothers" in the Soviet Union, while the Pushtuns and

182

Baluchis on both sides of the border would be united in their own states, "free" from the "domination of the imperialists." Pakistan, of course, would also cease to exist.

The second step can be subdivided into two stages or components; the first would involve Soviet actions up to the border of Pakistan, while the second could be described as movements toward the gradual dismemberment of Pakistan itself. Since most of the Pushtuns and Baluchis are in Pakistan, the establishment of such "national entities" as "Pushtunistan" and "Independent Baluchistan" cannot be accomplished without the end of the Pakistani state. Thus, the Soviet design on Afghanistan could be described as the contemplated "Polandization" of Afghanistan, but with the difference that in this case such encroachments upon the neighbor, Pakistan, would for all intents and purposes amount to the dissolution of the latter country.

It seems probable that the Soviets do not attach equal significance to each of these objectives, or to the steps involved in attaining them, at least not at this point. The absorption of northern Afghanistan should be seen as a core objective, while the creation of new, weak, and smaller buffer states (entailing the dismemberment of Pakistan) constitutes---for now---a secondary, less proximate objective.

What is of significance, however, is that Moscow has moved from not considering actively the continued existence of Pakistan (a relatively passive mode) *to actively planning for its eventual disappearance.* Pakistan has become a target of opportunity. The first steps described above reflect a certain determination, while the second step is now at a probing stage.

Moscow's distinctly different policies regarding northern Afghanistan and the rest of the country make little sense outside of the larger Soviet design outlined above, especially when they are viewed against both the changes in Soviet military tactics in Afghanistan and the steps taken with regard to Pakistan in 1985 and since. The systematic destruction of Afghan towns and villages in south and west, the depopulation of a belt of territory around the north, the exclusive development of resources in the north, the pronouncements by Babrak---these policies do not fit in well with a supposed Soviet intention to control all of Afghanistan but to go no further.

These policies do, however, make a great deal of sense in the context of the creation of weak buffer states from the Hindu Kush south to the Indian Ocean---states that would be almost entirely dependent on Moscow not only for development but for their very existence. The irredentist pressures being generated within the Pushtun communities in both Afghanistan and Pakistan would further heighten Pushtun dependency upon Moscow for the realization of these irredentist goals. (The Soviet government has been on record since at least 1955 as supporting Afghan demands for a plebiscite through which the Baluchis and Pushtuns of Pakistan would determine their political future, including the option of "rejoining" Afghanistan.*)

The gradual approach followed by Moscow in pursuit of its objectives raises some interesting questions. Why should they not, for instance, attempt to incorporate (or, as the Soviets would like us to believe, reassert control and "pacify") all of Afghanistan? Why take a differentiated approach that builds the north and kills the south? Why not go about wider Soviet objectives in an even more open and blunt manner?

The Soviet Union, conscious of charges that it seeks to establish a land route to the Persian Gulf and therefore aware that there may well be significant opposition to moves in that direction, is attempting to arrive at such results without arousing that kind of opposition. Moscow is aware that even India would resent having the Soviet Union itself as a neighbor, and that too abrupt and direct an approach might jeopardize the very relationship with New Delhi that the Soviets have established over a period of many years and at significant cost. (The argument advanced by some that Moscow and New Delhi together might conspire to divide up Pakistan and launch coordinated military operations toward that end does not have much to support it. If such temptations ever existed on the Indian side, they must have dated to the period antedating the Soviet invasion of Afghanistan.)

The Soviet leadership is therefore purposefully laying the groundwork for the establishment of several smaller states that would *appear* to be the creation not of outside forces but of indigenous political aspirations---states that would be under total Soviet influence while providing India and the rest of the world with the illusion of buffers between the Soviet empire, the Indian subcontinent, and the Indian Ocean. The analogy between Afghanistan and Outer Mongolia, which is sometimes used to describe Soviet intentions in Afghanistan, might be somewhat applicable---but not to Afghanistan *per se*. Rather, in the above scenario, it would apply only to the southern portions of Afghanistan plus all the component parts of Pakistan (not only those contiguous to the Afghan border).

However, it is important to realize that the above analysis is meant to point to trends in Soviet policy and intentions. *It is not meant to be taken as a description of predetermined, inevitable future_reality.* It is meant to illustrate the *intended direction* of Soviet actions, not to indicate that the goals of these policies are certain to become fact.

There are a number of factors militating against the potential success of such a Soviet approach. To begin with, Soviet success with regard to

---

* Between 1748 and 1813/43 their areas were at times part of an Afghan empire.---ed.

Afghanistan is itself far from assured. Continued improvements in Resistance armaments, training and capabilities can go a long way toward frustrating Soviet designs inside Afghanistan and even forcing a Soviet withdrawal. So can greater and better international media and diplomatic attention. In Pakistan, it is far from clear that Soviet efforts at subversion and at winning over the Pushtuns and the Baluchis to the Soviet way of seeing things can make significant headway. From all appearances, the majority of Pushtuns and Baluch see their future as being tied to that of Pakistan rather than in some association with a Communist Afghan puppet. And, while Soviet attempts to buy off some of the tribal chiefs in Pakistani border areas constitute a nuisance, they do not materially change a way of doing business there that has traditionally proven inconclusive for those engaging in it.

In the final analysis, then, whether or not Soviet attempts to subvert the region while swallowing up Afghanistan will succeed will depend in large part upon how determined and forceful the other interested parties are in their resistance to Soviet designs. Karl Marx's observation regarding nineteenth-century Tsarist imperialism applies equally well if not better to twentieth-century Soviet imperialism: "The Russian bear is certainly capable of anything so long as he knows the other animals he has to deal with to be capable of nothing."

NOTES

1. A. Yepishev, in a review of Brezhnev's book *Standing Guard for Peace and Socialism*. *Soviet Military Review*, No. 9 (September 1980).

2. Compare, for instance: *Soviet Military Power* (U.S. Department of Defense, 1982) as well as subsequent editions, and "Who Endangers the Peace?' (USSR Ministry of Defense, 1982).

3. Hua Di, "The Soviet Threat to the Northern Pacific Region from an Overall Point of View," (Symposium on Regional Balance of Power in the Pacific Basin, sponsored by the National Defense University, Honolulu, 21-22 February 1985).

4. Foreign Broadcast Information Service, *Daily Report: People's Republic of China* (Washington, D.C., 26 Sept. 1980): C/3. See also, for a good analysis of Chinese views on this subject, Yaakov Vertzberger, "Afghanistan in China's Policy," *Problems of Communism* (May-June 1982): 1-23.

5. Hua Di, op.cit.

6. Ibid.

7. *Washington Post* (23 March 1986).

8. *Wall Street Journal* (19 November 1985).

9. *Tears, Blood and Cries: Human Rights in Afghanistan Since the Invasion (1979-1984): A Report from Helsinki Watch* (New York: Helsinki Watch, 1984). The statement quoted there was made by Vitaly Smirnov, the Soviet Ambassador to Pakistan, to Olivier Warin of French television and the Agence France Presse correspondent in Islamabad, on 5 October 1984. It reads: "I warn you, and through you, all of your journalist colleagues: stop trying to penetrate Afghanistan with the so-called mujahidin. From now on, the bandits and the so-called journalists---French, American, British and others---accompanying them will be killed. And our units in Afghanistan will help the Afghan forces to do it."

10. See, for instance, *Les Nouvelles d'Afghanistan,* No. 24-25 (Paris: October 1985): 10-11. See also Bennigsen; Rubin; and Amin, this volume.

11. Aside from the basic distinction discussed here between the northern portion and the rest of the country, some other distinctions have been made by the Soviets in their treatment of Afghanistan's various regions. For example, central Afghanistan, the area known as the Hazarajat, has remained essentially untouched by the war, largely due to its lack of strategic importance to the Soviets, while the territory abutting Pakistan has been subjected to particularly heavy attacks because of its strategic importance and in order to interdict Resistance supply routes.

"...[the Afghans] would all sacrifice every drop of blood till the last man was killed, in fighting for their God, their Prophet, their religion, their homes, their families, their nation...their liberty and independence."
   ---Amir Abdur Rahman

Cultural Wellsprings of Resistance in Afghanistan

Fredrik Barth

AFGHANISTAN AND the Afghans have fascinated Westerners who have had the opportunity to visit them: we have been charmed by their hospitality, or impressed with their force and style, or sympathetic to their egalitarian ideals. But if we wish to understand persons of another culture we need to focus not on what happens to be most appealing (or objectionable) to us in terms of our own ideals, but on what is most important to *them*. By identifying the values which Afghans themselves cherish above all, we also identify the wellsprings of their will to independence and cultural survival. We may then better understand their remarkable strengths, and characteristic weaknesses, in their present struggle against Soviet domination.

The Afghan Resistance differs from most resistance and liberation movements in other parts of the world in that it is not based on a shared political ideology. It is not a centrally organized movement, and it is not animated by a vision of a new and reformed society. From what then does the Resistance arise, what gives it the characteristics it has?

Its roots are deep in folk culture, and consist of three major components:

• A clear and demanding conception of individual honor and self-respect as a necessary basis for personal identity and value;

• A desire to live by one's own local, highly diverse traditions and standards;

• An Islamic conviction.

The intensity and heroism of the Afghan Resistance, as well as the painful divisions that have weakened it, both derive from these sources and are deeply and genuinely Afghan. Three hundred years ago the Pushtun national leader and poet Khushhal Khan Khattak lamented that same divisiveness and promised that "the day the Pushtuns unite, old Khushhal will arise from the grave!" Today, many who work to provide relief or to support the Afghan struggle have shared his frustrations, though expressing them less poetically.

Yet one needs only the barest glimpse of what is taking place within Afghanistan today to recognize the powerful motivation which permeates the resistance to the Soviets. As year after year of resistance fighting progressively molds Afghan awareness, they are developing new conceptions both of their struggle and of themselves. Nevertheless these same profound spiritual and cultural roots continue to shape and sustain their struggle.

An inward-looking society?

Most accounts of Afghanistan emphasize the country's underdevelopment and isolation, and identify its distinctiveness with conservatism and Islam. The American anthropologist Louis Dupree (whose description has been widely and uncritically accepted) characterized Afghanistan as an "inward-looking society," and described its population as predominantly composed of illiterate, self-sufficient villagers set on defending their traditional outlook behind the "mud curtain" of their compound walls, thereby rejecting progress, social reform, and their own (previously non-Communist) government's development initiatives.[1]

And so it may have appeared from the outside. But this is not how life seemed to the Afghans themselves in the years before the Soviet invasion. Nor does it seem so to them now. To share their conception, we must make the imaginative effort to transport ourselves from where we stand to where they stand: away from what *we* unconsciously view as the center of the world---our own Western society---and over to where *their* world inevitably has its center, in the middle of Asia.

Afghans look out at the world from a vast land of mountains and plains, surrounded by world powers and teeming millions of other and different Asians. Throughout history they have stood at the crossroads of the world, traversed by caravans, conquerors and migrations, in close commerce and interchange with great cities and civilizations from the Mediterranean to China. (See Appendix II for details.)

It is true that much of their local history is taken up with the story of the inhabitants of each village defending the rocky glen where their forefathers settled. But even the most inaccessible groups picture themselves as parties to world history: the tribes of Nuristan maintain traditions (probably entirely incorrect) of descent from the troops of Alexander the Great, while the Hazara tribes in the central mountains claim to hail from Genghis Khan's Mongol armies. And all of them see themselves as contemporary actors on a world stage. With limited resources at home, it was always in that larger world that wealth and fame could be won: as conquerors in India and Persia; as labor migrants throughout the Indian subcontinent; as scholars influencing the entire Muslim world; as wandering traders, nightwatchmen, moneylenders or artisans; and, for more than a fifth of them, as pastoral nomads, ever on the move across the borders of nations in search of pastures.

This cosmopolitan outlook is also a product of the makeup of Afghan society itself. The Afghan people are not one nation in the cultural sense: they are a commonwealth of peoples and cultures. By one count[2] they belong to twenty-two different ethnic groups, speaking more than thirty different languages of several distinct language families, mainly Indo-European and Ural-Altaic. Every Afghan town and most Afghan villages serve as meeting places of people with different cultures. It is not mud walls but an active inner fortitude and a proud awareness of one's own heritage that provide the basis for every Afghan's identity, both men and women.

For most Afghans, that identity is tied to the culture of the countryside rather than the towns or the state. This is an orientation unlike that of most of Asia and Europe, where cities have usually been the center of civilization, but in some ways it is reminiscent of the United States. Americans tend to find the essence of American culture, and true human virtue, in life in rural areas of Iowa or Maine rather than in "the mess in Washington" or the great cities which, since Jefferson, have been viewed as essentially corrupt. Most Afghans have likewise distrusted the towns and big government: their ideals of courage, integrity and the good life thrive best in the village and the countryside, whereas cities make one at least soft and devious, and at worst dissolute and godless.

Honor and society

Why should honor and self-reliance have such an important place in this identity? This question reflects the problems with which every Afghan has had to cope, and the structure of the society of which every Afghan has been part.

The world of Central Asia in which they have survived has been a harsh and pitiless world, and so have been the valleys and villages into which the individual Afghan has been born. Neither the state nor your neighbor could be counted on to defend your life and your rights if you were weak. Any property or privilege an Afghan claimed, he would have to secure and defend for himself; and any assistance he obtained from others would depend on what he could offer in return. The strong person, the one who had honor and self-respect, was best able to defend himself and had most to offer as a friend and ally. Such have been the formative life experiences which have, over the centuries, shaped Afghan values and self-reliance: in the last instance, your life and security---and that of your family---depend squarely on your own force and standards.

No wonder that these same sources of toughness serve as the wellsprings of strength when Afghans are forced to resist foreign domination. A people's specific ideas of what constitutes honor and self-respect make sense only in the context of the particular society which has shaped them: to understand the Afghan code of honor we must know something more of Afghan society.

In looking for the unique aspects of Afghan society and psychology, one must, for several reasons, focus first of all on the Pushtuns. The seven million or so Pushtuns living in Afghanistan* make up nearly half of the total population. Moreover, the Pushtuns are the historical founders of the Afghan state, its rulers, and its backbone. Although the other ethnic groups in Afghanistan organize social life on somewhat different principles, Pushtun culture has exerted a powerful influence on all of them, giving them in one degree or another the characteristics one can call "Afghan."

Where the state is weak, as it traditionally has been in Afghanistan, family and tribe become the mainstay of human society. The Pushtuns probably compose the largest tribally organized people in the world today. Fifteen million people claim to be related in one immense patrilineal family through known genealogies in a paternal line like those of the Tribes of Israel. (The mythical figure Qais, who, according to legend, travelled to Mecca and was converted to Islam by the Prophet Mohammed himself, is supposed to have been their common ancestor about twenty-five generations back.)

Genealogies serve to order all Pushtuns into families, lines and branches, systematically related to each other and corresponding to the territorial divisions of eastern and southern Afghanistan and northwestern Pakistan. In large areas of the countryside, people live in their ancestral

---

* An approximately equal number of Pushtuns (Pathans), tribally related, live in Pakistan, most of them concentrated in the Northwest Frontier Province and the semi-autonomous Administered Tribal Territories. It was this circumstance that gave rise to the perennially troublesome issue of "Pushtunistan."

homelands. Their roots in these specific territories form the base of their tribal organization: the population of neighborhoods and districts compose families and clans of the tribe. Defense of ancestral home territories and retribution for the killing of relatives are not matters for chiefs and government courts to deal with but the responsibility of these families and clans. In such conflicts, the basic rule is that close relatives should support each other against distant relatives, and that all relatives should support each other against outsiders.

This structure has two important implications:

• A Pushtun's rights as a citizen of a tribal community can only be exercised if he lives among his relatives, i.e., on the land of his forefathers.[3] His inherited plot of land, or his share in the commons, is thus irreplaceable for him as the basis for his political participation in the group. No purchased field or residence elsewhere can give him tribal rights. Every person is thus closely tied to his place of birth and its defense is always his first concern.

• The family and clan unite to defend their common interests against outsiders---but only then.

The rest of the time they are one another's perpetual competitors and rivals. (Just as the word "rival" derives from the Latin term for those who shared an irrigation channel, so also the Pushto word for paternal cousin means "rival" and "enemy" as well as a relative.)

This, then, defines the context within which the Pushtun male ideology of courage, honor and independence has been bred and exercised. (In different forms and degrees, women partake of it too.) To succeed in such a society demanded great force and self-reliance; it fostered an individualism that we, even in our individualistic Western societies, can hardly conceive of and certainly not practice. A reputation for force and violence is a great asset in such a society; it discourages others from trying to take advantage of you. But friendliness and hospitality are also valued as long as they do not make you dependent on others but make them appreciate you more, and make them readier to support you when you need that support.

Security and influence in such a society depend on personal strength, conceptualized in terms of an honor that the individual himself defends well enough to allow him to believe in himself; a confidence that he is brave, independent and unblemished; and a reputation that he is one whom others must respect and fear to challenge. Only the man who succeeds in creating and perpetually defending such a reputation can rest assured in his self-respect and his confidence that others must also respect him. The result is a marked ideology of individualism. Pushtuns often represent life as a perpetual struggle of all against all for honor, wealth and land (*zin, zer, zamin;* literally: "women [in whom the honor of the family resides to a significant degree], gold and land." Every boy is trained to carry arms and to fight---not for abstract ideas of freedom or big collectives like nation and state, but for himself, his honor and his property, in revenge or defense or self-aggrandizement.

This is a good background for guerrilla fighters. But it also carries the seeds of some of the weaknesses that are apparent in the present Afghan Resistance. Self-respect and individualism foster toughness and bravery, but they provide poor guidance for participation in collective action and they make it difficult to take orders. Previous experience of a social pattern in which cousins support each other against outsiders but fight among themselves when left alone develops political practices that encourage factionalism, divisiveness and rivalry.

It was this divided, segmentary character of tribal society which initially prevented Pushtuns from reacting *collectively* to Soviet infiltration in 1978-79 and to the Soviet invasion in 1980. Each clan and district reacted only when directly provoked. It is inherent in the traditional tribal system that one may even like to see other groups weakened and destroyed---but also that there will be competition to prove oneself and one's clan "the bravest," and to reap the fame that follows from spectacular exploits. Accustomed as they were to plowing and herding with the rifle on their shoulder always ready for use, the Pushtuns have exceptional potential as guerrilla fighters; but their ideas of group structure and individual self-assertion create difficulties in coordination and discipline, and have produced an internal divisiveness which continues to plague them.

Naturally, in the struggle for honor in Pushtun tribal society, not everyone could succeed. Through the generations, poverty or overwhelming force often drove the losers from their patrimony and thereby from their place in the clan. Some of these persons drifted into the cities. Others sought shelter as servants of a stronger man. These *hamsaya* ("people who live in the shade of others") had no political identity of their own, but formed an expanded quasi-family around the leader or strongman they followed. In some parts of Pushtun areas (for example, in the semi-arid regions around Kandahar), land became concentrated in the hands of leaders of this kind, while the propertiless became their tenants. But even tenants, bodyguards and servants remain jealous of their honor and seek to defend it, not least because their reputation is their main asset when seeking employment. Thus, the same ideals of toughness, bravery and self-reliance are also cultivated by them.

As mentioned above, all of the other ethnic and cultural groups in the Afghan population have been significantly influenced by Pushtun culture and values, and show similar characteristics to a significant degree---although not all of them are tribally organized, and each is powerfully shaped by the specifics of its own culture, history and social structures.

We shall return briefly to the character of this diversity; here it is enough to emphasize that, as mountain and desert farmers and nomad herdsmen and traders surviving in this turbulent part of Asia, all the cultural groups have had to cope with the same hardships and have shared similar historical experiences, which have bred the same kinds of toughness into them. If anything, the physical and mental stamina of Tajik, Nuristani and Hazara mountaineers exceeds even that of Pushtuns, though lacking some of the Pushtun egalitarian arrogance.*

The defense of local culture and custom

If a high valuation of individual honor and self-respect is one wellspring of Afghan strength in their fight for independence, their high valuation of local custom and culture is another. Like their concepts of honor and integrity, these values are strong on creating the will to resist, but weak on creating unity. The different peoples of Afghanistan are culturally diverse and have had---at least before the invasion---little consciousness of a common destiny; between some groups there is a history of long-standing enmity, discrimination and suppression. Some of the minorities also embrace heterodox sects of Islam: a sizable minority is Shi'a, and there are small scattered communities of Ismailia adherents who are subject to discrimination from a Sunni majority. Moreover, throughout the whole country there runs a deep division between town and countryside. Townspeople---only about ten percent of the prewar population---are largely Farsi speaking, nontribal, and more closely identified with government and the State.

The villagers in the countryside---who, before the war, made up about 90 percent of the population---generally speak Pushto, Farsi, Uzbek, or one of the other communal languages as their mother tongue. (Farsi [Persian] is the *lingua franca,* spoken as a second language throughout the country by those who have other mother tongues.) The majority are tribally organized,

---

* One of the clearest expressions of a nation's character is seen in its favorite sport. For Afghans, this is *buzkashi,* a kind of equestrian football in which dozens or even hundreds of horsemen, in a grand melee, struggle to seize a hundred-pound goat carcass and carry it at full speed a mile or more around a goal while fighting off all comers. It calls for superb skills, team defense, toughness, and imperviousness to injury. Of Turkoman and Uzbek origin, it has been universally adopted as the Afghan national game.

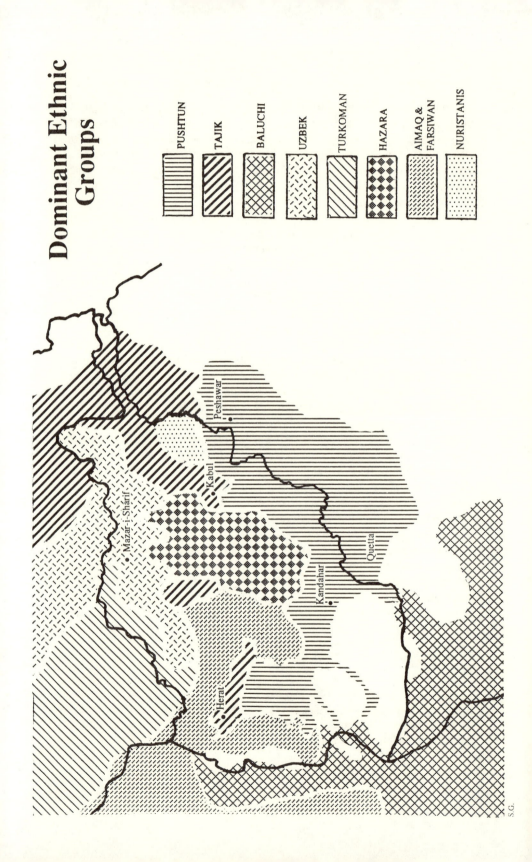

Dominant Ethnic Groups

PUSHTUN

TAJIK

BALUCHI

UZBEK

TURKOMAN

HAZARA

AIMAQ &
FARSIWAN

NURISTANIS

Mazár-i-Sharíf

Kabul

Peshawar

Kandahar

Quetta

Herat

S.G.

and they are universally independent, self-sufficient, and proud.   For them, each individual's identity is closely tied to his or her membership in their ethnic group---and, needless to say, each group considers itself to be culturally and morally superior.

Ethnic groups

The main ethnic groups, or clusters of related groups, can be divided into those that are tribally organized and those that are not. (See facing map) Since no complete census was ever taken, all figures are approximate and have been rounded off in this article. And all data, of course, refer to the population before the war, which has created a massive exodus of refugees predominantly to Pakistan, Iran and the comparative safety of cities, changing the demographics.

Tribally Organized Communities

• *Pushtuns*. As previously noted, the nearly seven million Pushtuns were the largest group. Concentrated in the south and the east, they are closely related to the Pathans of Pakistan.   Almost all Pushtuns are orthodox Sunni Muslims of the Hanafi school; many are adherents of the Sufi religious orders, particularly Qadiriya Sufiism.

• *Hazaras*. About one million mountain farmers who speak a Persian dialect and live in the central massif, the Hazarajat.   Perhaps of Mongol origin, claiming (probably mistakenly) to be the descendants of the soldiers of Genghis Khan, they are the largest Shi'a community in Afghanistan.

• *Aimaq*. Almost a million nomads and farmers in the western mountains. Like the Hazaras, their culture is basically Central Asian, but they are orthodox Sunni Muslims.

• *Nuristanis*. About 100,000 people of ancient Indo-European origin speaking a number of different but related languages live in the high mountains north of Jalalabad.   The Nuristanis were converted to Sunni Islam less than a century ago and are now ardent Muslims, although they retain many unique characteristics of their extremely ancient culture.

• *Baluch*. About 100,000 nomads and farmers in various regions of the southwest who speak Baluchi, a language related to Persian. (The majority of Baluch live in Pakistani Baluchistan and Iranian Baluchistan, where they are dominant.)

Non-Tribal Communities

• *(Mountain) Tajiks*. About two million people, largely small farmers, concentrated in northeastern Afghanistan.   They speak various Iranian languages and are related to the Tajik peoples in the Soviet Union. Most

Tajiks are Sunni Muslim, though a small number are adherents of Shi'ite or Ismailia Islam.

• *Uzbeks and Turkomans.* About one million people of Central Asian origin who speak Turkic languages and are very closely related to the Uzbeks and Turkomans in the Soviet Union. (Indeed, a number of them came to Afghanistan to escape first the Tsarist and then the Soviet takeovers in Central Asia.) Mostly farmers and herdsmen, it is they who produce the famous Afghan carpets and Persian lamb (karakul). They too are Sunni.

• *Farsiwan.* In the West, toward the Iranian border, one million or so Persian (Farsi)-speaking farmers and townsmen in Herat and its surrounding countryside, who are often---mistakenly---called "Tajiks." This area was often, in the course of history, part of Persia, and the Farsiwan are for the most part Shi'a.

• Another several hundred thousand villagers in the areas between the Pushtuns and the Nuristanis speak various languages of the Indian (Dardic) family and, sometimes, Pushto. Also Sunni, they do not form a single coherent group but are often lumped together as *"Kohistanis."*

• Other *"Tajiks."* Finally, there is a large, widely distributed population of various origins, Sunni Muslims who speak Farsi as their mother tongue, who are also generally called "Tajiks," although they are not culturally related to the Tajik community of the northeast, mentioned above, or to the Tajiks in the USSR.

All of these groups---and their various subgroups---maintain their distinctive cultures and sense of identity. It would seem that the contacts between groups have only served to nurture each person's awareness of his own separate identity, and have taught him to value and cherish it---and therefore to want to retain it. Thus, in Afghanistan no one speaks his mother tongue, follows his ancestors' customs, or lives in accordance with his tribal or community organization from a mere ignorance of alternatives (as may be the case in some extremely isolated areas of the world). On the contrary, in Afghanistan these are conscious choices.

All Afghans have for centuries been aware of alternatives. They have been, and are, bilingual or multilingual; they have known change and development. When the Afghans have rallied around tribal institutions, this has not been a rejection of progress but a form of collective defense against domination by an encompassing state which they did not want to have overpower them.

There have of course been deep historical conflicts between some of the ethnic and cultural groups. The Nuristanis, before their final forcible conversion to Islam in 1895, fought a relentless war with all their neighbors. Pushtuns have encroached on the pastures and lands of the

Hazaras, and have forced them and various Tajik groups to become their tenants. Sunnis have persecuted Hazaras and certain Mountain Tajik villagers for their Shi'a beliefs.

Yet despite these historic internecine conflicts, neither the Communist governments nor the occupying Soviet Army seems to have had much success in broadening and exploiting these divisions. Afghans are divided, yes, by cultural differences and by personal ambitions and rivalries; and they may---in the brutal realities of war and genocide of which they are the victims---sometimes even sell each other out to win tactical advantage and survival. But their customs and cultural identity are above all a thing of crucial positive value to them. In the struggle to defend that, they know that the enemy is the Soviet Army and the Soviet-backed regime, not other cultural groups. So they seek alliance and unity rather than conflict with other Afghans, and do not wish to be played off against each other even if the positive loyalties are sometimes weak.*

The importance of Islam

This is where, Islam, the third major wellspring of the Afghan liberation movement becomes particularly important. It is a striking fact that nearly all the different Afghan resistance organizations use religious symbols in their names and in their rhetoric. Because of the conspicuous but fortuitous coincidence in the timing of the upheavals in both countries, Westerners have made comparisons between the Afghan Resistance and the resurgence of Islam in Iran, and have tried to understand them as expressions of the same basic forces. In my judgement, this is an error that only serves to foster a false interpretation of the character of the Afghan Resistance. Islam is important to Afghans in their struggle, but in a way that is very different indeed from the role it has played in Iran, with which it is now often confused.

To all Afghans, Islam is a self-evident part of everyone's culture and identity---more so than was Christianity in nineteenth century Europe, and perhaps even more so than Catholicism in Poland today (which, like Islam in Afghanistan, serves as a national rallying point). Lacking since medieval times a critical native tradition of science and written history, with little else than oral history to enhance their cultural awareness, and practically without written literature in most of their own languages---except of course

---

* The impact of the Soviet invasion has been a significant stimulus to the development of a sense of nationhood and national identity, but circumstances make it impossible to measure this and, in any case, local and ethnic identities continue to underlie it.---ed.

in Persian, and that ancient---their cosmology, their knowledge of history, and their understanding of the human condition have of necessity been firmly based on Islam.

A pure and abstract monotheism has thus provided both the foundations of their world view and the source of their ethics and their law---the Sharia in the Hanafi interpretation---which contains rules for all human intercourse and for the very basis of society. In such a context, atheism not only represents a ridiculous denial of the existence of God, and thereby of the world and His creation: atheism is also a dangerous and amoral denial of the basic preconditions for all human and social standards.

Yet Afghans have rarely been other-worldly in their orientation but instead are highly secular and pragmatic. A folk story nicely reveals, and lampoons, their attitudes: "A mullah came to our village and started upbraiding us for our ignorance and laxness in observing Islam. We didn't like the disrespectful way he spoke to us, so we shot him---and now we have a fine holy grave where we can pray!"

In the stateless politics of Afghanistan's countryside, religious men, specifically *because* they are outside of the structure, have traditionally been important as arbiters of Muslim law and as mediators to negotiate local settlements between independent tribesmen. They are outside the tribal system; they can therefore unite the different tribal branches and communities and command a combined army without threatening the parity of the temporarily united clans and ethnic groups. When the land has been threatened by external enemies, such religious figures have also taken on extended functions as leaders of jihad, "holy war." Throughout several centuries of resistance to British and Russian expansionism, such leaders arose again and again to head a defensive jihad.

In many parts of Afghanistan there is also a contemporary pattern of local Sufi brotherhoods under the leadership of one or another religious scholar. On a relatively small scale, such brotherhoods too can unite persons of different classes, ethnic groups or tribal branches. In Afghanistan these brotherhoods have never fused into large, hierarchical organizations under the leadership of divines like the Ayatollahs of Iran. For that, Afghans have always been too democratic and too independent-minded. Thus, among the Afghans, Islam has never been the basis for a permanent, formal and hierarchical religious or political organization.

In the present crisis, when symbols of unity are desperately needed, these historical experiences and shared sentiments become invaluable in forging organization. This explains why a few of the Resistance organizations are built on the foundations of Sufi religious brotherhoods; others are led by widely respected religious scholars who can unite patriots across traditional lines of cleavage; and all the Resistance movements find in Islam a unifying moral force around which they can rally in defense of everything that Afghans value.

The state and the central government

Why could not the nation, the state of Afghanistan, serve them equally well as such a unifying symbol? The Afghan resistance movements all aim to re-establish an independent Afghan state, and this sense of independence and statehood is important to Afghan consciousness. To an outsider, that might seem to be motive enough. But we must not misjudge the character and force of Afghan nationalism; it is not itself the major force behind their resistance.

Through its 2500 years of history, Afghanistan was at times the center of great empires, at other times part of various Greek, Mongol, Turkish, Persian and Indian empires. The modern kingdom of Afghanistan, as we know it today, emerged only in 1747 through a confederation and election after a brief Persian empire fell apart. A group of Afghan tribal chiefs who broke away from the dissolving Persian army chose as their king the young Ahmed Shah, a member of the Durrani tribe of Pashtuns. His descendants, always confirmed by public consent through the *jirga* system, ruled in Kabul until Taraki's coup in 1978; but in those 231 years Afghanistan never knew strong centralized kingship.

Kabul's control of the provinces was always precarious, even though several of the rulers were indeed notable statesmen who secured Afghanistan's existence and maintained its independence throughout the two centuries of European colonialism and imperial conquest. "How can a small power like Afghanistan, which is like a goat between these lions [British India and Tsarist Russia], or a grain of wheat between the strong millstones of the grinding mill, stand midway of the stones without being ground to dust?" asked Abdur Rahman, perhaps the greatest nationbuilder among Afghan rulers. The answer, which legitimate Afghan governments have always followed, was, in external affairs, neutrality and a policy of balance--- and internally, a slow and careful unification. Every regime had to secure the support of, at the least, many or most of the different cultural groups and tribes within the nation's territory. This forced them to observe a cautious balance of power between the center and provinces, the state and the tribes and communities---i.e., a de facto confederate structure.

Since the provinces were inhabited by an armed, freedom-loving population, it was a military and political necessity for the government always to be sensitive to the wishes and interests of the population, with or without benefit of the specific legal techniques of modern, Western-style democratic elections.* Thus, although the King was, legally speaking, an absolute monarch until 1963, in actuality the society was both decentralized and permeated by the Afghans' egalitarian ideology. Even the most humble citizen insisted on his right to speak his mind, simply and directly, to anyone, regardless of differences in status and wealth; and if he gave respect to the king, he expected---and got---respect in return.

Despite the overall modernization which began after the Second World War, these traditional features of Afghan society were largely retained. In contrast to developments in many other Asian countries, the influential and propertied Afghan families never coalesced as a national elite or distinctive upper class. There certainly were sharp material differences in Afghan society. Both around Kabul and in some other parts of the country, much land became concentrated in few hands, but the estates never reached the size characteristic of other parts of the Middle East at the time and most of the land was held by small independent farmers.

Education also made for important differences: some persons obtained the highest modern training and degrees while most remained illiterate. But high levels of education could not easily be transformed into *political* influence unless an individual was also able to gain the support of local people in a district and make himself their spokesman.

Given the way local and national politics interacted, anyone who wished to wield influence---or even just to secure his position and properties---had to find ways to rally local support in a district, usually in or near his birthplace. Otherwise, no matter how modern an education he had, he would remain simply a bureaucrat, a government servant. In order to achieve influence, would-be leaders had to cultivate their contacts with the common people of their own tribe, town or district rather than concentrating on their contacts with one another within a national elite.

As in traditional times, modern political divisions continued to run vertically---i.e., between different leaders with their groups of followers---and not horizontally along class lines. Because of this absence of class divisions and class-consciousness and the strength of a profoundly egalitarian spirit, revolutionary and Marxist rhetoric had (and has) little appeal to the population at large. It suited only those who had a modern education and developed the ambitions that go with it, but who had failed for various reasons to develop a local base or following, and therefore felt frustrated as mere government servants without influence on policy.

The relatively small membership of the two radical movements---Khalq

---

* Amanullah, who tried to rule without such consensus, was overthrown in 1929.---ed.

(The People) and Parcham (The Banner)---was overwhelmingly composed of such junior civil servants, army officers, teachers, and students---usually urbanized, even if village-born---who had become estranged from their own culture through modern education and perhaps studies abroad and who no longer had much contact with, and indeed little knowledge of, their own people. When they suddenly obtained power in 1978 they impatiently dispersed through what had become to them an alien countryside to "liberate" and "modernize" it on the basis of dogmatic Marxist political and ideological schemata of what was "progressive" and what was "reactionary."

Suddenly every Afghan found that his or her chance to realize an honorable, independent and cherished life was threatened by an expansive central government they had never desired or supported. No wonder that, particularly as the ranks of Soviet advisors swelled in 1978-79 and finally the Red Army moved in, Afghans shortly found themselves more united that they had ever been since they defeated the British Empire one hundred years earlier.

But the Afghan dream of independence remains as much a dream of personal freedom *from* government as it does freedom *of* government. Therefore, the image of nationhood, though enormously strengthened since the invasion, is not enough to serve as the sole emotive banner of their national resistance: Islam is needed as a unifying symbol and emotive force.

The destruction of a balance

Every nation and every people has its culturally distinctive dreams and hopes, its shared ideals of the good society and the good life---ideals in terms of which their actual society must always fall short, but which certainly cannot be realized for them by other people with other cultures.

Central to every Afghan's consciousness are his or her standards of honor and self-respect, with a particularly great emphasis on individual self-reliance, autonomy, equality and courage. Far more emphatically than even we, with our Western tradition of individuality, Afghans emphasize the necessity always to fight to defend self-respect, to take responsibility for oneself and one's dependents, to meet force with counter-force.

Together with this, despite a great gusto for life, goes a rejection of luxury and comfort, a denial of materialism as an index of value. The stark and pure have much deeper appeal than the elaborate and luxurious. "It is almost impossible for a rich man to be honorable, and to be happy," a Pushtun once explained to me. "He will always be worried that he may lose his wealth, he will compromise himself to try to defend it, he will be pursued by flatterers who deceive him, thieves who rob him, and enemies who threaten him. Better a poor man, who has only one loaf of bread. He can be generous and hospitable, share his bread with his fellow, and then be free. He never needs to be afraid and suspicious. He can walk with his head high, and look any man in the eye!" With such a view of the good life, the fact of poverty gives little incentive to revolutionary enthusiasm and cooperation with the occupying power.

To a greater extent than many other societies, both industrialized and undeveloped, Afghan society gave its people a pattern of daily life whereby individuals could realize a meaningful existence, and could live, work and die with pride and integrity. It is tragic to see such a life shattered. Certainly it is always tragic when violence and death strike as blindly and senselessly as they do in war, but it becomes even more tragic when there is reason to believe that the destruction is irreparable, that the values being destroyed can probably never, even under the most fortunate circumstances, be restored.

The balance that existed in Afghanistan---between state and tribe or group, and between the encompassing nation and tribe and the autonomous individual---was never institutionalized in constitutions and laws, and cannot be recreated. The struggle of the Resistance movement, of the whole Afghan nation fighting against an overwhelming modern power, necessitates political and social changes and a degree of coordination and hierarchization of power which, if the Afghans survive the struggle, will have deprived them of some of the most cherished things that motivated the struggle. A world in which local traditions and cultures could live and assert themselves, unregulated by majorities and minorities, a world in which every person could enjoy many of the freedoms that were ours before any state existed, has now been laid in ruins; and the whole world is poorer for the loss.

Notes

1. Louis Dupree, *Afghanistan* (Princeton University Press, 1973): 248 ff.

2. Dupree, op. cit., 57 ff. See also other works cited in the bibliography under "General History and Background."

3. In 1983, the former chairman of a department in the Faculty of Letters at Kabul University, educated at Columbia University and the University of London and now living in exile in the United States, wrote to a friend, "[The Russians] invaded my country. The country where I was born, my father was born, his father was born....My graveyard was there. My mosque was there. My land...everything that I owned and inherited... I was obliged to leave my country---my beloved country... Now I am a man without a homeland, without culture and values. Now I am a man of no identity."---ed.

"I believe...that a people must never value anything higher than the dignity and freedom of its existence ...under most circumstances, a people is unconquerable if it fights a spirited struggle for its liberty..."
---Karl von Clausewitz

The Afghan Resistance: Its Background, Its Nature, and the Problem of Unity

Abdul Rashid

THE HISTORICAL traits that inspired the rising of the Afghan people against the Communist government in Kabul and the Soviet invasion---fierce individual and communal independence conditioned by geography, livelihood, culture, and social and religious codes---have also been disruptive to the unity of the Afghan Resistance. The divisions among the mujahideen issue from such contradictions as individualism versus group cohesion, the time-honored openness of Afghan institutions versus the secrecy entailed in combat operations, religion versus nationalism, and mutual suspicions among leaders. Those internal factors have been exacerbated by increasing reliance on outside assistance and the resulting influx of outside influences, and by intensive efforts of Communist agents to penetrate and subvert Resistance organizations at all levels. Yet, greater unity is essential not only to the Resistance's survival but also to its effective representation in international forums and in negotiations affecting Afghanistan's fate.

To understand both the successes and the problems of the Afghan Resistance, it is necessary to glance briefly at its origins, the society and culture from which it springs, the path of its development, and the nature of its organization and its problems. Then perhaps one can look at possibilities for its future.

The background of the Resistance

Geography and history have combined to create in Afghanistan a decentralized and fiercely individualistic society, which traditionally has resisted the attempts of any central government to impose control over local, tribal and social affairs. These characteristics suggest that a central government---and especially a hated Communist regime---may never be able to impose strict control over the country and its populace. Yet these same characteristics have also strained the Resistance, leading to competition for resources and feuding in the field.

Notwithstanding these time-honored barriers, traditional Afghan institutions do provide the basis for a potential unification of Afghan clerical and secular leaders against occupying Soviet armed forces. Without such operational---if not political---unity, the Resistance may not be able to survive long. With it, and with the help of centrifugal forces operating on the Soviet Empire, Afghanistan may yet escape becoming another Soviet Socialist Republic.

The Afghan Resistance is an expression of the distinctive Afghan character, which has been shaped in turn by the country's geography. Land-locked Afghanistan is at the hub of South and Central Asia. The massive Hindu Kush mountain range cuts across the country and, with its many offshoots, dominates most of the terrain, determining the character of the people as well as the socioeconomic conditions in the country.

Most of the Afghan terrain is rocky, barren and sharply divided by mountain ranges and ridges, and much of the land of the south and west is desert. Many of the semi-arid areas are dependent on ancient and elaborate irrigation systems. Its inhabitants have subsisted traditionally from small agricultural plots cut along the slopes and stream banks in the valleys, and from pastures on mountainsides. Despite the scarcity of arable land, roughly 95 percent of Afghanistan's population is rural. Urban centers are few: Kabul, Herat, Mazar-i-Sharif, Jalalabad and Kandahar are the only notable towns. The other towns are merely markets or administrative centers comprising government offices and a few shops.

The difficult living conditions have created a decentralized tribal culture that fiercely protects itself through a tribal social code. There are numerous ethnic groups, hundreds of tribes and subtribes in Afghanistan.* Many of these are mini-nationalities which in the past largely practiced self-rule.

---

* See: Barth.

Maliks (landowners) and *khans* (local or tribal leaders, mostly landowners) were predominant in the cultural life.

Within the community, the family was a cohesive unit that normally resisted any external interference. Inter-family or wider disputes were resolved in the local *jirga* (council), where judges were selected from among the local maliks. Because the judges were appointed by the families involved and every concerned individual was present and could express his opinion, people had faith in the system. Religious leaders were often consulted to confirm the legality of the decision in *Shari'a* (Islamic law) but in a dispute, the tribal tradition often prevailed over religion. Jirga proceedings, therefore, were essentially secular in approach.

The pre-Communist national government essentially followed a similar system. The national parliament and provincial assemblies---some of whose members were popularly elected, some appointed---were called jirgas, as was the ultimate national body, the Loya Jirga, called as needed to deal with exceptional matters of national importance. In these national jirgas, maliks and khans usually represented their communities or tribes. The national parliament *(majlis)* did include a specified, limited number of representatives of the religious leadership and other special interest groups, but it was on the whole considered a secular, nationalist body rather than a religious one.

Individual character of Afghans

The individual Afghan is as rugged as the terrain he inhabits, fiercely independent in his personal and community life. Beyond the battle for survival, he is governed by a social code based on honor *(nang)*, revenge *(badal)* and hospitality *(malmastia)*. While this code has its origins among the Pushtuns, it has permeated the culture of the other ethnic communities in Afghanistan as well.

Afghans tend to resist the pull of a central government: the rigid centralization that the Soviet Union has attempted to impose in recent years runs completely counter to the Afghan social code as well as to the religious code of Islam. An Afghan's honor extends to family, clan, tribe, nation and religion. The Communist takeover in 1978 threatened all of these. Resistance therefore became a matter of honor, incorporating the requirement of revenge. The code of revenge is basic to Afghan (and especially Pushtun) society. Any harm to an Afghan's family or its interests is avenged, often violently, on a scale at least commensurate with the offense. Failure to seek revenge is tantamount to loss of honor, and honor is at the very core of Afghan self-identity.

In recent years, the *jihad* against Soviet and Afghan Communist forces has supplanted many internal and local feuds. Soviet brutality inspires revenge, drawing ever larger numbers of Afghans to the Resistance. The Soviets have attempted both to divert this thrust of revenge and to undermine the Resistance by recreating internal feuds. Thus far the code of revenge has been a major source of strength for the *mujahideen,* although growing Soviet skill in exploiting the Afghan social system presents a potentially serious problem for the Resistance.

The code of hospitality provided another important early element of the strength of the Resistance. The feeding and protection of anyone who walks into a home is a sacred responsibility of the host. Fighting groups of the Resistance were therefore welcomed in every Afghan home and were provided food, shelter and other material support. In fact, in accordance with religious and cultural tradition, 10 percent of all agricultural produce and 2.5 percent of all other yearly earnings were set aside by each Afghan family as the share for the mujahideen.

This Afghan social code made the rapid early growth of the Resistance possible. Each mujahideen group supplied its support needs from local sources and could purchase a limited quantity of arms and ammunition from the donations of cash. In an emergency, all the villages in a given rural area provided sanctuary and responded to calls for help by sending men to fight. Although all groups preferred to operate on or close to their home bases, the code of hospitality ensured support for fighters throughout the country.

Over the years, however, extensive Soviet bombing has devastated the countryside, reducing the population's ability to support itself, let alone support the Resistance. Approximately five million people, roughly one-third of the prewar population, have been driven out of the country into Pakistan or Iran. The remaining population of many rural areas has been compelled to seek shelter in the relatively safe mountain regions or in Kabul. This has progressively forced the Resistance to seek external support for its survival.

Religion and communal tradition in the Resistance

Islam is the central bond among Afghanistan's diverse and independent ethnic groups. Afghans, especially in rural areas, generally practice a Muslim devotion stronger and stricter than those prevalent in some other Islamic societies. Religious preachers and other theologians have large followings and play a preeminent role in the social and political affairs of the countryside.

After the Communist takeover in 1978, government courts and ministries of the new regime began deciding matters that had traditionally been the monopoly of the community or tribe and religious men. Communist attempts to impose a centralized regime clashed with the free, decentralized and religious traditions of Afghan society, threatening individual freedom, tribal independence and religious beliefs. Hence, they ignited a spontaneous, nationwide rebellion led by mullahs which was eventually proclaimed a *jihad* by religious leaders with the authority to do so.*

The relative Afghan religious homogeneity, due to the predominance of the Sunni sect, tended to unify the religious groups. However, although Islam provided a basis for national mobilization against atheistic Communism, religious leaders lacked a cohesive nationwide organization as well as experience in organizing the population. The uprising, although powerful, became fragmented and localized along village and tribal lines: every mosque became a center for a village fighting group led by mullahs, operating according to the doctrines of Islamic religion and adopting Islamic law rather than secular tradition to regulate their routine affairs.

But while fighting groups, led mostly by religious leaders, thus fought on the slogan of Islam, in reality they, too, operated along tribal lines. The system suited the initial situation (in 1978-79), but created major problems for the future. Religious leaders who fiercely oppose secular, nationalist trends inadvertently ended up by strengthening them.

The Soviet invasion in December 1979 broadened the rebellion against the Communist regime by rousing nationalist and anti-Communist elements in the society who until then had stood aside from the struggle. The rebellion then became a national freedom movement as well as a jihad. Nevertheless, religious figures continued as the backbone of military

---

* Although the term *jihad* (holy war) is very often used loosely in any conflict in the Muslim world—for example, in the war between Iraq and Iran—it has a very specific doctrinal meaning: a jihad is a war in defense of Islam against enemies of the faith; and it must be declared by religious authorities. Since Communism is actively atheistic, and since the Communist regime imposed in 1978 immediately began active measures against religion, the Afghan resistance against the Soviet Union and the Communist regimes it has installed is in fact a genuine jihad.—ed.

and ideological power, relying on the Shari'a and religious doctrine and, as its instrument, the *shura,* the religious assembly.*

Simultaneously, however, among the emerging traditionalist and nationalist groups, the traditional secular jirga system was the basis for decision or for resolving internal disputes. The jirga was favored by these groups because, unlike the Shari'a, which has fixed rules, the jirga follows social trends and can be molded by community elders.

The new nationalist groups participating in the rebellion lacked the unifying doctrinal elements that Islamic ideology provided to the religious groups and were all the more tightly restricted to village or tribal boundaries. The mountainous terrain and lack of communications systems further isolated them from one another. The new groups also depended on the relatively meager material resources provided locally. Therefore, these groups initially were not strong enough to challenge the domination of the religious leaders, who were already receiving outside aid.

These differences between the religious and the nationalist organizations created a bipolarity in the Resistance---a phenomenon that, beyond Afghan individualism, is responsible for the present division in the Resistance. Moreover, the slowness of the nationalists to rise to rebellion brought them into conflict with the mullahs, who had condemned their hesitation and branded them as accomplices of the Russians. Nevertheless, in the early stages of the war there was a basic sense of harmony of purpose among the various localized groups that made up the Resistance inside Afghanistan---

---

* The shura is a distinctively Islamic governmental institution found throughout the Muslim world---a consultative and advisory body whose members are drawn from the religious community, particularly those well-versed in Islam. Their role as advisors to a government or ruler has distinctly religious overtones.

The *jirga,* on the other hand, is a uniquely Afghan political institution which may be on the village level or on a larger scale---regional, tribal or communal. The jirga is called to deal with specific issues, and all adult male members of the concerned community participate in decision-making in accordance with conventional codes. While of course Islamic law is always implicit in societal decisions, and religious figures may participate in a jirga, it is, as indicated, essentially communal and secular.

In the Afghan political context, it is perhaps worth noting that before 1964, the houses of the Afghan parliament were called Shuras. Following the adoption of the new constitution of 1964, the two houses were identified as Jirgas (while the term *majlis*---"elected assembly" or parliament---was used for the whole).---ed.

notwithstanding the emergence of various political parties that came to represent the Resistance outside the country.

Increasing dependence on outside resources for combat needs, however, has also brought into the Resistance a greater influx of disruptive outside influences.

The Afghan Resistance parties and efforts at unity

In order to understand the multiplicity of Afghan Resistance organizations and parties and the problems involved in the search for greater unity, one must look at the history of the Resistance, at earlier unification efforts, and at factors stimulating greater diversity. This history begins in the years preceding the Communist coup of 1978, the period of Daoud's Republic.

Before the Soviet invasion

When Daoud seized power in 1973 with the help of the Parcham faction of the Afghan Communist party and brought the Parchamis into his government, he aroused the angry opposition of Islamic groups associated with the international Muslim Brotherhood *(Ikhwan ul-Muslimi)*. Centered around Kabul University, and especially its faculties of engineering and theology, these groups were already loosely allied in a party led by Engineer Gulbuddin Hekhmatyar.

Soon after the Daoud coup, many of these students left Afghanistan for Pakistan, where they regrouped their party under the new name *Hezb-i-Islami* (Islamic Party or Group) and were soon joined by a number of religious leaders and mullahs. Among them were many of today's Resistance leaders, including (in addition to Hekhmatyar) Prof. Burhanuddin Rabbani, Maulawi* Younos Khalis, Maulawi Mansoor, Commander Jalaluddin and Commander Ahmad Shah Massoud. Led by Hekhmatyar and Qazi Amin,† the Hezb organized active opposition to Daoud and made at least one attempt (in Panjsher in 1975) to raise an armed insurrection against his government with the aid of Zulfikar Ali Bhutto of Pakistan.

The Communist takeover in Kabul in 1978, the subsequent general unrest, and the beginnings of widespread grassroots resistance enhanced the prestige and political influence of this Islamic movement. It had, after all, been struggling for years against increasing Soviet and Afghan Communist influence in Afghanistan. Therefore, when the call to jihad mobilized the Afghan people against the atheist regime, the nation understandably looked to the Hezb-i-Islami leadership for guidance and support.

---

* "Maulawi" is a religious title.

† "Qazi" means "judge."

As Muslim organizations and supporters in Pakistan and the Middle East began to send economic and material aid to their struggling Afghan brethren, it was initially channeled though a religious political party in Pakistan, the Jamaat-e-Islami, and through the Muslim Brotherhood. In disbursing such aid, both of these organizations favored the Hezb-i-Islami, which shared many of their ideas.

The Hezb had been strongly influenced by several modern Muslim thinkers, including Syed Mawdoodi, the founder of Jamaat-e-Islami Pakistan and leader of a movement for a "more Islamic" Pakistan; Syed Qutab and Hassan ul-Bana, the founders of the Egypt-based Muslim Brotherhood; and Ali Shariati of Iran. Their ideas appealed to the educated Afghan Muslim activists who formed the Hezb. In line with these intense Islamic revival ideas, the party tended to adopt a strong centralized organizational approach, with power within the party concentrated in the hands of a few men.

This tight centralized power structure clashed with the traditional Afghan social system based on individual freedom and equality. The Hezb therefore did not appeal to the ordinary Afghans from the villages who were increasingly involved in the fighting, and the concentration of power in a few hands also created antagonism among the rank and file within the party itself. Thus the ground was laid for organizational fragmentation.

The first to break away was Prof. Burhanuddin Rabbani, a former professor in the Faculty of Islamic Law of Kabul University, which was the breeding ground of radical Islamic ideology among educated Afghan youth. In Afghanistan, Rabbani had been one of the leaders of the Muslim Brotherhood, but when he moved to Pakistan he was relegated to an unimportant job in the Hezb-i-Islami office. Apparently fed up with the impractical and extremely hardline approach of younger men who had more influence than he, he quit the Hezb soon after the 1978 coup in Kabul and founded the *Jamiat Islami Afghanistan* (Islamic Society of Afghanistan). Many others followed him out of the Hezb into the Jamiat, including Ahmad Shah Massoud.

Rabbani, of Tajik origin and from Badakhshan province in the northeast, attracted in particular many of the non-Pushtuns; many Resistance groups in northern and western Afghanistan switched their connections from Hezb to Jamiat. Soon the Jamiat had captured much of the political and military turf, influence, and personnel that had formerly belonged to Hezb, creating hostility between the two organizations---a hostility which has continued and intensified over the years and which has been one major cause of the consistent failure of all efforts to unify the Resistance.

Meanwhile, as resistance to the Communist regime sprang up throughout the country, the uneducated Afghan villagers (who form the majority of the Resistance) were for the most part led by their local mullahs. These traditionalist mullahs opposed the influence of the new interpretations of Islam that dominated the Hezb and the Jamiat, viewing such ideas as a deviation from true Islam. In particular, they opposed the ideas of Syed Mawdoodi of the Pakistani Jamaat-e-Islami, branding him a revisionist and denouncing his followers as *kafirs*---unbelievers and atheists.

Rejecting the basic concepts embodied in the political platforms of the Hezb and Jamiat, the mullahs began to organize their own platform and party, *Khudam ul-Furqan* (The Servant of the Koran).

A few months after the April 1978 Communist coup in Kabul set off the grassfire of nationwide resistance, the first effort at unity was made. By then, Jamiat Islami and Kudam ul-Furqan had been formed, in addition to the original Hezb-i-Islami. The three factions agreed to merge into a single party, *Harakat-i-Inqilab-i-Islami Afghanistan* (Movement for the Islamic Revolution of Afghanistan) to be headed by Maulawi Mohammad Nabi Mohammadi, a religious leader who had been a member of the Afghan parliament before the 1973 coup. It was hoped that, as a religious leader who also had practical political experience, Mohammadi would be able to bridge the gap between the two political positions and unite the three factions. The new combined party adopted the Shari'a---the Islamic legal code---as its governing rule, with political power concentrated in Mohammadi's hands.

Representing a unified Resistance and serving as the sole conduit of outside aid to the fighting men, the Harakat drew most of the mujahideen into its fold and quickly became dominant throughout Afghanistan. But, although the ranks of the party swelled very rapidly indeed, there was no organizational structure to establish administrative control and insure party discipline. Disorder soon set in. In addition, the leadership failed to provide clear plans and strategy for fighting the war. As a result, they lost control of the fighting inside Afghanistan as well as the political and administrative activity outside the country.

In this disorganized situation, the latent internal frictions resurfaced. Through the Harakat, the mullahs, who were already dominant inside Afghanistan, had also gained political importance. The result was that the non-mullahs---mostly the educated young men of Hezb and Jamiat--- felt suffocated in Harakat. Moreover, most of the aid came from Jamaat-e-Islami Pakistan and the Muslim Brotherhood, sources which the Hezb and Jamiat leadership considered exclusively theirs by right; but now it

212

was going to Mohammadi and the mullahs instead. Various others---nationalists and others---also felt themselves repressed within the Harakat framework.

Within a few months the alliance evaporated, as Hezb and Jamiat pulled out and returned to independent status. A number of mullahs from Kandahar and other areas, however, opted to stay with Mohammadi, who kept the Harakat alive as a separate party---a third one (incorporating Kudam ul-Furgan). A few days after this split, three more parties emerged:

The mullahs who had remained in Hezb-i-Islami announced that they were withdrawing and forming their own party under Maulawi Younos Khalis from Nangrahar province. To add to the confusion, they too took the name of Hezb-i-Islami, leading to the existence of two separate parties with the same name, customarily identified by their leaders' names as *Hezb-i-Islami/Khalis* and *Hezb-i-Islami/Hekhmatyar*.*

The mullahs from the provinces near the Pakistani border and those who had been educated in Pakistan joined the Khalis faction. Because of their ethnic ties to the Pushtuns of Pakistan, their understanding of official Pakistani procedures, and their control of sensitive areas along the Pakistan-Afghanistan border, the Khalis Hezb was advantageously placed to draw maximum support from Pakistani and other supporters and it soon became an important factor in the eastern border area.

Meanwhile, at about the same period, two entirely new Resistance organizations had been established by prominent religious leaders who already had significant national and even international prestige: Pir Sayed Ahmad Gailani and Prof. Sibgatullah Mojadidi, both of whom brought to bear a very different background and approach, thus inserting into the situation a new political element: nationalism.

Mojadidi, a theologian educated at the famous al-Azhar University in Cairo and a former professor of Islamic law at Kabul University, arrived from Copenhagen, where he had spent several years as leader of the small Muslim community in Denmark. He was a member of a well-known family of prominent religious leaders associated with the Naqshbandi Sufi order. The Mojadidi family had been active in public affairs in Afghanistan for a century or more; one of its members was instrumental in the overthrow of King Amanullah in 1929. Soon after the 1978 coup, more than thirty leading members of the family were arrested and executed by the Taraki/Amin regime; Sibgatullah inherited the family leadership and moved

---

* For outside observers, this confusion is compounded by the tendency, especially among foreign journalists, to refer only to "Hezb-i-Islami," without identifying the party referred to.---ed.

to set up the *Jabba-i-Nejat-i-Afghanistan* (The Front for the Rescue of Afghanistan).

Unfortunately for his organization, most followers of his family were mullahs (who had been educated at the religious schools organized and run by the Mojadidis) but these mullahs were already affiliated with the Khudam ul-Furqan, which was then a member of the first Harakat; since Mojadidi himself was not a mullah, they chose to remain with the Harakat rather than leave it and join him. He was therefore able to win only a small following, mostly among the villagers of certain areas, although his prestige as a leader of Naqshbandiya Sufism made him a figure to be reckoned with.

Around the same time, Gailani got out of Kabul and established another party, *Mahaz-i-Milli Islami Afghanistan* (The National Islamic Front of Afghanistan, sometimes known by its English-language acronym NIFA). Gailani is the hereditary spiritual leader *(pir)* worldwide of the Qadirya Sufi order founded by his ancestor, to which a very large number of Afghans---especially Pushtuns---adhere. Gailani transformed this spiritual following into military and political influence.

The Gailani family had been wealthy and influential in Kabul and, before the overthrow of the monarchy in 1973, were close to the king. They had similar close connections with senior military officers and high-level government officials. As a result, after 1978 most of those officers and former officials who survived and escaped to Pakistan joined Gailani's Mahaz.

To summarize: by late 1979, on the eve of the Soviet invasion, there were six Afghan resistance parties established in Pakistan. Four of them had emerged from splits and recombinations in the original group, and shared in varying degrees political ideas rooted in the ideas of the Muslim Brotherhood and other radical modernist Muslim movements and/or traditional views held by locally trained mullahs. The other two parties, established independently, came from a very different background: their political views were derived from traditional Islam and traditional Afghan political and social structures.

Since the Soviet Invasion

Following the Soviet invasion in December 1979, the increased strength of Communist forces in Afghanistan heightened the need for Resistance unity on the battlefield. Increased pressure for such unity came from outside supporters of the Resistance, primarily Muslim sources in the Middle East and Pakistan.

In early 1980, Abdul Rasul Sayyaf, who had been a ranking member of the Muslim Brotherhood in Afghanistan, was released from prison in Kabul. His arrival in Pakistan renewed hopes that at least the various religious factions could be reunited, and perhaps all six could be brought together. As a result, a new alliance emerged, the *Ittehad-i-Islami* (Islamic Alliance or Islamic Unity), headed by Sayyaf with Hekhmatyar as his deputy. Five of the six parties joined. (Gailani's Mahaz initially agreed to join but ultimately did not do so.) Like its predecessor (the 1978 Harakat "unity"), the 1980 Ittehad was organized on the principles of the Islamic shura, with all power vested in the leadership---this time, Sayyaf.

But the formation of this alliance brought out into the open another source of intra-party conflict which had previously remained below the surface: friction between those who supported (for a free Afghanistan) an essentially nationalist and traditional political system based on the uniquely Afghan and basically secular jirga, and those who demanded its replacements by a shura system based on Islamic religious law under the authority of religious leadership.*

All of the party leaders who joined this first Ittehad were either educated in Islamic theology at al-Azhar University (Mojadedi, Rabbani and Sayyaf), mullahs trained at traditional mosque schools (Khalis and Mohammadi), or militant members of the Muslim Brotherhood (Hekhmatyar and Sayyaf). All of them believed in the practicality of Islamic ideology as a working system that could form the basis of a modern nation state and were willing to adopt Islam as the ideological basis for the struggle against atheistic Communism.

Gailani and his associates in Mahaz, however, rejected this position in favor of a more traditional Afghan structure, a confederation of communal groups and tribes under a monarchy. They wanted to fight against the Soviet Union and its Communist puppets in the name of Afghan nationalism as well as in the name of Islam.

---

* For the purposes of this article, the terms "nationalist parties" and "religious parties" are used to refer to this division. Needless to say, all Afghan parties and leaders, like almost all Afghans, are devout Muslims and recognize the religious authority of Islam. None is anti-Islamic. These two groupings are frequently referred to in the world press by the erroneous and misleading terms "moderates" and "fundamentalists," by analogy with Protestant Christian denominations. Even without a detailed analysis of the differences in Islam, it should be clear from this article alone that such terminology simply does not apply and indeed such labels are misleading. The situation is far more complex than that. See also: Bodansky; "fundamentalist Islam" in the Glossary---ed.

Leaders of the religious parties---and especially the mullahs who held both military power and an ideological mandate---despised the secular nationalism which left power in the hands of khans, maliks and other secular leaders, while the latter, led by Gailani, were reluctant to accept religious leadership and abandon their traditional roles as spokesmen for their communities.

Despite these differences and flaws, the effort to form the Ittehad was seen by outside observers as a token of the willingness of the Resistance groups to create some order in their own house. It increased good will for the Resistance inside Afghanistan as well as among the various outside supporters. It was especially appreciated in the Middle East, where Sayyaf had good contacts, both as a result of his years at al-Azhar and because he had been the last of the pre-war leaders of the Afghan branch of the Egypt-based Muslim Brotherhood. Many Middle Eastern well-wishers even acclaimed Sayyaf as Amir-ul-Momenin---"Chief of all Muslims." As a result, the flow of aid from the Middle East increased many times over.

The aim of the Ittehad was the creation of coordination in the field among the various groups and units fighting inside Afghanistan, but the organizational structure defeated the attempt. The Ittehad leadership concentrated on political issues, diplomatic and propaganda efforts, and the creation of an administrative infrastructure to handle outside aid. Many senior fighting commanders who had come to Peshawar to participate in setting up the Ittehad were appointed to administrative positions at reasonably good salaries; as a result, a large number of commanders needed on the battlefield were lured to the Ittehad infrastructure instead.

Not only was the battlefield drained of its most effective manpower but it also suffered from an economic drought. Although more support was coming in, control was entirely in the hands of Sayyaf, who chose to channel the money to his own favorite groups. Most of the fighting groups that did not offer personal loyalty to Sayyaf could not get economic support. The result was increased tension within the alliance. Sayyaf lost the good will of most of the military commanders who had been the main sponsors of the Ittehad in the first place. The individual party leaders, too, were dismayed by the situation, and slowly they made their way out of the Ittehad.

This second attempt to bring about unity did not survive long. It not only failed outright to fulfill hopes of unity but, when it collapsed, it increased factionalism. As the other parties dropped out of the Ittehad, Sayyaf held onto the organization's name and, like Mohammadi before him, transformed it into a party. He drew most of his members from the older Muslim Brotherhood factions, Jamiat and Hezb/Hekhmatyar, creating a rift between them that has continued---and has frequently erupted in active interparty feuding inside Afghanistan, particularly around Kabul, where Sayyaf's Ittehad took over turf previously held by Hekhmatyar's Hezb.

As a result of the consistent failure of the Islamic religious alliances, many members now abandoned them and turned instead to the nationalist parties: Gailani's and, to a lesser extent, Mojadidi's. This fragmentation produced new examples of the Afghan religious/nationalist polarity.

In 1981, the two political outlooks became visible in the complicated interplay and realignment among the many parties. This time, the result was not one but two alliances, both of them, confusingly, using almost identical names. To differentiate between them, people began calling them simply "the Seven-Party Alliance" (religious) and "the Three-Party Alliance" (nationalist).

The nationalist or three-party Alliance consisted of Gailani's Mahaz, Mojadidi's Jabba, and the Harakat party headed by Mohammadi.

The religious or seven-party Alliance consisted of the four previously established religious parties (Jamiat, Hezb/Hekhmatyar, Hezb/Khalis, and Sayyaf's Ittehad) plus three splinter groups from Harakat and Mahaz. (These splits and realignments, though not an unfamiliar phenomenon in Afghan politics, were quite unusual for the Resistance at that stage. A large group of mullahs led by Maulawi Mohammad Mir had left Gailani's Mahaz to join the religious alliance as a new party, but keeping the same name, Mahaz-e-Milli Islami Afghanistan. The Khudam ul-Furqan faction led by Maulawi Mohammad Mansoor pulled out of Mohammadi's Harakat to become a party in the religious Alliance, as did another group led by Maulawi Mozin, a former Harakat commander in central Afghanistan.)

The departure of these mullahs from the nationalist parties reduced the latter's religious component and increased their nationalist image.

In reality, of course, neither of these alliances was fully "nationalist" or fully "religious." Although one called its central body a jirga and the other proclaimed theirs to be a shura, both worked on much the same principles and had a roughly similar ratio of religious leaders and maliks among their members. The leaders of the three parties in the nationalist alliance---Gailani, Mojadidi, and Mohammadi---all drew legitimacy for their leadership from religious credentials, while in the religious alliance the second echelon of leadership was made up of maliks and khans. And the combat groups of *all* the parties in *both* alliances were organized along tribal or village lines, and were for the most part led by mullahs.

However, their differing conceptions of the *political* role of religion did approximate the two political poles. The leaders of the three-party nationalist alliance had all been part of the regular political process in Afghanistan before the Daoud coup and they opted for a similar, basically secular government structure based on the jirga formula, a confederation of tribes and communities, a loose central government, and an executive monarchy, working in semi-religious, semi-nationalist style. The leaders associated with the seven-party religious alliance would not---and will not---have anything to do with either the jirga or a monarchy, and want a greater if not a decisive role for religion in overall government affairs.*

In 1985, as the need for increased unity and pressures to achieve it increased, the two separate alliances were dissolved in order to form, once more, a wider alliance encompassing all the major parties.† This new alliance is, again, called the *Ittehad* (literally, "unity"). This time, however, the constituent organizations have retained their individual identities and structures, merely coordinating their activities under the new Ittehad umbrella; this coordination is intended to pave the way for eventual consolidation. The leadership of the present Ittehad is rotated among the party leaders. (See Appendix III for further details.)

The 1985 Ittehad has held together thus far, and a very limited progress has been made in the crucial aspects of coordinating military and political activity among the various members. Without such coordination, the Alliance can hardly be expected to make progress toward its goal: the streamlining and consolidation of Resistance activity, both politically and military, inside Afghanistan and on the world stage. But, the 1985 Alliance has at least survived.

The Iranian factor

Comparatively little international attention has been paid to Iran's role in the Resistance, particularly in the Hazarajat---the central massif in which most of Afghanistan's Shi'a Muslim minority, only about fifteen percent of the population, eke out a living among the arid mountains. Since most of the Afghan Resistance parties based in Iran come from the same region (the Hazarajat), are members of the same ethnic group (Hazara), and are Shi'ites who---unlike the Sunni majority---have a tradition of unified, doctrinaire religious-political leadership, it might seem that they could more readily

---

* There were, however repeated rumors that Khalis was considering shifting to the three-party alliance.---ed.

† Many splinter parties and effective fighting groups of mujahideen are still outside the umbrella.

achieve unity. This has not proved to be the case. Although the government of Iran has made strenuous efforts to impose unity among them, they remain as factional as the groups based in Peshawar---largely as a result of those ill-conceived Iranian efforts.

The 1978 Communist coup in Afghanistan and the subsequent rise of anti-Communist resistance occurred more or less simultaneously with the Iranian revolution and the overthrow of the Shah, carried out under the banner of Islam. For the triumphant clergy in Iran, the massive swell of Afghan resistance following the Soviet invasion was a favorable development: it reinforced their ideological belief in the ultimate supremacy of the *'Umma,* (the entire body of Muslim faithful), united in a theocratic nation-state (of which Afghanistan of course would be an integral part) and all under Iranian Shi'a leadership. They therefore offered all-out support for the Afghan cause. Initially, all of the Resistance parties were willing to accept Iranian help, even the Pakistan-based groups which were predominantly Sunni, although most of the latter were gradually disillusioned and eventually drew away.

In any case, Iranian Shi'a leaders naturally favored the Afghan Shi'as of the Hazarajat and their local ayatollahs (clergy leadership), many of whom had been trained in Iran and had personal ties with the Iranian leadership. The Hazara population had always had strong ties with their co-religionists in Iran. The Hazarajat is extremely isolated, the Hazaras were for many years in conflict with the dominant (and Sunni) Pushtuns, and as a result they played little part in political affairs in Kabul. Because the rugged, waterless Hazarajat offered little economic hope, large numbers of its men went to work elsewhere, many of them in Iran. It was therefore natural now for them to look to Teheran for support.

With the prospect of abundant support in the offing, many Hazara religious leaders formed their own resistance organizations: by 1979, there were at least thirty-seven different factions operating in the region, most of them local village or tribal groups, often based on kinship. Each of these set up offices in Iran, where their numbers were swelled also by ideological groups of intellectuals who had no representation on the ground inside Afghanistan but whose activities flourished in the Iranian revolutionary environment.

By 1979, many of the local groups had come together in the *Shura-i-Inqilab-i-Ittefaq-i-Islami* headed by Sayed Ali Beheshti, which established, in effect, an independent government in the Hazarajat. It ran schools, operated the only functioning telephone network remaining in Afghanistan and provided a relatively safe base of operations   for several European medical organizations. The pre-invasion Khalq regime had an extremely limited presence in central Afghanistan: its isolated battalion and company-size posts in the region, no match for even the small village mujahideen groups, were soon wiped out and, until after the Soviet invasion, the Kabul regime did not replace them. The Hazarajat seemed to have won its independence; there was little active stimulus to unify and reorganize. Following the Soviet invasion, however, Iranian leaders began pressuring Afghan Shi'a representatives in Iran toward greater unity, and some began to form at least nominal combined organizations. (For example, nine combined to form yet another Harakat-i-Islami.)

When the Iran-Iraq war broke out in the fall of 1980, however, Iranian interest and support for the Afghans diminished sharply. Hundreds of small groups, unable to survive independently, were finally forced to form combined alliances, and Beheshti's Shura emerged as the dominant umbrella organization. Moreover, Soviet forces began to conduct large-scale search-and-destroy operations in the Hazarajat, increasing the need for Resistance operational unity.

Nevertheless, by 1982 the Shura was under severe attack by two organizations, *Sazman al-Nasr* (Organization for Victory) and the *Pazdaran-i-Jehad-i-Islami* (Protectors of the Islamic Holy War), both of which have links to extreme leftwing Iranian organizations (the Spahi Pazdaran, better known in the West as the Revolutionary Guards), as does a third group, the Harakat-i-Islami headed by Sheikh Mohseni.*

Eventually, Nasr and Mohseni's Harakat emerged the survivors; they then turned against each other in a vicious struggle which still continues.

The case of the Iranian-based Afghan Resistance organizations is particularly interesting as a demonstration of how external influences affect internal unity. Initially, Iran was extremely well-placed to influence the Resistance leadership and forge unity; all the Afghan Resistance leaders were receptive to the newly successful Iranian leadership and ready to benefit from its experience. But Iranian favoritism toward Shi'a groups and leaders drove away the Sunni leaders, reducing Iranian influence with the main Afghan Resistance organizations and the Sunni majority of the Afghan population. Unconcerned about the negative results of this favoritism, the Iranian leadership tried to forge unity by channeling all aid and political coordination through a single office via Mohseni. This too backfired: it

---

* This Shi'a organization is *not* connected with the Harakat organizations based in Peshawar and headed by Mohammadi and Mansoor respectively.

was seen by other Afghan leaders as an attempt to impose Mohseni on them and reduce them to subordinate roles. This created antagonism toward both Mohseni and the Iranian leaders.

Moreover, it was the attempt to impose Mohseni that set off the fighting between his Harakat and the equally important Nasr organization, fighting which has claimed thousands of lives and continues to divert energies from the struggle against Communist forces who are the only beneficiaries of the feud. A later attempt by Iran to redress the balance by aiding Nasr only aggravated the situation further, enraging the Fedayeen, the Hizbullah, and other groups that joined the fray, with disastrous results, as noted above.

Thus the Iranian attempt to use aid as an instrument for controlling and influencing the direction of the Resistance proved in the end to be destructive and self-defeating.

At present, a number of so-called "umbrella" parties (composed of many mini-parties) have offices in Iran, but at least 70 percent of the Shi'a mujahideen belong to either Nasr or Mohseni's Harakat. Mohseni's base is essentially rural, perhaps comparable to the Sunni Harakat based in Pakistan and headed by Mohammad Nabi Mohammadi. Nasr is modeled more along the lines of Hekhmatyar's Hezbi Islami, i.e., based on ideological radical Islam---but adhering to the ideology of the Ayatollah Khomeini instead of that of the Muslim Brotherhood.

A third group in Iran, the *Hezb-i-Illahi* (Party of God) is only a political forum with a mixed and sometimes confused program, more a literary/intellectual circle than a combat organization. Its main activities are publications, propaganda, and political/ideological combat, in all of which it is highly successful in the Muslim world, especially in Iran and Pakistan, and among Muslims in Europe. A fourth group, the Jabba Mutehid-i-Inqilab-i-Islami (Combined Friends of the Islamic Revolution) is made up of small independent Shi'a groups such as Pazdaran, Fedayeen-i-Islami, FAMA, RAJA, etc., which are not very active any more.

These and a number of other small groups all operate under the auspices of the offices of the Islamic Revolution of Afghanistan (Inqilab-i-Islami-i-Afghanistan) in Teheran, itself a branch of the Iranian office that oversees Islamic revolutionary affairs outside as well as inside Iran, and which is controlled by the Iranian Revolutionary Guards.* On the whole, the Iranian-based parties are very small compared to the mainstream organizations based in Pakistan. Being weak, they play only a small direct role in the fighting or the political affairs of Afghanistan and the Resistance, although

---

* See entry for *Jundullah* in the Glossary.

some of them--especially the Hezb-i-Illahi---have secretly infiltrated many of the mainstream groups and may exert influence indirectly.

Obstacles to unity

The Soviet invasion created an urgent need for unity. Extensive bombing displaced much of the population, which had been the main source of support for the Resistance. Combat equipment also became increasingly scarce as the Afghan Army, the sole source of equipment in 1978-79, came under tighter Soviet control. The freedom fighters were increasingly forced to rely on external sources whose aid might be selective and conditional; this in turn compelled them to create wider political organizations for funnelling the outside assistance. Thus logistics and other requirements for continuing the struggle encouraged the Resistance to unite, while external as well as internal factors aggravated differences and forestalled that unity.

The extremely independent character of Afghans, the very quality which has inspired the battle against great odds in the war against the Soviet invaders, is at the same time a basic hurdle to permanent unity. Afghan organizations, even today, are essentially collections of individuals and far from the systematic structure that the word "organization" evokes in modern Western societies.* The jihad pits the individual, not the nation or an organization, against Communism and the Soviet Union. Inside Afghanistan the commander of a battle group spends much of his time keeping the group together. Party leaders operating outside the country have similar problems on a larger scale. Within the groups, fighters move freely, joining and quitting the battle front at their wish and convenience. This problem is compounded by the Afghan love of openness. Afghans traditionally have been free to voice their opinions and participate in a jirga. The Afghan demands such participation and is averse to, and suspicious of, decisions made or deals struck by others on his behalf.

The problems this creates in fighting a war are obvious. The demand for mujahideen military leaders to share their plans with their troops creates security problems: the larger the group, the more difficult it is to maintain the secrecy essential to combat operations. In fact, there is little within the Resistance that is secret. Meanwhile, political leaders try to use secrecy both for security and to maintain control. As a result, the ordinary fighting men, not being part of the inner workings of the parties, do not feel any kind of permanent party attachment; they consider the parties merely as conduits for aid.

---

* This is true not only of the Resistance but of the Afghan Communist Party as well. See: Arnold and Klass.

The competing demands of traditional openness and of the battlefield have thus created barriers between the political and military leadership and the people.

In addition, outside influences have exacerbated Resistance divisions, as the detailed example of Iran demonstrates---and that is only one example among many. The very creation of international channels of support stimulated disunity as different villages, tribes, and ethnic groups aligned themselves with various parties represented in Pakistan in hopes of receiving aid through them. As a result, cooperation in the field was reduced.

Insofar as the Resistance and its parties are dependent on international support, they are also susceptible to the influences of their main foreign supporters. For example, the lure of Saudi Arabian support was responsible for the creation of a strong group of converts to the Wahhabi sect of Islam (which is the official Saudi sect but was not previously present in Afghanistan) in the eastern provinces; this added a new religious dimension to the already diverse and divided Afghan social system. Aid from the Muslim Brotherhood goes only to those who support its positions. On the other hand, some Western supporters are uncomfortable with what they call the "fundamentalists" and prefer traditionalists, i.e., supporters of the jirga system.

These differing preferences among the supporters have insured the continuing presence---and indeed, the increase---of factions with different individual party platforms: the party that shifts its political positions in order to improve unity through compromise risks losing its particular outside supporters. Moreover, each group is concerned that, in a unified organization, it might be dominated by one or more of the others. These apprehensions do not leave much room for the development of greater unity.

Subversion

And finally, in considering the obstacles to greater Resistance unity, one must take into account the widespread and constant efforts of the Soviet KGB and GRU, and their Afghan counterpart WAD (formerly KhAD), to create friction, disunity and conflict within the Resistance, to exacerbate existing problems and create new ones, and to create a gulf of distrust within and among the Resistance organizations and between the Resistance leadership outside the country and the fighting men and general population inside Afghanistan. Even taking into account all of the other problems cited above, almost 70 percent of the feuds and frictions among the mujahideen are initiated by KhAD agents who have infiltrated the Resistance organizations.* The presence of a number of political factions in the Resistance facilitates these infiltration efforts, as does the lack of adequate communications systems among Resistance groups inside Afghanistan and between those inside and the leaders outside. This lack of communication between the leaders and the led also makes it difficult to counter KhAD's divisive tactics.

In 1981, for example, after a minor confrontation between local commanders of the Hekhmatyar and Mojadidi groups in Nangrahar Province, KhAD circulated a fake letter supposedly written by Hekhmatyar instructing his groups to attack and wipe out those of Mojadidi. Luckily the letter first appeared in Nangrahar, only one day's walk from Peshawar; the commanders were able to contact their leaders about it speedily, the forgery was exposed and the situation was defused---in Nangrahar. Nevertheless, although this was neutralized locally without much physical damage, the loss of good will between the parties could not be repaired and suspicions lingered elsewhere inside Afghanistan, where the letter is still mentioned by mujahideen as an example of friction between the leaders.

Another such example occurred in 1982, after a temporary cease-fire was arranged between the Soviets and Commander Massoud in the Panjsher Valley. KhAD and the KGB circulated a rumor that, in exchange for a large sum of money, Massoud had agreed to stop fighting and had gone to Kabul to submit and join the regime. A few faked photographs showing Massoud meeting with Babrak Karmal and Soviet officers were effectively circulated to confirm the story. Many mujahideen who had been apprehensive about the ceasefire in the first place swallowed the story, and its damaging effects could not be neutralized for many months, not until the truce ended and Massoud resumed fighting.

These are merely two comparatively elaborate examples out of a multitude. In addition, on a local scale, KhAD agents spread rumors of all sorts inside Afghanistan and out (and in Pakistan, Europe and the United States as well) via fighting groups in the field, refugees in the camps, and---when they can---the press and other public agencies. In addition, there have been numerous efforts---some of them successful--- to assassinate Resistance leaders and have the blame laid to other Resistance organizations.

Dr. Najibullah, trained by the KGB and brought back to Kabul immediately after the invasion to head KhAD, has extensive tribal and other contacts in Pakistan as well as Afghanistan and was (and still is) notably active in developing efforts to subvert the Resistance. In May 1986 he

---

* See Bodansky.

replaced Karmal as head of the puppet regime, and all indications are that such activities have increased.

In short, every effort to develop greater unity is faced with a determined attempt to subvert it, often cleverly and skillfully carried out.

Possible developments

The Afghan Resistance leadership has thus far not been included in any of the several efforts by the United Nations and others to negotiate a solution to the Afghanistan issue, and they have spoken out harshly against any "settlement" that might be reached without the participation of representatives of the Afghan freedom movement, which has sacrificed more than a million people in its battle to rid the country of Soviet control. Since 1984, the Resistance has intensified its efforts to gain international recognition,* but it is unlikely that it will make much headway in this endeavor as long as it remains disunited. Even in order to survive and to outlast the Soviet occupation forces in their war of attrition against the Afghan people, the Resistance critically needs the bonds of political and operational unity that it has so far failed to fashion. Yet, despite all the problems discussed above, such functional unity, although difficult to achieve, would not be impossible.

I have outlined elsewhere a detailed set of proposals that might serve as a framework for such unity.[1] Here I will note only a few basic elements that must be considered in any such efforts:

The problem in unifying the Afghan Resistance is to reconcile the sometimes conflicting interests of Islam, democracy, Afghan tradition, and ethnic groups.

Religion was the basis for the uprising against Communist rule from Kabul. It also represents the only possible cement for a national unity of purpose. However, it bespeaks the complexity of Afghan affairs that religion cannot be the sole foundation for government, because Islamic law requires centralization, which is resisted by Afghans.

On the other hand, unification of the Resistance cannot be based solely on nationalism, a weak element at best among the mujahideen.

Nor can it be based on a confederation of tribes and ethnic groups, which would encourage separatist attitudes detrimental to the ideological basis of the jihad. Yet those groups cannot be ignored: neglecting the interests of the maliks and khans who lead the tribes and communities would further weaken the Afghan social system, which is already decaying due to the mass dislocation of the Afghan population.

---

* In November 1986 it received the support of the *New York Times*.

Efforts aimed at the merger of nationalist and religious-oriented groups must therefore alleviate the distrust between the religious and communal poles of Afghan society. Rubber-stamp shuras, jirgas or national assemblies like those of the past will not attract the population. Many religious figures would not join a traditional jirga, while a shura would be seen by traditionalists as a tool of clerical power.

However, choosing the form of government for a future free Afghanistan should not be allowed to become an obsession that interferes with the priority of Afghan independence. Instead, an interim form of government should be devised that combines features of traditional governmental forms and does not bear the name and the political associations of either shura or jirga. This political organization cannot be along religious lines because tribal leaders would fear domination by mullahs. Nor can it be modeled on Western-style parliamentary lines, for then they would fear domination by some of the current leaders of the Resistance. Therefore, a new form needs to be created in order to inspire a popular response, make for broad participation by all elements, traditional and emerging, in the overall process and allow for the cultivation of a new breed of Afghan leadership.

While openness is required of the political system in order to involve ordinary Afghans, secrecy obviously is essential to the conduct of military operations. Parallel structures therefore must be designed to enable political leaders to participate both in the open political forum and in closed military councils. From one they can gain a sense of the will of the people, while in the other they can participate in decisions on political matters and on broad military strategy. Attempts at unity must consider traditional Afghan openness and individual freedom. By giving ordinary Afghans a sense of involvement and belonging, the Resistance leadership can expect willing sacrifices from the proud Afghans for as long as necessary. While including the noncombatant population in an open political and administrative process, the fighting groups and other military-oriented affairs can be organized in relative secrecy without undue interference from the engaged population.

Islam must remain the ideological bond of the Resistance because it is the only available bond; but the friends of the Resistance in other Islamic countries need to keep sensitively in mind that the Afghans must be allowed their own version of Islam.

Refugee needs can be better served by appointing "open councils" in place of the present maliks, who tend to heed their own interests more than those of the refugees. To strengthen unity, control of the refugee camps should be invested in the Alliance leadership. This can help restore faith in Afghan leadership and in the ability of Afghans to administer themselves, even though the affairs of the external committees must of course be coordinated with host governments.

A collective leadership body should be created around the individual leaders. A consortium of all party leaders can act as the central body, regulating the affairs of the military committees and the political forum and through them exercising control over the administrative and combat affairs of the provinces. Proportionate sharing of power and the right of veto will help check the excessive influence of any one individual leader, reducing suspicions and enhancing unity. Outside assistance which is now given to individual party leaders should be channelled through this central body.

Meanwhile, efforts should be made to cultivate and develop the second line of leadership from the present battlefield commands in order to prepare for a more modern democratic political system.

The demands of a people's war

Supporters of the mujahideen must recognize above all that the Afghan jihad is a people's war against an occupying force, inspired by deep wellsprings in the Afghan culture. While drawing strength from that culture, the Resistance is also susceptible to its weaknesses. In any case, outside supporters cannot shape the Resistance to their predilections without regard for the character and the desires of the people of Afghanistan. Unless the Resistance remains rooted in the culture of Afghanistan, it is destined to fail.

Notes

Much of this chapter is based on close personal observation and experience as well as extensive contacts with many of the participants, and thus is not susceptible to documentation. Of those documentary sources that do exist, most are in local languages, were of limited distribution when published and are to come by later (e.g., publications of various Resistance organizations), are scattered in private files or archives, or are otherwise inaccessible to researchers.

However, a number of scholarly studies and general press coverage over an extended period of time provides data congruant with and supportive of this chapter, particularly in its broad outlines of trends and developments---e.g., the forming and dissolution of alliances, the differences among Resistance organizations, the situation in the Hazarajat, etc.---and field investigation will turn up still more.

See also chapters in this volume by Bodansky, Barth and Amin and works listed in the bibliography, esp. Fullerton, Girardet and Roy as well as research centers listed.

Parts of this chapter appeared in an article by the author, "The Afghan Resistance and the Problem of Unity," in the Summer 1986 issue of *Strategic Review,* Vol. XIV, No. 3, and are reprinted with the permission of the United States Strategic Institute.

1. *Strategic Review,* Vol. XIV, No. 3 (Summer 1986): 58-66.

"To reveal the direction in which the cognitive process will develop further, it is necessary to detect in it the remnants of the past, fundamentals of the present and embryos of the future."
     ---General of the Army I. Ye. Shavrov

"Asiatics respect only visible and palpable force."
     ---Prince Gorchakov, Imperial Chancellor
     of Russia

"I hold it a principle in Asia that the duration of peace is in direct proportion to the slaughter you inflict on the enemy."
     ---General M. O. Skobelev, conqueror
     of Turkestan, 1881

Soviet Military Involvement in Afghanistan*

Yossef Bodansky

SINCE THE Soviet Army invaded Afghanistan at the end of December 1979, there has been widespread speculation that Moscow is "bogged down" in its own "Vietnam." It is reported that Soviet leaders regret their "error" and wish only to find a face-saving way to pull out.

But as early as 1982, analysis of internal Soviet material on Afghanistan, and particularly Soviet military sources, revealed a far different picture---one which, five years later, appears to be more accurate than ever.[1] The Soviet military appears to be delighted with its strategic and tactical gains resulting from the seizure of Afghanistan, and unconcerned about the costs. All indications point to the conclusion that the Soviets intend to remain there. Indeed, they have already incorporated Afghanistan into the Soviet military structure and consider it a permanent forward base for future actions.

---

* The acronyms and specialized military terminology used in this chapter can be found in the special section *Soviet Military Terms* in the Glossary, p. 470.

The military advantages of the Soviet presence in Afghanistan are many. Strategically, the invasion brings the Soviets 200 rugged miles closer to the Persian Gulf (400 counting return distance) and control of the oil fields there. Operationally, the Soviet fighting in Afghanistan has initiated the most profound and far-reaching changes in the Soviet armed forces since the introduction of nuclear weapons to the Soviet arsenal.

Overall, the military and strategic benefits the USSR has gotten from Afghanistan since 1980, and those it expects to obtain in future, have increased and solidified with the passage of time. The Soviets are now much closer to achieving their long-range goal: the control of Afghanistan's territory with or without the active use of military force, and its conversion into a base for further regional expansion. This essay will attempt to survey briefly and in summary form a few of the key military aspects of Afghanistan and their effect on the Soviet regional position and the Soviet Armed Forces.

The historic context

The current Soviet presence in Afghanistan needs to be examined in its historical context. Under Tsars and Soviets alike, the relentless drive of Russia into Central Asia and toward the warm waters of the Indian Ocean and its strategic periphery has been one of the most persistent empire-building efforts in history---and is the only one still in progress. Current Soviet activities in Afghanistan in the name of Marxism-Leninism and progress can be seen to be an integral part of a more than 200-year-old drive to the east and south. This relentless advance into Asia emerged from the struggle of the Slavic population for fertile lands, and from the legacy of the Mongol conquest of Muscovy in the thirteenth century---"the Tatar Yoke"---to eventually become the focal point of Russian and Soviet expansionism and imperialism. These elements still determine Soviet perceptions of threats and challenges in the Near and Middle East.[2]

The quest of the Russian and Soviet leadership for legitimacy is a complex one. Tsarist Russia sought recognition and legitimacy as "the Third Rome" and the dominant power in the Christian world, on the grounds that it had eradicated the Mongol threat to the West; for this Christian claim, the Soviet Union has substituted Marxist dogma of "the course of history." But whatever the ideology, both Tsarist and Soviet elites have moved consistently to express their power and authority by outward expansion. The ruling elites have always sought, above all and as Russia's historic destiny, the political and economic submission of Europe and the

West. The current Soviet advance into Southwest Asia is perceived by the Great Russians and the USSR as a continuation of their historic struggle for the very existence of the Russian people, as well as for their ability to fulfill their historic destiny. Today as always, they consider an advance into Central and Southwest Asia to be the primary means by which their land-based military might can be translated into tangible strategic gains, and the key to eventual success in Europe. As Prince Gorchakov, the Imperial Chancellor and one of the architects of the Russian drive into Central Asia, remarked in 1864, "The greatest difficulty is in knowing where to stop."[3]

The continuity of Tsarist and Soviet policy

Militarily, the Russians consider "the Oriental Question" to be a component of the global issue of the domination of Europe and the civilized world. Fully aware of the military capabilities of Western powers, and wishing to impose a solution politically rather than fight for it, Russia has long sought to gain leverage over Europe through relatively low-risk operations in areas such as the Dardanelles and Central Asia, where this global quest can be pursued under the conditions of a contained localized war---for, since the mid-1820s, the Russians have believed that the major powers will acquiesce in the occupation of any Central Asian country, considering none to be worth a European war.

Unlike the British, who built their empire through naval operations and the consolidation of bases and secured lines of communication, the Tsars sought to compensate for British naval superiority by challenging England on land---"The Great Game"---creating the Russian Empire by acquiring masses of land connected by interior lines of communication. By the end of the century, Russian land power was so strong that the "Eastern Question" (and consequently the European balance of power) could no longer be determined by British naval power. In November 1899, after the outbreak of the Boer War, Tsar Nicholas II wrote: "I do like knowing it lies with me to change the course of the war in Africa. Telegraph an order for the whole Turkestan army to mobilize and march to the frontier. The strongest fleet in the world can't prevent us from settling our scores with England precisely at her most vulnerable point."[4] Yet the Russians were still afraid to attempt such decisive moves; they preferred instead to continue a steady, persistant encroachment into Central Asia and consolidate their gains.

The Tsarist ruling elite claimed to perceive itself as being reluctantly forced to advanced into Central Asia, a justification formalized in 1864 in the famous Gorchakov memorandum.[5] A British visitor to St. Petersburg observed, "The opinion that Russia cannot but advance into Central Asia when attacked by nomadic tribes, and that the only sound policy in dealing with such tribes is to permanently occupy their country, is held by everyone..."[6] Another observer was more reluctant to accept the claims of Prince Gorchakov and his contemporaries as to their altruistic motives and methods: "The promotion of discord amidst their neighbours was much more likely to be the policy pursued by the conquerors of Turkestan than the promotion of peace, commerce, and civilization."[7] In any case, the armed forces and the military doctrine developed for these "defensive" campaigns were in fact offensive in character.

Since the Bolshevik Revolution, the traditional Russian aspirations summarized above have been coated by and mingled with Marxist-Leninist ideology but they have otherwise remained unchanged. The Soviet ruling class---the *nomenklatura*---has pragmatic reasons of its own to expand the areas under its control.

Ideology aside, the *nomenklatura* has established its legitimacy and consolidated its power and control very much along traditional Russian lines, and has systematically pursued the expansionist policy of the Tsars. Having failed to establish a domestic system that can support it, the *nomenklatura* "aims at external expansion, the establishment of its rule over foreign countries and the exploitation of their wealth"[8] and economic-industrial potential. Their primary commitment is to the preservation and enhancement of their own power and privileges, so, like the Tsars, they remain reluctant to confront the West directly and instead use indirect approaches. "The vast expanses of the countries of the Third World lie to the south of Europe and the Soviet republics of Central Asia, and the 'nomenklatura' is on the offensive there" in order to change the global correlation of forces in their favor.[9] They are pragmatic and persistent. The Soviets want not war, but victory.[10]

Like their Tsarist predecessors, they have always perceived their position in Central Asia in terms of global strategy. In August 1919 Leon Trotsky wrote to the Central Committee, "...the road to Paris and London lies via the towns of Afghanistan, the Punjab and Bengal."[11] In the secret protocol to the 1939 pact in which Nazi Germany and the Soviet Union agreed on the future division of the world, the USSR declared that "[Soviet] territorial aspirations center south of the national territory of the Soviet Union in the direction of the Indian Ocean," and that "the area south of Batum and Baku in the general direction of the Persian Gulf is recognized as the center of aspirations of the Soviet Union."[12]

The Soviet Union has therefore always looked upon its involvement in Afghanistan as a long-term strategic investment and has examined each and every step accordingly. All Soviet military assistance to Afghanistan, and especially the training of Afghan officers, was always designed to establish a useful infrastructure for possible Soviet use. In 1925, when the USSR a-greed to help the Afghan government suppress a rebellion in Khost province by providing ten Soviet aircraft for aerial bombing, they internally explained the significance of this deployment: "...our Red Army High Command had in effect a strategic base in Afghanistan."[13] The air bases the Soviets built for the Afghans from the 1960s on exceeded by far the requirements of the Afghan Air Force, but were optimized for potential use by the Soviet Air Force. Even economic aid to Afghanistan was guided by strategic conside-rations: as Khruschev explained, the Soviet-built Afghan road network "had great strategic significance because it would have allowed us to transport troops and supplies in the event of war with either Pakistan or Iran."[14]

Sixty years after Trotsky, in the wake of the invasion of Afghanistan, Konstantine Chernenko made it clear that the regional and global ramifications of the Soviet position had not changed: "Iran, Afghanistan, the Near East, and the Indian Ocean are all links in the same chain---a chain that is pulling in the direction of war for all states and people."[15]

If the Russian/Soviet advance into Asia is the expression of the ongoing quest for power by the ruling elite, the legacy of the "Tatar Yoke"---the Mon-gol conquest---has determined its ferocity and persistence. The Muslims and the Russians have been in contact for a thousand years, during which rela-tions have been mostly hostile. As a result of this bitter legacy, the Great Russians have always perceived their struggle with the peoples of Central Asia in terms of *"kto kogo"* ("who gets whom"), an all-or-nothing contest in which there can be no compromises or even pauses. A century ago General Skobelev declared that "our position in Central Asia can only be considered comparatively secure so long as our influence meets no rival."[16]

After the Revolution, pervasive Marxism-Leninism, far from solving the Soviets' Central Asian problem peacefully (as they had expected), further exacerbated it. The Soviets therefore still view any conflict in Central Asia as an integral part of their historic anti-Tatar crusade, and raise the threat of a renewed "Tatar Yoke" should the Muslim population ever slip free of Russian control.

Russian/Soviet strategy in Central Asia, past and present

Since the beginning of Russian expansion into the Muslim territories in the early eighteenth century, a unified Russian-Soviet military strategy has emerged, based on the disparity between the speed with which superior military force can take a territory and the extremely long period needed thereafter to bring the local population to submission.

In its relentless drive into Muslim Central Asia (and its repeated wars with Turkey), Russia/the USSR has been interested only in the acquisition of territory and strategic-geographical assets. The essence of Russian/Soviet military strategy is the rapid consolidation of control over local strategic objectives; they advance through a process designed to "encage" the populations they seek to dominate. Only after an extended subjugation process can the Russians claim to control the entire territory; but when advancing into Muslim territories, Russian-Soviet strategists are sure of their ability to establish such control eventually and are prepared to let it wait for a later stage, meanwhile concentrating on their initial strategic goals.

On the basis of accumulating experience over nearly three centuries, they have defined the preconditions for the successful occupation of Muslim territories and the suppression of local resistance as:

1. The effective isolation of the region.

2. The destruction of the local leadership, and especially its ability to achieve unity.

3. The erosion of popular support for any resistance through the destruction of the local social and economic infrastructure.

The achievement of these preconditions is the key to Soviet success in Afghanistan. These Russo/Soviet techniques have developed cumulatively: the suppression of the Chechen resistance under Shamil in the Caucasus in the 1850s saw the first systematic Russian use of the persecution of a civilian population as the major counterinsurgency tactic. It was eminently successful. Hunger and ruin led to the collapse of popular support for Shamil and the rebellion died out without any major military clash. This technique was subsequently refined and extended in further moves into Central Asia, first by the Tsars and later by the Soviets.

When Central Asia attempted to regain its independence in 1917, the Soviets established the Muslim rebellion as an internal problem by obtaining non-intervention treaties with Turkey, Persia and Afghanistan and isolating the insurgents ("Basmachi") from organized outside help (Precondition #1). Except for a brief period under the leadership of Enver Pasha, a Turkish general committed to Pan-Turkism (under whom the Basmachi even seized Dushanbe), there was no unity among the Muslim forces; they not only lacked unified leadership but, as a result of existing ethnic and national hostilities, did not cooperate beyond their immediate localities. Soviet control of the regional strategic and communication infrastructure further fractured them (Precondition #2). Precondition #3---intensive destruction and suppression of the civilian support base---was applied simultaneously.

The Soviets demonstrated to their own satisfaction that Tsarist techniques worked: when Enver was assassinated by a special detachment of the OGPU* in 1922, the Basmachi were doomed. The insurgents still had strong military forces; major actions continued for another decade and sporadic clashes continued as late as the 1940s; but the Soviets knew that, in the absence of a credible leadership capable of unifying the insurgents, it was only a question of time before they were forced to submit. Once Afghanistan decided to deny the Basmachi the use of its territory for sanctuary (following a series of Soviet raids on northern Afghanistan in 1929-1930), thereby isolating them from outside support and completing the combination of the three preconditions, the revolt collapsed as an effective force within a year and the lengthy process of pacifying the rural Muslim population began.

Soviet authorities had no illusions about the extreme hostility they faced, but they were in no hurry. It took them more than twenty years to bring the Muslims of Soviet Central Asia to heel by "encagement" (surrounding and isolating problem areas) and the suppression of remaining isolated pockets of resistance (some of which survived till the late 1940s[17])---but they did it.

Today the USSR is using the same approach to consolidating control over Afghanistan. As early as the spring of 1980, the Soviets committed themselves to the policy of minimal internal military involvement. Their primary goals, dictated by strategic considerations, are to secure and maintain their power-projection-oriented strategic infrastructure in Afghanistan, to secure a show-case "safe" Kabul, and to prevent the escalation of Resistance activities from Pakistan.

In their analysis of the current situation in Afghanistan, the Soviets point out that the Afghan Resistance has no central capable leadership and is widely fragmented among diverse organizations, so that it is only a question of time until it collapses as an effective force. They compare the present situation in the more volatile areas of Afghanistan to that of the Basmachi revolt in the mid-1920s, a few years after Enver's death; the situation in other areas is already being compared to Central Asia in the late 1930s.

---

* A predecessor of the KGB. (The Soviet secret political police, originally the Cheka, has been repeatedly reorganized and renamed with various acronyms: GPU, OGPU, GUGB/NKVD, NKGB, and currently KGB.)

They acknowledge that clashes with the Resistance will probably continue for the forseeable future, but they consider that, from a historical point of view, the fate of the Afghan Resistance has already been decided---that it is doomed. In their view, current combat actions may influence the timing and the price of suppressing the Resistance but cannot decide the ultimate outcome.

They themselves admit that they do not control the entire country: they claim---fairly accurately---to control only 25 percent of the territory, concede that the Resistance controls some 10 percent, and define the rest (65 percent), as no man's land.[18]   They have not attempted to capture that uncontrolled terrain: their military strategy has been formulated not to control the entire territory and its population but only to facilitate the rapid consolidation of control over the militarily significant infrastructure, denying it to the enemy. The Soviets point out that, during the Basmachi revolt, for long periods of time the Red Army chose not to enter large areas of Central Asia, leaving them to Basmachi control because they were strategically insignificant and penetration would have cost high Soviet casualties without speeding up the suppression of the rebellion. They are pursuing the same policy in Afghanistan.

Meanwhile, Afghanistan is the first major protracted involvement of Soviet combined-arms forces in a local war. It takes place at a time when, in the Soviet world view, local wars are increasingly significant: the Soviets emphasize the growing importance of using military power to decide crises in the Third World in favor of their interests,[19] and they consider the acquisition of credible power projection capabilities to be a high-priority challenge for their defense establishment. Afghanistan is therefore an extremely useful testing ground for them in many ways.

Militarily, the present direct Soviet involvement in the conduct of combat operations in Afghanistan actually started soon after the April 1978 coup---the so-called "Saur Revolution." (The invasion of December 1979 was actually more an escalation which captured world attention rather than a fundamental change in Soviet policy; see below.) After more than nine years of direct Soviet military involvement, it is possible to outline the impact that combat actions there have had on the Soviet strategic position, Armed Forces and Art of War.

Accumulating experience from their military involvement in the Third World has proven to the Soviets that, as a direct outcome of the weapons sale and military assistance policies of all the major powers involved, the techno-tactical challenges of contemporary local wars do not differ greatly from those of major wars. Furthermore, they believe that local wars and other forms of military involvement in the Third World are not only becoming decisive *elements* in their confrontation with the West, but that such engagements may even become *the decisive form* of confrontation. Therefore, in deriving lessons from their experience in Afghanistan, they have emphasized the testing and development of Art of War and the proving of weapons systems as they are applicable to the entire Soviet Armed Forces, not simply for their use in overcoming specific problems in Afghanistan.

Special attention should be paid to the *Soviet* perception and analysis of their lessons: it is on the basis of their own analysis of their accumulating experience and lessons that the Soviets will decide the future of their Armed Forces. Moreover, their prolonged stay in Afghanistan has exposed them to the full range of complexities and challenges in the contemporary Muslim world. As a result, Soviet Islamic policy has undergone its most fundamental changes since Lenin's 1917 "Call for the Peoples of the East." Furthermore, Soviet analysis of Afghanistan concentrates on deriving lessons applicable not only to the entire Muslim world but to the Third World as a whole. The cumulative impact of Afghanistan's military and social lessons on the Soviet defense establishment will determine Soviet policy and military activities in the Third World for the foreseeable future. They have made a great effort to insure the dissemination of all of these lessons, and the acquired experience, throughout their entire Armed Forces. The initial impact of the lessons of Afghanistan is already apparent in the activities of the Soviet Union and its allies in such diverse places as Nicaragua, Angola and southern Africa.

They believe that in any conflict, regardless of its size or intensity, the final victory belongs to the side with the better Art of War, demonstrated primarily through the quality of the mid-rank and senior commanders and determined primarily by their military education and ability to implement what they know by accumulating experience in exercises or actual fighting. Soviet military writings designated for the education of their commanders are therefore of crucial significance: the analysis of combat operations in Afghanistan in such writings reflects accurately the lessons and the messages they want to deliver to their commanders and officers.

The discussion below is based in large part on these Soviet writings.

Soviet intervention in Afghanistan
The Turning Points

Since the beginning of Moscow's direct intervention in Afghanistan, the magnitude and level of combat operations have been determined primarily by the Soviet perception of the Democratic Republic of Afghanistan (DRA). Since 1978, three major turning points have determined policy:

238

• *Spring 1978*---The recognition of Afghanistan as a Socialist state immediately following the Communist coup, and the extension of the Brezhnev Doctrine to the DRA. This quickly led to escalating Soviet involvement, including military involvement, which in turn led eventually to the invasion in December 1979.

• *Spring 1980*---The realization that Soviet forces would have to remain in Afghanistan indefinitely---and the decision that the main goal of their deployment there is to further Soviet strategic and global interests. This has determined the nature and organization of Soviet deployment in Afghanistan.

•*Winter 1983/84*---The realization that Afghanistan is not in fact a "socially developed" state ripe for Socialism but rather a developing, traditional Muslim society---and that the intensifying Muslim insurrection might become a threat to the stability of the Muslim population of the USSR itself. This determined the subsequent nature and ferocity of the campaign against the Resistance.

The essence of these changing perceptions of Afghanistan is the key to understanding the Soviet approach to Afghanistan and to Central and Southwest Asia as a whole:

Decision #1:

The Russians have been deeply involved in internal Afghan politics for more than 150 years, always---until 1978---seeking to subvert the local ruling elites in order to further their regional interests.* Throughout this entire period, the Russians have always looked on Afghanistan as a major stepping stone to their ultimate goal---total victory in the Great Game.

At first the Soviets viewed the overthrow of the King in 1973---and even more, the "Saur Revolution" in April 1978 and the signing of the Soviet-Afghan Friendship Treaty seven months later---as stages in the social awakening and development of the Afghan people, a process coinciding with the growing involvement of the Soviet Union in the Third World and the emergence of other new Socialist countries.† As of the mid-1970s,[20] the Soviets had already extended the Brezhnev Doctrine (i.e., their obligation to intervene to keep a Socialist regime in power) beyond the Warsaw Pact.

In combination, the immediate recognition of the DRA as a Socialist state, the expansion of the Brezhnev Doctrine to include it, and the initial

---

* See: Poullada, Noorzoy, Arnold, and numerous works listed in the bibliography.
† Ethiopia, Nicaragua, South Yemen, Mozambique, Angola, Grenada, et al. See: Krakowski.

Soviet perception of the Afghan Resistance as a political movement challenging the Socialist regime together formed the first major Soviet decision, which led to a direct and escalating military involvement: instead of the subversive manipulations of the past, the Soviet military would henceforth be involved in the establishment and support of a national government of Afghanistan. Soviet troops soon became directly involved in Afghanistan.

Once committed to the survival of a Socialist regime, the Soviet Union had no alternative but to deepen direct intervention on its behalf, even to the point at which, in December 1979, such involvement had to become massive and overt---the "invasion," actually more an escalation. In January 1980, Moscow justified the Afghan invasion by declaring that "the international solidarity of revolutionaries" goes beyond "moral and diplomatic support and verbal wishes for success" and that "rendering material aid, including military aid"[21] was an obligation of the Socialist community to its member-states: "To refuse to use the potential which Socialist countries possess would mean in fact to avoid fulfilling an international duty and returning the world to the times when Imperialism would stifle any revolutionary movement with impunity as it saw fit."[22]

At the time, the Soviets considered the invasion to be merely a further development of a predetermined process. They expected the Afghan Army to go over to the offensive, while the insurgents would be reluctant to take on such odds. Soviet troops were supposed only to provide the initial stiffener[23] and were therefore organized for a brief stay of a few months among a friendly and safe population which would welcome the new leadership they brought in.

The first turning point, then, was not the invasion itself but the decisions made twenty months earlier.

Decision #2:

In the months following the invasion, the opposition of units of the DRA Armed Forces and especially the widespread hostility of the "liberated" population soon made it clear to Moscow that if they wanted to secure the Babrak Karmal regime, they were in Afghanistan to stay. Simultaneously, the unfolding crisis in Iran and the growing U.S. awareness of the strategic significance of the region made the consolidation of regional strategic military capabilities the Soviet Union's top priority. Soon after the invasion, the Soviets began to explain their presence in Afghanistan in terms of Soviet strategic interests: by May 1980, Marshal SU N.V. Ogarkov was justifying the invasion in global terms as "a timely and far sighted step which ruined the insidious scheme of imperialism and its helpers to convert

Afghanistan into a beachhead on the southern borders of the Soviet Union."[24]

Counterinsurgency (COIN) combat operations by the Soviet Armed Forces against the Afghan Resistance were intensified---but the primary Soviet military effort in Afghanistan was thereafter directed toward the consolidation of a permanent strategic deployment and the building of a vast strategic infrastructure, especially airbases. Since then, the bulk of the Soviet forces and assets have been confined to well-secured installations which are out of reach of the Resistance and have little or no involvement in the routine anti-Resistance operations, but from which offensive operations against the Resistance are conducted at will.

This was the second turning point: the decision to remain militarily in Afghanistan and transform it into a base for Soviet power projection elsewhere in the region.

Decision #3:

By mid-1983, the Soviets had realized that changing the leadership of any centralized Communist government in Kabul made no difference---that they were confronted with an indigenous Muslim insurgency whose strength derived from the inherent strength and cohesion of the various tribal and ethnic groups ("nationalities"), making their erosion the key to the collapse of resistance. Drawing on 200 years of highly successful past experience, the current Soviet campaign in Afghanistan since then has been based on exploiting longstanding differences among these groups, completely distorting them in order to further Soviet designs.

Soviet covert and propaganda operations play a crucial role in this campaign. Abdul Majid Mangal, the former DRA chargé d'affaires in Moscow who recently defected, has pointed to the growing significance of intelligence and special operations, stating that "the Soviets have now diverted their attention to further strengthening the espionage and spying department of KhAD. The KGB experts now extend special training for inhuman atrocities and brutalities. The purpose of such merciless practices is on the one hand to intimidate the masses and on the other hand to infiltrate their agents and spies into the lines and ranks of mujahideen and to create disunity among them."[25] Successful Soviet efforts range from spreading mutual suspicion and mistrust among segments of the Afghan population to the running and manipulating of complete Resistance organizations.

The significance of current Soviet moves is fully comprehensible if they are examined in the light of Soviet ethnographic studies. The Soviets believe that there are two types of "nationalities:" traditional, "socially under-developed" nationalities, in which friction stems from the differences between classes; and the Socialist, "socially developed" nationalities which have emerged since the Bolshevik Revolution, characterized by tendencies to unify and identify with "mature" political concepts. The Soviets insist that a single brief event, the Bolshevik Revolution, was sufficient to transform their own Muslim minorities from separatist backwardness to their current status of Socialist nationalities and that other such brief monumental events can similarly transform other peoples.

At the same time, however, they acknowledge that such a transformation met with stiff resistance from "backward and counterrevolutionary elements" in Central Asia. In discussing the Basmachi Movement, they provide insight into their understanding---and their expectations---of the Afghan Resistance: they define the Basmachi Movement as an "armed, counter-revolutionary nationalist movement" which was totally dependent on external assistance and "operated from the territory of neighboring countries and carried out surprise bandit raids against Soviet establishments, military sub-units, industrial, agricultural, and other targets."[26] They emphasize that, once Enver was eliminated, the continuation of popular resistance for more than twenty years presented no challenge to the consolidation of Soviet control and sovereignty over Central Asia and required no significant Soviet effort to eliminate it.

In stating that "the tactics of the Basmachi are being used by counterrevolutionary bands in the struggle against the Democratic Republic of Afghanistan"[27] the Soviets also define their attitude toward the solution of their Afghan problem, even though the situation is somewhat more complex in Afghanistan because of the universally Muslim nature of the country.* The Soviets emphasize that in developing Muslim countries awareness of religious community often takes the place of national self-awareness, and the public sense of identity is based on common heritage and especially on linguistic affinity.† In mid-1983, the Soviets concluded that the Afghan population had not in fact undergone in 1978 "the brief monumental event that can transform nationalities from one status to another," namely, a genuine revolution---that the Afghans still develop, perceive and define their identity through similarities of religion, language and cultural behavior.

This, then, was the third turning point: the Soviet conclusion in mid-1983 that the "Saur Revolution" had had little or no impact on the social development and behavior of the Afghans, followed by the realization that

---

* During the Tsarist period, large numbers of Russians, other Slavs, Armenians, etc., had settled in Central Asia.

† Hence the importance of language policy. See: Amin.

the intensifiying Muslim insurrection in Afghanistan might even become a threat to the stability of the Muslim population in the USSR. This was the most significant of the turning points, because it represented a Soviet realization that, contrary to Leninist doctrine, a Communist revolution could be rejected, combined with a Soviet decision to proceed nevertheless with the consolidation of control.

This third conclusion has determined the subsequent nature and increased ferocity of the campaign against the Resistance. The realization that in Afghanistan they were confronted with the most basic traditionalist Muslim social order led the Soviets to adopt completely the age-old, proven Russian solutions to the challenges of Muslim rebellions. Moscow is currently committed to a strategic-regional solution which is bound to have a profound impact on its own Muslim population---for any demonstration of Soviet lack of resolve or any indication that Soviet military supremacy is not unchallengeable will encourage Soviet Muslims to reassert their submerged desires for autonomy and independence.

Soviet analysis of the role of the "limited contingent" of Soviet troops in Afghanistan is revealing. They recently explained that "the presence of the limited contingent of Soviet troops...combines functions of defending Soviet borders from the approach to them of hostile imperialists and pro-imperialist forces with the function of rendering international assistance to the Afghan national-democratic regime which has repeatedly asked the Soviet Union for assistance in the struggle against foreign intervention."[28] They define U.S. assistance to the Resistance in similar strategic terms, explaining "that it is precisely anti-Soviet military-strategic designs, and not platonic feelings for Afghan rebels, that prompt the actions of official Washington."[29]

The Soviets believe that the source of instability throughout all of Muslim Central and Southwest Asia lies in the mismatch between the political frontiers and actual ethnic boundaries. They believe that, in view of the low level of "social awareness" among the Afghan "nationalities," the only chance for stability lies in the unification of political (statehood) and ethnic identities in a regional solution, and that growing contact between Farsi (Persian) and Turkish speakers in northern Afghanistan and their brethren in the USSR will result in unified national identities which will self-evidently determine revised territorial boundaries, i.e., the incorporation of northern Afghanistan into the respective Soviet Republics.

...and Soviet Perspectives

After many years of direct involvement in combat operations against the Afghan Resistance, the Soviets are fully aware of its qualities and deficiencies. They recognize the growing hostility of the population towards the Communist regime and the strong Muslim and nationalist sentiments of the rural population, especially the Pushtuns. They know that the Resistance is not only committed to fighting them but does its best to escalate the war. Soviet sources point to recent improvements in the capabilities and performance of some Resistance groups as an indication of escalation potential, singling out the use of radio communication as an indication of growing Resistance "militarization," and emphasizing increased Resistance efforts to insert more supplies and personnel into the country since May 1984. (They claimed to have destroyed twenty-five major mujahideen caravans in 1984 alone, when they began a highly successful interdiction campaign which has since intensified; see below). They also point to the growing quality of weapons captured from the Resistance---heavy machine guns, mortars, grenade launchers, artillery pieces, recoilless rifles, rockets, and anti-aircraft missiles. "Judging by appearance, the militarist circles supporting the Afghan counterrevolution want to make the undeclared war against the young DRA even bloodier and more brutal; they want to add fuel to its flames."[30]

However, this Soviet awareness of the Resistance should be examined in the proper perspective. Since mid-1980, the Resistance has never constituted more than a tactical inconvenience to the Soviets. For the Soviets, it is already doomed, just as the Basmachi movement was doomed after the assassination of Enver Pasha. Even the introduction of improved weapons systems---including sophisticated air defense systems---has never amounted to more than a temporary techno-tactical challenge and harassment. In strategic terms---the consolidation of Soviet control over Southwest Asia---the Afghan Resistance has had little or no impact. Currently the Resistance is a negligible factor in Soviet calculations of the regional dynamics.

The Soviets are also fully aware of the rapidly deteriorating situation of the civilian population inside Afghanistan. They know that the population, though dedicated to the cause of resistance, can no longer readily support Resistance operations, either from fear of brutal reprisals or because of an acute shortage of food---and that as a result the Resistance is ever more dependent on open lines of communication with Pakistan for its very survival. "Without the constant injections from the outside, without the large-scale material and military support, the counterrevolution would have completely failed long ago; it would have suffered a final and unconditional defeat."[31] They point to the historical precedents: Russian and Soviet forces have completely crushed all past Muslim insurrections the moment they managed to isolate them from external support.

It is the willingness to confront Afghan realities, and then to adopt classic Russian and Soviet solutions in pursuit of classic Russian and Soviet goals and aspirations, that makes the Soviets so devastatingly effective against the Afghan Resistance.

The USSR, the Muslim Revival
and the Afghan Resistance

The accumulating lessons of their experience in the Middle East, Afghanistan and Iran have provided the Soviets with new perceptions of the threats and challenges of the Islamic world, and their intimate and protracted confrontation with a conservative Muslim society in Afghanistan has been a watershed in their comprehension of Islam. The most significant new factor is the Soviet realization that two movements---radical-revivalist Islam (commonly but misleadingly called "fundamentalist") and traditionalist Islam---have become the most decisive trends in the Muslim world, and that if Moscow is to have any influence there, it must find a way to exploit and manipulate them---particularly the radical-revivalists, who are most useful to them.

The Soviets are well aware of the uncompromising and irreconcilable hostility between the Communist USSR and both Islamic revival movements. They are also fully aware of the threat presented by an activist Islamic revival of any sort among the Soviet Muslim population: they know that any activist Islam increases the activities of secret religious orders and conspiratorial sects (Sufi orders and various sub-organizations of the Muslim Brotherhood, etc.), and that inside the USSR it is next to impossible for Soviet agents to penetrate the Sufi orders (which in Central Asia are based on family ties).

The Soviets have concluded, however, that these trends are inevitable, and they have made a clearcut decision that, despite the threat that all activist Islam and especially its radical-revivalist forms present *inside* the USSR, the opportunities and gains to be gotten from penetrating and manipulating such movements *outside* the USSR (where they are differently organized and vulnerable) outweigh the dangers.

The Soviets have further concluded that, although radical-revivalist Islamic movements are more dangerous than the traditionalists, they are also more useful, because they are intensely anti-Western. They have therefore concluded that their only practical option is to make such movements dependent on the USSR. They know that their hopes for success lie in persuading the radical-revivalist Muslims to see the Soviets as an instrument to be used against a common enemy, the West. Moscow therefore seeks to create situations in which the radical-revivalists will accept a "temporary" condition of dependency on the Soviet Union (or its allies) because they believe that this is merely a useful expedient to be exploited in their fight against what the radicals see as a greater evil and a greater threat to Islam: the United States and the West, the sources of earthly temptations, i.e., goods and technologies.

The Soviets also realize that there is only one way by which they can gain access to the militant radical-revivalist groups, develop a degree of penetration, establish data bases, and influence and manipulate these groups so that they will bypass Soviet Central Asia and concentrate on objectives beneficial to Soviet goals---and that one way is by making the radical Muslims dependent on the USSR for what they want and cannot get elsewhere: military training, weapons support and intelligence. They also know that some of this access is best achieved through Muslim proxies in order to make the contacts with the USSR more palatable to the radical-revivalist groups.

So this is what the Soviets do throughout the Muslim world, including Afghanistan.

The social upheaval in Afghanistan, and especially the massive movements of refugees, have allowed the Soviets to establish major intelligence penetration of the Resistance. They are fully aware of the crucial significance of the traditional Afghan and Islamic values and sense of identity to the continued defiance by the Resistance and the Afghan population as a whole, both of which are generally traditionalist. (Many of the more effective Resistance organizations, and especially the groups focussed around locally active commanders and leaders, are organized along nationalist-traditionalist lines and are, to a degree, less accessible than the radicals.)

Therefore, although they have been successful in penetrating and exploiting all groups, they have been most successful in fully exploiting the commitment of radical-revivalist organizations and commanders---and especially that of Gulbuddin Hekhmatyar---to the radicals' conviction that the purge of apostates at home, including traditionalists and nationalists, takes precedence over any struggle against an external infidel enemy. As a result, they have been able to create conditions in which the most radical-revivalist elements of the Resistance will consider cooperating with the Soviet Union and the DRA, believing such cooperation to be a temporary measure that will expedite their purge of apostates and a necessary evil on the road to the utopian Islamic State they envisage.[32] Through this approach, the Soviets have neutralized major components of what are ostensibly the most anti-Soviet elements of the Afghan Resistance, just as they have facilitated their penetration and consolidation of effective control over Khomeini's Iran.[33]

The Soviet military in Afghanistan
The operational approach

The Soviet military operational approach stems from the Mongol conquest of Russia: under the "Tatar Yoke" (1240-1480) the local nobility and military elite were exposed to the Tatar Art of War, fighting in mixed formations of Slavs and Turkic troops. This lengthy exposure to and close cooperation with the Tatars had a profound impact on the Russian Art of War, and the Soviets fully appreciate the Mongol military legacy.

In the late eighteenth century, the Russian army began to incorporate many of the tenets of the Tatar heritage into its own Art of War. Aleksander Vasilevich Suvorov, the father of the modern Russian Art of War, integrated many of them into the new concept of maneuver warfare he introduced to the Russian army. Indeed, to one of his Westernized contemporaries, "it seemed that his style was that of a Cossak or Tatar chieftain, rather than the commander of a European army."[34] General Suvorov himself attributed the essence of his victories to the "ability to judge by eye, speed and onslaught," the instinctively grasped Mongol style of war.[35] Preparations for the Turkish War of 1787 gave him the opportunity to develop and test his concepts and to define the essence of the rapid deep offensive which still characterizes the Soviet Art of War.[36]

Because Russo-Soviet operational art is determined by strategic requirements, the continuity of strategy in Central Asia has resulted in a continuously evolving development of operational art, the outcome of generations of refinement and techno-tactical changes. On the basis of this cumulative experience, the Soviets define the following military conditions as the key to success in suppressing Muslim insurgencies:

1. Deep intelligence penetration and manipulation of the hostile population.

2. Deep raiding capabilities and the ability to conduct surgical strikes against priority objectives.

3. The ability to rapidly inflict massive collateral damage on the civilian infrastructure in order to erode popular support for the enemy.

In their first encounters with Muslim uprisings two centuries ago, the Russians realized that intelligence is the key to interdicting flexible, elusive forces. Since then, they have always made a concentrated effort to develop a thorough intelligence picture of the areas in which such forces operate; this intelligence data has then been utilized by highly mobile small detachments---

from the Cossak cavalry to today's heliborne SPETSNAZ---to interdict and destroy enemy caravans and raiding groups.

After the Soviets consolidated their control in Central Asia in the 1920s, one of their first moves was the establishment of comprehensive intelligence networks in all the neighboring countries, including Afghanistan. These networks gathered data on the local governments and anti-Soviet activities, and fomented and assisted local anti-government movements mainly based on nationalistic and ethnic grounds. Ismail Akhmedov, a former GRU officer posted in Azerbaidjhan, described the thoroughness of their work: in 1930 he was assigned to "very serious study" of Turkish and Iranian Kurdistan which "involved obtaining intimate and detailed knowledge of the character and background of chieftains of...tribes, of routes and paths, of sources of water, of local history and folklore, of the origins and current reasons of the hatreds separating the many tribes and people of the Middle East, the struggle between the various political parties. The smallest detail was not neglected. For example...how Soviet advisors should appeal to and play on the national and religious feelings and customs of individual local populations."[37]

From the early 1920s on, Moscow also developed elaborate subversive means in Turkey, Persia* and Afghanistan, including both Russian and local armed detachments. By 1927, the OGPU could kidnap defectors from the middle of Persian cities in broad daylight and ship them back to the Soviet Union.[†] Since then, the Soviets have improved their regional intelligence and subversive infrastructure, achieving an unprecedented degree of deep penetration and manipulation of both governments and local populations.

Throughout Russian/Soviet campaigns in Central Asia and Eastern Turkey, they refined their Art of War, optimizing it for the conduct of swift military operations in rugged desert-mountain terrain against numerically superior enemies. By 1880, the Russians had further refined their conduct of deep offensive operations in Central Asia with extremely small units, basing their methods on intimate knowledge of the special conditions of the theater and the extremely efficient use of available troops and weapons. The British were fully aware of the sophistication and capabilities of Russian forces in Central Asia, and of the great value of the accumulating operational experience of the Russian Army there.[39] Describing Russian

---

* The name of the country was not changed from *Persia* to *Iran* until 1935.
† When Boris Bajanov, then Stalin's secretary, defected to Persia in early 1928, the OGPU resident in Turkey organized and led an armed chase for more than 600 miles from the Soviet border into British Indian Baluchistan.[38]

military doctrines and tactics, Lord Curzon remarked in 1889 that "repellent though they be to nineteenth century notions, and discreditable to the Russian character, they do not stand alone in the history of Russian conquest in Central Asia, but are profoundly characteristic of the methods of warfare by which that race has consistently and successfully set about the subjugation of Oriental peoples."[40]

The initial Soviet military operations against the Basmachi in the 1920s did not differ much from Tsarist operations in Central Asia forty or even seventy years earlier. The remoteness of Basmachi mountain redoubts prevented the Soviets from using their relatively modern artillery so, as of the mid-1920s, they based their counterinsurgency combat operations on long-range raids, using cavalry as a mobile force, and, once again, on the destruction of the social and economic infrastructure supporting the insurgents. The Soviets increased the number and size of attacks on civilians, destroying villages and killing most of the people; although the Basmachi forces and their supporters tried to withdraw into isolated mountain hideouts, they could no longer escape Soviet fire power once the Soviets started to use aircraft in growing numbers.

To further enhance the effectiveness of their fire strikes, the Soviets also began to use chemical weapons. According to a Soviet chemical officer, "At the end of the 1920s, during the suppression of the rising in the Caucasus, chemical shells were used to destroy the defenders and the population of the mountain villages....In the 1930s, during the actions against the Basmachi tribesmen in Central Asia, Soviet aircraft sprayed Yprite---mustard gas..."[41] The cumulative effects of fire power and chemical attacks led to the collapse of support for the insurgents and forced them to reduce their level of resistance to sporadic and insignificant skirmishes.

By the late 1920s, however, the remaining Basmachi forces had become increasingly flexible, operating in small groups and concentrating their forces only for major attacks. In 1929, the Soviets therefore introduced a new element in their operations---the tactical aerial *desant:* infantry detachments transported to combat zones and landed or dropped in the rear of the enemy by aircraft which then provided them with fire support.[42] From the 1930s on, aerial strikes and desants became the decisive element in Soviet counterinsurgency operations, enabling the Soviets to insert forces and firepower into the depth of the Basmachi safe havens and catch them by surprise. Desants were also used as the decisive component in complex large-scale operations: Soviet cavalry units would start a major sweep into a Basmachi area; the insurgents would withdraw into what they believed to be safe areas; aerial desants and strikes would then attack them unexpectedly from their rear. Trapped between the Soviet cavalry and the desant, the

Basmachi force would eventually be eliminated. (In 1928-1931, Soviet aerial strikes and desants were also used inside northern Afghanistan against Basmachi safe havens there.)

Developments in Afghanistan since 1979/80

The Soviet military involvement in Afghanistan is extremely low key. The invasion itself was based on the lessons of the operations of the 6th GTA during the Manchurian Campaign in 1945 and was conducted by a reduced-size Army. For political reasons and because of logistical challenges, the then-ad hoc Southern TVD and the Turkestan Front command echelons were directly involved, primarily to deal with local surprises of strategic significance which could come only from other countries in the region, not from Afghanistan itself.* As noted above, the major national-strategic decision making did not take place until April-May 1980, when the Soviets realized that they were in Afghanistan to stay and that its greatest value for them was its geographical location as a starting point for a possible advance into the Persian Gulf. They then changed their regional military priorities accordingly.

Since 1980, the regional Fronts inside the USSR have been reorganized into the now fully operational Southern (Near Eastern) TVD, while the forces in Afghanistan, ostensibly still under the command of the 40th Army, have in reality been reorganized into a Front-level command. The building of a diversified strategic infrastructure, especially air bases, has become the regional priority, and this determines the nature and size of the Soviet deployment in Afghanistan and the conduct of combat operations there.

The chief purpose of those Soviet forces dedicated to confronting the Resistance has been to deny it access to Soviet strategic assets, using the least possible Soviet force in order to avoid casualties and wastage of Soviet military assets. In this they have been highly successful. As of this writing, the Resistance has been unable to hit any major Soviet installations, to interrupt the economic exploitation of Afghanistan, or to prevent major troop movements and maneuvers. The Soviets can move anywhere in the country as long as they are willing to pay the price. As Prof. Rabbani, head of the Jamiat Islami Resistance party, has admitted, "the Soviets feel comfortable in Afghanistan."[43]

---

* Because of the turmoil in Iran, the Soviets did not rule out the possibility of a U.S. reaction in or from Iran; the prime role of the Southern TVD was to confront such a development, highly unlikely as it might have been.

The next strategically significant decision did not take place until 1983. By then, the Soviets had realized that the establishment of the DRA regime had had no impact on Afghanistan because the country was not yet prepared to accept a "progressive socialist regime." Therefore, as a result of direct confrontation with the Afghan Resistance, they took the pragmatic decision to resume the policies which had crushed the Basmachi, adopting Tsarist means to achieve traditional strategic goals with resultant changes in military operations.

Militarily, the operational level is the most critical and challenging level of warfare and the ongoing development of Soviet operational art in particular has been a cohesive, continuous evolutionary process---in essence, the integration of novel, even daring, combat forms employing the newest weapon technologies into traditional Russian operational art, as Afghanistan clearly demonstrates. There have been two major development cycles in Afghanistan: the development first of direct---and later of indirect--- approaches to confrontation with the Resistance. Both have been characterized by a rapid and very efficient adaptation of the local military system both to directives from Moscow and to the specific conditions, especially in eastern Afghanistan.

The first approach---direct confrontation---resulted from the initial Soviet misperception of Afghanistan as a developing society engaged in a civil war over the consolidation of an "advanced" form of regime, and from the initial Soviet misperception of the nature of the Resistance. These determined the structure and organization of Soviet combat operations from November 1979 to March 1980. The Soviets expected both sides to be heading toward the consolidation of organized national fronts. They believed that after the "Saur Revolution," the Afghan population was ripe and eager for social progress and that the Resistance represented merely a few narrow social strata---the rich and the clergy. They expected the population to cooperate with their Soviet "liberators" if they quickly transferred the control over the population to Afghan authorities (Babrak Karmal and the PDPA, with massive KGB penetration and control).[44] The Soviets also envisaged the "partisanization" of the Afghan Resistance, i.e., the emergence of an organized and unified irregular military force capable of engaging major regular forces.

Consequently, the invasion was a swift two-pincer advance designed to throw the Resistance off balance, depriving them of control of the population centers and the transportation and military infrastructure. Since the Soviets expected to be dealing with a cooperative population and a competent DRA force capable of taking over the longterm control of urban centers, the first Soviet forces to enter Afghanistan had little or no capacity to leave garrisons behind and maintain a protracted logistical support. Reality was totally different, and the Soviets ran into massive problems, straining their lines of communications to the point that their logistical support collapsed in January 1980; but by rushing in reinforcements, including counterintelligence experts from East Germany, they quickly solved their immediate problems.

Expecting the "partisanization" of the Resistance, the Soviets initially sought to confront it. This notion lay behind the first offensives of the Spring of 1980: the Soviets were seeking direct engagements with the Resistance in the belief that, following a series of defeats on the battlefield, Resistance leaders would accept the futility of their struggle and come to terms with the Babrak government. They soon realized that they were not going to confront an organized Resistance force---simply because there wasn't any. Soviet military policy then became the prevention of the partisanization of the Resistance through attrition and denial of access to strategically significant locations. This policy has been highly successful, preventing the development of the Resistance as an armed movement.

These early combat operations involved the use of combined-arms units and subunits, since the essence of victory was the capture or denial of territory. The accumulating lessons pointed to the growing significance of integrating combined-arms and combat arms, including the most modern weapons systems, into a unified force. This in turn led to organizational changes and the development of the combined-arms formation in ways relevant both to the specifics of the Afghan theater and to the potential combat performance of Soviet forces against an organized army elsewhere. Assets available to combined-arms units were redistributed to subunits, creating flexible forces small enough to maneuver freely in the most demanding terrain while still containing components of all the combat arms under a unified combined-arms command. These developments occurred rapidly: the first CARBs were operating in Afghanistan by the summer of 1980, and the retraining of battalion commanders began in the Soviet Union at about the same time. By 1985, as a result of the Afghan experience, the bulk of divisions throughout the entire Soviet Armed Forces had been reorganized to operate Combined-Arms Reinforced Battalions (CARBs) as their core subunits; their commanders and staffs had been given far greater authority and combat autonomy than ever before; and the quality of the officers nominated as CARB commanders had improved.

The Soviets believe that the rapid extension of fighting into the deep rear of the enemy is a prime factor in securing speedy victory. Special attention is paid to the use of outflanking and enveloping forces during a deep offensive in mountainous terrain. The adoption of the CARB for combat operations provides the main forces with unprecedented performance and operational flexibility.

Once the Soviets were confident of the ability of their commanders to fully exploit the unique combat capabilities of the CARB, they started to extend the flexibility and performance of the all-too-crucial supporting "quality edge" measures, i.e., those forces and weapons whose combat effectiveness exceeds that of the main forces and which are brought in as the decisive element in combat. Helicopters have been particularly significant.

During the 1979-1980 invasion/escalation, the Soviets deployed helicopter regiments with extensive experience in mountain flying, operating in close cooperation with both special and regular troops. The Soviets seem to have been surprised by the effectiveness of these measures, and rapidly reinforced their helicopter force in Afghanistan with other units with little or no experience in mountain flying. As a result, more than 75 percent of the Soviet helicopter losses in Afghanistan are---even now---a result of pilot errors or mechanical malfunctions; but in view of the amount of flight time and sortie ratio, the losses are negligible. In Afghanistan, the helicopter has developed from one indispensable component of Soviet combined-arms subunits to the core component of highly flexible deep offensive operations and the embodiment of Soviet ability to out-maneuver any force the Resistance could muster, hitting or confronting them in their deepest sanctuaries.

The Soviets have also derived valuable lessons about the technical reliability, accuracy and performance of most of their major weapon systems under harsh conditions and have examined the validity of their tactical procedures under conditions of extreme pressure on their troops. They have demonstrated that the Soviet soldier is properly trained for the most demanding combat operations, the only major exception being the Muslim reservists pressed into service in early 1980 who, despite popular beliefs, proved to be mostly loyal but poorly trained and inefficient.

Afghanistan's most important contribution to Soviet tactics is the emergence of innovative concepts of troop control, especially the role of the junior officer and the senior NCO. This seems to have resulted from necessity: many young officers were killed in action and sergeants and NCOs had problems taking over the command. Tactical procedures became more complex, demanding more from the junior commanders. (The Soviets had previously relied on their experience with the development of the

Egyptian "War Officer" concept prior to the 1973 Yom Kippur War, limiting the role of squad and platoon commanders while increasing the role and autonomy of the commanders from company level up.[45]) Small unit combat operations in Afghanistan have led to the refinement of the role and authority of junior commanders, including the growing role of the professional sergeants and senior NCOs as combat commanders.

At the height of their routine military operations, only 15 percent of the Soviet troops in Afghanistan were committed to fighting the Resistance. As a result of growing Soviet emphasis on special operations and improvement in the performance of the DRA Armed Forces, an even smaller number of Soviet troops---only about 5 percent of the total deployment in Afghanistan---are actually involved in the conduct of such combat operations.[46] The Afghan Resistance as presently constituted is incapable of inflicting substantial damage to Soviet strategic assets and infrastructure.

Developments regarding Soviet military personnel

The Soviets consider the quality of their troops, and especially their commanders---i.e., their ability to carry out the demands of the Soviet Art of War---to be the decisive factor in warfare. Afghanistan has provided the USSR with a pool of seasoned veterans of troops who will go into the reserves throughout the USSR; they are defined as the core of any future mobilization and their potential capacity to crystallize other reservists around themselves under extreme pressure is valued highly. Since 1978, more than half a million Soviet servicemen have served in Afghanistan, although only about 50,000 troops have actually been involved in combat. A similar number of technicians have been able to exercise their expertise under combat-related conditions.

A close examination of the troops in Afghanistan points to a healthy military population. Despite the harsh living conditions in the country, combat casualties, and exposure to vices ranging from defection to drug use, the Soviet enlisted population is very cohesive and stable. The current casualty level in Afghanistan (from all causes) is well within the average of the Soviet Armed Forces. Indeed, it is below the casualty rate occurring during the exercises and routine activities conducted by the most active Soviet Fronts (in the Far East and Belorussian Military Districts and the GSFG), and it is therefore acceptable to the Soviet authorities.

It is impossible to know actual defection rates because all Russian soldiers caught by the Resistance declare themselves to be defectors; but even if this were true, the defection rate in Afghanistan would be only about one to two percent of the defection rate of Soviet troops during The Great

Patriotic War.* There is little or no statistical evidence to support reports of massive drug consumption.

The several thousand career NCOs who have combat experience in Afghanistan are indispensable to the effort to increase the role of NCOs throughout the Soviet Armed Forces, where, as a result of the growing reliance on small units and formations, the role of the senior NCO as a combat commander has been dramatically enhanced. But the most important veterans of Afghanistan are the officers, both commanders and pilots. The Soviets are making a special effort to ensure that the best of their officers will serve in Afghanistan, and that their acquired expertise will subsequently be fully and effectively utilized.

As regards senior officers, very few have actually served in Afghanistan and even fewer have been involved in the conduct of military operations; the significant element is that group of senior officers entrusted with the control-management of military operations and the procedure of deriving and learning lessons from them. Most of the senior officers involved in operations in Afghanistan have been promoted or moved to higher positions. A few have already reached national prominence, most notably General of the Army Dmitri T. Yazov, whose appointment as Minister of Defense in May 1987 capped a series of rapid promotions and advancements, far ahead of schedule. This was in recognition of his successes in Afghanistan where, as commander of the Central Asian Military District from late 1980 to mid-1984, he was directly involved in the conduct of the war against the Afghan Resistance, in the lesson-learning derived from it and in the resulting innovations in Soviet operational art and tactics discussed above. Similarly, then-Gen. Col. Yuri P. Maximov, who from 1978 to 1984 commanded the Turkestan Military District (which, as indicated above, was activated as a Front at the time of the invasion), was in 1982 promoted to the rank of General of the Army in recognition of his successes in Afghanistan. He was given command of the entire Southern TVD in mid-1984, and a year later was given command of the entire Soviet Strategic Rocket Forces.

The junior commanders and NCOs get the most actual combat experience. A period of service in Afghanistan counts double in time-accumulation for promotion and command authority so, for the junior officer, a successful tour of combat duty in Afghanistan can be a major career boost. Their morale and dedication are very strong. They lead their

---

* The Soviet term for World War II *after* 22 June 1941, when Nazi Germany invaded the USSR. Prior to that date, the Soviet Union called it "The Second Imperialist War" and joined with Germany in the dismemberment of Poland.

men in combat and fight to the end, refusing to be captured; some have blown themselves up, taking Resistance fighters with them. It is already possible to notice the emergence of subunits throughout the USSR operating with "the Afghanistan style" introduced by a few experienced junior commanders.

The most important officer population---the one whose impact on the Soviet Armed Forces is bound to be long-term and decisive---is that of the mid-rank commanders, most of whom were among the cream of the Soviet Armed Forces even before their deployment to Afghanistan. The Soviet High Command makes special efforts to ensure their optimal utilization after they complete their combat tours in Afghanistan. Many or most of them are sent as either students or faculty to the higher military schools, military academies, and the Vystrel, the group of institutions which improve the entire officer corps and prepare the future high command. The growing attendance by prime mid-rank commanders from Afghanistan in the Vystrel provides a clear indication of their growing significance and perceived role in the future of the Soviet Armed Forces. If current trends continue, in a few years they will have a noticeable impact. Eventually, one should expect to see many of them becoming the core of the future leadership and High Command of the Soviet Armed Forces.

Special operations

Space does not permit a detailed analysis of Soviet military operations but a brief look at key elements may be useful. As of early 1983, the Soviets moved gradually from confrontation to the indirect approach---a growing reliance on special operations, leaving most of the ground operations to the DRA while conducting daring but sporadic separate surgical strikes against safe havens and sanctuaries of the Resistance on the basis of accurate intelligence.

A major development occurred in Spring 1984 when the Soviets adopted special operations as the *prime* method of countering the Resistance: since then these operations have brought the Resistance close to a breaking point through the cumulative effect of the diversified but well coordinated, well-timed, extremely sophisticated, and ruthless use of deep-raiding special forces, airpower (helicopter and combat aircraft), and especially irregular warfare occasionally supported by airpower.

The Russo-Soviet approach to the conduct of COIN (counterinsurgency) combat operations calls for three essential elements: the operational flexibility and autonomy of the small unit; the availability of superior and flexible fire power; and a complete intelligence picture. The moment the Soviets succeeded in integrating these three elements into their COIN combat operations in Afghanistan in 1983, the Resistance began to suffer serious defeats, culminating in the 1986 attacks on their key bases from which they have not yet recovered.

The key to the success of the Soviet special operations is their ability to exploit their intimate intelligence picture of the Resistance in a correct and timely fashion which the Resistance is unable to counter. For example, when it is known that a village is actively cooperating with the Resistance, the Soviets use special forces which destroy the entire village in order to (a) not give away intelligence assets, and (b) demonstrate to the Resistance that the Soviet special forces can get everywhere, and by surprise.*

The Soviets started sophisticated, smallscale COIN operations in Afghanistan in mid-1980. Soon afterwards, it became clear that routine methods of reconnaissance, mainly by helicopters and aircraft, could not supply all the data needed. Reconnaissance helicopter patrols subsequently intensified and the proficiency of their pilots has increased, but in addition the Soviets realized that there is no substitute for subversive and special operations. The goal is to put the insurgent organization constantly on the defensive through devastating surprise strikes on its very deep sanctuaries; to succeed, such operations require extremely detailed and up-to-date intelligence which must be collected on the ground and covertly, so that the subjects are unaware.

The Soviets conduct deep reconnaissance themselves in order to guarantee its accuracy. Patrols of various sizes penetrate deeply into the targeted area, operating independently and in isolation, walking through the most rugged terrain. Some are violent, but most are covert and quiet--- planting mines, stealing documents, sabotage, killing, etc.---conducted by specially trained teams and detachments. One reconnaissance commander who received the Hero of the Soviet Union award "for his courage and valor in fulfilling his internationalist duty" described his work: "For these one and a half years I have crawled all around on my belly."[48] Some operations are conducted to enable DRA troops to reliably attack and achieve surprise; others locate DRA units lost or under fire, so they can be aided.

---

* In a letter, one man described the recent exploits of a friend in a desant unit, probably the KDB (Punitive Desant Battalion): "He participated in 29 punitive expeditions... He took part in torture which is used to get information about the rebels... The commandos usually work at night. They surround a village that has been designated for destruction. The inhabitants are killed silently, knives and bayonets only. Shooting is allowed only if armed rebels appear."[47]

Their own Muslim population provides the Soviets with a manpower pool ideal for insertion into both DRA and Resistance forces. In the KDB (Punitive Desant Battalion) which is maintained in Kabul for special operations, most personnel are Soviet Muslims who wear DRA uniforms. By cautious estimates there were some 6,000 specially trained Soviet Muslim troops in Afghanistan in early 1984 (in addition to those in the general units.)[49] The Soviets also insert their own troops into KhAD and the DRA Border Guards, the most loyal and efficient DRA anti-resistance forces, trained by the Soviets in Kabul and Bagram from basic training to preparation for special operations.[50]

Currently, KhAD and Border Guards forces carry out most of the highly successful interdictions and pursuits of the Resistance, using extremely accurate intelligence data, often supplied by the Soviets. Local Soviet commanders "advise" KhAD forces on the timing and location of ambushes.[51] Resistance leaders acknowledge the growing effectiveness of such operations and their increasing difficulty in maintaining open lines of communication deep into Afghanistan.

In early 1984, the Soviets began to use specially trained VDV (Airborne Troops) and SPETSNAZ detachments to interdict Resistance caravans. Special attention is paid to night operations using very small forces against very specific objectives; it is therefore safe to assume that the raiding forces have real-time guidance of some sort. These operations are extremely effective, killing both mujahideen and pack animals. When the Resistance attempts to run several caravans simultaneously, the Soviets often intensify their interdiction efforts, launching four or five heliborne-helicopter strikes simultaneously to paralyze all Resistance transportation in a selected region; these operations obviously are able to rely on specific, extremely accurate intelligence, including real time guidance.

The most significant special operations are those conducted in the deep rear of the enemy by three-man SPETSNAZ teams which include at least one member of a local ethnic group and operate at night, usually on the basis of general intelligence data gathered by aerial reconnaissance.[52] Resistance leaders admit that these selective and accurate deep raids are the most effective of all Soviet tactics: their highly accurate strikes against seemingly invulnerable targets have a devastating effect on the entire Resistance over vast areas.

For the conduct of deep surgical strikes, the Soviets rely heavily on helicopters, both to transport troops and weapons and as a major source of fire power. The mobility of the helicopter is fully utilized to land raiding parties of varying sizes in the deepest sanctuaries of the Resistance, sometimes on the objectives themselves. The accuracy and lethality of the firepower of the fire support helicopters are used against point targets, usually from extremely short range.

Even large scale raiding forces are deployed in the deep rear of the enemy, and for as long as a week or more. Comprised of diversified helicopter regiments, an Airborne Troops battalion (with artillery) and a SPETSNAZ detachment, they are used against major targets like large villages, to attack diversified regional targets simultaneously, to seal valleys in which they expect to find large Resistance forces, and to deny the Resistance the approach to vast areas simultaneously and for a long period. In 1984-85, the Soviets often used them for the final strike in a significant area after a series of small-scale deep raids had brought the local Resistance near to collapse.

Their significance lies in their operational flexibility and the diversity and fire power of troops and weapons. The Soviets have acquired the ability to deploy high performance helicopter-heliborne units and formations in the rear of the enemy for extended periods without logistical resupply. The assignment of such units to the maneuver (mobile) groups provides them with the quality edge that turns them into a highly potent weapon capable of rendering the enemy rear combat ineffective. (In recent exercises of the GSFG, helicopter pilots who had served in Afghanistan played important roles with an operational maneuver group, demonstrating the significance of their combat experience.)[53]

In accordance with their traditional strategy, Soviet forces in Afghanistan do not attempt to pacify areas where they encounter resistance; instead, they clear the area of civilians. When they want to create collateral terror to produce a massive flight of refugees, the KDB (Punitive Desant Battalion) as well as regular regiments are sent to provide the population "with an example."[54] Whole villages are destroyed beyond recovery and the population is slaughtered with extreme cruelty. Rape and the throwing of women from helicopters are frequent. Special chemicals are used to cause rapid decomposition of the corpses,[55] a very effective means of deterrence for Muslims.* The attacks on civilians are neither accidental nor a goal in themselves; they are simply a pragmatic and highly effective tactic.** By

---

* Islamic religious doctrine makes the mutilation of a body especially abhorrent to Muslims, as the Soviets well know.

** After hearing of German atrocities in the USSR during World War II, a Soviet veteran of such a unit remarked that the Germans "had a lot to learn." Told of surviving evidence of German atrocities and war crimes, he "grinned maliciously" and added that "they did not know that everything can be burnt."[56]

such means, the Soviets have not only emptied whole areas, sending waves of refugees into Pakistan and Iran, but have also created forced migration within Afghanistan, resulting in artificially created famine, and have intensified internal feuds and ethnic separatist notions.

Chemical Weapons†

Soviet chemical warfare (CW) operations in Afghanistan began as early as April 1979, when Soviet helicopters fired rockets filled with toxic smoke and non-lethal agents to suppress the uprising in Herat. Since then, and especially since the invasion, there have been increasing reports of Soviet use of both lethal and non-lethal chemical agents (including several toxins and mycotoxins ["yellow rain"]) against both Resistance forces and civilians. These weapons are disseminated by the professional operators of the delivery platforms (Ground Forces, Air Force, Rocket and Artillery Troops, etc.) with the direct participation, professional assistance and supervision of the Chemical Troops (KhV).

Although the Soviets have tested chemical agents on live prisoners in the past,[57] those tests were carried out in confined testing facilities. Afghanistan provides them with the opportunity to test entire chemical weapon systems (including the delivery platform, the dissemination weapon and the agent itself) under field conditions and against a live population.

Since 1980, the Soviets have tested and used in Afghanistan at least two generations of chemical weapons, including all the previously known lethal agents in the Soviet arsenal as well as a family of previously unknown "super nerve agents" which have become the backbone of the Soviet chemical arsenal.[58] They have tested and discovered the operational usefulness of non-lethal agents, especially incapacitants (knock-out weapons), and have subsequently put them to massive use.[59] They have also tested a series of incendiary munitions and weapons ranging from solid cluster elements to new chemical substances and delivery modes.[60] Since 1984, there have been growing indications of the ongoing fielding of yet an additional generation of chemical weapons, the outgrowth of the lessons derived from the use of CW in combat operations.[61]

According to Brigadier Watay, Chief of the Chemical Department of the 99th Rocket Regiment of the DRA army until his recent defection, the

---

† By Soviet definition, all weapons which are not nuclear, biological or based on high explosives are chemical weapons, including lethal and non-lethal agents, smoke, incendiary munitions, defoliants, etc. For sources in this section, see esp. footnote 59. The Soviets define toxins as chemical weapons.

chemical weapons are kept and used only by the Soviet units, and have been used repeatedly: "The Russians used chemical weapons at a time when their strategic tactics and the operations of their air and ground forces did not bear any result and they failed to beat back the assault of mujahideen and break through their resistance."[62]

Currently available reports by Resistance, Soviet and DRA personnel provide a clear picture of the persistent, efficient and effective use of chemical weapons by the Soviets. These reports and others point to the conclusion that chemical warfare has become an integral component of Soviet combined-arms small-unit military operations: chemical weapons are used whenever deemed necessary by the combat commander.[63]

The most important impact of the Soviet use of chemical weapons in Afghanistan is on the Soviet commanders and troops: they have learned to enjoy the operational benefits of using chemical weapons, and have realized that these can be integrated safely and effectively into combined-arms units and subunits. This will have a great impact on the willingness of the Soviet Union to introduce chemical weapons in future wars.

Subverting the Resistance

The Soviets started intensified covert operations in Afghanistan in the early 1970s, long before the 1978 coup, making a concentrated effort to penetrate the most conservative, traditionalist sectors of society. By mid-1980, when COIN operations intensified, the Soviets had already long had a widespread network of deep moles inside the Resistance, assets they have continued to use to home in on its elusive forces. The agents in place are controlled by the local COIN commander so that he can make use of the real-time tactical intelligence they provide, which can determine the outcome of an offensive sweep (in which agents may also actively participate).

As a result of massive efforts to penetrate Resistance caravans, the Soviets seem to have a pretty accurate picture of the situation of Resistance LOCs at any given moment. According to well-informed sources in Kabul, one source of Soviet success in the 1984 Panjsher offensive was the excellent intelligence data available to the Soviet commander and his Afghan counterpart, who knew the exact whereabouts of Resistance forces throughout the offensive. These sources claimed that "the Soviet-Kabul authorities...succeeded in infiltrating government agents among the mujahideen of Panjsher; they [were] informing the Russians about the Resistance's positions, its supply routes and its weapons."[64]

The Soviets also rely on such intelligence penetration to conduct deep raids into Resistance sanctuaries, usually to seize newly arrived weapons and supplies before they are distributed or to capture or assassinate effective commanders. The case of Qari Samad, the general commander for Hezb-i-Islami/Khalis in Shinwar and Nangrahar, indicates the speed and accuracy of Soviet intelligence: on 28 January 1985, Qari Samad sent most of his forces on diversified missions in the Shinwar area, then entered the village of Siaghok to await results. According to a Hezb/Khalis source; "The enemy learned of his whereabouts and a heliborne commando attacked the village. The commander and his four companions, knowing that they had no chance of escape, did not surrender and fought to the last. Commander Qari Samad and the four fighters were killed and the civilians suffered heavy casualties."[65]

Since mid-1983, the KGB/KhAD has intensified its efforts to turn Resistance commanders around, making use of disillusioned commanders who have lost power and position as a result of internal feuds and have consequently defected to the DRA, as well as KhAD deep penetration agents who have returned to overt KhAD service after operating for a long time under cover as mujahideen. (There have been quite a few cases in which a Resistance commander who was in reality a KhAD agent knowingly led his entire force into a devastating Soviet-DRA ambush, then openly joined the DRA forces.[66])

Growing pressure on the Resistance has intensified internal feuds, thereby increasing such defections. These defectors are extremely dangerous, since they have details and current data on local Resistance forces and seek revenge against the rivals who unseated them. The Soviets are fully aware of their intelligence value, so the KGB/KhAD has intensified its efforts to stimulate defections, spreading disinformation and creating provocations and internal feuds. As of this writing, hundreds of mid- and high-rank Resistance commanders have defected, leading DRA security forces against their former mujahideen forces. Many Militia troops are former Resistance fighters who know a specific Resistance infrastructure thoroughly. Masquerading as mujahideen, their job is to infiltrate, spread rumors, issue false orders, carry out sabotage, and assassinate capable leaders. The cumulative effect is chaos in Resistance lines, infighting, mistrust and disunity.

The 1986 Offensives and their impact

The occupation and destruction of the key Resistance complexes at Zhawar in Paktia Province by Soviet and DRA forces in the spring of 1986 was a grave blow to the Resistance and an integral component of a larger drive to sever Resistance lines of communication which began with an offensive in the Kunar Valley in late 1985.

In mid-February 1986, the Soviets and their Afghan allies escalated the fighting just as the Resistance began to organize a massive spring resupply effort for the northern and western provinces. The Soviets knew that as a result of their Kunar strikes the Resistance was hard-pressed: the Soviets had severed vital lines of communications and severely disrupted Resistance ability to recover and launch summer operations.

In late February, the Soviets launched their offensive into Paktia. Seventy-five percent of their forces were DRA troops and militia, many of the latter former Resistance fighters who had operated in these regions, supported by elite Soviet forces---primarily artillery, special forces (VDV and GRU SPETSNAZ detachments) and air power. (Resistance sources admit that the DRA troops have begun to fight effectively; in the 1986 offensives, there were no reports of units deserting or collapsing.) By mid-March, Soviet-DRA forces were advancing in three axes eastward toward their key objectives, especially Zhawar. They launched the second stage of their offensive in mid-April; the vast majority of the troops were still DRA, reportedly reinforced by an elite regiment combining VDV and GRU SPETSNAZ. The Soviets landed air-assault troops on local ridges to encircle Resistance forces or ambush advancing caravans and units; these included units of Afghan militia, spearheaded by GRU SPETSNAZ in local civilian clothes, most of them Central Asians who could easily pass as Afghans,[67] and who insured optimal exploitation of the intelligence material retrieved.

The Soviets manipulated the Resistance into taking active part in its own self-destruction by confronting it with a threat it could neither ignore nor absorb: the assault on its most important base, Zhawar. Consequently, the Resistance activated---and exposed---all its assets in the region. Because of its dismal coordination capabilities and almost total lack of real-time (radio) communication, the Resistance cannot concentrate and coordinate the attacks of its diverse forces, so the Soviets, with the superior mobility provided by helicopters, were able to destroy them piecemeal.

The Soviet-DRA advance was characterized by a vast use of helicopter strikes and heliborne desants; a massive use of fire power involving tube artillery, multiple-barrel rocket launchers, tanks, helicopters and aircraft; and the spreading of wide mine-fields by artillery and aircraft. Rahim Wardak, a senior commander of NIFA, described these strikes as "the heaviest since the invasion," adding, "This is the worst fighting we've ever seen. The air attacks are terrible."[68]   Those attacks blocked Resistance freedom of movement and denied the mujahideen access to much of Paktia province, compelling them to operate along limited axes of transportation vulnerable to interdiction and ambushes.

This primary reliance on fire power for denial rather than destruction reflects the pragmatic Soviet approach to confronting the Resistance. In no way can any military system, no matter how excellent its tactical intelligence, accurately predict and follow every movement of irregulars in rugged terrain like Paktia; even if they could, it would be impossible to deal with all of them. The Soviets therefore maneuvered most of the local Resistance forces into advancing into designated "hunting zones" where they could be dealt with, while those who stayed behind were destroyed by the relentless fire strikes.

For all intents and purposes, the Soviet goal---the destruction of the Resistance infrastructure and its functioning command and control organization near the Pakistan border---was achieved. At Zhawar, the Soviets destroyed the Resistance's primary strategic reserves and storage, a large portion of its heavy weapons and special equipment, and its primary command and control center inside Afghanistan, drastically reducing Resistance ability to initiate and mount sizable operations, to support large scale logistical efforts, and to react on a timely basis to a Soviet-DRA drive. The destruction of Zhawar made the Resistance vulnerable to Soviet initiatives and exposed its already damaged lines of communication and logistics to interdiction and disruption.

The Soviet-DRA force captured huge quantities of weapons (including surface-to-air missiles and other heavy weapons, many of which are reported to have been of Western manufacture), communication systems, and intelligence data (documents, reports, correspondence of commanders, Resistance analysis of its own combat operations, names of commanders and assets, etc.). After destroying the installation, they departed, leaving behind them wide areas of mine fields and booby-traps. Because it lacks mineclearing equipment, the Resistance was forced to use its Afghan prisoners to clear the minefields by hand; several were killed or wounded.

During the summer months the offensive continued to widen. The Resistance lost the initiative and was pushed into a strategic defense, with unbearable attrition of trained commanders and fighters.

In 1986, Soviet-DRA forces also destroyed twenty other Resistance bases and positions, capturing large quantities of weapons and ammunition. The most severe loss to the Resistance was large quantities of diversified anti-aircraft weapons, including Western-made anti-aircraft cannons and a large number of surface-to-air missiles of several types. The Resistance suffered heavy casualties---1,500-2,500 killed plus an undetermined number of wounded, most of whom were unable to make it to hospitals across the border because of Soviet mining and interdiction of every movement, resulting in many more deaths for lack of medical care.

The long-term impact of the loss of Zhawar can best be understood in the context of established Russian strategy for the suppression of Muslim insurgencies, which still constitutes the essence of Soviet military doctrine in Afghanistan and which, as I have noted, predicates three preconditions for victory: (1) the neutralization of the leadership; (2) the destruction of popular support by inflicting unbearable suffering on the civilian population; and (3) the effective isolation of the insurgency from outside support.

Currently, the Soviets are very close to accomplishing the first and second preconditions, especially in areas remote from the Pakistan border. As just one example, the 1984 assassination of Commander Zabiullah of the Jamiat resulted in the total collapse of the Resistance in the Mazar-i-Sharif area. In the interior, the economy and civilian population are shattered to the point of starvation. Exposed to highly effective Soviet psychological warfare, civilians and the locally based Resistance in such areas tend to cease fighting and concentrate on the revival of the social and economic infrastructure, under only loose control by the DRA but completely out of reach for the Resistance. Meanwhile, the southern border areas have been emptied of population: there the Resistance is now totally dependent on continued contact with Pakistan.

The very existence of the entire Resistance effort depends primarily on the ability of the political leadership in Peshawar to insert commanders, instructions and weapons into the interior so that it is possible to incite the suppressed population into reviving and maintaining the jihad. This vital operation is entirely dependent on a few logistical centers in Paktia, especially Zhawar; without them, it would be next to impossible to support and sustain the Resistance.

The destruction of Zhawar and other forces and facilities in Paktia did not seal the border completely. The Soviets know perfectly well that is impossible. Moreover, since they never intended to leave behind substantial standing forces at Zhawar, the Resistance was eventually able to resume some resupply---but by the time the Resistance was able to rebuild its stockpiles and resume supplies to the interior, it was too late for a major escalation in 1986. That left the hard-pressed mujahideen and the civilian population even more vulnerable to the Soviet suppression and pacification effort.

To date, despite their rapidly intensifying interdiction campaign, the Soviets have been unable to completely isolate the Resistance in Afghanistan from its leadership and safe haven in Pakistan, and as long as the Resistance can maintain some organized communication between Peshawar and the interior, the third precondition to victory cannot be attained---but the 1986 Soviet offensive in Paktia, designed to further this third precondition, was a major step toward that goal.

Soviet strategic deployment in Afghanistan

As noted above, the bulk of the Soviet "limited contingent" in Afghanistan is not involved in local fighting. Instead, it operates and is deployed along all the lines of a Soviet permanent strategic deployment.[69]

The ten to twelve MRDs, organized in three CAAs[*]; the assortment of Front- and TVD-level units and formations (especially the VDD, the 10th TVA, and an Armiya PVO); the training complex in Mazar-i-Sharif; and the troop control installations in Kabul and Bagram---all these suggest that what is offically titled "40th Army" is in reality a Front headquarters. The identity of the local senior commanders and their relationship with other regional senior commanders also fit into the structure of a regional power-projection-oriented strategic organization.[70]

These forces are not involved in routine fighting but are garrisoned near the major air bases and communications centers, mainly south of a line from Herat to Kabul. The bulk of Soviet forces are power-projection forces deployed in unpopulated areas in which there is hardly any Resistance activity. (Combat operations against the Resistance take place in mountainous terrain, but these Soviet forces deploy and exercise in an area they describe as "...semidesert. Stone-hard, cracked earth, flat as a table...There would seem to be nothing living around. It is stifling and dusty. Even the breeze offers no joy: if it does blow, then it burns rather than refreshes. The temperature in the sun is over 50 degrees. [122° F.]"[71]) In populated areas like Kandahar, the Soviets deploy anti-Resistance forces along with power-projection deployments so that the latter will not get involved in local skirmishes.

In the Soviet Army, the true significance of a force is manifested first and foremost in its command echelon and its Troop Control authority. In the organization and functioning of its command echelons, the Group of Soviet Forces in Afghanistan (GSFA) has all the characteristics of a Soviet wartime Front. It is not only a formidable combat force in constant readiness but is entrusted with missions of strategic significance. In late 1981, General of the Army M.I. Sorokin, the senior commander in Afghanistan, was identified as being in "a leadership assignment in the field."[72] He is directly in charge of the overall conduct of military

---

* For this and other references in this section, see *Soviet Military Terms*, Glossary.

operations; the GSFA is his second Front command and it is considered to be a major promotion.

Although there is seemingly only a single Army-level headquarters in Afghanistan, the routine troop-control functioning points to the actuality of a Front-level command structure and three Armies. Soviet command and control facilities in Bagram include a direct satellite communication center with Moscow;[73] such command and control systems are installed only in Front- and TVD-level headquarters. Soviet deployment in Afghanistan includes other Front-level autonomous formations. Aerial assets are organized in the 10th TVA (Tactical Air Army) and operate under a centralized command structure. The airborne formations at Bagram were upgraded and reinforced in mid-1983 and now constitute a VDD (Airborne Division---a TVD-level formation). In addition, there are a growing number of other VDV (Airborne Troops) elements in Afghanistan, including at least two BONs (Special Duties Brigades---Front-level assets) and the strategically significant SPETSNAZ of the GRU (TVD- and Front-level assets).[74] The air defense assets---both missiles and electronic systems---now deployed in Afghanistan (aside from the specialized deployment in the Wakhan, which was annexed by the USSR in 1980) constitute an Armiya PVO, which is also a Front-level formation.

At the Shindand airbase south of Herat, the Soviets maintain a vast array of C3I (Command, Control, Communication and Intelligence) installations and specialized air force installations, including the routine deployment of strike aircraft, bombers and electronic warfare and intelligence aircraft.[75] There are repeated reports that at Shindand the Soviets have already completed the support systems required for absorbing a fast deployment of the highly mobile SS-20 missiles (which can be speedily deployed by the new An-124 CONDOR transport aircraft)---and for their launch.[76]

All these assets are special TVD-level installations *which are not under the command of the GSFA*.[77] They point to the growing strategic significance of Afghanistan in the Soviet global strategy. (From Shindand, for example, the SS-20s, with a range of over 5,000 kilometers, can hit the U.S. base on Diego Garcia, out of range from the Soviet Union itself.)

A Soviet wartime Combined-Arms Army (CAA) must include the headquarters and combat elements of four motorized-rifle divisions (MRD) in order to carry out its mission, which is to operate in the operational depth of the enemy along a main axis of advance; and there are indications that the GSFA includes all these elements.

In war, the GSFA will be expected to operate along two main axes from

Afghanistan into Iran (toward Shah-Bahar in the south and the Straits of Hormuz in the west), plus a third single thrust into Pakistan toward Islamabad and Karachi.[78] This implies that the GSFA must include at least three CAAs, thus answering all the criteria for a front---and in fact, it does. As of mid-1984, elements of ten to twelve or even fourteen MRDs (i.e., three CAAs) were positively identified in Afghanistan (in addition to an MRD and a Command and Control facility in the Wakhan Corridor which answer directly to the Central Asian VO). Each of these MRDs includes a complete divisional headquarters (with the appropriate decision-making authority, a complete command, and control-management skills and capabilities) as well as several subunits and formations which the Soviets believe would suffice to accomplish the wartime roles of these divisions.[79] They believe that these MRDs, although much smaller than the standard TO&E, are sufficient to successfully perform the wartime role of divisions.

Should the need arise, these divisions will be reinforced by local DRA forces and reserves from the USSR (see below). All of these developments and changes are earmarked for operations outside of Afghanistan---specifically, for Iran and Pakistan.[80]

It should be emphasized that the Soviet Union does not expect to encounter significant resistance in Iran because it already controls or manipulates large segments of the local regular and paramilitary forces there; therefore, the Soviet divisions deployed to Afghanistan are assigned only a fraction of the regular TO&E. As a result, the Soviets have been able to streamline and vastly improve their operations, increasing the number of their small, highly mobile task forces in, and therefore potential separate operations from, Afghanistan without increasing the overall number of Soviet troops there---a number which has for some time fluctuated between 120,000 and 180,000, averaging about 150,000.*

As mentioned above, Soviet deployment in Afghanistan is organized

---

* These figures change constantly as a result of the Soviet policy of rotating troops regularly every six months throughout their Armed Forces. The old troops are not withdrawn until the new ones have been trained; as a result, every few months there is a period of overlap when the number of troops is temporarily increased. Press reports that the Afghan Resistance has "pinned down" more than 100,000 Soviet troops are based on a misunderstanding of how these troops are deployed and what they are doing. This misunderstanding enables the Soviets to use their standard troop rotations for propaganda claims that they are "withdrawing" forces, as they did in the fall of 1986 (and earlier, in 1980), bringing the foreign press in to view the "withdrawals" but not of course the arrival of the replacements.

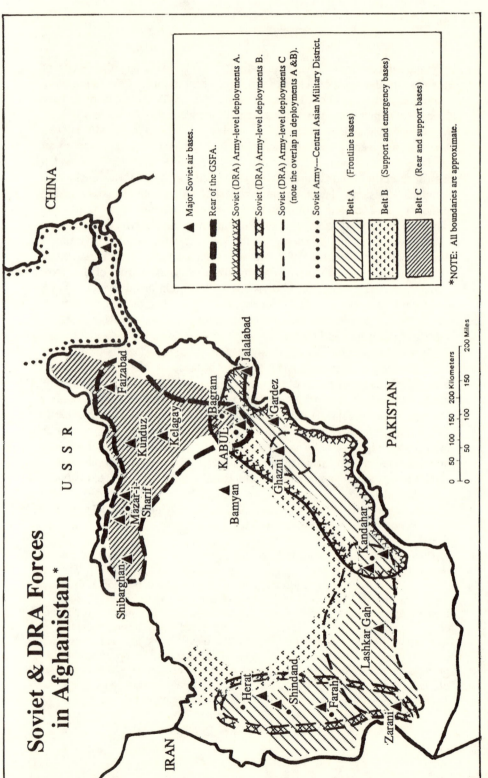

Soviet & DRA Forces in Afghanistan*

CHINA

U S S R

IRAN

PAKISTAN

Shibarghan
Mazar-i-Sharif
Kunduz
Faizabad
Kelagay
Bamyan
Bagram
KABUL
Jalalabad
Gardez
Ghazni
Herat
Shindand
Farah
Lashkar Gah
Kandahar
Zarani

| 0 | 50 | 100 | 150 | 200 Kilometers |
| 0 | 50 | 100 | 150 | 200 Miles |

▲ Major Soviet air bases.

▬▬ Rear of the GSFA.

XXXXXXX Soviet (DRA) Army-level deployments A.

XX XX Soviet (DRA) Army-level deployments B.

▬ ▬ Soviet (DRA) Army-level deployments C
(note the overlap in deployments A &B).

• • • • • Soviet Army—Central Asian Military District.

Belt A   (Frontline bases)

Belt B   (Support and emergency bases)

Belt C   (Rear and support bases)

*NOTE: All boundaries are approximate.

S.G.- with Yossef Bodansky

around the primary airbases, which by early 1983 had been completely rebuilt and modernized. Since then, the Soviets have doubled or tripled the sortie-generating capability of the frontline bases by constructing additional runways, storage, and support installations (see map p. 268, Belt A). They have also improved and enlarged rear and support airbases (Belt C) and have embarked on a massive buildup of support and emergency airbases, most of which are already operational (Belt C).

By mid-1985, the Soviets could support some 500 fixed-wing aircraft in Afghanistan for at least a month without re-supply of POL, ammunition and spares, providing the West did not conduct massive strikes against them.[81] Once completed, the Soviet aerial infrastructure in Afghanistan will be able to support 700 fixed-wing aircraft for a shorter period under similar conditions---or, alternatively, it will be able to support some 500 fixed-wing aircraft even under the conditions of Western massive air attacks.

This infrastructure is optimized for the support of strategic military operations against Iran.

Should the occasion arise for a Soviet attack on Iran, they will attempt to launch it with maximum surprise and their forces in Afghanistan will play a key role. Such an invasion will be spearheaded by the massive dispatch of airborne and heliborne units to key positions, massive airstrikes, and the dispatch of KGB, SPETSNAZ and other special units to urban areas to secure a takeover by friendly local groups as well as to carry out "wet jobs" (assassinations and sabotage).

Units and formations of the ground forces will immediately break into Iran from Afghanistan (without having to go through the Zagros mountains which lie between the USSR and the Persian Gulf), moving swiftly on traditional, proven routes* to consolidate gains, relieve the airborne and heliborne units, and reinforce Soviet and friendly forces in need. Their major objectives will be the permanent securing of the Straits of Hormuz and the Shah-Bahar/Konarak military and port complex in Iranian Baluchistan, both of which are to be captured by airborne troops on the first day of the attack, probably with the active assistance of Baluchis loyal to Soviet agents. If there is no indigenous chaos in Iran when the Soviets choose to invade, their controlled and manipulated "national liberation" organizations (Baluchis, Kurds, various political groups, et al.) can effectively create it.

In the fall of 1981, the Soviets conducted a major penetration into Iran from Afghanistan, intended to verify the axes of transportation between their

---

* Used at least as early as Alexander the Great.

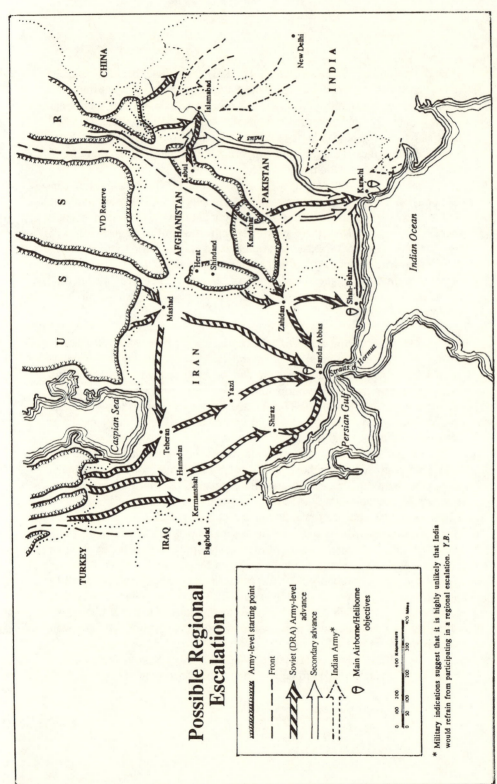

Possible Regional Escalation

xxxxxxxxxx Army-level starting point

— — — Front

Soviet (DRA) Army-level advance

Secondary advance

Indian Army*

Main Airborne/Heliborne objectives

0 50 100 200 300 400 Miles
0 100 200 300 400 Kilometers

* Military indications suggest that it is highly unlikely that India would refrain from participating in a regional escalation. *Y.B.*

S.G.- with Yossef Bodansky

deployment zones in Afghanistan and the routes to the Persian Gulf and the Indian Ocean. They reported that "in two weeks, scattering the remainders of counterrevolutionary bands, [Soviet troops] drove about 1,300 kilometers [815 miles] across the stony desert and the quicksand of Seistan in 50-degree [122° F.] heat."[82] With similar performances, it will take the Soviets just over a week to reach both the Straits of Hormuz and Shah-Bahar† /Konarak with major units of the ground forces [See map p. 270]. The Soviet-trained (and pro-Soviet) Egyptian General Saad el-Shazli has pointed out the significance of Afghanistan as a route to the Persian Gulf:

> As for the lure of the Indian Ocean, Iran and not the Gulf provides the Soviets with a logical route to those warm waters. The Indian Ocean lies 1,500 kilometers from the borders of the Soviet Union, but only 600 kilometers from Afghanistan, where the Soviets already have troops. To pass through the Gulf states on their way to the Indian Ocean, Soviet forces would have to travel through---bluntly, invade---Turkey, Iraq, and on southward: a route of 3,600 kilometers....Why should the Soviets want to do that? A Soviet invasion of Iran would no doubt invoke a full-scale crisis, but nothing approaching the convulsion that would follow a Soviet takeover of Turkey and six Arab states. Turkey is a member of NATO, and the Arab Gulf states are friendly to the U.S., whereas Iran proclaims America the "Great Satan." Unlike an invasion of the Gulf, moreover, a Soviet seizure of Iran would not be a mortal threat to the West: Iranian oil does not go to the U.S. or Western Europe.[83]

Assume, however, that the Soviets would initially elect not to block the Straits of Hormuz, declaring instead that they would not interfere with the flow of oil; in that case the USSR can reach the Persian Gulf with little or no opposition, only to "surprise" the West by a change of policy later on.

In order to facilitate this rapid drive, the Soviets intend to use units of the Baluchi People's Liberation Front (see below) as well as special elements of the Afghan Armed Forces. Both forces have wide popular support in Iranian Baluchistan, and they will portray the Soviet advance as a regional "liberation" mission.

As of mid-1981, thanks to their growing emphasis on the regional aspects of their presence in Afghanistan, the Soviets had built and trained *in the USSR* a 20,000-man Afghan Armed Forces.[84] It was to this that

---

† Renamed Bandar Beheshti in November 1985 but still generally known as Shah-Bahar.

Babrak Karmal referred in May 1981 when he declared, "Our army will become a strong and energetic army capable of defending peace and security not only in Afghanistan, but in the region as well."[85] In early 1982, the acting DRA Defense Minister, Gen. Abdul Qader, told a journalist that "the Afghan Army will have a significant role in the future, like that played by the Cuban and Vietnamese armies."[86] Currently, most of these Afghan forces are still in the USSR, and all of them are kept out of routine fighting.[87]

Regional considerations

The Russians have always considered Afghanistan to be a natural continuation of their Muslim territories. In May 1888, General Skobolev wrote that "the time is approaching when the Hindu Kush, the natural boundary of India, will form the boundary of Russia, and when Herat will probably also be incorporated with the Russian Empire."[88] Little wonder, then, that since 1918---when, even before the consolidation of the Bolshevik Revolution, Moscow clandestinely began inserting instructors and weapons into Afghanistan and training Afghans for subversive actions against their own government and the British in India---the Soviet Union persistently penetrated the country. Since 1978, the Soviet Union has had the opportunity to begin realizing those historic aspirations. When he was in Moscow, Abdul Majid Mangal learned that "the Soviets intend to bring the northern provinces of Afghanistan closer to the Republics of Soviet Central Asia under a special program...the Minister of Cultural Affairs of the Soviet Union spoke about the coordination of cultural affairs of the Soviet Muslim Republics and the northern provinces of Afghanistan."[89] Through a series of economic, cultural and educational projects, the northern provinces of Afghanistan have indeed been virtually incorporated into their "neighborly" Soviet Republics.*

The Soviet attitude towards pacification and propaganda among the rural population of northern Afghanistan is very ambivalent. The classic, highly effective Russian/Soviet military solution calls for a ruthless suppression of the "liberated" population without any effort to win hearts and minds, and the Soviets believe that the key to the final destruction of a Muslim guerrilla movement lies in devastating its popular support through the destruction of the social and economic base of the population and the creation of forced migration by means of famine and atrocities. Only *after* segments of the population in a certain area have been completely subjugated, terrorized into passivity and total submission, are the remainder

---

* See: Amin. also Shroder and Assifi, Krakowski, and Noorzoy.

to be reeducated to provide a certain level of cooperation with the authorities.

But the growing success of Soviet-DRA military operations in Afghanistan has provided the Soviets for the first time with areas in northern Afghanistan where they believe the Resistance has been so thoroughly and devastatingly crushed that its chances for recovery are nil. To a degree, they judge those areas ripe for the introduction of the second stage of pacification and have gradually begun to increase direct propaganda efforts among the population there in an effort to recruit and educate Farsi and Turkish speakers and condition them for their eventual unification with brethren north of the border.

Soviet expectations for southern Afghanistan are no less important and far reaching. For Russia---both before 1917 and since---Afghanistan has always been a temporary stop on the way to the Indian subcontinent, Iran and the warm waters; for the Soviets, the Afghan "revolution" is in addition a stage in the revolutionizing of the entire region. In his first interview after he became President of the DRA, Babrak Karmal reiterated the unyielding commitment of the DRA to such regional revolutionary change, especially in Pakistan. "The Democratic Republic of Afghanistan," he said, "principledly advocates the right of the fraternal Pushtun and Baluchi peoples to express their free will, which should themselves take decisions on their future."[90] Almost six years later, in a series of fierce speeches to an "Assembly of Border Tribes" (which included a large Pakistani delegation) in September 1985, he called explicitly for a unified and "autonomous" Baluchistan, Pushtunistan and Nuristan, declaring, "The unity of Pushtuns and Baluchis is also the guarantor of freedom, progress, unification and national maturity for the Pushtuns and Baluchis," and asserting that DRA policy would be directed toward attaining of "the unity of all the people among the Pushtun tribes and clans, and toward unity with Baluchis."[91]

In short, Babrak revived---and since 1986 Najibullah has intensified---the policies of Greater Pushtunistan and Baluchi independence which, if implemented, would mean the dismemberment of Pakistan and Iran as well as Afghanistan. The DRA initiative has been favorably received in some quarters: in November 1986 a series of uprisings occurred in Pakistan's Administered Tribal Territories, culminating in a major clash with the Pakistan Army and the closing of the Khyber Pass.

Throughout the Near East, the Soviets train, support and manipulate a series of ethnically-based "national liberation" movements and organizations. Some of them (in Iran, for example) fight against their governments, including governments friendly to the USSR, as well as among themselves; but the Soviets recognize that, as a practical matter, it is impossible to have 100 percent control over all of these groups, and are in most cases content to manipulate and exploit them to Soviet benefit.

However, Soviet control over and manipulation of the Baluchis in both Pakistan and Iran are of unprecedented depth and sophistication. Russian encouragement and support for Baluchi nationalism started in the mid-nineteenth century as part of the Great Game. The Soviets intensified this support considerably after the Bolshevik Revolution and even more from the early 1970s on. They have by now persuaded the Baluchis to regard them as their future liberators. A former Pakistani diplomat said, "We Baluchis would not mind if the Russians came in from Afghanistan. We have no love for Pakistan and have never been given a fair deal, although we voted for Pakistan in 1947..."[92]

Although Ataullah Mengal, who is based in London but spends time in Kabul, is believed to be a longtime KGB agent, he is ostensibly an influential non-Communist Baluchi nationalist leader and his rhetoric is representative of many or most Baluchis in Pakistan. Mengal has declared: "The Communists frequently claim that they believe in the rights of nationalities. We believe that within this overall situation, the Russians will have no objection as far as the emergence of an independent Baluchistan is concerned, unless they feel it is against their interest....There is no doubt the Soviets are a big power and like all big powers they wish to extend their influence....But we have objectives and we would certainly accept any aid that comes from any quarter without committing the integrity of Baluchistan or allowing ourselves to be used as anyone's pawn."[93]

The Baluchis in Pakistan have not yet recovered from the excessively violent crushing of their 1973-77 rebellion by Pakistan's Zulfikar Ali Bhutto, aided by the Shah of Iran, whose armies are perceived to have been U.S. trained, equipped and controlled. The Soviets have capitalized on the growing U.S. involvement in Pakistan and the strengthening of its armed forces, enhancing tensions between the Baluchis and the Punjabis who dominate Pakistan, in order to encourage deep overall anti-U.S. sentiments. Currently, the Baluchis, especially in Pakistan, watch with horror Pakistan's growing U.S.-supported military strength. Mengal and other tribal leaders say that with the influx of Afghan refugees into Baluchistan they now fear for their very existence as a people, and that they have given up any hope for a peaceful solution in the context of Pakistan. According to Mengal, their only solution is an independent Baluchistan, and the Soviets, as reliable allies and friends, are the only hope for Baluchi national liberation.[94]

Currently, the Soviets manipulate and have at least some control over the entire territory dominated by the Baluchis: Iranian Baluchistan is actually under the control of the pro-Soviet Baluchi People's Liberation Front (BPLF) and the Baluchi Tudeh Party.[95] Pakistani Baluchistan is deeply penetrated by the KGB; the BPLF is also very active there, and enjoys widespread popular support.[96] In southern Afghanistan there are some ten BPLF training camps and supply installations between Kandahar and Gardez.[97] Run by Soviet agents, these existed without the knowledge of the Kabul authorities for years before the Afghan Communist coup; since mid-1978 they have been considerably enlarged and improved. Since early 1981, the Soviets have intensified the training of the BPLF in southern Afghanistan and the BPLF is allowed to keep their weapons and ammunition in these bases.[98] The Baluchis have repeatedly demonstrated their loyalty to the Soviet-DRA authorities---Baluchi fighters based in Qalat-i-Ghilzai in southeastern Afghanistan and in Kandahar province have frequently clashed with Resistance forces operating in these areas; BPLF detachments operating inside Pakistani Baluchistan have clashed with Afghan Resistance forces based there and have attacked Afghan refugee camps; Baluchi fighters also participate in the operations of the DRA People's Militia in Afghanistan's southern provinces.[99]

Currently, Afghanistan, although it has only an insignificant Baluchi population, is the only country in the world in which Baluchi is an official language.

Conclusions

Since the seventeenth century, the "Great Game" has been the essence of Russian and Soviet foreign policy and imperialism. The Tsarist ruling elite sought to legitimize and enhance its power and authority through expansionism; the Soviet elite continues to do so. Since the seventeenth century, they have publicly pretended to have been reluctant to advance deeper into Central Asia. By their own definition, when they have consolidated control over the vast lands and huge Muslim populations of Central Asia, the Russians (under the Tsars) have been selfless and loyal to their Christian moral commitments and later (under the Soviets) to their "internationalist duties." Each and every additional advance has been explained as a reluctant move imposed upon the State in order to protect the Muslim population which had already become "civilized" and/or Socialist from external intervention and aggression.

The Russian/Soviet Armed Forces have refined a highly effective Operational Art in order to meet strategic requirements. The Soviets believe in the crucial significance of experience accumulated in actual fighting, emphasizing that "although the opportunities for practice in peacetime conditions have greatly improved, this is still no substitute for practice in wartime."[101] For this, they find Afghanistan highly valuable. They are proud of their success in the development of the combined-arms small unit and helicopter and heliborne combat operations in Afghanistan, and even prouder of the tremendous combat experience accumulated by their forces, especially the special forces. More and more officers, warrant officers and senior NCOs with combat experience in Afghanistan are being reassigned to higher military academies or command posts throughout the Soviet Armed Forces, from the GSFG to the Far East. Their promotions are faster than any other Soviet soldiers of the same rank. Emphasis is put on the paramount importance of their sharing their combat experience with their comrades. Discussing a daring VDV commander in Afghanistan who had led many raids, the Soviets emphasize that "his considerable experience in the mountains is even now being studied as part of officer training."

The Soviet Union has brought its expansion into Central Asia to new heights of pragmatism and cynicism. Quoting Clausewitz, Lenin emphasized that "the conqueror is always peace-loving; quite gladly would he march into our state without disturbance." Lenin also declared that the relations between Soviet Russia [sic] and the people of Turkestan were of "gigantic universal-historical significance. For the entirety of Asia, and for all the world colonies, for thousands and millions of people, there would be practical meaning in the relations of the Workers-Peasants Soviet Republic with the until-now oppressed weak peoples." The truth in Lenin's understanding of the historic geopolitical significance of Central Asia has come to the fore in Afghanistan.

The Soviets are in no hurry in Afghanistan. Experience tells them that time is on their side. They claim that "historical experience shows that the forces of reaction cannot withstand the irrepressible desire of peoples for progress and happiness." They rely on the experience of over a thousand years of fighting with the Turkic peoples and more than 200 years of relentless advance into the Muslim territories of Central Asia, which has always met stiff and protracted resistance from the population. It took the Russians many years to solve the Central Asian problem completely and the pacification was extremely harsh and violent, but currently there is no challenge to Soviet rule there. They find the situation in Afghanistan no different. They are employing proven methods and solutions with considerable success---and unless the West provides the Resistance with the required assistance, the Soviets will solve the Afghan problem too.

Soviet long-term geopolitical strategy should not be confused with ongoing military strategy, but their military strategy facilitates the eventual attainment of their geopolitical strategy. Soviet long-term solutions are regional and include the dismemberment or destruction of Pakistan.

History shows that the turning point in the Russian/Soviet struggle for the control of Muslim territories has always occurred when they succeeded in effectively isolating the population and cutting off external support to the local resistance. Currently, the cumulative effect of Soviet special military operations has brought both the Resistance and the Afghan civilian population near to a breaking point and almost total collapse, while the logistical problems of the Resistance amount to its virtual isolation. Taken together, these two trends constitute the key to Soviet success. If these current trends continue, Afghanistan cannot be saved---and the clock will start ticking for Pakistan, for the Soviets will be encouraged to continue their persistent advance towards the warm waters and the oil of the Near East.

The Soviet Union is presently winning in Afghanistan and is closer than ever before to total victory in the Great Game. Afghan courage and fighting spirit are not enough to counter the effective employment of proven Russian/Soviet military methods, which have brought the Soviets very close to crushing the Resistance. This will happen soon provided Western assistance does not speedily become effective. The Soviets are correct when they identify the current situation in Afghanistan as a component of a historical process leading to a regional solution. The West cannot alter historical realities---but it can, and should, capitalize on existing developments to affect the nature of that solution and to bring about results favorable for the entire region and the broader international situation.

Afghanistan is not lost if---*but only if*---Western assistance becomes more effective, and soon. To paraphrase Lord Curzon, the hourglass of destiny is once again turned on its base---and the sands are fast running out.

Notes

To fully document sources for this chapter would require hundreds of notes, far more than space allows, and many of them Russian-language sources accessible only to the specialist. Citations are therefore given only for direct quotations and a few major points. Regarding the undocumented sources, a word on methodology may be useful:

This chapter is entirely based on open sources, primarily Soviet doctrinal writings, military and political; other published Soviet sources, particularly military sources; the writings of various regional movements (Afghan, Iranian, Baluchi, et al.); interviews and communications with numerous defectors from the DRA and other relevant

278

movements and agencies; and interviews and communications with commanders and officials of the variousAfghan Resistance movements and organizations. In addition, of course, sources include a wide range of standard histories, analyses, and other publications, Western and Russian, from both the Tsarist and Soviet periods.

Those who wish to pursue this subject further can take direction from the sources described above and those cited below.

1. Yossef Bodansky, "The Bear on the Chessboard," *World Affairs,* vol. 145, no. 3 (Washington, D.C., winter 1982-1983).

2. S.M. Seredonine, "Historical Perception of the Occupation of Asiatic Russia," *Aziatskava Rossia* [Asiatic Russia] (Petrograd: State edition, 1913): 1. Quoted in René Cagnat and Michel Jan, *Le Milieu Des Emoires* (Paris: Editions Robert Laffont, 1981): 113.

3. Quoted in G. Morgan, *Anglo-Russian Rivalry in Central Asia: 1810-1895* (London: Frank Cass, 1981): 120.

4. Quoted in Anthony Verrier, *Through the Looking Glass* (New York: W.W. Norton & Co., 1983): 12.

5. Quoted in E. Ollier, *Illustrated History of the Russo-Turkish War* (London: Cassell & Co., 1890), 358-359, vol. II. See also: W. K. Fraser-Tytler, *Afghanistan* (London: Oxford University Press, 1953), 319-323.

6. C. Marvin, *The Russian Advance Towards India* (London, 1882), 243.

7. F. Burnaby, *A Ride to Khiva* (London: Cassell, Petter & Galpin, 1877), 373.

8. Michael Voslensky, *Nomenklatura* (New York: Doubleday & Co., 1984): 320.

9. Ibid., 327.

10. Ibid., 353.

11. J.H. Meijer, *The Trotsky Papers, 1917-1922* (London: 1964), 623-625.

12. R.J. Sontag and J.S. Beddie, eds., *Nazi-Soviet Relations 1939-1941* (Washington, D.C.: Department of State, 1948), 257.

13. G. Agabekov, *OGPU: The Russian Secret Terror* (New York: Brentano's, 1931), 66. Before his defection, Georges Agabekov was the head of the OGPU Near Eastern section, in charge of all field activities from Turkey to India.

14. Nikita S. Khrushchev, *Khrushchev Remembers: The Last Testament* (Boston: Little Brown, 1974), 299.

279

15. *Pravda* (30 May 1980).

16. Quoted in Sir C.M. MacGregor, *The Defense of India: A Strategical Study* (Simla, India, 1884), 140-141.

17. Cagnat & Jan, op. cit., 139.

18.*Guardian*, London (16 June 1981). Citing a Polish paper *Zycie Gospodarcze*.

19. Col. V.M. Kulish, *Military Forces and International Relations* (Moscow: Mezhdunarodnyye Otnosheniya, 1972); I. Ye. Shavrov, General of the Army, *Local Wars: History and the Present* (Moscow: Voenizdat, 1981).

20. Kulish, op. cit.; A.A. Yepishev, General of the Army, *The Powerful Weapons of the Party* (Moscow: Voenizdat, 1973); D.A. Volkogonov, *War and Army* (Moscow: Voenizdat, 1977); P.A. Zhilin, *On War and Military History* (Moscow: Nauka, 1984).

21. Editorial, *New Times* (January 1980).

22. Ibid.

23. Former KGB Major Vladimir Kuzichkin cited in *Time* (22 November 1982).

24. N.V. Ogarkov, Marshal SU, *Oktybr* No. 5 (8 May 1980).

25. Material provided by Resistance sources.

26. "Basmachi" entry in *Military Encyclopedia Dictionary* [*VES*], N.V. Ogarkov, Marshal SU, ed. (Moscow: Voenizdat, 1983), 68.

27. Ibid.

28. Editorial, *Pravda* (14 February 1985).

29. Ibid.

30. G. Ustinov, *Izvestiya* (4 October 1984).

31. Ibid.

32. Material provided by Resistance sources, including former DRA secret service officers with direct knowledge of Gulbuddin Hekhmatyar's activities. See also: John Fullerton, *The Soviet Occupation of Afghanistan* (Hong Kong: SCMP, 1983), 68-71; Edward R. Girardet, *Afghanistan: The Soviet War* (New York: St. Martin's Press, 1985), 170-171.

33. *Jane's Defense Weekly* Vol. 4, No. 21 (23 November 1985).

34. C. Duffy, *Russia's Military Way to the West* (London: Routledge & Kegan Paul, 1981), 188.

35. C. Bellamy, *Journal of RUSI* (March 1983).

36. P.A. Zhilin, et al., *History of Art of War* (Moscow: Voenizdat, 1986); Gen. Col. M.A. Gareyev, *M.V. Frunze---Military Theorist* (Moscow: Voenizdat, 1985); B.A. Panov, V.N. Kiselev and I.I. Kartavtsev, *History of Art of War* (Moscow: Voenizdat, 1984).

37. Ismail Akhmedov, *In and Out of Stalin's GRU* (Frederick, Maryland: University Publications of America, Inc., 1984), 84.

38. Agabekov, op. cit., 132-137; Bajanov; G. Brook-Shepherd, *The Storm Petrels* (New York: Ballantine, 1982 [1977]), 5-24.

39. MacGregor, op. cit., 51.

40. G.N. Curzon, *Russia in Central Asia in 1889 and the Anglo-Russian Question* (London: Longmans Green & Co., 1889); Quoted in Gerald de Gaury and H.V.F. Winstone, eds., *The Road to Kabul* (New York: Macmillan, 1982), 182.

41. V. Pozdnyakov, Col., "The Chemical Arm," *The Red Army* (B.H. Liddell Hart, ed., New York: Harcourt, Brace and Co., 1956): 385.

42. V. Verstakov and T. Gaydar, *Pravda* (11 September 1981).

43. Based on the Soviet analysis of the situation. Prof. Rabbani's statement provided by Resistance sources.

44. Material provided by several Afghan defectors through Resistance sources.

45. Saad el-Shazli, Lt. Gen., *The Crossing of the Suez* (San Francisco: American Mideast Research, 1980), 94.

46. Estimate calculated on the basis of the Resistance's combat record and detailed material provided by Resistance sources, especially former DRA officers and NCOs, as well as Soviet prisoners (defectors) held by the Resistance or in the West.

47. Cited in *National Review* (2 November 1984).

48. V. Sukhodol'skiy, *Krasnaya Zvezda* (31 December 1983); Lt. Col. A. Nekrylov, "The Salt of the Earth," *Stars of Valor: In the Land of Afghanistan* (Col. I.M. Dynin, ed., Moscow: Voenizdat, 1985): 164-180.

49. Interview with former Soviet soldiers now in the West; also material provided by several Resistance sources, including testimony of former DRA Border Guard troops who defected.

50. Interview with former Soviet soldiers now in the West.

51. V. Sukhodol'skiy, *Krasnaya Zvezda* (21 April 1984).

52. Material provided by Resistance sources, especially former Afghan Commando officers who defected. These characteristics are fully corroborated by the extensive Soviet doctrinal literature on SPETSNAZ operations.

53. V. Verstakov, *Pravda* (16 February 1984); Lt. Col. N. Panyukov, *Krasnaya Zvezda* (27 August 1986).

54. Interviews with former Soviet soldiers now in the West.

55. Material provided by Resistance sources.

56. Information provided by a recent Soviet emigre.

57. Q. Crommelin, Jr. and D.S. Sullivan, *Soviet Military Supremacy* (Los Angeles: University of Southern California, 1985), V.

58. Material provided by Resistance sources, especially the testimonies of two KhV soldiers, Y. Povarnitsyn and A. Sakharov, captured by the Resistance, and of Brig. Watay, formerly Chief of the Chemical Department of the 99th Rocket Regiment of the DRA Armed Forces, who defected to the Resistance. See also: E.M. Spiers, *Chemical Warfare* (Urbana, Illinois: University of Illinois Press, 1986), 105-112; J. Fullerton, op. cit., 110-118.

59. Ibid.

60. Ibid.

61. Ibid.

62. Testimony of Brig. Watay provided by Resistance sources.

63. See note 59 above.

64. Material provided by Resistance sources.

65. Ibid.

66. Ibid.

282

67. Material provided by Resistance sources.

68. Material provided by Resistance sources.

69. Viktor Suvorov, *Inside the Soviet Army* (London: Hamish Hamilton, 1982), 116-117 & 122; Comparison with the organization, deployment and routine operations of the Soviet forces in Eastern Europe.

70. Deployment constructed on the basis of material provided by Resistance sources, especially former DRA officers and NCOs, as well as Soviet prisoners (defectors) held by the Resistance or in the West.

71. V. Skrizhalin, Lt. Col., *Krasnaya Zvezda* (19 August 1983).

72. "Sorokin" entry, *VES,* op. cit., 691.

73. Material provided by Resistance sources, especially former DRA officers and NCOs, as well as Soviet prisoners (defectors) held by the Resistance or in the West.

74. Ibid.

75. Ibid.

76. R.A. Mason, Air Vice-Marshal, and J.W.R. Taylor, *Aircraft, Strategy and Operations of the Soviet Air Force* (London: Jane's, 1986), 188-189.

77. Material provided by Resistance sources, especially former DRA officers and NCOs, as well as Soviet prisoners (defectors) held by the Resistance or in the West.

78. Material provided by former Afghan senior officers. See also: J.B. Curren and P.A. Karber, *Armed Forces Journal International* (March 1985); Saad el-Shazly, Lt. Col., *The Arab Military Option* (San Francisco: American Mideast Research, 1986), 103 & 207.

79. Material provided by Resistance sources, especially former DRA officers and NCOs, as well as Soviet prisoners (defectors) held by the Resistance or in the West. Soviet textbooks on manpower management and unit organization during the Great Patriotic War (World War II subsequent to 22 June 1941) explain that reorganization and partial building of units around divisional and brigade headquarters in accordance with the prevailing missions were one of the keys to the Soviet operational-level successes, and emphasize that such procedures are still applicable.

80. Material provided by Resistance sources, especially former DRA officers and NCOs, as well as Soviet prisoners (defectors) held by the Resistance or in the West.

81. Material provided by former DRA Air Force officers and *Jane's Defense Weekly* (7 July 1984).

82. I. Shchedrov, *Pravda* (4 October 1981).

83. Saad el-Shazli, Lt. Gen., op. cit., 103.

84. Material provided by Resistance sources, especially former DRA officers and NCOs who trained with and belonged to this force.

85. TANJUG (Belgrade, 27 January 1982).

86. Ibid.

87. Material provided by Resistance sources, especially former DRA officers and NCOs who trained with and belonged to this force.

88. Cited in J. Biggs-Davison, *NATO's Fifteen Nations* (February-March 1981).

89. Material provided by Resistance sources.

90. Statement to TASS (30 December 1979).

91. The "high jirga of the frontier tribes" held in Kabul 14-16 September 1985 included a sizable number of delegates from Pakistan's Administered Tribal Territories; reportedly, they were offered significant inducements of cash and weapons to attend. In any case, all of the officially-reported speeches and statements of the gathering referred repeatedly and pointedly to "the deputies of *all* tribes" representing "the *entire* frontier areas" as well as, specifically, the *"free tribes"* and *" free tribal areas, "* code words for Pakistan's Administered Tribal Territories [emphasis added].

In his opening address on 14 September, Babrak called upon *all* the tribes to defend "the soil of our ancestral homeland and the traditional freedom of the tribes, safeguarding the frontiers of our *united* homeland Afghanistan" [emphasis added], declaring that the "High Jirga of the frontier tribes will initiate efforts for emancipating the Pushtun and Baluch people from the clutches of national and social oppression being continued since the era of British colonial administration times [code words for Pakistan, the successor state to British India]." (FBIS, *South Asia*, 16 September 1985).

"It is our expectation from you tribal frontier elders," he declared, "to realize that the enemies of the new Afghanistan are your enemies and the enemies of the Pushtuns and Baluchi tribes in particular. The Pakistani militarists who are incited and provoked by the diabolical U.S. imperialism strive to encroach upon the freedom of the tribes and to undermine their ancient traditions and customs. They try to occupy your areas..." (ibid., 17 September 1985).

The high tribal assembly issued a resolution emphasizing "the common national and historical identity of the tribes with the people of Afghanistan" and declaring that "The great historic role of the border tribes in the destiny of the country has been revealed and expressed in all documents of the DRA Government. The high tribal

284

assembly firmly supports the principled policy of the DRA State vis-a-vis the Pushtun and Baluch brothers and declares that the Pushtuns and Baluch have a common national and historical destiny with all the Afghan people... [and] strongly condemns the conspiracies and intrigues of international imperialism, especially of the reactionary military regime of Pakistan, against the Pushtuns and Baluchi, aimed at eliminating their traditional freedoms and historical identity... Cursed be the internal and external enemies of the national democratic April Revolution! ...Long live the PDPA!" (ibid., 20 September 1985).

On 21 September, Babrak reported to the PDPA Politburo that "The high jirga of the tribes showed and emphasized that the Pushtuns, *wherever they are,* consider Afghanistan their common historical home... [and that] ...without an independent, free *and powerful* Afg hanistan, the freedom of the Pushtuns and Baluchis is impossible ...The participation of the representatives of the *free border tribal areas* in the jirga points to the *international authority and influence* of Afghanistan and the constructive essence of the PDPA's and DRA's policy. They confirmed the statement of the PDPA leadership concerning support for the struggles of the Pushtun and Baluchi tribes *residing in the free tribal areas* for their independence and freedom." [emphasis added] (ibid., 23 September 1985).

The rhetoric, appeals and exhortations of the 1985 tribal assembly are typical of the constant stream of propaganda directed into Pakistan and Iran. See: FBIS, ongoing.

92. Quoted in General Sir Walter Walker, *The Next Domino?* (Merrimac, Massachusetts: Destiny Publishers, 1980), 98-99.

93. Lifshultz, op. cit.

94. Ibid.

95. Material provided by Afghan Resistance, Baluchi (Pakistani and Iranian) and Pakistani sources. Also diverse material in *Jabal* (The organ of the BPLF); Lawrence Lifshultz, *Economic and Political Weekly, Annual Number* (May 1983); A.B. Awan, *Baluchistan: Historical and Political Process* (London: New Century Publishers, 1985); Tariq Ali, *Can Pakistan Survive?* (London: Verso, 1983); Selig S. Harrison, *In Afghanistan's Shadow: Baluch Nationalism and Soviet Temptations* (Washington D.C.: Carnegie Endowment for International Peace, 1981).

96. Ibid.

97. Ibid.

98. Ibid.

99. Ibid.

100. Yu. V. Chuyev and Yu. B. Mikhaylov, *Forecasting in Military Affairs* (Moscow:

Voenizdat, 1975), English translation: USAF's "Soviet Military Thought Series," Washington, D.C. (USGPO, vol. 16): 60.

"Surely it is within the Central Asian regions of Russia, and the Central Asian borders of Russia, that the real problems of the immediate future are going to develop."

---Chester Wilmot, 1952

Afghanistan & The Muslims of the USSR

Alexandre Bennigsen

TOO OFTEN we in the West hear that the Soviets are waging a "cheap war" in Afghanistan; that their losses are relatively moderate; that the economic pressure of the war is negligible; that there is no public opinion in the USSR and therefore no "Vietnam syndrome" in Moscow; that it may even be for them a "useful" war, an excellent testing ground for new weapons and a training ground for the arms. In brief, we are given to understand that, sooner or later, the Soviets are certain to win the war.

While there may be some truth in the specific points, it is not the whole truth, nor can such a conclusion be so easily drawn. It is impossible to accept such an oversimplified approach, primarily because it does not take into account what may be called the Central Asian dimension of the Afghan war---i.e., the impact of the Afghan war on the Muslim population of Soviet Central Asia---and its corollary: the influence of Soviet Islam on the war in Afghanistan, and the effect of both on the Soviet Union itself. To appreciate this "Central Asian dimension" fully, we must keep in mind a few well-known factors, look at others not so well known, and consider the implications of all.

Today, there are 50 million Muslims in the Soviet Union, with 35 million of them in Central Asia and the remainder divided between the Caucasus and the Volga-Urals. This Muslim population is presently undergoing what demographers call a "demographic explosion," while ethnic Russian population growth is stationary. Thus, by the end of this century,

Muslims will number between 75 million and 80 million out of a total Soviet population of a little less than 300 million: one out of every four Soviet citizens will be a Muslim. Everybody in Central Asia knows that time is on the Muslim side.[1]

The relations between Russians and the Muslim peoples of the Soviet Union are typical colonial relations. And that is a fact. Despite all the efforts of Soviet *agitpropaganda* to prove the opposite, the reality is that the Russians are colonisers and rulers, while the Muslims, who have been conquered by force, are the colonized.[2] Relations between the Russians and the Muslims are the same everywhere, whether it be in areas such as the Volga Tatar region, which was conquered by the Russians more than four centuries ago, or in Turkestan, occupied only a century ago or even less. (Indeed, anti-Russian xenophobia is even stronger among the Volga Tatars than it is in Central Asia.) Between Russians and Muslims, there is neither biological (i.e., through intermarriage) nor cultural assimilation.[3]

Islamic power: past and present

These colonial-type relations are aggravated by the fact that the Muslim territories of the Soviet Union---Central Asia, the Caucasus, Kazan---were in the past among the most prestigious centers of world culture at a time when the Russians were obscure and primitive. Some years ago Samarkand celebrated the 3000th anniversary of its foundation. Tashkent was built 2000 years ago. Persian literary language and literature, one of the world's greatest, was born in Bokhara in the ninth century. In fact, for more than three hundred years---from the thirteenth to the fifteenth century---the Russians were actually vassals of the Muslim Khans of the Golden Horde.

Today, the magnificent architectural monuments of past Islamic power in Samarkand and Bokhara are among the major attractions in the Soviet Union touted by Intourist; tourists flock to admire them. For the Muslims who live their daily lives among them, they are a constant reminder of their own past glories and high culture, in vivid contrast to the stolid concrete-block constructions of their present rulers. All this adds to the continuing undertone of Muslim humiliation.

Ever since Russia, under the Tsars, began its eastward expansion [See map, p. 36.], Muslims have strenuously resisted Russian conquest. It took the Tsars almost a century (1783-1859) to conquer the northern Caucasus and, following the Communist Revolution in 1917 and the collapse of Tsarist control, the Soviet regime was not accepted there without strong resistance. Indeed, throughout the Muslim areas of the Russian empire, many revolts and independence movements broke out after the Revolution. The Basmachi movement in Central Asia, comparable in some of its aspects to the Afghan Resistance, lasted for ten years, from 1918 to 1928 (when Afghan sanctuary for the fighters was cut off), and it was not finally defeated until 1936. Another major revolt broke out again in the North Caucasus during World War II, and was followed by an attempted (though ultimately unsuccessful) Soviet genocide of more than one million North Caucasian Muslims who were brutally deported to Siberia.[4]

For a better understanding of the real relationship between the Russians and the Muslims, we must also recall that between 1932 and 1938, practically the entire brilliant prerevolutionary Muslim intelligentsia was physically exterminated (as the Afghan intelligentsia has been exterminated since 1978). Last, but far from least, it must be kept in mind that since 1928, over a period of sixty years, Moscow has tried---and is still trying, unsuccessfully---to wipe out the Islamic religion. (In 1917, in Tsarist Russia's Muslim areas, there were 30,000 mosques, each with its attached Koranic school. Today fewer than 450 mosques remain to serve 50 million people).[5]

There is a deep and solid reservoir of mutual hatred between Russians and native Muslims in Central Asia, and even more in the Caucasus. Russians are hated and despised. We find this feeling at all the levels of the indigenous Muslim society, but it is particularly strong among the intellectuals. They know that South Yemen, say, or Uganda is independent and sovereign, while the glorious kingdom of Bokhara is not. Muslims in the Soviet Union are neither free nor equal to the Russians, who monopolize all the key positions in the Communist Party, the Army, the K.G.B., and the economy---and the Muslims know it. Even those Muslims who appear to have power have only the appearance, an illusion of power. In the USSR, everybody understands---and nobody better than the Central Asian Muslims---that Soviet rule in Central Asia is maintained not by a special unifying political doctrine, as officially claimed, but by the strength of the Russian armed forces, and by the police.

For more than half a century, the Muslim population, with its ancient and brilliant Irano-Turkic culture, has been isolated from the rest of the Muslim world by a tight Iron Curtain* and has been subjected to the sterilizing influence of Marxism-Leninism in its worst Russian model,

---

* The enforced substitution of the Cyrillic alphabet for the Arabic alphabet that is universally used throughout the Muslim world (except in Turkey where a modified Roman alphabet is used) effectively cut off Muslims in the USSR not only from contemporary thought and life in the Muslim world but from their heritage of poetry, philosophy, and tradition---the entire rich heritage of Islam accumulated over 1200 years. And, of course, it cut them off from the Koran itself, except in the few heavily edited official editions. This single stroke severed them from their religious, cultural, and historic roots.---ed.

particularly debasing in the eyes of Muslims because of its militant atheism. As a consequence, Soviet Muslims, who have lived for such a long time in an intellectual void, are eager and ready to accept any ideology coming from outside that is based on Islam, from the most reasonable to the most extravagant.

This point must be constantly recalled when talking about the impact of the Afghan war on the Soviet Union. Russian Marxism-Leninism might appear attractive to some Western intellectuals or Third World radicals who have not tasted it, but to the Muslims of the Soviet Empire it is nothing but an alien doctrine imposed by foreign conquerors.

Raising an Iron Curtain

In December 1979, however, the Iron Curtain that protected Soviet Central Asia along its political border, artificially isolating Soviet Tajiks, Uzbeks, and Turkomans from their brethren in Afghanistan and Iran, was raised by the Soviet army itself when it invaded Afghanistan. Although Soviet Muslims are no longer used in fighting units---they were pulled out immediately after the invasion---there are thousands of them in Afghanistan as workers, truck drivers, interpreters, etc. Moreover, thousands of Afghans have been sent to Soviet Central Asia as students, technicians, military personnel, and in innumerable delegations. We know that not all of them are Communists or admirers of the Russians.

Oral and written propaganda from Afghanistan and other Muslim countries is now received on a massive scale in Central Asia.[6] As a result, the war in Afghanistan is well known there, and it is followed with an intense and passionate interest by all levels of the Central Asian population. Today, more than seven years after the invasion of Afghanistan, we can begin to appreciate how Soviet Muslims react to the genocide being committed against their Muslim brethren across the border, and what message the Afghan resistance brings to them. It may be summed up by what a Central Asian intellectual told me last year while visiting Western Europe. This man, an academician and a high-ranking Communist Party member, said: "The resistance of the Afghans is for us the first gleam of hope since the Russian conquest."

Indeed, the Afghan resistance brings to the Muslims of the Soviet Union--- first to the Central Asians and then, through them, to the Caucasians, the Tatars, and all the other Muslims of the USSR---a number of important messages:

• The first message is practical: the Soviet Army, presented by official propaganda as the First Army in the world, invincible and irresistable, and possessing crushing technical superiority, is unable to overcome the determined resistance of poorly armed bands. The Russian soldier appears as a poor fighter; the officers as worthless; the high command as inept, unable to devise appropriate strategies and tactics. In short, it turns out to be possible to challenge the Big Russian Brother.

This is a message full of hope: "Resistance is possible." Its impact is, without exaggeration, comparable to the impact that the defeat of Russian armies at the hands of the Japanese in Manchuria in 1905 had on the development of national liberation movements---Polish, Finnish, Caucasian, Tatar---in the Tsarist empire of the time.

• The second message is the rediscovery---the sudden and dramatic rediscovery after a three-generation-long isolation---of the Muslim 'Umma, "the Community of Believers": of a kinship and solidarity with the Afghans, more *religious* than ethnic or national, and, through them, with the entire Muslim world. For the first time since the October Revolution, the Muslims of the Soviet Union are thinking in terms of "Us/Muslims" as opposed to "Them/Russians."

Thus we are back to the pre-1917 situation, with the sole but exacerbating exception that today the average Russian is no longer a Christian, i.e., a believer in God, but an atheist---a difference which, in the eyes of Central Asian Muslims, degrades him to the level of an animal.[7]

• The third message is probably the most ominous for the stability of the Soviet Empire: the war in Afghanistan is understood by the Soviet Muslims (at least by a number of intellectuals) both as a Holy War, a jihad, and as a national liberation movement---*but a national liberation movement in which Islam represents the essential element of ideology.* In other words, for the Central Asians, because the Afghan resistance is successful, Islam--- which Soviet propaganda has for the past seventy years portrayed as an outdated medieval survival---now appears to be younger, more dynamic, and with a higher mobilizing capacity than the aging, dusty and bureaucratic Marxism-Leninism.[8]

In their attempts to explain and excuse the Soviet invasion of Afghanistan, Soviet propaganda and its Western apologists (and conscious or unconscious "relayers") present the occupation of Afghanistan as a purely defensive operation: Soviet troops were sent to Kabul in order to protect Central Asia from the nefarious influence of militant fundamentalist Islam coming from Afghanistan. This is of course an absurdity---first, because before 1978 no organized fundamentalist trends played a significant role in Afghan Islam and second, because Afghan Islam was not aggressive or militant before 1978. Radical Islamic currents and organizations certainly existed in Soviet Central Asia both before and after the 1917 Revolution, but these were purely domestic phenomena which needed no outside influence to grow and develop by themselves.

However, if this was the case *before* the Soviet-backed Communist coup of 1978, it is now true that Soviet invasion and the consequent genocide of the Afghan nation have helped to transform the traditional liberal Islam of Afghanistan into a militant and dynamic political ideology. It is also true that this spirit of the Afghan jihad is slowly but steadily spreading first into the neighboring countries and then into the entire Muslim world, including Soviet Muslim territories. In other words, by their inept actions in Afghanistan the Soviets themselves have created the very threat they claimed to fear, a tiger on which they are now riding.

The shifting political climate

Today it is no longer possible to ignore the positive aspect of the Afghan war on the political climate in Soviet Central Asia. Soviet borders are crossed by Afghan Resistance propagandists;[9] written and published propaganda, both religious and political, is regularly smuggled into the Muslim republics of the USSR. In 1984, 1985, and 1986, the Soviet Central Asian press revealed that booklets printed in Peshawar were circulating all through Central Asia, as far north as Frunze in Kirghizia.[10] Foreign broadcasts are regularly recorded on cassettes by well-organized groups of local "fanatics," a term generally used by the Soviets to designate members of Sufi groups.[11]

(Sufism, the mystical search for God, represents today an important spiritual and also political aspect of Islam throughout the world. It is becoming increasingly important within the context of Islam in the Soviet Union as well. The adepts are grouped in brotherhoods *(tariqa)*---secret and closed societies forbidden by Soviet legislation---which are bound by a complicated sets of compulsory rules that regiment every aspect of an adept's life, and by a common ideology: the defense of Islam against the rule of the unbelievers and against the bad Muslims who serve them is part of their creed. Today these brotherhoods are active in the USSR: the Naqshbandiya (founded in the fourteenth century) in all Muslim republics; the Qadiriya (founded twelfth century), especially active in North Caucasus; and the Yassawiya (also twelfth century) centered around the Ferghana Valley.

In the last two years, we have had strong evidence of a number of acts of solidarity between Central Asian Muslims and the mujahideen of the Afghan Resistance, although this has seldom been reported in the world press. In May 1984, a reliable emigre publication[12] reported that a group of Soviet Tajiks were arrested in Dushanbe for maintaining contacts with the Afghan

Resistance. In April 1984 widespread demonstrations of Uzbek students on behalf of the Afghans occurred in the region of Termez in southern Uzbekistan. As a result, villages in Soviet Uzbekistan---inside the Soviet Union itself---were bombed by Soviet aircraft and attacked by Soviet troops. Following these incidents, a number of Soviet Muslims---Uzbeks, Tajiks and Turkomans---escaped to Afghanistan; some have joined Afghan Resistance guerrilla units. One of the demonstrators, a young Uzbek teacher and former member of the Communist League (Komsomol) from Termez who escaped to Afghanistan and joined the mujahideen, was interviewed by an Afghan journalist in the Wardak area in 1985.[13]

In central Afghanistan the same journalist has also seen several Tajik and Turkoman families who escaped from the Soviet Union after the April 1984 incidents in Termez. Some of the refugees from Uzbekistan settled in the liberated areas of Afghanistan; others made their way to the refugee camps in other countries.

But the most spectacular and, from the Soviet point of view, the most dangerous impact of the war in Afghanistan is the religious revival which, according to all Soviet mass media, is being manifested in all Muslim republics of the USSR. This revival---which, according to the Soviets themselves, is a direct consequence of the Afghan war---involves not the well-domesticated and loyal "official Islam" paraded before the Muslim world, but the strongly anti-Communist and anti-Russian "parallel Islam" represented by Sufi brotherhoods.[14]

All Soviet media link the burgeoning Islamic revival to the growth of anti-Russian nationalism among the Muslims of Central Asia. Several official statements have been made by Soviet rulers, including a statement in January 1986 by Usmankhojaev, the new First Secretary of the Central Committee of the Communist Party of Uzbekistan. Speaking at the 21st Congress of the Communist Party of Uzbekistan and denouncing the dangers of religious revival in his republic, Usmankhojaev warned: "Religion clears the way for nationalism, chauvinism, and xenophobia."[15] In August 1986, K.M. Makhkamov, First Secretary of the Central Committee of the Communist Party of Tajikistan, told those in charge of ideological work in his republic that "during the last few years . . . the level of religiosity has increased perceptibly" and that a new category of "religious fanatics" has recently appeared in Tajikistan, which he called *the adepts of Wahhabism*, "an extremely reactionary religious-political movement."[16] In November 1986, First Secretary Mikhail Gorbachev himself, on his way to New Delhi, paused in Tashkent to talk to Uzbek Party leaders and launched a vicious attack on Islam, calling for a "resolute and uncompromising struggle against religious phenomena."[17]

If the Afghan resistance continues---and nothing allows us to imagine its imminent end---the deterioration of the political climate along the entire southern "soft belly" of the USSR may become a real threat to the unity of the Soviet Empire. This threat is especially serious if we remember that by the end of this century (only fifteen years hence), the Muslim population in Central Asia alone will be more than 50 million, and that in this area the Russians will be reduced to the status of a small minority. It is obvious that the destabilization of Central Asia (or, even more modestly, a serious deterioration in Russian-Muslim relations) and the growth of local nationalism and xenophobia would be among the most powerful factors that might oblige the Soviets to put an end to their adventure in Afghanistan and force them to look for a genuine political solution.

Early in December 1986, bloody anti-Russian ethnic riots took place in Alma Ata, the capital of Kazakhstan. The official reason given for the disturbances---the replacement of the Kazakh local Communist Party leader by a Russian---is hardly a full explanation. According to Soviet press reports, the rioters were Kazakh students (members of the Communist Youth Organization) and professors at the Alma Ata University (members of the Communist Party), manipulated by "nationalists, hooligans, anti-social elements, and parasites." "Anti-social elements" and "parasites" are, in the Soviet political literature of Central Asia, synonymous with "religious fanatics" and fundamentalists. Those who have a personal knowledge of the political situation in Kazakhstan---the "most nationalist" republic of Central Asia---and who know the intense, passionate interest of the young Kazakh intellectuals in the cause of the Afghan mujahideen, cannot doubt that the riots in Alma Ata are an indirect backlash from the war in Afghanistan.

The ideological conflict

Recently, Soviet propaganda has been insisting on the desire of the Kremlin to find a "political solution" to the war in Afghanistan. Many Western journalists and "experts," as well as outright Soviet apologists, help to relay and disseminate this message. Some of them support its acceptance and implementation, often insisting that the final Soviet victory is inescapable, that it is only a matter of time. For instance, in May 1986 Heléne Carrére d'Encausse, a French specialist on the USSR, expressed this position in an interview given to *Le Monde* in which almost every statement is a misinterpretation of the facts, and which can only be explained by an abysmal ignorance of the real situation in Afghanistan. She said,

> The Soviet aim in the long run is not military victory but the "Mongolization" of Afghanistan. With all the appearance of independence, it will be an unconditional ally, a kind of Sixteenth Soviet Re-

> public. [The Soviets] are counting on time. There are Afghan children in Soviet schools. Soviet administration covers Afghan territory. Karmal was unable to liquidate the Resistance, but his successor has succeeded "in a Soviet way" to "pacify" Afghanistan. He has demoralized the population and a portion of the Resistance. The process of normalization will be accelerated and it will allow the Soviet Union to pull out it troops. . . .[18]

In reality, Kabul administration covers only an insignificant portion of the Afghan territory, and the Afghan children in the Soviet schools are far from becoming---as too many Western "experts" imagine---dedicated partisans of the Communist system. On the contrary, we have plenty of evidence that they are authentic Soviet/Russian haters.[19]   And it is an absurdity to talk about the "Mongolization" of Afghanistan after more than eight years of genocide.

In fact Moscow will be obliged to find a genuine political solution to the Afghan war and pull out of Afghanistan, even at the cost of sacrificing the geopolitical advantages they sought to gain there, *only if and when the war in Afghanistan becomes politically too expensive---which is not yet the case.*

However, a growing number of Muslims in the Soviet Union and in the Muslim world abroad are beginning to understand that the war in Afghanistan is first of all an ideological conflict. It is in the realm of ideology---the conflict between Islam and Marxism---that its long-term effects could be felt throughout all Soviet Muslim republics, where "Marxism" is perceived not as an internationalist philosophy but as a technique devised by the Russians to protect their colonial rule. It would be foolish to imagine that such ideological forces, once set in motion by the war in Afghanistan, can be easily restrained, even in the event of a very unlikely Soviet military victory.

It is therefore not unreasonable to conclude that the "contamination" of Central Asia has already begun, and it is difficult to imagine how Soviet leaders can stop it.

For the time being, two factors can make the war in Afghanistan more costly to the Soviets: the worsening of Russian-Muslim relations in Central Asia (a process already begun, as shown by the 1986 riots in Alma Ata) and a more active support by the Muslim world abroad both for the cause of the Afghan resistance and for Soviet Muslims' attempts to reestablish contacts with their brethren in Islam beyond Soviet borders.

There is plenty of evidence that both factors are beginning to emerge. The struggle of the Afghan mujahideen is becoming a question of growing concern for public opinion in many Muslim countries, especially among the younger generation. The Russian is steadily acquiring the profile of the "Greatest Devil," even worse than the American.

After more than half a century of total isolation from one another, the Muslim world is rediscovering its forgotten Soviet brothers. These in turn are discovering that they belong not only to the Communist empire dominated and subjugated by the Russian *kafir* ("infidel") but also to a much larger world of Islam.

NOTES

1. This problem has been analyzed in detail by several American demographers. See esp.: Murray Feshbach & Stephen Rapawy, "Soviet Population and Manpower: Trends and Policies,"*Soviet Economy in a New Perspective*, Joint Congressional Economic Committee of the U.S. Congress, 14 Oct. 1976; Godfrey S. Baldwin, "Population Projections by Age and Sex for the Republics and Major Economic Regions of the USSR, 1970 to 2000,"*International Population Report*, Series P-91, No. 26; Foreign Demographic Analysis Division, U.S. Bureau of the Census, Washington, D.C., Sept. 1979; Edmund Brunner Jr., "Soviet Demographic Trends and the Ethnic Composition of Draft Age Males, 1980-1995," Rand Publications Series, #N61654-NA. Los Angeles, Feb. 1981.

2. Space does not permit a detailed analysis here of the mechanisms which maintain Russian domination in the Muslim republics. Suffice it to say that all key positions in the Soviet Army, the K.G.B., the Border Guards (which are part of the K.G.B.), the Department of Economic Planning, and the ministries of Irrigation and Finance are controlled by Russians. The "natives" have only the facade and illusion of power, in such non-substantive roles as (for the individual republic) Chairman of the Council of Ministers, Minister of Foreign Affairs [!], President of the Supreme Soviet, etc.

The same holds true for the Communist party hierarchy: at all levels (republic, region, district, city), the second secretary, who is the man who actually controls the selection and promotion of cadres---in other words, the actual Party boss---is always a Russian or other Slav.

3. In all Soviet Muslim republics, the "native" Muslim and Russian communities co-exist separately but do not mix. Mixed marriages remain as rare today as they were seventy years ago. According to Muslim Shari'at law, a marriage between a Muslim woman and a non-Muslim man is illegal. A Muslim man is permitted to marry a non-Muslim wife, but the children must be brought up as Muslims. A recent survey taken in the Caucasian Republic of Daghestan illustrates the fact that these Muslim legal taboos remain in force despite the permissive Soviet law that formally prevails: although by 1973 twelve percent of the population of Daghestan was Russian, out of 7,495 marriages in 1973 in which the bride was Muslim, only a total of 54 (i.e., .007 percent) involved an ethnic Russian partner. See: S. Gadzhieva & Yankova, *Daghestanskaya Sem'ia* ("The Daghestani Family"); Makhach-Qala, 1979.

4. During the winter of 1943/44, the entire Chechen, Ingush, Karachay, and Balkar population of North Caucasus, together with a number of Muslim Ossetians, Daghestanis, and Western Cherkess, were rounded up and deported to camps in Siberia and North

Kazakhistan. These were followed in Spring 1944 by the entire population of Crimean Tatars.

The deported Muslims were accused of collaboration with the invading German army; but since the Wehrmacht never reached the borders of the Chechen-Ingush Republic, it is totally absurd to pretend that the deported Chechens and Ingushes had collectively--- or even individually---collaborated with the invaders.

It has been estimated that 20 to 30 percent of a total of more than one million members of these minorities died during the deportation. See: A. Avtorkhanov, *Narodoubiistvo v SSSR* ("Genocide in the USSR"); Munich, 1952.

5. There are no official figures on the total number of functioning mosques in the Soviet Union. This estimate of 450 mosques for the entire USSR is based on combined fragmentary statements from various official sources, e.g., 143 mosques in Uzbekistan in 1979 (personal communication of a high-ranking Soviet *ulema* to the author) to serve a Muslim population of more than 13 million; 18 mosques in Tajikistan as of 1964 (*Nauka i Religiia;* Moscow, January 1964, p. 22) for a Muslim population which reached approximately 3.5 million in 1979; 4 small village mosques in Turkmenistan in 1979 (several concordant Soviet sources) for a Muslim population of 2.5 million; etc.

6. See: A. Bennigsen and S. Enders Winbush, *Mystics and Commissars: Sufism in the Soviet Union,* London: C. Hurst; and Berkeley: University of California Press, 1985: 88-93.

7. For Muslims, Christians and Jews as well as Muslims belong to the same revelation, received by their common ancestor, the Prophet Ibrahim (Abraham). Despite their "incomplete faith," Christians and Jews are nonetheless "People of the Book" (*Ahl al-Kitab)*---very different indeed from the unbelievers (kafirs or *bidin).* Even today, for Central Asian Muslims the words "atheist" (in Tajik Persian, *bidin;* in various Turkic languages, *dinsiz)* and "Godless" (*Allasyz)* are still synonyms for "scoundrel."

To a Muslim, even an "unbelieving" one, an atheist is not a romantic rebel against convention but simply an idiot.

8. This is illustrated by the passionate interest shown by all Soviet Muslims, and particularly by the intellectuals travelling abroad, in recent Islamic publications. We scholars in the West have all seen our Central Asian colleagues, while visiting American or European universities, rush---whenever they can escape the control of the KGB watchdogs who accompany them---to the bookstores and libraries, to read the forbidden writings of Pakistani, Iranian, or Egyptian Islamic revivalists.

9. The crossings are especially frequent along the borders of Turkmenistan and Tajikistan, if we judge by the number of references in the Soviet Central Asian press. To list only the most significant among many articles, see:

For the Turkmenistan border: Maj. General G. Zgerskii in *Turkmenskaiia Iskra,* Ashkhabad, 7 December 1982; Lt. E. Kharchenko, *id.,* 15 March 1983; Iu. Podzolov, *id.,* 6 April 1983; V. Orlov, *ibid.,* 16 July 1983; M. Andreev, *ibid.,* 28 July 1984; M. Andreev, *ibid.,* 7 April 1985.

For the Tajikistan border: M. Andreev in *Kommunist Tajikistana,* Dushanbe, 29 May 1982; V. Volkodav, *id.,* 4 December 1983; M. Andreev, *ibid.,* 4 October 1984; Maj. General Britvin, *ibid.,* 28 May 1985.

For the Uzbekistan border: Maj. General V. Shliakhtin in *Pravda Vostoka,* Tashkent,

28 May 1985.

Several foreign travellers inside Afghanistan have witnessed the crossing of Soviet borders by mujahideen. The most interesting testimony was given recently by two Turkish journalists who crossed the border into Soviet Turkmenistan with a group of mujahideen. See: Hayrettin Kalyomen in *Hürriyet,* Istanbul, 30 March 1986, and Mim Kemal Öke in *Tercuman,* Istanbul, 6, 7, 8, 9, and 11 April 1986.

10. Pamphlets printed in Russian in Peshawar in 1982-83 by the Afghan mujahideen and smuggled into Central Asia included: *The Life of the Great Muhammad; How to Pray; Is Religion No Longer Necessary?* (this, by the Egyptian revivalist Muhammad Kutab); and *Islam and Social Justice* (by the Pakistani radical theologian Sayed Abul-Ala al Mawdoodi. The appearance of these pamphlets in Kirghizia was denounced in 1984 by M. Abdyldaev, Director of the Institute of Philosophy and Law of the Academy of Science of the Kirghiz SSR, in an article entitled "Behind the Screen of Islam" (*Sovetskaia Kirghizia,* Frunze: 30 June 1984.) The same pamphlets, translated into Uzbek, appeared the same year in several cities of Uzbekistan: Tashkent, Samarkand, and Namangan; see *Soviet Özbekistoni,* Tashkent, 20 June 1984. See also: Bennigsen, "Mullahs, Mujahidin, and Soviet Muslims," *Problems of Communism,* Washington, D.C., November-December 1984: 28-44.

11. Among many other evidences, see the report by K.M. Makhkamov, First Secretary of the Central Committee of the Communist Party of Tajikistan at a meeting of ideological workers of Tajikistan, in which Makhkamov mentioned "the appearance in the republic of obnoxious religious literature, recorded, written, and on video films from abroad"; *Agitator Tadjikistana,* Dushanbe, 20 October 1986: 9.

12. *Possev,* May 1984; see also Julia Wishnevetsky, "References to Afghanistan in Samizdat", *Radio Liberty Research Bulletin, RL 143/84,* 6 April 1984.

13. The interview was tape-recorded, and I have a copy of the audio cassette tape.

14. Two Sufi brotherhoods, the Naqshbandiya and the Qadiriya, are especially active in the Muslim territories of the USSR. Both are also well-represented in Afghanistan and take an active and significant part in the Resistance. Pir Sayed Ahmad Gailani, leader of the Qadiriya Sufi brotherhood founded by his ancestor, heads the National Islamic Front of Afghanistan (NIFA, or its Persian nickname, MAHAZ), one of the most important Resistance groups fighting in southern Afghanistan, particularly in Paktia and Paktika provinces. Prof. Sibgatullah Mojadidi, an important leader of Naqshbandiya Sufism in the region, heads the small but significant National Front for the Liberation of Afghanistan. A huge Soviet literature exists on the recent development of Sufi brotherhoods in the USSR. See: A. Bennigsen, "Sufism in the USSR: A Bibliography of Soviet Sources," *Central Asian Survey,* Vol. 2-4: 81-107; Oxford, December 1983. Also: A. Bennigsen and Ch. Lemercier-Quelquejay, "Muslim Religions: Conservation and Dissent in the USSR," *Religion in Communist Lands;* Keston, Vol. 7-3: 148-159, Autumn 1979. Also: Bennigsen and Winbush, *op. cit.*

15. *Pravda Vostoka,* Tashkent, 31 January 1986. For a recent analysis of Usmankhojaev's report, see: "Muslims in USSR---Tough Times Ahead," *Arabia,* Vol. 5, No. 56: 45. London, April 1986.

The same alarm was sounded in almost identical terms by K.M. Makhkamov, First

299

Secretary of the Central Committee of the Communist Party of the Tajik SSR at the 20th Congress of this party, held in Dushanbe on 24 January 1986. See: *Kommunist Tajikistana*, Dushanbe, 25 January 1986.

16. *Agitator Tadikistana*, Dushanbe, 20 October 1986, p. 13. In Soviet political literature, the term "Wahhabism" is synonymous with "Islamic revivalism." This statement confirms the claim of the Jamiat Islami Afghanistan and Hezb-i-Islami Afghan Resistance organizations to have established contacts with various national-religious groups within Soviet Tajikistan.

17. *Pravda Vostoka*, Tashkent, 25 November 1986.

18. *Le Monde*, 11/12 May 1986.
Mme. d'Encausse is not alone. Editorial and Op Ed pages of most major journals in Europe and the U.S. provide other examples. For a sampling, see: Jonathan Steele in*The Guardian*, 17-19 March 1986; Antero Pietila in the *Baltimore Sun*, 9 13 March 1986; Selig S. Harrison, numerous articles including: *Foreign Policy*, No. 41, 1980-81; *Parameters*, Summer 1985; *Washington Post*, 13 May 1984; *South, The Third World Magazine*, March 1985; *New York Times*, 12 July 1982; *USA Today*, 27 December 1982; *New York Times*, 17 March 1986, etc., plus widely quoted lectures and interviews.
Moreover, it seems that hardly any parliamentarian, Congressman, or other distinguished visitor to Moscow returns without announcing that one or another important Soviet official has confided to him that Moscow is eager to find a political solution that would enable Soviet forces to withdraw from Afghanistan. These hopeful messengers are apparently unaware that Moscow has been disseminating such rumors in almost identical form via other "unofficial channels" since February 1980, less than two months after the invasion began, when Dr. Armand Hammer reported on Brezhnev's eagerness to withdraw. Usually these returning visitors deliver their message as a new development and urge that a political settlement be explored while the opportunity offers. See, for example: Flora Lewis, "No Peace for the Afghans," *New York Times*, 5 June 1986.

19. The removal of Muslim children from their parents is a technique used by the Tsars as well, as early as the eighteenth century in the Middle Volga territories. There, young Tatar children aged eight to twelve were forcibly converted to Orthodoxy and placed in special boarding schools run by Orthodox missionaries from Kazan. The Tsarist regime hoped that these new converts---Christians, but speaking Tatar---would become middlemen between the Russian administration and the Muslim masses. The results were disastrous. Galimjan Ibragimov, the best Soviet Tatar historian, comments on this first attempt to create a "Russified Muslim": "The results were exactly the opposite of what the administration expected. Instead of assimilating the Muslims, this policy created among them a deep and long-lasting hatred for everything Russian."*Tatary v Revoliutsii 1905 goda* ("Tatars in the 1905 Revolution"); Kazan, 1926: 27.
The ruthless methods employed in the eighteenth century were not very different from those used under Stalin and his successors in the Soviet schools where Muslim children were---and still are---subjected to relentless anti-religious propaganda from the age of four. But once again the results are far from the expectations of the authorities. Today, sixty years after the beginning of the Soviet educational experience, it is among the younger Muslim generation---educated under Stalin, Khrushchev, and Brezhnev---that one finds the most dedicated and outspoken nationalists and anti-Russian xenophobes. It is doubtful that the Soviets will obtain better results with Afghan children.

"Marxism is incompatible with national-ism...Marxism replaces any kind of nationalism with an internationalism which fuses all nations in greater unity."

--Joseph Stalin

The Sovietization of Afghanistan

A. Rasul Amin

SINCE THE Soviet invasion of Afghanistan, international attention has been mainly focused on the war, the refugees in Pakistan, the "indirect negotiations" conducted under U.N. auspices by Pakistan and the Kabul regime, and statements by Soviet leaders. It is unfortunate that at this crucial juncture the world media and even the Resistance have paid little attention to the Sovietization policy now being carried out inside Afghanistan itself, a policy which has important implications for Soviet intentions regarding any possible "political solution," and for the future of Afghanistan.

There is a great difference between controlling a country by military means, and transforming it into a committed member of the Communist bloc. A basic step in accomplishing such a transformation is to gain control of the minds of an invaded people through an absolute dominance over the sources of information available to them, thereby regulating what they read, what they hear and, over a time, what they think and how they view their history, their society and themselves.

The cogs of the mechanism designed to sovietize the minds of the Afghan people are the research studies institutions, curriculum departments and compilation and translation centers in Moscow, Tashkent and Kabul. Here Soviet-oriented ideology, political, historical and economic tracts, text books and literary works are prepared in Pushto, Farsi and other Afghan languages by Party-directed state scholars who "reconsider" Afghan history, society, religion, culture, politics, et al in the light of Marxist-Leninist thought in order to legitimize an unpopular regime and an illegal occupation. In so doing, the occupiers are laying the ideological foundation for reconstructing Afghan society in the image of the Soviet model.

The production of this gigantic propaganda machine already floods the book stalls, educational institutions and propaganda centres in Kabul and other occupied cities, spreading Soviet-style Communism and explaining each dimension of the Afghan crisis in the light of the Party line. In addition, electronic and printed media and official agencies are busily at work using all possible means to gain converts to Communism and providing disinformation about the war, the invasion, the occupation, the regime, the refugees and current international developments relating to the Afghan crisis.

Through these materials and the efforts of Soviet personnel working in Afghanistan both as "advisors" to DRA agencies and in direct contact with the population, and with the assistance of their Afghan Communist subordinates, the sovietization program now permeates all aspects of Afghan social structure, education and cultural life in Kabul, Mazar-i-Sharif and the other areas under Soviet control. Through radio, publications, clandestine penetration and other means, efforts are being made to extend it into unoccupied areas as well.

The Central Asian model

Even before the Bolshevik Revolution, unrest among Central Asian Muslims directed against the Russian conquerors and colonists was widespread. Between 1905 and 1916, a movement for independence and the restoration of their age-old cultural heritage spread to all strata of the Muslim communities, leading to efforts to regain their freedom from the tottering Tsarist colonial empire.

In this crucial period, Lenin recognized both the immediate usefulness and the long-range dangers of Muslim separatism and appealed to the Muslims (with some success) through three manifestos: *On the Socialist Revolution and The Rights of Nations to Self-determination, On the Nationalities Question* and *Rights of the People of Russia,* which promised self-determination for all non-Russian nationalities in a new Socialist union, including the right to secede.

After seizing power in 1917, he soon went back on his word; but the new Bolshevik regime, faced with continuing Muslim demands for independence and self-determination, had to reckon with the danger that the Muslims would join the anti-Bolshevik forces. In 1918, Lenin therefore embarked on a two-track policy. To pacify Muslim opposition, he created a Commissariat for Internal Muslim Affairs with a Tatar as its nominal head;

important religious books and objects were ostentatiously presented to a regional congress of Muslims as a gesture of goodwill from the new Bolshevik regime. But soon the Muslim Commissariat was replaced by the Commissariat of Nationalities, headed by Joseph Stalin, who soon made Soviet policies clear: "Marxism is incompatible with nationalism, even the most just, pure, and civilized nationalism."[1]   Another member of the Commissariat spelled it out further: "National culture is for backward countries and we are a Communist country."[2]

In 1918, a commission under Stalin's chairmanship reorganized the entire administrative structure of Central Asia on a new cultural basis: Turkestan was fragmented into various republics and areas, named for the majority ethnic community in each---Uzbeks, Turkomans, Tajiks, Kazakhs, Kirgiz, etc.---but incorporated into the Soviet Union under the strict centralized control of the Communist Party.

This reorganization, ostensibly intended to grant the Muslims full autonomy in cultural and educational fields, was in fact designed to divide the residents of the previous larger political units and alienate them from one another. In each new SSR, the majority language was recognized as the official and academic language of the particular republic but the other ethnic and cultural minorities in the republic were not required by law to learn it. Instead, each ethnic group was supposed to run its own schools and cultural institutions in its own mother tongue, isolating them from one another. The Russian language was given the status of *lingua franca* among all of them, used in the schools and offices as the official and diplomatic language of the entire Soviet Union.

The Commissariat of Nationalities launched this campaign to russify and sovietize the Muslim communities, eradicate the local languages, and gradually replace them with Russian, in order to eliminate the national characteristics of the Muslim communities and mold them in the image of the new Communist society. Their dialects (of Persian and Turkish, for the most part) were declared to be separate languages---Tajik, Uzbek, etc.---while after some time the Cyrillic alphabet replaced the traditional Arabic script in which they had been written, cutting them off from their own ancient literature as well as from contact with the rest of the Muslim world and making them dependent on Soviet cultural sources. Espionage networks were established in each locality; those who spied on their fellows were honored as true patriots, loyal activists, and the guardians of Communist ideology, the Party, and the State.

That Central Asian policy is the model for Soviet policy in Afghanistan today. The principle strategic objectives are as follows:

1. To divide the country on an ethnic and cultural basis by giving each

unit cultural autonomy and its own language for official transactions and schooling. In due course, this fragmentation will necessitate the adoption of Russian (instead of Farsi) as the *lingua franca* and the medium of instruction in all Afghan schools from primary schools to higher studies. Certainly the KGB personnel experienced in this craft will be the real administrators of the new institutions, either in the guise of advisers or as technical supervisors.

2. To disintegrate the cultural and religious ties between different tribes and ethnic groups according to the Central Asian model, thereby reshaping the country's structure along lines based on Lenin's policy as expressed in *On the Nationalities Question.* If effectively implemented, this would certainly lead Afghanistan towards increased fragmentation, atomization, alienation, and ultimate social disintegration under centralized Soviet domination.

Rewriting Afghan history

In order to legitimize an unpopular and unacceptable regime and an illegal invasion, and to lay the groundwork for permanent ongoing Afghan acceptance of Soviet control and domination in whatever form it may take, Afghan history has been not merely reinterpreted but actually rewritten to promote two basic themes:

1. The Soviet Union and, before it, Tsarist Russia, are portrayed as having been for the past 200 years the main defenders and supporters of Afghan liberty and independence against repeated and continuing attacks by imperialist aggressors of the West, which is depicted as the sole source of any threat;

2. The historical primacy of Afghanistan's cultural ties with the Indian subcontinent, Persia [Iran], and the Muslim Middle East are downgraded in order to emphasize, enhance, and if necessary manufacture primary ties to Turkestan (now Soviet Uzbekistan, Turkmenistan and Tajikistan) and its peoples as the essential basis of Afghan culture.

These themes are constantly reiterated in the press, the broadcast media, films, poetry (a major cultural medium among Afghans), songs, stories, and of course the speeches of Afghan Communist leaders; they are elaborated in the rewritten textbooks of the schools.

To reinforce the first of these themes, Soviet and Afghan propagandists strive to keep alive the national memory of the two nineteenth-century British invasions, elaborating on those bits of national history that are known to every Afghan from the cradle: the British invasions of 1839-42 and 1878 (which ended in British withdrawal and, in 1842, a disastrous defeat), plus the Third Anglo-Afghan War of May 1919 [which, unknown to many Afghans, was initiated by Afghanistan and lasted less than a month, but which has been mythologized into a third triumph over British power.---ed.].

These long-gone conflicts are treated as though the British threat had continued until recently and the United States is introduced as the present-day successor to British imperialism, with U.S. policies the continuation of nefarious British designs on Afghanistan, while a good word is said even for the Tsars in order to depict Russia and the Soviet Union as the historically staunch friends and allies of the Afghan people:

> For the last century and a half British imperialism was *the only constant threat* to the disintegration and occupation of Afghanistan. But contrary to this policy, the Tsarist regime and the Soviet Union have *always been* determined to keep the solidarity and sovereignty of the country intact. [Emphasis added][3]
> The principled policy outlined by Lenin himself has been the main factor in establishing good neighborly relations with Afghanistan.[4]
> The Soviet Union gave great support to the struggle of the Afghans against the British and it was the first country to recognize Afghanistan's independence in March 1919. The Afghan-Soviet Treaty of Non-Aggression and Neutrality, signed in 1926, laid the foundation of good neighborly relations in the years to come. This treaty strengthened the national independence and international status of non-aligned Afghanistan. After the Second World War, the United States paid great attention to the strategic position of Afghanistan in order to bring it under its political influence through economic investment, just to destroy its years-old traditional non-aligned status.[5]

The Soviet Union is constantly identified as "our old faithful friend" and never mentioned without such epithets as "brotherly," "generous," "principled," "valiant," and "fraternal." No mention is made, of course, of the Russian seizure of Panjdeh, of Tsarist and Soviet military incursions into Afghan territory, or of Moscow's secret annexation of the entire Wakhan a few months after the 1979 invasion.

King Amanullah, who established friendly relations with the Soviet Union and whose overthrow in 1929 the USSR tried to prevent by sending Soviet troops into Afghanistan in Afghan uniforms, is hailed as the farsighted precursor of the PDPA in recognizing the "brotherly" nature of Afghan-Soviet ties.

Afghanistan's present enemies, constantly linked to the British, are "the interfering American imperialists," "Chinese chauvinists" (or alternatively, "hegemonists"), "the Pakistani military junta" and "other reactionaries" who would like to "destroy the integrity" of the Soviet Union's southern neighbor.

As in all such Communist contexts, the Party is given the leading heroic role. With each change of leadership, Party history is rewritten to explain away all inconsistencies and disguise internal power struggles. Particular emphasis is given, of course, to justifying the Soviet invasion and the subsequent restoration of the Parcham faction to power. For this purpose, Hafizullah Amin is portrayed as the source of all evil, labelled a CIA agent and a betrayer of the revolution from whom the Afghan people were saved with the benevolent aid of their friendly and brotherly northern neighbor:

> The April revolution was staged under the leadership of the People's Democratic Party of Afghanistan by active revolutionary participation of the overwhelming majority of the proletarians, peasantry, toilers, intellectuals and patriots* in the hope of bringing prosperity, affluence, comfort and welfare to the oppressed masses, but while usurping political power, Hafizullah Amin, the CIA agent, and his collaborators let loose the era of terror against loyal Party members, spiritual leaders, intelligentsia, proletariats, peasants and patriotic personages in civilian and military establishments. The traitor was determined to strangle the revolution and its basic achievements just to pave the way for outside intervention. Despite all his terror and suppression, the vigilant patriots in the Party and armed forces were ready to topple his murderous regime at the appropriate time as they did...
> After repeated requests by Mr. Taraki and his successors (including Amin, the traitor and CIA agent) the Soviet Union, in accordance with the Leninist policy of 'peaceful co-existence' and 'good neighbourly relations' decided to send her limited contingents to Afghanistan to help the Afghan people in their struggle to defend the sovereignty of their homeland against the *basmachi*....bands of killers, terrorists, bandits, robbers, plunderers and marauders who are trained in camps in Pakistan...the representatives of Afghanistan's external enemies.
> The Soviet military action is a legal as well as a friendly development based on good neighbourly relations as envisaged in the treaties of non-interference (1921), neutrality and non-aggression (1931), and of friendship (1978). This military action must not be

---

* See: Arnold and Klass for details of actual coup participation and party membership.

considered a threat to the national interest of any country; whenever the limited contingents fulfill their duties of socialist internationalism to help the revolutionary regime eliminate the causes of disturbances and intervention and maintain the territorial integrity of the country, then they will be immediately withdrawn.*[6]

In a society like Afghanistan with a low level of literacy, the historic memory of the nation is transmitted primarily through the oral tradition; but as literacy rises, printed material rapidly displaces it as the primary source of knowledge. By constantly hammering home the falsified Communist version of history through every broadcast, visual and print medium, and by flooding the bookstalls, educational institutions and propaganda centers of Kabul with it, the Soviets and their Afghan agents hope to rapidly confuse the Afghans' memory of their own history and, as the older generation with pre-Communist historical knowledge dies out, to assure a thoroughly propagandized population with access to no other knowledge of themselves and their identity.

The attempt to bind the Afghans (particularly the non-Pushtun groups) to the peoples of the Soviet Republics of Uzbekistan, Turkmenistan and Tajikistan also has a significant historical aspect, and this history too is being rewritten. Historically, Afghanistan's most profound ties over several thousand years have been with the two great cultures of the area: those of Persia and the India subcontinent---plus, over the last thousand years, the Islamic world. [See: Chronology, Appendix II.] As detailed below, major Soviet efforts are devoted to transforming the historical record to downgrade these primary elements in Afghan culture and to magnify instead the less significant connections with Turkestan, particularly those of the Timurid period and since.

Reinterpreting Islam

Islam, as a religion and a culture, is an inseparable part of Afghan identity and society and the binding force that unites all of Afghanistan's ethnic communities today in their fight against an atheistic Communist regime and the Soviet invaders.

Immediately following the 1978 coup, the new regime immediately launched a virulent campaign against religion. Islamic doctrine and the belief in God were denounced, mocked and ridiculed in the schools, in public gatherings, and in the mosques as the PDPA campaigned to replace "outmoded superstition" with "scientific Marxism." Numbers of religious

---

* Compare: "A Soviet Ambassador...Writes Us a Letter."

leaders and scholars were humiliated, arrested, imprisoned, tortured and killed---more than thirty in the prominent Mojadidi family alone. Village mosques were defiled, Korans destroyed and desecrated. Among the Party elite in Kabul, drunkenness and sexual license were cultivated in a flamboyant flaunting of Muslim moral values. This frontal attack on the faith of a fervently devout people backfired: it was a major factor in igniting the nationwide fires of resistance. Following the invasion, the Soviets and the new puppets they installed attempted to undo the damage, blaming the anti-religious campaign on Amin and loudly proclaiming their devotion to Islam while in fact, through techniques already tested in Central Asia, they moved to control and manipulate religious institutions, using the secret police (then KhAD, now WAD) as the KGB had been used in the Soviet Union.

The purpose of post-1980 policies is to reinterpret Islam *in order to harness it as a means of controlling the country*. The older generation is to be deceived into thinking that Islam is not under attack while, among the younger generation, a Sovietized Islam is spread---an Islam that omits God, and instead stresses passivity and the obligation to cooperate with a benevolent "progressive revolutionary" regime and its inspired mentors, i.e., Marxism itself, the Afghan Communist regime, and especially the Soviet Union.

In the wake of the invasion, the newly-installed Babrak Karmal moved quickly to establish a Department of Islamic Affairs (later raised to the status of a ministry) under the control of KhAD with direct ties to the Muslim Board of Central Asia and Kazakhstan in Tashkent headed by Siyanuddin Babakhanov. In addition to providing an Islamic image for the regime and promoting Sovietized Islam, this ministry controls the mosques, religious schools and holy places and maintains contacts between Afghan and Soviet Islamic institutions, organizing frequent exchanges of delegations.

The staff of the ministry, from the beginning, has had only rudimentary religious education---if indeed they have any. Many have none: their credentials are political. The Minister of Islamic Affairs from 1982 till late 1986, Maulawi Abdul Wali Hojjat, is typical: a member of a religious family in Takhar province in the north, he studied at a *madrassa* in Kabul but was accused of blasphemy. In the 1960s he was arrested for his involvement with Setem-i-Milli, an anti-Pushtun Marxist separatist organization based in the north.[7] Until the 1978 coup, he was an official of the Ministry of Justice, not involved in religious affairs.

Soon after the founding of the Department of Religious Affairs, a meeting of (ostensibly) religious scholars and spiritual leaders attended by Babrak Karmal and other party figures adopted a resolution declaring that "With the uprising [sic] on December 27, 1979, the Saur Revolution has entered a new phase. Therefore it is the sacred obligation of every Muslim

Afghan to support the government...misguided elements hired by bloodthirsty American imperialism exploit Islam against Islamic principles...these murderers and terrorists are ignorant of God's commandments...[The mujahideen] are not Muslim and every true Muslim must strongly condemn them...We ask all religious scholars and spiritual leaders to expose the falsehoods and allegations of the enemies of the Saur Revolution through their sermons...and lead the people toward rendering their honorable services to revolutionary and Muslim Afghanistan...On the Soviet part, [the invasion] was a humanitarian and friendly act not only in the interest of all Muslims of our country but in the interest of all peaceloving peoples the world over."[8]

A new regulation gave the government full control of the previously independent finances and endowments of all mosques and other religious institutions. At a stroke, this destroyed the autonomy of mullahs and religious leaders and made them totally dependent on the regime, subject to direct control and manipulation. They are now paid by KhAD/WAD via the Ministry of Islamic Affairs, thus becoming, willy-nilly, agents of the secret police. More than 20,000 mullahs are on the Ministry payroll. They received salaries of 1,200 to 4,000 afghanis a month, are exempted from military service (a major motivation), receive special allowances to make the pilgrimage to Mecca, and may benefit from land redistribution. In return they serve as propaganda instruments for the regime and the Soviets. In the mosques and on radio and television these hired mullahs now call upon the people to join in constructing a new revolutionary Afghanistan "with the fraternal help of the Soviet Union" and denounce the freedom fighters and their supporters---the United States, Western Europe, China, and many of the Arab countries. They deliver the message that Islam and Marxist Socialism are not in opposition but that, on the contrary, they share common goals: that both work for the uplift of humanity.

Despite such compliant behavior, in the last few years the Ministry has begun to remove many of the older mullahs---those who received traditional training before the Communist takeover---from their mosques and educational institutions, replacing them gradually with mullahs newly trained in KhAD-controlled schools who spread a Sovietized version of Islam that stresses the obligation of a Muslim to the Islamic community without any reference to God, let alone to *jihad*, Islamic antipathy to atheism, the Soviet invasion, or other embarassments.

The Ministry makes a great show of whitewashing, repairing and building mosques, particularly in Kabul and the major cities, and Najib, like Babrak Karmal before him, is photographed in mosques in a effort to counter his well-established reputation as an atheist, a blasphemer, and a cruel and brutal torturer. Meanwhile, in villages under Communist attack, mosques are not only destroyed but regularly and systematically desecrated: mosques are used as latrines, Korans are torn up for use as toilet paper. Mosques are also used as military and political headquarters, prompting Resistance attacks which are then denounced as "anti-Islamic."

The Ministry maintains contacts with controlled Islamic institutions in the Soviet Union and sends delegations of Afghan religious personnel to visit them, selecting for these delegations the oldest, poorest, most apolitical and least sophisticated mullahs from rural areas, who are likely to be impressed by the Soviet standard of living. These delegations, accompanied by members of WAD, are introduced to official religious figures, shown mosques under restoration, and taken to staged assemblies of Muslims and religious services. (Nonreligious delegations of villagers, workers, and tribal elders from similarly unsophisticated backgrounds are also chosen for such guided tours.) When they return home, the Ministry arranges press conferences and radio and television interviews for them, using them to support propaganda to the effect that the Soviet Union is a land of religious freedom, a land of light, a land of Islam.

It is the primary function of the Ministry of Islamic Affairs to provide an Islamic image for the Communist regime, to persuade the public that Communism and Islam are not only not incompatible but are actually similar, and to disseminate a pseudo-Islam that will, over a period of time, defuse and undermine religious opposition to Soviet control and to whatever regimes Moscow may install as a facade.

The legal system

In those areas under Soviet occupation and Communist control, the legal system has been completely wiped out. As part of the effort to demonstrate the compatibility of Communism and Islam, matters pertaining to marriage, divorce and inheritance have thus far been left to the Islamic courts, but all other legal matters are covered by special decrees and handled by the Special Revolutionary Tribunal, which in turn is under Soviet control. Former jurists and lawyers report that Soviet advisers supervise all court proceedings and dictate the verdicts.

Attention is focussed almost entirely on "political crimes," i.e., opposition to the regime; little or no attention is paid to common crimes (robbery, assault, etc.). Even civil suits are judged in political terms. Torture is routinely used. Sentences, including death sentences, are passed and carried out with the merest semblance of a trial. [See: Rubin.]

One former judge of the Supreme Court stated, "As a consequence of the entry of the Red Army into Afghanistan, it is not proper any longer to speak of such things as courts, lawyers or judicial proceedings in our country."[9]

Press and media

The press (including books) and media are totally controlled. Possession of unauthorized publications is grounds for arrest. Non-Communist publications have disappeared from the bookstores, which have instead been flooded with materials from the USSR and especially from Soviet Central Asia.

The press and media use only Soviet sources for international news, while the official Bakhtar News Agency provides all domestic news. A 1983 Bakhtar brochure declares that its function is "to be a true mirror of revolutionary gains...to strengthen the political and ideological consciousness of the people. The revolutionary regime has directed this agency to establish close cooperation, through treaties and protocols, with...Tass, Novosti, and other agencies of the socialist countries...Bakhtar News Agency shall strengthen the friendship of the DRA with the Soviet Union..."[10]

Soviet advisers hold key positions in the press as well as in radio, television, and telecommunications---apparently on a 24-hour basis, since they reportedly issue directives at all hours. Russian publications translated into Farsi and Pushto are widely distributed, as are numerous publications from Soviet Tajikistan, Uzbekistan, and Turkmenistan, all of which constantly emphasize Afghan ethnic and cultural ties with the people of Central Asia. Considerable attention is given to shaping Afghan journalists to fit the socialist mold: under a series of agreements, the training of Afghan journalists is under the direction of the USSR, East Germany and Czechoslovakia and a number of journalists have been sent to those countries for training.

The Soviets have provided a new land-based satellite communications system which improves Soviet transmissions into Afghanistan and also enables Kabul radio to broadcast not only domestically but to Europe, the Middle East, Pakistan, Iran, and other parts of Asia in English, French, German, Russian, Arabic and Urdu as well as Farsi and Pushto. With the new satellite system, a dozen or more new radio and television stations have been installed in Herat, Mazar-i-Sharif, Nangrahar, Ghazni, Paktia, Farah, Badakhshan, Kandahar, and other provinces, particularly those along the Pakistan border from which their transmissions reach the refugee camps and potentially the Pakistani public as well. A program called Watan Ghazh, "Voice of the Homeland," is specifically beamed at Afghan refugees in Pakistan and Iran. In September 1986, Kabul Radio announced that the USSR would help set up twenty television stations as part of a nationwide network "to bring Afghan and Soviet programs to all parts of the country." In addition to these Afghan stations, Radio Tajikistan and Radio Moscow beam more than eight hours of daily programming into Afghanistan in Farsi and Pushto.

The programming follows a consistent line, subject to close scrutiny by Soviet advisors. The Soviet Union is constantly portrayed as invincible, the nation that (single-handedly) defeated the Nazis in World War II, the defender of Afghan freedom and the historic friend of the Afghan people. Ties between the Afghans and the peoples of Soviet Central Asia are stressed and exaggerated. Dramas are adapted from old Central Asian themes. All programming is ideological, hammering home the message that pre-Communist days were dominated by grasping feudal chieftains and tyrannical tribal chiefs, that the Resistance are bandits, murderers, plunderers, and tools of the imperialists, and that Afghanistan's enemies are Iran, Egypt, Saudi Arabia, France, West Germany, the United Kingdom, and above all the United States, Pakistan and China, all of whom have evil designs on the Afghan nation against which only the friendly Soviet Union is protecting them.

At least once a week there are Soviet films dealing with Soviet heroism, progress under Communist leadership (particularly in Central Asia), and the victories of the Red Army: small children are shown waving Soviet and Afghan flags while singing in praise of the Soviet Union. Illiterate villagers are put on television to mouth bombastic phrases about "imperialist reactionary enemies," "the Great Saur Revolution," and "Soviet friendship and brotherhood." Not even love songs on the popular musical programs are immune: a woman sings of her lover who goes to the front and "fights for the revolution."

A movie production company has been set up to produce propaganda films; its directors and actors are invited to Communist bloc cinema festivals where they and their films are feted and given awards.[11] By early 1987, according to official sources, Afghan Films had produced fifteen features "and a number of documentaries," some of them in color. Their content can be gauged from a report by the Bakhtar Information Agency in late 1986: "Production of a number of documentary films relating to the revolutionary transformation in Afghanistan is...underway. The subject of [a new feature film] is the gains of the April Revolution...[Another] depicts the miserable life & the tragic destiny of the deceived Afghans who had been compelled to abandon their homeland as a result of the criminal acts of the counter-revolutionary bands."

Molding the new generation

The most extensive efforts at Sovietization are concentrated on children and young people, in the expectation of creating an acquiescent future Communist Afghan public.

Afghan educational institutions have been transformed into agencies of Sovietization under the direction of Soviet and East European advisers, directors and teachers. The curricula have been completely replaced, as have the textbooks. Large numbers of non-Communist teachers have been jailed, executed, or become refugees, and those who remain are under intense pressure to join the Communist party. In September 1986, Najibullah told Afghan teachers bluntly, "The demand to politicize the entire educational process is on [your] agenda."

Before assessing the changes in the Afghan education system, it may be useful to look at its prewar structure:

Modern education in Afghanistan began in the early years of the twentieth century with the establishment of a prestigious secondary school in Kabul. In the 1920s and 1930s a number of others were added, more or less modeled on the French lycée system. A number of these schools established connections with European educational organizations and were partly staffed, and sometimes directed, by French, British, German, and Indian instructors to whom were added, after World War II, Americans. The curriculum was particularly strong in mathematics and languages, with algebra, geometry, trigonometry, calculus, Arabic, Persian (Farsi), Pushto, and a European language in addition to literature, history, geography, biology, chemistry, physics and Islamic studies.

During these decades, a few secondary schools were opened in other major cities and towns and teacher training schools were established. The government undertook to extend at least elementary education to villages throughout the country which had hitherto had only the mosque schools, which taught literacy and religion, and not always even those.

From the 1920s on, merit scholarships were made available to top-ranking graduates of secondary schools, who were sent to England, the United States, France, Germany, Italy, Switzerland, Egypt, Turkey, and India for advanced education. By the late 1940s, a significant number of highly educated Afghans had returned and many of them were put to work in the Ministry of Education to upgrade domestic schooling.

After World War II, the Afghan government intensified its educational efforts significantly, opening more schools, including technical schools, and sending many more students abroad. By the early 1950s, the government was spending nearly 40 percent of its limited budget on education.

Beginning in the late 1950s, the Ministry of Education, with the assistance of Columbia University Teachers College, overhauled its teacher training programs and prepared a complete series of modern textbooks in Farsi and Pushto for grades 1-12.

Meanwhile, Kabul University had been established in 1932; in the late

1950s it was made coeducational.* In the 1960s a second medical school was established at Jalalabad, later developing into a university. Most of divisions of Kabul University had international connections† and many senior university faculty had one or more degrees from such institutions as Harvard, the University of Chicago, the Sorbonne, the University of London, and al-Azhar University in Cairo.

The educational effort continued to pick up steam, though the limited national budget was a severe handicap. By the 1970s, approximately 200 elementary schools were being opened annually.

Since 1978, the entire educational system has been politicized, turned into a conduit for Communization, and ruined. The universities are dealt with separately below; here, a few statistics demonstrate the impact on primary and secondary education[13]:

	1978	1984	% decline
Primary schools	1154	210	-82%
Village schools	1451	†zero	-100%
Middle schools	350	78	-78%
High schools	163	44	-73%
Technical schools	17	8	-53%
Teacher training schools	26	6	-78%

---

* Primary and secondary schools were not coeducational.

**Kabul University affiliations as of the 1970s: Faculty of Medicine/University of Lyons; Faculty of Law and Political Science/University of Paris; Faculty of Science/Bochum and Bonn Universities; Faculty of Economics/Bochum, Bonn and Cologne Universities; Faculty of Theology/al-Azhar University; Faculty of Agriculture/University of Wyoming; Faculty of Education/Teachers College, Columbia University; Faculty of Engineering/ a consortium of American institutions including Carnegie Institute of Technology (Carnegie-Mellon), Georgia Institute of Technology, Lehigh University, Notre Dame University, Purdue University, et al. In 1967, the Soviet Union was for the first time permitted to participate in education and the Soviet-built Polytechnic Institute was attached to the University. [See: Dupree, *Afghanistan*. (Princeton, 1973): 598.]

† This refers to government-established schools. In areas of Resistance control, Resistance organizations and local villagers are trying to provide at least basic schooling with whatever personnel and facilities they can scrape together. These range from the simplest instruction in reading, writing, arithmetic, and Islam to a few schools with trained teachers and English or French language instruction.

Most of the surviving schools are in Kabul; the remainder are in the few other areas under the control of the Kabul regime and Soviet forces.

Nor do these figures tell the full story. Many of the male teachers have been jailed and some killed; others have fled into exile to avoid conscription into the DRA army. Since boys as young as fourteen or fifteen are pressganged into military service, many of the male students have also vanished. As a result, both the teaching staffs and the student bodies are now greatly reduced and in the upper grades many classes are composed almost entirely of girls.

Transforming primary and secondary education

Under the Khalq regimes of 1978-1979, efforts to transform and Communize the schools were crude, improvised, and often clumsy; since the invasion such efforts have been systematically organized under Soviet control; Afghan education now conforms to the Soviet model. In addition to the Soviet personnel who dictate the policies of the Ministry of Education, Soviet advisers and instructors supervise curriculum and instruction in all educational institutions from kindergarten through the university. Every secondary school is under the control of an official Soviet adviser. In primary schools, advisers from the curriculum department of the Ministry visit the schools regularly to see that the curriculum is implemented and classroom instruction is being carried out as ordered.

In 1980, the First Congress of Teachers was held in Kabul with high-ranking education specialists from the USSR and other Communist-bloc countries in attendance, and plans were announced for the new curriculum. Among the changes: the Russian language was made mandatory in all schools, replacing English (by then the most widely taught foreign language), French and German. According to the Teachers Congress, "Teaching the Russian language is an urgent need. By mastering this language in earlier schooling, the student will be able to read useful materials in Russian and will also have a useful means of communication, bringing the younger generation closer to the friendly Soviet Union."[14]

In February 1985, the DRA severed its last remaining ties with Western educational institutions---the Germans and the French, whose educational and cultural activities in Kabul had begun fifty years earlier. Since there are few Afghans qualified to teach Russian, instruction has been intensified in the Department of Russian Language at Kabul University and courses have been made available free of charge at Afghan-Soviet Friendship Centres. Eventually a newly-trained teaching staff educated in the Soviet Union as well as in Afghanistan is to be put in charge of Russian language instruction and perhaps other subjects considered important.

Schools in the north have begun to use local mother tongues [Uzbek and Turkoman Turkish dialects] as languages of instruction in place of Farsi. Over a period of time, this will isolate the members of the various ethnic groups from one another, forcing them to depend on Russian as their sole medium of communication.

The textbooks in Afghan schools have been completely replaced by new ones prepared under the strict supervision of Soviet advisers. Many are simply translations of Soviet textbooks; some are specially prepared and published in Soviet Central Asia and shipped in. All of them contain the same preface:

> Dear Children:
> Your revolutionary regime has firmly resolved to bring deeprooted change in the infrastructure of your society. The education and training of the younger generation is the first goal of your democratic regime whose Party leadership has already laid the foundation of a new progressive education system that will help to train the "new man."

The new curriculum reduced the teaching of Islamic subjects from four to two class hours per week. A new subject, Politics, has been introduced, starting in the seventh grade and occupying five hours per week, for which students in grades seven through ten study *The Textbook for Learning Politics* [Da Siyasi Siwad Darsi Kitab] published in both Farsi and Pushto in 1980 by Novosti, Moscow. Eleventh and twelfth graders use *Scientific Sociology* [Jamia Shinasi Elmi], a textbook published in Kabul in 1983 by the DRA Ministry of Edication.

Between the seventh and twelfth grades, this new course covers the following topics: the general definition of political science; socio-economic formation; socialism and its success in the world; class and class struggle; imperialism as an exploiting system; revolutionary movements of the proletariat class; socialist revolution; the history of the Communist Party of the USSR; how public property is geared toward public production; Communism, the higher form of socialism; state and revolution; just wars [i.e., Socialist/Communist] and unjust wars [i.e., Western]; Maoism---its deviation from Scientific Socialism; the history of the People's Democratic Party of Afghanistan; and the history of Soviet-Afghan friendship.

Apparently even this is not enough. In 1985, the Central Committee of the PDPA notified all schools that *every* teacher (of whatever subject) is duty-bound to lecture his or her classes about Afghan-Soviet friendship, the Soviet system, and the "fruitful endeavor" of the PDPA.

Compulsory military training begins in the ninth grade: Afghan army officers teach military tactics and provide basic hands-on training. Severe pressure is exerted on male students to join the army and fight against the mujahideen, as well as inducements to do so: diplomas granted without the completion of courses or examinations, easy entry into the university, etc.

Every teacher is under intense pressure to join the Communist Party; failure to do so is considered highly suspicious, and has led to the arrest of many teachers, women as well as men.

Orphans

In addition to the regular school system described above, special institutions known as Fatherland Training Centers [*Parwarishgah-i-Watan*] have been established in Kabul and other occupied cities for orphaned children, including those who have lost only one parent, the father.* Ostensibly these are primarily homes for the orphans of Party members and DRA soldiers, but there are widespread and reliable reports of children taken by force from villages attacked by Soviet/DRA forces, of the seizure of children of Resistance fighters, of house-to-house searches in Kabul for the children of widowed mothers, and of parents persuaded to send their children to these centers on the basis of misinformation. [See: bibliography, sources under "Atrocities/Human Rights Violations."]

The Fatherland Training Centers are under the control and direction of the secret police, KhAD (WAD), and have their own schools and a separate curriculum even more stringently designed to turn them into Communists and eventually agents, since the children have no relatives to object to their textbooks or to the openly anti-religious atheist doctrine taught them.

Large numbers of these children---as well as others from the Pioneer and DYOA youth organizations described below---are being sent to the Soviet Union and other Communist bloc countries for periods of up to ten years or

---

* In the extended family which is the basis of Afghan society, a child who has lost both parents is taken in by relatives; so long as any relative remains alive, the child is not considered orphaned. The concept of institutional arrangements is completely alien to Afghan social thinking. In the Afghan social structure, therefore, the taking of any child with surviving adult relatives is tantamount to kidnapping. In any case, in all societies this would apply to taking a child from a surviving parent. Other aspects of this program of course reinforce that view.---ed.

even more to be raised there and molded into a hard-core cadre group for the future control of Afghanistan without the need for Soviet forces.

Student organizations

At the age of ten, all children---girls as well as boys---are enrolled in the *Sazman-i-Peshahangan* [Pioneers], modeled on its Soviet counterpart; some may be enrolled even younger. Children of PDPA members may join willingly, but others are recruited by inducements, persuasion, or if necessary coercion of the child or the parents.

In each school, the Pioneers are organized into groups of seven children under adult leaders whose purpose is to undermine their family ties and replace them with loyalty to the PDPA, the regime, and the Soviet Union. The children are taught that the Party and its leaders are more important and more benevolent than their parents and relatives; that true virtue consists in working for the national good as embodied in the Party instead of for the benefit of their families; and that the Soviet Union is their one true friend. They are trained as informers and assigned to report to their adult leaders on the opinions of their parents, relatives and friends regarding the regime and the Soviet Union, as well as the identity of visitors to their homes, unusual behavior among their neighbors, and the arrival of newcomers in their neighborhoods; in school, they spy on classmates and non-Communist teachers; and they are used to spread disinformation.

Once a week, groups from various schools gather at Pioneer centers---in Kabul, the Pioneer Palace---where women from Tajikistan, Uzbekistan and Russia (and some Afghans) teach them folk music and dances. Eventually, they may be sent on holiday to the Central Asian SSRs, accompanied by teachers selected by KhAD.

At age fifteen, students are recruited into the Democratic Youth Organization of Afghanistan [DYOA/Sazman-i-Jawanan]. Its newspaper, published in Kabul and distributed in other occupied areas, is devoted to glorifying the PDPA, the Soviet Union, and young people in Communist countries, to reminders of the members' duty to serve a "progressive society," and to other Soviet-style literature.

The DRA claims to have 1,100 "professional cadres" working to develop the DYOA. Leaders divide members into small groups and assign their responsibilities, which include guarding schools and government buildings, persuading others to join the DYOA and/or volunteer for the army, transmitting decisions made by the regime and its leadership to their classmates and the community, and conducting intensive spying and surveillance in the community. They arrange and carry out demonstrations on behalf of the regime and its policies and against its opponents.

Official sources admit that DYOA members are used in labor brigades, characterized of course as "volunteer" effort, during their holidays; labeled "social and production brigades," these admittedly have included work in the coal mines of Baghlan province and on the Lashkari canal among other "contributions to the task of consolidating the gains of the Revolution."[15]

DYOA members of both sexes frequent the Afghan-Soviet Friendship Centers, where Soviet acquaintances induce them to drink alcohol and dance with members of the opposite sex, violations of Islamic doctrine and Afghan social mores; the result is to stimulate them into sexual indulgence and promiscuity, further cutting them off from their own society and giving them a sense of no return.

The DYOA is a constituent of the Fatherland Front, and membership in the youth organizations is designed to lead to eventual adult Party membership.

Higher Education

Immediately following the April 1978 Communist coup, Soviet advisers arrived in numbers at Kabul University, Jalalabad University, and the technical institutions and began their transformation. The figures on Kabul University alone[16] tell the story of the destruction of higher education:

	1978 Pre-coup	1984	% change
Tenured faculty (Assistant professor and above)	750	432	-42%*
Students	14,000	6,000	-57%†

The first Soviet advisers arrived at Kabul University in June 1978, and speedily eliminated Islamic subjects from the curriculum on the grounds that they were not "scientific." The history of Islamic art was henceforth to be subsumed under "archeology" (i.e., treated not as a living subject but as

---

* This includes 36 faculty members executed, 6 jailed with sentences of up to 12 years, and 276 forced to flee into exile.

† Since male students are subject to draft or impressment into DRA forces, a high proportion of teenage boys have gone into hiding, joined the Resistance, or fled into exile; the majority of the remaining student body are women (as many as 80 percent in some classes), along with male Party members and other favored groups who are exempted from military service. Moreover, hundreds of students have been arrested or killed.

part of the ancient past); the history of Islamic civilizations was first abolished, then restored after faculty protests but reduced to minimal significance.

Fundamental changes were made in the curricula of the Faculties of Letters, Theology, Economics and Law. New courses introduced in the Faculty of Letters include Historical Materialism, The Revolutionary History of Workers, The History of Russia, The New History of Afghanistan, Dialectical Materialism, Scientific Sociology, and History of World Literature. World Literature, taught by a Soviet Tajik, covers the writings of Marx, Lenin, Fidel Castro and other Communist writers of Eastern Europe and Latin America. The text for the "New History of Afghanistan" was prepared by Politburo member Ghulam Dastagir Panjsheri; this course and "Scientific Sociology" have been made mandatory in all thirteen faculties of the university.

Departments of Russian and Spanish languages have been established, the latter taught by Cuban instructors; both languages were made compulsory.[17] Short-term scholarships for Russian-language study in the USSR have been instituted for teachers, students, officials and workers, Russian being the essential language for every administrative section of the Afghan government.

The syllabus of the history department was radically revised by a Soviet Tajik "advisor" to conform to the prospectus of Moscow University.

The Faculty of Theology was eliminated. The study of Arabic was transferred to the language section of the Faculty of Literature; the study of Islamic law *(Fiqah)* to the Faculty of Law. The study of the Koran and *Hadith* [Traditions] was downgraded and revised to omit all references to jihad and all denunciations of godlessness, while the syllabus was revised to promote the presumed similarity and compatibility of Islam and socialism.

The ties between the Faculty of Economics and the universities of Bonn, Bochum and Cologne in West Germany were severed and replaced by East German affiliations. Although the formal curriculum in this faculty remains largely unchanged, all subjects are now taught from a Soviet perspective on the basis of the Moscow University syllabus and in 1982 a dozen East German instructors joined the teaching faculty. The ties of other Faculties to other Western institutions were similarly cut off.

Parts of the Faculty of Medicine were abolished, the length of medical education was reduced from seven years to five, and oral examinations replaced written exams.

The Faculty of Engineering, which had enjoyed a particularly high reputation, was abolished, incorporated into the Russian-built Polytechnic Institute.

A Russian pre-examination system called *zarchod* ["satisfaction"] was subsequently been introduced: every student must "satisfy" his teacher in order to qualify for final examinations. Every institution maintains a complete and minutely detailed record of both the academic and extra-curricular activities of each student; under the *zarchod* system, the teacher checks each student's record of attendance for political indoctrination classes, participation in Party-directed demonstrations and parades, and above all for information on his or her private views of the regime and the Soviet Union. A student who successfully passes *zarchod* is guaranteed high marks, a scholarship to one of the Communist countries, exemption from military service and other privileges. Those unsatisfactory in *zarchod* are failed. For a male student, two failures result in his being drafted and sent to fight against the mujahideen in a far-off province, to avoid which he has only two further alternatives: to join the PDPA or WAD, or to flee the country. The *zarchod* system is obviously an invitation to widespread irregularities, and is the source of much bitterness among the students.

Every Faculty has its own Afghan-Soviet Friendship Room, hung with photographs of Engels, Marx, Lenin, and the current DRA leadership and filled with publications from the Soviet Union, Eastern Europe and Cuba.

Beginning immediately after the 1978 coup, many members of the university administration and faculty were arrested and imprisoned for varying periods (in addition to those still serving long terms), as were hundreds of students. Many were tortured, some were killed, and all were threatened and pressured; many subsequently fled the country. Those remaining are under intense pressure to join the Communist Party; those who fail to do so are constantly subject to humiliation as well as dismissal, arrest, and possible execution. They are under constant observation: spies are present among the students in every classroom as well as among Communist and pro-Communist faculty members who infiltrated the university before 1978 and since. Party membership has replaced academic qualification as the requisite for appointment to the teaching faculty or the administration and large numbers of Soviet and East European instructors have been brought in.

The Polytechnic, now attached to the university, has reportedly been transformed into an affiliate of Patrice Lumumba University in Moscow, but with an emphasis on technical rather than social science training. Little information is available about the current situation at the University of Jalalabad, which has come under frequent attack by the mujahideen: most of its faculty and students have either joined the Resistance or gone into exile. Reportedly, its faculties are now being used as a training center for

322

terrorists, drawing a "student body" from Pakistan, Iran and the Middle East as well as Afghanistan.[18]

Adult reeducation

Although primary attention is focussed on transforming the younger generation, adults are also subjected to systematic propagandizing, manipulation and Marxist instruction in structured classes.

In the army, all troops and NCOs are required to spend four hours a week in political courses for Marxist indoctrination, and political officers are attached to all units to ensure ongoing ideological reinforcement and prevent backsliding.

Among civilians, Marxist indoctrination programs are carried out in the guise of literacy classes. The regime makes grandiose claims for this literacy campaign (for which they received an award from UNICEF in September 1986) but their figures appear highly inflated and unreliable. The "literacy campaign" was one of the first programs announced by the new regime after the 1978 coup; under Amin, the DRA was boasting of hundreds of thousands, even millions, of new literates. In September 1984, Karmal claimed that 1.5 million had become literate. In April 1985, he said that 380,000 people were attending 20,000 literacy courses throughout the country, but his claims had dropped to only one million new literates. A few weeks later he was using the figure of only 95,000 new literates in Kabul, where regime programs are most actively implemented.[19] Later claims returned to million or more.

In reality, once their ideological nature became apparent---almost immediately following their inception---the "literacy classes" were widely rejected. Indeed, armed resistance to the Communist regime erupted in 1978 in part in reaction to efforts to force village women into these classes in which religion was ridiculed and Marxism preached and glorified.

While official information is inflated and unreliable and the current extent of the programs is therefore unknown, some specifics can be gleaned from personal testimony by refugees and defectors from the regime. These indoctrination programs obviously are conducted in the areas under regime control---primarily in Kabul and a few other cities---and appear to be concentrated in factories, offices, and other workplaces where employees can be forced to participate; even so, participation appears to be fairly low. [A film seen on American television several years ago, taken by a camera crew admitted to Kabul to show what the regime wanted seen, showed a purported literacy class in a Kabul factory: a handful of rather glum women clustered at the front of a large and otherwise empty room, twiddling pencils and flipping pages.---ed.] The classes are too brief to effectively teach literacy---

often only an hour or two altogether. In any case they are primarily devoted to propaganda and indoctrination. If the participants do learn reading skills, the only reading materials available to them are totally-controlled Marxist propaganda.

Sending Afghans to the USSR for indoctrination

Faced with the intransigent hatred of the populace, the Soviets and the DRA regime early on began to send numbers of Afghans to the Soviet Union in an effort to create a favorable impression and develop a body of pro-Soviet supporters even among non-party members. These early efforts concentrated on comparatively short visits (a few weeks to a few months) designed to impress high school students, cultural leaders and others with the friendliness, high standards of living, and overall benevolence of their northern neighbor.

Faced with widespread failure in their effort to change the attitudes of older children and adults, the Soviets turned to younger children. Children returning from the USSR report being placed in Russian families and told to think of those families as having replaced their own. Older students and adults tell of being pressured to drink alcohol and eat pork in violation of religious taboos.

In addition, high school and college level students were (and still are) offered extended scholarships (which are also open to selected Pakistanis who are first given scholarships to Kabul and Jalalabad Universities where their potential is assessed).

In early 1985, one source[20] estimated (on the basis of information from sources inside the regime) that between July 1980 and December 1984, more than 60,000 Afghans of all ages had already been sent to the Soviet Union and its satellites for long or short visits, including six thousand sent to East Germany, Bulgaria and Cuba. This figure was broken down as follows:

• About 1,400 of those sent were party members or their relatives rewarded with Soviet holidays. Two thousand or so were party members or selected government employees sent for training and indoctrination.

• Another 19,000 party members and army officers, both active duty and retired, were sent for "special training," including, specifically, training in explosives, as were 300 "special police" and 1,080 regular police, while 740 party or front organization members were sent to learn "special information."

• Approximately 1,800 members of KhAD were sent for "special training" *each year* until 1984; in that year the number doubled to 3,600; in other words, by 1985, more than 10,000 members of KhAD had received special training by Soviet or Soviet-bloc KGB organizations. (More recent figures are not available, but presumably the training of KhAD in skills and organization have continued at the higher rate since 1984.)*

• Aside from these trainees, adult groups sent to be impressed, flattered, propagandized, and won over included nearly 200 musicians and others from Afghan radio, television and films; 669 mullahs, elders and personnel from the Ministry of Islamic Affairs; 569 tribal figures and personnel from the Ministry of Tribes and Nationalities; and 900 more identified simply as "workers."

These efforts have continued apace since 1984 but the results continue to be disappointing among adults and older students. Soviet efforts have therefore been further focussed on the more malleable young children.

By the end of 1984, 19,992 children between the ages of four and eight had been sent to the USSR for varying periods of time, along with nearly 1,500 more children between eight and fourteen---with or without their parents' voluntary approval. (Many parents, under severe pressure to send their children to the USSR, choose instead to flee the country.) But even this had not proven successful in transforming Afghan hearts and minds.

As a result, in November 1984 the Soviets began a program described by Babrak Karmal in the official DRA announcement as a "magnificent friendly gesture by the Soviet Union toward Afghan people": beginning in 1984, *two thousand young Afghan children are to be sent to the Soviet Union each year for the next ten years and are to remain there for at least ten years* "for schooling." Press reports[21] describe weeping parents gathered at the airport as the first flight of 870 children between the ages of seven and nine took off for ten years in Soviet Central Asia. There are reports of children as young as three or four being sent off, and in the case of the orphanages (Parwarishgah), of infants and toddlers as well. Parents are threatened and coerced into giving permission for their children to be sent; there are reports of children sent without parental permission--- or kidnapped and sent without parental knowledge.[22] This program continues, designed to create an eventual hard core of thousands of deculturized, deracinated, trained Communist cadres to be used in the control of an eventual Communized Afghanistan.

Meanwhile, the other programs continue, including short-term (six months) and medium-term (three years) training in the USSR. A number of children have been taken to the Soviet Union, trained in espionage, weapons use, deception and terrorist techniques, and sent back to infiltrate the

---

* Former police sources report that at least some of that training is in torture techniques.---ed.

Resistance, thereby exploiting the Afghan cultural tradition by which a child is regarded as "mahsoom" (innocent), hence immune and protected in wartime. The Resistance has captured a number of these child agents and is on the whole at a loss as to how to deal with a trained, crafty and dangerous enemy who may be only nine or ten years old.[23]

On an ongoing basis, it is difficult to find out the exact numbers of students and others being dispatched to the Soviet Union and other Communist countries every year, either as totals or categories; the transactions are now being carried out by the Statistics Processing Department in close collaboration with the KGB. It is clear, however, that the number is large and is not decreasing.

Central Asia: A conduit for sovietization

The Soviet Union is attempting to use the Central Asian Soviet Republics as a conduit to transform Afghanistan's historical relationships by severing the younger generation from their age-old cultural ties with the Persian, Indian and Islamic civilizations and convincing them instead that Afghanistan is---and always has been---an inseparable component of Central Asian culture. This effort is directed in particular at the non-Pushtun ethnic minorities and aims at separating them from the majority Pushtuns.

To implement Soviet policy on the "nationality question," large numbers of educators, teachers, writers, specialists in various fields, and propagandists from Soviet Central Asia have been sent to Afghanistan.

The people of Herat, Balkh and Badakhshan, and other Afghans as well, have always been familiar with the great Turkic rulers, poets and scholars of centuries past (most of whose writings were in Persian, the great literary language of the area, or were Persian-influenced). Until very recently, Soviet media and propaganda condemned and ridiculed these famous figures as semi-civilized feudals, fanatics and reactionaries. Since the 1978 coup in Afghanistan, however, many of them have suddenly been resurrected in the Soviet media as great men of history and contributors to civilization. The most effusive recognition is given to those who at one historic period or another ruled parts of northern Afghanistan from Central Asia: these rulers are eulogized and their statesmanship and foresight are pronounced to be the main source of "existing friendly and good neighborly relations" among the "nationalities" on both sides of the Oxus.

Preparations are busily under way, for example, for a celebration in Kabul in 1991 of the fifth centenary of Ali Sher Nawai, a poet and

326

statesman of the Timurid period who was born and lived in Herat. His poetry was modeled on that of the great Persian poets Nizami and Jami (also of Herat), but he attempted to prove the superiority of Chagatai Turkish ["Uzbek"] over Persian as a poetic language. The PDPA has honored Nawai with several literary gatherings, at one of which Babrak Karmal declared, "Ali Sher Nawai had the greatest impact on the development of culture, literature and science in Afghanistan and Central Asia. His services to friendship and solidarity between the Afghans and Central Asian people were outstanding. Since the fifteenth century, his contributions to social justice have not lost their value; therefore we are obliged to hold this immortal scholar in the highest esteem."[24*]

The Soviet press has also begun to single out for tribute Babur, a prince of a Timurid Mongol dynasty who established himself in Kabul and from there in 1526 embarked on the conquest of India and the founding of the Moghul empire. Babur wrote brilliantly in both Chagatai Turkish and Persian, and is buried in Kabul. According to a recent Uzbek journal, "Through his contributions to the literary, artistic and cultural life of this barren [sic] land, Babur rendered a great service to the Afghan people."[25] His fifth centenary too is soon to be celebrated. The same journal uncovered the more obscure figure of a long-gone ruler of Bukhara who in their words sounds remarkably like a modern fellow traveller: "Abdul Aziz, the founder of peace, friendship and solidarity in the region, ruled Bukhara and the northern parts of Afghanistan from 1680 till 1702 and had cordial and friendly relations with the Indian Moghul and Iranian Empires. He deserves a great celebration."[26]

Newspapers, magazines, pamphlets and books eulogizing more recent Central Asian thinkers of the nineteenth century are lavishly distributed among the Afghan minorities with the express objective of reminding them of their ethnic and cultural ties with Central Asian peoples in the past. Moscow has arranged numerous gatherings in Kabul to which large numbers of Uzbeks are sent from Tashkent, loaded with abundant propaganda materials, in an effort to fragment Afghanistan via such comrades-in-arms from across the Oxus. Fabricated statistics purport to show that the minority populations in Afghanistan are much larger than they actually are: according to such published figures, in northern Afghanistan there are three

* Nawai and some others coming in for belated official praise were indeed significant figures, but were minor influences in comparison to such towering Persian poets as Saadi, Hafiz, Firdausi and Nizami, several of whom lived and worked in Afghanistan and whose poems are known to every Afghan.---ed.

million Uzbeks, three million Tajiks, and one million Kirghiz and Kazakhs.*

Soviet propaganda also attempts to exploit and exacerbate minority resentment against the dominant Pushtuns, reviving memories of Pushtun-minority conflicts since the founding of modern Afghanistan in 1747. While glorifying Leninist policies as the only path for remedying the "depressed state of oppressed nationalities," an Uzbek historian named Nishanov, in his book *The Constructive April Revolution*, claims that the "brutal regimes" of Zahir Shah and Daoud launched a "Pushtunisation" movement in order to "liquidate the very identities of other nationalities and their valuable traditions." This, he says, accounts for the use of a single term---Afghan---for all citizens irrespective of their ethnic identities, citing in evidence the statement in the 1964 constitution, "The people living in Afghanistan shall belong to the Afghan nation."** According to Soviet propaganda, in contrast to past "brutal regimes," the April Revolution put an end to the prevailing "liquidation process" and other racial abuses. Now, goes the line, Uzbeks, Turkomans, Tajiks, Baluch and others have their own local schools where their children are taught in their mother tongues, whereas in the past no such schools or appropriate publications existed. One Mr. Zahidov, a member of the Academy of Sciences of Uzbekistan who visited Afghanistan with a group of Soviet-bloc correspondents, concluded that "...the then exploiting class of big landlords had imposed a miserable state of poverty, slavery, lawlessness and exploitation on the toiling masses ...The Democratic Republic of Afghanistan has geared all its national resources to give them a bright future..."[27]

The newspapers *Yuldis* (The Star), *Girash* (The Struggle) and *Sab* (The

---

* The most widely accepted prewar figures are approximately one million Uzbeks and approximately two million Tajiks. The entire Kirghiz population, numbering only a few thousand (most of whom had earlier fled the USSR) fled Afghanistan en masse following the 1978 coup and have been resettled in eastern Turkey. The number of Kazakhs in Afghanistan is too negligible to appear in standard statistics. See Barth---ed.

** *Afghanistan* means "the land of the Afghans" The word "Afghan" was originally a synonym for "Pushtun" but as nationalism developed, it came to mean any citizen of the country, of whatever ethnic origin; the 1964 constitutional clause (Article 1) was of course an effort to cement this sense of nationality and confirm the equality of all ethnic groups. In the official English translation it reads: "The Afghan nation is composed of all those individuals who possess the citizenship of the State of Afghanistan in accordance with the provisions of the law. The word Afghan shall apply to each such individual."---ed.

Revolution), published in Soviet Uzbekistan, are sent into Afghanistan in quantity and widely distributed. According to the monthly *Eastern Star*, "By distributing the newspapers and literary works of the Uzbek poets, playwrights and dramatists among the nationalities, we have two objectives to work for: firstly, we must keep our Uzbek brothers in northern Afghanistan informed about the greatest material and cultural achievements of the Central Asian peoples under communism; secondly, we must extend help to our *backward brothers* on the other side of the Oxus to enrich and develop their *primitive* literature and culture."[27] [emphasis added.]

Uzbeks, Tajiks and Turkomans from the Central Asian republics and fugitive Iranian members of the Tudeh Party (Iran's communist party) work in various official Afghan agencies. They are required to study these materials and carry out the indoctrination of young Afghans along the lines of prescribed dogma. In the Ministry of Education and the Academy of Sciences, the Soviets have established a Research Studies Institute for Uzbek Literature and Culture, headed by a Mr. Osmanov who was for many years an adviser to the Soviet Embassy in Kabul. And, although Suleiman Layeq, Minister of Tribes and Nationalities, is the nominal head of the Academy of Sciences, in reality the Academy is directed and controlled by a Mr. Azimov, the president of the Academy of Sciences of the Uzbek SSR.

Manipulating the Tribes

Following the 1978 coup, Moscow advised Nur Mohammad Taraki to first eliminate anti-Communist elements inside Afghanistan and then to penetrate both the tribal and settled Pushtun areas across the border in Pakistan. The instrument for this penetration is the Ministry of Tribes and Nationalities, which was originally a Directorate of Tribal Affairs established in 1934 to deal with problems of the tribes inside Afghanistan.

In 1895, the Durand Line, which fixed the boundary between Afghanistan and British India, was drawn through the midst of a number of Pushtun tribes, splitting them; tribal members on both sides of the border always have generally ignored it. As a result, the 1934 Tribal Directorate soon found itself involved on both sides of the border. The sons of tribal leaders from both sides of the border were educated at special schools in Kabul. That cross-border involvement intensified as a result of the Pushtunistan dispute that emerged with the creation of Pakistan in 1947, and under Daoud, Afghan efforts to cultivate tribal leaders on the Pakistani side of the border further increased.

During this period, KGB agents working in the guise of expert advisers to many parts of the Afghan government made contacts and carried out clandestine Communist indoctrination of the students at the special tribal leadership schools in Kabul, who came from influential families in strategic areas and might someday be useful. From 1964 on, Taraki and Amin gave special attention to recruitment in those schools.

After various name changes and transmogrifications, the Ministry of Frontiers (as it was called under Amin) was in 1981 renamed the Ministry of Tribes and Nationalities; Suleiman Layeq was named as its head. Its administrative and functional structure was remodeled to replicate the Soviet Commissariat of Nationalities (with a few slight adaptations to Afghan circumstances) and it is now in actuality under KhAD/KGB control. While it handles matters involving the minorities in the north and elsewhere, it is in particular the primary instrument for the manipulation of the Pushtun tribes in southern Afghanistan and Pakistan. Its name in Pushto---Ministry of *Aqwam* (Afghan tribes), *Gabayal* (tribes on the Pakistan side of the border), and *Millatuna* (nationalities, i.e., non-Pushtuns) clearly reveals the scope of its involvement.

Operationally it is organized into "desks" or directorates for each tribe and nationality zone. General directorates are located in the border provinces of Kunar, Nangrahar, Paktya, and Kandahar. Those in Paktya and Kandahar deal with tribes and ethnic groups on both sides of the Pakistan border. Deputy ministers are appointed for each region, with full authority to meet with tribal members, spend money, and do whatever is necessary to persuade tribal chiefs and elders in Pakistan as well as Afghanistan to back the Kabul regime.

Dr. Najib, as head of KhAD from 1980 to 1986, was in charge of tribal affairs via the Ministry; as head of the regime, he still retains specific overall authority in tribal affairs. (His membership in one of Afghanistan's two largest Pushtun tribes, the Ahmadzai, adds to his usefulness.) The financial and political policies of the Ministry and the implementation of its programs through various departments are strictly planned and directed by the KGB using the KhAD organization and its agencies.

The multiple functions of the Ministry, carried out with full political support from other agencies, can be briefly categorized as tactical (pacification) and strategic (sovietization).

Tactically, the KGB has developed tribal and KhAD organizations to penetrate Resistance groups, sabotage Resistance operations, spread rumors and disinformation, and create suspicions and enmity both within and among the various Resistance groups and between the Resistance and local tribes and communities. These agents set one tribe against another, encouraging (and bribing) influential tribal chiefs, spiritual leaders and dissidents of all sorts to exploit their personal rivalries; and they also persuade or bribe them to restrain their respective tribes and communities from anti-Communist activities.

KhAD has formed extensive networks of spies and informers, and establishes militia and tribal units close to the border to observe Resistance activities, to interdict Resistance lines of supply and movement, and to guard offices and homes of regime personnel. KhAD agents carry out bombing and other active measures inside Pakistan, designed to prove to the refugees and Pakistani population that active opposition to the Communist regime in Kabul brings ruthless reprisal while passive acquiescence wins leniency. They also carry out operations in the Afghan refugee camps, spreading propaganda and misinformation and sowing dissension and mistrust.

The long-range intentions of the tribal manipulations among the Pushtuns are, for obvious reasons, not discussed as openly as are the efforts at establishing cross-Oxus ties in the north. However, from the first days of the first Communist regime in 1978, every leader in Kabul has pointedly spoken of DRA support for "the oppressed Pushtun and Baluch people"; and Pakistani Baluch and Pushtun separatist leaders like Khan Abdul Ghaffar Khan, his son Khan Abdul Wali Khan, Ataullah Mengal and others spend significant portions of their time in Kabul and Moscow. When Abdul Wali Khan, who heads Pakistan's Awami National Party, visited Kabul in September 1986 at the invitation of the PDPA Central Committee, Nur Ahmad Nur, in a speech, "assured" him that his visit would "play a significant role [in] the ever-further consolidation of the links between the PDPA and the ANP."[29]

Conclusions

The USSR has designed and is implementing a massive program intended to deprive the Afghans of their cultural heritage and their very identity, and to transform Afghanistan into a passive future instrument of Soviet policy. When Soviet leaders hint at a possible willingness to withdraw military forces, they say nothing about withdrawing their second army---the army of social and cultural transformation, spearheaded by the KGB---or dismantling the programs designed to a accomplish this end. Indeed, both Moscow and Kabul constantly repeat that, whatever cosmetic modifications may be made, "the revolution is irreversible." The sovietization policy is one of the major ways through which they intend to make sure of that.

Notes

The following notes are citations only of published sources and, with a few exceptions, sources that are available without too much difficulty.

A great deal of this chapter is however based on personal experience and observation, monitoring of broadcasts, and numerous interviews with Afghan refugees from all walks of life with direct experience of the situation. Much of this is unpublished, and therefore does not readily lend itself to documentation; however, supportive material is available in a number of sources, including publications of WUFA, the *Central Asian Survey*, bulletins issued in Peshawar, FBIS reports, human rights reports, etc., as well as occasionally in the general press.

1. E.H. Carr. *The Bolshevik Revolution* (London: vol. 1): 432.

2. Ibid., 376.

3. *Englistan da Afghanistan Pa Zad* [Britain Against Afghanistan] (Moscow: Novosti, 1980): 5. In Pushto.

In contradiction to their usual pattern of condemning the Tsarist regime, the Soviet propagandists now defer to their predecessors for their colonization of Central Asia and even praise them as great rulers. For this purpose, in July 1982 the Kremlin encouraged the celebration of the anniversary of the Tsarist occupation of Kazakhstan in Alma-Ata. For this celebration, the Russians and the local Communist Party fabricated and forged many documents which contradicted the historical facts of the brutal occupation of Kazakhstan. Mr. Konayov and Mr. Rashidov, respectively the general secretaries of the Communist Parties of Kazakhstan and Uzbekistan, thanked the "Great Russian regime" for allowing the Uzbeks "voluntarily" to join the union of the "civilized community." According to Mr. Konayov, "For a long time, the oppressed Central Asian masses had been struggling to rid themselves of their oppressive rulers, and Great Russians carefully watched all these brutal oppressions by the semi-civilized rulers in Central Asia. When it became unbearable, Great Russia had no alternative except to respond to the wishes of the masses to put them under a civilized administration. Kazakhstan was also voluntarily annexed to the Union of Great Russia in 1732 and since then the Great Russians have always given due respect to the general will, hopes and expectations of their Kazakh brothers. After the voluntary annexation to Great Russia, a special importance was given to the right of self-determination and political status of our free Kazakhstan." (*Soviet Ozbekistani,* 12 June 1982). At the end of this historical mockery, the Kremlin sent Mr. Victor Grishin, member of the Politburo and secretary of the Moscow Communist Party, to Alma-Ata to bestow the Lenin Medal upon the Soviet Republic of Kazakhstan for its "voluntary union" with Great Russia 252 years earlier.

4. U. Gangovsky and Mucil, *Tarikh Naween-i-Afghanistan* [New History of Afghanistan], translated into Dari. (Kabul University, Department of Social Science, 1984): 3.

5. Ibid., 41.

6. The Soviets attempt to twist the well-established facts concerning two important events: firstly, they acquit the dominant KGB agents working under the guise of police advisers of complicity in the genocide during the Taraki-Amin period, and, secondly they claim that it was the Afghans and not Soviet forces who killed Amin, the pawn in the Soviets' first-round chess game in Afghanistan. See *Da Afghanistan Pa Vara Rishtia Sanaduna, Haqayaq aw Shawahid* [The Truth About Afghanistan: Documents, Facts, Eyewitness Reports] (Moscow: Novosti, 1980): 3-6. In Pushto; available in English.

7. Chantal Lobato. *Central Asian Survey,* vol. 4, no. 4 (Oxford, 1985): 114. See: Krakowski; also Appendix IV, this volume.

8. *Da Islam Nanga* [In Defense of Islam] (Kabul, 1980): 45-46. In Pushto.

9. Judge Omar Babrakzai. Statement to the Bar Association of the City of New York, 28 January 1983. *World Affairs,* vol. 145, no. 3 (Washington, D.C., Winter 1982-83): 303. See also for details of court operations since 1978. Judge Babrakzai is a graduate of the University of Paris and was formerly a judge of the High Court of Appeals in Kabul.

10. Agence-i-Italati Bakhtar (Kabul, 1983): 2. In Farsi.

11. "Medals to Afghan Actor." *Afghanistan Today* (Kabul: Journal of Peace, Solidarity and Friendship Organization of the Democratic Republic of Afghanistan. Sept.-Dec. 1985): 30.

12. FBIS *South Asia* (10 October 1986): C2.

13. Sayed Mohammad Yusuf Elmi, "Education As an Instrument of Sovietization," *The Sovietization of Afghanistan,* S.B. Majrooh and S.M.Y. Elmi, eds. (Peshawar: Afghan Jehad Translation Centre, 1986): 90-91.

14. The First Congress of the Teachers (Kabul, 1980): 158. In Farsi.

15. "Kabul Students Join Work Brigades," *Afghanistan Today,* (Kabul: March-April 1986): "Over 2,000 students of Kabul city, boys and girls, joined last winter the labour and construction brigade of Democratic Youth Organization of Afghanistan...contributing to the socio-economic development of the country. Of them, 1,400 were assigned in the productive, construction and transport institutions of Afghanistan's capital. Fifty boys were sent to Karkar coal mine in Baghlan province. Another group of 50 worked at Lashkari canal, Nimroze province. The procedure of admission, payment of salary, food allowance and transportation of the brigades was in conformity with the contracts concluded between the DYOA district and the concerned institutions..."

16. Elmi, op. cit., 80. Prof. Elmi provides extensively detailed information on the university situation and the faculty.

17. Elmi, op. cit., 75.

18. Rosanne Klass, "Pushing and Pulling Pakistan Apart," *The Wall Street Journal* (New York, 2 October 1984).

19. For constantly varying and inconsistent literacy claims, see numerous FBIS *South Asia* reports since 1979.

20. *Afghan Realities,* No. 34 (Peshawar: Afghan Information and Documentation Centre, 1 June 1985).

21. See: Michael Goldsmith, "Report Soviets Ship Children to Russia for Decade of Indoctrination," Associated Press (13 November 1984) and other widely published reports in the general press. See also: Rubin, op. cit., pp. 80-82, and Jeri Laber, *To Win The Children* (New York: Helsinki Watch, 1986): 10-12.

22. Barnett R. Rubin, *To Die in Afghanistan* (New York: Helsinki Watch, 1985): 71-87.

23. Rubin, op. cit., 83-87. See also: John Barron, "Trained As a Terrorist—At Age Nine," *Reader's Digest* (August 1985):69-73.

24. *Ozbekistan adabieti va san'ati* (25 December 1981).

25. Ibid.

26. Ibid.

27. Ibid.

28. *Yuldis* [The Star] (Tashkent: September 1980).

29. Agence-i-Italati Bakhtar (Kabul, 1 September 1986).

"The Communists promised us bread, clothing, and houses.
For bread, they gave us bullets; for clothing, shrouds; and
for houses, the grave."
               ---Common saying among Afghans since 1979.

Human Rights in Afghanistan

Barnett R. Rubin

> When half the population is uprooted and a third driven into exile,
> when infant mortality reaches plague levels, when half a million
> civilians die and uncounted millions of others are maimed and
> malnourished, when the situation is getting worse, all this moves
> Soviet conduct well beyond what is ordinarily called "human rights
> violations." The word that comes to mind when one reads this
> report is genocide...Moscow is committing one of the great
> crimes.
>   ---*Washington Post*, 15 December 1985, commenting on the
> November 1985 report of the Special Rapporteur on Afghanistan of
> the United Nations Commission on Human Rights.

WHEN HEARING accounts of the atrocities committed in Afghanistan, some
Westerners wonder whether the current level of human rights violations
there is a continuation of a longstanding pattern that now attracts attention
only because of the involvement of the Soviets. Historical studies of the
treatment of prisoners and of dissident elements of the population are few,
but the available evidence suggests that the level of abuses since 1978 is
unprecedented, and that it reflects the widespread disaffection from a government bereft of legitimacy, the unparalleled technology of violence available to that government and the occupation forces, and the sophisticated
counterinsurgency and institution-building techniques introduced by the
Soviets.

    Until the late nineteenth century Afghanistan's political structure
remained medieval. Political conflict and the administration of justice could
be harsh and violent, but much depended on the personality of the ruler. As

336

elsewhere, the establishment of a modern state proceeded with considerable violence. Amir Abdur Rahman Khan (reigned 1880-1901), founder of the modern state of Afghanistan, repressed rebellions ruthlessly and summarily executed thousands of his opponents.

His successors, however, tried, gradually and haltingly, to modernize the consolidated state they inherited from him. The rulers tried to erect a legal system and promulgated constitutions that limited the powers of the rulers. Torture was outlawed in 1904 and, although it occasionally continued, sometimes at the behest of the ruler himself, it did not become institutionalized again until 1978. Prison conditions gradually improved from the medieval horrors of Amir Abdur Rahman's time to a rudimentary but modern regimen, including rights to see visitors and to receive packages of food, books, and writing materials. Political arrests occurred at several times: in the 1930's, following the assassination of a king, and at the end of the first constitutional period (1949-1952), when the royal establishment became alarmed by the growth of a small radical group. The protection of human rights improved notably during the second constitutional period (1963-1973) under King Mohammed Zahir.

After the coup of 1973, which (with the aid of army officers linked to the Parcham faction of the People's Democratic Party of Afghanistan [PDPA]), brought former Prime Minister Daoud back to power, there was a relatively small number of arrests. A former prime minister, Mohammed Hashim Maiwandwal, died in prison under mysterious circumstances and, after an unsuccessful uprising by Islamic revolutionaries in 1975, several hundred were arrested, and some executed. Daoud then distanced himself from Parcham and, according to some opposition groups, entered into contact with SAVAK, the secret police of the Shah of Iran, to help train his security forces. Nevertheless, repressive measures applied only to active political opponents, and were usually undertaken with some measure of legality. There were no disappearances and at most a handful of unexplained deaths that might have been summary executions.[1]

The Khalqi Period: April 1978 to December 1979

After the PDPA coup of 27 April 1978, the Khalq ("Masses") faction initially emerged as dominant.[*] [†] The two Khalqi leaders, Nur Mohammad

---

[*] See: Arnold and Klass.

[†] However, during the first months after the coup, Parcham controlled the Ministry of Interior (police), headed by Nur Ahmad Nur. The arbitrary arrests, torture and secret executions which began immediately after the coup were therefore carried out with, at the least, Parcham's complicity.---ed.

Taraki and Hafizullah Amin, surprised Afghans with a level of repression they could hardly have imagined.[2]

The repression was not simply a response to resistance. Although repression intensified in response to the growth of armed resistance in various regions of the country, it preceded, and indeed helped to inspire, the revolt. The summary execution of certain real or suspected political opponents grew directly out of Khalqi ideology, according to which a small band of feudalists and reactionaries exploited the people of Afghanistan by keeping them in ignorance. Killing these real or suspected opponents went hand in hand with the "literacy" and "land reform" programs as part of a strategy for revolutionary change.[3] As conflict broke out both within the ruling party and between the government and population, the repression extended to those even suspected of opposition as a result of family or ethnic ties, and also became an instrument for settling personal or family scores under cover of political action. Thousands, perhaps tens of thousands, were arrested and tortured; many were executed without trial and just disappeared.

Those arrested and killed included political leaders of the constitutionalist period (such as former Prime Ministers Moussa Shafiq and Nur Ahmad Etemadi); members of Daoud's family and other branches of the royal family; religious scholars and spiritual leaders (including, for instance, all the men of the Mojadidi family still in Kabul, by birth the leaders of the Naqshbandiya Sufi order); high school teachers and students, university students and professors, including leading scholars; lawyers and judges; government and diplomatic officials; military officers, members of the Parcham faction of the PDPA, members of other parties (including several anti-Soviet Marxist parties oriented towards Maoism; Afghan Mellat, a Pashtun nationalist group identifying itself as social democratic; and Islamic political organizations); members of the Hazara and Nuristani ethnic groups (whose regions were among the first to revolt); and local dignitaries in many parts of the countryside.[4]

During this period arrests were carried out at night, sometimes by the army and sometimes by the newly established security police, called AGSA under Taraki and KAM under Amin. The major detention centers in Kabul at that time were the Interior Ministry and Pul-i-Charkhi prison. All prisoners were tortured and many executed, sometimes in horrendous and brutal ways. There does not seem to have been even a pretense of judicial procedure. Testimonies collected by Michael Barry, an American anthropologist with long experience in Afghanistan, suggest the atmosphere in the prisons. Testimony of a professor:

> Torture began at ten o'clock at night, and lasted until four in the morning.
> It was electric shocks, and also a sort of electric chair....There was a

man there, the commander of Pul-i-Charki, his name was Sayyed 'Abdollah. He could decide death for people, he could have them shot at once, he could bury them alive...in the earth.

Especially at night they put people against the wall, and turned on them a sort of blue light. Then they shot them. Collectively. Ten persons. Twenty persons. Sometimes 45. One night 120 persons were killed under the wall.

Someone's cell was searched, and they found a ballpoint pen. That was the most dangerous weapon there. The prisoner was brought before the line of inmates. The commander told them: "He has done something very serious. He has had a pen reach him inside the prison. We are going to teach you a lesson. If any one of you does the same thing, he will be punished the same way." The prisoner was thrown into the pool of filth [excrement---the professor had drawn a map showing the location of the cesspool]. He tried to get out, but it was soft, he sank, the soldiers around pushed him with sticks, and drowned him.[5]

As, one after another, various parts of the country passed into resistance, the regime responded with massive reprisals against civilians. In March 1979 the army collected 1200 men in the village of Kerala [Chagaserai] in Kunar Province, and asked them why they were helping the Resistance. When the villagers denied giving such help:

The godless Commander Nezamuddin said, "Lie down!" . . .There were perhaps twelve hundred people who lay down. Then he gave the order: "Fire!" Twelve hundred people, all the Muslims, were killed in this firing. And then there was a tank, what you call a bulldozer. This tank drove over the Muslims and lifted them up in the air and threw them in the ground. Some were still alive, but they were buried. The others were dead. They were buried.[6]

In April-May 1979 soon after members of the Hazara ethnic group had overrun government posts near the northern town of Samangan, witnesses reported that Afghan troops with Soviet advisers rounded up all the males from one village and drowned them in the Oxus River (Amu Darya). Several independent reports speak of 1500 dead. Other Hazaras were thrown off a cliff into a nearby ravine, where they were machine-gunned.[7] In August 1979 the police arrested about 300 Hazaras living in Kabul, half of whom were burned to death with gasoline and half buried alive.[8]

There are various estimates of the number killed under the Khalqi regime, most of them dealing only with those killed in prisons in Kabul. After Hafizullah Amin had Taraki killed and took sole power in September

1979, the Ministry of the Interior announced that it would publish the names of 12,000 people who had died *in Kabul jails* since April 1978. It is not clear, however, whether the list was ever published. After the Soviet invasion the Karmal regime and other sources gave various numbers for those killed by its predecessors, ranging from 4,854 (given by the Kabul government to Amnesty International) to 32,000 (reported by Michael Barry). Oliver Roy, a careful scholar, summarized as best he could: "The number of executed and missing persons in the countryside was also very great, although these victims received less publicity than those at Kabul. In all about 50,000 to 100,000 people disappeared...Partial inquiries have been made, but the story of this wave of repression has yet to be written."[9]

Human rights: Soviet occupation, 1979 to date

When the Soviets invaded, killed Amin, and installed Babrak Karmal, part of the justification given by Babrak and his associates was a vigorous denunciation of the atrocities of the Khalqi regime, all of which they attributed to the person of Hafizullah Amin. The new government proclaimed an amnesty for some prisoners on 28 December 1979; the extent of the amnesty and the precise events surrounding the release of prisoners are disputed.[10] What cannot be disputed is that, in the words of Ghausuddin, Afghanistan's leading artist, "although they released some of the prisoners, they have filled the prisons again and again."[11]

Under the Soviet-Parcham regime, the pattern of human rights violations has changed, as a result of a change in political strategy. Since 1980 repression has been part of a counterinsurgency program to provide the security necessary for a longer-term policy of building a new, Sovietized Afghanistan. The pattern of repression in the countryside, where the insurgents operate openly, differs from that in the cities, especially Kabul, where open opposition has been suppressed and the process of sovietization is being carried out.[12] The program of "national reconciliation" announced by Najib in January 1987 could lead to further changes. In February 1987 the Kabul regime announced the release of four thousand political prisoners from jails throughout the country, including 1,300 from Pul-i-Charkhi prison; but Western reporters present at the Pul-i-Charkhi release estimated only several hundred released, and their identities could not be verified, nor could the reported release of others elsewhere. No information was available as of March 1987 regarding other changes in the human rights situation. The fifth report of the Special Rapporteur to the U.N. Commission on Human Rights, presented in Geneva in February 1987,

340

concluded that the announced policy of "national reconciliation" had done little to produce an immediate improvement in the human rights situation in Afghanistan.

Attacks on the Rural Population

Probably the largest single cause of civilian casualties in the war is Soviet bombardment of populated areas under the control or influence of the Resistance. The frequency and intensity of the bombing vary with the strategic importance of the area and the level of fighting, but many observers echo Dr. Juliette Fournot of *Médecins sans Frontières* [Doctors Without Borders], who reported in September 1984 other observations during repeated visits to different areas of the country:

> Each village in Afghanistan has been bombed at least one time since four years ago...Everywhere that I have been, in all the villages, there was a story that it had been bombed, six months ago, two years ago, four years ago, even six years ago, at a time when we were not aware of the war, before the official invasion.[13]

After visiting several Afghan provinces in December 1985, *Washington Post* reporter James Rupert found that all of the thirty-two villages he visited had been bombed: "We walked through the abandoned ruins of a dozen villages [in the plain of Zormat, on the route from Pakistan]. Moonlight shone through the shell-shattered walls of homes and mosques."[14] A British art historian, Nick Danziger, reported similar sights on the other side of the country, between the Iranian border and Herat:

> I stayed in a village where they claimed there had been 5,000 inhabitants. There remained one building intact in the whole village. I didn't see more than 10 inhabitants there. To destroy this place the bombers came from Russia. And there were craters everywhere, even where there were no buildings, so there was no pretense about, "We're trying to hit the mujahideen." It was a complete blitz. All the way from there on into Herat there was no one living there, absolutely no one. The town that I stayed in, Hauz-e Karbas, looks like Hiroshima.[15]

Besides the continuing bombing, designed to keep military and psychological pressure on the Resistance base areas, the Soviets have a clear and consistent policy of taking reprisals against civilians for military actions by the Resistance. Afghans in Resistance-held areas have observed this, and defecting Soviet soldiers and former government officials from Kabul confirm it. According to a Soviet defector, Garik Muradovich Dzhamalbekov, "If the mujahideen set fire to trucks on the road, they [the Soviets] carry out strikes against civilian houses. They don't bomb the mujahideen, they bomb the houses."[16] An Afghan who formerly worked in military communications reported, "When the mujahideen ambushed a convoy, we got certain orders....They send a message to the nearest air base to ask for help and also to the nearest brigade or military post. Then maybe 10 to 20 helicopters and MIGs appear and troops move in about two hours and destroy completely all the villages in the area. [Afterwards] in reports they mentioned, we killed 20 ashrar [bandits], 30, even 100 ashrar."[17]

Bombing civilians is clearly intentional, as the Soviets have shown themselves capable of bombing military targets with great precision when they so desire. Furthermore, the bombing is a key part of pacification strategy: the government tells the villagers that if they join pro-government organizations and prevent the Resistance from operating in their area, they will be safe from bombing.[18]

In the countryside, Soviet aircraft and ground troops also distribute anti-personnel mines in inhabited areas, in areas used for grazing, cultivation, and other agricultural activities, and along roads. After sweeps through villages, the troops leave mines in food storage bins, in mosques, under furniture, in fruit trees, and in fields. The most common type of mine is the so-called butterfly mine, which comes in two camouflage colors, brown and green, and which has cost many children their fingers, hands, and feet. (Many of these mines have been seen, photographed and displayed.)

Even more clearly aimed at the civilian population, especially children, are mines disguised as toys and everyday objects, such as toy trucks, watches, pens, and knives. There have been many reports of such disguised mines over the years from refugees (often with serious injuries resulting from them) and from Western medical personnel and journalists inside Afghanistan. Until recently no unexploded sample of these toy mines had been produced; the refugees who described these mines said it was too dangerous to pick them up to bring them to outside observers. In July 1985, however, the Kabul government displayed a selection of such mines at a press conference, claiming that they had been introduced into Afghanistan by "imperialism," and in December 1986 one was shown on American television.[19]

Soviet troops, sometimes assisted by Afghan officials acting as guides or interpreters, kill unarmed civilians during sweeps through villages. The killings take many forms. Sometimes soldiers kill individuals as part of pillage (which is also frequent):

> In October [1985] the Soviets and Afghan Army troops staged a four-day sweep through Barakat [Ghazni Province] and nearby villages, killing 20 people and taking 12 young men to serve in the Afghan Army, villagers said.
>
> The villagers said the Soviets had entered the nearby hamlet of Gabrubr and killed Abdul Gul, 55, and Niaz Gul, 70. "They were just farmers," Bismullah (Khair Mohammad, a villager) said, "and they took their money from their house to keep the Soviets from stealing it. When the Soviets searched them and found the money, they stole it and strangled them. We found their bodies two days later, when the Soviets left," he said.
>
> A young man from nearby Bedmoshk told a horrifying tale of Soviets who held a fourteen-year-old boy and slowly killed him when his parents would not pay a ransom. "They tied him to a tree and beat him and stabbed him with a bayonet," the man said. "Finally they shot him."[20]

Larger massacres of civilians, including the virtual annihilation of entire villages by special commandos, have occurred with increasing frequency since 1984, although they started as early as the Kerala massacre in 1979, mentioned above. A Soviet soldier now with the Resistance in Baghlan Province told the *New York Times,* "Our officers said we must go into a village and kill all the people and animals, sheep, horses, even dogs and cats." Another, who had been stationed near Kandahar, reported, "We were ordered by our officers that when we attack a village, not one person must be left alive to tell the tale. If we refuse to carry out these orders, we get it in the neck ourselves."[21]

The first such massacre to be documented in detail after the Soviet invasion was the killing of 105 people in Padkhwab-e Shana, Logar Province, on 13 September 1982 by Soviet soldiers who ignited an explosive material they had poured into an underground irrigation tunnel *(karez)* where the villagers were hiding.[22] Since then many more incidents involving deaths in the hundreds have been reported. The following account by Mohammad Taher, a forty-year-old graduate of the Engineering Faculty of Kabul University, describes the destruction of his own village, Haji Rahmatullah, in Chardara District, Kunduz Province, on 22 December 1984:

> It was 10 A.M. when some Russians and Parchamis entered the village. We were sitting---we didn't know---and suddenly they started killing our people. Some of our neighbors were killed at that time. Then they came

to my house. My mother, my brother, my mother's brother, in all eight members of my family were killed....They killed all four members of my uncle's family at once with bullets. Our neighbors, Mohammad Akbar, his wife, his mother, and his one-year-old son were killed. [He gave names and ages of those killed in his family and with the help of village elders he provided a list of heads of households in the village and the number killed in each family. The total was 250.]

After the Russians had finished their massacre, we loaded the dead bodies of children and old people and sent them to the capital, Kunduz, for the Governor. And the Governor didn't care about the dead bodies, and he said, take your dead bodies away, I can't do anything about it....When we brought the dead bodies back to the village to bury them in the graveyard, at 4 o'clock in the afternoon, they shelled the village again, and we couldn't bury the bodies. We had to postpone and bury them at night. We had no time, so we put six people, ten people in each grave.[23]

At about the same time, the Soviets apparently attacked other villages in the area; Dr. Fournot of MSF has supplied a list prepared by the Jamiat Islami resistance organization of Kunduz Province giving names of 629 people killed in five nearby villages on 24 December 1984.[24] Such massacres continue: refugees arriving in Pakistan in December 1986 told of the killing of over 600 people on 10 November in five villages on the Amu Darya in the Imam Saheb district of Kunduz Province, apparently in relatiation for the destruction of two helicopters by the Resistance.[25]

One of the purposes of such attacks is to force people to abandon certain areas of the country.[26] One effective way of driving people out of their homes is to deprive them of their livelihood, and the intentional destruction of food, agriculture, and pastoralism has been one of the Soviets' main counterinsurgency tactics. Farmers working in the fields are frequently gunned down by Soviet helicopter gunships or jets. Much of the agricultural work is now done by women, who are forced to reverse the traditional working day, sleeping by day and working in the fields after dark. Virtually every Soviet attack includes the burning of foodstuffs, especially wheat, the main staple of Afghanistan. The Soviets have a variety of specialized incendiary weapons for burning wheat from the air or from the ground, for grain standing in the field, gathered on the threshing floor, or stored in the home.[27]

Even more ominous than destroying food is the Soviets' policy of destroying all the parts of the delicate agricultural and pastoral system that undergirds food production in this semi-arid country in which agriculture is heavily dependent on irrigation. Bombing has destroyed carefully terraced hillsides in the Kunar Valley. Grenades and bombs have destroyed the delicate underground irrigation channels. Soviet aircraft and ground forces systematically bomb, strafe, and slaughter the livestock that is not only the main source of protein and fiber but also the principal means of storing wealth. Five-hundred-pound fragmentation bombs, artillery, and napalm have devastated carefully tended orchards and vineyards. Finally, Soviet forces steal and destroy the personal possessions of the peasants---their teapots, blankets, money, and homes. Such offensives create scenes such as that described by a refugee who fled an April 1985 attack in Laghman Province:

> They used napalm bombs and burned all the crops. My house was bombed, and all the property in the house was destroyed. They burned the ripe wheat fields in the month of Saur [April-May]. In the Kats area of Laghman they destroyed about 2,000 houses. And they totally destroyed the area. Until now there is no one living there. Until now the empty beds are sitting on the rooftops, because there is no one left their alive.[28]

The Soviet-Afghan authorities systematically try to prevent relief or treatment from reaching victims of such offensives. They have bombed medical clinics run under Resistance auspices by foreign or Afghan doctors.

Until recently, they completely forbade the International Committee of the Red Cross to treat the war-wounded or otherwise maintain a presence in Afghanistan. In late 1986 the ICRC announced that it had reached agreement with the Soviets and the Kabul government to establish a hospital in Kabul. As the U.N. Special Rapporteur noted, however, "even if ICRC hospitals were installed in government-controlled areas, they would not admit wounded or sick persons belonging to or suspected of belonging to opposition movements."[29]

Urban Strategies

The generalized violence directed against civilians in the countryside is a sign of lack of control over these areas; the regime remains external to most of Afghanistan's rural society, capable of punishing it or negotiating with it but not, as yet, of penetrating it. The exact opposite is true in Kabul, where the Soviets and their Afghan allies are concentrating their efforts on constructing a new Afghan society. The new society, an extremely repressive variant of the Soviet model, places all social institutions under the control of the state and party, which are dominated by Soviet advisers.[30]

The rulers maintain this control in the short run through a system of spying, torture, prisons, and executions; they hope to retain it in the long run by sending thousands of young Afghan children to the Soviet Union for education in order to form them into a loyal, Sovietized elite. The single largest state institution appears to be WAD, formerly KhAD, the State Information Services, a new agency which was established under KGB supervision in January 1980 to replace KAM and oversee the vast apparatus of intelligence, counterinsurgency, and repression. The importance of KhAD became even more evident in 1986 when it was upgraded to the status of a ministry and its former director, Najib(ullah), succeeded Babrak Karmal as First Secretary of the PDPA.[31]

All newspapers, magazines, and book publishing and sales are under the direct control of the state. Only publications from Soviet bloc countries are available in Kabul. Criticism of the government by citizens is forbidden. Private conversations are monitored by an extensive network of informers. Meetings and even informal gatherings without government approval may be grounds for arrest. All political parties except the PDPA---anti-Soviet Marxists, Pushtun nationalists, Islamic revolutionaries, Islamic reformers, royalists---have been outlawed, and although the "national reconciliation" program announced in January 1987 offers government positions to members of political organizations who renounce armed struggle, it provides no effective safeguard for the free operation of such organizations. Membership in the PDPA, however, confers privilege in every area of life.

While the government states that it encourages Islam, it penalizes religious observance among employees and students in government institutions.[32]

The educational institutions are a major force for the Sovietization program. Soviet advisers arrived at the university in 1978; the curricula at all levels have been changed to reflect Soviet interests, and Soviet-written texts have replaced Afghan and imported textbooks. In the high schools, teachers of "politics" classes pressure students to join the Party's Youth Organization. Party members teach the officially approved ideology, and frank discussion can lead to arrest, as in this incident recounted by a former student at a vocational high school:

> In the politics class we were talking about Sabra and Shatila in Palestine. One of the students said that he would rather learn about our own country, where there were hundreds of Sabras and Shatilas that no one was talking about. After class he was arrested by two guards, students who were members of the [Youth] Organization. He was imprisoned for four months and after four months he signed a paper saying he would no longer speak in class.[33]

At the universities, between 50 and 70 percent of the pre-1978 faculty have been killed, imprisoned, or driven into exile. Party members without academic qualifications have been appointed deans of the faculties, and Soviet and other Eastern bloc advisers and teachers dominate curriculum decisions. The student body, which led mass demonstrations against the Soviet invasion in early 1980, has also been decimated by arrests. Surveillance by KhAD creates an atmosphere of distrust and fear for teachers and students alike. Ideological conformity is required. In 1982 an attempt by a group of professors to create an Organization for the Defense of Human Rights and Academic Freedom led to the arrest of five of them. The four who refused to recant remain in prison, some suffering mentally and physically from the effects of torture, serving sentences of seven to twelve years.[34]

Indoctrination of Children

The methods described above have not managed to produce enough ideological change in the Afghans, however. As a result, in 1984 the Soviet-Afghan government introduced a new program designed to mold a new generation from the earliest school years. They established "National Training Centers" (Parwarishgah-e Watan) ostensibly for "orphans of the revolution," namely children of party members or soldiers killed in the war. Children living in the Centers receive a more thoroughgoing Soviet-style education than in the regular schools. Some of the children remain in the Centers in Afghanistan, but for many of them the Centers are simply gathering points on the way to the Soviet Union. Under an agreement between the USSR and the DRA signed in 1984, at least 2,000 and possibly many more children aged seven to nine are to be sent *each year* to the Soviet Union for ten years of education.[35]

While some of the children gathered into these Centers and sent to the Soviet Union may indeed be orphans or children of Party members who send them there voluntarily, others are taken by other means. The army collects children who survive bombing attacks and transfers them to the Centers. Principals and teachers in the schools put pressure on parents to send their children to the Soviet Union, offering both economic incentives and threats. Sometimes children are simply collected in the school and sent away without informing the parents. A few testimonies illustrate the various methods used:

A former military communications specialist reported: "When they bomb some village and the parents lose their lives, if some children survive, they collect them and take them to the Soviet Union...The military commanders in the political headquarters had to report, 'In this area we have completed the operation, and so many villages were destroyed, and so many children captured by the "forces of friendship" [quwa-ye dost, the term used to refer to Soviet forces] and transferred by helicopter to the Soviet Union.' "[36]

While touring Wardak and Ghazni Provinces, *Washington Post* reporter James Rupert met a man he called Omar. Omar had brought his son to his village to prevent him from being sent to the Soviet Union: "'In Kabul the Soviets are taking the children,' Omar explained....Omar said that many children who had gone to the Soviet Union were those of Afghan Communist Party officials who he thought might have sent them willingly. But, he said, 'I know many families who did not know their children would be taken. The government sent people into the schools, and they took children away. The children's fathers only heard when someone came from school to tell them.' "[37]

A woman doctor, formerly one of Kabul's most prominent obstetricians, reported: "Last year in the month of Sunbulah (August-September 1984) one of my colleagues who was working for me was forced with some other girls and three or four boys to go to the alleys of Deh Mazang and Jamal Mina (neighborhoods). They had the duty to search the houses and find all those children who had no fathers and were being kept by their families. Their families were very sad and unhappy, and the mothers were crying. They took some kind of note from all of them and made a list. Then some soldiers came with a vehicle and took the children out of the houses by force, took them to the airport, and flew them to the Soviet Union."[38]

A former teacher described what happened to the watchman in her school, a poor man who had two sons: "They asked him to send his sons to Parwarishgah-e Watan. They told him, 'You are poor, and they will be well taken care of there.' Finally he agreed and took them to Parwarishgah-e Watan. One day I greeted him and asked, 'How are your sons?' He said, 'Madam, a misfortune has struck me. They have sent my sons to the Soviet Union.' "[39]

Arrests and torture

It is the job of KhAD to uncover and punish those who oppose the new order. The first wave of new arrests began in late February 1980, after the series of demonstrations that began on 21 February (popularly known as the "Night of 'Allahu akbar'") when thousands of Kabul residents shouted "Allahu akbar!" ("God is great") from their rooftops throughout the night and took to the streets by day. Demonstrations, many of them led by schoolgirls, led to hundreds of deaths and thousands of arrests until June, when they were finally brought under control.[40] Since then wave after wave of arrests have again hit virtually all the same groups that were previously targeted under the Khalq---although, since the killing, imprisonment, or emigration of most of the old elites has left relatively few of them to be targeted, the subsequent repression has concentrated more on those suspected of current opposition.

Reasons for suspicion can be quite diverse: a past friendship with an American Peace Corps volunteer, possession of an opposition leaflet, having relatives suspected of opposition, or being named by a paid spy or a prisoner under torture. In June 1983 a group of handicapped teenage boys who had been cared for by a French priest were arrested and interrogated under torture about their alleged work for French intelligence.[41]

The treatment of prisoners has definitely changed since the establishment of the KGB-controlled KhAD, and it continues to evolve as Kabul comes under ever stricter Soviet control. Under the Soviets, systematic torture of virtually all political prisoners continues, but it is now part of a scientific system of intelligence rather than just a form of sadistic punishment. Amnesty International found that "although Amnesty International has received reports of torture under all three governments since the 'Saur revolution' of April 1978...it was only after the formation of the KhAD in late 1979 that the practice was reported to have become systematic."[42] The Soviets have introduced increasingly sophisticated equipment as well as more techniques of psychological torture. Prisoners who have been arrested more than once corroborate the changes:

An engineer arrested for membership in Afghan Mellat reflected: "I was arrested three times, once under Taraki, once under Amin, and once under Babrak and the Russians. Before, they were killing a lot of people without any investigation. Many of them just disappeared. But the third time they did a really deep investigation. It is much better organized, because of the Russians."[43]

A woman high school teacher arrested in 1981 and again in 1984 reported: "The main difference the second time was the increased dependence of the Afghan KhAD on the Soviet advisers. The last time it was much more pronounced than the first time. For example, the Afghans bragged to each other about being close to the Soviet advisers. They competed with each other for their attention. The first time I clearly distinguished the Soviet advisers from the Afghans, but this time the Soviets were in direct contact with the prisoners. I also heard that the Soviets give torture themselves sometimes for more suspect, more dangerous prisoners. I especially heard this the last time."[44]

The pattern of interrogation is standardized. The KhAD officers first take the prisoner to one of the many preliminary interrogation centers established throughout Kabul (Amnesty International lists seven) for the first round of questioning. Most prisoners eventually continue their interrogation in the KhAD's Central Office in the Prime Ministry, located in the Sedarat Palace. When the KhAD is satisfied that the "file is complete," they transfer the prisoner to Pul-i-Charkhi prison. Some prisoners report continued interrogation in Pul-i-Charkhi, but for most it is merely a detention center.

The methods of torture are those familiar throughout the world: beatings, death threats, pulling out of hair and fingernails, near-drownings, sleep deprivation, strangling, and, most common of all, electric shocks. The electric shock equipment has been upgraded since the Soviet invasion; prisoners have described a number of contraptions that go beyond the original supply of shock batons. Several sources tell of a new equipment introduced in 1984, such as the chair that was used to torture an eighteen-year-old girl who had distributed anti-Soviet leaflets in October of that year:

> For the electric shocks there was a new machine brought from the Soviet Union. They fixed wires around the wrist. There was a chair on which they made you sit. They tied us to it and connected the wires to the electricity. Then they pushed a switch. The chair turned around in a circle. When they connected it to the electricity, the chair moved so fast it made me dizzy.[45]

All prisoners, as well as defectors from KhAD, report that Soviet advisers control and permeate KhAD. While Soviet officers rarely give the torture themselves (at least not to prisoners insignificant enough to have been released and to have reached refuge outside the country where they can report their stories), virtually all former prisoners report in identical terms that their interrogators periodically reported to Soviets for instructions. Some report interrogation directly by Soviet officers.[46]

Trials and Legalistic Forms

A major change from the Khalqi period is that most former prisoners report receiving a sort of trial by a Revolutionary Court. But prisoners are not informed in advance of the sessions of the court and are not allowed to have defense representation. The courts meet in secret and invariably confirm the verdict already determined by KhAD. Prisoners are no longer subject to execution without trial in the jails, but the Revolutionary Courts appear to hand out the death penalty frequently, mostly for charges having to do with participation in armed resistance. The government does not announce most executions, so the total is not known. Prisoners at Pul-i-Charkhi report several dozen men a week being taken out blindfolded for execution.

Prisoners sentenced to jail generally serve out their terms in overcrowded

Pul-i-Charkhi prison under conditions that breed lice and disease; these conditions led to a revolt by the prisoners in June 1982 which was severely repressed.[47]   The number of prisoners is unknown; the United Nations Special Rapporteur stated that "according to one source, over 50,000 political prisoners are distributed as follows between Kabul and the provincial prisons: 70 per cent men, 15 per cent women and 15 per cent young people, the latter two categories being held for the most part in the provincial prisons."[48] Estimates of the number of inmates of Pul-i-Charkhi alone have ranged from 12,000 to over 20,000; a 1986 estimate by Amnesty International put the number at over 10,000 prisoners, of whom not more than 1,000 were common criminals.

The Soviet and DRA forces do not accept Resistance fighters as prisoners of war. As noted by the U.N. Special Rapporteur, despite regular reports of defeats in which "bandits" are reported to be "crushed," there are no known prisoner of war camps in Afghanistan. According to many reports, Soviet troops frequently (although not invariably) execute captured fighters. Soviet defectors have described captives being crushed by tanks, stabbed to death, and blown apart by artillery.[49]

Human Rights Violations by the Afghan Resistance Groups

The parties and groups engaged in the fight against the Soviets and their Afghan allies vary in their treatment of prisoners, civilians, and members of rival parties. The most consistent allegations of violations of human rights are made against the Hezb-i-Islami organization led by Gulbuddin Hekmatyar.

Some of the Afghan Resistance parties have allowed the International Commission of the Red Cross (ICRC) access to Soviet prisoners, a limited number of whom have been transferred to Switzerland under an agreement between the ICRC and the Resistance parties. (This agreement is currently not being implemented further because the Resistance expected the ICRC to be allowed some visits with Resistance prisoners held in Kabul, which the Soviets continue to refuse.)   Some Soviet prisoners are undoubtedly executed on the orders of local commanders. The Resistance releases captured Afghan conscripts, but generally keeps DRA officers. Some groups try to use the officers to bargain for prisoner exchanges, but most execute them if they are found to be Communists after some type of investigation or trial. Suspected spies may be tortured and executed as well. The Islamic trials held by Resistance groups vary from summary procedures to elaborate hearings with considerably more judicial safeguards than those of the Kabul government.

Conflicts among the Resistance parties, most often between the

Hezb/Hekhmatyar and the rest, lead to various abuses. The Hezb/Hekhmatyar has captured and executed rival fighters and attacked villagers belonging to other groups. Resistance groups sometimes attack civilian targets associated with the Kabul government, notably during operations inside the capital.[50]

Consequences for the population

The extent of death, hunger, disease, and depopulation as a result of the invasion of Afghanistan place it among the great disasters of the twentieth century. Nevertheless, accurate figures are hard to come by. In his first report the United Nations Special Rapporteur noted "certain estimates," according to which bombing and massacres have "resulted in the killing of approximately 500,000 Afghans since 1979, most of them civilians." In his second report he cites other statistics according to which "32,755 civilians were reported to have been killed [during the first nine months of 1985]....1,834 houses destroyed, 74 villages destroyed and 3,038 animals killed."[51]

No one has yet undertaken the demographic work necessary to arrive at more precise estimates of those killed. This author can note from his own experience in interviewing about 200 Afghan refugees in Pakistan that it is rare to find anyone who has not lost at least one family member.

There is anthropometric and other evidence that the destruction of agriculture has created pre-famine conditions in certain regions of the country. In some areas the diet is limited to bread and tea (without sugar). The peasants have consumed their livestock and may be on the verge of consuming seeds. Infant mortality, always high, has skyrocketed to 300 to 400 per thousand. Food is readily available in Kabul and other government controlled cities, but villagers may lack funds to buy it. The long-term result of the famine conditions may be further depopulation through emigration from the affected regions.[52]

The extent of depopulation can at least be estimated. The United Nations High Commission for Refugees counts 2.8 million Afghan refugees registered in Pakistan, and there are estimated to be about 400,000 more unregistered. The government of Iran claims that there are 1.8 million Afghan refugees registered in Iran, and there, too, many others are unregistered.[53] Out of a prewar population estimated at 15.5 million, therefore, about a third have left the country. Several million more have abandoned their homes while relocating for greater safety elsewhere inside Afghanistan: since 1979 the population of Kabul has grown from around 600,000 to perhaps two million. Thus as many as half of all Afghans may have been forced to leave their homes. In the autumn of 1985, a team from the International Humanitarian Enquiry Commission on Displaced Persons in Afghanistan, in a survey of portions of Paktia, Logar, Wardak, and Ghazni Provinces, found 56.4 percent of all dwellings abandoned.[54]

The violation of human rights in Afghanistan is a challenge to the world community. One can do no better than to repeat the appeal of Professor Ermacora, who in his third report foresees a situation "approaching genocide":

> In view of the worsening situation in the country that every day claims victims among the civilian population, in particular among women and children, governments and representatives of international organizations have an urgent responsibility to find ways and means to ensure respect for and guarantees of human rights throughout the country. The Special Rapporteur is convinced that every hour lost is detrimental to the population and to the human rights situation in the country.[55]

Notes

1. For historical background on human rights in Afghanistan, see: works listed in the bibliography of this volume by Kakar, Gregorian and Dupree.

For Daoud's republic (1973-1978) see: Henry Bradsher, *Afghanistan and the Soviet Union* (Durham, N.C.: Duke University Press, 1983); *The Disappeared: Report on a New Technique of Repression.* (London: Amnesty International, 1980); Louis Dupree, "Red Flag Over the Hindu Kush," *American Universities Field Service Report No. 28*, Part V, 1980; A. Rasul Amin, "The Saur Revolution," *WUFA*, vol. 1, no. 2. (Peshawar: Writer's Union of Free Afghanistan, 1986): 11.

2. Olivier Roy, *Islam and Resistance in Afghanistan* (New York and London: Cambridge University Press, 1986): 84-97.

3. Ibid.

4. Amnesty International lists categories of the population who were arrested in Kabul (op. cit.: 64-65), as does Roy (op. cit.: 126-128). Dupree also gives a partial list of religious figures in Kabul ("Red Flag Over the Hindu Kush," Parts V & VI) but, as he notes, "The arrests and executions never stopped."

5. Michael Barry, "Afghanistan—Another Cambodia?" *Commentary* (August 1982): 29-37. A prison testimony from the same period is that of American anthropologist Louis Dupree, arrested in Kabul in November 1978 during a purge of the universities. See his "Red Flag Over the Hindu Kush," Parts V & VI.

6. Michael Barry, "Repression et Guerre Sovietiques," *Les Temps Modernes* (July-August 1980): 227. Interview with an eyewitness. This well-documented incident was first reported by Edward Girardet in *The Christian Science Monitor* (4 February 1980). According to Girardet's witnesses, as well as an eyewitness who testified in Oslo in March 1983, a group of Soviet advisors accompanied the Afghan unit and approved (or

gave) the order to shoot. See also: Girardet, *Afghanistan: The Soviet War* (New York: St. Martin's Press, 1985): 107-110.

7. Barry, op. cit.: 211-213, gives several independent accounts.

8. Testimonies in ibid., 204. Also reported in *Le Monde* (17 August 1979).

9. For reports on the lists published and estimates of numbers killed, see: *Amnesty International Report 1980:* 177-179; Barry, "Afghanistan---Another Cambodia?": 29; Roy, op. cit.: 95-97; Dupree, "Red Flag Over the Hindu Kush," Part IV: 9.

Amnesty International reports that the Khalqi list of the dead was never published, but states that during a visit of an AI delegation to Kabul in February 1980, after Babrak had replaced Amin, "The Ministry of the Interior revealed that it possessed a list of 4,854 people killed whose names it had not published; the list was far from complete. Many inquiries had been received about the fate of 9,000 individuals who had 'disappeared' after arrest in the Kabul area."

Roy writes, "In February 1980, the government of Babrak Karmal acknowledged 12,000 'official' killings, but these were only those who disappeared in Pul-i-Charkhi prison."

According to Dupree, however, "The Amin regime attempted to place blame for the repressions on Taraki by announcing a list of 12,000 persons executed prior to September 15 [1979]...The announcements stopped abruptly after about half the names had been released, because 10,000 demonstrators in front of the Ministry of the Interior demanded more details, and government feared an outbreak of violence."

Barry also claims that the list was published, but puts the number of names at 15,000. To this figure he adds an additional 17,000---which he says is the number of prisoners found to be missing when Pul-i-Charkhi was briefly opened following the Soviet invasion---to obtain a total figure (32,000); even if these figures are accurate, some of those counted as missing might have figured on the earlier list, in which case it would be a mistake to add them.

Clearly an accurate count may never be possible.

[Amin blamed the killings on Taraki. The Babrak regime, having rehabilitated Taraki and obliterated reference to its own early participation in the Taraki regime, placed all blame for the acknowledged executions on Amin, who, it claimed, was a CIA agent. Who will be blamed by Babrak's successors remains to be seen.---ed.]

10. For the post-invasion Soviet view of human rights under the Khalq regime echoed by Kabul, as well as the official depiction of the "complete amnesty for political prisoners," see: *The Truth About Afghanistan: Documents, Facts, Eyewitness Reports* (Moscow: Novosti Press Agency, 1980).

Barry, in "Afghanistan---Another Cambodia?," describes the amnesty differently: "On January 5, 1980, President Karmal freed Parcham faction members from the Pul-i-Charkhi concentration camp. Then, pressure from rioters at the prison gates forced the freeing of all inmates." On the other hand, Anthony Hyman, in *Afghanistan Under Soviet Domination*, p. 177, describes the release of a mere 118 prisoners, after which crowds of relatives stormed the prison gates, seeking family members. [According to many sources, including some who were in the prison at the time, not all prisoners were released.---ed.]

The Kabul government itself gave several different figures for the number of prisoners released, ranging from 6,146 to 15,084; the government explained the difference to Amnesty International as the number of prisoners released outside Kabul. Independent sources estimated to AI that 3,000 to 4,000 prisoners had been released from Pul-i-Charkhi. See: *Amnesty International Report 1980:* 180, and Henry Bradsher, *Afghanistan and the Soviet Union:* 187-188.

Many observers describe scenes such as that recorded by Hyman, op. cit.: 177: "A Kabul engineer went [to Pul-i-Charkhi prison], armed with a list of 134 professional men and intellectuals who had disappeared, and found to his horror that not one was alive. Many families at last realised that they could expect no better news, and out of their frustrations and anger a mood of defiance developed in the capital."

11. Barnett R. Rubin, *To Die in Afghanistan: A Supplement to "Tears, Blood, and Cries": Human Rights in Afghanistan Since the Invasion, 1979 to 1984* (New York: Helsinki Watch and Asia Watch, December 1985): 103.

12. For reasons of space, this summary is necessarily oversimplified in a number of ways. The various provinces and regions have fared differently, depending on such factors as their political and strategic importance, the location of natural resources, topography, and Resistance activity. The eastern and northeastern parts of the country---which include major supply lines from the Soviet Union, Resistance infiltration and supply routes from Pakistan, major Soviet bases, and rich agricultural areas like Baghlan and Nangrahar---have received especially harsh treatment. So has the region between Herat and the Iranian frontier, for similar reasons. The northern steppes (including the heavily-protected gas fields which supply Soviet Central Asia), accessible by land from the Soviet Union, and lacking mountain redoubts for the Resistance, are under more stable occupation than some other areas.

Aside from Kabul, Kunduz, Mazar-i-Sharif, and one or two other towns on major Soviet supply routes or adjoining major Soviet bases, most of the towns are contested to some degree; the Resistance operates openly, if sporadically, in Kandahar and Herat, the second and third largest cities. It appears that while certain government institutions---at least KhAD, the secret police---function in most towns, it is only in Kabul and possibly Mazar-i-Sharif that a complete Sovietization program is underway. Moreover, Soviet strategy and tactics vary to some extent at different times. Under Andropov, direct military attacks on civilians decreased and efforts at pacification were favored, while under his successors Chernenko and Gorbachev, counterinsurgency terror in rural areas has returned and increased.

13. Jeri Laber and Barnett R. Rubin,*"Tears, Blood, and Cries": Human Rights in Afghanistan Since the Invasion, 1979-1984* (New York: Helsinki Watch, 1984): 26. Médecins Sans Frontières is one of several European humanitarian organizations that have operated medical clinics inside Resistance-held territory in Afghanistan. Dr. Fournot has directed the MSF program in Afghanistan since 1980; she spent part of her chidhood in Afghanistan and is fluent in Farsi.

14. James Rupert, "Depopulation campaign brutally changes villages," *Washington Post* (15 January 1986).

15. Laber and Rubin, op. cit.: 23.

16. Tim Cooper, "Inside Afghanistan: the plight of a prisoner," *Financial Times* (London. 23 May 1984).

17. Rubin, op. cit.: 16-17.

18. On both these points see the testimony of two MSF nurses who spent six months in Balkh province: Rubin, op. cit.: 13-15.

19. Many reports about the war have described these mines. For a selection of testimonies and some further references, see Laber and Rubin, op. cit., 55-63. For more recent information see Rubin, op. cit.: 33-39, which also contains information on the Kabul press conference. See also: listings in the bibliography, especially Girardet and Fullerton.

The Kabul press conference was reported by Lt. Col. V. Skirzhalin, "V. Kogo Oni Tselyatsya: Press-konferentsiya v Kabulye" ("At Whom Are They Aiming: Press Conference in Kabul") *Krasnaya Zvezda.* (Moscow: 12 June 1985): 3.

[In December 1986 one of the red plastic toy mines was shown for the first time outside Afghanistan on the CBS Evening News, where it was shown both intact and exploding. On 30 December 1986 *Izvestia,* denouncing an advertisement by the Afghanistan Relief Committee in the *Washington Post,* acknowledged that such toy mines exist but claimed that they are manufactured by the U.S. and provided to the "bandits."—Ed.]

20. Rupert, op. cit. See also Barry, Lagerfelt et al, in bibliography. The press-ganging into the army reported during this campaign is quite common, as the Afghan Army quickly loses new recruits through desertion. See Laber and Rubin, op. cit.: 63-65. Extra-judicial executions of individual Afghans occur during house searches (especially when weapons are found), in the course of robbery, looting and rape, as part of interrogation, or as random terror or revenge. See ibid.: 41-55.

21. Arthur Bonner, "Five Defectors, turned Afghan, fight 'Holy War'," *New York Times* (1 November 1985); see also Christina Dameyer, "Afghan guerrillas may turn Soviet deserters into a fighting force," *Christian Science Monitor* (10 August 1984). See also the account of a massacre in Tashkurghan given by Soviet defector Garik Dzhamalbekov in Laber and Rubin, op. cit.: 34-35.

22. See: Richard Bernstein, "Afghans in New York Tell of a Massacre by Russians," *New York Times* (28 January 1983); Patrick E. Tyler, "The Horrors and Rewards of the Soviet Occupation of Afghanistan," *Washington Post* (13 February 1983); Rosanne Klass, "Lifting the Curtain on Afghanistan's Horror," *Wall Street Journal* (24 January 1983). This massacre was documented by a team led by Michael Barry and sponsored by the People's Tribunal.

23. Rubin, op. cit.: 18-23, provides the complete testimony as well as several other independent accounts of the same incident.

24. Ibid.: 32-33. Members of the International Humanitarian Inquiry Commission met refugees from some of these villages inside Pakistan on 27 September 1985. They described massacres in their villages on the same date given in Dr. Fournot's report, part of which is included in: Rosanne Klass, "The New Holocaust," *National Review* (4 October 1985): 29. See also: Michael Barry, "Les Chemins de l'Exode," *Defis Afghan* no. 5 (January 1986): 9-10.

25. Interviews with refugees by the author, and subsequently also by Jan Goodwin, Executive Editor, *Ladies Home Journal.*

26. See: Claude Malhuret, "Report from Afghanistan," *Foreign Affairs* (Winter 1983/84) vol. 62, no. 2. See also: Krakowski, this volume. The systematic destruction of agriculture is limited to the strategic areas targeted for depopulation in eastern, northeastern, southern and western Afghanistan and in apecific districts targeted for various reasons,e.g. they support the Resistance, the area is required for Soviet use, etc. See also: Bodansky.

27. Some of the destruction of agriculture is collateral war damage, but the pattern of specific targeting of agricultural infrastructure and food indicates that much of it is intentional. Laber and Rubin, op. cit.: 74, describe some of the various weapons used to burn wheat. [Dr. Johan Lagerfelt, a member of the International Humanitarian Inquiry Commission mentioned above, reported at the second Oslo hearing, March 1986, that Soviet troops urinate and defecate in villagers' food stores to render them inedible.---ed.]

28. Rubin, op. cit.: 48. For full documentation of the pattern described above see Laber and Rubin, op. cit., 70-82. See also: Claude Malhuret, op. cit.

29. Felix Ermacora. Fourth report, 9 January 1987, para. 92: 21. See full citation in the bibliography.

30. Beginning in November 1985, the PDPA, under pressure from Moscow to try to broaden its base, began to appoint non-Party people to an enlarged Revolutionary Council and as deputy ministers. Members of parties other than the PDPA remain excluded, as all such parties are illegal and will remain so "unless they support the revolution." Since policy making remains effectively in the hands of the Soviets, these changes cannot lead to changes of policy. As of this writing (March 1987) there is no apparent change in respect for human rights.

31. On the formation of KhAD (and its predecessors under Khalq, KAM and AGSA), see: Hyman, op. cit.: 177; Laber and Rubin, op. cit., 84-85; Anthony Arnold, *Afghanistan's Two-Party Communism: Parcham and Khalq* (Stanford: Stanford University/Hoover Institution Press, 1983): 84, 90. On 10 December 1985, Dr. Najibullah, head of KhAD since its founding, was appointed deputy prime minister with overall responsibility for security forces; and on 4 May 1986, he replaced Babrak Karmal as General Secretary of the PDPA and effective head of the regime.

32. On Islam, see Rubin, op. cit.: 54-56. [Numerous other references are also available, *passim,* in other sources listed in the bibliography, in general press reports, and in Resistance publications.] On the educational system, see Laber and Rubin, op. cit.: 86-122. See also: Amin.

33. Laber and Rubin, op. cit.: 99. The acronym KhAD stands for Khedamat-i Etela'at-i Dawlati (State Information Service). When it became a ministry in January 1986, its name was changed to Wizarat-i Amaniat-i Dawlati (Ministry of State Security), with the acronym WAD. Afghans nevertheless continue to refer to it as KhAD, and that general usage is followed in this volume.

34. On the universities in general and these professors in particular, see Laber and Rubin, op. cit.: 86-90 and 103-111; Rubin, op. cit.: 52-54; and in this volume, Rasul Amin. One

of the professors imprisoned was Dr. Hasan Kakar, Afghanistan's most distinguished historian, whose work is cited above in Note #1 and in the bibliography of this volume. Dr. Kakar was adopted as a prisoner of conscience by Amnesty International. As of early March 1987, he was released from Pul-i-Charkhi.

35. Rubin, op. cit.: 76-82. For an extensive description of this program, based on a visit to Kabul and illustrated with photographs of the centers, see: "Diese Krieg is langst Entschieden," *Der Spiegel* (15 January 1986): 180 ff.

36. Rubin, op. cit., 75.

37. James Rupert, "Soviets try to Reshape Afghan Culture," *Washington Post* (13 January 1986). For a virtually identical story from a former woman high school teacher, see Rubin, op. cit.: 82.

38. Rubin, op. cit.: 80.

39. Ibid.: 82.

40. Laber and Rubin, op. cit.: 96-98.

41. Ibid.: 95, 124-130.

42. "File on Torture," Amnesty International (12 December 1984).

43. Laber and Rubin, op. cit.: 132.

44. Rubin, op. cit., 66. For the most complete description of torture in Afghanistan available as of June 1987, see: *Afghanistan: Torture of Political Prisoners* (Amnesty International, November 1986).

45. Rubin, op. cit.: 58. Former police officials who have defected report that these chairs and other torture equipment are actually manufactured in East Germany.

46. On the role of Soviets in KhAD, see Laber and Rubin, op. cit.: 137-149; Rubin, op. cit.: 64-66. See also: Report on Oslo Hearings and other listings in the bibliography.

47. Laber and Rubin, op. cit.: 149-163; Rubin, op. cit.: 66-70. [Pul-i-Charkhi prison was designed and begun under Daoud as a modern replacement for the old Kabul jails; construction was not finished at the time of the 1978 coup and many parts of the prison lack heat, water, toilet facilities, etc. It was designed to house up to approximately 6,000 common criminals, but all sources report much higher prison populations under the various PDPA regimes, almost all of them political prisoners; estimates range as high as 23,800. See: Thomas Hammond, *Red Flag Over Afghanistan* (Boulder, Colorado: Westview Press, 1984): 77, n. 26.---ed.]

48. Felix Ermacora. First report, 19 February 1985, para. 85: 25. See full citation in the bibliography. By March 1987 he had presented five reports; his mandate has been renewed, and further reports are expected. Reports on provincial prisons are beginning to emerge, and appear

358

to replicate those on Kabul prisons. See: various issues of the Bulletin of the Afghanistan Information Center, Peshawar.

49. Laber and Rubin, op. cit.: 170-174; Ermacora, op. cit.: 28.

50. Laber and Rubin, ibid.: 195-210; and Rubin, op. cit.: 89-98.

51. Felix Ermacora. Second report, 5 November 1985, para. 82, 86: 26.   See full citation in the bibliography.   The latter set of statistics was complied by the Bibliotheca Afghanica Foundation in Liestal, Switzerland.

52. Dr. Frances D'Souza, *Threat of Famine in Afghanistan: A Report on Current Economic and Nutritional Conditions* (London: AfghanAid, 1984); James Rupert, "Depopulation brutally changes Villages," *Washington Post* (15 January 1986): A26; Barry, "Les Chemins de l'Exode": 9; Ermacora, ibid.: para. 103-111: 30-31.

53. These numbers may include the approximately 600,000 Afghans working in Iran before 1978. U.S. intelligence sources place the number of Afghan refugees in Iran much lower, at around 750,000, but many observers believe this figure is too low. Figures given are for late 1986 in all cases.   The refugee populations continue to grow.   In 1987, Pakistan was reporting about 8,000 new refugess per month.

54. Michael Barry, Johan Lagerfelt, and Marie-Odile Terrenoire, "International Humanitarian Enquiry Commission on Displaced Persons in Afghanistan: Mission to Afghanistan and Pakistan (September/October/November 1985)," *Central Asian Survey* (Incidental Paper No. 4, 1986).

55. Felix Ermacora, ibid., para. 132: 36.

Appendix I

A Summary of Selected Treaties, Customary International Law and the Laws of War Applicable to the War in Afghanistan*

Guy B. Roberts

FOR THE purpose of this summary, international law is divided into two major categories: customary international law, whether codified or not; and codifications explicitly stated in specific treaties, which in turn are governed by general principles.

I. Relevant principles of customary international law

International law is generally defined as the law of nations. That is, "the system of rules and principles, founded on treaty, custom, precedent, and the consensus of opinion as to justice and moral obligation, which civilized nations recognize as binding upon them in mutual dealings and relations."

International law is primarily based on multinational treaties reflecting the consensus of nations and the customary practice of nations which determines the rights and regulates the intercourse of independent states in peace and war. Customary international law develops over a period of time and is, in effect, a codification of the practice of states and the norms they ascribe to as a reflection of the civilized status of nations.

If a rule or principle is considered to be part of customary international law, it is binding on all states irrespective of whether or not a state has signed a treaty, convention, or other instrument which incorporates or codifies that custom.

During the conduct of armed conflict, populations and belligerents remain under the protection of the basic principles of international law. The first and most important principle regarding conduct during armed conflict is contained in the preamble to the Hague Convention No. IV (discussed below), and is commonly referred to as the Marten's Declaration or Clause. It provides that:

> Until a more complete code of the laws of war has been issued, the
> High Contracting Parties deem it expedient to declare that, in cases

---

* The opinions and views expressed herein are those of the author and do not necessarily reflect the views of the United States Government or any of its component agencies.

not included in the Regulations adopted by them, the inhabitants and the belligerents remain under the protection and the rule of the principles of the law of nations, as they result from the usage established among civilized peoples, from the laws of humanity, and the dictates of public conscience.

This principle has been codified and endorsed in numerous other instruments including the 1874 Brussels Declaration Concerning the Laws and Customs of War; the 1880 Oxford Manual on the Laws of War; the Preamble to the 1899 Hague Convention II (Laws and Customs of War on Land); and in the four Geneva Conventions of 1949.

In essence, the necessities of armed conflict must be balanced against the laws of humanity. In traditional terms, this balance requires a consideration of three basic principles: chivalry, military necessity, and humanity.

Chivalry has proven to be an ineffective deterrent to prohibiting conduct in warfare but the other two remain viable.

Military necessity has been variously defined, but it, in general, is a principle which "permits a belligerent to apply only that degree and kind of regulated force, not otherwise prohibited by the laws of war, required for the partial or complete submission of the enemy with the least possible expenditure of time, life and physical resources." *Military necessity does not justify the violation of the laws of war* and previous attempts to assert the supremacy of military necessity over all other principles have been specifically rejected in numerous forums.

The principle of humanity is sometimes referred to as the avoidance of unnecessary suffering. All use of force not actually required by the "exigencies of war" is prohibited. Inherent in this concept is the principle of *proportionality*, which requires a balancing between military and humanitarian considerations. Loss of life and damage to property must not be excessive in relation to the concrete and direct military advantage expected to be gained. Obviously, in the absence of gaining a military advantage it would be prohibited to wantonly attack civilians or objects traditionally considered civilian.

In addition there are accepted definitions of war crimes and crimes against humanity which are reflected in the prohibitions contained in both the Hague and Geneva Conventions (described as grave breaches of the laws of war), the 1946 Judgment of the International Military Tribunal in Nuremberg, the 1948 Genocide Convention, and the prohibition contained in the United Nations Charter against wars of aggression. Examples include:

• *War crimes: Violations of the laws or customs of war.* Such violations include, but are not limited to, murder; ill-treatment or deportation of the civilian population in occupied territory for slave labor or for any other purpose; murder or ill-treatment of prisoners of war; killing of hostages; plunder of public or private property; wanton destruction of cities, towns, or villages; devastation not justified by military necessity.

• *Crimes against humanity.* These include murder, extermination, enslavement, deportation, and other inhumane acts committed against the civilian population in part or as a whole.

II. Basic Treaty Principles

1. The first is a principle of customary international law which has also been codified in Article 18 of the Vienna Convention on the Law of Treaties; it applies to a state which has signed a treaty but has not yet ratified it:

> Once a state has signed a treaty, it is obliged to refrain from acts which would defeat the object and purpose of that treaty until such time as it either ratifies (becomes a party to the treaty) or makes clear its intentions not to ratify.

In essence, states which have signed a treaty have thereby placed certain limitations upon their freedom of action during the period which precedes its entry into force and/or the time when the state ratifies the treaty.

2. The second is codified in Article 26 of the Vienna Convention on the Law of Treaties and also incorporates a principle of customary international law:

> Once a state has both signed and ratified a treaty, the customary international legal principle of *pacta sunt servanda* applies, i.e., "every treaty in force is binding upon the parties to it and must be performed by them in good faith." This is a fundamental principle of the law of treaties requiring states *not* to rely on technicalities to defeat the object and purpose of the treaty to which they are party.

3. Finally, Article 60(5) of the Vienna Convention on the Law of Treaties provides that a material breach of the treaty by one of the parties (i.e., when a state violates its obligations under the treaty) does not operate as a ground for termination or suspension of the treaty and its obligations in cases in which the breach concerns provisions relating to the protection of the

human person which are contained in treaties of a humanitarian character. This particularly applies to provisions prohibiting reprisals against persons protected by such treaties (see the discussion of the Geneva Conventions below). The reason for this is that treaties of this nature are intended not so much for the benefit of the state as they are directly for the benefit of the individuals concerned, as human beings and on humanitarian grounds.

III. Applicable Treaties Relating to the Conduct of Armed Conflict

1. **The 1907 Hague Convention IV** (Conduct of War on Land) (USSR became a party on 7 March 1955.)

Relevant Articles:

Article 4: Prisoners of war must be humanely treated.

Article 21: The right of belligerents to adopt means of injuring the enemy is not unlimited. (This recalls the Marten's Clause, discussed above, and general principles on human rights.)

Article 23: It is prohibited to:
> • Employ poison or poisoned weapons;

> • Kill or wound treacherously (e.g., by indiscriminate use of mines);

> • Employ arms, projectiles, or material calculated to cause unnecessary suffering.

Article 25: It is prohibited to attack or bombard undefended villages, dwellings, or buildings.

Article 26: Belligerents have the duty to warn before bombardment occurs.

Article 28: Pillage is prohibited.

Article 44: It is forbidden to force inhabitants to furnish information about the forces of the other belligerent(s).

The majority of nations and scholars of international law consider the above to be a codification of customary international law.

2. The 1925 Geneva Protocol

(Ratified by the USSR on 5 April 1928---with the reservation that they would accept the prohibition on the use of gas only as regards its use against those states which have accepted the Protocol. Afghanistan has not signed or ratified the Protocol.)

The Protocol prohibits the use of all chemical weapons.

Despite the Soviet Union's reservation, there is a large body of legal authority which holds that the prohibition on the first use of gas (and other chemical weapons) and bacteriological weapons is customary international law and therefore binding on all states without reservations. The Soviet Union has acknowledged that the prohibition is customary international law.

3. The 1948 United Nations convention on the prevention of genocide

(Ratified by the USSR on 3 May 1954. Afghanistan became a party on 22 March 1956.)

Genocide is defined as acts committed with intent to destroy, in whole or in part, a national, ethnic, racial, or religious group by means of:

• Killing members of the group;

• Causing serious bodily or mental harm;

• Deliberately inflicting on the group conditions calculated to bring about its physical destruction in whole or in part (e.g., starvation tactics, deportations).

4. The four 1949 Geneva conventions

(Ratified by the USSR on 10 May 1954. Afghanistan ratified on 26 December 1956.)

(a) *Common Article 3* (identical in all four conventions) concerns persons sick and wounded, prisoners of war, civilians, medical personnel, etc., and requires that they shall be treated humanely. It applies in all situations involving armed conflict whatever the characterization (e.g., undeclared war, police action, civil war, etc. are all covered under Common Article 3). The following acts are specifically forbidden:

  • The committing of any type of violence to life and person, particularly murder, mutilation, torture and cruel treatment;

  • The taking of hostages;

  • Outrages upon personal dignity; and

  • Executions without trial.

(b) *Geneva Convention III* (Protections of Prisoners of War): Relevant articles include:

Article 13: Prisoners of war must at all times be humanely treated. They may not be subjected to physical mutilation or to medical or scientific experiments, acts of violence or intimidation, or reprisals.

(c) *Geneva Convention IV* (Protection of Civilians): Relevant articles include:

Article 16: The wounded and sick shall be the object of protection and respect;

Article 18: Hospitals shall not be attacked;

Article 49: Individual or mass transfers of peoples are prohibited.

(d) In addition to the four Conventions mentioned above, there are also two Additional Protocols to the Geneva Conventions which the USSR has signed but not ratified. However, as noted above, the USSR is nevertheless bound by the principle requiring a state to do nothing to defeat the object and purpose of the treaty it has signed unless it makes clear its intention not to ratify (which the USSR has not done). Additionally, many of the provisions contained in Additional Protocol I are reflective of customary international law.

Major relevant provisions of Additional Protocol I are:

Article 15: Civilian medical personnel are to be protected;

Article 35(1): Incorporates the Marten's Clause as set forth above;

Article 35(2): Prohibited to employ weapons, projectiles and material and methods of wrfare of a nature to cause superfluous injury or unnecessary suffering.

Article 40: Prohibited to order that there shall be no survivors, to threaten an adversary therewith or to conduct hostilities on this basis.

Article 51: The civilian population shall not be made the object of attack. Indiscriminate attacks are prohibited. Reprisals against civilians are prohibited.

Article 52: Civilian objects (e.g., stores, warehouses, residences, etc.) shall not be made the object of attack.

Article 54: Starvation as method of warfare is prohibited. It is prohibited to attack, destroy, remove or render useless objects indispensable to the survival of the civilian population. These include crops, livestock, water installations, silos, etc.

Article 55: It is prohibited to use methods or means of warfare which may cause widespread, long-term and severe damage to the environment.

Article 59: It is prohibited to attack non-defended localities.

5. The 1972 Biological Weapons Convention
(Ratified by both the USSR and Afghanistan.)

Prohibits the development, production and stockpiling of bacteriological (biological) and toxin weapons.

6. 1980 Conventional Weapons Convention
(Ratified by the USSR on 10 June 1982 but with a reservation stating that it will apply only to those states that have accepted the restrictions contained in the Convention. The Democratic Republic of Afghanistan signed but has not ratified. Under international law it has a good faith obligation to comply with the convention unless it makes clear a decision not to ratify.)

This means that the USSR agrees to apply the Convention to Afghanistan, and Afghanistan also is required to abide by it unless it

366

specifically indicates otherwise. Also, many of the provisions of the Convention are considered a reflection of customary international law.)

Protocol I: Prohibits the use of any mines or other weapons which might cause injuries undetectable by x-rays (e.g., the use of plastic mines).

Protocol II: Prohibits the following:
- Indiscriminate use of mines and boobytraps;

- Booby-trapping the dead or wounded;

- Booby-trapping children's toys (or making mines that look like toys), booby-trapping kitchen utensils, food, drink, or appliances;

- The use of booby-traps made in the form of an apparently harmless portable object but specifically designed and constructed to contain explosive material.

Protocol III: Prohibits the use of air-delivered incendiary weapons on any military objective when it is surrounded by a concentration of civilians. The use of incendiaries on civilians or civilian objects (e.g., living quarters, shops, work places, any object not directly involved in war production or war fighting) is specifically prohibited.

* *

The texts of the above referenced treaties and other applicable documents can be found in following general reference books:

Ian Brownlie, ed., *Basic Documents in International Law,* 3d ed. (Oxford University Press, 1967).

A. Roberts and R. Guelff, eds., *Documents on the Laws of War* (Clarendon Press [UK] and Oxford University Press [U.S.], 1982).

D. Schindler and J. Toman, eds., *The Laws of Armed Conflicts* (Rockville, Md., and the Netherlands: Sijthoff & Noordoff, 1981).

Leon Friedman, ed., *The Law of War, A Documentary History*, vols. I-II (New York: Random House, 1972, original publication.   Currently, Greenwood Press).

Appendix II

A Summary Chronology of Afghan History

Some general information about modern Afghanistan:
Afghanistan (including Wakhan) is about fifteen percent larger than France. It lies roughly in the same latitudes as Colorado, New Mexico and Arizona, and its topography and climate are much like theirs.

Although no complete census was ever taken, official estimates put the pre-war population at 15.8 million. Approximately 85 percent of the population is of Caucasian stock, primarily of the Mediterranean type; in some areas blond or reddish hair and blue, hazel or green eyes are common. The other 15 percent are mostly of Mongol stock [see Barth].

Aside from about 30,000 Sikhs and Hindus, mostly merchants and moneylenders concentrated in the major cities, the entire population is Muslim, predominantly Sunni. A small but ancient Jewish community has entirely emigrated in recent years. No indigenous Christian community existed.

Prehistoric Period
Afghanistan played a key role in the spread of civilization from its earliest beginnings. Arnold Toynbee describes it as one of the two great crossroads of cultural dispersion from prehistoric times until the Renaissance.

There is archeological evidence of Paleolithic and Neolithic cultures: the earliest known piece of Asian portrait sculpture, carbon-dated to c. 20,000 B.C., was found in Afghanistan. By 3000 B.C., Afghanistan was the crossroads between Mesopotamia, Persia, and the civilizations of the Indus Valley. Numerous finds indicate a vigorous Bronze Age civilization, and it has been speculated that bronze may even have been invented there.

Certainly Afghanistan had ties to the pre-Aryan Indus Valley civilizations, and the lapis lazuli in the mask of King Tutankhamen indicates that there was trade between Afghanistan and Egypt at least as early as the fifteenth century B.C. Afghanistan was the base from which the Indo-European (Aryan) peoples invaded the Indian subcontinent c. 1300 B.C., bringing with them Sanskrit and the basis of Hindu civilization; there are some indications that the Rig Veda may have been created in Afghanistan. Before 1979, sixty years of archeological exploration had begun to reveal an increasingly rich record of numerous high civilizations, and many more sites remained to be explored.

Historic Period

Pre-Islamic Period

c. 600 B.C

Zoroaster (Zarathustra) is born in Bactria (northern Afghanistan), founds a monotheistic religion which still survives today (that of the Parsis).

c. 500 B.C.

Afghanistan is part of the Achaemenid Persian empire of Darius the Great and Xerxes.

329-326 B.C.

Afghanistan is invaded by Alexander the Great on his way to India. Beginning of the historic record.

According to Greek and Roman historians, in southern and eastern Afghanistan the Macedonian army met fierce resistance from a people known as the Paktues or Paktuike who had also fought in the Persian army at Thermopylae 150 years earlier, and who are widely identified with the modern Pakhtuns/Pushtuns. In eastern Afghanistan, Alexander's troops adopted the local flat felt hat which they wore as a badge of honor from their Indian campaign, as shown in Hellenistic sculptures; this appears to be the same flat cap that has today become the badge of the Afghan Resistance.

Alexander founded or enlarged a number of cities both north and south of the Hindu Kush, naming most of them for himself, i.e., Alexandria (Sikandra); one of these, Kandahar, still retains his name in variant form. Alexander also left behind satrapies that developed into various Graeco-Bactrian empires in the centuries that followed.

323 B.C-
c. 125 A.D.

During the milennium between Alexander's campaign and the coming of Islam, the historical record is full of gaps and confusions.

For several centuries after Alexander's death in 323 B.C., Graeco-Bactrian Seleucid satrapies and kingdoms ruled north of the Hindu Kush, while south of the mountains lay the kingdom of Gandhara, part of the Maurya empire of India. Half a century after Alexander, the Mauryan emperor Ashoka proclaimed

Buddhism as the official religion of his empire, bringing Buddhism into contact with Hellenistic art in Afghanistan; as a result of this contact, Buddhist iconography, previously abstract, developed the full panoply of art forms and symbols. From Afghanistan Buddhism spread across central and northern Asia to China and Korea.

Major known surviving Buddhist sites in Afghanistan include Bamian, where the world's largest Buddhas are carved into the face of the cliffs, and Hadda; others continue to be unearthed.

2nd-7th centuries A.D.

At various times parts of Afghanistan are invaded or ruled by the Scythians, the Kushans, the Parthians, the Suren kings, the Yueh-Chih, the Huns, the Sassanids, and other Persian and Indian empires, while local Afghan kingdoms at other times expand to conquer northern and western India.

During the 500-year reign of the Kushans, which began c. 50 A.D., and particularly under the great Kushan king Kanishka, the Graeco-Buddhist Gandharan culture reached its zenith. Afghanistan was a renowned center of religion, art and scholarship and a magnet for pilgrims from all over Asia, as well as the crossroads of trade between the Roman empire, India, Persia, and China, until the invasion of the White Huns (450-475 A.D.) destroyed the high Buddhist culture, leaving much of the country in ruins.

Islamic era

7th-12th centuries A.D.

Islam reaches Afghanistan in the seventh century but does not become universally dominant for another 300 years.

The Islamic era can be said to have really begun with the Ghaznavid dynasty (962-1160) founded by Muslim Turkish invaders who built their capital at Ghazni. Sultan Mahmud incorporated much of northern India into the Ghaznavid empire, and for two centuries Ghazni was a major literary and artistic center, influential throughout the Islamic world and south Asia. Poets and scholars flocked to the Ghaznavid court. The great Persian epic poem, Ferdausi's *Shah Nama* ("Book of Kings") with its stories of Sohrab and Rustum, was completed at Ghazni and dedicated to Sultan Mahmud. Further north, the physician and philosopher Avicenna (Ibn-i-Sina) was born to a family from Balkh c. 980. The greatest name in medieval medicine in Europe and the Arab world, he was also influential for his combination of Aristotelian and Neo-Platonic thought. During this period, Afghanistan became firmly and solidly Muslim.

In the twelfth century, the Ghaznavids were overthrown by an indigenous Afghan dynasty originating in Ghor, in the central mountain massif. The Ghorids went on to conquer India, establishing their capital at Delhi, where they and their successors ruled until the Delhi Sultanate fell to Tamerlane in 1398. In Delhi, they built the Qutb Minar, the world's tallest minaret. The sole surviving monument of their original capitol in Ghor is the Jam Minar, second highest minaret in the world, solitary in the Afghan mountain wilderness.

1219-1221

Genghis Khan and his Mongol horde invade Afghanistan.

Meeting resistance, the Mongols laid the country waste, completely wiping out Herat, Balkh, and other cities, slaughtering the population, and systematically destroying the irrigation systems---developed over many centuries and necessary for agriculture in this semi-arid land---thus turning historically fertile cropland into permanent desert. This was the single most catastrophic event in Afghan history prior to the Soviet invasion. For a century and a half, Afghanistan lay under the Mongol yoke. (During this period, Marco Polo visited Afghanistan en route to the court of Kublai Khan via the Silk Road, which passed through northern Afghanistan and Wakhan.)

1370-c. 1500

Repeated invasions by the Mongols under Tamerlane (Timur-i-lang) (1336-1404; crowned in Balkh in 1370) and incorporation into the Timurid empire, which stretched from the Caucasus to the Ganges.

Afghanistan had barely begun to recover from

Genghis Khan's devastation when Tamerlane again inflicted ruin upon it. This sealed its doom as a dynamic cultural center, although the Timurid capital at Herat became for a few decades the greatest center of Persian painting of all time and one of the greatest centers of Islamic architecture, poetry, literature and scholarship, often compared to Renaissance Florence.

The Mongol invasions not only undermined Afghanistan's leading historical cultural role but permanently impoverished it. In the wake of the Mongols, Afghanistan lay depopulated and ruined, with neither the people nor the economic means to generate energetic revival. Its one hope of recovery lay in the trade routes which had been the main arteries of commerce between Europe, the Mediterranean, China and India for thousands of years. But when Magellan circumnavigated the globe in 1520, commerce shifted to sea routes, the overland routes fell into comparative disuse, and Afghanistan was left with no significant economic base. As a result, the area ceased to be a major center of culture and commerce and began its decline into stagnation as a backwater of the modern world, with a minuscule economic and a small population base.

1504-1709

Babur, the founder of the Moghul dynasty, establishes himself in Kabul. From there, beginning in 1526, he and his descendants mount the conquest of India and the creation of the Moghul empire.

Throughout the period of the Great Moghuls (1526-1701), Kabul remained the northern seat of the empire: Babur chose to be buried there; Akbar, the greatest of the Moghuls, was born there and frequently returned. Over the next 200 years, most of Afghanistan was attached either to the Moghul empire (Kabul and the east) or to the Safavid Persian empire (Herat), or was disputed between the two (Kandahar).

Modern National Period

1747

Founding of the modern nation of Afghanistan.

When the Persian general Nadir Shah died on his march homeward after sacking the declining Moghul empire, a number of his Afghan commanders opted for independence, elected a young Durrani Pushtun, Ahmad Shah, as their king, and established the modern state of Afghanistan, which at one time included the Peshawar Valley and other areas which are today parts of Pakistan and India. Ahmad Shah's collateral descendants held power until the overthrow of President Mohammed Daoud in the Communist coup of 1978.

19th Century

Gradual coalescing of the Afghan kingdom and definition of its borders.

A period marked by internecine power struggles within the royal clan and attempted manipulations by agents of an expansionist Russian empire on the north and forces of the expanding British empire in India on the south and east, where the British were determined to keep Russian influence out of their Hindu Kush defense perimeter.

1839-1842

The first Anglo-Afghan War: the worst British defeat in modern history until Dunkirk in World War II.

In 1841, a British expeditionary force, sent to prevent the establishment of Russian influence in Kabul, was wiped out during its withdrawal through the gorges of the Kabul River.

1864

The Gorchakov Memorandum justifies Russian expansion in Central Asia as a civilizing mission.

1865

The Russians take Bokhara, Tashkent and Samarkand.

1873

Russia agrees to a fixed boundary between its newly conquered Central Asian territories and Afghanistan, much of it demarcated by the Oxus River. St. Petersburg also formally acknowledges that Afghanistan is and will remain outside the Russian sphere of influence, and promises to respect Afghanistan's territorial integrity.

1878-1880	Second Anglo-Afghan War. Once again, the result of British efforts to prevent the establishment of Russian influence in Kabul. A weak ruler, susceptible to manipulation by active Russian agents, was deposed, and replaced by a strong ruler, Abdur Rahman.
1880	Abdur Rahman takes the throne of Afghanistan as Amir with the reluctant acquiescence of the British, who fear that, after more than a dozen years in exile in Russia, he will be pro-Russian. Instead, he turns out to be shrewdly cognizant of Russian ambitions and determined to resist them. Abdur Rahman established the policy of careful neutrality between the competing powers of Russia and Britain which remained the cornerstone of Afghan independence until 1955, and strove energetically to establish fixed borders, even at the cost of some territory. Abdur Rahman acquiesced in British demands for control of Afghanistan's foreign relations, while keeping full power internally. He devoted the twenty-one years of his reign to the effort to pull his disparate people into nationhood, using often brutal methods to impose central authority: Nuristan was forcibly converted to Islam, rivals were eliminated, rebellions crushed. But he looked forward with prescience to future modern development and the entry of Afghanistan into the comity of nations.
1884	Russians take Merv, which brings them to the northern border of Afghanistan along its full length.
1885	The Panjdeh Incident. In violation of the 1873 agreements, Tsarist forces seized the Panjdeh oasis, a piece of Afghan territory north of the Oxus River. Afghanistan was finally forced to allow Russia to keep Panjdeh, on the Russian promise to honor Afghan territorial integrity in the future.
1893	The Durand Line fixes the southern and eastern

borders of Afghanistan with British India [now Pakistan].

Despite Abdur Rahman's warnings, the boundary was drawn on the basis of topography to meet British defense requirements: it runs through the midst of the Pushtun tribal areas, splitting the tribes without regard to their relationships and connections. The Durand Line left roughly half of the Pushtuns in Afghanistan and half in what is now Pakistan, paving the way for post-1947 problems of "Pushtunistan."

1895   Afghanistan's northern border is fixed and guaranteed by Russia.

1901   Death of Abdur Rahman; his eldest son, Habibullah, peacefully succeeds him as Amir and continues to pursue the neutralist policies laid down by his father.

Less harsh than Abdur Rahman, Habibullah was anxious to begin bringing his country into the modern world. He established the first modern high school (Habibia), hired an American engineer to build a power plant, employed European and Indian teachers and experts, and moved cautiously toward modern development.

1907   Russia and Great Britain sign the Convention of St. Petersburg, in which the Russian government again formally declares that Afghanistan is outside Russia's sphere of influence.

1914-1918   World War I. Afghanistan remains neutral despite strenuous efforts by the Central Powers, including Ottoman Turkey, the seat of the Caliphate, to win its aid for an attack on Britain's Indian empire.

January 1919   Habibullah is assassinated---possibly by pro-Turkish elements angry at his refusal to abjure neutrality and support the Central Powers in World War I or by Afghan enthusiasts for the Young Turk movement.

He was succeeded by his third son, Amanullah, who is believed by some to have had a hand in his assassination. Amanullah was energetic, willful, impetuous, impatient to bring Afghanistan into the modern world. He changed his title from "Amir" to "Shah" (king), developed friendship with the newly-established Soviet government in Moscow.

May 1919

Third Anglo-Afghan War. Amanullah attacks India, expecting support from a planned uprising in the Northwest Frontier Province, which, however, fails to materialize.

The British airforce dropped a few bombs near Kabul---Afghanistan's first and, until 1978, only experience of modern warfare. Minor fighting went on fitfully for a few weeks. In August, the Treaty of Rawalpindi granted Afghanistan full control of its foreign relations, an event thereafter celebrated as Afghan independence day. The Afghan government immediately sought recognition from major governments. The new Soviet regime became the first to grant such recognition; the U.S. declined to do so.

1921

Afghan-Soviet friendship treaty.

The USSR promised to return the Panjdeh territory seized in 1885 but did not do so. Moscow also assured Afghanistan that it had no intention of keeping its troops in Bukhara and Khiva permanently.

1929

Amanullah is overthrown in May as a result of his ill-conceived attempts to emulate Kemal Ataturk's transformation of Turkey by modernizing Afghanistan---but unlike Ataturk, to do it overnight by fiat without first developing support in any sector of society.

Some of his efforts were of lasting significance, e.g., founding modern schools and sending students abroad for study. Others were simply silly---e.g., insisting that provincial leaders wear western formal dress (top hats, morning coats, striped trousers) for a Loya Jirga. Unable to differentiate between the trappings of modernity and it foundations, he managed to alienate almost everyone among his subjects. Strongly anti-British, he looked to the new Soviet regime for support. In mid-1929, Soviet forces in Afghan uniforms entered northern Afghanistan in a brief effort to reinstate Amanullah and set up a pro-Soviet government, but Amanullah abdicated and fled to permanent exile in Italy. (In 1940, Hitler and Stalin together toyed briefly with the idea of restoring him to the throne.)

The Tajik rebel who led the uprising against Amanullah, a Kohistani known as Bacha-i-Saqao (Son of the Water-Carrier), took the throne as Habibullah II for a few chaotic months but was overthrown (October) and executed by Gen. Mohammed Nadir Khan, former Afghan Ambassador to France and a member of another branch of the royal family. Nadir took the throne as Nadir Shah and began restoring order. In reaction to Amanullah's disastrous efforts to achieve instant modernity, many of his reformist edicts were abrogated and an anti-modern mood set in.

1933

Nadir Shah is assassinated by a student whose family was involved in leftwing movements and the Soviet attempt to keep Amanullah on the throne; Nadir's 19-year-old son takes the throne as Zahir Shah (and rules till 1973). The young king's uncles serve as his prime ministers and advisers until 1953.

In reaction to the upheavals of the Amanullah period and Nadir Shah's assassination (initially believed to be part of a conspiracy), there was a harsh authoritarian clampdown under Prime Minister Hashim Khan, who, childless, began grooming his nephew, Sardar (prince) Mohammed Daoud, for eventual power.

Although the Amanullah fiasco put a brake on social change, careful efforts at modernization continued, especially in education, and gained momentum after World War II. A number of modern high schools were opened in provincial cities as well as in Kabul; several of them were staffed and directed by French, German, English, Indian, and

American teachers (but Russian offers were declined). High schools for girls were opened in Kabul, and a university (eventually co-educational) was established. Increasing numbers of students were sent to Europe and the U.S. for higher education on government merit scholarships. Telephones, power lines, banks, small industries, and other elements of a modern infrastructure were gradually added.

1934	U.S. recognizes Afghanistan.

1939-1945   World War II. Afghanistan remains neutral but friendly to the Allies despite inducements from the Axis powers to aid an attack on British India.

Refugees from Nazi Germany were given sanctuary. First U.S. representation in Kabul, 1942.

1946-1952   Shah Mahmud Khan becomes prime minister and experiments with cautious liberalization: parliamentary elections, independent press, etc.

Leftwing opposition groups emerged, some possibly with secret Soviet connections [see Arnold and Klass]. As a result, political and press freedoms were curtailed again and, in a crackdown, some liberals as well as radicals were jailed.

1947   Britain withdraws from India, which is divided along religious lines into two new nations: predominantly Hindu India and the new Muslim nation of Pakistan. Afghanistan takes the opportunity to raise the question of Pushtun self-determination and "Pushtunistan", strongly supported by Daoud as Minister of Defense, thereby setting off bad relations with Pakistan from its birth.

The Soviets supported the Pushtunistan issue, and, through agents, perhaps even helped to create it. The leader of the Pushtunistan movement in Pakistan, Khan Abdul Ghaffar Khan, was and is openly Marxist; he was believed by British sources to have had Soviet ties as early as the 1920s; today, in his late 90s, he spends much of his time in Kabul, Moscow and Prague, as does his son and successor, Khan Abdul Wali Khan of Pakistan's Awami National Party.

Late 1940s-early 1950s

Afghanistan, left without a powerful British presence to balance Soviet pressures on the north, turns to the United States to fill its need for a counterweight; Washington rejects Afghan overtures.

1953

Prince Mohammed Daoud becomes prime minister, ending the era of government by the royal uncles.

The king now emerged as a political power in a triumvirate with Daoud and Daoud's brother, Prince Naim, the foreign minister. Some of the jailed leftists were released and brought into Daoud's cabinet.

1954

The U.S. finally and unequivocally rejects Afghanistan's requests to purchase military equipment to modernize the army.

1955

Daoud turns to the Soviet Union for military aid, violating the basic principle of Afghan foreign policy laid down by Abdur Rahman sixty years earlier. The Pushtunistan issue flares up.

1956

Khrushchev and Bulganin visit Kabul, offer a generous "da" to Afghan requests, and the widespread Soviet penetration of Afghanistan begins.

Hundreds of Afghan army officers were sent for training in the USSR, where the KGB and GRU selected promising candidates for special attention and recruitment as Soviet agents, among them several who were later to play key roles in the 1973 and 1978 Communist coups and subsequent Communist regimes.

1959

Liberation of women: purdah is made optional. Women begin to enter the professions and work force, go abroad for education, enroll in increasing numbers at the university, which becomes coeducational. Several enter government, including the cabinet and later parliament; in 1963 women participate in writing the new constitution which gives full rights and legal status to women. [Note: The resumption of the veil after 1978 is a response to the Communist takeover, a silent gesture of protest which DRA regimes claiming to support Islam have found difficult to prevent.]

1961

The Pushtunistan issue erupts again, bringing Afghanistan and Pakistan to the verge of war.

1963-1964

Zahir Shah, alarmed at the enormously increasing Soviet influence and Daoud's adventurist policies regarding Pushtunistan, demands Daoud's resignation. For the first time, the King turns to someone outside the royal family and appoints Dr. Mohammad Yussof, a German-educated engineer and educator and not a Pushtun, as prime minister.

Yussof put together a cabinet dominated by highly educated, pro-democratic, experienced liberals. In 1964 a new constitution was accepted by the Loya Jirga, adapted in many respects---including a bill of rights---from the American and British constitutions. Freedom of speech, press, and religion were guaranteed. A key provision barred members of the royal family in certain close relationships to the king from participating in political parties or serving in the parliament or the cabinet; this was in large part designed to prevent Daoud from returning to power. Elections were scheduled for 1965.

1 January 1965

The Afghan Communist party (PDPA) is formed secretly at the home of Nur Mohammed Taraki. Babrak Karmal is one of the founders.

The party was apparently formed to take advantage of the electoral process under the new constitution. Both Parcham and Khalq were already active; the unified party may have been set up at the instigation of KGB officers in the Soviet embassy, with whom key members are known to have been in regular contact.

| September 1965 | First nationwide parliamentary elections under the new constitution, by secret ballot and universal suffrage (including women). |

Four Communists from the Parcham faction of the PDPA, including Babrak Karmal, were elected to parliament.

| October 1965 | The King asks Dr. Yussof to form a second government. |

When the parliament met to approve the new cabinet, riots were instigated by Babrak Karmal and the PDPA. The first political riots in Kabul since 1929, they profoundly shocked the city and the nation. Dr. Yussof resigned and was succeeded by a former ambassador to the U.S., Mohammad Hashim Maiwandwal. From the podium in Parliament, Babrak told his followers, "Today is ours, the future is ours." For the next dozen years, the PDPA continued to instigate and orchestrate riots, strikes and student unrest.

| 1969 | Second nationwide elections for Parliament by universal suffrage and secret ballot. |

The Communists, by now split, lost two seats: only Babrak and Hafizullah Amin were elected.

| 1970-1971 | Drought creates famine in parts of the Hazarajat and Ghor; U.S. aid is sent. |

| December 1972 | Mohammad Moussa Shafiq, the foreign minister and the primary author of the 1964 constitution, becomes prime minister. Energetic, educated at al-Azhar, Columbia and Harvard, he offers promise of the dynamism needed to move the country forward domestically and internationally. |

Shafiq had already resolved a dispute over water rights which had long been a source of friction with Afghanistan's western neighbor, Iran; he moved immediately to resolve the Pushtunistan issue and establish permanent friendly relations with Pakistan. His long-term goal was a loose regional economic confederation of Iran, Afghanistan, and Pakistan along the lines of the Benelux countries; since the resources and capacities of the three were complementary, he anticipated significant benefits to all and had apparently already received indications of interest from the other two governments. He quickly initiated contacts with Pakistan. The third nationwide parliamentary elections were scheduled for late 1973.

17 July 1973

While the King is vacationing in Europe, the constitution and the monarchy are overthrown in a military coup headed by Daoud and carried out with the assistance of the Parcham faction of the divided PDPA through Parchami officers, notably Lt. Col. Abdul Qader (air force) and Major Mohammed Aslam Watanjar (tank corps).

Daoud abolished the monarchy and declared himself president of a new Republic of Afghanistan. He brought numerous Parchami Communists and other leftists into the cabinet (including some of whose communist leanings he was not aware); but within a few years, disillusioned, he began to jettison them--- at least those he knew about. Most of the public was unaware of Daoud's leftist ties and accepted the coup as a mere fight within the royal family.

1974

UNESCO names Herat, along with Athens, as one of the first cities officially designated as part of the world's cultural heritage and given international concern and preservation.

1975

Constitution of Daoud's one-party republic is adopted.

It formally reconfirmed the granting of equal rights to women which had begun in 1959 and been codified in the constitutional period.

1975-1977

Daoud, finally alarmed at the extent of Russian influence and control, begins to oust known Communists from his government and initiates overtures to Iran, Saudi Arabia, India, and Egypt, asking for support to enable him to loosen his dependence on Moscow and re-establish Afghan nonalignment.

The Shah of Iran agreed to provide major credits. Daoud was unaware that at least one, and possibly more, of his trusted confidantes were Soviet agents who kept Moscow informed of his plans.

1976-1977

The Soviet embassy in Kabul works to heal the rift between the two Communist factions in preparation for a coup.

The two PDPA factions---Khalq, headed by Taraki, and Parcham, headed by Babrak Karmal--- though bitter enemies, were temporarily glued together. The coup was planned in detail, rehearsed, and scheduled for August 1978.

Early 1978

Daoud takes further steps to loosen overwhelming dependency on the USSR.

He visited several capitals to confirm and strengthen support for his change of policy. Significantly, he also initiated moves aimed at resolving tensions with Pakistan. The Non-Aligned Movement, of which Afghanistan was a charter member, was scheduled to hold a meeting in Kabul in early May; Daoud spoke openly of his intention to return it from its pro-Soviet orientation to genuine non-alignment.

17 April 1978

Mir Akbar Khaibar, a Parchami ideologue, is murdered---probably by Khalq.

Mass protests organized by the PDPA accused Daoud of Khaibar's murder. On April 26, Daoud ordered the arrest of PDPA leaders; but security agents who were secret PDPA sympathizers allowed Hafizullah Amin, the Party liaison with the military plotters, several hours to send messages that activated the preplanned coup.

27 April 1978

Bloody Communist coup, carried out by Qader, Watanjar and other officers, possibly with Soviet aid.

Several thousand were killed in the fighting; Daoud and his family, including children, were machine-gunned to death in the palace. A government under a Revolutionary Council headed by Qader was declared while the fighting continued. On May 1, with Daoud dead, Taraki was named president and prime minister with Babrak Karmal as first deputy prime minister and Amin as deputy prime minister and foreign minister. The 1978 coup is known to the PDPA, Moscow, and their supporters as "The Great Saur Revolution." (It occurred in the month of Saur in the traditional Afghan lunar calendar.)

Post-Communist Coup

May-June 1978 (and thereafter)

Measures for a doctrinaire Marxist transformation of the nation are announced even as the regime heatedly denies Communist leanings; reign of terror begins.

Mass arrests, torture, and secret executions began immediately following the coup. Pul-i-Charkhi was turned into a political prison; the secret political police (AGSA, later KAM, after 1979 KhAD, now WAD) was established. Soviet advisors began to pour in. Land redistribution and other measures were proclaimed. Religion was derided. An all-red flag replaced the traditional Afghan tricolor.

As the population began to realize that Communists had taken over, sporadic incidents of resistance broke out---primarily in the provinces but also in Kabul---and began to spread. As organized resistance developed, more Soviet military personnel poured in, eventually commanding down to the brigade level in the field; according to French Communist and DRA sources, the USSR had 15,000-20,000 troops in Afghanistan *before* the invasion.

The new regime immediately began signing hundreds of new agreements with the Soviet Union and Soviet satellites, giving Moscow increasing economic control and benefits, plus significant influence in all aspects of Afghan society. The ministries of defense and interior were reportedly soon under Soviet control.

Summer 1978

In June/July, the patched-together PDPA splits again: the Khalq faction emerges the winner, with

Taraki and Amin in power, Babrak Karmal and his associates out.

Six leading Parchami, including Babrak and Najib(ullah), were shipped off as ambassadors, a traditional Afghan method of disposing of political opponents; several more soon followed. In late summer, the Khalq regime uncovered a Parchami plot (with possible Soviet complicity) to oust Khalq and seize power. Large numbers of Parchami were arrested and tortured, some killed. The Parchami ambassadors abandoned their posts and fled to Moscow. In Kabul, Watanjar, Gulabzoy and others implicated in the plot were given sanctuary in the Soviet embassy until the invasion.

5 December 1978

Taraki and Brezhnev sign a Treaty of Friendship, Good Neighborliness and Cooperation, one clause of which opens the way for the presence of Soviet forces in Afghanistan if the Afghan government requests them; this treaty is used by Moscow as justification for the invasion a year later.

Late 1978-1979

Nationwide resistance to the regime spreads and intensifies; major Resistance organizations emerge. Massive army desertions.

Mutiny in Kabul army headquarters had to be put down by helicopter gunships. In an uprising in Herat against the Soviet presence there, fifty Soviet personnel were killed; in retaliation, Soviet aircraft massacred an estimated 20,000-30,000 civilians in Herat city. Kerala massacre of 1,100 villagers in Kunar. Atrocity reports began to trickle out, received with disbelief by the Western press. More than 250,000 Afghan refugees had already fled to Pakistan. Regime control was crumbling; the possibility of Resistance success emerged.

February 1979

U.S. ambassador Adolph Dubs is kidnapped from his car and is killed when Afghan police under a Soviet adviser open fire and storm the hotel where he is held, despite pleas of U.S. embassy staff to negotiate him free.

Much about this event remains obscure,

including the identity and motives of Dubs's kidnappers; the results of the official U.S. investigation have not been made public. Washington did not send another ambassador to Kabul and has since maintained a chargé d'affaires as head of mission.

April 1979

A high-level Soviet military team headed by General Aleksey Alekseyevich Yepishev \ 'sits Kabul.

Yepishev (a major figure in the 1968 invasion of Czechoslovakia and a trusted associate of Andropov, then head of the KGB) was sent to assess the "political reliability" of the Afghan armed forces, i.e., their loyalty to the regime and to Soviet connections. When, as a result of his visit, he concluded that Afghan forces were not "politically reliable," plans were set in motion for massive intervention by Soviet forces. By midsummer, military preparations in Central Asia were detected by Western intelligence.

August 1979

A Soviet delegation of nearly fifty high-ranking officers headed by Gen. Ivan G. Pavlovskiy, commanding general of all Soviet ground forces, visits Kabul, staying nearly two months.

September 1979

En route home from a meeting in Havana, Taraki stops in Moscow, receives instructions to eliminate Amin, and meets with Babrak Karmal. On Sept. 14, a forewarned Amin escapes a trap set with the aid of the Soviet ambassador, turns the tables, eliminates Taraki (who is killed then or a few days later), and takes sole control as president, foreign minister and minister of defense.

Parchami exiles met in Eastern Europe and began a clandestine campaign to win support from Afghan exiles in Western Europe for Parchami's return to power. In the next few months, as Amin became increasingly isolated and desperate, Soviet agents inside the Khalq regime also began paving the way for the invasion.

December 1979
Soviet invasion.

Under the guise of support for Amin, heavily-armed Soviet forces began arriving in early December. On December 24, two airborne battalions secured Kabul airport for the subsequent massive airlift of infantry and armor. Meanwhile, Afghan forces were immobilized on various pretexts (e.g., tank batteries were removed on the excuse of winterizing). On December 27 Soviet forces seized the city and a special assault unit killed Amin and his family.

On the same night, a speech by Babrak Karmal, claiming to be in Kabul and announcing his takeover of the government and the PDPA, was broadcast from Tashkent on the Radio Kabul frequency. On or about January 1, Babrak arrived in Kabul (though he later claimed to have been there secretly since October). Having killed the pre-invasion head of government without obtaining from him any scrap of paper to document a request for Soviet forces, Moscow fell back on a variety of contradictory explanations to justify the invasion under the terms of the 1978 treaty and the United Nations Charter.

While the international press was present in Kabul, a number of prisoners were freed from Pul-i-Charki prison, most of them Parchamis though some non-Communists; meanwhile, other arrests continued secretly.

Afghan refugees began to pour into Pakistan and Iran.

January 1980
Amin's secret police, KAM, is replaced by KhAD, organized with the assistance of the KGB and East German secret police; Dr. Najibullah is brought back from the Soviet Union to run it.

April-May 1980
USSR decides it is in Afghanistan for a long campaign, alters strategy accordingly.

June 1980
In secret treaties ostensibly covering "clarification" of Soviet-Afghan borders, Afghanistan cedes the Wakhan salient to the Soviet Union, giving the USSR a direct border with Pakistan.

June 1981	Founding Congress of the National Fatherland Front (NFF)
	An umbrella organization comprising numerous front organizations (women, youth, workers, etc.) and modeled on a similar East German organization, the NFF was intended to replace the Parliament and Loya Jirga for the purpose of bestowing legitimacy on government actions. (At the second Congress, held in January 1987, the word "Fatherland" was dropped from the name.)
1982	"Indirect" negotiations for a political solution begin between Pakistan and the Kabul regime under United Nations auspices.
	Neither the Resistance nor the Soviet Union are participants, although the USSR is kept directly informed and involved, as is the United States. The Resistance is informed only via other governments. As of 1987, talks continue, deadlocked over the question of a timetable for Soviet troop withdrawal. The requirement for Afghan self-determination has been quietly dropped from the schedule of issues to be negotiated. The Resistance, rejecting the Kabul regime as a puppet without legitimacy, continues to call for direct Resistance talks with Moscow and to declare that it will not accept any solution negotiated without the participation of the representatives of the Afghan people, i.e., the Resistance. The DRA and USSR consistently refer to the purpose of negotiations as being the solution of problems "*around* Afghanistan," never "in" or "of" Afghanistan.
1984	The UN Commission on Human Rights appoints a Special Rapporteur to investigate the situation in Afghanistan---the first time such an inquiry has ever been made into human rights in any Communist country. Kabul denounces the action and rejects any results in advance.
Late 1985 early 1986 ---to date	Campaign for "national reconciliation" launched by Kabul regime. Massive Soviet attack on key Resistance bases in Paktia province in February

1986. In Pakistan, terrorist bombings by KhAD agents increase noticably throughout 1986-1987.

May 1986
Babrak Karmal resigns as Secretary General of the Central Committee of the PDPA (i.e., party boss), and is replaced by Dr. Najib; Najib is replaced as head of KhAD by Gen. Yakubi but still retains unofficial oversight control of KhAD, now raised to the level of a ministry (WAD) and oversight of tribal affairs.

November 1986
Babrak resigns as president, is replaced by Acting President Haji Mohammed Chamkani, a non-Party member and tribal leader with tribal power and connections in key areas of the provinces bordering Pakistan, extending inside Pakistan as well. Resistance Alliance leaders visit the UN, call for international recognition of the Resistance as representatives of the Afghan people.

December 1986
Campaign for "national reconciliation" picks up steam as Najib announces a unilateral six-month cease-fire to begin 15 January and offers to admit non-Communists to regime if they will accept the irreversable nature of the "revolutionary process." Rejected by Resistance as a manipulative ruse.

The number of Afghan refugees outside Afghanistan totals more than five million by the end of 1986.

Pakistan reported 3.2 million refugees registered. Thousands more were unregistered, and more continued to arrive at a rate of roughly 6,000-10,000 per month, depending on fighting and food conditions inside. Refugees have begun to arrive from remote northern areas like Kunduz. Iran reported approximately two million. Another 100,000 or so were scattered in Europe, the United States, India and elsewhere. Inside Afghanistan, an estimated two million have fled their home villages for safety in the mountains or in Kabul. The death toll since 1979 has been estimated at one million. In sum, by the end of 1986, nearly 50 percent of the total pre-war population had been killed, driven into exile, or displaced from their homes as "internal refugees."

15 January 1987

Unilateral "ceasefire" proclaimed by DRA if the Resistance will stop fighting.

Three weeks later, a massive Soviet attack was launched in Paktia Province, followed by others elsewhere. Attacks on refugee camps in Pakistan escalated in 1987.

June 1987

The DRA announces a six-month extension of its unilateral "ceasefire" but steps up campaigns against the Resistance and attacks on Pakistan territory.

Kabul also published the law governing "independent" (i.e., non-PDPA) political parties. No such party can exist without permission from the Revolutionary Council; to apply for permission (which may not be granted), any would-be party must submit the names of all members (minimum: 500) and identify all sources of financing.

Appendix III

Who's Who in the Afghan Resistance
Parties, Party Leaders and
some of the well-known Commanders

Abdul Wakil Akbarzai	Director of refugee affairs for the Ittehad (q.v.).
Nasim Akhundzada	A Harakat commander in the Helmand area.
Said Alam	Commander of urban guerrillas in Kabul (killed August 1984).
Mohammad Anwar	A Jamiat commander in the Jagdalak area.
Sheikh Sayed Ali Beheshti	A Hazara religious leader and head of the *Shura-i-Inqilab-i-Ittefaq-i-Islami Afghanistan* [Revolutionary Council of the Islamic Union of Afghanistan; *Shura* for short], the Shi'a resistance organization in the Hazarajat which was from 1979 to 1982 the effective government of the central massif. When Beheshti refused to give allegiance to Khomeini in Iran, the Shura was destroyed by Nasr and Pazdaran, extremist leftwing Shi'a groups armed and supported by Iran's Revolutionary guards. Beheshti is now with Sayed Jaglan (q.v.). Party program was nationalist-oriented.
Pir Sayed Ahmad Gailani	Head of *Mahaz-i-Milli Islami Afghanistan* [National Islamic Front of Afghanistan; *Mahaz* for short; also known by the English-language acronym NIFA]. A religious leader of international importance in the Muslim world, Gailani is the hereditary leader of the Qadirya Sufi order founded by his ancestor in the twelfth century, of which many Afghans (especially Pushtuns) are adherents (murids). Now in his mid-fifties, he was trained in

theology at Kabul University and served as religious advisor to the former king before the 1973 coup. Mahaz is one of the larger parties, and since 1983 has become well organized and effective. Represented in London.

Party program: Traditionalist-nationalist. Calls for a basically secular government incorporating Islamic law and Afghan tradition, preferably with a parliament based on free elections.

Dr. Shah Rukh Gran

A Mahaz commander in the Kabul-Sarobi area and a medical doctor.

Abdul Haq

An important Hezb/Khalis commander in the Kabul area.

Maulawi Jalaluddin Haqani

A Hezb/Khalis commander in Paktia province.

Harakat

See: *Mohammadi* and *Mohseni.*

Engineer Gulbuddin Hekhmatyar

Head of *Hezb-i-Islami/Hekhmatyar* [Islamic Party/Hekhmatyar Faction.] A highly controversial figure. Hekhmatyar, like Sayyaf (and Hafizullah Amin), is a Kharruti Pushtun, but from Baghlan province. Now in his late thirties, he first studied at the military academy, then abruptly switched to the Engineering Faculty of Kabul University, where he became a leader in the Afghan branch of the international Muslim Brotherhood (Ikhwan ul-Muslimi). He reportedly spent about four years in the PDPA before shifting to radical Islamic politics. According to Girardet, he was jailed in 1972 in the killing of a Maoist student and subsequently fled to Pakistan to join other exiles in founding the original Hezb and instigating the anti-Daoud insurrection in Panjsher in 1975.

Since 1979 Hekhmatyar has been consistently singled out by Kabul as the leader of the entire Resistance and is the only leader accused of being "an instrument of the C.I.A." Nevertheless, since

1979 many in the Resistance have accused him of secret collusion with the DRA and even with the Soviets. Resistance commanders repeatedly charge his units with undermining their military operations and even cooperating with Soviet forces, and Hezb forces are involved in most conflicts among Resistance groups in the field. (Cf. Girardet.) (One recent example, reported by a Western eyewitness: On 1-7 October 1986, Hezb/Hekhmatyar forces attacked a village under other Resistance control housing a French-run clinic then being inspected by a representative of the Paris aid organization. The attack was repulsed. The captured attackers stated that the assault had been ordered by their commander. Three days after the Hezb attack failed, Soviet jets targeted and destroyed the clinic.)

The Hezb/Hekhmatyar is widely accused of killing many effective commanders affiliated with other parties and is held responsible for the murder of a large number of political opponents and party defectors whose bodies have been found, bound and shot, in the river near Peshawar since 1982, as well as for the disappearance of others, including the Afghan husband of a U.S. citizen. The existence of private Hezb prisons has been verified and reported in the press. Reliable sources among Afghan moderates both inside and outside of Resistance organizations report receiving death threats from the Hezb, and Hekhmatyar is widely feared.

He has at one time or another attacked every other Resistance organization vituperatively. When the Alliance sent a delegation to Washington in 1986, Hekhmatyar, together with Sayyaf, not only refused to participate but called a press conference to denounce the mission.

In addition to operations from his base in Peshawar, Hekhmatyar reportedly operates out of Iran, where his organization, said to be managed jointly by the Hezb and the leftist Iranian Revolutionary Guards, is called *Jundullah* (q.v.).

Once one of the largest Resistance parties, the

Hezb/Hekhmatyar has lost much of its support among both mujahideen and civilians, most of whom do not share its extremist views, and its numbers have declined significantly in recent years. Nevertheless it remains important, in part because of ties to Pakistan's influential Jamaat Islami political party and to the Muslim Brotherhood and its supporters. It is widely reported to be a favored recipient of Middle Eastern and other foreign aid. The Hezb/Hekhmatyar is very skillful at dealing with the international press; it maintains offices in New York, London, several Asian countries, and possibly Australia, and attempts to present itself as the voice of the entire Resistance.

Party program: Most extreme radical-revivalist Islamic theocracy. Pro-Khomeini (although Sunni); pro-PLO, despite PLO support for the Kabul regime. Violently anti-American and anti-Western as well as anti-Soviet. Has acknowledged receipt of money from Libya's Qaddafi in the past and is reliably reported to maintain continuing ties with him. Generally allied with Sayyaf against the other Resistance parties.

For additional details on this extremely controversial leader and his organization, see: Roy; Girardet; Fullerton; also general press. (See bibliography.)

Hezb-i-Islami See *Hekhmatyar* and *Khalis.*

Jalaluddin Hokani An independent commander allied with Hezb/Khalis, operating in Paktia and provinces in the south.

Ismail Khan A Jamiat commander in the Herat area; the most important commander in that region.

Ittehad The Alliance (literally, "unity") of the seven major Resistance organizations based in Peshawar. Sometimes referred to as "The Unity." Founded in early 1985, this Ittehad, unlike previous efforts, has held together. Within the Alliance, each party maintains its individual identity and the role of spokesman for the Ittehad is rotated among the seven leaders. Joint medical, education and other committees have been set up and other steps are being taken to promote increasing unity of action. As of 1986, the Alliance began lobbying for recognition of the Resistance as the representatives of the Afghan people in the Islamic Conference, the United Nations, and other international bodies.

Sayed Jaglan

A major in the pre-Communist Afghan army, he was formerly military commander for Beheshti's Shura in the Hazarajat. Since the destruction of the Shura by Khomeinist forces, he has continued to operate independently in the area but has a formal agreement of cooperation and coordination with Mahaz.

Jamiat Islami Afghanistan

See *Rabbani*.

Jundullah

The Iranian branch of Hezb-i-Islami/Hekhmatyar (see *Hekhmatyar*), reportedly managed jointly by the Hezb/Hekhmatyar and the leftist Iranian Revolutionary Guards (the organization that seized the U.S. embassy in Teheran in 1979).

Maulawi Mohammad Younos Khalis

Head of *Hezb-i-Islami/Khalis* [Islamic Party/Khalis Faction]. A Pushtun from Nangrahar province and a mullah trained in traditional Afghan religious schools, Khalis was a university lecturer and the editor of a journal in Kabul. Direct, forthright, and to the point, he is widely respected even by opponents. Although he was nearly sixty at the time of the Soviet invasion, he has regularly gone inside Afghanistan to command in the field. His son was executed by the Soviets. Hezb/Khalis maintains an office in Essen, West Germany.

Party program: Though one of the Islamist parties, Hezb/Khalis appears to be more traditionalist and less radical than some of the others and has at times reportedly moved closer to the nationalist groups headed by Gailani, Mojadidi and Mohammadi. Its strength is in significant measure tribally based. One of the better organized parties with strength in strategic areas, its importance is greater than its size would indicate.

Mahaz See *Gailani*.

Ahmad Shah Massoud A commander for Jamiat. Perhaps the best-known of Resistance commanders, he received considerable international press attention while heading operations in the Panjsher Valley. After 1985, he shifted most of his attention to the northern provinces. Nicknamed "the Lion of Panjsher." ("Panjsher" means "Five Lions" and according to legend is named for five heroes; Massoud was popularly acclaimed as another.)

Kandahar Mawlawi A Hezb/Khalis commander in Nangrahar (killed September 1986).

Qari Taj Mohammad A Harakat commander in Ghazni province.

Maulawi Mohammad Nabi Mohammadi Head of *Harakat-i-Inqilab-i-Islami Afghanistan* [Movement for the Islamic Revolution of Afghanistan; the *Harakat* for short.] A graduate of al-Azhar University in Cairo now in his early sixties, Mohammadi combines religious authority with political experience. A theologian who established and headed an influential religious academy, he also served in the pre-Daoud parliament, 1969-1973. An Ahmadzai Pushtun, he has considerable backing from both tribal leaders and mullahs, especially in the Kandahar and Helmand regions, combined with support from the urban middle class. The Harakat is one of the largest Resistance parties but is very loosely organized, usually under local leadership. Has representative in Washington.

Party program: Centrist, traditional, nationalist. Supports a popularly elected government with a system based on Islamic law (but not theocracy or radical Islam) and on the traditional Loya Jirga rather than a Western-style parliament.

Sheikh Asaf Mohseni

Head of the Iran-oriented Shi'a *Harakat-i-Islami* [Islamic Movement] in the Hazarajat. (Do not confuse with the Harakat headed by Mohammadi.) Khomeinist; connected with, supported and armed by Iran's left-wing Revolutionary Guards (who seized the American embassy in Tehran in 1979). Engaged in a struggle with Nasr for power in the central massif, pays little or no attention to the fight against the Soviets and the Communist regime.

Prof. Sibgatullah Mojadidi

Head of *Jabba-i-Milli Najat-i-Afghanistan* [National Front for the Rescue of Afghanistan]. In his early sixties, Prof. Mojadidi comes from one of most prominent religious families in Afghanistan, one which has been highly influential for a century or more and which has suffered greatly from the Communist takeover: more than thirty members of the family were executed shortly after the 1978 coup. Heir to his family's mantle of religious leadership, he is also an important figure in the Naqshbandiya Sufi brotherhood, which has many adherents (murids) in Afghanistan and Soviet Central Asia.

A graduate of al-Azhar University in Cairo, a theologian, and a teacher, Prof. Mojadidi was imprisoned under Daoud. After his release, he served as religious leader of the Muslim community in Copenhagen, Denmark, for several years. Following the 1978 coup he returned to Pakistan and founded the National Front. His party is small and maintains only a modest military presence, but is politically influential.

Party program: Traditionalist-nationalist orientation. Constitutional monarchy, based on the traditional institutions of pre-Communist Afghanistan and possibly involving the former king.

Nasr

Full name: *Sazman al-Nasr* [Organization for Victory]. An extreme Khomeinist Shi'a organization connected with and armed by the leftist Iranian Revolutionary Guards. Nasr, together with *Pazdaran,* first destroyed Beheshti's indigenous moderate *Shura* Resistance organization in the Hazarajat, then crushed Pazdaran, and is now fighting with Mohseni's Harakat for power in the central massif. Nasr has devoted little or no attention to the struggle against the Soviets and the Communist regime, which have been the chief beneficiaries of the infighting in the Hazarajat.

NIFA

See *Gailani.*

Pazdaran-i-Jihad-i-Islami

[Protectors of the Islamic Holy War]. Extreme Khomeinist Shi'a group in the Hazarajat; like Nasr and Mohseni's Harakat, armed and supported by the Iranian Revolutionary Guards. Helped to destroy the moderate Shura in the Hazarajat but lost out in the subsequent power struggle with Nasr and Mohseni's Harakat.

Prof. Burhanuddin Rabbani

Head of the *Jamiat Islami Afghanistan* [Islamic Society of Afghanistan]. A Tajik born in Badakhshan in 1940 and a graduate of al-Azhar University in Cairo, Rabbani was a professor in the Faculty of Islamic Law at Kabul University, a writer on religion and literature and a leading figure in the Ikhwan ul-Muslimi (Muslim Brotherhood) movement at the university before fleeing Daoud's crackdown in 1973. Once associated with Hekhmatyar, he broke with him to establish the Jamiat c. 1978.

With a non-Pushtun leadership, the Jamiat has special appeal for Tajiks and other minority ethnic groups, although some Pushtuns in the north have accepted its leadership as well. The Jamiat is one of the largest parties, particularly in northern Afghanistan; it gained international prominence through press coverage of fighting in the Panjsher Valley led by Ahmad Shah Massoud. The Jamiat emphasizes organization in the field---social and political as well as military. Jamiat spokesmen maintain offices in Paris, Washington, and elsewhere.

Party program: Originally almost identical to that of Hezb/Hekhmatyar (radical-revivalist Islam) but, although not repudiating those positions, it appears to have reduced the radical ideological components somewhat since about 1984. Rabbani led the 1986 Alliance delegation to Washington.

Brig. Gen. Rahmatullah Safi

Director of military operations for Mahaz. A general and Chief of Special Forces in the pre-Communist Afghan Army, he received advanced training in the U.S., Britain and the USSR.

Abdul Rasul Sayyaf

Head of *Ittehad-i-Islami B'rai Azad-i-Afghanistan* (Islamic Union to Free Afghanistan). A leading member of the Muslim Brotherhood (Ikhwan ul-Muslimi) in Kabul before the 1978 coup, Sayyaf was imprisoned under the Khalq regime but survived, probably because he had family ties to Amin (both of them being Kharruti Pushtuns from the village of Paghman). Released after the Soviet invasion, he reached Peshawar and, because he had no party ties, was chosen as a non-partisan independent to help unify the alliance formed in 1980. Fluent in Arabic (he studied theology in Cairo and Saudi Arabia) and an eloquent speaker, he also seemed an excellent choice to win support from Saudi Arabia and other Muslim states. In this latter function he proved eminently successful but arranged for the funds to be paid into his personal account, maintaining total control over, reportedly, many millions of dollars which he has refused to distribute. Far from encouraging unity, this led to a breakdown of the 1980 alliance.

When the 1980 Ittehad collapsed, he retained the name and transformed it into a personal power base. Having neither an organization nor followers, he proceeded to buy the adherence of groups of mujahideen by providing the arms they needed in exchange for nominal allegiance. In his effort to gain a following, he has also reportedly given weapons to extremely dubious groups that are little if anything more than bandits taking advantage of the chaotic conditions of wartime; this has led to numerous problems for civilians and mujahideen inside Afghanistan. His support in the field remains small and almost solely dependent on his funding power but his financial resources remain very large, thanks to his eloquence before Arab audiences and his close connections with the Muslim Brotherhood. Their support and the funds he has accumulated have kept him in the leadership circle, but his activities are divisive. In 1986 he joined Hekhmatyar in denouncing the Alliance delegation to Washington.

Party program: Unclear. Indeed, Sayyaf does not seem to have a real party. His positions are radical-revivalist and largely coincide with those of the international Muslim Brotherhood. Generally allied with Hekhmatyar, with whom he has tribal ties, against the other Resistance parties.

For additional details on this controversial figure, see: Roy; also Fullerton. (See bibliography.)

Maulawi Shafiullah	A Harakat commander in Koh-i-Safi (killed April 1985).
Haji Mohammad Shah	A Harakat commander in Farah province.
Shura	See *Beheshti*.
Gen. Abdul Rahim Wardak	Deputy director of military operations for Mahaz. A colonel in the pre-Communist Afghan Army and liaison to the Indian Army, he received advanced

training in the United States and Egypt in the early 1970s.

Amin Wardak	A Mahaz-affiliated commander in Wardak and Ghazni provinces.
Zabiullah Khan	A very able Jamiat commander in Mazar-i-Sharif and the north (killed 1984). Though not so well known internationally as Massoud, Zabiullah was one of the most effective field commanders in the entire Resistance. His assassination by KhAD was a major Resistance loss.

Note: For security reasons, many effective field commanders maintain a low profile and anonymity, and are little known to the outside world. Those listed here are already publicly known.

Appendix IV

Who's Who in the DRA and the PDPA:
A Selected List

The following short biographical sketches and identifications provide summary information on most of the more prominent figures who are or have been significant in the People's Democratic Party of Afghanistan (PDPA) and the Democratic Republic of Afghanistan (DRA) regimes, and on some who may perhaps be prominent in the future. Because of the secretive nature of both the PDPA and the DRA regime, it is not possible to know all of those who may play significant roles behind the scenes---or whether all of those who are visible are in reality significant, or in what way. Still, this provides a starting point.

Most of those listed here are known to be party members---but not all. Some may have unknown or concealed party connections, or may be collaborators whose connections can only be speculated on. Not all factional affiliations are known.

The list is divided into three sections:

I. The four men who have thus far headed the DRA: Dr. Najib, who came to power in 1986, and his predecessors Babrak Karmal, Hafizullah Amin, and Nur Mohammad Taraki.

II. Others of past or present significance, most of whom are still alive and may continue to be important.

III. A number of others holding official positions who at present appear to be minor players, some of whom may be more important than appearances indicate or may become more important in the future.

For known party members, factional affiliation, if known, is indicated by (P) for Parcham and (K) for Khalq.

The names of the twenty-one who have been identified as being present at the founding Congress of the PDPA on 1 January 1965 are marked with an asterisk (*).

The names of those with suspected links to Soviet intelligence (usually KGB, possibly GRU) are marked with a dagger (†).

Known non-party members are so identified in *italics*.

The information given below is drawn from numerous sources: the general press, the daily Foreign Broadcast Information Service reports, DRA publications, various other publications (most of which are listed in the bibliography), personal observations and interviews, and Afghan sources. Special recognition is due the invaluable help of Anthony Arnold, both in his writings (which are an essential source for any inquiry into the PDPA) and his advice. Thanks are due also to Ruth L. Arnold of the Hoover Institution and Steven L. Ginsberg of Freedom House, who researched and maintained files on which Part III in particular, and some of Parts I and II, are based.

NOTE: Many extreme leftists adopted *noms de plume*, usually expressing patriotism or noble motives; these served to conceal their ethnic origins and identities, which are ordinarily revealed by many Afghan surnames. The best known of these is, of course, Babrak Karmal.

I. Party Leaders

Dr. Najib (ullah)† (P) [uses one name only]

General Secretary of the PDPA since 4 May 1986: party boss and de facto head of the DRA. Head of KhAD from its establishment at beginning of 1980 until November 1985; now holds the rank of lieutenant general.

He was born near Gardez in Paktia province in August 1946 (or 1947), one of six children of a middle class family "of average wealth." During the 1960s, his father was trade representative for the Afghan government in Peshawar, Pakistan---and allegedly an agent for Daoud, establishing ties with tribal figures which Najib may have later built on and may now be using. He began student radical activities while still in Habibia High School and joined the PDPA immediately after graduation in 1965. That same year he entered Kabul University Faculty of Medicine but took ten years to get a medical degree because of extensive time spent organizing demonstrations, strikes, and student radicalization (including the riots of 1965 and later), plus two periods in jail for his activities. He joined the PDPA Central Committee 1977 and the Revolutionary Council 1978. He often drops the ending "-ullah" (which refers to God) from his name, using only "Najib" (which means "honorable"). Not visibly prominent under Taraki but was one of six Parchamis exiled as ambassadors in mid-1978 for plotting to overthrow Khalq. Posted to Iran, he subsequently fled to Eastern Europe and Moscow, absconding with embassy funds. Five days after Babrak arrived in the wake of the Soviet invasion, Najib returned to Kabul and was immediately made head of KhAD, the secret police, which was then reorganized from KAM under KGB direction. He was thoroughly trained by the KGB.

An Ahmadzai Pushtun, Najib has extensive tribal connections and remains active in efforts to buy or subvert Pushtun tribes on both sides of the border and plant agents in Pakistan's Frontier Province and Peshawar. Reportedly headed the Tribal Department of the Ministry of Tribes and Nationalities while also head of KhAD. Reportedly still maintains oversight of secret police, now upped to ministry status as WAD under his former deputy Maj. Gen. Farooq Yaqubi; also unofficially oversees tribal ministry, which is nominally headed by Layeq.

As a physician who made a profession of---and personally carried out---torture, he provides an interesting parallel with the Nazi Dr. Joseph Mengele. As chief of KhAD, he has been automatically subordinate to the KGB since 1980. Now in the leader's chair, he should enjoy KGB protection at least in the short run.

Najib's wife Fatana, headmistress of a school, is a member of the Amanullah branch of the royal family (pre-1929 royal line), giving him a valuable network of social contacts. He has several children.

Babrak Karmal † *
(P)

Former General Secretary of the PDPA, President of the Revolutionary Council, and founder of Parcham and its leader from its inception, installed by Soviet power in 1980 but deposed from all leadership positions in 1986 after he had failed to pacify the country and win public acceptance. The Afghan Communist *par excellence* and, according to KGB defector Vladimir Kuzichkin, a paid agent of the KGB for many years before the 1978 coup. "Karmal" is a *nom de plume* adopted early on, possibly for its double meaning: it means "friend of labor" but can also be interpreted as "Kremlin." He is frequently referred to by his first name alone (but not by his last name alone).

Babrak was born in 1929 near Kabul, the son of an Army officer (his father retired with the rank of general) and a member of the wealthy Kabul elite. Claims to be a Pushtun but may in fact be of Tajik origin. Educated at the elite German-language Nejat School where he may have come under pro-Nazi influence as well as that of former members of radical Jawanan Afghan movement. Early involvement with clandestine radical movements began at least by late 1940s if not earlier; active in Daoud's Cloob-i-Milli.

A mediocre student, he failed his first entrance examinations for the Faculty of Law and Political Science at Kabul University but established himself on campus. Finally admitted to the university in 1951; by then, he was already a committed, more or less fulltime radical activist who at one point in his career was disowned by his father. He was active in stimulating student unrest at the university, a good public speaker, and a gifted demagogue. (Boyish in appearance, as late as the 1960s he continued to rally university students as "we.")

Jailed in the 1952 crackdown on leftists, but given the comforts of home in his cell. Released in 1956, he worked as a translator, did his military service, and in 1960 finally completed his degree. After various minor jobs, he went into politics fulltime in 1964. The point at which he established KGB connections is uncertain, but he was a regular visitor to the Soviet embassy in Kabul from the late 1950s on and arranged Soviet favors for potential followers.

Between 1956 and 1963, Babrak kept a low public profile, conducting private meetings with students and others, clandestinely organizing Parcham. Later he helped pave the way for the establishment of the PDPA on 1 January 1965. Elected to parliament in 1965, he and his agents instigated riots that forced the resignation of the new cabinet; thereafter they kept the political process in turmoil until the 1973 Daoud coup. Under Daoud, a number of secret as well as overt Parchamis entered government (especially the key security ministries), many of them with the help of Babrak's close associate Nehmatullah Pazhwak; a number of clandestine Parchamis and sympathizers remained in official positions after Daoud ousted the known leftists.

[Party developments, the Parcham/Khalq conflict, activities in the intervening years, Parcham involvement in the coups of 1973 and 1978, and Babrak Karmal's role in all of these are covered elsewhere in this volume. See Arnold and Klass]

After eighteen months in exile in Czechoslovakia and Moscow, Babrak returned to Kabul in January 1980 after Soviet forces had secured the city and killed Hafizullah Amin; his speech laying claim to power was in fact broadcast from Tashkent. The Soviets apparently expected that in a classic bad cop/good cop maneuver, Babrak, by contrast to the brutal Amin, could gain public acceptance and pacify the country; moreover Babrak had long since proved himself an obedient instrument of Soviet policy. (During the 1965 parliamentary elections, the editor of this volume interviewed Babrak, who expounded "revolutionary principles." A few questions elicited the fact that he had never heard of the French or any other revolution other than the Bolshevik Revolution.)

Such Soviet expectations were however doomed to failure from the start: Babrak had for years been known throughout the country as a Soviet tool; and in any case, his installation by the USSR plus the

Soviet presence in Afghanistan inevitably aroused more, not less, public resistance. Beginning in 1982, rumors periodically circulated that he was about to be replaced. In 1986 he was finally removed---in stages, resigning first the party leadership and then the presidency. That he was bitter at being cast aside after so many years of loyal service was indicated by his refusal to throw the flowers provided to him during ceremonies surrounding the highly publicized Soviet troop "withdrawal" (actually a troop rotation) in the autumn of 1986; but he offered no more concrete public protest nor has he thus far given overt support to protesting supporters. In 1987, however, he departed for Moscow "for reasons of health." He is the first Afghan Communist leader to lose power without losing his life.

Babrak is married and his wife has played a ceremonial role in the DRA (e.g., inaugurating orphanages); but his connection with his reputed mistress Anahita Ratebzad has been an open scandal since at least the early 1960s.

Hafizullah Amin (K) (1929-1979)

A Ghilzai Pushtun of the Kharrut clan born in Paghman, the mountain resort just outside of Kabul, Amin was the son of a minor government clerk. After graduating from Kabul University, he became a teacher of mathematics and physics at the main teacher training institution in Kabul, a boarding school to which the brightest boys from the provincial villages were sent and where he himself had studied. Intensely ambitious, he worked his way up to become principal of another school for provincial boys. About this time he became involved in the Afghan Mellat (q. v.), a Pushtun supremacy organization promoting Pushtun dominance and a "greater Pushtunistan" policy, which was strongly influenced if not dominated by Afghans educated in Germany who had absorbed elements of Nazi racial thinking and identified the Pushtuns as the "original Aryans."

In 1957 he won a scholarship to Teachers College of Columbia University in New York, where he earned an M.A. in education. Returning to Kabul, he taught at the university, again headed a high school, and became involved with Nur Mohammad Taraki, already probably a member of the Communist Party of India. Although he later claimed to have become radicalized while taking summer courses at the University of Wisconsin during his second stay in the U.S., it seems likely that in fact his conversion to Marxism was already under way much earlier.

By the time he returned to New York in 1962 to take a Ph D. at Columbia, he was belligerently political, neglecting his studies in favor of radical anti-government politics and trying to radicalize the Afghan Student Association. He was in the U.S. when the combined PDPA was formed in January 1965 but returned to Kabul (via Moscow) without his degree in time to run for Parliament in September 1965: he had lost his scholarship and been expelled from Columbia, either because the Afghan government complained of his political activities (his explanation) or because his politicking left him little time for study and he flunked out.

In 1966, Taraki added Amin to the PDPA Central Committee as an alternate member; in 1967 he became a full member. In 1969 he won election to parliament, the only Khalqi ever to do so. *[His role in the party, in the 1978 coup, and in office is discussed elsewhere in this volume. See Arnold and Klass]* His naked and unbridled ambition made him many enemies inside the party and out, and when in 1978 power finally came into his hands, he took vengeance on his enemies, personal and political, with ferocity and guile. Almost from the beginning of the Khalq period, it was apparent that genuine power lay in his hands rather than with the relatively ineffectual Taraki.

It has been suggested that Amin adopted

Marxism simply as the most effective way to the power he openly coveted. That is possible; but in any case, once in power, he attempted to carry out a rigidly doctrinaire, textbook Marxist-Leninist transformation of Afghan society without concern for the realities of his nation, his Soviet backers, or his own best interests.

Amin was an able and clever man but under a veneer of Afghan good manners, he was essentially a brutal murderous thug. A French journalist who interviewed him just after he had killed Taraki and taken total control in September 1979 described him succinctly as "*un mafioso.*" In his last months, as he became increasingly isolated---aware that Moscow intended to get rid of him, that the Resistance was growing stronger, and that the army on which he had once depended was deserting in droves---he reached out frantically in any direction, contacting Resistance leaders with whom he had tribal connections, vainly attempting to contact the U.S. embassy, drinking heavily, constantly on the alert for assassins. On the night of 27 December 1979, when a Soviet special forces team assigned to kill him attacked the presidential palace, he reportedly went down fighting.

Nur Mohammed Taraki †? * **(1917-1979) (K)** The first known Afghan member of the Communist party, Taraki was a Ghilzai Pushtun from a small town in Ghazni province. He came from a poor family, the first member of his family to become literate. After schooling in Kandahar, he got a job with an import-export company owned by the head of the national bank, Abdul Majid Zabuli, and in 1934 or 1935 was sent to Bombay. There he took night school courses in English and Urdu and met Khan Ghaffar Khan (leader of the Pushtun Red Shirt movement in British India and after 1947 of the Pushtunistan movement and the Awami National Party in Pakistan, an avowed Marxist and admirer of Lenin) and important members of the Communist Party of India. He reportedly joined the CPI before returning to Kabul in 1937.

Back in Kabul he became a private secretary to Zabuli, who may have introduced him to Soviet officials, and took a degree in law and political science in 1941. Through Zabuli he got a job with the Ministry of Economics but was fired after his patron discovered that Taraki was stealing not only from the government but from Zabuli himself.

Taraki then joined the government press office and eventually became deputy chief of the official Bakhtar news agency. He began to establish a reputation as a writer and poet and became involved in radical politics in the late 1940s, by which time he was certainly a committed Marxist if not in fact a party member. When the government cracked down on radicals in 1952, Taraki was banished to Washington as press and cultural attaché in the Afghan embassy. Recalled by Daoud a few months later, he denounced the Afghan government to the American press as a brutal tyranny and asked for political asylum in the U.S. Five weeks later he repudiated his statements and said he was going home.

His whereabouts during the next three years are uncertain. He may have travelled in the Soviet Union and Eastern Europe; he may or may not have gone to Kabul. In any case, in 1956 he was back in Kabul and was hired as a translator by the U.S. aid mission there. In 1958 he quit that job to open a translation business but returned in 1962 to work as a translator in the U.S. embassy itself until he quit again in 1963 to devote himself fulltime to laying the organizational groundwork for the PDPA. In an embassy in which almost none of the diplomatic personnel spoke the local languages and were therefore dependent on translators, Taraki was in a position not only to obtain confidential information but also to manipulate the information received by American officials and to plant disinformation. Moreover, as a capable and trusted translator, he was in a position to recommend others for the staff.

In short, as a committed Communist, he twice took jobs at the U.S. embassy. At the least, he was an ideological opponent whose manipulations may have lingered long in the reports and assessments made by American diplomatic staff, influencing American policy decisions even many years later. Beyond that, he may have been a controlled KGB agent.

[His role in the formation and development of the PDPA and in the DRA is discussed elsewhere in this volume. See Arnold and Klass] He reportedly had a pleasant, softspoken, unassertive manner, and was able to play a mediating role between more aggressive and ambitious figures like Amin, Babrak Karmal and others; his low-key personality, his gray hair and his fatherly appearance may well have contributed to his selection first as head of the glued-together PDPA and then as president of the new Communist regime immediately after the 1978 coup. By then he was an alcoholic, almost never seen without a teapot before him---a disguise for his liquor supply--- from which he poured and sipped all day long. Members of the diplomatic community thought he was ill and on medication but according to Afghan sources he was constantly drunk.

Long before Taraki was killed, it was apparent that the reins of power were in Amin's hands; and when he died, he was forgotten immediately.

II. Prominent Figures

The Central Committee of the PDPA had 79 members, including 8 Secretaries, until July 1986, at which time membership was enlarged to 147 in order to include more members from the provinces; the number of Secretaries remained the same.

The Politburo has 11 members.

The Revolutionary Council, which has little actual power, had 69 members until January 1986, when another 79 members were added in order to "broaden the base" by "giving greater representation to workers, peasants, businessmen, clergy and intellectuals." Most of the new members are described by official DRA sources as being "non-party."

These numbers may of course change in the future.

Abdur Kashid Arian * (K)	A Pushtun born in Kandahar, 1941. Began PDPA activities there in 1964, before official party founding. Alternate member, Khalq Central Committee, 1967; full member, 1977. Member, Revolutionary Council, and Deputy Minister of Information and Culture, 1978. Ambassador to Pakistan, late 1978. After the Soviet invasion installed Parcham leadership, Arian remained on the Revolutionary Council and PDPA Central Committee, became Minister of Justice, Attorney General, and president of High Judiciary Council. In August 1980 he became Deputy Prime Minister. In June 1981 shakeup he lost ministerial and judicial posts but was elected to Revolutionary Council Presidium. In June 1982 he was vice president of the Revolutionary Council, possibly as a token Khalqi. Named head of the PDPA Central Committee's Control and Auditing Commission, July 1986.
Mohammed Aziz	Appointed Minister of Light Industries and Foodstuffs March 1984. Appointed Deputy Prime Minister, June 1986 and Chief of State Planning Committee. Full member, PDPA Central Committee, July 1986.
Taher Badakhshi * (P) (d. 1979)	His name indicates northern and non-Pushtun origin. A member of the original PDPA Central Committee, he switched back and forth between Parcham and Khalq, and in 1968 quit the PDPA to found Settem-i-Milli, a northern-based anti-Pushtun Marxist party initially calling for northern autonomy but now calling for secession and working actively with Soviets and regime. [See Krakowski] Badakhshi was killed by Amin in 1979.

Mahmoud
Baryalai * (P)

Babrak Karmal's half-brother, an economist married to a daughter of Anahita Ratebzad, hence a brother-in-law of Nur. Chief PDPA ideologist under Babrak, responsible for the ideological committees of the armed forces. A secretary of the PDPA Central Committee for some time. His role is reputedly diminishedsince Babrak's ouster as party chairman in May 1986, and rumors abound: he ispromoted, he is arrested, etc.; but he was promoted to full Politburo membership in July 1986 and was deputy chairman of the Central Committee's Permanent Commission on Foreign Affairs as of December 1986. Present and any possible future roles unclear.

Haji Mohammad
Chamkani
(not a Party member)

In May 1986, following the ouster of Babrak and the elevation of Najib to the party chairmanship, Chamkani, a Pushtun tribal leader, suddenly surfaced as Vice President of the Revolutionary Council and chairman of Central Council of the High Jirga of Tribes. In November 1986, when Babrak was stripped of the presidency, Chamkani was named as Acting President of the Revolutionary Council. Also deputy head of the Supreme Extraordinary Commission for National Reconciliation, created by the Revolutionary Council, 3 January 1987.

A Pushtun from Paktia, Chamkani was a member of parliament and a senator before 1973, and governor of Kunar province under Daoud; as a *non-Party member,* his appointment as Acting President of the DRA was apparently part of the effort to validate the "national reconciliation" campaign floated in late 1985, which picked up steam in 1986 and 1987. His use of the honorific "haji" indicates that he has made the pilgrimage to Mecca, hence is ostensibly a devout Muslim. His appointment has other important implications as well: the Chamkani tribe which he heads, though relatively small, is strategically located along Resistance lines of communication in Afghanistan's Paktia provinceand, in Pakistan, from Miram Shah into Peshawar; the tribe is said to be loyal to his leadership. His tribe can therefore provide a major base for tribal penetration in key areas on both sides of the border as well as hampering the Resistance movement and logistics; this may be a major factor in his elevation to the presidency.

Mohammad Ismail Danesh (K) *

An engineer educated in the U.S. and the Soviet Union. Pushtun. An alternate member of the PDPA Central Committee and Minister of Mines and Industries under Taraki and Amin, he survived Parcham/Khalq infighting and was the only minister to hold on to his post under Karmal. In mid-summer 1986, Najib sent him into diplomatic exile as ambassador to Libya. His brother lives in the U.S.

"Disappeared" Khalqis

A number of Khalqis who played important roles in the Taraki and Amin regimes disappeared shortly after the Soviet invasion and Parcham's return, and were initially reported killed but later reported to be alive and being held incommunicado in Pul-i-Charkhi prison but receiving good treatment. This was confirmed in May 1987 when several, though not all, were released, possibly in connection with the campaign for a "government of reconciliation." Their survival is due to Soviet intercession: in future they should be beholden to their protectors and vulnerable to recruitment, perhaps for service in some kind of "government of reconciliation." Resurrecting them would infuriate the Parchamis, however, and their utility in any future government is questionable.

They include: Faqir Mohammed Faqir, Abdul Quddud Ghorbandi, Mohammed Mansur Hashemi, Abdur Rashid Jalili, Abdul Hakim Sharayee Jauzjani, Khayal Mohammed Katawazi, Mohammed Salem Masoodi, Abdul Karim Misaq, Mahmoud Alamgul Suma, Dr. Akbar Shah Wali and possibly others; see individual listings. Ghorbandi, Hashemi, Jauzjani, Suma, Dr. Wali, and possibly others were released in 1987.

Ghorbandi, Hashemi, Jauzjani, Suma, Dr. Wali, and possibly others were released in 1987.

Shah Mohammed Dost (P)

Foreign Minister under Babrak Karmal regime from January 1980 to November 1986, when he was named Minister of State for Foreign Affairs and packed off as DRA representative to the United Nations. Under Taraki and Amin, he had served as Deputy Minister for Political Affairs, according to his official biography. Member of the Revolutionary Council and PDPA Central Committee. A Farsi-speaking Kabuli and a career diplomat, he earlier held posts in the Afghan embassies in Washington and Islamabad, served as consul in Peshawar, and in 1965 was appointed *chef de cabinet* in the office of Prime Minister Maiwandwal. Presumably his political sympathies were not public at that time. In New York in June 1987, he deliberately ran down a pedestrian in a dispute over a parking place.

Faqir Mohammed Faqir (K)

A member of the PDPA Central Committee and Minister of the Interior for a few months after Amin took full power in the wake of Taraki's death. See *"Disappeared" Khalqis* (above).

Brig. Gen. Mohammad Faruq

Member of the PDPA Central Committee. Head of the Political Affairs Department of the Ministry of Internal Affairs [Interior].

Mohammed Foruq

General Commander of Border Forces as of July 1983 since July 1983. Member of PDPA Central Committee.

Abdul Quddud Ghorbandi (K)

Minister of Commerce under Taraki and Amin, and a member of PDPA Central Committee from late 1978. See *"Disappeared" Khalqis* (above).

Goldad (K)

A literacy teacher trained in India, he has been flexible enough to hold posts under Taraki, Amin, Babrak and Najib. Appointed to the PDPA Central

Committee by Amin, he has remained there under Babrak and Najib. In 1980 he was made Vice President of the Afghan-Soviet Friendship Society, deputy head of a Central Committee Sub-committee, and Minister of Higher and Vocational Education, and soon thereafter, Deputy Prime Minister. In June 1981 he was appointed Deputy Chairman of the Council of Ministers, a position he still held as recently as November 1986 even though he lost his ministerial post in September 1982.

Lt. Gen. Sayed Mohammed Gulabzoy (K) †

A Pushtun from Paktia province and an air force major who participated in Daoud's 1973 coup, Gulabzoy was the first person Amin contacted to activate the 1978 coup. There are indications that direct ties to the Soviet Union may be more significant in his career than his PDPA connections. Minister of Communications under Taraki, he was implicated in the Soviet plot to get rid of Amin in September 1979 and was one of four who took refuge from Amin's vengeance in the Soviet embassy in Kabul, where he remained until the invasion and Amin's overthrow. Although a Khalqi, he was immediately named to the sensitive post of Minister of the Interior by Karmal and was promoted steadily, reaching the rank of Major General in 1985, Lt. General and alternate member of Politburo in 1986, full member June 1987. His steady climb suggests Soviet backing. A member of the PDPA Central Committee; but he could not become top man in the PDPA or regime without mortally offending the Parchamis.

Mohammed Mansur Hashemi*

From a tiny village in Badakhshan, Hashemi was one of Amin's students in high school and later was associated with him at Columbia University, where Hashemi was taking an M.A. in education. After the Parcham/Khalq split, Hashemi was made an alternate member of the Khalq Central Committee. He served as Minister of Water and Power under

420

Taraki and Amin, and was reportedly particularly brutal in putting down resistance to DRA policies in his home district. See *"Disappeared" Khalqis* (above).

Abdur (Abdul) Rahim Hatif

Member of Revolutionary Council Presidium; chairman of the National (Fatherland) Front; also head of Supreme Extraordinary Commission for National Reconciliation (created 3 January 1987). A Pushtun from Kandahar, former teacher, former member of parliament and businessman.

Mohammad Khan Jalalar †
[not a Party member]

Minister of Commerce since 1980. A suspected Soviet agent of long standing. He served in pre-Daoud cabinet of Moussa Shafiq and in Daoud's cabinet, and is widely believed to have been a KGB agent who reported the plans of both Shafiq and Daoud to affect a rapproachment with Pakistan and Iran and loosendependency on the USSR, leading to the coups of 1973 and 1978. He is the only non-Parchami member of Daoud's cabinet to survive in the DRA cabinet, and direct Soviet ties are indicated. Jalalar is a first-generation Afghan of Turkoman origin born in Andkhoi in 1935 to immigrants from Soviet Central Asia; his paternal great-uncle was a Soviet general and he reportedly has family in the USSR. He is a member of the Revolutionary Council, but as a n*on-party member* is not eligible for the PDPA Central Committee. His sons, daughter and son-in-law live in the U.S. and are active as DRA agents among the Afghan refugee community.

Dr. Abdur Rashid Jalili (K)

Rector of Kabul University before becoming Minister of Education under Taraki in October 1978. Member of PDPA Central Committee, he became Minister of Agriculture and Land Reform in 1979 and was elected to Amin's eight-man Politburo in October 1979. Holds a Ph. D. earned in the USSR. See *"Disappeared" Khalqis* (above).

Abdul Hakim Sharayee (Sherai) Jauzjani * (K)	Born in Shibarghan in 1935, he studied first theology, then journalism, in Kabul, then went to the USSR for further studies. Worked for Kabul Radio and various publications, ran for parliament unsuccessfully in 1965 and 1969. Minister of Justice and Attorney General under Taraki and Amin, Politburo member under Amin. See *"Disappeared" Khalqis* (above).
Khayal Mohammedi Katawazi (K)	Member of PDPA Central Committee and Minister of Information and Culture under Taraki and Amin from March 1979 on. According to Male (see bibliography), one of Amin's most trusted associates and one of those he utilized to activate the April 1978 coup. See *"Disappeared" Khalqis* (above).
Najmuddin Akhgar Kawiani	A secretary of the PDPA Central Committee as of July 1986. Also on Revolutionary Council Presidium and a vice chairman of National Front. Named candidate member of Politburo, June 1987.
Sultan Ali Keshtmand (Kishtmand) * (P)	Prime Minister since 1981, Chairman of the Council of Ministers, member of the PDPA Central Committee and the Politburo, Keshtmand has long been one of the top Parchamis and at one time appeared slated to replace Babrak Karmal. Since Najib's accession to power, Keshtmand has been put in charge of ministries, administration, and economic policy. Born in 1935, he is a Shi'a of Hazara origin, an economist, sociologist and writer. Served briefly as Minister of Planning under Taraki but was implicated in Parchami plot, arrested, tortured (by Sarwari) and sentenced to death. Amin commuted his sentence to imprisonment, possibly under Soviet pressure. Released from Pul-i-Charkhi when Karmal returned in January 1980, he immediately became Deputy Prime Minister. May have been wounded in a shoot-out with Sarwari when both were in the cabinet in 1980. His wife, **Karima Keshtmand,** is

secretary of the Democratic Organization of Afghan Women.

Most Afghans began to adopt family names only in the late 1950s and 1960s, so Keshtmand may have chosen his own surname; the name "Keshtmand" means "peasant."

Abdul Ghaffar Lakanwal (P)

Since 1981, a member of the Presidium and Minister of Agriculture and Land Reforms. Chairman of the Agricultural Cooperatives Council.

Suleiman Layeq (Laiq, Laeq) * (P)

A renegade member of the Mojadidi family and a poet who turned to radical political writing. He apparently tried to switch to Khalq in 1978, changed sides again after the invasion. Minister of Radio and Television for a few months under Taraki, he was removed from power in 1980 but returned to the PDPA Central Committee and Revolutionary Council. Seems to have been mistrusted by Parcham but slowly regained Party's trust. In 1980 was made President of the Academy of Sciences; in 1981 was made Vice-Chairman of the National Fatherland Front and given the sensitive post of Minister of Tribes and Nationalities. Became a full Politburo member in 1986.

Gen Ghulam Mohammad Mahfouz

As of July 1984, head of the Department of Political Affairs of the State Information Agency (KhAD).

Sayyed Nassim Shah Maihanparast †

Named as a Deputy Chairman, Council of Ministers, December 1985, and on election commission. Head of the Northern Zone 1983-85. (See Alburz, below) Alternate member, PDPA Central Committee as of July 1983. Reportedly received sixteen years of training in Moscow and Tashkent before returning to Afghanistan in 1982 to take over running the north. Almost unknown to outside observers but has held highly important posts;

obviously trusted by Moscow. Maihanparast is a *nom de plume* of the sort adopted by many Afghan leftists: it means "intense patriot."

Mohammed Salem Masoodi * (K)

Ambassador to Bulgaria under Taraki, then Minister of Education for last six months before the invasion. Full member of the PDPA Central Committee under Amin. See *"Disappeared" Khalqis* (above).

Sher Jan Mazdooryar † (K?)

Born 1945, a Pushtun from Paktia province. A lieutenant colonel in the tank corps, he played a key role in both the 1973 and 1978 coups. Member of Central Committee, Minister of Interior, and then Minister of Frontier and Tribal Affairs under Taraki. Involved in plot to assassinate Amin in September 1979, took refuge in the Soviet embassy in Kabul until the invasion along with Watanjar, Gulabzoy and Sarwari. Unobtrusive as Minister of Transportation and Tourism since 1980. Believed to be more pro-Soviet than pro-PDPA faction, hence conceivably acceptable to Parchamis in leadership role, but would be obedient to Soviet commands in any capacity.

Abdul Karim Misaq * (K)

A bookkeeper, mechanic and writer. Minister of Finance, member of Politburo and PDPA Central Committee under Taraki and Amin. See *"Disappeared" Khalqis* (above).

Lt. Gen. Nazar Mohammad (K)

Initially General Commander, Air Force and Air Defense. Studied at Soviet General Staff Academy 1981-82. Replaced the less disciplined Abdul Qader as Minister of Defense in December 1984. Replaced by Mohammad Rafi and named Deputy Prime Minister by Najib, December 1986. Chief of General Staff. Member, PDPA Central Committee; candidate member of Politburo.

Dr. Niaz Mohammad Mohmand

Since June 1981, a secretary of the PDPA Central Committee. Named head of Revolutionary Council's Permanent Commission for

Budget and Planning, January 1987. Named candidate member of Politburo, June 1987. Mohmand Pushtun.*

Abdul Hamid Mohtat

Appointed Deputy Prime Minister, June 1987, after serving as ambassador to Japan. He is one of five known to hold the position of Deputy Prime Minister.

Nur Ahmad Nur *
(P)

Born in Kandahar 1937, educated in Kabul, worked as archivist in Ministry of Foreign Affairs. Claims PDPA membership before formal 1965 founding. Elected to parliament 1965, lost seat in 1969. Member of Central Committee 1960s and again Central Committee and Politburo as of 1977. Under Taraki,Minister of Interior and member of Revolutionary Council for several months following the 1978 coup but exiled as ambassador to Washington in mid-1978, later fled to the Soviet Union. Checkered Parcham career since invasion. At one point was member of Politburo and a Secretary of PDPA Central Committee and was considered second to Karmal, but left suddenly for the Soviet Union with family in January 1984 and dropped from sight amid rumors of attempted defection and/or falling out with Babrak and/or drunken denunciation of Soviet forces in Afghanistan. Returned to Kabul in September 1985. Was dropped without comment from Revolutionary Council Presidium in January 1986 but five months later was still identified as a Secretary of the Central Committee and Politburo member. Married to one of Anahita Ratebzad's daughters, hence a brother-in-law of Baryalai and relative of Babrak Karmal by marriage.

---

* The Mohmand are a major presence not only in the Nangrahar region but in Pakistan where they dominate the region around Peshawar. (See Mohmand, Part III below.)

**Mohammad Zahir
Ofuq
(Ofagh) * (K)**

Sided with Khalq in 1967 but at some point thereafter resigned and allegedly organized "Revolutionary Society of Afghanistan's Toilers," which merged with PDPA in August 1986 and turns up under the rubric of National Front organizations. Made full member, PDPA Central Committee, July 1986.

**Dr. Mehrabuddin
Paktiawal (P)**

President, Central Bank of Afghanistan, a cabinet post created in 1982; Chairman, Afghan-Bulgarian Friendship Society. Under Daoud, was president of Budget Department, Ministry of Finance. Deputy Minister of Finance 1978-80. Deputy head of State Committee for Planning. A Pushtun; his name indicates Paktia origin.

**Ghulam Dastagir
Panjsheri †? ***

Journalist and teacher, member of original PDPA Central Committee. Jailed, presumably for political activities, 1969-1972. Played both sides of Parcham/Khalq fence, even started his own breakaway Communist party in late 1960s; eventually returned to PDPA fold but factional affiliation is unclear. Periodically disappears from attention, resurfaces. Under Taraki and possibly Amin, was Minister of Education, later Minister of Public Works. Headed PDPA Central Committee's Party Control Commission, 1981-83. Head of Union of Writers and Poets since 1983; also head of Workers Movement. Retired from Politburo November 1985 "for reasons of health" but heads cultural delegations. Named head of Central Inspection Commission of PDPA in July 1986. A Tajik villager from the upper Panjsher Valley, he, like Hashemi and Suma, came under Amin's influence as a student at the teacher training institution; so did numerous other smaller fry. His ability to survive all political shifts suggests Soviet ties.

**Nematullah Maruf
Pazhwak †?**

Perhaps best described as a "closet Parchami"; close friend and associate of Babrak Karmal since their school days; though never an acknowledged party member, his PDPA sympathies were open. A Ghilzai Pushtun, the nephew and son-in-law of a well-known diplomat (the longtime Afghan ambassador to the UN), he has top social connections and holds an M.A. and Ph. D. from Columbia University. Was principal of several major Kabul high schools and for several years headed the department of secondary education in the Ministry of Education. Cultural attaché in Moscow. As Minister of Interior in Shafiq cabinet (1972-73), he was responsible for infiltration of secret Parchamis and other leftists into police and other key positions then and also later under Daoud. Participated in 1973 Daoud conspiracy. Minister of Education under Daoud, helped increase PDPA influence among teachers and students. In eclipse during Khalq period, he became advisor to the Prime Ministry under Babrak in 1981, subsequently returned to private life but re-emerged again as an adviser to the cabinet in January 1987, promoted as an example of "non-Communist" participation in Najib's "national reconciliation" program for "coalition government." May have direct Soviet connections.

Lt. Gen Abdul Qader †? (P)

Air Force officer trained in USSR; played a key role in the coups of both 1973 and 1978. Headed air defense under Daoud. Headed interim military junta 27-30 April 1978, and announced the "revolution." Taraki's first minister of defense, but was accused of involvement in 1978 anti-Khalqi plot, sentenced to death (commuted to prison sentence by Amin, probably through Soviet pressure). After the Soviets installed Babrak Karmal, Qader was made a member of PDPA Central Committee and head of its defense and judicial sections, named to Revolutionary Council Presidium, and in 1981 made Presidium Vice-President. In 1982 became at first Acting, then permanent, Minister of Defense. Reportedly involved in frequent brawls with other cabinet members and staff. In 1984 was replaced as Minister of Defense and demoted tofirst Deputy Chairman of the Revolutionary Council Presidium. Retired from Politburo November 1985. Reportedly very close to Soviet GRU in Kabul, others in Soviet embassy---at least in the past. A Tajik, born in Ghor in 1944.

Maj. Gen. Mohammed Rafi (P)

Minister of Defense 1980; replaced by Qader 1982; re-appointed Defense Minister by Najib, December 1986. A Pushtun born in Paghman c. 1946, he is a Soviet-trained tank officer who participated in 1978 coup. Minister of Public Works under Taraki, but jailed August 1978 for involvement in anti-Khalq coup. Freed after Soviet invasion as a lieutenant colonel, he was a major general only three months later and was one of four officers sent to Moscow for special training 1981-1982. Member of PDPA Central Committee and Politburo; Deputy Chairman, Council of Ministers, even when no longer a minister.

Dr. Anahita Ratebzad * (P)

DRA's top woman politician, commonly known only by her first name (Anahita). Reportedly Babrak Karmal's mistress for many years A Kabuli, born c. 1930. Claims to have taken a degree in nursing in the U.S., later took M.D. at Kabul University. Elected to parliament 1965; reputation as effective speaker. Founded (1965) Democratic Organization of Afghan Women which she headed until 1986. Effective organizer and agitator before 1978 coup, after which she was Minister of Social Affairs and Tourism until exiled as ambassador to Belgrade in July 1978. Returned with Babrak after Soviet invasion; became Minister of Education, member of Politburo, PDPA Central Committee and Revolutionary Council Presidium, head of Afghan-Soviet Friendship Society and the Peace, Solidarity and Friendship Organization. Invited to Stockholm by Swedish Socialists in

1985, promoted image of DRA as agency of progress for women. Since Babrak's ouster in 1986 her position is probably in decline. Dropped from Politburo June 1987. One of her daughters is married to Nur Mohammad Nur, another to Mahmoud Baryalai.

Maj. Gen. Mohammad Yasin Sadiqi (P)

Close friend and relative of Babrak Karmal, under whom he was a Secretary of the PDPA Central Committee, head of local organs department of Council of Ministers and chief of Political Affairs section of the army from August 1982 until fired from all positions by Najib in July 1986. A Tajik from Kabul.

Abdul Majid Sarboland (P)

Minister of Information and Culture, 1980; ousted September 1982 along with Guldad but remained as Deputy Chairman of Council of Ministers and reportedly spent time in Moscow. Named ambassador to Cuba, September 1986. A Pushtun.

Assadullah Sarwari † (K)

Cold, brutal chief of secret police (AGSA) under Taraki; called "King Kong" by the public. After the 1979 plot against Amin failed, Sarwari took refuge in the Soviet embassy with Watanjar, Gulabzoy and Mazdooryar. Hardliner, reportedly wants complete Sovietization of Afghanistan. Personally tortured several top Parchamis imprisoned in 1978/79, including Keshtmand. Named Deputy Prime Minister by Karmal immediately after invasion but soon left for Moscow and thence was sent directly to Mongolia as ambassador; fired from PDPA Central Committee by Najib July 1986. Like Najib, he undoubtedly has a special relationship with the KGB but Sarwari is totally unacceptable to Parcham and has no future inside Afghanistan. A Kabuli.

Mohammed Hassan Bareq Shafiee * (K)

Writer, editor, poet, a Pushtun from a Laghman family. A political chameleon born in Kabul c. 1932. Khalqi 1966, Parchami 1967-77, in

Politburo by 1978, repudiated Parcham. On PDPA Central Committee under Khalq. Held two cabinet posts under Amin and Taraki. Worked his way back into Parchami good graces, achieved full PDPA Central Committee membership again and high posts in National Fatherland Front in 1984, but sent to Libya as Second Secretary of embassy in December 1985, an apparent demotion.

Mahmoud Alamgul Suma (K)

Like Hashemi and Panjsheri, a provincial boy who came under Amin's influence as his student. Became an alternate member of the PDPA Central Committee in 1968 when Amin became a permanent member, according to Male. Minister of Higher Education under Taraki and Amin; member of Amin's eight-man Politburo, October 1979. See *"Disappeared" Khalqis* (above).

Abdul Wakil * (P)

Born in Kabul, 1947. Educator and economist. A member of the Central Committee 1977-78, he was exiled in 1978 as ambassador to the United Kingdom, subsequently fled to Moscow, returned to Kabul with Babrak. Minister of Finance but reportedly an ineffective administrator; posted as ambassador to Vietnam in 1984. Returned to Kabul 1986, and was made Foreign Minister and full member of PDPA Central Committee and Politburo. May be even more important in the future than presently appears.

Dr. Akbar Shah Wali *(K)

Medical doctor. Elected as candidate member of first PDPA Central Committee in 1965, full member in 1967. Joined Politburo in 1977. Arrested under Daoud. Prominent under Amin, in 1978 Wali became Minister of Public Health and also Minister of Planning. In March 1979 named Deputy Prime Minister; in July, became Minister of Foreign Affairs also. Reportedly criticized Soviet involvement in anti-Amin plot. See *"Disappeared" Khalqis* (above).

Mohammed Aslam Watanjar †

Tank commander, a Pushtun born in Paktia, 1946. A key figure in the 1973 nd 1978 coups and the plot to overthrow Amin in 1979, after which he found refuge in the Soviet embassy with other plotters. Under Taraki and Amin, served as Minister of Defense and (twice) as Minister of Interior. Said to have played a significant role in Soviet invasion, after which he joined PDPA Central Committee, Revolutionary Council and Politburo. Immediately made Minister of Communications, clear indication of Soviet trust: Soviets consider the Ministry of Communications in any subordinate country to be a key element in controlling events there, and have left Watanjar in that position since 1980. He has not openly participated in the Parcham/Khalq conflict and is probably more pro-Soviet than pro-PDPA faction. A possible "comer" in DRA politics.

Lt. Gen. Ghulam Faruq Yaqubi †
(P?)

When Najib became party chairman in May 1986, Yaqubi, his deputy, replaced him as Minister of State Security (head of WAD, the new acronym for KhAD after it was raised to ministry status.) Rapid rise in PDPA: full member of PDPA Central Committee, November 1985; alternate Politburo member, July 1986; full Politburo member, November 1986. A Pushtun. Any head of WAD can be presumed to have KGB connections.

Mohammad Farid Zarif

Counsellor, DRA Mission to the United Nations, before November 1981, then ambassador until replaced by former Foreign Minister Shah Mohammed Dost in December 1986. Returned to the foreign ministry in Kabul. Born in Kabul 1947; graduated from Kabul University and Oxford. Joined Ministry of Foreign Affairs 1974 and served in Havana. While in New York, Zarif proved skillful at handling press and television, and may well play an up-front role in future. Authorized assault on Resistance delegation in New York, November 1986.

Saleh Mohammed Zeary * (K)	A medical doctor born in Kandahar, 1937. A Pushtun, nicknamed "Quicksilver" for his adroitness in shifting positions and allegiances. Ran for parliament in 1969. Jailed 1969-75. Top Khalqi activist under Taraki and Amin. Immediately after the coup, he was made Minister of Land Reform, put in charge of "people's organizations," and joined Politburo. Only member of Amin's Politburo to retain membership after Amin's overthrow and Parcham return; also retained Revolutionary Council membership. Named to Babrak's early three-man Secretariat and to Presidium. In 1981 became first chairman of new National Fatherland Front, retained position till replaced in 1985. Power appeared to be in decline: he was apparently dropped from the Revolutionary Council Presidium in 1986; but in January 1987 he was reinstated, so may be on upswing as a major Khalqi proponent of party unity.

III. Less prominent members of the regime and the PDPA

In addition to the more prominent members of the PDPA and the regime listed above, there are a number of figures who often play multiple roles: in lesser cabinet and party positions, sub-cabinet positions, the party structure, and the National Front (formerly National Fatherland Front/NFF) and its constituent organizations, particularly the Democratic Youth Organization of Afghanistan [DYOA]. Many are members of the Central Committee of the PDPA.

Some of them may exert more influence behind the scenes than is visible to the outside eye. Moreover, it is always possible that some of these obscure figures may eventually emerge to displace those who are presently more visible.

The following list does not pretend to be comprehensive. It is based on published materials, in large part on the broadcasts and announcements of the DRA as published in the Foreign Broadcast Information Service's daily reports [See bibliography]. It is therefore incomplete and occasionally confusing, particularly in terms of the succession of individuals in a given office. The dates given indicate reports mentioning individuals as holding particular offices; they may have been appointed earlier.

a careful study does offer glimpses of some other pointes of interest: e.g., the number of Hazara (and probably other minority members) given significant positions; the tribal significance of some appointments; (see entries for *Chamkani, Mangal, Mohmand, Safi,* and *Waziri,* among others); and the installation of religious figures to try to present a pro-Islamic appearance. Also interesting, in view of the intense DRA propaganda to the effect that they are liberating women, is the minuscule number of women on the list; any such list of prominent figures in government, parliament (for which the NFF is a substitute), education and community organizations compiled before 1978 would have included many women.

Also of interest is the introduction of an increasing number of non-party members into prominent positions, starting in 1984 and increasing significantly in late 1985 and 1986. This coincides with the theme of "national reconciliation" which was introduced in 1985, intensified in 1986, and made the centerpiece of Najib's international publicity campaign in December 1986 and January 1987, and which continues as this is written. Obviously, preparations for the campaign were begun far in advance.

On the list below, factional affiliations are given if known, but many are obscure. Known non-party members are so identified, as are members of the Central Committee of the PDPA.

Dr. Khalil Ahmad Abawi	As of 1982, Deputy Chairman, Council of Ministers, and head of the State Planning Committee. Reportedly out of the government by 1984. *Not a Party member.*
Mawlawi Abdourrauf	An Uzbek from Badghis. As of January 1986, a member of the Revolutionary Council Presidium and Vice Chairman of the Central Council Executive Board of the National (Fatherland) Front. *Not a Party member.*
Dr. Wali Mohammed Abdyani (P)	One of six deputy chairmen of the Central Council of the National Front. Since 1980 was president of the Herat cement plant, then governor of Kandahar province. In April 1983 made head of the PDPA Central Committee's department of Local Organs of State Power. Made mayor of Kabul in 1984. Pushtun.

Maulawi Gol Mohammad Ada

Member, High Council of Ulema and Clergy.

Maj. Gen. Juma Mohammed Ahsaq (Atsak)

Formerly commanded 17th Division, Herat; lost both legs in combat. Deputy Chief of Staff as of July 1986; acting head of Northwest Zone October 1986. Member, PDPA Central Committee.

Mohammad Na'im Ajmal

As of 1984, head of civil aviation, which is now, in Afghanistan as in the USSR, integrated with military aviation.

Brig. Gen. Mohammad Akram

Head of Department of Propaganda and Popularization of the Army Political Affairs Section.

Maj. Gen. Nurulhaq Alami

Member, PDPA Central Committee; commander of Kandahar Army Corps, 1985.

Faizullah Alburz

An Uzbek. Governor of Faryab 1980-1986. Rapid rise since then: named to expanded Revolutionary Council January 1986, replaced Maihanparast as head of the Northern Zone June 1986, and named directly to full membership on PDPA Central Committee July 1986.

Mohammed Alem

An electrical engineer in the construction Department of the Ministry of Defense. Full member of PDPA Central Committee November 1986.

Maulawi Mohammad Salem Almi

Executive Board, National (Fatherland) Front. *Probably not a Party member.*

Sayyed Amanuddin Amin

A Tajik, educated in West Germany. Headed Afghan Textiles; then deputy minister of Light Industries and Foodstuffs. Appointed Deputy Chairman of the Council of Ministers in December 1985 and later also Chairman of the Economic Consultative Council. *Not a Party member.*

Brig. Gen. Gol Aqa
Member, PDPA Central Committee and Vice-Chairman of the Revolutionary Council Presidium. Until August 1982 he was in charge of Political Affairs section for the Armed Forces.

Abdul Qader Ashna (P)
Head of State Cultural Committee and alternate member, PDPA Central Committee.

Abdul Qader Azad
Former member, PDPA Central Committee and Secretary of the Party Committee of Herat province under Babrak, removed from Central Committee by Najib in July 1986.

Maj. Gen. Mohammad Nabi Azemi (P)
Appointed First Deputy Minister of National Defense after completing General Staff course in Moscow. Member, PDPA Central Committee and Revolutionary Council. Took part in both 1973 and 1978 coups. Tajik.

Brig. Gen. Mer Azimuddin
Made Brigadier in April 1985.

Mohammad Aziz
Under Babrak, Minister of Light Industries and Foodstuffs; under Najib, named Deputy Prime Minister, head of State Planning Committee, and full member of PDPA Central Committee.

Mohammad Bashir Baghlani
Minister of Justice and Attorney General under Babrak.

Abdul Karim Baha
Full member of PDPA Central Committee.

Abdullah Bahar
Member of PDPA Central Committee and head of Agricultural Land Reform and Cooperatives Department.

Abdul Rahim Basam
A candidate member of PDPA Central Committee as of January 1987.

Khodaidad Basharmal	Member of PDPA Central Committee. Under Babrak, Secretary of Nangrahar Provincial Party Committee, head of the Eastern Zone, and Deputy Minister of Foreign Affairs.
Brig. Gen. Basmillah	Promoted to Brigadier in April 1985.
Khoda Nur Bawar	Pushtun. Former Chief of Southwest Zone, now chairman of the Central Council of Peasantry Cooperatives, member of PDPA Central Committee and Revolutionary Council Presidium.
Mir Afghan Bawari	Candidate member of PDPA Central Committee as of January 1987.
Jura Beg	Candidate member of PDPA Central Committee as of January 1987. His name indicates that he is of Uzbek or Turkoman origin.
Dastagir	As of November 1985, Secretary of Paktia Provincial Party Committee. In July 1986, head of Southeast Zone and full member of PDPA Central Committee.
Feda Mohammed Dehnishin (P)	Following the 1978 coup, served briefly as governor of Balkh before being ousted from PDPA Central Committee for participation in anti-Khalq plot. In 1980 he was back on the Central Committee and head of its Publicity, Extension and Instruction Commission. By November 1984 he was presidentof the State Committee for Printing and Publications. In June 1985 appointed chief of the National Fatherland Front Central Council.
Yazi Qilich Dehqan	A peasant. Candidate member of PDPA Central Committee as of July 1983.
Sayyed Muhammad Naderi Esmaili	Member of the Executive Board of the National Fatherland Front Central Council as of January 1986. Of Hazara origin. *Not a Party member.*

Muhammad Anwar Eysar	Secretary of the Provincial Party Committee for Nangrahar province as of March 1985, and member of PDPA Central Committee.
Sayyed Rasul Fakur	Member of the Executive Board of the Central Council of the National Fatherland Front as of January 1986. Former member of parliament. Tajik origin. *Not a Party member.*
Abdul Wahed Farahi	Full member of PDPA Central Committee, November 1986; in charge of Central Committee administrative affairs.
Anwar Farzam	Member of PDPA Central Committee. Secretary of the Revolutionary Council under Babrak but was fired by Najib in July 1986.
Feroza Fedaie	A Pushtun village woman from Wardak, born 1940. A widow, she joined the PDPA in 1984 and led her Gulkhana village group of Defenders of the Revolution, made up of 50 women. Member of the Revolutionary Council and alternate member of PDPA Central Committee in 1986. In August 1986, she was named president of the new All-Afghan Women's Council [AAWC], the successor front group to the Democratic Organization of Afghan Women, which was led by Anahita Ratebzad before Babrak's ouster.
Brig. Gen. Abdul Ghafur	As of July 1982, Deputy Chief of the General Staff of the Armed Forces of the DRA.
Hanur Ghairat	Party Secretary for Kabul's 5th Ward in 1978 and chief of customs at Kabul Airport under Taraki, on PDPA Central Committee since 1980 and deputy head of its Organizational Department s ince 1981.
Borhanuddin Ghiasi	As of 1982, Minister of Higher and Vocational Education. Previously was First Secretary of the Central Committee of the Democratic Youth

Organization of Afghanistan [DYOA]. Member, PDPA Central Committee.

Gol Jan

Member of the Executive Board of the Democratic Women's Organization of Afghanistan [DWOA].

Assadullah Habib (K)

A personal friend of Babrak, though identified as Khalqi. Secretary of the Farah Provincial Party Committee. Affiliated in some way with the "Work Movement" headed by Dastagir Panjsheri. Former head of Writers' Union, now Rector of Kabul University. Alternate member of PDPA Central Committee, July 1986.

Brig. Gen. Mohammad Hakim

As of October 1984, commander of the Southern Zone. Named to PDPA Central Committee, July 1986. Named a Deputy Prime Minister, November 1986.

Mir Abdul Halim (Jalal?)

"Non-professional Deputy" member of the Executive Board of the National Fatherland Front as of January 1986. Governor of Herat province. A Tajik. Named alternate member of PDPA Central Committee, July 1986.

Gen. Mohammed Hashim (K)

Active in the 1978 coup, he served as deputy chief of the Political Affairs Department of the Ministry of Defense under Amin and again under Babrak Karmal. By July 1981 his title was Attorney of the Armed Forces. In September 1981 he was one of four top-ranking officers sent to the USSR for advanced training. PDPA Central Committee.

Emtiaz Hassan (P)

Active in PDPA since 1965. Ambassador to Japan and Bulgaria in early 1980s. As of 1984 he was apparently back in Kabul as Vice Chairman of the DRA Peace, Solidarity and Friendship Society, Afghan-Soviet Friendship Society. In 1985 was secretary of Herat Provincial Party Committee.

Maj. Gen. Hesamuddin (Husamuddin)	Member of the Revolutionary Council as of April 1985, and in January 1987 a Candidate Member of PDPA Central Committee. Ambassador to Pakistan.
Maulawi Abdul Wali Hojjat	Headed Department of Islamic Affairs, later upgraded to Ministry of Islamic Affairs and Endowments, from 1982 till October 1986. The appointment of a *maulawi* to this post was clearly intended to gain the support of mullahs. Since his ministry has seized all religious endowments hitherto administered by individual religious institutions and mosques, it now has total control over the finances of all mosques, religious schools, and religious personnel. A Tajik from Takhar, Hojjat was born into a middleclass religious family in 1935 and attended a madrassah but was accused of blasphemy. Career was totally secular before 1978. Reportedly involved with Dastagir Panjsheri; active involvement with Setem-i-Milli separatist party (q.v.); arrested and jailed for four years in 1960s. President of Afghan-Libyan Friendship Society as of December 1985. Joined Revolutionary Council January 1986. *Officially not a party member* but follows the party line.
Nasim Joya	Secretary of the National Committee of the National (Fatherland) Front. Made full member of PDPA Central Committee in July 1986.
Mohammed Kabir	Minister of Finance as of July 1984, replacing Abdul Wakil. Alternate member, Central Committee.
Hashmat Kaihani	Special Revolutionary Attorney General of the DRA as of December 1984. As of March 1985, Special Revolutionary Prosecutor. (Possibly the same job.) Formerly head of Political Affairs Department of KhAD. Alternate member, Central Committee.

Dr. [Ghulam or Mohammad] Nabi Kamyar	Minister of Public Health from May 1982 to March 1987, when replaced by Dr. Sher Bahadur.
Abdul Wassi Kargar	Member, PDPA Central Committee. Formerly a worker at Jangalak Workshops, now chairman of Kabul City trade union council.
Hayatollah Karim	Secretary of the Central Council of Trade Unions as of March 1985.
Mohammad Zarin Karimzada	Deputy Minister of Communications as of January 1985. Pushtun.
Mohammed Faruq Karmand	Candidate member of PDPA Central Committee as of January 1987. Ambassador to Poland 1983-86; appointed ambassador to Vietnam December 1986. Born in Paghman, 1948. Studied engineering in Leningrad.
Mir Sahib Karwal	Pushtun from Khost. A secretary of PDPA Central Committee. Led a delegation to Bucharest, i.e., earned a trip to Europe. Formerly Secretary of Kabul Provincial Party Committee and head of Central Zone. Named alternate member of Politburo July 1986.
Muhammad Daoud Kawian	Head of Bakhtar News Agency, the DRA information agency, as of June 1985.
Sayd Mansur Kayhani	A Tajik and leader of the Isma'ilia community, adherents of the Muslim sect headed by the Aga Khan. As a tiny minority group in Afghanistan, the Isma'ilia have reportedly found it expedient to cooperate with the regime. *Not a Party member* but elected to the Presidium in January 1986.
Abdullah Keshtmand (P?)	As of 1984, chargé d'affaires of the Afghan embassy in Paris. A plum for a relative of high-ranking PDPA member, combining nepotism with the placement of a reliable man in an important

slot: Paris is the most important center of European support for the Resistance.

Maj. Gen. Khalil(ullah) (P)

Implicated in anti-Khalq plot in 1978; Commander of Central Garrison in 1980. Went to USSR in 1981 for advanced training. By December 1982 he was Deputy Minister of Defense but reportedly quarreled with the Minister, Gen. Abdul Qader, and in 1984 was shifted to head of Northwest Zone. Reportedly was involved in 1973 coup, has spent much time in the USSR, and has a Russian wife. PDPA Central Committee.

Maulawi Mohammed Rabani Khatebi

Member or possibly official of the High Council of Ulema and Clergy.

Abdul Shokar Khushachin (?)

Associated with the Vanguard Workers Organization of Afghanistan; full member of PDPA Central Committee, November 1986.

Abdul Latif

Minister of Revenue under Babrak. Killed in Kabul early 1984.

Shahzar Lewal

A vice president of the Kabul City Party Committee and PDPA Central Committee in early 1981, he was head of the Southeast Zone by September 1981 and accompanied Babrak Karmal to Hungary in 1982. By January 1987 he was a deputy Minister for Nationalities and Tribal Affairs.

Engineer L'mar Ahmad L'mar (Lemar)

Began as president of the consumer's co-op for government officials and employees; rose to head a department and by January 1986 to head the State Control Committee, both in the Council of Ministers. In June 1986 became Minister of Light Industry and Foodstuffs. Pushtun.

Maj. Gen.
Muhammad Afzal
Ludin

Member, PDPA Central Committee. Promoted to Major General, April 1985. Commander, 1st Army Corps, 1986. Commander of the 3d Army Corps in Paktia province, 1983-85. Pushtun.

Abdul Aziz
Majidzada

By August 1981, he was deputy chairman of the PDPA Central Committee's Party Control Commission, became chairman by January 1987. Pushtun.

Aqel (Aga?) Shah
Mangal

Member of the Central Council Executive Board of the National (Fatherland) Front. As a retired general and a member of the Mangal tribe located in the Khost area of Paktia province, his participation can be very useful to the DRA. *Not a Party member.* The presence of so many members of the Mangal Pushtun tribe is significant, for reasons noted below. (See entry for *Suleiman*.)

Dr. Habib Mangal
(P)

DRA Ambassador to Moscow since November 1980. Born 1946 in Paktia. M.D. degree, Kabul University. Active PDPA member since 1965. Jailed by Khalqis November 1978. Mangal Pushtun. Member of PDPA Central Committee and Revolutionary Council since 1980.

Manukif
(Manuchir?)
Mangal

Head of Political Affairs in the Sarandoy (police); full member of PDPA Central Committee, November 1986.

Sarwar Mangal (P)

Promoted from Deputy Minister to Minister of Higher and Vocational Education in September 1982. Named to PDPA Central Committee in 1983. A vice-chairman of the Council of Ministers and head of the State Planning Committee. Mangal Pushtun.

Maulawi Ghulam
Sarwar Mansur

Deputy Minister of Islamic Affairs, 1985; head of High Council of Ulema and Religious Leaders. Member, Revolutionary Council, January 1986. The maulawi most involved in receiving foreign religious delegations; led delegation to the USSR in 1985. A Pushtun from Nangrahar. *Not a Party member.*

Ahmad Marufi

President in charge of external relations and developmental planning in the State Planning Committee. This means that he deals with the governments of the Soviet Bloc, which are signing numerous agreements to provide personnel and direction for various phases of Afghan development. Pushtun.

Dr. Najibullah Masir (or Masud, or Wakil)

In August 1982, appointed head of administrative department of Council of Ministers (with rank of minister); named Minister of Mines and Industries in June 1985.

Haydar [Haidar] Masud

As of July 1986, a secretary of the PDPA Central Committee. Formerly Deputy Minister of Information and Culture.

Farid Ahmad Mazdak (P)

Secretary of the Central Committee of the Democratic Youth Organization of Afghanistan [DYOA] as of June 1982. Elected to Presidium, January 1986. Named alternate member of Politburo, November 1986.

Brig. Gen. Abdul Qader Miakhel (K)

Reportedly Soviet-trained. Governor of Kunar in January 1980; then commander of army corps in Jalalabad and later Paktia. Named Chief of Operations in January 1984, Deputy Chief of Staff in June 1984. By June 1985 he was back in the field as head of the Northwest Zone (Herat). Pushtun. Member of PDPA Central Committee as of July 1986.

Abdul Hamid Mobarez

As of May 1986, Deputy Minister of Education. Previously an important figure in the Afghan-Soviet Friendship Society, an editor, and head of Bakhtar (official news agency). *Not a Party member.*

Col. Abdul Fattah Mohammed

In September 1981 was chief of logistics in Ministry of Defense and one of four top-ranking officers sent to USSR for advanced training. A pilot, by July 1983 he was commander of the air force and an alternate member of the PDPA Central Committee.

Dip. Eng. Lt. Col. Dost Mohammed

Head of the Political Affairs Department of the Air Force by January 1981, he was Deputy Minister of Defense in charge of civil defense in July 1986 when he was promoted from alternate to full member of the PDPA Central Committee.

Eng. Nazar Mohammed (P)

Born in Paktia 1948, joined PDPA in 1965. Studied engineering and electric power at Kabul University and in West Germany. Spent most of Khalq period as ambassador to Bonn. In January 1980 named to PDPA Central Committee and made Minister of Public Works (later changed to Construction Affairs).

Fazl Rahim Mohmand

Named Minister of Agriculture and Land Reform in 1980. Shifted to head of Central Statistical Organization, August 1982. Studied in the U.S. Was deputy Minister of Agriculture in 1974 under Daoud and again under Taraki in July 1978. Mohmand Pushtun (see Mohmand, Part II, above). *Not a Party member.*

Gen. Gol Muhammad Mohmand

In charge of the Justice and Defense Department of the Party Committee for Nangrahar Province (see Mohmand, Part II, above). Promoted to Deputy Brigadier General in April 1985.

Abdurrahim Morad

A Turkoman. Member of the PDPA and, as of January 1986, of the Executive Board of the Central Council of the National Fatherland Front.

Maj. Gen. Ghulam Nabi

As of October 1984, mentioned as Deputy Minister of Nationalities and Tribal Affairs. May be the same person as Nabizada (below).

Mohammad Ewaz Nabizada	As of July 1983, Deputy Minister of Nationalities and Tribal Affairs and governor of Baghlan province in the north. His name suggests Pushtun ethnic identity, interesting in view of his posting to Baghlan. Alternate member of PDPA Central Committee, 1983; full member 1986.
Najibullah	*Not Dr. Najibullah* but another man with the same name; full member of PDPA Central Committee, November 1986.
Mohammed Aziz Negahban	As of April 1986, head of newly-formed Ministry of Civil Aviation. (See above: Ajmal.)
Ni'amatollah (single name only)	As of July 1983, a candidate member of the PDPA Central Committee and head of the Central Zone.
Abdul Jamil Nooristani	As of August 1982, removed from position as Prosecutor in KhAD. As of July 1986, Deputy Minister of Interior. Made alternate member, Central Committee, July 1986.
Abdul Qayum Nurzay (K)	Member, PDPA Central Committee. As of November 1982, Chairman of the Central Council of the Union of Agricultural Cooperatives. Former editor of *Khalq*. Deputy Minister of Education and Information under Taraki and Amin.
Qazi Mohammad Omar	Preacher for the official mosque of the Revolutionary Council. *Not a Party member.*
Abdurrahim Oral	A member of the Revolutionary Council Presidium and Assistant to the Chairman of the National Front in Fariab Province. A Turkoman.
Dr. Raz Mohammad Paktin (K)	Born 1938, Paktia; joined PDPA 1966. Took Ph D. in engineering in USSR. Under Taraki and Amin, was deputy minister, then ambassador to Moscow. Named Minister of Water and Power after invasion; when ministry was split, he became

Minister of Electric Energy. Member of PDPA Central Committee since 1980.

Mohammad Hasan Payman (K)

Member of PDPA Central Committee. Member of Khalq Central Committee since 1967. Deputy Minister of Agriculture in the Ministry of Agriculture and Land Reforms.

Sayyed Tahar Shah Paykargar

Member of PDPA Central Committee. Deputy Chairman of the Afghan-German Friendship Society as of October 1984. Deputy head, Organizational Department of PDPA Central Committee since April 1981.

Abdus Sattar Purdelli

Baluch from Nimroz. President of Trade Unions since March 1980. Elected to Presidium, January 1986. On National (Fatherland) Front Central Council.

Haji Abdul Qayum

President of the National (Fatherland) Front as of May 1986. The honorific "haji" indicates that he has made the pilgrimage to Mecca, is ostensibly a pious Muslim. *Not a Party member.*

Abdul Samad Qayumi

Engineer. Minister of Education and Training since April 1983. Previously headed Department of Local Organs and State Power. As of November 1986, alternate member of PDPA Central Committee.

Maulawi Rahmatullah Rahmat

Member of the High Council of Ulema and Clergy.

Abdul Bashir Ranjbar

General president of the Afghanistan Central Bank since June 1985. Candidate member of PDPA Central Committee as of December 1986.

Mohammad Esrail (Esmael?) Rasi

Member of PDPA Central Committee. Secretary of the Provincial Party Committee in Badakhshan.

Zohur Razmjo (P) Member of PDPA Central Committee and as of December 1986, full member of the Politburo. Secretary of the Party Committee for Kabul City. (As of 1984 Governor of Kabul province?)

Brig. Gen. Abdul Sabur In charge of air defense rocket-artillery exercises conducted by DRA forces in early 1985. The Resistance, of course, has no air force.

Maj. Gen. Mohammad Yasin Sadiqi (P) Under Babrak (a close friend and relative) , head of Local Organs Department of the Council of Ministers, a secretary of PDPA Central Committee, and director of the Main Political Affairs Section of the Afghan People's Army from 1982 until July 1986, when Najib fired him.

Meftahuddin Safi Deputy Minister of Frontier and Tribal Affairs (now Nationalities and TribalAffairs) since 1980; also head of Eastern Zone since February 1985. Named directly to full membership in PDPA Central Committee in July 1986. A Safi Pushtun. The Safi are a major tribe strategically located in Eastern Afghanistan.

Mohammad(-ullah) Safi Alternate member of PDPA Central Committee, 1981. On the staff of the Afghan embassy in Moscow from 1982 till appointed ambassador to South Yemen, October 1985. A Safi Pushtun. (See above)

Abdol Wahab Safi (P) Named Minister of Justice and Attorney General, June 1981. Replaced, October 1983. Now on High Council of Supreme Court and on Constitutional Drafting Commission. A Safi Pushtun. (See above)

Abdul Salem As of 1982, Secretary General of the Afghan Red Crescent Society and a member of the Executive Board of the National (Fatherland) Front.

Dr. Shams Samadi	As of 1982, president of AFSOTR ["Afghan-Soviet Transport"].
Brig. Gen. Abdul Qayum Samadi	Commander of the Afghan Air Force, October 1984-July 1986.
Abdullah Sangar	Heads the Department of Training, Publicity and Propaganda of the PDPA Central Committee.
Adina Sangin	Member of PDPA Central Committee and head of its Department of Economics. Former mayor of Kabul.
Hassan Sepahi	As of March 1985, Vice Chairman of the Central Council of Trade Unions. The surname Sepahi (or Sepoy) means "soldier" and is used by several DRA officials.
Sher Aqa Sereshk	Head of Northeast Zone since February 1985. Made member of PDPA Central Committee in July 1986.
Shah Ali Akbar Shahrestani	Member of the Revolutionary Council Presidium and Dean of Faculty at Kabul University. A Hazara and a Shi'a. *Not a Party member.*
Mohammed Sharif	As of March 1983, Secretrary of Balkh Provincial Party Committee. Named to PDPA Central Committee July 1986. As of November 1986 head of Northern Zone, replacing Maihanparast and Alburz (q.v.).
Qari Sirat	Deputy head of the Kabul City Council of the National Fatherland Front as of December 1984.
Mohammed Shah Sorkhabi	As of 1982, Minister of Irrigation and Water Resources. Full member of PDPA Central Committee since July 1983.

Abdul Wahid Sorabi	Member of the Revolutionary Council and as of February 1986, Ministerial Adviser for Social and Culture Affairs. A Hazara Shi'a, born 1926, he is also deputy chairman of Central Council of Hazara Workers. Has a Ph. D. in economics from West Germany. Before 1978, he served (1969-1972) as Minister of Planning in two Cabinets during the constitutional period and Dean of Economics Faculty at Kabul University. *Not a Party member.*
Abdullah Spantgar (Sangar?)	Went from acting to permanent head of Publicity, Extension and Education Department of PDPA Central Committee in November 1984.
Sayyed Muhammad Ali Shah Sujadi	Member of the Central Council Executive Board of the National Fatherland Front as of January 1986. A Hazara Shi'a. *Not a Party member.*
Haji Abdurrahim Suleiman (Soleymankhayl)	According to a January 1985 report, a leader of the Suleimankhel Pushtuns *and* also representative of the Khejo clan of the Mangal tribe* who is cooperating with the DRA.
Maj. Gen. Shahnawaz Tanay	Chief of Staff as of October 1985. Member of PDPA Central Committee. Born 1950. A graduate of military schools, he participated in the 1978 coup. Commander of the Central Army Corps. Promoted to Major General April 1985; led forces in Panjsher and Khost offensives.
Fazl Ahmad Toghyan	Tajik. Member of PDPA Central Committee. As of July 1983 Governor of Kabul province; "Non-professional deputy" in the National Front as of

---

* The Mangal are concentrated in the key strategic southern region of Khost in Paktia Province, while the Suleimankhel and some Mangal are widely located in key border areas of Pakistan. Much of the Mangal tribe on both sides of the border has been coopted by the DRA. See also *Chamkani* (Part II), *Mohmand, Safi,* and *Waziri.*

January 1986. Secretary of Kabul Provincial Party
Committee as of January 1987.

Mohammed Is'haq
Tokhi

Aide to the General Secretary of PDPA Central
Committee, Dr. Najib. Full member of PDPA
Central Committee, Novmeber 1986.

Brig. Gen. Abdul
Haq Ulumi

As of October 1984, head of the Justice and
Defense Department of the PDPA Central
Committee. Secretary of the Central Committee of
the Democratic Youth Organization of Afghanistan.
Made full member of PDPA Central Committee
July 1986.

Maj. Gen. Nur-ul
Haq Ulumi

As of August 1982 was chief of Southern Zone.
As of July 1983 commander of the Kandahar Army
Corps. Alternate member of PDPA Central
Committee, 1981; full member, 1983.

Rahimullah Usoli

Governor of Uruzgan in January 1980. Head of
Southwest Zone in 1986 when he became a
member of the PDPA Central Committee.

Taza Khan (or
Ihan) Wayand
(or Wial or
Deyal)

Ph.D. student in USSR. Spokesman for the
Vanguard Organization of Working People [Toilers]
of Afghanistan, which merged with PDPA in
December 1986. Elected to PDPA Central
Committee November 1986.

Abdul Rashid
Waziri

Deputy Minister of Nationalities and Tribal Affairs.
Member of the Revoltionary Council and PDPA
Central Committee. A Pushtun from Paktia. As
his name indicates, he is a member of the
extremely important and fractious Waziri tribe
and in a position to influence its dealings
with the Resistance. The Waziri are a comparatively small group inside Afghanistan but a
major group in Pakistan, where they dominate
some of the key routes through which the
Resistance must move men and supplies across the
border.

Faqir Mohammad Yaqubi	Promoted from deputy to Minister of Education in June 1981. By April 1983 was listed as Minister-Adviser and president of Afghan-Mongolian Friendship Society.
Ghulam Sarwar Yuresh (P)	Deputy Minister of Foreign Affairs since 1982. Member of PDPA Central Committee and Deputy director of its International Relations Department. Was president of publications department in Ministry of Information and Culture 1980-81, and head of Eastern Zone/governor of Nangrahar Province 1981.
Maj. Gen. Ghulam Nabi Yusofi	As of February 1985, commander of the Southeastern Zone (Ghazni).
Sayed Amir Shah Zara	First Deputy Minister of Health, 1980-82. In January 1983 named head of Bakhtar, the DRA information agency; replaced by Kawian as of 1985. Deputy Chairman of the DRA Peace, Solidarity and Friendship Organization and Afghan-Soviet Friendship Society as of June 1981. Member of Revolutionary Council and alternate member of PDPA Central Committee since 1980. Posted as ambassador to Iraq November 1985.
Maulawi Abdul Jamil Zarifi	A Tajik from Balkh, he replaced Hojat as Minister of Islamic Affairs in October 1986. "Non-professional deputy" in the Central Council of the National (Fatherland) Front and Chairman of the NFF Executive Committee for Balkh province. Member of Revolutionary Council as of January 1986. *Allegedly not a Party member.*
Brig. Gen. Zabiullah Ziarmal	Named head of political affairs for the armed forces, July 1986. Member, PDPA Central Committee.

Appendix V

Significant Afghan Political Movements of the Constitutional Period*
[1963-1973]

Not including the PDPA (Parcham and Khalq).

NAME OF ORGANIZATION	ORIENTATION	COMMENTS
Jamiat Demokrati-i-Mottaraqi (Progressive Democratic Society)	More or less social democrat	Maiwandwal was arrested in 1973 and killed in prison, reportedly by Parchamis without Daoud's prior knowledge. Party no longer exists.
Early leadership		
Former prime minister Mohammad Hashim Maiwandwal		
Jamiat Islami (Islamic Party)	Islamic	Reconstituted now as one of the major Resistance organizations, headed by Prof. Burhanuddin Rabbani.
Early leadership		
Menhajuddin Gahiz		

* Based on combined information from a number of sources.

(continued on next page)

NAME OF ORGANIZATION	ORIENTATION	COMMENTS
Ikhwan al-Muslimi (Muslim Brotherhood)	Radical-revivalist Islam; ties with the international Muslim Brotherhood based in Egypt.	Leading members included Gulbuddin Hekhmatyar, Abdul Rasul Sayyaf and Prof. Burhanuddin Rabbani, all of whom now head Resistance organizations.
Afghan Mellat (The Afghan Nation) *Early leadership* Ghulam Mohammed Farhad, Mohammad Amin Wakman	Pushtun supremacy; Pushtunistan; ultra-nationalist, "national socialist." In recent years, lays claim to social democratic identity and positions, but program still includes elements of original Pushtun supremacy positions.	Possibly founded as early as the 1940s. According to Afghan sources, key elements were German-educated and pro-Nazi. After the 1978 PDPA coup, Mellat leadership inside Afghanistan was decimated. Remainder is now fragmented and operating primarily in India, Europe and the U.S. as a Social Democratic party seeking admission to the Socialist International with the support of Willi Brandt and Bruno Kreisky. Wakman is now chairman and most visible figure.
Setem-i-Melli (The Oppressed People). Founded 1968. *Early leadership* Taher Badakhshi (d. 1979), who was also a founding member of the PDPA.	Marxist/Leninist, anti-Pushtun, separatist, appealing to ethnic minorities.	Communist splinter group focused on northern provinces, now collaborating openly with the PDPA regime. Before 1978, demanded northern non-Pushtun autonomy; now calls for complete independence from "Pushtun domination." *See Krakowski.*

NAME OF ORGANIZATION	ORIENTATION	COMMENTS
Shola-i-Jawid (Eternal Flame). Action arm inside Afghanistan: **SAMA.** Action arm outside Afghanistan: **FASA** *Early leadership* Dr. Rahim Mahmudi and Dr. Hadi Mahmudi; SAMA (Farsi acronym) was founded by Majid Kalakani (d. 1980)	Marxist. Ostensibly Maoist but Chinese officials disclaim any connection. Main faction reportedly has ties to North Korea. Some of several splinter factions have ties with Albania.	Doctrinally, overtly Maoist and violently anti-Soviet, at least initially. SAMA action arm conducted guerrilla warfare against the DRA until 1980 and was probably involved in kidnapping of U.S. Ambassador Dubs; but after Kalakani's death the organization began secret collaboration with DRA regimes though it still represents itself to be a resistance organization. The women's arm, The Revolutionary Organization of Afghan Women, is or was headed by Farida Ahmadi, also known as Kishwar Kamal and "Mina" (real name uncertain). External political arm is active in Europe, the U.S., Latin America and elsewhere under various names and acronyms, including FASA, GUAFS, GUDSPA, others. European headquarters in Aachen and Karlsruhe, West Germany; publishes glossy, expensively-produced German-language magazine, *Afghanistan Tribune.* Quite successful in promoting a resistance identity in Europe, especially West Germany, Austria, Switzerland, and Scandinavia, and to a lesser extent also in Belgium, France, Netherlands, Brazil, possibly Spain and Italy. Efforts in Iceland, Argentina, Colombia, possibly elsewhere in Latin America. Also active in refugee camps. In 1985, identified by Pakistani intelligence as a KGB operation.

A Short Glossary

A note on pronounciation and terminology:
A few basic comments on pronunciation: "a" is always broad, as in "father." The letter "q" *not* followed by "u" indicates a very hard "k" sound, as in "Inqilab." "Kh" is a gutteral, pronounced like the German "ch" in *Aachen.* The accent is usually on the last syllable, e.g., muja*hid,* mujahi*deen;* Is*lam,* Islami.

For reasons of precision and accuracy this book uses the term "resistance" and not the word "rebel." A check with any unabridged dictionary or thesaurus will show that the term "rebel" implies action against duly constituted authority; indeed, one standard reference gives as synonyms for "rebel" the terms "mutineer," "renegade" and "traitor." Such implications are obviously inappropriate in reference to the Afghan people, who are fighting an alien invader and a regime imposed on them by a bloody coup and a foreign power and maintained by force---just as the French, Dutch, Norwegians, Danes and others fought under similar circumstances in World War II. As the word "Resistance" was appropriate for those forces then, so it is for the Afghans today.*

The term "mujahideen" has not been used here as a proper noun because it is widely used by many others throughout the Muslim world, both generically and specifically by various political groups, hence could lead to confusion. The term "Freedom Fighters" simply becomes awkward with frequent repetition. "Resistance" is both succinct and accurate. (All three are of course technically accurate in the Afghan context.)

Since the Afghan *people* are opposed to the Afghan *regime,* the acronym DRA rather than the term "Afghans" has been used for the regime except for contexts in which there is no likelihood of confusion (e.g., "Soviet-Afghan treaty.") In general, then, the term "Afghan," in reference to the post-1978 period, refers to the Afghan people unless otherwise indicated by the context.

And since those holding official titles in Kabul have no independent authority and do not actually govern but are instead under the direct orders of Soviet occupation officials, the term "regime" has been used instead of "government."

---

* Journalists and copy editors may find it useful to note that the *New York Times* decided to cease using the term "rebel" in 1986.

Terms that appear frequently in this book and in the general press:

Administered Tribal Agencies (tribal territories)

An administrative area in Pakistan between the Northwest Frontier Province (NWFP) and the border of Afghanistan, inhabited by a number of historically fractious Pushtun tribes and holding special status in the administrative structure of Pakistan. The Tribal Agencies are administered by the Federal Government through the Governor of the NWFP (using a long-established system of Political Agents drawn from the civil service) but are administratively separate from the NWFP. The Tribal Agencies have their own seats in the National Assembly and maintain a degree of local autonomy under a unique and complicated system developed over many years in which the respective areas of government and tribal authority are carefully delineated. Although the Tribal Agencies are part of Pakistan and their inhabitants are Pakistani citizens, in large part the tribes in the Agencies manage their own affairs through their jirgas, with minimal government interference. They do not pay regular taxes; on the contrary, they are in large part supported by subsidies from the Government of Pakistan.

It is from these semi-autonomous districts that the Afghan Resistance conducts many of its activities, and it is here too that Soviet and Afghan Communist agents seek to cultivate support among what they call the "free" Pushtun tribes for the regime in Kabul. Such often-mentioned locales as the Khyber Pass, Parachinar and Miramshah are in the Administered Tribal Agencies.

Afghan

Originally a synonym for "Pushtun," it has come to mean a citizen of Afghanistan of whatever ethnic origin. The adjectival form is also "Afghan," not "Afghani" or "Afghanistani."

afghani	The unit of currency of Afghanistan.
AGSA	Acronym for the first Afghan secret police set up by the Taraki/Amin/Babrak regime after the 1978 coup; see KhAD, KAM, WAD.
Amir (Emir)	A commander, leader, minor ruler, prince, king. Usually refers to a ruler of a lesser kingdom. From 1826 to 1930, Afghan kings used the title "Amir"; thereafter, the title was changed to "Shah."
Amu Darya	Oxus River. (*darya* means river.)
Baluch/Baluchi	A tribally organized ethnic group living in southeastern Iran, western Pakistan and marginally in southwestern Afghanistan; not related to the Pushtuns, as Kabul at times has claimed. Also, their language.
Basmachi	Literally, "bandits;" the term used by the Soviets to describe the Muslim groups in Central Asia who fought to gain independence from the USSR in the 1920s-1930s; now sometimes used by Moscow to refer to the Afghan Resistance. See *dushman*.
chai	Tea. A *chaikhana* is a teahouse.
correlation of forces	A term used in Soviet geopolitical analysis, referring to the relative strength of socialist and non-socialist powers; according to Soviet doctrine, it is historically inevitable that the "correlation of forces" will inexorably shift in favor of the socialist powers led by the USSR. Similar to---but not identical with---the term "balance of power."
Dari	See *Farsi*.
darra	A mountain pass. The village of Darra Adam Khel is a well-known gun-making center in Pakistan's Administered Tribal Agencies.

DRA

Democratic Republic of Afghanistan. The official title used by the regime since the Communist seizure of power in 1978. In July 1987, the regime announced its intention to drop the word "Democratic" upon the adoption of the proposed constitution and to revert to "Republic of Afghanistan," the name used under Daoud (1973-1978). This habitual Communist newspeak has turned numbers of unsophisticated Afghans and others elsewhere against democracy, which they understand to be Communist oppression; the new name may have a similar effect on their understanding of the term "republic." The DRA is neither democratic nor a republic.

Durrani

One of the major divisions of Afghan tribes, and the tribal identity of the rulers of Afghanistan from 1747 to 1978. See: *Ghilzai*.

dushman

Literally, "enemy." Term used by DRA and Soviet sources for the Afghan Resistance.

DYOA

Democratic Youth Organization of Afghanistan.

Farsi

The Persian language, one of the world's great literary languages and the *lingua franca* from eastern Iraq to northern Pakistan, including Afghanistan and much of Central Asia. In the 1960s, a few Afghan scholars coined the term "Dari" in an effort to differentiate the Afghan dialect of Farsi from the dialect spoken in Iran, but the term has caught on only with a limited number of academicians; the public still call their language *Farsi*. The Afghan dialect differs from other dialects of Persian about as much as American English differs from British English. The Soviets, however, support and promote the use of the term "Dari" in an effort to establish it as a separate language (as they did with Tajik, another Persian dialect) in order to forward their "nationalities" policies and encourage separatism.

fundamentalist Islam	A misnomer and a highly misleading term widely used in the Western media to identify any of a wide range of extremist, radical Islamic movements. Apparently introduced, in a false analogy with Protestant Christian fundamentalism, by Western observers unaware of the complex differences between Islam and Christianity, but there is no such parallel: the term "fundamentalist" distorts and falsifies the positions of these Muslim movements. In fact, the doctrines of these radical movements are comparatively recent products of the twentieth century, and are enunciated as a political ideology, not as religion per se. Except in Iran, with its special Shi'ite hierarchy, their leaders are drawn not from among the clergy or other religious leaders but from modern universities, technical schools, and the urban laity. The radicals reject the Shari'at (q.v.) and the entire historic development of Islam since the death of the Prophet Mohammad in the seventh century, repudiating the whole of Muslim tradition and thought and demanding an entirely new beginning. As Olivier Roy points out, they seek "the total reconstruction of political relations... [and the creation of] a political model capable of competing with the great ideologies of the Western world...utopia, the millenium and revolution." These movements are more accurately described as *radical-revivalist* (q.v.), extremist, or, in a term they themselves sometimes use, *Islamist*. [For a fuller discussion, see Roy (bibliography).]
Ghilzai (Ghalji)	A major division of the Pushtuns; historically rivals of the Durrani Pushtuns for power in Afghanistan. The *kuchis*, or Pushtun nomads, are predominantly Ghilzai.
GRU	Intelligence branch of the Soviet Armed Forces.
Hanafi code	The most important Sunni school of Islamic law (shari'a), named for its founder, Abu Hanifa. Among the Sunni majority in the Islamic world,

there are four schools of legal thought, all based on Koranic law but differing significantly in interpretation and methodology. The Hanafi code is the Islamic legal system which obtains in much of the Muslim world and particularly in southwest Asia, including Afghanistan, Pakistan and India.

haji

One who has made the pilgrimage *(haj* or *hegira)* to Mecca.

hezb

Party, group.

Hezb-i-Islami

Islamic Party. Name used by two different Afghan Resistance organizations, headed by Maulawi Younos Khalis and Eng. Gulbuddin Hekhmatyar. See: Who's Who in the Resistance.

Hindu Kush

The western-most ranges of the Himalayas, which cover much of eastern and central Afghanistan, stretching 600 miles on a roughly east-west axis and dividing the Central Asian steppes from the plains of the Indian subcontinent. The Hindu Kush includes the western ranges of the Karakorum, the Koh-i-Baba in central Afghanistan, and the Safed Koh in the Khyber area. More than 100 peaks rise to 20-25,000 feet (6,000-7,600 meters or more) and hundreds of others rise above 14,000 feet (4,270 meters). The origin of the name "Hindu Kush" ("Killer of Hindus") is unknown but may be a corruption of the earlier "Hindu Koh"; in any case, it has no modern significance.

-i suffix

Added to a noun, indicates possessive; approximately the equivalent of the prepositions "of" and "from" (e.g., Kabuli = from Kabul; Panjsheri = from Panjsher.) Also indicates other relationships (e.g., "khaki" = colored like dust [khak]). Pronounced as "ee."

ikhwan

Brotherhood. The *Ikhwan al-Muslimi* ("Muslim Brotherhood") is an international radical-revivalist organization based in Egypt, where it was founded in the 1930s.

India

References to "India" *before 1947* refer to the entire Indian subcontinent, which has been divided into the modern nations of Pakistan, India and Bangladesh only since the withdrawal of British rule in 1947. In most cases, the context indicates whether the reference is to the entire subcontinent or to the post-1947 nation.

Inqilab

Revolution.

Iran

New name for *Persia,* adopted in 1935.

Islami

Islamic, Muslim

Isma'ilia

A non-orthodox Shi'a sect headed by the Aga Khan.

-istan

Suffix meaning "the place or land of"---which may refer to a nation state (e.g., Afghanistan) but can also refer to a province or district, or an undefined territory (e.g., Baluchistan, Turkestan, Nuristan, Arabistan, etc.). The suffix may be attached to the name of the inhabitants or to significant features--- land of deserts, of mountains, etc., e.g., Kohistan.

Jamaat-i-Islami

A Pakistani radical-revivalist Islamic political party founded c. 1941 by Maulana Syed Abdul Ala Mawdoodi. Not to be confused with the Afghan Resistance organization (see below).

Jamiat Islami Afghanistan

An Afghan Resistance party founded by Prof. Burhanuddin Rabbani c. 1979. See: Who's Who in the Resistance.

jerib

A measure of farmland, about one-quarter acre.

jihad

In Islam, a war in defense of the faith, against enemies of the faith. Although the term is sometimes used loosely by non-Muslims to refer to any war in the Muslim world, and by Muslims to try to gain support and religious authority for war even against other Muslims, this is inaccurate. Jihad has a very specific meaning, and a struggle or war must be declared a jihad by appropriate religious authorities. Since the Soviet Union actively promulgates atheism and attempts to suppress religion, the Afghan struggle is correctly and properly identified as a jihad, and is recognized as such throughout the Islamic world. One who fights in a *jihad* is a *mujahid* (plural, *mujahideen*).

jirga

An Afghan social institution, Pushtun in origin. A general meeting of all adult men in a community, a tribe, a region, etc., or of all parties to a dispute, or of a leadership group, in which disputes or problems are discussed, all those present are allowed their say, and a decision is reached (by consensus if possible) that is acceptable to all concerned. See *Loya Jirga.*

kafir

Infidel, unbeliever, especially an idolator.

KAM

Acronym for the renamed secret police under Amin in 1979; see *KhAD, AGSA.*

karez

Underground water tunnel used in irrigation systems in Afghanistan and Iran. An ancient technique essential to agriculture in this semi-arid land. Villagers now also use the tunnels as shelters from Soviet bombardments and search missions.

KhAD

Acronym for *Khedamat-i Etela'at-i Dawlati* [State Information Agency]. The DRA secret police set up under Soviet KGB direction in 1980 as the successor to Taraki's AGSA and Amin's KAM; headed until late 1986 by Dr. Najib. Raised to the level of a ministry in January 1986, with a new acronym, WAD, but still usually referred to as

KhAD. These two terms are therefore used interchangeably in this volume for the post-1986 period. Still under KGB direction.

Khalq Literally, "people" or "masses." A faction of the Afghan Communist Party, originally headed by Taraki and Amin; in power 1978-1979. Pushtun-dominated. *Khalqi:* a member of Khalq.

khan An honorific or courtesy title added after a man's name. (Not ordinarily a surname.) A khan is a man of importance, substance, power, or achievement---usually though not always a property owner (no matter how tiny the scrap of land). A man who has won respect or prestige by other means, or an elder, may however be addressed as a khan whether or not he has property.

khel Pushtun clan or sub-tribe. Lineage (tribal sub-group). Pronounced to rhyme with "mail."

longhi Turban cloth, wrapped around a the head to form a turban; the ends may be used to cover the face against dust or cold.

Loya Jirga Great Assembly. The supreme Afghan political institution: a national assembly of leaders and representatives from every part of the country, called to decide on matters of grave national import, e.g., confirming the legitimacy of a ruler, accepting a constitution, etc. Only a handful of Loya Jirgas have been called in this century.

madrasa In Sunni Islam, a higher religious school, an academy of advanced Islamic studies.

Mahaz See: Who's Who in the Resistance.

malik A village or tribal leader.

masjid Mosque.

maulawi/ mawlawi	In Afghanistan, a term used for someone who has completed a higher degree in a *madrasa;* an Islamic scholar. A religious title indicating an important cleric. (See 'ulema.)
millat/mellat	The nation, i.e., the people of the nation (as differentiated from the state).
milli/melli	National.
minar	Minaret.
mohafiz	Local militia, raised in the area where they serve. The word literally means "protection."
Mohammadzai	The clan of the royal family of Afghanistan; the extended royal family. Includes through marriage such other extended families as Etemadi, Seraj, Tarzi, Ziayee, Zikria, etc.
Mohd.	Standard abbreviation for the name Mohammad. *Never* used for the Prophet Mohammad, however.
mujahid	One who fights in a jihad (see above) in defense of the Faith. Plural: *mujahideen.*
mullah	A Muslim cleric; often mistranslated as "priest," but a mullah does not have priestly authority or functions; he leads the prayers, teaches, etc.
murid	A follower or disciple of a *pir,* a religious leader, esp. in one of the Sufi mystical orders. Many Afghans are murids, esp. of Naqshbandiya and Qadiriya leaders. See *Sufiism.*
Naqshbandiya	Sufi order (tariqa) founded by Bahauddin Naqshband. Prof. Sibgatullah Mojadidi is a prominent Naqshbandi leader. See *Sufiism.*
National Fatherland Front [NFF]	An umbrella organization set up in 1981 by the DRA to provide a controlled alternative to the

parliament, Loya Jirga and other traditional Afghan agencies of social and political participation. Made up of various other DRA-established organizations and Party front groups---of Youth, Women, Writers, Toilers, etc.---to provide a facade of popular support and involvement for the DRA. Modeled on Fatherland Front organizations in Eastern Europe. Participants appear to be mostly Party members adopting one or more roles as "delegates" representing other Party front organizations. For reasons as yet unclear, the word "Fatherland" was dropped from the name in January 1987 at the Second Congress of the NFF, which was also attended by representatives of Pakistan's Awami National Party, Iran's Tudeh and Revolutionary Guards, the Congress Party of India, and several international Communist front organizations.

NIFA
See: Who's Who in the Resistance.

Nuristan
A region of eastern Afghanistan, including parts of the Kunar Valley, which was not converted to Islam until 1895 and received the name *Nuristan* ("place of enlightenment") at that time. Previously known as *Kafiristan* ("place of the unbelievers"), it had an ancient religion and culture whose origins are still obscure.

NWFP
NorthWest Frontier Province (of Pakistan). The major Afghan Resistance organizations have their headquarters in the capital of the NWFP, Peshawar. [Peshawar, incidentally, rhymes with "flower."]

Parcham
Literally, "flag" or "banner." The faction of the Afghan Communist Party that was installed by Soviet forces in December 1979 and remains in power. Leadership: Babrak Karmal, Najib. *Parchami:* a member of Parcham.

Pathan
Pushtoon, Pukhtun.

466

PDPA	People's Democratic Party of Afghanistan: the Afghan Communist Party comprising both Parcham and Khalq factions.
Persia	The historic name for Iran; the name *Iran* was adopted only in 1935.
pir	A spiritual master, esp. in Sufiism; a title indicating a holy man.
Pushto	Language of the Pushtuns (or Pukhtuns, depending on dialect: the -sh form is dominant in the south, the -kh form in the east and in Pakistan's Northwest Frontier Province). Numerous variant spellings: Pashtu, Pushtu, Pakhtu, etc.
Pushtun	The dominant ethnic group in Afghanistan and in Pakistan's Northwest Frontier Province; also: Pukhtun (see above). Widely known by the Indian form, Pathan. Also: an individual member of this ethnic group.
Pushtunwali	The social code of the Pushtuns.
Qadirya	Sufi order (tariqa) founded in the 12th century by Abdul Qadir Gailani; now headed by Pir Sayed Ahmad Gailani, leader of one of the Afghan Resistance organizations. Qadirya Sufiism is noted for tolerance and a philanthropic spirit. See: *Sufiism.*
qazi	Judge, esp. a judge who applies the shari'a(t) or Islamic law.
radical-revivalist Islam	A more accurate term for the extremist modern Islamic movements widely but mistakenly labeled "fundamentalist" in the Western press. See *Fundamentalist Islam* (above).
sardar	Prince.
sarandoy	Police.

Saur	In the Afghan lunar calendar, the month that begins on 21 April of the Gregorian calendar. (Rhymes with "power.")
"Saur Revolution"	The coup that brought the Communists to power in Afghanistan on 28 April 1978, referred to by the PDPA and its supporters as "the Great Saur Revolution" by way of analogy with the 1917 Bolshevik October Revolution.
shabnama	Literally, "night letter": clandestine political leaflet distributed secretly at night by opponents of the regime.
shah	King.
shahid	Martyr; specifically, one who has died fighting for the Faith, especially in jihad.
shari'a/shari'at	The totality of Muslim law. There are four major schools of legal thought and codification, of which the most liberal, the Hanafi code (q.v.), was until 1978 the official legal system of Afghanistan.
sheikh	A revered religious figure, similar to a pir. Among Afghan Shi'a, it refers to 'ulema who have studied in Iran or Iraq.
Shi'a/Shi'ite	The largest heterodox minority sect of Islam, with centralized religious authority (ayatollahs); dominant in Iran since the seventeenth century. The Shi'a-Sunni conflict goes back to a struggle over the leadership succession to the Prophet Mohammed thirty years after his death. Unlike the Sunni majority, Shi'ites have a tradition of hierarchical and authoritarian religious political leadership.
shura	A council or consultative assembly, primarily of religious authorities.
Sufiism	Islamic mysticism, emphasizing a direct personal

relationship with God. There are four major schools of Sufi thought *(tariqa,* q.v., usually translated as "orders" or "brotherhoods"), two of which are particularly significant in Afghanistan: Qadirya and Naqshbandiya. A large number of Afghans are adherents (murids) of Qadirya Sufiism, whose head is Pir Sayed Ahmad Gailani, one of the leaders of the Afghan Resistance. Many others are adherents of Naqshbandiya Sufiism (which is even more widespread in Central Asia), in which Prof. Sibgatullah Mojadidi, another Resistance leader, is an important figure. Sufiism is famous as a source of art and poetry; in the West, the most famous Sufi figure is probably the poet Omar Khayyam. In recent years, Westerners have shown increasing interest in Sufi thought; internationally, its best-known explicator today is Idries Shah, an Afghan. For the political significance of Sufiism today, see: Bennigsen.

Sunni/Sunnat

The orthodox Muslim majority (worldwide). About 85 percent of Afghans are Sunni Muslims. *Sunnat* means "tradition"---specifically, tradition(s) of the Prophet Mohammed.

syed

An honorific indicating a descendant of the Prophet Mohammed through his daughter Fatima. [Also: sayed, sayyid, said, etc.]

Tajik

A Persian-speaking ethnic group living in Afghanistan and Central Asia. In the USSR the Soviets, in accordance with their divisive "nationalities" policies, replaced the modified Arabic alphabet used by these people with the Cyrillic alphabet and labeled their dialect as a separate language, "Tajik." It is however a regional dialect of Persian, comprehensible to speakers of other Persian dialects.

tariqa

Literally, "path"; one of the Sufi orders.

Tudeh party   The official acknowledged Communist Party of Iran.

Turkoman   A Turkic people in Central Asia. Also their dialect of Turkish, which is in the Soviet Union labeled a separate language and transliterated into the Cyrillic alphabet.

'ulema   In Afghanistan, a group of *maulawis*.

'Umma   The Muslim community; the totality of Muslims in the world.

Uzbek   A Turkish dialect spoken by the Uzbek people and formerly known as Chagatai Turkish. In conformity with Soviet "nationalities" policies, this dialect was transliterated into the Cyrillic alphabet and labeled a separate language. Uzbek has a rich literature which, like other aspects of Central Asian culture, was historically strongly influenced by Persian literature.

WAD   Acronym for *Wizarat-i Amaniat-i Dawlati* [Ministry of State Security], the Afghan KGB, formerly KhAD, which was raised to ministry status in January 1986. Still widely referred to as KhAD. The two acronyms are therefore used interchangeably in this volume for the post-1986 period. See *KhAD*.

wali   A governor.

Wahhabi Islam/ Wahhabism   An extremely strict, rigid, severe, and puritanical Islamic sect founded in the 18th century, which aims to do away with all innovations more recent than the third Islamic century (10th century A.D.). Wahhabism is the official sect of Saudi Arabia but is rarely found elsewhere. However, the term "Wahhabism" is used by the Soviets to refer to all activist Islamic movements. (See Bennigsen).

zamindar	Landlord, i.e., a landowner with tenant farmers working his land. N.B., not all land *owners* (khans) are landlords (zamindars), although DRA propaganda tries to blur the distinction. In prewar Afghanistan there were relatively few zamindars; most land was worked by small independent farmers who owned their small farms.

Soviet Military Terms and Acronyms

Armiya-PVO	Air Defense Army; a command unit in charge of air defense for entire regions or campaigns.
Army	The permanent command unit immediately below the level of a Front.
Art of War	Over hundreds of years, the Russians have developed a unique approach to all military matters which is subsumed under the name "Art of War" and which has no precise equivalent elsewhere. Defining and describing it occupies entire volumes. Art of War is briefly defined as "Theory and practice of preparing and conducting military operations on land, sea, and in the air. Theory of Art of War is part of Military Science. Art of War includes military strategy, operational art, and tactics, which are closely interlinked." [*Military Encyclopedic Dictionary*. Marshal SU N.V. Ogarkov, ed. (Moscow: Voenizdat, 1983).] For further details of this highly complex term, see the above and other specialized sources. (Cf. Military Science).
BMP	Infantry Fighting Vehicle.
BON	Special Duties Brigade. Heliborne units of the Airborne Troops (VDV), highly trained and considered thoroughly reliable, used for especially difficult and sensitive operations, often as advance forces. BON forces are often confused in the Western press with SPETSNAZ forces, but they are different.

CAA	Combined-Arms Army. An army that includes all types of weapons systems and personnel.
CARB	Combined-Arms Reinforced Battalion.
COIN	Counter-insurgency.
C3I	Command, Control, Communication and Intelligence.
desant	The insertion of forces, especially infantry, behind enemy lines, usually carried out by air drops; also, forces so inserted.
Front	A permanent command level just below TVD, comprising several Combined-Arms Armies and an assortment of dedicated units including a Tactical Air Army, an Air Defense Army, BON, etc. Authorized to determine and conduct major campaigns.
Group (of Soviet Forces: GSF)	In peacetime, for Soviet forces *outside* the Soviet Union, the command level equivalent of a Military District within the Soviet Union; transformed in time of war into one or possibly two Fronts.
GRU	Soviet Military Intelligence. The intelligence arm of the Soviet General Staff.
GSFA	Group of Soviet Forces [in] Afghanistan.
GSFG	Group of Soviet Forces [in] Germany.
GTA	Guards Tank Army.
KDB	Punitive Desant Battalion.
KhV	Chemical Troops.
LOCs	Lines of communications.

Marshal SU	Marshall of the Soviet Union
Military District	See: VO.
Military Science	Russian term, briefly defined as "A system of knowledge on the character of and laws governing war, preparation of a country and its armed forces for war, and modes of its conduct." [*Military Encyclopedic Dictionary.* Marshal SU N.V. Ogarkov, ed. (Moscow: Voenizdat, 1983).] For further details of this highly complex term, see the above and other specialized sources. (Cf. Art of War).
MRD	Motorized Rifle Division.
POL	Petrol, oil & lubricants.
PVO	See: Armiya-PVO
Real time	Immediate; simultaneous. Real time knowledge or guidance enables forces to respond to events as they are occurring.
ShVDB	Air Mobil Assault Brigade, made up of regular Motorized Rifle Troops with heliborne training. Should not be confused with BON or SPETSNAZ.
SPETSNAZ	Special Purpose Troops. The most elite of all specially trained troops, with unique characteristics---most importantly, absolute trustworthiness, enabling them to be entrusted with intelligence-related activities and independent operations. Much misunderstood by Western observers who often confuse them with BON and other specialized units. Each branch of the Soviet military has its own SPETSNAZ. In Afghanistan, the most efficient SPETSNAZ are those answering to the GRU and VDV. (See Suvorov, bibliography.)

TO & E	Table of Organization and Equipment.
TVA	Tactical Air Army.
TVD	Theater of Military Operations. The top Soviet combat command level, comprising several Fronts.
VDD	Airborne Division.
VDV	Airborne Troops.
VO	Military District. In peacetime, the managerial command level for Soviet troops on Soviet territory; transformed in time of war into one or two Fronts.
Vystrel	An institute of advanced education for Soviet and allied officers who are marked for promotion to senior ranks. The Soviets consider the quality of officers (not enlisted men) to be the key element in war. The Vystrel is designed to insure that officers are of top quality and fully aware of the newest concepts, weapons systems, etc., and it serves as a major testing ground for innovations.

Selected Bibliography

The following is an introductory bibliography, not a comprehensive one. Most of the works listed should be available through most research or college libraries and at least some of them may be available in a large public library or in bookstores, or from sources indicated. They provide a starting point for further research; as indicated, many of them contain extensive, detailed and scholarly bibliographies and sources for those who wish to pursue aspects of the Afghanistan issue in depth. Other research guidance is also listed.

For convenience, they are organized in the following categories:

I.   General history and background
II.   The Communist takeover and after
III.   Journalists' reports on the war
IV.   Strategic/military analysis
V.   Atrocities/human rights violations
VI.   Economics & natural resources
VII.   Soviet regional policy
VIII. Central Asia
IX.   Institutional sources
X.   Selected periodicals
XI.   Specialized research centers
XII.   General interest, travel, description
XIII. Photo books
XIV.   Afghan art
XV.   Works of fiction
XVI.   A guide to research

Very few individual articles in periodicals are included here; those listed cover material not yet available in book form. However, several periodicals that regularly cover Afghanistan on an ongoing basis are included. Needless to say, the general press, and particularly the *New York Times, Washington Post, Christian Science Monitor, The Economist, Time, Newsweek,* the *Telegraph* (London), *Washington Times,* and *New York City Tribune* are also continuing sources of general news reports. Since 1983 *Reader's Digest* has occasionally published reports on aspects of the issue, especially human rights violations.

Unless otherwise indicated, all works listed are in English.

476

I. GENERAL AFGHAN HISTORY & BACKGROUND

Abdur Rahman. *The Life of Abdur Rahman, Amir of Afghanistan.* London: John Murray, 1901. 2 vols.

The memoirs of the most important Afghan ruler of modern times (1880-1901), who set Afghan policy for the next 75 years. This is a rare book, available only in specialized research libraries; but it is often quoted in this volume and others and is so highly useful for historical research that it is included in this list. Particularly interesting for Abdur Rahman's observations regarding his twelve years of exile in Russia.

Adamec, Ludwig W. *Afghanistan's Foreign Affairs to the Mid-Twentieth Century.* Arizona: University of Arizona Press, 1974. Paperback: 324. Maps, illus., sources and readings.

------ *Afghanistan 1900-1923: A Diplomatic History.* Berkeley and Los Angeles: University of California Press, 1967: 245. Appendices (texts of treaties, correspondence, and documents), bibliography.

------ *A Biographical Dictionary of Contemporary Afghanistan.* Graz, Austria: Akademische Druk-u. Verlagsanstalt, 1986: 280.

Covers the period from World War II to 1986, with 1,600 entries of officials, religious figures, writers, artists, military officers, etc. Special indexes of selected categories and other useful research information. 400 photographs.

Cambridge History of India, especially Vol. IV.

Caroe, Sir Olaf. *The Pathans.* St. Martin's Press, 1958: 521. Maps, diagrams, illus., glossary, transliteration table, appendices.

The standard one-volume history of the Pathans (i.e., Pushtuns/Pakhtuns).

Curzon, George N. *Russia in Central Asia.* London: 1889.

Lord Curzon was a close and often prescient observer of Russian expansionism in Central Asia both before and during his service as Viceroy of India. He traveled widely in Central Asia, Afghanistan and Persia. This and other of his works are very useful.

Dupree, Louis. *Afghanistan.* Princeton, N.J.: Princeton University Press, 3rd ed., 1980: 760. Charts, maps, graphs, illus., appendices, bibliography.

A standard reference, the only one-volume compendium with a little on everything.   Useful for data of many kinds, e.g. dates, treaties, dynasties, statistics, agricultural data, etc.   Less useful for analyses.   Written before the Communist coup and invasion.

Fahimi, Fatima. *Women in Afghanistan/Frauen in Afghanistan.* Liestal, Switzerland: Stiftung Bibliotheca Afghanica, 1986. Originally published in 1977, now reissued with an update by Nancy Hatch Dupree: 111. Bilingual: English and German texts on facing pages. Photographs.

The work of an Afghan woman journalist, originally published in Kabul; a useful source on the situation of modern Afghan women, particularly urban women.   It covers historical background, education, health, government and diplomacy, social welfare, sports, journalism, law, entertainment, constitutional status before 1978.   An annex to the 1986 edition reports on the treatment of women in the political prisons of the DRA since 1978.

Fletcher, Arnold. *Afghanistan: Highway of Conquest.* Reprint. New York: Cornell University Press, 1982: 325.

A one-volume history drawing more on Afghan source materials than does Fraser-Tytler.

Fraser-Tytler, Sir Kerr (W.K.).   *Afghanistan.* 2d ed. London: Oxford University Press, 1953: 348.   Maps, illus., bibliography.

The standard one-volume history, with emphasis on the political history from the 19th century on, particularly British and Russian competition for influence in Kabul.

Gregorian, Vartan. *The Emergence of Modern Afghanistan: Politics of Reform and Modernization, 1880-1946.* Stanford, California: Stanford University Press, 1969: 586. Illus., bibliography.

Kakar, Hasan Kawun. *Government and Society in Afghanistan: The Reign of the Amir Abd al-Rahman Khan.* Austin, Texas and London: University of Texas Press, 1979: 328. Appendices, glossary, bibliography.

An important study of the most significant formative period of modern Afghan history (1880-1901) by the distinguished Afghan historian.

McGrory, Patrick. *The Fierce Pawns.* Philadelphia and New York: J.B. Lippincott Company, 1966: 252. Illus., maps, bibliography.

A modern account of the First Anglo-Afghan War (1839-1842).

Poullada, Leon B. *Reform and Rebellion in Afghanistan, 1919-1929.* New

York: Cornell University Press, 1973: 318. Illus., maps, appendices, including information on Afghan tribal distribution, bibliography.

Sykes, Sir Percy. *History of Afghanistan.* London: Macmillan, 1940. 2 vols.

A standard history.

II. THE COMMUNIST TAKEOVER AND AFTER

Because many developments were clandestine, many documents have been destroyed or are now unavailable, and many of the key figures are dead, the full story of the course of events leading up to the Communist takeover, the Soviet invasion, and its ongoing aftermath will probably never be known with absolute accuracy. Therefore all of the accounts listed below have slight variations and possible errors of detail in addition to differences of interpretation. Taken together, however, they probably offer as accurate a picture as can be known, and the overall development of events is clear.

Amstutz, J. Bruce. *Afghanistan: The First Five Years of Soviet Occupation.* Washington, D.C.: National Defense University, 1986: 545. Illus., maps, appendices, bibliography, and index.

The author served in the U.S. embassy in Kabul 1977-1980 and observed many of the key events preceding and surrounding the Soviet invasion. A detailed reference, full of information and statistics, and surveying the political, diplomatic and military aspects of events up to early 1986, with emphasis on the Afghan Resistance.

Arnold, Anthony. *Afghanistan: The Soviet Invasion in Perspective.* Revised ed. Stanford, California: Hoover Institution Press, Stanford University, 1985: 179. Selected bibliography.

The author traces the pattern of Soviet economic penetration and political subversion leading up to the invasion, and makes recommendations for changes in U.S. policy.

------ *Afghanistan's Two-Party Communism: Parcham and Khalq.* California: Stanford University Press, 1983: 242. Appendices, bibliography.

The only detailed study of the Afghan Communist party (PDPA), its origins and its development both before and after seizing power. Extremely useful appendices include biographies of PDPA members, the public platform and secret constitution of the PDPA at its founding, the official party history, and charts of PDPA and cabinet membership, showing factional relations and developments.

Banuazizi, Ali and Weiner, Myron. *The State, Religion, and Ethnic Politics: Afghanistan, Iran, and Pakistan.* Syracuse University Press, 1986: 390. Maps, tables of ethnic groups, topography, etc.

Papers given by a dozen scholars at a 1982 symposium, comparing developments in the three countries under discussion.

Bradsher, Henry S. *Afghanistan and The Soviet Union.* 2d ed. North Carolina: Duke Press Policy Studies, 1985: 384. Bibliography.

Bradsher is a specialist in Soviet affairs and a journalist with experience in Afghanistan. A standard one-volume overview of events.

Farr, Grant M. and John G. Merriam. *Afghan Resistance: The Politics of Survival.* Boulder, Colorado: Westview Press, 1987: 235. Maps, bibliography.

A collection of essays by several scholars on various aspects of the Resistance and the situation of Afghan refugees, with emphasis on social and cultural impact and changes. Includes specific discussion of refugee women.

Griffiths, John C. *Afghanistan: Key to a Continent.* Boulder, Colorado: Westview Press, 1981: 225. Illus., maps.

A short history and overview of the region, British and Russian maneuvers, diplomatic history, culture and ethnic background, etc. Includes a section on Afghan natural resources and potential for Soviet exploitation.

Hammond, Thomas T. *Red Flag Over Afghanistan: The Communist Coup, The Soviet Invasion and the Consequences.* Colorado: Westview Press, 1984: 261. Maps, appendix, bibliography.

Hammond is an authority on Soviet affairs and Soviet coups. Although his lack of background in South Asia and, specifically, in Afghan affairs weakens his analysis, his expertise in Soviet policies provides useful insights. Appendix includes the secret constitution of the PDPA, with notes.

Howard, Norman F. and Colleen Sussman, eds. *Afghanistan: Seven Years of Soviet Occupation.* Washington, D.C.: United States Department of State, Bureau of Public Affairs, (Special Report No. 155, December 1986): 19. Maps, photographs. See **Institutional Sources,** below.

Hyman, Anthony. *Afghanistan Under Soviet Domination, 1964-81.* New

York: St. Martin's Press, 1982: 223. Maps, illus., chronology, documents on land reforms, Resistance *shabnama* (clandestine publications).

Hyman is a journalist who has published several valuable reports on human rights violations.

Jones, Allen K. *Afghan Refugees: Five Years Later.* Washington, D.C.: U.S. Committee for Refugees, January 1985: 24. Illus., bibliography.

A succinct overview of the situation of the Afghan refugees in Pakistan, who already numbered 2.5 million at the time this was published. Gives information on the reasons for refugee flight, impact on the host country, refugee conditions, aid programs of the Pakistan government and the UNHCR, resettlement, etc. Still useful although statistics may be out of date.

Klass, Rosanne, ed. *World Affairs, Special Issue on Afghanistan,* vol. 145, no. 3, (winter 1982-1983).

Contains articles by various experts on aspects of the Afghanistan issue, some of which supplement material in this book.

Majrooh, S.B., and Elmi, S.M.Y., eds. *The Sovietization of Afghanistan.* Peshawar, Pakistan: Afghan Jehad Works Translation Centre, GPO Box 417, Peshawar, 1987: 195. Bibliography.

Reports by eight well-known Afghan scholars in exile. Some of the essays are very good and the book includes a great deal of useful data not available elsewhere: tables, lists of university faculty ousted and killed, details of the press and industrial development, etc. First volume of a projected series.

Male, Beverly. *Revolutionary Afghanistan.* New York: St. Martin's Press, 1982: 229. Bibliography.

An apologia for the Khalq regime and for Hafizullah Amin by an Australian sympathizer who was reportedly a personal friend of Amin. This is in many respects a highly unreliable work full of factual errors, distortions and propaganda, with a very selective bibliography. However---precisely *because* the author had close ties to Amin and Khalq, had access to DRA and PDPA materials, and was strongly anti-Parcham---it contains some "insider" materials that may be of interest to knowledgeable scholars. It also provides a picture of PDPA party infighting and the Soviet invasion from the Khalq point of view.

Newell, Richard and S. Richard. *The Struggle for Afghanistan.* Ithaca and London: Cornell University Press, 1981: 236. Appendices give resolutions of the Islamic Conference, 1980; illus.

A succinct overview of Afghanistan's modern history up to the Soviet invasion by two well-known specialists.

Roy, Olivier. *Islam and Resistance in Afghanistan.* London, New York, etc.: Cambridge University Press, 1985: 253. Glossary, chronology, appendix on the Resistance parties, bibliography. A study of the role of Islam and its transformation in the context of the Afghan struggle by a leading French scholar who makes extended journeys inside war-torn Afghanistan every year. Unlike most observers, Roy's sympathies lie primarily with the non-Pushtun elements and the radical religious Resistance parties, particularly Prof. Rabbani's Jamiat, providing a somewhat different perspective. Roy includes detailed discussions of the various Resistance parties, their origins, programs, activities and international connections.

Pennar, Jaan. *The USSR and the Arabs: The Ideological Dimension.* New York: Crane, Russak, 1973.

Shahrani, M. Nazif and Canfield, Robert L., eds. *Revolutions and Rebellions in Afghanistan: Anthropological Perspectives.* Berkeley, California: Institute of International Studies, University of California (Research Series no. 57, 1984): 394. Glossary, maps, bibliography, index. Thirteen contributors analyze local-level resistance in Afghanistan since 1978 from the cultural/historical perspectives of the groups that make up the heterogenous Afghan society.

Staar, Richard F., ed. *1987 Yearbook on International Communist Affairs.* Stanford: Hoover Institution Press, 1987.
[Note: earlier editions of this annual report also have information on the PDPA.]

III. JOURNALISTS' REPORTS ON THE WAR

Chaliand, Gerard. *Report from Afghanistan.* New York: Viking Press/Penguin Books, 1982: 112. Maps, bibliography.
A French writer on foreign affairs, Chaliand made two clandestine visits to Afghanistan in 1980. Interesting for a moderately left-wing European view of Afghanistan in the context of East-West relations.

Fullerton, John. *The Soviet Occupation of Afghanistan.* Hong Kong: South China Morning Post *(Far Eastern Economic Review)*, 1983: 205. Illus., ethnographic map, glossary, bibliography.
Paperback, available through *Far Eastern Economic Review.* Fullerton

covered Afghanistan for more than three years for the London *Telegraph.* Historical background is flawed but his reporting and analysis of the events he himself covered from 1980 on is excellent.

Gall, Sandy. *Behind Russian Lines.* London: Sidgwick & Jackson, 1983: 194. Maps, illus.

A popular British television journalist's account of his visit to the Panjsher Valley in 1982 in the midst of a major Soviet attack.

Girardet, Edward R. *Afghanistan: The Soviet War.* New York: St. Martin's Press, 1985: 259. Maps.

As correspondent for the *Christian Science Monitor,* Girardet has made numerous trips inside Afghanistan since 1979, particularly into the Panjsher Valley. He is a sharp observer and an outspoken reporter, and his book contains much useful information.

Goodwin, Jan. *Caught in the Crossfire.* New York: E.P. Dutton, 1987: 330 Photographs.

A vivid first-person view of the war by a journalist who spent several months inside Afghanistan with the Resistance in 1985, then went to Kabul and interviewed DRA figures.

Lessing, Doris. *The Wind Blows Away Our Words.* London: Picador/Pan Books, 1987: 172.

The distinguished British writer visited Peshawar in 1986, visiting the refugee camps, talking with Resistance commanders, and eliciting their experiences and observations. Particularly useful for its information on Afghan women. Excerpts were published in *The New Yorker,* 16 March 1987.

Van Dyk, Jere. *In Afghanistan: An American Odyssey.* New York: Coward McCann, 1983: 253. Photographs.

A personal account by an American reporter who went into Afghanistan with the Resistance in 1981 for the *New York Times;* his reports were nominated for a Pulitzer prize. A sensitive picture of the Afghans as a people under fire, both civilians and Resistance fighters.

IV. STRATEGIC/MILITARY ANALYSIS

Relatively little expert in-depth information and analysis is available in published form on these important aspects of the issue. Reports in the general press are superficial, contain many inaccuracies, and may often be misleading, resulting in faulty analysis by commentators dependent on them. Some military and technical journals such *Aviation Week & Space Technology* occasionally publish articles on the subject, but most relevant resource material is either inaccessible to the public or hard to come by (e.g., Soviet internal military journals). Centers for strategic studies in the United Kingdom and several other countries do sometimes issue relevant papers.

Afghanistan Reports. Crisis & Conflict Analysis Team, Institute of Strategic Studies, Islamabad, Pakistan.
    Monthly reports cover military issues in detail and also include information on economic and civilian conditions and other aspects of the war. Available through the embassies of Pakistan or by subscription.

Agabekov, George. *OGPU: The Soviet Secret Terror.* Translated by W. Bunn. New York: Brentano's, 1931.

Collins, Joseph J. *The Soviet Invasion of Afghanistan: A Study in The Use of Force in Soviet Foreign Policy.* Lexington, Massachusetts/Toronto, Canada: Lexington Books, 1985: 195. Map, tables, bibliography.

Krakowski, Elie D. "Defining Success in Afghanistan." *Washington Quarterly,* vol. 8, no. 2 (Spring 1985): 37-46.

Rashid, Abdul. "An Afghan Resistance Commander Looks at The War and Its Strategic Implications." *Strategic Review.* Washington, D.C.: United States Strategic Institute, vol. XIII, no. 1 (Winter 1985): 30-39.
    A detailed analysis of the military situation of both the Afghan Resistance and Pakistan.

------ "The Afghan Resistance and the Problem of Unity." *Strategic Review.* Washington, D.C.: United States Strategic Institute, vol. XIV, no. 3 (Summer 1986): 58-66.
    A somewhat different approach to the question of Resistance unity from that taken in this volume, this article includes detailed policy recommendations.

Stahel, Albert A. and Paul A. Bucherer. *Afghanistan 1985/86: The Effects of Soviet Occupation and Warfare.* Liestal, Switzerland: Bibliotheca Afghanica, 1986: 34. Originally published in German; English translation prepared by Congressional Research Service, Library of Congress. Available from Foundation Bibliotheca Afghanica (See Section XI below); $5.00.

Includes detailed military analyses, including disposition of Soviet troops, deployment and tasking of air-to-ground units and special forces, combat assignments of DRA forces, tactics and equipment, operations, etc., with charts, maps and diagrams. Also includes extended discussion of Resistance parties, commanders, equipment and tactics, specific operations, and atrocities against civilians, with diagrams and photographs. Bibliography.

Suvorov, Viktor. *SPETSNAZ: The Story of the Soviet SAS*. London: Hamish Hamilton, 1987: 213.

Suvorov, a Soviet defector, was formerly an officer in the GRU directly involved in control and planning of *SPETSNAZ*. He provides a detailed report on *SPETSNAZ* organization and functions. Several sections are relevant to Afghanistan, which is mentioned.

Jane's Defense Weekly. See "Selected Periodicals" below.

V. ATROCITIES AND HUMAN RIGHTS VIOLATIONS

Major Reports, Books and Monographs

Afghanistan: Torture of Political Prisoners. New York: Amnesty International, November 1986: 51.

Issued after many complaints about Amnesty's failure to give adequate attention to Afghanistan. Limited in scope, but within those limitations, very good. Largely the work of Anthony Hyman.

Barry, Michael. [forthcoming] *Afghanistan...The Destruction of a Nation.* Revised and updated English edition. London: Collins, Special publication, 1988. (Published in French as *Le Royaume de l'Insolence.* Paris: Flammarion, 1984.)

Michael Barry, an Islamic scholar and Afghan specialist, has made repeated trips inside Afghanistan since 1982 to investigate and verify atrocity reports and has developed evidence on a number of specific incidents.

Barry, Michael, Johan Lagerfelt, and Marie-Odile Terrenoire. *Mission to Afghanistan and Pakistan,* International Humanitarian Inquiry Commission on Displaced Persons in Afghanistan. Oxford, England: Central Asian Survey (Incidental Paper No. 4, 1986).

Report on a mission to Afghanistan and Pakistan from September to November 1985, to inquire into the situation of Afghans who are refugees within their own country.

Ermacora, Felix. *Report on the Situation of Human Rights in Afghanistan---Prepared by the Special Rapporteur, Mr. Felix Ermacora, in Accordance with Commission on Human Rights Resolution 1985/88.* U.N. Document No. E/CN.4/1985/21. 19 February 1985.

The first report by the U.N. Special Rapporteur on Afghanistan. 57 pp. Submitted to the Commission in Geneva.

This and all subsequent reports by the Special Rapporteur are available from the U.N. Commission on Human Rights, Center for Human Rights, Room 3660, United Nations, New York, NY 10017, and Geneva, Switzerland. When ordering, give document numbers and dates.

------ *Report on the Situation of Human Rights in Afghanistan---Prepared by the Special Rapporteur, Mr. Felix Ermacora, in Accordance with Commission on Human Rights Resolution 1985/88.* U.N. Document No. A/40/843. 5 November 1985.

Second report of the Special Rapporteur, with cover note by the Secretary-General. 43 pp. Submitted to the General Assembly.

------ *Report on the Situation of Human Rights in Afghanistan---Prepared by the Special Rapporteur, Mr. Felix Ermacora, in Accordance with Commission on Human Rights Resolution 1985/88.* U.N. Document No. E/CN.4/1986/24. 17 February 1986.

Third report of the Special Rapporteur. 28 pp. Submitted to the Commission in Geneva.

------ *Report on the Situation of Human Rights in Afghanistan---Prepared by the Special Rapporteur, Mr. Felix Ermacora, in Accordance with Commission on Human Rights Resolution 1985/88.* U.N. Document No. A/41/778. 9 January 1987. (Originally issued 31 October 1986.)

Fourth report of the Special Rapporteur. 25 pp. Submitted to the General Assembly. Only part of this report was initially issued but, following public outcry, the full report was made available.

------ *Report on the Situation of Human Rights in Afghanistan---Prepared by the Special Rapporteur, Mr. Felix Ermacora, in Accordance with Commission on Human Rights Resolution 1985/88.* U.N. Document No. E/CN.4/1987/22. 19 January 1987.

Fifth report of the Special Rapporteur. 12 pp. As of April 1987, not yet available from New York offices. Deals largely with policy changes announced by the PDPA.

Final Report, International Afghanistan Hearings, Oslo 13-16 March 1983.

Introduction by Bjørn Stordrange, Chairman. Published by the Hearings Committee, Oslo, 1983: 274.

The transcript of testimony given by eyewitnesses, victims, and investigators during the four-day hearing held in Oslo. To obtain a copy, contact: Afghanistanhjelpen, P.O. Box 1922, Vika 0125 Oslo 1, Norway.

Laber, Jeri. *To Win the Children: Afghanistan's Other War*. New York: Helsinki Watch, 1986: 21. Photographs.

A summary essay on what is happening to Afghan children as a result of the war and Soviet policy. Largely based on data developed in the Helsinki Watch reports of the two previous years. (See below).

Laber, Jeri and Barnett Rubin. *Tears, Blood and Cries: Human Rights in Afghanistan Since the Invasion, 1979-1984*. New York: Helsinki Watch, 1984: 210. A Report from Helsinki Watch. Paperback.

The most detailed single report on atrocities. (See also Rubin, below).

Rubin, Barnett R. *To Die in Afghanistan*. New York: Helsinki Watch and Asia Watch, 1985: 106. (A supplement to *Tears, Blood and Cries*). Paperback.

Taken together, the two Helsinki Watch reports provide the fullest detailed reporting thus far available of atrocities of all kinds, with numerous reports by eyewitnesses, victims and survivors. Based on extensive interviews conducted among refugees in Pakistan, Europe, and the United States.

Seagrave, Sterling. *Yellow Rain: A Journey Through the Terror of Chemical Warfare*. New York: M. Evans & Co., 1981.

In the book that gave currency to the term "yellow rain," Seagrave presents firsthand evidence of the use of new Soviet chemical weapons in Afghanistan.

Thorne, Ludmilla. *Soviet POWs in Afghanistan*. New York: Freedom House, 1986: 40.

Interviews with Soviet defectors to the Resistance.

Articles

Barron, John. "From Russia With Hate." *Reader's Digest* (November 1985).

The use of boobytrapped toys in Afghanistan.

------ "Trained as a Terrorist---At Age Nine." *Reader's Digest* (August 1985).
Soviet use of children as KhAD agents.

Barry, Michael. "Afghanistan---Another Cambodia?" *Commentary* (August 1982): 29 - 37.
A detailed account of atrocities, secret executions, torture, and other violations from the Communist coup of April 1978 until the Soviet invasion of December 1979.

Klass, Rosanne. "The New Holocaust." *National Review* (New York. 4 October 1985).
Details of the massacre of 631 villagers in northern Afghanistan reported by a French doctor in late 1984, and discussion of lack of press interest.

Kucewicz, William. Series of eight articles on chemical warfare. *The Wall Street Journal* (New York. 24 April - 18 May 1984).
An extensively-researched in-depth survey of available information.

Malhuret, Claude. "Report from Afghanistan." *Foreign Affairs,* vol. 62, no. 2 (Winter 1983-1984): 426-435.
A valuable analysis of Soviet strategy in Afghanistan and the deliberate use of civilians as targets. Dr. Malhuret was formerly executive director of Médecins Sans Frontières [Doctors Without Borders] and in 1986 became Secretary of State for Human Rights in the French government.

Perkins, Samuel. "Massacre in the Tunnel." *Reader's Digest* (August 1983). The first major atrocity to gain international attention.

Revel, Jean-François. "The Awful Logic of Genocide." *National Review* (New York. 4 October 1985).
Details of recent atrocity reports and analysis of lack of public attention to them.

VI. ECONOMICS AND NATURAL RESOURCES

Agnew, Allen F. *Mineral Resources of Afghanistan.* Washington, D.C.: Congressional Research Service, Library of Congress, 7 August 1980.

Bullis, L.H. "A Congressional Handbook on U.S. Materials Import Dependency/Vulnerability: Report to House Banking, Finance, and Urban

Affairs Subcommittee on Economic Stablization." U.S. 97th Congress First Session Committee Print 97-6, September 1981.

Glassner, M.I. *Access to the Sea for Developing Land-locked States.* The Hague, Netherlands: Martinus Nijhoff Publishers, 1970.

Hannigan, J.B. and C.H. McMillan. *The Soviet State in Afghanistan and Iran: Rationale and Risk of Natural Gas Imports.* Ottawa, Canada: Institute of Soviet & East European Studies, Carlton University, August 1981.

Jensen, R.G., T. Shabad and A.W. Wright, eds. *Soviet Natural Resources in the World Economy.* University of Chicago Press, 1983.

Khairzada, Faiz M. "Western goods a Soviet weapon in Southwest Asia," *Wall Street Journal,* 1 January 1984.

Shafer, M. "Mineral Myths." *Foreign Policy* (Summer 1982): 154-171.

Shareq, Abdullah, et al. *Mineral Resources of Afghanistan: Afghanistan Geological and Mines Survey.* 2d ed., translated from Russian by G.M. Bezulov. (Kabul: Ministry of Mines, 1977): 419. 12 maps.
    Extremely rare. Available in the library of the University of Nebraska at Omaha.

Shroder, John F. *Physical Resources and the Development of Afghanistan.* Omaha, Nebraska: Dept. of Geography-Geology, University of Nebraska at Omaha, 1981.

------ "The USSR and Afghanistan Mineral Resources." *International Minerals: A National Perspective* (A.F. Agnew, ed. AAAS Selected Symposium 90. Boulder, Colorado: Westview Press, 1983): 115-153.

Strauss, S.D. "Mineral self-sufficiency---the contrast between the Soviet Union and the United States." *Mining Congress Journal* (November 1979): 49-54 and 59.

Thomas, John R. *Natural Resources in Soviet Foreign Policy.* New York: National Strategy Information Center, Agenda Paper #15, 1985.

"Dossier: Les intérêts économiques de l'URSS en Afghanistan." *Les*

Nouvelles d'Afghanistan no. 7, November 1981. Paris: Afrane. In French. See **Selected Periodicals** below.

VII. SOVIET STRATEGIC POLICY IN THE REGION

Relevant works are far too numerous to list; therefore only three recent books of special interest and one basic work are noted. [Note: Anyone doing research on this subject must regard as essential reading those portions of the works of V.I. Lenin dealing with Central Asia, Soviet Asian and nationalities policies, and related subjects; Lenin specifically discusses Afghanistan and what are now Pakistan, India and Iran. Other Soviet sources are also vital. For advanced research, the records of the India Office in London would also be invaluable if not essential.]

Brzezinski, Zbigniew. *Game Plan.* Boston/New York: Atlantic Monthly Press, 1986: 288. Maps.
    The former National Security Adviser assesses the U.S.-Soviet global contest through a focus on the Eurasian land mass. He gives particular attention to the role of Afghanistan in Soviet strategic planning. Illustrated with a series of unusual and extremely useful maps showing strategic factors as they appear from the Soviet point of view.

Hopkirk, Peter. *Setting the East Ablaze: Lenin's Dream of an Empire in Asia.* New York and London: W.W. Norton, 1984: 254. Maps, illus.
    The first general study of Soviet efforts to undermine British control of India via upheavals in Central Asia immediately following the Russian Revolution.

Mackinder, Halford, "The Geopolitical Pivot of History," *The Geopolitical Journal,* vol. 23, no. 4 (London, 1904), 421-444.

Parker, W.H. *Mackinder: Geography as an Aid to Statecraft* (Oxford: Clarendon Press, 1982).

VIII. CENTRAL ASIA

Only a small sampling of the multitude of works in this field is given here. Most of those listed have extensive bibliographies.

Bennigsen, Alexandre and Marie Broxup. *The Islamic Threat to the Soviet State.* London. 1983.

Bennigsen, A. and S. Enders Wimbush. *Muslim National Communism in the Soviet Union. A Revolutionary Strategy for the Colonial World.* Chicago. 1979.

------ *Mystics and Commissars. Sufism in the Soviet Union.* London. 1985.

Blanch, Lesley. *The Sabres of Paradise.* New York: Viking Press, 1960: 495. Illus., bibliography.
A recounting of the Shamil uprising in the Caucasus in the 1850s, a testing ground and model for subsequent Tsarist and Soviet campaigns in Central Asia. Not a scholarly book but well-researched and readable, but no index or notes.

Central Asian Survey (See **Selected Periodicals**, below)

Encyclopedia of Religion. New York: Macmillan, 1987.

Hambly, Gavin., ed. *Central Asia.* New York: Delacorte Press, 1969: 388. Maps, illus., selected bibliography.
A historic overview, with essays by the leading scholars in their fields.

Prawdin, Michael. *The Mongol Empire: Its Rise and Legacy.* New York: Macmillan, Free Press Paperback, 1967.
Genghis Khan, Tamerlane, their successors, and their impact on history. An introductory survey.

Rywki, M. *Moscow's Muslim Challenge.* London. 1982.

Wheeler, Geoffrey. *The Modern History of Soviet Central Asia.* London: Weidenfeld & Nicolson, 1965: 272. Maps, photographs, bibliography.

Wimbush, S.E., ed. *Soviet Nationalities in Strategic Perspective.* London. 1985.

IX. INSTITUTIONAL SOURCES

Statements and papers are presented at ongoing hearings held periodically since 1985 by the **Joint Senate-House Task Force on Afghanistan.**

These include analyses and reports on many aspects of the issue by a wide range of high-level experts and eyewitnesses; additional hearings continue to be scheduled. Copies of testimony are available from the office of Senator Gordon J. Humphrey, 531 Hart Senate Office Building, Washington, D.C. 20510. Address requests to: Afghanistan Task Force.

A survey report on Afghanistan entitled "Afghanistan: __ Years of Soviet Occupation," is issued each December by the **Bureau of Public Affairs, Department of State**, Washington, D.C.

In addition, occasional reports on specific topics are issued from time to time. Available on request.

The **British Foreign and Commonwealth Office** issues several short reports on Afghanistan each year as events warrant.

Available on request from the British Embassy or the British Information Services.

The office of the **United Nations High Commissioner for Refugees** (UNHCR) publishes the journal *Refugees*, which frequently reports on the Afghan refugees, and in addition issues occasional special materials.

Available on request from: UNHCR, Palais des Nations, CH-1211 Geneva 10, Switzerland; or Office of UNHCR, United Nations, New York, N.Y. 10017.

The **International Committee of the Red Cross** (ICRC) issues regular reports on the medical situation among Afghan refugees and other aspects of their situation that come under the purview of the ICRC.

Available on request from: ICRC, 17, avenue de la Paix, CH-1202 Geneva, Switzerland; or ICRC, 780 Third Avenue, 28th floor, New York, N.Y. 10017.

X. SELECTED PERIODICALS

Foreign Broadcast Information Service (FBIS) Daily Reports: Near East and South Asia edition. (Previous to 1 June 1987, entitled *South Asia* edition.) Washington, D.C.: National Technical Information Service of the Department of Commerce.

Published Monday through Friday, these reports contain current news and commentary monitored from foreign broadcasts, news agency transmissions, newspapers and periodicals around the world. An invaluable resource available in many research libraries. Other editions, including the *Soviet Union* series, are also useful.

By subscription only: National Technical Information Service, Department of Commerce, 5285 Port Royal Road, Springfield, Virginia 22161.

Central Asian Survey. London, Oxford: The Journal of the Society for Central Asian Studies. Distributed by Pergamon Press.

Useful articles related to Afghanistan in almost every issue, and monographs in the Occasional Papers series.

By subscription. Pergamon Journals: Maxwell House, Fairview Park, Elmsford, NY 10523 (for the U.S.); Headington Hill Hall, Oxford 0X3 0BW, England (for other countries).

Jane's Defense Weekly. New York and London.

Regularly carries detailed military reports and analysis on the Afghan war.

Monthly Bulletin of the Afghanistan Information Centre. Peshawar, Pakistan.

Usually about 25 pages. The Centre is a non-affiliated independent Afghan-run news service that is widely considered to be the most reliable Resistance news source. Frequently cited by the international press. Analyses of the economic situation, political developments, etc., as well as reports on fighting. Bulletins appear monthly with up-to-date news from inside Afghanistan.

By subscription only: P.O. Box 228, Peshawar, Pakistan. Subscription rate: U.S. $50 p.a.

Afghan Realities. Peshawar, Pakistan: Afghan Information and Documentation Centre.

Bi-weekly bulletin. Usually about 16 pages. Considered a generally reliable independent source. Focus on battle reports, photos; less emphasis on integrated analysis. *Suspended publication on 1 February 1987 but may resume in early 1988.*

WUFA. Peshawar, Pakistan

Quarterly English-language journal of the Writers Union of Free Afghanistan, an association of Afghan writers, scholars, and intellectuals in exile. Analyses and essays on various aspects of the Afghan situation.

By subscription: P.O. Box 867, Peshawar University, Peshawar, Pakistan. Subscription rate: U.S. $40 p.a.

Les Nouvelles d'Afghanistan. Paris: Afrane.

Monthly magazine issued by Afrane, a French humanitarian support organization. Regularly publishes extremely useful reports by European scholars, analysts, and aid personnel returning from clandestine visits inside Afghanistan. French language only.

By subscription: Afrane, BP 254, 75524 Paris, France. Subscription rate: FF 80 p.a. For selected back issues and reprints, inquire.

Afghanistan Forum.

Bimonthly roundup of coverage from many sources, including the *Kabul New Times* and other DRA publications. Calendar of recent developments, book reviews, information on organizations and events, etc.

By subscription only: 201 East 71 Street, New York, N.Y. 10021. Subscription rate: $20 p.a. in U.S.; $24 overseas; $35 institutions.

Note: Most of the Resistance organizations (and their offices and supporters in various countries) issue publications which usually concentrate on reports of fighting and political activities. These vary widely in quality and reliability, ranging from some which attempt to check their data and provide a degree of objectivity to others that are rife with unverified and often erroneous reports and propaganda. In all cases, these publications represent party positions rather than independent reporting, and as sources of information they should be checked against other, more objective independent sources.

An effort is presently being made to train Afghans in the basics of professional-quality journalism and to enlarge and improve present independent, non-party sources of reliable information and establish new ones, in order to better serve the international media and scholars. At this writing, the results cannot yet be assessed.

XI. SPECIALIZED RESEARCH CENTERS

Afghanistan Information Center. Freedom House, Inc., 48 East 21 Street, New York, NY 10010.

Provides information assistance to the press, policy makers, researchers, and the general public. No library facilities. Director: Rosanne Klass.

Bibliotheca Afghanica Foundation [Stiftung]. Benzburweg 5, CH-4410, Liestal, Switzerland.

An extraordinary private archive of materials on Afghanistan established twenty years ago. Not open for general public use but provides assistance for scholarly and other serious research, e.g., its director provided assistance to the United Nations Special Rapporteur on Afghanistan. Issues occasional publications in German only. Director: Paul Bucherer-

Dietschi. Associate: Prof. Albert Stahel (specialist in strategic and military studies).

Center for Afghanistan Studies. University of Nebraska at Omaha, Omaha, Nebraska 68182.

The only academic center in the United States devoted entirely to Afghan studies. Director: Prof. Thomas Gouttierre. The Arthur Paul Afghanistan Collection in the University Library is perhaps the most extensive collection on Afghanistan in the U.S. It includes several thousand books plus thousands of papers, documents, monographs, journals, unpublished materials and other resources and is one of the few major resources for economic information. (Arthur Paul was adviser to the Afghan Ministry of Finance in the 1960s.)

CEREDAF (Centre de recherches et d'études documentaires sur l'Afghanistan). 8, rue Christine, 75006 Paris, France.

A research center established a few years ago by several French scholars and organizations. Has accumulated significant resource materials, many of them first-hand reports. Largely but not exclusively scholarly orientation.

South Asia Collection, Perkins Library, Duke University, Durham, North Carolina.

The Louis and Nancy Hatch Dupree Inner Asian Collection comprises several thousand items, including rarities. Already accessible to researchers on request, the collection will be fully open to the public in 1988 and a catalog is planned for publication in 1989.

Additional useful sources include:

In the United States: Library of Congress; Oriental Division, New York Public Library; Asian Library, University of Illinois; Center for Middle Eastern Studies, Harvard University; Hoover Institution on War, Peace and Revolution, Stanford University; Middle East Collection, University of Texas Library; and the libraries of the University of Wyoming, University of Indiana, University of California at Los Angeles, University of Arizona, University of Connecticut, State University University of New York at Buffalo, and Teachers College, Columbia University.

In England: School of Oriental and African Studies, University of London; India Office Library, London.

XII. TRAVEL & DESCRIPTION, GENERAL INTEREST

Byron, Robert. *The Road to Oxiana.* New York and London: Oxford University Press, 1982: 292.

Recently rediscovered, this description of a journey in 1933 through Persia, Afghanistan, and Central Asia is considered a classic. Byron was especially intrigued by the city of Herat.

Chaffetz, David. *A Journey Through Afghanistan: A Memorial*. Chicago: Regnery Gateway, 1982: 254.

The author recalls a trip he made around much of Afghanistan in the mid-1970s, when trouble had begun to simmer but Afghan life had not yet been changed by it.

de Gaury, Gerald and H.V.F. Winstone, eds. *The Road to Kabul*. New York: MacMillan, 1982: 235. Maps, illus.

An anthology of writings by authors as diverse as Marco Polo, Rudyard Kipling, Lord Curzon, Gonzales de Clavijo, and Theodore Roosevelt, Jr.

Klass, Rosanne. *Land of the High Flags*. New York: Random House, 1964: 319. Map, photographs.

A picture of Afghanistan and its people just as modernization and development began to set in, in the form of a descriptive memoir by an American writer and teacher who spent several years in Kabul in the 1950s.

Stark, Freya. The Minaret of Djam. London: John Murray, 1970: 99. Photographs, sketches, map.

The famous travel writer's description of a journey to the newly-rediscovered Ghorid minaret, Bamian, Balkh, the Helmand Valley and Kabul.

Toynbee, Arnold J. *Between Oxus and Jumna*. New York and London: Oxford University Press, 1961: 211. Maps, photographs.

Toynbee adds historical insights to personal impressions in describing a journey through an area he considered pivotal to modern as well as ancient history.

XIII. PHOTO BOOKS

Kessel, Joseph and K. Flinker. *Afghanistan*. London: Thames & Hudson, 1959. 182 black and white photographs, 19 color plates.

Text by the prizewinning French author of *The Horsemen*.

Michaud, Roland and Sabrina. *Afghanistan: Paradise Lost*. Paris: Vendome Press, 1980. Distributed by Viking Press, New York.

98 full-color plates of northern and western Afghanistan. Introductory text, map.

------ *Caravans to Tartary.* New York: Viking Press, 1978.
76 full color plates of northern Afghanistan. Introductory text, map.

------ *Memoire de l'Afghanistan.* Paris: Chêne/Hachette, 1985. Preface by Michael Barry. Paperback. 98 color plates.
Concentrating alternately on landscape and on Afghan faces, the Michauds conceived this as a valedictory tribute to the country and the people they so often photographed. Text in French.

Nicod, M.R. *Afghanistan.* Innsbruck: Pinguin-Verlag, 1985: 144. 60 color plates, several dozen black and white photographs, maps, chronology.
Color photographs, capturing details often overlooked by others. Text in German.

XIV. AFGHAN ART

Auboyer, Jeanine. *The Art of Afghanistan.* Middlesex: Paul Hamlyn, 1968.
140 plates, many of them in color, of major works of Afghan art and architecture from pre-history on.

------ *Rarities of the Musée Guimet.* New York: Asia House Gallery.
Includes an essay and 9 plates on Gandhara art in Afghanistan.

Bunker, Emma C., Bruce C. Chatwin, and Ann R. Frakas. *"Animal Style" Art from East to West.* New York: The Asia Society, 1970. 185 pp.
145 black and white photographs plus engravings and drawings. Bibliography. Bronze and Iron Age art of northern and central Asia, including Afghanistan, which reveals cultural ties and Asian nomad influence on classical Greek art.

Hallade, Madeleine and Hans Hinz. *Gandharan Art of North India and the Graeco-Buddhist Tradition in India, Persia, and Central Asia.* New York: Harry N. Abrams, 1968.
225 plates, many of them in color. Maps, drawings, glossary, bibliography, chronological tables and notes in addition to text. A large number of the works shown come from Afghanistan.

Hallet, Stanley I. and Rafi Samizay. *Traditional Architecture of Afghanistan.* New York and London: Garland STPM Press, 1980: 202.

Several hundred black and white photographs, drawings, architectural diagrams, etc., glossary, bibliography. Detailed discussion of various types of Afghan domestic architecture, from adobe and brick houses to yurts and nomad tents, some of which anticipate twentieth century design.

Klass, Rosanne. "Missing in Action: Treasures of Afghanistan." *Asia.* New York: The Asia Society. April 1981.

A report on the damage and loss of collections of the Kabul Museum, Tillya Tepe and other Afghan art in 1979-80. (See also the "Letters to the Editor" columns of the June and August 1981 issues.)

Rowland, Benjamin, Jr. *Ancient Art from Afghanistan: Treasures of the Kabul Museum.* New York: The Asia Society, 1966.

Catalogue of the first major exhibit of Afghan art in the United States. Covers prehistoric period through the Ghaznavid empire. 137 black and white plates, introduction, bibliography.

Sarianidi, Viktor. *Bactrian Gold.* Leningrad: Aurora Publishers, 1985: 259.

166 color plates, 260 black and white photographs. The sensational discoveries made in 1978-79 by Soviet archeologists digging at Tillya Tepe near Shibarghan in northern Afghanistan. Unearthed in the first Greco-Bactrian royal tombs (c. 3d century B.C.) ever found, the dazzling hoard of more than 20,000 objects exquisitely worked in gold has been compared to the treasures of Mycenae and King Tutankhamen's tomb.

Sarianidi, director of the Soviet archeological team, with the assistance of staff from the Musée Guimet in Paris, gives all details except one---the present whereabouts of the treasure. It was reportedly taken to the Soviet Union, although under pre-Communist Afghan law it is a protected national treasure; the text subtly implies that the Afghans are not capable of protecting such art works. Photographs in a DRA publication [*Afghanistan Today,* no. 3, May-August 1986] show only a negligible handful of minor objects from this treasure as belonging to the collection of the Kabul Museum.

The above-listed works are just a sampling. For a wealth of additional sources on Afghan art and architecture, search under periods and styles listed in the "Guide to Research" section below.

XV. WORKS OF FICTION

Novels set in Afghanistan, with the war in the background or the foreground as the case may be, have begun to appear. They are, of course, of no value for research or reference but, since many readers assume---often wrongly---that novelists research their backgrounds carefully, they are briefly assessed here *in terms of their portrayal of the Afghan scene only.*

Kipling, Rudyard. *Kim.* 1901. Many editions, hard cover and paperback.
Not new, but far and away the best. This classic provides a wonderful sense of the nineteenth-century background to the events that culminated in the 1970s-1980s. The plot is "The Great Game," a phrase Kipling popularized if not coined. One of the characters, the Afghan horsetrader Mahbub Ali, is a fine portrait of the characteristic Afghan personality.

Shah, Idries. *Kara Kush.* New York: Stein and Day, 1986.
Uniquely a novel by an Afghan who is a skillful writer in English. Idries Shah, who has lived in England for many years, is internationally known as a leading writer on Sufism. As an Afghan, he was able to combine access to numerous sources with understanding of the people and the society, and the book is reportedly based in part on actual incidents.

Hirsch, M.E. *Kabul.* New York: Atheneum, 1986.
A romantic novel of the conflict between tradition and modernity in an Afghan family on the eve of the Communist coup, described as "an epic tale of the exotic East, a sweeping saga of civil war, political intrigue and family tragedy." The author's knowledge of the subject has been questioned.

Follett, Ken. *Lie Down With Lions.* New York: Signet, 1986.
Follet's usual formula of sex and spies, this time set in the Panjsher Valley. It could as easily be set anywhere else in the world. Poorly researched, it gives a false and distorted picture of the war and the participants. Pure fiction in all respects.

XVI. A GUIDE TO RESEARCH

Because Afghanistan has historically been a crossroads, a pivot, and a seedbed of many cultures and empires, and because the modern nation of Afghanistan was formed only in 1747, those interested in further research into its history and culture will find much of the information they seek listed under other headings, particularly in works on history, art and art history. The following is a list of entries under which such information on Afghanistan and its people is likely to be found.

General History, Art, Culture

Achaemenids, Afghanistan, Alexander the Great, Aryans, Babur, Bactria, Balkh, Buddhism, Central Asia, Darius, Delhi Sultanate, Gandhara, Genghis Khan, Ghaznavids, Ghorids, Greco-Bactrians, Herat, India, Indus Valley civilizations, Islam, Kushans, Marco Polo, Moghuls, Mongols, Nuristan (Kafiristan), Parthians, Pathans, Silk Route, Sufism, Vedas.

Also Persia, Safavids, Sakas, Samanids, Sassanians (Sassanids), Seleucids, Seljuks, Tamerlane (Timur-i-lang), Timurids, Uzbeks (Uzbegs), White Huns, Xerxes, Yueh-Chih, Zoroaster (Zarathustra).

Art:

Listings under the above. Also under topical listings:

Animal Style, Bihzad (Bezad), calligraphy, carpet art, coins/numismatics, Greco-Buddhist, Islamic, Mauryan, miniature painting, Moghul, North Indian, Parthian, Persian, School of Herat, Steppe art, Turkish.

Political History (Nineteenth century to date)

Afghanistan, India, Pakistan, Persia (Iran), Central Asia, Russia, Soviet Union, Basmachi, Turkestan, Samarkand, Bukhara, Khiva, British Empire.

Under the rubric of the British period in India see esp.: Forward Policy, Northwest Frontier, Peshawar, Afghan Wars, Lord Curzon, Lord Roberts, Pathans, Russian-British relations, Panjdeh incident, Herat, Persia, Kandahar, Central Asia. *Note:* For this period many entries are found under the term "Pathan" and under other variant spellings of "Pushtun" (e.g., Pashtun, Pakhtoon, Pashtoon, etc.).

Contributing Authors

A. Rasul Amin is a political scientist and historian, and the author of several studies on aspects of Afghan society. He was chairman of the Department of Social Sciences at Kabul University before the Communist coup. Arrested in 1978 and imprisoned in Pul-i-Charkhi, he was released and emigrated to Pakistan after the Soviet invasion. He is now director of the Writers Union of Free Afghanistan, an independent association of scholars and intellectuals established in Peshawar in 1985.

Anthony Arnold served in Afghanistan and elsewhere in Asia and Europe as an intelligence officer specializing in Soviet affairs. After his retirement from government service in 1979, he became a visiting scholar at the Hoover Institution. He is the author of two books and numerous articles and essays on the Communist takeover of Afghanistan, including a detailed study of the Afghan Communist Party.

Abdul Tawab Assifi, who holds degrees in engineering from Cornell University and Colorado State University, served as Afghan Minister of Mines and Industries from 1975 to 1978 and observed at first hand Soviet techniques of negotiating and implementing economic aid and development agreements. He had previously served as president of the Rural Development Department, governor of Herat Province, and chief engineer of the Helmand and Argandab Valley Authority. Following the 1978 Communist coup he spent two years in Pul-i-Charkhi prison. He left Afghanistan in 1981 and now lives in the United States.

Fredrik Barth holds a chair of Social Anthropology at the University of Oslo. A graduate of the University of Chicago and Cambridge University, he has held visiting professorships at Columbia, Yale and Johns Hopkins Universities, the University of California at Berkeley, and the University of Khartoum, and has published numerous books and articles. A specialist on the area stretching from Oman to Pakistan, he has for many years concentrated much of his attention on Afghanistan and its neighbors.

Alexandre Bennigsen is a historian and Orientalist, and the leading specialist on Soviet Islam. Born in St. Petersburg, Russia, in 1913, he took his doctorate at the Sorbonne and is presently professor of Turkic history at the École des Hautes Études en Sciences Sociales in Paris. He has been a visiting professor and scholar at universities in several countries, including the University of Chicago (1972-1982), and is the author of numerous books, articles and papers.

Yossef Bodansky is a specialist on Soviet military affairs with a special focus on Soviet operations in Afghanistan and the region, on which he is one of the leading Western authorities. He has been a visiting scholar in the Security Studies Program of the School of Advanced International Studies, Johns Hopkins University, and is a consultant to the U.S. Department of Defense. He writes regularly for *Jane's Defense Weekly, Defense & Foreign Affairs,* and other publications.

Rosanne Klass is the director of the Afghanistan Information Center of Freedom House. She lived and taught in Afghanistan for several years in the 1950s and returned there in 1965-1966 to cover the first free elections and the first Communist riots for *The New York Times.* A writer, editor, journalist, and lecturer, she is the author of a book and many articles on Afghanistan, including predictions of the Soviet invasion, and has been following affairs in that country closely for many years.

Dr. Elie Krakowski is the head of the Office of Regional Defense of the United States Department of Defense, and previously served as advisor to the Undersecretary of Defense for Policy. Before joining the government, he was a professor of international relations and Soviet foreign policy.

M. Siddieq Noorzoy is professor of economics at the University of Alberta and a Visiting Fellow at the Institute of International Studies and the Center for Middle Eastern Studies at the University of California at Berkeley. Born in Kabul, Afghanistan, he is a graduate of the University of California at Berkeley and the University of Washington, has taught at the University of Washington and the Naval Postgraduate School, and has held research posts with the Federal Reserve Bank and at Stanford University. He has published widely and is presently working on a book on the Afghan economy before and since the Soviet invasion.

Ambassador Leon B. Poullada worked and wrote extensively on Afghanistan and Pakistan for more than thirty years. As a career Foreign Service officer he served in Pakistan and Afghanistan in the 1950s, was Counselor for Economic Affairs in the U.S. Embassy in Kabul 1954-1958, and later served in supervisory positions dealing with Afghan affairs in the Department of State. After serving as Ambassador to Togo, he retired from the Foreign Service and took a doctorate at Princeton, writing his thesis on

Afghanistan, and taught at Northern Arizona University. In the 1960s and 1970s he returned to Kabul for extended periods as a Fulbright professor. At the time of his death in 1987, he was working on a book on Afghanistan since the Communist coup. Parts of chapter three appeared in the Winter 1982-1983 issue of *World Affairs* and are reprinted with the permission of the American Peace Society.

Abdul Rashid is the *nom de guerre* of a field commander in the Afghan Resistance with a distinguished combat record and more than six years of experience in the field. He is a member of the Harakat-i-Inqilab-i-Islami organization headed by Maulawi Nasrullah Mansoor. His writings have previously appeared in *Strategic Review* and other publications. Parts of chapter nine appeared in the Summer 1986 issue of *Strategic Review* and are reprinted with the permission of the United States Strategic Institute.

Guy B. Roberts holds a J.D. from the University of Denver, an M.A. in international relations from the University of Southern California (with the London School of Economics), and an LL.M. in international and comparative law from Georgetown University. He is presently Assistant Staff Judge Advocate for Commander-in-Chief, U.S. Pacific Forces.

Barnett R. Rubin is assistant professor of political science at Yale University, specializing in South Asia and India. He is the author and co-author of two major books and many articles on human rights violations in Afghanistan and is a leading authority on the subject. A graduate of Yale University and the University of Chicago, he has published a book and numerous articles and chapters in his field of specialization.

Dr. John F. Shroder is Nebraska Foundation Professor of Geology and Geography at the University of Nebraska at Omaha. A specialist in landforms and resources, he has done extensive research and taught widely in Afghanistan, Pakistan, East Africa, and the American West. Dr. Shroder served as Director of the National Atlas Project of Afghanistan from 1976 to 1978, when he was thrown out of Afghanistan by the new Communist regime---an event he regards as a badge of honor. He is the author of four books, nearly forty articles, and numerous published abstracts.

Index

Note: There are various ways to transliterate the Arabic, Persian and Pushto terms used in any discussion of Afghanistan. This book uses standard English transliterations. Personal names are transliterated as their owners choose. Some publications have begun to use Russian spellings for Afghan names, using *V* (which does not exist in the modified Arabic alphabet used in Afghanistan) for the standard and more accurate Afghan transliteration *W* (e.g., *Vardak* for *Wardak*), *dzh* for *j* (e.g., *Tadzhik*), and *ts* (as in *Tsamkani* for *Chamkani*). Such russifications are not used here.

"DRA" is used for "Afghanistan, Democratic Republic of"; "PDPA" is used for "People's Democratic Party of Afghanistan."

Appendices have not been indexed.

Freedom House Books

Yearbooks

Freedom in the World: Political Rights and Civil Liberties, Raymond D. Gastil; annuals for 1978, 1979, 1980, 1981, 1982, 1983-84, 1984-85, 1985-86, 1986-87

Studies in Freedom

1. *Strategies for the 1980s: Lessons of Cuba, Vietnam, and Afghanistan*, Philip van Slyck; 1981.
2. *Escape to Freedom: The Story of the International Rescue Committee*, Aaron Levenstein; 1983.
3. *Forty Years: A Third World Soldier at the UN*, Carlos P. Romulo (with Beth Day Romulo); 1986. (*Romulo: A Third World Soldier at the UN*, paperback edition, 1987.)
4. *Today's American: How Free?* James Finn & Leonard R. Sussman, (Eds.); 1986.
5. *Will of the People: Original Democracies in Non-Western Societies*, Raul S. Manglapus; 1987.

Perspectives on Freedom

General Editor: **James Finn**

1. *El Salvador: Peaceful Revolution or Armed Struggle?*, R. Bruce McColm; 1982.
2. *Three Years at the East-West Divide*, Max M. Kampelman; (Introductions by Ronald Reagan and Jimmy Carter; edited by Leonard R. Sussman); 1983.
3. *The Democratic Mask: The Consolidation of the Sandinista Revolution*, Douglas W. Payne; 1985.
4. *The Heresy of Words in Cuba: Freedom of Expression & Information*, Carlos Ripoll; 1985.
5. *Human Rights & the New Realism: Strategic Thinking in a New Age*, Michael Novak; 1986.
6. *To License A Journalist?*, Inter-American Court of Human Rights; 1986.
7. *The Catholic Church in China*, L. Ladany; 1987.
8. *Glasnost: How Open? Soviet & Eastern European Dissidents;* 1987
9. *Yugoslavia: The Failure of "Democratic" Communism;* 1987

Focus on Issues

1. *Big Story: How the American Press and Television Reported and Interpreted the Crisis of Tet-1968 in Vietnam and Washington*, Peter Braestrup; Two volumes 1977; One volume paperback abridged 1978, 1983.
2. *Soviet POWs in Afghanistan*, Ludmilla Thorne; 1986.
3. *Afghanistan: The Great Game Revisited*, edited by Rossane Klass; 1987
4. *Nicaragua's Continuing Struggle: In Search of Democracy*, Arturo J. Cruz; 1987